each individual contracts with every other individual to transfer his or her natural right to all things to an artificial person, the sovereign (whether monarchic, aristocratic, or democratic), which is the artificial creation of political life.[22] The state begins with the creation of an artificial difference that is so great, so unequal that it can be called a "mortal god," or perhaps more precisely, an artificial god. The artificial person that is the sovereign is so different that it fills the subjects who have created it not only with fear but also terror. Through the creation of this fundamental artificial difference that establishes civil life, there are now two ways in which many other differences can become interesting, significant, and relevant to justice—through law and through the silence of law.

Law is an "artificial chain."[23] There are no natural limits, so law must be created artificially through the creation of the artificial person that is the state, and the will of the sovereign is law. Law establishes which differences are significant and a matter of justice; legally sanctioned difference—for example, the division of property—artificially divides all things and thus limits the desires of individuals according to justice. By nature, each has the right to everything; by law, each has the right to his own.[24] Where the law is silent, justice becomes once again individual desire.[25] This is not, however, a return to the state of nature because this liberty or right is granted by the sovereign, not nature. Individual liberty is the choice of the sovereign not to limit. Nevertheless, in this silence of the law, the vast differences of individual desire can flourish—a multitude of tastes, diversions, and differences, all of which are just.

In the example of affirmative action, Hobbes's sovereign would be free to enact or not to enact such a law. It could be enacted because Aristotle's notion that the innocent—that is, the one whose merit is overlooked for the sake of justice to an individual from an oppressed group—is harmed by affirmative action would be nonsensical to Hobbes. Indeed, for Hobbes there would be no need for a narrative that explains how the one whose merit is based on performance has unfairly benefitted from some privilege such as race or gender or economic background; the sovereign is incapable of harming the subject, since the subject has transferred to the sovereign (thus creating the sovereign) the individual's natural right to all things. The "innocent victim" of affirmative action has already authorized the sovereign's decision. Moreover, the diversity to be sought at a university would not be primarily intellectual because knowledge is not something distinct from power. Access to knowledge is access to the natural basis of distributive justice in merit, which prioritizes differences that stem from the properly human activity of reason.

Thomas Hobbes rejects Aristotle's distinction between form and matter, and, if there is no form, there are no formal or final causes.[12] Aristotle's distinction between nature and artifice becomes, for Hobbes, a distinction between two human conditions, a state of nature and a state of political life, each of which has a unique account of diversity and justice. Contrary to Aristotle, reason is incapable of governing the passions; reason is always an instrument of the passions, and the subordination of reason to the passions is due to nature rather than a poor habituation.[13] The dominance of the passions renders the natural condition of human beings a state of absolute individuality; what is good is what I desire, and what I desire is constantly changing.[14] The only constancy and commonality in human desire is the passion for power, but power is a means rather than an end, and so there is no final cause that unites human desire.[15] Naturally there is no law to limit human nature; there is only a natural right (*jus naturale*), which is a liberty that extends to all things.[16] If each individual has the natural right to everything, and if individuals are governed by the passions, then there is a certain sameness to human beings without that sameness leading to unity. What distinguishes human beings is power, the ability to attain and keep what they desire. Knowledge, for example, is a type of power that distinguishes individuals' capacity to attain and keep what they desire.[17] The natural differences in power are not, however, very significant. Human beings are by nature equal, which is proven by the ability of anyone to kill anyone,[18] which leads to the war of each individual against every other individual.[19] Life in the state of nature is "solitary, poor, nasty, brutish and short" because of the combination of absolute individuality and the lack of natural difference.[20] Each individual desires and has the right to everything without having the power to achieve it. Thus war is natural and political life unnatural. While Aristotle's natural difference between male and female leads to political life, and the differing ways that the passions and reason can be related through habituation grounds justice, in the Hobbesian state of nature all differences are "just"; whatever the individual desires is just, and if there is no injustice, justice loses its significance.[21] The equality of all differences in nature renders justice meaningless.

If there are no naturally significant differences, then differences must be established artificially. Escape from the state of nature occurs when division of labor that makes possible wealth and leisure but also principally for the development of reason through speech about justice.

Political life begins within the family in the speech between husband and wife and between parents and children. The human potentiality for reason is actualized through such speech, but that can never be a complete achievement of human reason because the speech is limited by the privacy and sameness of the family. There is a difference of male and female, parent and child, but the children speak like the parents, look like the parents, and, more or less, come to think like the parents. Reason requires diversity to develop, and the diversity of the family is limited. The limitations of similarity in physical appearance, speech, and reason are less in the tribe, but only in the city is the maximum difference achieved that allows for the full development of reason. Speech in the city moves beyond the easy familiarity of speech in the family, where each can finish the sentences of the other, and beyond the dialect of the tribe, where speech is used to exclude the noninitiated; in the city, speech requires a kind of formality that makes possible argumentation across family and tribe. Differences that arise from the particularity of moral reasoning and from all the particularity of ethnic and linguistic roots in the city force reason to argue to a justice that is aware of both the universality and sameness of human nature and the accidentality and diversity that is inseparable from materiality and from the exercise of human reason in action. One can, in fact, well imagine Aristotle agreeing that diversity is essential to the university and having sympathy with the intention of affirmative action admissions because reasoning about justice cannot flourish where students are too homogeneous, but a diversity that fails to produce debate and intellectual diversity would not be reasonable or human; tribal allegiance must be surpassed by the formal argumentation of the "city." Aristotle would, however, have a more basic objection to affirmative action—that it necessarily entails a confusion of distributive and corrective justice. Past discrimination based on differences such as race or gender would be a failure of distributive justice that should be remedied through corrective justice. Affirmative action, on the other hand, corrects past injustice by distributing according to race or gender or other factors; that is, it undermines the grounding of distributive justice in merit. In other words, the artificiality that is inherent in the devising of punishments according to corrective justice cannot, for Aristotle, negate the mean and with reasonable feeling—is something that must be achieved; it must happen through external force in habituation and eventually through inner choice when the habit is fully developed. For Aristotle, the most significant differences among human beings are moral characters, which are a stable relationship between reason and the passions caused by habituation. There are four main moral characters: vice, incontinence, continence, and virtue.[8] Virtue is reason and the passions in harmony with each other and with human nature, so a good action is done with pleasure. Happiness, at least for the majority of human beings who live without philosophy, is moral virtue—a life of human actions done reasonably and with pleasure; for those with the requisite leisure and education, it is primarily philosophical contemplation—intellectual virtue, and secondarily moral virtue.[9]

The differences, then, that Aristotelian justice highlights are differences in moral character, which concern success or failure in habitually acting and feeling with reason. Aristotle's *Politics* adds that reason, and especially reasoning about justice, can only develop fully in a context of differences that arise from the complexity of the city (*polis*), which represents the maximum particularity and multiplicity that is compatible with the unity of political life and the capacity of moral reason. Human reason develops through speech (*logos* means both reason and speech), and this is especially true of reasoning about justice:

> Now, that man is more of a political animal than bees or any other gregarious animal is evident. Nature, as we often say, makes nothing in vain, and man is the only animal whom she has endowed with the gift of speech [*logos*]. And whereas mere voice is but an indication of pleasure or pain, and is therefore found in other animals, . . . the power of speech [*logos*] is intended to set forth the expedient and the inexpedient, and therefore likewise the just and the unjust. And it is a characteristic of man that he alone has any sense of good and evil, of just and unjust, and the life, and the association of living beings who have this sense makes a family and a state [*polis*].[10]

Political life begins in the family through the complementary diversity of male and female in reproduction, and so the family is the smallest political unit.[11] The family develops naturally into the tribe or village and the tribe into the city, which is necessary not only for defense and for a different accounts of justice determine which differences are most important and what is owed to them? Conversely, which differences are most real, and how does the answer to that question determine what justice is? We can illustrate the philosophical debate in more detail through three emblematic philosophers—Aristotle, Thomas Hobbes, and Jean-Francois Lyotard—who represent, respectively, an ancient, a modern, and a postmodern approach to justice and diversity; more important than the historical sweep, however, is their exemplification of some irreducible philosophical differences concerning the relationship between justice and diversity. We can further illustrate the importance of the philosophical debate by posing to each of these philosophers the question of affirmative action.

For Aristotle, there are four fundamental distinctions in material being that the human mind must acknowledge: substance/accident, matter/form, potential/actual, and nature/artifact.[2] What is owed to these differences? Aristotle defines justice as a mean of equality. There are two kinds of equality, and thus two kinds of justice. Distributive justice equalizes different distributions based on merit.[3] Corrective justice equalizes unjust distributions; that is, corrects distributions that were not merited.[4] What each thing merits depends upon the natural activity that follows from its form or kind. Nature is hierarchical, inasmuch as the higher can perform the activity of the lower and another activity that the lower cannot perform.[5] What is owed to an animal is essentially different than what is owed to a plant or rock because they have essentially different activities, and the activity of an animal (sensation) is superior to that of a plant (life) or a rock (mere existence). Within a natural kind, there are accidental differences, but the individuals are essentially the same. The activity that is proper to human beings is reason; essentially human beings are the same, and they differ accidentally. Distributive justice would require, then, that human beings be treated essentially the same—that is, equally, and essentially different than animals, plants, and inanimate things—but what about the accidental differences among human beings? Which accidental differences in human nature are important in justice?

Although the activity that is proper to human beings and that distinguishes human from animal is reason, it is complicated by the presence of the passions, which are in themselves irrational.[6] The passions, however, are capable of listening to reason, and the passions become reasonable through habituation.[7] The habit of acting humanly—that is, according to ple, famously ignores the differences between male and female, even to the point of having men and women performing military exercises together naked; justice would have us ignore the difference of gender. On the other hand, the differences between the work performed by merchants, warriors, and philosophers are essential to Plato's hierarchical definition of justice. One may say that justice and diversity are always conjoined, but their meanings and the manner of their conjunction must be a matter of debate in philosophy and theology.

Justice through diversity is, therefore, not merely a problem for the university but a question—that is, it is not clear that the university can survive without the debate provided by philosophy and theology. Jean-Francois Lyotard identifies efficiency with dissent, and so in 1979 he prophesied the collapse of both the Soviet Union and the modern university based on the inefficiency that follows from the stifling of dissent.[1] In twenty years, his prophesy about the Soviet Union would be fulfilled, and that should give us pause about the future of the university. The university arose in the Middle Ages around public disputation; the university was a creation of and for public debate, and the method of the "disputatio" dominated university teaching, examination, and publication. Descartes saw postmedieval scholasticism and the university as sterile, and so he moved philosophy outside university disputation and toward consensus. As Lyotard shows, the modern university, exemplified by the University of Berlin, sought to replace debate with consensus, but that was only possible through the silencing of dissent. If justice through diversity is only a problem for the university and not a question, then dissent about the most important issue for the university is impossible. For debate about justice through diversity to be as central as the issue itself, philosophy and theology must have a voice, and that is the purpose of this volume. To the problem solving of the social sciences, this volume adds the questioning voices of philosophy and theology concerning justice through diversity.

THE DEBATE WITHIN PHILOSOPHY AND THEOLOGY

Philosophy

The questions within the philosophical debate concerning justice and diversity are fundamental in their simplicity. What is justice, and how do held by different races, ethnicities, sexual identities, cultures, religions, and so on. If justice is equality, and power is unequally distributed among these differences, one can see through social sciences how to equalize power by weighting and ranking differences; social science points the way to justice. A philosopher such as Michel Foucault has much to say about power and institutions, but he cannot match the empirical verification, the ready translation into practice, and the accessibility of the social sciences. In brief, the social sciences seem to provide a more reliable method by which power and privilege can be calculated and equitably distributed.

As justice through diversity became central to the mission of the university, philosophy and theology fell somewhat from their privileged positions, especially in Catholic universities. Philosopher kings and theocrats in the university would give way to empirical investigations of privilege and techniques of countering that privilege. Although Catholic universities may claim in their mission statements that their commitment to justice through diversity derives from their religious commitments, it is left to the social sciences to interpret the relationship between justice and diversity and to provide the prescriptions for how justice through diversity is to be implemented. The meanings of justice and diversity become less a matter of debate and more a matter of scientific investigation. Universities emphasize their commitment to action—to enacting justice through diversity—rather than their commitment to debate. Philosophical and theological debate thus appears a relic of a time when the university lacked commitment to justice through diversity and of a power structure that ignored the most pressing issue for academia.

Nevertheless, besides being a problem to be studied by the social sciences and solved by a corresponding policy, justice through diversity is also a question, the roots of which are so deep that they can be reached only by philosophy and theology. The relationship between justice and diversity is a question of first principles, which are irreducible, multiple, and therefore competing; it is a question that has to acknowledge irreconcilable differences about what constitutes a meaningful difference and a question that therefore must be posed within the context of debate. Consensus in philosophy and theology about which differences among human beings are most real and what is owed to which differences is impossible. To which differences must justice be blind, and upon which must justice shine its bright light? Plato's account of justice in the *Republic*, for exam-

INTRODUCTION

Michael J. Sweeney, Xavier University

JUSTICE THROUGH DIVERSITY AS A QUESTION

Perhaps the most transformative force in the contemporary university is the commitment to justice through diversity. This commitment has changed who enters, teaches, and administers the university. It has changed the content of what is taught and the mission statements that define the purpose of higher education. What is rarely defined, however, is justice and how it is related to diversity. A commonsensical understanding of justice as equality generally suffices because the most basic commitment is to make higher education equally accessible. Nevertheless, if that were the limit of the commitment to justice through diversity, the transformation of the university would stop at the admissions office. Moreover, the problem with the simple definition of justice as equality is that it does little to explain the relationship between justice and diversity. If justice is equality, are all differences equal? Are all differences in race, gender, sexual orientation, national origin, ethnicity, religion, and culture equal? Should such differences be weighted differently and thus hierarchically? On what basis are those differences to be weighted and ranked to ensure equality?

The answers that have dominated the interpretation of justice through diversity have come from the social sciences. Social sciences dominate the publication of material for courses in justice and diversity, as they dominate that portion of the curriculum. The appeal of the social sciences here is plain: they provide an empirical analysis of power and how it is

20 Unity and Religious Diversity in Islamic Theology, Shariah
Law, and Tradition 407
*Muhammad Zia-ul-Haq, University of Islamabad, and
Waleed El-Ansary, Xavier Univerisity*

IV: PARTICULAR ISSUES IN JUSTICE AND DIVERSITY: THEOLOGY 439

21 From Benevolent Tolerance to Humble Reverence: A Vision
for a Multicultural Church 441
Virgilio Elizondo, University of Notre Dame

22 The Common Good, Freedom, and Difference 455
Shawn Copeland, Boston College

23 Ordered Justice and the Diversity of Rights and Nations in
Pacem in terris 487
Russell Hittinger, University of Tulsa

24 Was National Socialism Political Religion?: The
Transformation of Christianity into a Nazi Religion during
the Third Reich 509
Susannah Heschel, Dartmouth University

25 Vattimo, Diversity, and Catholicism 533
Thomas G. Guarino, Seton Hall University

26 Respecting Gay People: Justice and the Interpretation of
Scriptural Traditions 551
Kwame Anthony Appiah, New York University

27 Homosexuality and the Word of God 573
Mary Healey, Sacred Heart Seminary

28 How (Not) to Debate Christian Sexual Ethics 601
Mark D. Jordan, Harvard University

29 Not Just Love: The Anthropological Assumptions of Catholic
Teaching on Same-Sex Attraction and Activity 615
John Grabowski, Catholic University of America

Index 639
About the Contributors 649

II: PARTICULAR ISSUES IN JUSTICE AND DIVERSITY: PHILOSOPHY   157

8 Diversity: How Far?   159
Rémi Brague, University of Paris

9 Intolerance and Diversity in Three Cities: Ancient Babylon, Renaissance Venice, and Nineteenth-Century Philadelphia   175
Camille Paglia

10 Essentializing the Classed Other   187
Gayatri Chakravorty Spivak, Columbia University

11 Racist Disrespect in Moral Theory: Dialogue with Glasgow   207
Jorge Garcia, Boston College

12 A Feminist Defense of The Complementarity Between Men and Women   237
Laura L. Garcia, Boston College

13 Immigration and American Exceptionalism   277
Robert P. George, Princeton University

14 What Marriage Can Be   285
John Corvino, Wayne State University

15 Marriage: Whose Justice? Which Diversity?   309
Sherif Girgis, Princeton University

III: JUSTICE AND DIVERSITY FROM DIVERSE THEOLOGICAL PERSPECTIVES   333

16 *Dignum et Iustum*: Justice, Diversity, and the Mystery of Catholicity   335
Peter A. Huff, University of Mary

17 Diversity in Eastern Christianity: Historical Traumas and Cultural Dislocations   359
Dr. Paul L. Gavrilyuk, University of St. Thomas

18 Justice and Diversity: A Homogenous Protestant Project?   373
D. Stephen Long, Southern Methodist University

19 Justice, Diversity, and Tolerance in the Jewish Tradition   395
David Novak, University of Toronto

CONTENTS

Introduction   ix
   Michael J. Sweeney, Xavier University

I: JUSTICE AND DIVERSITY FROM DIVERSE PHILOSOPHICAL PERSPECTIVES   1

1. Justice and Diversity in Virtue Ethics   3
   Peter Simpson, City University of New York

2. Thomas Aquinas on Justice and the Diversity of Goods   19
   Thomas Hibbs, Baylor University

3. On Deontology: Is Diversity for Real?   39
   Aaron Szymkowiak, Xavier University

4. Utilitarianism on Justice (and Diversity)   59
   Raymond Hain, Providence University

5. Systems of Justice and Role of the Moral Prophet   81
   James Campbell, University of Toledo

6. Justice through Diversity from an Analytical Perspective   99
   Paul Weithman, University of Notre Dame

7. The Dilemma of Diversity: Rawls, Derrida, and Political Justice   123
   Fred Evans, Duquesne University

Published by Rowman & Littlefield
A wholly owned subsidiary of The Rowman & Littlefield Publishing Group, Inc.
4501 Forbes Boulevard, Suite 200, Lanham, Maryland 20706
www.rowman.com

Unit A, Whitacre Mews, 26-34 Stannary Street, London SE11 4AB

Copyright © 2016 by Rowman & Littlefield

All rights reserved. No part of this book may be reproduced in any form or by any electronic or mechanical means, including information storage and retrieval systems, without written permission from the publisher, except by a reviewer who may quote passages in a review.

British Library Cataloguing in Publication Information Available

Library of Congress Cataloging-in-Publication Data

Names: Sweeney, Michael J., editor
Title: Justice through diversity? : a philosophical and theological debate / edited by Michael J. Sweeney.
Description: Lanham, Maryland : Rowman & Littlefield, 2016. Includes bibliographical references and index.
Identifiers: LCCN 2016012239 (print) | LCCN 2016017295 (ebook) | ISBN 9781444227116 6 (cloth : alk. paper) | ISBN 9781442271173 (electronic)
Subjects: LCSH: Justice (Philosophy) | Religion and justice. | Plurilism.
Classification: LCC B105.J87 J87 2016 (print) | LCC B105.J87 (ebook) | DDC 172/x2--dc23. LC record available at http://lccn.loc.gov/2016012239

∞ ™ The paper used in this publication meets the minimum requirements of American National Standard for Information Sciences Permanence of Paper for Printed Library Materials, ANSI/NISO Z39.48-1992.

Printed in the United States of America

JUSTICE THROUGH DIVERSITY?

A Philosophical and Theological Debate

Edited by Michael J. Sweeney

ROWMAN & LITTLEFIELD
Lanham • Boulder • New York • London

JUSTICE THROUGH DIVERSITY?

power, and the diversity to be sought concerns the range of power in society—the range that extends from the powerless to the powerful.

For Jean-Francois Lyotard, justice is diversity. Which differences? All of them. In our postmodern condition, knowledge is electronic information and its control.[26] There is an inherently dehumanizing tendency to such a view of knowledge because knowledge is, in large part, outside the human being.[27] Machines hold more information than minds, and even the control over the information is largely in the machines through software and search engines. What is left for human beings is merely to know how to use the machines. We have no need to know, to hold within our minds, information; rather, we need to know how to access the information through technology. From the dominance of technology follows the supremacy of efficiency as the standard of judgment. Indeed, society is like a giant machine that processes information (knowledge), which is the principal product and which circulates like money.[28] The parts of this machine, individual human beings, are judged by the standard of efficiency.[29] Modernity understands efficiency as consensus, and thus dissent must be eliminated in the name of efficiency. The result of this modern understanding of efficiency has been the great totalitarian systems of the twentieth century that eliminated countless dissenting, and thus inefficient, individuals.

Descartes foresaw a technological society but did not foresee that technology would change the nature of knowledge itself, moving it, in large part, outside the human mind. Modernity also failed to foresee how language would fundamentally change, ushering in the postmodern period. Modernity's view of language aiming at consensus—for example, Descartes's metalanguage (method) and his metanarrative (the myth of a return to the Garden of Eden through science)—easily leads to totalitarianism because it cannot tolerate dissent.[30] Taking his cue from Wittgenstein, Lyotard says that in the postmodern condition language is now seen as a game.[31] As consensus among the players about the rules allows them to make moves in chess and compete, so language in the postmodern condition is a set of rules that allows utterances, which are moves that aim, not at consensus, but at dissent: "to speak is to fight."[32] In fact, this view of language aiming at dissent, a counter move in the game, is the key to overcoming the dehumanizing tendency of efficiency as the sole standard in postmodern society. Lyotard's response is not to object to efficiency as the sole standard but to show that each individual human being is efficient and therefore cannot be eliminated in the name of efficiency.[33] Dissent leads to disruption but also calls for a novel response, which ultimately leads to greater efficiency. Every individual human being can speak—every individual human being can dissent, and thus every individual human being is a contributor to efficiency—so every dissent is a significant difference. The more that difference and dissent are multiplied, the more efficient society becomes. Every difference, every dissent that is a move within the bounds of discourse, is an increase of efficiency; there are no inefficient individuals.

As truth is merely "a moment in the circulation of capital"—that is, subordinate to the standard of efficiency—justice is likewise efficiency.[34] "The normativity of laws is replaced by the performativity of procedures" in postmodern society.[35] Justice is the result of dissent—for example, a fair fight that is conducted according to the rules of the courtroom. If "to speak is to fight," then justice is the result of the fight that is spoken according to rules that allow the maximum possible dissent. The result is efficient and just; there is no difference between them. Justice is diversity, and the only limit to that identification of justice with diversity is the need for consensus about the rules for the game. Even that consensus, however, is local (no Cartesian method or metalanguage) and subject to cancellation (the rules can be changed by a new consensus).[36] Justice is the maximizing of difference: "Let us wage a war on totality; let us be witnesses to the unpresentable; let us activate the differences and save the honor of the name."[37]

Lyotard would find affirmative action, especially with regard to entrance to the university, a woefully inadequate means of diversification. He would want to increase the diversity of education by privileging all differences, not merely some; in fact, he would want to increase the diversity of the university to the point that the modern university is nullified. The university is organized around modern notions of sameness and consensus; it is a place where the individual is to be indoctrinated into modernity's metalanguage and metanarrative.[38] Since in the postmodern condition we no longer believe or need the metanarrative, and since a metalanguage is now impossible, there is no longer a need for the university to unify knowledge. The university is also no longer needed for research—for new knowledge.[39] Finally, the university is no longer needed for the transmission of knowledge that is already possessed, since it is possessed by machines, which can teach one how to access the information.[40] Professors and the university as a whole are replaceable by the computer, and technology rather than law is the chief vehicle to diversity. Real diversity in education is achieved by the removal of the monopoly that the university has to grant access to knowledge, not through legal refinement that leaves the monopoly. Real diversity will be achieved through a democratization of knowledge in which knowledge is accessed through technology rather than through institutions.

It is thus evident that the differing accounts of diversity and justice by Aristotle, Hobbes, and Lyotard are not simply historical but irreducible philosophical differences. Aristotle's justice emphasizes what is owed to natural differences, especially to differences in the achievement of reason. It stresses the natural and complementary differences of male and female as the beginning of political life and intellectual differences as essential to the end of political life, since moral reason cannot develop fully without complexity and diversity beyond that of the family and tribe. These differences are made possible by the sameness that is human nature. Hobbes's justice emphasizes that what is owed to artificial—that is, legally sanctioned—differences. Differences to which something is owed are artificial and emphasize power and positive law. It is the primacy of the artificial over the natural—of law over human nature, of desire over reason, and of individual differences over the differences of male and female. Intellectual diversity is reducible to differences in power. Justice requires a degree of sameness, but it is the artificial equality of subjects before the sovereign, not natural equality. Lyotard's justice is the maximization of diversity. Justice privileges linguistic differences—dissent—and language is artificial; what results from the human creation of rules, though, as we shall see, Lyotard has difficulty avoiding the natural character of language. With Aristotle, Lyotard emphasizes the importance of language, but without emphasis on natural reason. Hobbes stresses the importance of power, but for Lyotard the power is language, which is a game that aims at efficiency, dissent, and the increase of power, all of which are equivalent. Efficiency from digital (postmodern) technology (as opposed to Hobbesian-Cartesian mechanics) is subordinated to the efficiency of language games; knowledge as electronic information is an instrument of language rather than directly a tool of an individual's desires. Lyotard takes the individuality of the Hobbesian state of nature, but "war" is linguistic; it is dissent. Language games are civilized war, a war with rules and, contrary to war in Hobbes's state of nature, one that is efficient and that produces the highest level of civilization. The sameness that Lyotard acknowledges as grounding dissent is consensus about the rules, although even that is local and subject to cancellation. Nevertheless, the question arises whether, if each individual is efficient because each has the capacity to speak, the natural human capacity for language grounds Lyotard's dissent. Lyotard wants to save the individual without a return to human nature or to form and final causality, but is the universal capacity to speak and dissent an unacknowledged return to human nature? Lyotard's reply would point to how language has changed in postmodernity—how, in a game, language aims at dissent rather than consensus. Even granting that change, however, it is difficult to deny that something constant and natural remains with regard to the human capacity for language.

In conclusion, within philosophy there is no single account of diversity or justice. There is a diversity of diversities and a diversity of justices. The relationship between justice and diversity is a matter for argument and public debate. Indeed, that is one of the principal purposes of the university; whether the diversity of the university is ultimately intellectual, or whether it is to diversify power in society, or whether its purpose is to increase dissent (and thus efficiency) to the maximum, are questions that cannot be decided independently of this debate. The university cannot be a means of indoctrinating students into a particular account of justice and diversity; rather, it is the place where all accounts are questioned and the arguments for the various possible positions can be evaluated. This volume is intended as a means to that end. The philosophical section is divided into two parts: the first elaborates the irreducible differences in accounts of justice and diversity through seven philosophical perspectives; the second explores some particular issues in justice and diversity. Neither section is, of course, exhaustive; the purpose of the work is to introduce a debate, not end it. The health of this debate is a measure of the health, justice, and diversity of the university.

Theology

The theological meanings of justice and diversity are no less a matter of debate. Among the religions that are revealed, there is a fundamental difference between Christianity, which emphasizes dogma, and Judaism and Islam, which emphasize law. John Esposito sums up the differences:

> Islam is similar to Judaism in its emphasis on practice rather than belief, on law rather than dogma. The primary religious discipline in Judaism and Islam has been religious law; for Christianity it has been theology. Historically, in Judaism and Islam the major debates and disagreements have been among scholars of religious law over matters of religious practice, whereas in Christianity the early disputes and cleavages in the community were over theological beliefs: the nature of the Trinity or the relationship of Jesus' human and divine natures.[41]

If revelation is principally law, justice will be obedience to the law. If revelation is principally the person of Christ, justice will be the person and sacrifice of Christ. For Judaism and Islam, the answer to the question concerning what justice is is given by religious law; in Christianity, it comes from theology. There can be similarities but not identity in the understandings of justice by Christianity on one side and by Judaism and Islam on the other. The principal differences that concern justice for Islam and Judaism are between those under the law and those not under the law and then differences in merit among those under the law. In Christianity, the principal differences are between those who believe in Christ and those who do not and, among those who believe in Christ, the degree of one's likeness to Christ.

Thomas Aquinas exemplifies the difference that Trinitarian monotheism makes for justice because he looks at justice from both the perspective of monotheism and Trinitarian monotheism. Taking the perspective of monotheism, Aquinas asks whether there is justice in God.[42] Justice in God is distributive rather than corrective, and distributive justice requires an "other" to whom something is distributed according to the recipient's merits. Thus, distributive justice in monotheism is orientated toward creation. God gives to each created thing what is proper to its nature and activity. Justice is like truth; justice is the equality between the will and reality, and truth is the adequation (equalizing) of the intellect to reality. At the beginning of creation, God pronounces His justice and truth that creation is good, and at the end of the world He will pronounce His distributive justice according to the merits or demerits of each individual human being. More fundamental than justice, however, is God's mercy, for the act of creation is itself not owed according to justice. Aquinas compares mercy to liberality, and for Aristotle liberality is giving money to people to whom it is not owed. Creation is an act of liberality that produces natures to which God can be just. Human justice toward God is thus radically unlike God's justice toward human beings. God owed nothing to human beings until he chose to create them, but human beings by nature owe everything to God. Human justice toward God has to consist in worship and thanksgiving, and it must recognize the ultimate inability of human beings to be just to God because human beings cannot give to God equally—that is, justly, as God has given to human beings. Within monotheism, divine justice is externally focused because that is where the other to whom justice is owed can be found. For Trinitarian monotheism, the most significant "other" is within the divinity itself: "Now equality implies both—namely distinction of persons, for nothing can be said to be equal to itself; and unity of essence, since for this reason are the persons equal to one another, that they are of the same greatness and essence."[43] The essential identity of the divinity—monotheism—grounds divine justice, but it is also difference of persons that makes justice within the divinity possible. The Word alone is the perfect expression of what is, the perfect expression of the Father. Only the Word does justice to God; only the Son does justice to the Father through the Holy Spirit.[44] Justice in the complete sense is found only in God and among the relations and persons of the Trinity.

The most fundamental theological critique of justice through diversity, however, is the Christian questioning of justice itself. Christians are called to something superior to justice; namely, mercy.[45] As Aquinas explains it, in the Christian life, justice is subsumed under mercy. Mercy is a feeling of sorrow over the suffering of another. It is God's natural freedom from suffering that allows Him to be merciful, to take upon Himself the suffering of human beings. For Aristotle, mercy or pity is possible only if the evil is undeserved so that the cause of the suffering cannot be the moral evil of the one suffering; mercy is proper to one who suffers physical evil, which may be caused by the moral evil of another.[46] This is the principal difference with regard to Aristotelian mercy: whether or not the one suffering the evil is virtuous. According to Aquinas, Christian mercy is possible for the one who wills moral evil, if the moral evil is no longer willed; that is, if the moral evil is repented, mercy is fitting. The difference between guilty and innocent is no longer so significant in Christian mercy; one can pity the virtuous person who suffers evil and one can pity the "incontinent" person who suffers because he has committed a moral evil and regrets it.

The proper response to divine mercy is penance, which, for Aquinas, is a virtue as well as a sacrament. Penance is a virtue when there is contrition over an evil performed and one acts to "remove the act." The act itself, of course, cannot be removed, but the hope is to remove the punishment for the act. Penance is rooted in the hope that distributive justice can replace corrective justice. Correct justice would require an involuntary punishment that is equal to the offense. Penance substitutes a lesser punishment that is distributive inasmuch as based on the "merit" of contrition, the voluntary assumption of a lesser punishment, and hope in divine mercy. Whereas corrective justice focuses on the question of guilt or innocent, mercy focuses on the question of repentance that is expressed through the merit of voluntary punishment. "Merit" here is much different than Aristotelian merit based on virtue. This is the "merit" of the incontinent person who regrets the evil action that he has performed. Aristotle saw incontinence as typical but embarrassing; it was no more noble than the regrets of a sobered drunk. The conjunction of that repentance and divine mercy becomes, for Aquinas, the basis of a hope that leads to a new focus in the moral life—penance as a response to mercy; mercy to other human beings as a response to having received through hope divine mercy.

In sum, there are differences among Judaism, Christianity, and Islam concerning which differences revelation emphasizes and thus what justice is. This sketch takes no note of the differences between revealed and nonrevealed religion and none of the differences between Judaism and Islam or within Judaism and Islam. There are two sections in the theological part of this volume. The first elaborates the views of justice and diversity among Judaism, Islam, and Catholic, Orthodox, and Protestant Christianity. The second considers some particular theological issues of justice and diversity. It is the aim, then, of this volume to promote greater precision concerning which justice and which diversity is meant in the debate concerning justice and diversity and to highlight that the meanings of these terms and their relationship are a matter of debate. Since virtually all universities see justice and diversity as essential to their mission, a more precise and vigorous debate about justice and diversity is vital to the health of higher education.

THE CHAPTERS

Justice and Diversity from Diverse Philosophical Perspectives

Peter Simpson's account of justice and diversity in virtue-ethics stresses the diversity of justice in Aristotelian ethics that is made possible by the underlying unity of justice. Distributive justice is based on merit—that is, on virtue—and the mean relative to the agent can change from person to person and according to circumstances. Commutative justice can vary with the changes in supply and demand. There is a diversity of regimes that qualify as just, and while what is natural in justice is what happens spontaneously, for the most part, deviations from that are possible based on unique circumstances. Aristotle "steers a mean between the extremes of cultural imperialism and cultural relativism."

Thomas Hibbs's chapter on justice and diversity in Aquinas's natural law argues that "in contrast to the modern tendency towards a homogeneous account of justice, Aquinas recognizes diverse types of obligation." Aquinas's natural law ethics occupies a place between the abstract homogeneity of the Enlightenment and the radical otherness of postmodernity. Contrary to the focus on the excellence of the agent in virtue ethics, justice in Aquinas's natural law focuses on the good of others; it recognizes a diversity of goods and offers hospitality to the other. Justice is ordered to something superior—namely, mercy—and is thereby better able to account for the differing conditions of human beings. Religion, as justice toward God, highlights the difference between human being and God and thus gratitude.

Aaron Szymkowiak examines justice and diversity in deontology and argues that "[p]resent day writers on diversity work almost fully within concepts of self-rule inaugurated by Kant, while simultaneously endeavoring in late-Rawlsian fashion to give cultural identity its due." Although the universality of Kant's categorical imperative must ignore all differences rooted in the particularity of nation, ethnicity, gender, virtue, and nature, such differences remain as a source of conflict and will become the material for moral judgment in Rawls. In contemporary deontology, tolerance, understood as a distancing from all heritages, makes moral reasoning possible.

Raymond Hain treats justice and diversity in utilitarianism. For John Stuart Mill, diversity is subordinated to and judged by the greatest happiness principle. As Hain states, "Diversity is necessary if it promotes the overall greatest good, but if it frustrates that good, it must be suppressed." Peter Singer's utilitarianism argues that the equal right of all to happiness entails an equal claim to the means to happiness. Such justice highlights the sameness of human individuals. Nevertheless, since happiness is pleasure and animals feel pleasure and pain, justice extends to animals, although not equally, inasmuch as they are unable to experience the higher pleasures. Justice thus includes the diversity of humans and animals. Moreover, human individuals are equal only inasmuch as each counts as one, and therefore the happiness of the many can require the sacrifice of anyone.

James Campbell looks at justice and diversity in American pragmatism from the perspective of the moral prophet. James Hayden Tufts distinguishes between progressive justice and the justice of established rights, which considers social inequality as a difference between the naturally strong and the naturally weak. The progressive view sees justice as elimination of the difference between the weak and the strong. John Dewey similarly distinguishes between customary morality, which renders all social differences static, and critical morality, which questions social inequality. William James sees institutions as the great obstacle to such change, and "[f]or James the moral prophet is the determining factor in social change."

Paul Weithman sees John Rawls as the most important philosopher for the question of justice and diversity from an analytical perspective, and he treats current debate in analytical philosophy in relation to Rawls. Weithman describes the change in Rawls's thought as centered on the question of diversity: "In short, Rawls came to realize that while justice requires liberty, liberty would encourage diversity, and diversity would pose a challenge for his accounts of congruence and stability. To meet this challenge, Rawls recast justice as fairness as a political liberalism." A diversity of moral and religious perspectives about the good is compatible with stability, if each finds in justice as fairness a neutral political basis for unity that makes possible such diversity.

Fred Evans's chapter concerns justice and diversity in postmodernism. Rawls is again central, this time in contrast to Jacques Derrida. Rawls achieves unity by distinguishing between justice and the good, and yet his political liberalism is the unacknowledged imposition of the good of political liberalism. Evans argues that "[Rawls's] revised justice as fairness doctrine does not give equal emphasis to diversity let alone provide what is much stronger, a sense in which justice is diversity." For Derrida, justice is diversity. Democracy is always temporally incomplete, undecidable, and beyond all consensus. For Evans, postmodern democracy is like a multivoiced body whose voices never arrive at a unified understanding of justice beyond difference.

Particular Issues in Justice and Diversity: Philosophy

Rémi Brague treats the historical roots of diversity as a positive value in Greek democracy, the toleration that arose after the European wars of religion, modern political philosophy, and commerce. He describes Western culture as a synthesis of two diverse "cities," Athens and Jerusalem, into a third, Rome, and the role of Christianity, especially the Christian notion of law, in that synthesis. Brague argues that the Pauline understanding of law made possible the secular notion of diversity: "Something like profane culture was made possible by Pauline Christianity. . . . What I mean is that culture as such, culture that is only culture, and nothing more, in particular a culture that leaves aside the religious dimension, was made possible by the severance of the Greek *paideia* from its religious elements."

Camille Paglia also discusses three cities—ancient Babylon, Renaissance Venice, and nineteenth-century Philadelphia—as examples of intolerance (amid an overall atmosphere of tolerance) that leads to a heightening of group identity. Paglia sees tolerance and group identity in tension with each other; real tolerance leads to assimilation and a diminishment of group identity. Paglia argues for the necessity of intellectual diversity on college campuses: "Surely tolerance and diversity in regard to race, ethnicity, gender, and sexual orientation must also be extended toward ideological diversity, if colleges and universities are to succeed in their mission of fostering the free exchange of ideas."

Gayatri Chakravorty Spivak, on the one hand, rejects the request to address postmodern feminism: "I refuse to be interpellated as a single-issue visible minority feminist deconstructivist." On the other hand, she treats feminism within her broader understanding of postmodernism. Class, she argues, is the diversity that we are inclined to ignore, and so feminism must be understood within this wider context of social justice: "The right to intellectual labor, the right to abstraction, which is completely not allowed and to women even less, among these literate groups, the right to theorize rather than just apply theory, which is all that the feminism debate is about, and also the right to feel that intellectual labor is important in the face of poor education; these are to me more crucial that the struggle of dominant feminism against postmodernism by hearsay."

Jorge Garcia aims at a philosophical account of racism, which he calls VAR (volitional account of racism): "The appropriate objective of conceptual inquiry into racism is to explicate its nature. VAR is an ontic claim about racism's reality, its essence and nature, undertaken through examining our discourse to identify the assumptions and insights behind it." According to VAR, the primary locus of racism is an individual's attitude: "There is no racism merely in things—'structure,' 'systems,' 'cultures,' 'social imaginaries,' and more—as many today would have it, that has not gotten there from a deeper, more fundamental kind of racism in individuals' attitudes—as we say, in their hearts."

Laura L. Garcia defines feminism, provides a history of feminism, and ultimately argues for a feminism based on natural differences between male and female as complementary: "The complementarity thesis that I propose here consists of three claims: (1) There are significant, innate, gender-based differences between human males and females; (2) These differences complement each other so as to make collaboration between the sexes advantageous to both; and (3) Promoting and celebrating women's distinctive strengths is essential to an authentic feminism."

Robert P. George argues for the justness of immigration and the goodness of the diversity that it brings, which is rooted in the notion that "people really can, in the richest and fullest possible sense, *become* Americans" in a way that one cannot really become Greek, French, or Chinese. Gratitude for American liberty, security, and opportunity is opposed to entitlement, which prevents an immigrant from becoming fully American. The diversity of custom, tradition, and religious identity brought by immigrants is good so long as it does not deny "the fundamental goodness of American principles of political and civil liberty."

John Corvino argues for same-sex marriage and against the new natural law philosophers, who maintain that same-sex marriage is impossible and who are represented in this volume by Sherif Girgis. Corvino and Girgis exchanged drafts of their chapters. Corvino notes that legally "[t]he marriage debate is over, and the gays won." Nevertheless, significant political opposition remains, and a legal victory is not an end to philosophical debate. Corvino contends that Girgis's account of same-sex marriage is a straw man and that Girgis is unable is to define marriage in a way so as to exclude same-sex marriage. He argues that, if same-sex marriage is to be excluded, infertile heterosexual marriage would have to be excluded as well.

Sherif Girgis maintains that Corvino fails to present affirmative reasons for accepting same-sex marriage and that Corvino's definition of marriage is parasitic upon the heterosexual one. Girgis defines marriage by its comprehensiveness: "(a) in the basic dimensions in which it unites two people (body *and* mind); (b) in the goods with respect to which it unites them (with respect to procreation, and hence the broad domestic sharing of family life); (c) in the kind of commitment that it calls for (permanent and exclusive)." An infertile couple fails to meet the "strong" view of marriage thus outlined, but the state should continue recognizing such marriages because "excluding them would have social costs but not social benefits."

Justice and Diversity from Diverse Theological Perspectives

Peter A. Huff offers the acclamation *dignum et iustum* from the liturgy of the Catholic Church as a key to understanding justice and diversity in Catholicism. This liturgical perspective is necessary to balance an excessively soteriological or social justice approach to justice. It affirms the existence of a universal and objective standard of truth by which human acts attain meaning. This standard, through the incarnation of Christ, has a face that serves to unify the diversity of truths and goods and that incarnational presence is extended in history through the Church: "The Church is universal in space, embracing all nations, languages, ethnicities, and cultures. A stunning variety of orders, rites, vocations, charisms, apostolates . . . make the Catholic Church arguably the world's most diverse religious organization . . . and perhaps the world's most diverse organization of any kind."

Dr. Paul L. Gavrilyuk traces the diversity of the Orthodox churches through history from the fall of the Roman and Ottoman empires to national churches, communism, postcommunism, and Orthodoxy's minority status in America: "World Orthodoxy continues its recovery from imperial, colonial, and totalitarian past. The traumas of this past are deep and not likely to heal quickly." The unity of the Orthodox churches is based on adherence to the seven ecumenical councils, a common liturgical tradition, and the episcopacy. "Sobornost" expresses the unity-in-diversity that characterizes Orthodox Christendom—unity of faith and diversity of charism.

D. Stephen Long begins his treatment of justice and diversity in Protestantism by showing how diversity is, in fact, a homogenizing force: "From the military to government to corporations and universities, 'diversity' draws institutions into a common cultural project. . . . By that I mean that a primary function of the affirmation of 'diversity' is to insure sameness across cultural institutions." He traces the various uses of the term *diversity*, and then turns to the Book of Revelation for an understanding of justice and diversity in Protestantism. There he sees diversity as a theological mission of the church—one that is meant to bring healing to the nations. A Protestant understanding of justice is less inclined to turn these historical and cultural particularities into abstractions.

David Novak approaches justice and diversity in the Jewish tradition through the rabbinic discussion of the *ger toshav* or resident alien among the Jewish people, who was owed justice according the Noahide law, which reflects the natural law that guides all nations and that guided Jews before the revelation of the Torah. Until the mid- to late eighteenth century, Jews in Europe were not citizens but a foreign nation to be tolerated. With the emergence of secularized nations, European Jews could become citizens and were owed justice, not mere toleration. Natural law became the public standard for Jews as citizens; revealed law, the basis of their diversity, was a private matter.

Muhammed Zia-ul-Haq and Waleed El-Ansary examine justice and diversity in Islam. Diversity in creation and revelation, in contrast to the absolute unity of God, is the central fact, and pluralism is the central problem of our time: "Unfortunately, such religious diversity does not necessarily lead to religious pluralism, for the latter requires more than tolerance." Responses to this religious diversity range from the claim that (1) all religions are true, (2) none are true, (3) one is true and the others are false, and (4) one is fully true and the others partially true. The last is found in Islam: "Islamic doctrine asserts that all nations have received a prophet who both warns the community and bears glad tidings for fidelity to God. It is the confrontation of this universality of revelation with the multiplicity of race, nations and tribes that necessitates the diversity of revelation." They trace various Islamic legal, theological, and mystical schools in their interpretations of the supercession of Islamic revelation and the justice owed to other revelations.

Particular Issues in Justice and Diversity: Theology

Virgilio Elizondo looks at justice and diversity from the perspective of current immigration into American Catholicism, which is different than previous immigrations because it entails diversity at the level of the parish and not simply the establishment of national churches. Diversity was essential to the justice offered by early Christianity and explains much of its original appeal: "The early Christians were considered atheists because they refused to recognize the national gods of any nation." It was not merely that Christianity ignored national differences, it also ignored other differences that had traditionally been considered most important: "It is in this very radical acceptance of our personal and collective mystery of giftedness/lack, wealth/poverty, blessing/curse, health/sickness, understanding/blindness, saintliness/sinfulness, truth/ambiguity, knowledge/ambiguity, knowledge/ignorance, that we become truly human." A return to this original openness of Christianity requires recognition of the sin of dogmatic ethnocentrism.

Shawn Copeland writes about the relationship between the common good, freedom, and difference; that is, the question is how, from the perspective of political theology, the common good can be reconciled with individual freedom and cultural diversity. Freedom is contrasted with slavery, and slavery in America is understood against the background of the exodus narrative. The teleological view of the common good in classical thought is contrasted with modernity whereby "[p]olitical problems are recast merely as technical ones and a vocabulary of rights and self-interest circumvents concern for duties, obligations and the common good." She analyzes the oppressive differentiation of social groups and cultural imperialism, the universalization of a particular culture. The impact of divine grace on the reconciliation of the common good, freedom, and difference in social life concludes the chapter.

Russell Hittinger's subject is justice and the diversity of rights in Pope John XXIII's 1962 encyclical, *Pacem in terris*, for it encapsulates much of our contemporary debate over the relationship between justice and diversity through the question of the relationship between rights and order. The historical context of the encyclical was a disordered differentiation of the world into "the West" and the communist bloc, of first, second, and third worlds, and of new nations brought about by rapid decolonization. The encyclical asserts the existence of human or natural rights (twenty-five of them) that are based on six modes of order: (1) in the universe, (2) in individual conscience, (3) in human nature, (4) in a political community, (5) between political communities, and (6) in a world community. Rights depend on order, which is cosmological, metaphysical, and anthropological. Hittinger compares this notion of rights to Martin Luther King's *Letter from Birmingham Jail*; the two documents are close temporally, in sources and in their notion of rights. The central debate that the encyclical highlights is "whether human dignity is endowed (in an order prior to our choices) or whether it is constructed (socially, culturally legally)." In other words, are justice and right rooted in natural or artificial differences?

Susannah Heschel describes how Christian justice became the elimination of diversity in Nazi Germany. The German Christian Movement, under the leadership of Walter Grundmann, joined forces with National Socialism for the elimination of un-Germanic differences: "For its part, National Socialism was the military tool of the Institute's goal: eradication of Jews, Judaism and Jewishness." For the German Christian Movement and Grundmann, racial differences were most important, and German Christianity had to be racially distinct and pure. Heschel traces the Movement's attempt to purify Christianity of anything Jewish: Jesus became Aryan; Paul had to be banished. The end of the war was not the end of the Movement's work, and Grundmann remained the most important East German theologian.

Thomas G. Guarino looks at religion, diversity, and tolerance through the lens of Gianni Vattimo's postmodernism in which all truth is inseparable from its historical and cultural context with the result that all claims to truth must be recognized as a provisional hermeneutics. This weak understanding of truth mandates tolerance. Whereas modernity saw dogmatic religion as inherently intolerant and thus confined to the private sphere, Vattimo's postmodernism tolerates the return of "weakened" religion to the public sphere. Guarino considers a different basis for religious tolerance, which is exemplified by Pope Benedict XVI's notion of an autonomous, naturally intelligible world: "There exists a good deal of shared space between Christians and the secular world—a shared political order, shared learning and, at least to some extent, a shared social morality."

Kwame Anthony Appiah treats a central question for the tolerance of diversity within religion (and conversely for the tolerance of religion by secular societies); namely, the justness of homosexual acts. He approaches scripture through interpretation based on a coherentist epistemology: "Christians, who seek a proper understanding of homosexuality, must try to establish a reflective equilibrium among texts that seem to be about homosexuality, other texts, and our wider knowledge of the world beyond the texts." He traces the manifold difficulties in such an interpretation, such as the transcription of oral tradition into written text, canonicity, integrity of the text, and, most importantly, translation. He applies this method to relevant passages in the Old and New Testaments, until he reaches the one most problematic for the licitness of same-sex acts, Romans 1:26–27, where he concludes: "So it seems reasonable, at least, to read Paul as seeing the evidence of infidelity in men and women turning away in their lust from what is natural to *them* . . . . If that is so, then it is at least *possible* to read this passage as critical of homosexual acts only when it is not natural to the person who engages in it." In other words, natural differences are just, and for some homosexuality is natural; others engage in homosexuality from disordered lust rather than from their nature, and such (unnatural) homosexuality is unjust.

Mary Healey sees a consistent condemnation of homosexuality in the Bible and acknowledges that "[t]he biblical teaching on homosexual conduct, interpreted impartially, is deeply challenging to modern sensibilities." It is an obstacle to many accounts of the relationship between justice and diversity. Her interpretation of homosexuality in the Old Testament begins with the account of sexuality in Genesis 1–3, which demythologizes the sexuality of the surrounding pagan cultures and highlights the complementary differences of male and female. Marriage is a covenant, an image of the spousal love that defines the relationship between God and His people. Sin entails a loss of sexual innocence and marital discord. The Sodom story is about homosexual rape, and the Leviticus passages condemn the morality and not just the ritual uncleanness of homosexuality. In the New Testament, Jesus reaffirms the heterosexual complementarity of the Genesis account of marriage, holds his disciples to a higher standard of sexual purity, and sees mercy to sexual sinners as healing rather than acceptance. St. Paul's treatment of homosexuality in Romans 1:24–27 deems it unnatural.

Mark D. Jordan aims to recast debate about the justice of homosexual acts by focusing on two words, *toleration* and *diversity*, viewed in relation to Thomas Aquinas's *Summa theologiae*, and a third, *homophobia*. Aquinas argues that toleration, which is related to courage, allows (suffers) certain evils, including sexual ones, in order to avoid greater ones. Jordan extends the call for tolerance to homosexuality as a positive contribution to patience and spiritual growth. Diversity in nature, for Aquinas, is a finite reflection of divine perfection, and thus Jordan concludes: "So we should ask of sex—as of any created difference—what it shows us about God." By "homophobia," Jordan means the violent reaction to homosexuality that "is a sin against nature so far as it rejects what God intends in creating sexual diversity." In brief, the sin against nature is not homosexuality but homophobia.

John Grabowski considers three contemporary challenges to the traditional Catholic view that nature is the source of justice and that only heterosexuality is natural: (1) heterosexual complementarity can be replaced by personal or individual complementarity; (2) sexual dimorphism is not universal in nonhuman nature; (3) homosexual relationships can conform to the standard of justice as fairness. Grabowski responds that (1) this approach "reduces the category of nature and 'the natural' to an individually constituted reality." (2) Sexual dimorphism "is the basis of the continuation of almost all animal species—at least mammalian ones." (3) Justice is not, as the standard of justice as fairness would maintain, mere sameness; it cannot entail abstraction from the human body and the complementary differentiation of male and female.

Most of the authors in this volume were speakers in a series on "Justice, Tolerance and Diversity" that took place at Xavier University in Cincinnati, Ohio, between September 2011 and April 2014. Xavier University's Ethics/Religion and Society Program sponsored the series, which was supported, in part, by a grant from the National Endowment for the Humanities.

NOTES

1. For Lyotard's predictions about the collapse of the Soviet system, see *The Postmodern Condition*, trans. Geoff Bennington and Brian Massumi (Minneapolis: University of Minnesota Press, 1991[eighth printing]), 12–14 and 38–39. For his predictions about the university, see *The Postmodern Condition*, xxv, 39, 50, 53.

2. See Aristotle, *Metaphysics* XII.5, 1071a1; *Categories* 2, 1a24–25; *Physics* II.3, 194b24–27; *Metaphysics* VII.17, 1041b5–8; *Physics* V.2, 226a19–23; *Metaphysics* VII.10, 1035b28–32; *Metaphysics* IX.9, 1050b2–12; *Physics* II.3, 194b28–32; *Metaphysics* V.2; *Physics* II.1, 192b8–19.

3. Aristotle, *Nichomachean Ethics* V.3, 1131a10–26.

4. *Nichomachean Ethics* V.4.

5. Aristotle, *History of Animals* VIII.1, 588b1–23; *Nichomachean Ethics* I.7, 1097b1–18; Aristotle, *Politics* I.8, 1256b15–20.

6. *Nichomachean Ethics* I.7, 1097b23–1098a5.

7. *Nichomachean Ethics* I.13 and I.4.

8. *Nichomachean Ethics* VII.1.

9. *Nichomachean Ethics* X.6–8.

10. Aristotle, *Politics* I.2, 1253a7–17, in *The Basic Works of Aristotle*, ed. Richard McKeon (New York: Random House, 1941).

11. *Politics* I.1–3.

12. Thomas Hobbes, *Leviathan: Or the Matter, Forme and Power of a Commonwealth Ecclesiasticall and Civil*, ed. Michael Oakeshott (New York: MacMillan, 1962) IV.46.

13. *Leviathan* I.8.

14. *Leviathan* I.6.

15. *Leviathan* I.10, 11.

16. *Leviathan* I.14.

17. *Leviathan* I.8.

18. *Leviathan* I.13.

19. Ibid.

20. Ibid.

21. *Leviathan* I.15.

22. *Leviathan* I.17.

23. *Leviathan* I.21.

24. *Leviathan* I.13, 15 and II.24.

25. *Leviathan* I.21.

26. *The Postmodern Condition: A Report on Knowledge*, 4.

27. *The Postmodern Condition: A Report on Knowledge*, 4–5.

28. *The Postmodern Condition: A Report on Knowledge*, 6 and 11.

29. *The Postmodern Condition: A Report on Knowledge*, 12–13, 15.
30. *The Postmodern Condition: A Report on Knowledge*, 17.
31. *The Postmodern Condition: A Report on Knowledge*, 10.
32. Ibid.
33. *The Postmodern Condition: A Report on Knowledge*, 15.
34. *The Postmodern Condition: A Report on Knowledge*, 44–47.
35. *The Postmodern Condition: A Report on Knowledge*, 46.
36. *The Postmodern Condition: A Report on Knowledge*, 66.
37. *The Postmodern Condition: A Report on Knowledge*, 82.
38. *The Postmodern Condition: A Report on Knowledge*, 31–41.
39. *The Postmodern Condition: A Report on Knowledge*, 39.
40. *The Postmodern Condition: A Report on Knowledge*, 50–53.
41. John Esposito, *What Everyone Needs to Know About Islam* (Oxford: Oxford University Press, 2011), 77.
42. Thomas Aquinas, *Summa theologiae* I., q. 21, a. 1.
43. *Summa theologiae* I.42.1, ad 4, in *The Summa Theologica of St. Thomas Aquinas*, trans. English Dominicans (Benzinger Bros., 1948; Christian Classics, 1981). See also *Summa theologiae* II-II.58.2: "I answer that, As state above (Q. 57, A. 1) since justice by its name implies equality, it denotes essentially relation to another, for a thing is equal, not to itself, but to another."
44. Thomas Aquinas, *Summa contra gentiles* IV.11.
45. See, for example, Matthew 5.7, Matthew 9.13, Luke 6.36, Romans 9.14–29, and James 2.13.
46. See Aristotle, *Rhetoric* II.8–9 and *Poetics* 13.

I

Justice and Diversity from Diverse Philosophical Perspectives

I

JUSTICE AND DIVERSITY IN VIRTUE ETHICS

Peter Simpson, City University of New York

It might seem that there could be no diversity in justice for virtue ethics since justice is one of the virtues and to practice this justice is one thing, not many things. Specifically it would seem that it could never be the case that justice could be many and diverse. Particular just acts might be many and diverse, but what it is just to do here and now for this person in these circumstances would seem always to be one and the same, as it would seem also to be for the other virtues. For while the virtuous mean is relative to the agent, it is not relative to the opinions of the agent; it is relative rather to objective facts about the agent, as to his person, his emotions, his context, the object of his act, and the like. Two people similarly disposed and circumstanced would, one supposes, have the same virtuous mean in the same case.

But however it may be with the other virtues, in the case of justice there is in fact considerable diversity as to what things are just when and where. The evidence is best explored (because of limits of space and because of the excellence of his presentation) in light of the treatment of justice by Aristotle. In the justly celebrated book five of the *Nicomachean Ethics* (or book four of the *Eudemian Ethics*), Aristotle gives a comprehensive account of justice in all its forms, and his account has seldom if at all been bettered.

THE MAIN DIVERSITIES IN JUSTICE

One of the striking things about Aristotle's account is that he openly admits that the virtue of justice is not one but many. He has at least three kinds of justice: universal (or legal) justice as opposed to particular justice, and, within particular justice, distributive as opposed to commutative justice (*Ethics* 5, chapters 1–2). Universal justice is the practice of all the virtues in view of the community, the political community, and is, as Aristotle himself remarks, the perfection of virtue simply. Universal justice would therefore seem to be one thing—namely, the perfect virtue of the perfect man—and having made this point Aristotle leaves it aside because it has, in effect, been explained in the explanation of all the particular virtues in the previous books of the *Ethics*.

About distributive and commutative justice, which concern the distribution and the exchange of goods among persons in community, each again would seem to be one thing. Certainly each is explained in terms of one pattern of analysis, since distributive justice is a matter of proportional equality and commutative justice of numerical equality (chapters 3–4). Both equalities are equalities, to be sure, but very different equalities. So we have three kinds of justice but each kind is, in itself, single.

The matter, however, is not so simple. For, to begin with, Aristotle notes that there can be several different principles of merit for determining proportional equality (as wealth, virtue, freedom), and since each principle will determine proportion differently, there will be as many kinds of distributive justice as there are principles of merit. Within the *Ethics*, Aristotle does not decide between these principles. In the *Politics* he does, and there he says that only the principle of merit based on virtue is correct while those based on wealth or freedom are incorrect. By correct and incorrect he means, in the context, conformity to the common good, since the correct principle serves the common good while the deviant ones serve some private good. But still Aristotle seems willing to speak of kinds of justice in conformity with the deviant principles, as of democratic justice and of oligarchic justice. Are these deviant kinds of justice really justice or not? If they are deviant, how can they be just? If they are just, how, since they are deviant, can justice be one or, indeed, a virtue?

Analogous problems arise about commutative justice. First of all the principle is clear, that an exchange is just when the parties to the exchange have, after the exchange, equal to what they had before the exchange, as that if, to use Aristotle's example, five pairs of shoes are equal to one house, then cobbler and builder will have equality after their exchange if the cobbler gives the builder five pairs of shoes and receives from the builder one house. There are, however, two issues here. First, how to calculate the relative worth of different things, as shoes and houses, and second, since exchange presupposes an already existing partition of different goods (as that the builder has a number of houses and the cobbler a number of pairs of shoes) and aims only to preserve the equality of that partition, what to say of the justice of the partition in the first place? For could not some way of partitioning such goods be unjust, and if it was, how would we know and with what sort of injustice would it be unjust?

As to the first point, calculating the relative worth of different goods, Aristotle's answer is through the idea of reciprocity that he adapts from the Pythagoreans (chapter 5). So, in order to know what is equal in an exchange of shoes and houses, it is not enough to count the things (as five shoes against five houses); one must also proportion the things to the exchangers. A house is worth more than a pair of shoes, so in order to calculate equality of exchange between houses and shoes, one must first calculate the respective worth of house and shoe. The theoretical principle or reciprocity Aristotle gives here, that of diagonal conjunction, is clear. Shoes are to houses what a cobbler is to a builder, so that if, say, five pairs of shoes are to a cobbler what one house is to a builder (the example is schematic), then the equality of exchange will be secured if the cobbler gives the builder five pairs of shoes for one house. The exchange will now satisfy Pythagorean reciprocity, for the cobbler will do to the builder what the builder does to the cobbler, namely, give him his work back. Such reciprocity is, therefore, a case of commutative justice.

This theoretical principle as thus simply stated is clear, but its application to practice is not. For how does one measure a builder against a cobbler so as to calculate the relative worth of houses and shoes? Aristotle gives two answers, one immediate to practice and one more removed from it. The first answer is that money determines the worth (5.1133a19–24): a shoe is worth a certain amount in drachmas or dollars and a house is worth some other amount. So convert the shoes and the houses to their worth in the relevant currency and give for a house that amount of shoes whose denomination in currency is the same as the denomination for the house. Cobbler and builder will thus (as reciprocity requires) get their work back if they exchange with each other at the money rate (or, as is more likely, if they directly exchange money—money they have first acquired through selling their respective products).

Such monetary transactions are the way most people most of the time carry out exchanges with each other and exchanges that are, for the most part, to each party's satisfaction. But the recourse to money does not answer the question how to measure a builder against a cobbler, for it assumes this measuring has already been done and takes the existence and the function of money for granted. How then is the measuring done? Aristotle gives here his second and more removed answer that the determination is done by need or demand (5.1133a25–29, b6–13, 20). Houses and shoes are worth the need they satisfy, for the need determines how much people are willing to give to get what they need. If the need is great and the availability of the things small, the price will be high; if the need is small and the availability great, the price will be low. We know this phenomenon as the law of supply and demand, and though Aristotle does not use these terms or state the law, it is clear he has it in mind (it is obvious enough to reflection). Hence, supply and demand determine money values; money values determine equality in exchange; equality in exchange is commutative justice.

Coming now to the second point, about the partition of goods in the first place that form the elements of exchange, one may well raise a question about the justice of diagonal conjunction as Aristotle describes it. Or rather one might raise a question about the justice of the criterion of supply and demand used to apply it in practice. For if someone powerful were to manipulate supply and demand, so as to maximize his own profits and impoverish others, would he not be acting unjustly? With what sort of injustice, then, would he be acting (for he would not be acting against justice in exchange if justice in exchange follows the diagonal conjunction that is itself determined by supply and demand)? How, then, and by whom should his injustice be corrected?

Here Aristotle would no doubt have recourse to one of the other kinds of justice he has presented. In particular he would have recourse to universal or legal justice. For someone who exploited economic conditions for personal gain at the expense of others would be failing in the virtue of liberality or generosity, since he would be taking from where he should not (*Ethics* 4, chapter 1). So he would be failing in universal justice to the extent he was failing to use the virtue of liberality in view of the common good. But if the failure in liberality were not that of one or two individuals but of the political system, as we might say, because the system was arranged to benefit some and harm others, then distributive justice would come into play. For the system would not be directed to the common good but to the private good of some part or group in the political community. It would be the system of some deviant or incorrect political regime. Typically it would be the deviant regime of oligarchy or tyranny. Such a regime is simply unjust but it is, relative to its principle of merit, in a way just, for it would be distributing goods according to that principle. Correction here would require going back and behind the idea of distributive justice as such (which simply asserts proportional equality according to some principle or other of merit) to the idea of political justice or the idea of what the common good really is. For correct and deviant regimes, while they each accord with their own principle, do not each accord with the principle or nature of political community. This principle is the common good, and the common good, within virtue ethics, is precisely virtuous life. Those regimes that are ruled by the virtuous and that aim at virtue are correct, therefore, and those regimes that are not ruled by the virtuous and aim at something else are not correct.

Here, as is evident, the understanding of Aristotle's account of justice needs to be supplemented by his understanding of the kinds of political regimes. The three regimes of kingship, aristocracy, and polity are all correct regimes because they are ruled by the virtuous and aim at virtue. The three regimes of tyranny, oligarchy, and democracy are all incorrect because they are not ruled by the virtuous nor aim at virtue, but tyranny is ruled by one corrupt man and aims at the advantage of the tyrant, oligarchy is ruled by the corrupt wealthy and is aimed at the advantage of the wealthy, and democracy is ruled by the corrupt poor and aims at the advantage of the poor (*Politics* 3, chapter 7). Each of these six regimes (or of more than six, since Aristotle allows that there are subvarieties within these kinds, as that there are several varieties of democracy and of oligarchy, *Politics* 4) expresses a kind of justice, the distributive justice that accords with its chosen principle of merit (virtue, wealth, freedom). But not all these kinds of justice are equally just, but the justice of the correct regimes is just simply while the justice of the deviant regimes is just according to a supposition; namely, the supposition that the regime is deviant in one of the ways stated.

Here, indeed, is one striking way in which for Aristotle, and so for virtue theory in general insofar as it is dependent on Aristotle, there can be many and diverse kinds of justice, indeed kinds of justice that are diverse in justice since some are simply just and others only on a supposition. Aristotle's diversity of justice, then, is real since he has many and indeed conflicting kinds of justice (for democratic justice conflicts with oligarchic justice). But this diversity is not a bare or brute diversity. It is not a case of that being just for me that I think is just, and that being just for you that you think is just. On the contrary, while indeed justice does vary according to what we think (as that the justice of democracy varies from the justice of oligarchy according to what democrats and oligarchs think), there is nevertheless an objective way of judging the justice of the variations in justice. For there is an objective way of judging the justice of regimes—namely, by reference to the common good, or the perfect virtue of the perfect man. This objective way returns us in fact to the first justice Aristotle isolated; namely, universal or legal justice. This justice is first not only in order of presentation but also in logic. The other kinds of justice, distributive and commutative, while each has its own internal account of its own justice, is also measured as to its conformity to justice simply by reference back to the universal justice of complete virtue.

In the case of distributive justice, the measure is plain. Those regimes and those principles of merit are just which put virtue first, and those unjust which put something else in place of virtue. In the case of commutative justice the measure is similarly plain. For if there is some individual who is exploiting the laws of supply and demand, and so the concrete operation of commutative justice, to benefit himself at the expense of others, this individual will be adjudged unjust by reference to the virtue of generosity that is part of universal justice. If, however, there is some political system that exploits the laws of supply and demand, and so the concrete operation of commutative justice, to benefit one class in the community at the expense of others, that system and that class will be adjudged unjust also by reference to universal justice. For the system and the class will be unjust because they are based on and use a deviant principle of merit, and the principle of merit is deviant because it conflicts with the common good, which is universal justice.

Commutative justice is thus derivative first from distributive justice and second, and thereby, from universal justice; that is, the common good. The common good is virtue, and virtuous citizens, because they will have virtuous desires, will give a virtuous form to the operations of supply and demand on which commutative justice is based. Commutative justice will therefore in a way always be justice, for it will always ensure equality in exchange. But the equal exchange it ensures will not always be virtuous, or will only be as virtuous as are the people involved in the exchanging. For if the people are vicious and manipulate supply and demand to their own advantage, the equal exchange secured by commutative justice will be unjust. It will, if you like, be an unjust justice.

UNNOTICED DIVERSITIES IN JUSTICE

So much concerns the diversities of justice in virtue ethics that are fairly well known and fairly well recognized. But there is a further diversity which, while its existence has long been noticed, has not always been properly understood. It concerns the puzzling and cryptic remarks made by Aristotle when he distinguishes the political just into the natural and the legal. These remarks have seldom been properly understood because they are examined only in the form they take within the *Nicomachean* (or *Eudemian*) *Ethics*, and not also in the form they take within the *Great Ethics* (an exception is Dirlmeier,[1] but he does little more than refer to the fact).

There is, of course, a ready explanation for the neglect by scholars of this other discussion. For most scholars dismiss the *Great Ethics* as spurious. Fully to examine the reasons given for *GE*'s inauthenticity would here take us too far afield. Suffice it to note, first, that the majority of scholars who have devoted serious study to *GE* (notably Von Arnim and Dirlmeier) do think it genuine, and, second, that *GE* itself contains a passage that is almost a self-confession by the author that he is Aristotle. The passage (1201b24–26) is a reference to the *Analytics* and to something "we said" in that work. If the *Analytics* is the *Posterior Analytics* of Aristotle, then here is Aristotle saying directly in *GE* that he wrote *GE*. The reference can be explained away, for perhaps the *Analytics* is the lost work of the same name by Theophrastus. The burden of proof, however, is on those who deny *GE* to Aristotle, since, apart from the internal reference just mentioned, the work is universally attributed to Aristotle by the ancient tradition, and, as Rowe wisely remarks,[2] we should accept the tradition unless we have compelling reasons against it. But it will be enough for present purposes if the passage in *GE* gives us clues for making sense of the parallel passage in *NE/EE*, and indeed a sense that, on careful consideration, that passage itself can be seen to point to.

To begin with, then, here are translations of the relevant texts, first from *NE/EE* and second from *GE*.

> *NE* 5.7.1134b18–15a3: Of the political just there is the natural and the legal: natural being what has everywhere the same force and not because it is thought so or not thought so; legal being what makes no difference this way or that at the start but does after people lay it down, as to charge a mina for a ransom. . . . Some think everything is of this sort because what is by nature is unchangeable and has everywhere the same force, as that fire burns both here and among Persians, but they see just things changing. This is not how it is, except in a way, though at any rate with the gods perhaps it is not so at all. With us there is something that is by nature. Everything may be changeable but yet one thing is by nature and another not by nature. Which sort is by nature, given that things can also be otherwise, and which sort is not but is by law and contract, if indeed both are changeable, is likewise plain. In fact, the same definition will fit the other cases. For by nature the right hand is stronger, yet there are some who could become dexterous with both. What is by contract and what is of advantage in things just are like measures. For measures of wine and grain are not everywhere equal but greater for buying and less for selling.
>
> *GE* 1.33.1194b30–5a6: Among just things some are by nature and some by law. But one should not take this in such a way that they are things that never change. For even things that are by nature partake of change; I mean, for example, that if all of us were to practice always throwing with our left hand we would become ambidextrous. Yet by nature, at any rate, it is a left hand, and right-handed things are no less by nature better than the left hand even if we were to do everything with our left hand as with our right. Nor is it because things change that they are therefore not by nature. But if it is for the most part and for the longer time that the left hand stays thus being a left hand and the right hand a right hand, then this is by nature. The same with things that are just by nature: it is not the case that, if they change because of our use, therefore there is no just by nature. On the contrary there is; for what persists for the most part, that is on its face just by nature. For what we set down and accept as law, that is both precisely just and we call it just by law; therefore what is by nature is a better just than what is by law.

It is standard Aristotelian doctrine that things by nature are things that happen always or for the most part. Things that happen for the most part exist by nature even though sometimes they do not happen or happen differently. One is inclined to suppose that in the passage of *NE/EE* and in that of *GE* Aristotle has this point in mind. For he gives an example of things by nature that can change or happen differently; namely, the dexterity of the hands. The left and right hands are naturally different and are naturally fitted to do different things, but it is possible, by repeated practice, to make them do the same things and become ambidextrous. This point is, of course, not refuted by the existence of naturally left-handed people. For the same natural difference between the hands appears in them too, only the other way round, and it is their left hand rather than their right hand that is naturally more dexterous. Skill, we may say, naturally goes with one hand, and this natural differentiation remains the natural differentiation even if practice can bring the other hand up to the skill of the first. The reason, Aristotle adds in *GE*, is that the left and right hands are differentiated as left and right for the most part and for the longer time, or, in other words, that most people have the right hand more dexterous than the other and can only become ambidextrous after much practice. The same applies to justice as to hands, that the changes we make in naturally just things do not mean that there is no just by nature, for here as there what is for the most part is by nature.

The implication seems to be, then, that the just by nature is only what holds for the most part, so that occasions can arise where the just by nature no longer holds, or where, as it seems, what it is just to do here and now is other than what is naturally just. The further implication, then, seems to be that there is nothing that by nature is always and everywhere unjust to do, for occasions can arise where what it is just to do is what ordinarily or naturally it is unjust to do.

In fact, however, Aristotle's remarks do not have this implication. He has earlier in *GE* distinguished his discussion of justice into three topics: the "what" of justice, the "in what" of justice, and the "about what" of justice (1193a39–b1). As is made evident by how his analysis proceeds in the following pages, he means by the "what" of justice equality (1193b19–30): the unjust man wrongs by taking more of the good and less of the bad and the man whom he wrongs is wronged by having the opposite, so justice is the equal that brings the more and the less into the mean of the equal. The "in what" of justice is the persons and the things in which there is equality, and this equality, since it involves at least four terms (two persons and two shares), is an equality of proportion: as A is to B so C is to D. The "in what" of justice, therefore, is persons and things as equalized through this proportion (1193b30–94a18). The "about what" of justice, by contrast, turns on whether justice, which is a relation to another, is about relations to all others or only to some. For there are relations between masters and slaves and fathers and sons, and there is, by the same token, a just that exists in this relation. Aristotle dismisses justice in these cases as equivocal with the political just (1194b10–28). The political just exists in equality, which he then explains means the equality of the citizens in all being alike in their nature as citizens (even if they differ in other respects, 1194b5–10). He then adds (b28–30) that, since the just exists properly in the political community, justice is "about" the political just. Hence the "about what" of justice refers to what goes on between citizen equals and not, say, to what goes on between fathers and sons or masters and slaves.

But what is it that goes on between citizens? Or what are the things that citizens have political justice about? Here is where the extended passage quoted from *GE* above begins (and analogously where the parallel passage in *NE/EE* begins), and where Aristotle introduces his distinction between just things by nature and just things by law (1194b30ff.). His remarks are thus less cryptic than they may seem. For since he is not talking now of what justice is (equality), nor of what justice is in (persons and things related by proportion), but of what it is about, the just things that justice is about must be the things that citizens share with each other (and in respect of which they seek the equality of proportion that is the "what" and "in what" of justice). But there is clearly plenty of variation here. In some cities these things are shared and not those, and shared with these people and not those (or these people are treated as citizens to share with and not those), while in other cities the things shared and the persons sharing (those counted as citizens) are different, or at any rate include more or fewer people and things. The fact of such variation is obvious, and any study, even today, of comparative politics and comparative anthropology would be rich in discovering examples of it.

Now some of these variations will turn out to be rare and some to be more common, or to exist for the most part. These variations will also reflect the different usages of different peoples and places. But "it is not the case that, if they [things just by nature] change because of our use, therefore there is no just by nature," for "on the contrary there is; for what persists for the most part, that is on its face just by nature" (1195a1–4). Accordingly those customs about who shares what and with whom that exist for the most part in political communities will be the natural ones. When Aristotle continues, therefore, by saying that what we set down and accept as law "is both precisely just and we call it just by law; therefore what is by nature is a better just than what is by law" (1195a4–6), his meaning is that, while all communities lay down their own customs as law and call these customs just, yet the customs that are by nature (those that are for the most part) are better. Why are they better? Because they are in line with what holds for the most part; for thus they will not need any extra effort or time to develop. They will, on the contrary, arise spontaneously, as it were, in the way that people are for the most part right-handed and naturally develop skill in their right hand, becoming ambidextrous, if at all, only by some extra and unusual practice. But it does not follow that other customs, which are not by nature, are thereby not just or even that they are less just (or it does not follow for this reason). All that follows is that they are not the norm and require special effort and exercise in order to be established. The natural ones are therefore better (though not thereby more just) because they are easily and more effectively reached and are equally good or equally serve the purpose (as is also true of not bothering to become ambidextrous).

The passage in *NE/EE* about the natural and the political just can be seen to be saying the same thing. It follows a previous discussion of the "what" and "in what" of justice (5/4, chapters 1–6), and it also draws distinction between the natural just and the just by law. The distinction is multiple because, as emerges, some of the things by law are natural and some are not, and of those that are not natural, some are initially indifferent and some are not. The legal things that are not naturally just but are indifferent are mentioned first. They are distinguished in that the natural is what is unchangeable and has the same force everywhere, while the legal is what is initially indifferent but ceases to be so when a law is laid down (as about what religious sacrifices to make to whom). There is no problem about these legal justs, either about how they relate to the natural just or about their justice (they relate and are just by legal fiat). Such law-created just, while it will vary indefinitely from place to place, is not arbitrary but rationally related to the common good (as honoring past benefactors by sacrifice is for the common good because it is naturally just to give thanks).

There natural just, however, is not that which is unchangeable and has the same force everywhere. For there appears, in human affairs, to be no just of this sort but everything in them is changeable. The natural in this case is the normal, but nothing prevents this normal being changed in particular places and for particular reasons and being good, or even better, if so changed. The example of hands again makes the point. Normally people are right-handed (or are skilled only with one hand, which for some may be the left hand), but they could, by practice, become skilled with both. Being ambidextrous is not normal and so, to this extent, not natural. But it is not unnatural either, if by unnatural is meant bad or unjust, for there is nothing bad or unjust about being ambidextrous. Hence Aristotle adds a remark about contracts and advantage in things just, that there are variations here according to variations in utility. These variations are good because they enable us to go on achieving what is advantageous despite changes in need and circumstance. The end, we may therefore say, is everywhere the same—namely, the good of common life—but the ways of getting there, whether by sharing these things or also those, whether by using these measures or others, vary infinitely. Such variation in achieving the end is a feature of human life because human life is subject to change. It is not a feature, perhaps, of divine life (1134b28–30), for the gods are above the world of change and they and their state are always the same way.

Another part of what Aristotle means (and that is not in *GE*) can be discerned from his closing remark about regimes (1135a3–5), that these too are not everywhere the same though one is everywhere according to nature the best. Regimes vary from place to place, but some regimes are correct and others deviant. The correct regimes (kingship, aristocracy, polity) are correct because they pursue the common good, and they pursue the common good because the ruling body in each case is virtuous (with complete virtue in the case of kingship and aristocracy, with military virtue in the case of polity). The deviant regimes (tyranny, oligarchy, democracy) are deviant because they do not pursue the common good, and their ruling bodies are not virtuous (*Politics* 3.6–7). These rankings are everywhere the same, and among them kingship is always best. Hence Aristotle is presumably referring to kingship when he says that one regime is everywhere according to nature best. The regimes, however, that suit given cities are not everywhere the same, but for some kingship suits, for others aristocracy, for others polity; the deviant regimes may also suit some regimes, not by nature (for no deviant regime accords with nature [*Politics* 3.17.1287b39–41]), but because the citizens can only choose a deviant regime and not a correct one (*Politics* 6(4).12–13). In an extended sense, therefore, a deviant regime may be said to be natural for this or that city, if it will not tolerate a correct one.

A correct regime can, however, always in principle be set up, even in those cities that refuse a correct regime, for these cities will nevertheless have enough virtuous citizens in them to form the basis of a correct regime (whether a democratically leaning polity or an oligarchically leaning one [*Politics* 6(4).7–9, 11]). If they do not have enough virtuous citizens in them, then they are naturally slavish and may justly be subjected by force to a virtuous master (*Politics* 1.6–7), and under a master, if they do not have the political just, they will have the domestic just, for slaves share in the domestic just (earlier here, at 6.1134b8–17). Still, even where a correct regime can be set up, because the citizens are willing, the correct regime will not everywhere be the same. It will, however, everywhere be natural, for all correct regimes accord with nature.

Aristotle's position, then, on regimes and on the natural just steers a mean between the extremes of cultural imperialism and cultural relativism. It is not culturally imperialistic because it does not say that if some city does not have the regime that my city has, therefore I should say or think that that city is unjust or unnatural (for, on the contrary, if it has a correct regime, it will not be). The position is not culturally relativist because it does not say that all regimes everywhere are natural or just. On the contrary, it says that some are natural and just and others unnatural and unjust.

Aristotle has thus shown what the just and unjust things are and in how many ways and differences they exist (by nature, as in the correct regimes, by necessary concession, as in deviant regimes, and by order, as in laws about things originally indifferent). It is only by knowing what the just things are that we will also know what actions and persons are just or unjust. Without this knowledge we may, for instance, be tempted to say that those who sacrifice, say, to Brasidas are unjust because we do not sacrifice to Brasidas, and since what we do is just, what they do, if it is different, must be unjust. But it is not. On the contrary it is just; only it is just for them and not for us (for they have a law about it and we do not).

We may be likewise tempted to say that those who have a different regime from ours have an unjust regime, for our regime is just and since theirs is different it cannot be just. But, again, it can be just; only it is just for them and not for us (they have someone virtuous enough to be king, while we only have those virtuous enough to be aristocrats or rulers of a polity). And even if it is not just (for it is a deviant regime), it may be the closest to justice they are currently willing or able to go. Nevertheless, despite all these relativities, we will still be able to rank all the just things that we find in different times and places according to a standard that is everywhere the same: the standard of nature that ranks kingship best and the others after it, some as correct and others as deviant (and the deviant as some more and some less bad [*Politics* 6(4).4–6]).

Aristotle's discussion of justice thus expressly allows for a considerable amount of diversity, a diversity of things that are nevertheless all just, as that this thing is just here but not there, or just for me but not for you. But this diversity is not an anarchic relativism. It is a systematic devolution from a single first principle. That first principle is the perfect virtue of the perfect man that constitutes universal or legal justice and the common good. From this principle flow first, as regards distributive justice, the division of regimes into correct and deviant. Second, there flows the acceptability, indeed the justice, of deviant regimes in particular circumstances—not justice simply, but justice on the basis of a supposition (the supposition that a better regime is not practically possible). Third, there flows the variability of commutative justice according to the principles of exchange as determined by the law of supply and demand. Commutative justice is always justice if equality is observed after the exchange as before. But it need not be just with distributive or with universal justice if the equality preceding the exchange was a distribution against the correct principle of merit or against virtue. The injustices of commutative justice are understood and corrected, not by commutative justice, but by distributive and universal justice to which recourse must always ultimately be had.

Even so, despite this hierarchical systematizing of justice, there are many just and unjust things in community life that are just and unjust by mere convention, such as the cases mentioned of whom to make sacrifices to, or by what normally prevails, as the right hand being stronger than the left. The opposites of these things are not simply unjust even if they may be unjust for us here and us now. On the contrary, they could and would be unjust if they prevailed anywhere. But they would be just only there where they prevailed and not elsewhere.

Diversity in justice is real for Aristotle but it is not arbitrary. There is a hierarchy that establishes a final and objective standard, the standard of the perfect virtue of universal justice.

NOTES

1. F. Dirlmeier, *Aristoteles: Nikomachische Ethik, übersetzt und kommentiert* (Berlin,1956), 420–21, where he simply repeats, without comment, what *GE* says. His discussion directly of the *GE* passage (1958, 323–24) is brief and misses what, in this chapter, is argued to be its chief significance for understanding the *NE/EE* passage.

2. C. J. Rowe, *The Eudemian and Nicomachean Ethics: A Study in the Development of Aristotle's Thought* (Cambridge: Cambridge Philological Society, 1971), 12.

2

THOMAS AQUINAS ON JUSTICE AND THE DIVERSITY OF GOODS

Thomas Hibbs, Baylor University

Some years ago, Charles Taylor raised questions about the ability of the dominant Kantian and utilitarian schools of ethics to account for the "diversity of goods."[1] Similar criticisms of what might be called decision-procedure models of ethics can be found in the writings of a number of mid- to late-twentieth-century moral philosophers and date back at least to the concluding paragraphs of Elizabeth Anscombe's "Modern Moral Philosophy."[2] Virtue ethics arose in part as a way of offering a better account of the diversity of goods. Yet virtue ethics has been accused of not being diverse enough, as it seems to focus exclusively on goods of the agent and to downplay the goods of others. It also seems ill-equipped to address the needs of citizens in large and diverse societies in which there is little or no shared vision of the good. For Thomas Aquinas, who has both an account of the virtues and an account of the duties of the natural law, justice ranks as a preeminent virtue, whose focus is on the good of others. Moreover, diversity of types of obligation and complexity in the standards of the appraisal of human action enter into the very heart of Aquinas's account of justice; in contrast to the modern tendency toward a homogeneous account of justice, Aquinas recognizes diverse types of obligation.

There is an irony here. Decision-procedure models were constructed at least in part to accommodate widespread diversity of views about the good, to find a way of living politically that would allow for diversity, within limits whose scope and nature vary from thinker to thinker and regime to regime, to flourish or at least not be forced to conform to public-enforced visions of the good. Precisely because they seek, in the minimalist versions to which they naturally tend, a least common denominator, they foster homogeneity and uniformity.

Postmodern critiques of the Enlightenment have latched on to the way in which the universality and impersonality of its ethics marginalize diversity. Yet in the celebration of diversity and otherness, postmodernists create epistemological and ethical problems. How are we to recognize the radically other? And how are we to distinguish ethically between virtuous and vicious otherness? So modern conceptions of ethics and politics bring to the fore the demands of justice and diversity, yet the Enlightenment model too quickly abstracts from diversity while postmodernity tends to radicalize otherness in a way that undermines the possibility of a just response. Having attended to the dilemmas of otherness, we will turn to an account of justice; namely, that of Thomas Aquinas, which includes not only what is legally due to others but also what is due to others in a broader ethical sense best captured in notions of solidarity or hospitality.

THE DIVERSITY OF GOODS AND THE PROBLEM OF OTHERNESS

Attending principally to utilitarianism and secondarily to Kantianism, Charles Taylor's essay "The Diversity of Goods" underscores the way in which each of these theories promises an escape from the messy realm of qualitative ethical discourse, a realm in which various accounts of the good vie for our allegiance. Part of the appeal of utilitarianism and Kantianism is epistemological. The former purports to rest upon a conceptually uncontroversial expression of what constitutes human happiness and a calculus to guide deliberation about what is obligatory. Similarly, Kantian formalism offers a clear "underlying model of validation." Both "allow us to ignore the problematic distinctions between different qualities of action or modes of lie, which play such a large part in our actual moral decisions." They offer the "hope of deciding ethical questions without having to determine which of a number of rival languages of moral virtue and vice, of the admirable and the contemptible, of unconditional versus conditional obligation, are valid." Taylor calls these the "languages of qualitative contrast."[3]

Modern theories suggest ways of transcending or circumventing disputes over the good by recourse to an impersonal and abstract decision-procedure. In place of heterogeneity there would be uniformity; in place of diversity, unity. For all the appeal to the way these theories embody rigorous, scientific models of rationality, they also draw upon "substantive moral insights." Kantian views draw upon the "universal attribution of moral personality," while utilitarianism draws strength from the view that there is "no defensible distinction between different classes of human beings."[4]

That decision-procedure model of ethics draws upon substantive moral insights is instructive. They presuppose and never fully transcend ethical insights latent within every day, prescientific moral life. But that turns our attention back to what we might call following Husserl, the sedimented languages of moral contrast. As Taylor observes, we invoke a wide range of principles, ideals, and sources of evaluation. Among these are the insights that inform utilitarianism and Kantianism. Indeed, "'rational' as used by most utilitarians is a term in a qualitative contrast: it is the basis of moral admiration and contempt; it is a goal worthy of respect. The fact that it finds no place in their own meta-theory says a lot about the value of this theory."[5] The languages of qualitative contrast can generate not just different conceptions of what it means to lead a noble or admirable human life but divergent and incompatible accounts of obligation. We ponder not just what is right or wrong but what is "morally higher or lower, noble or base, admirable or contemptible."[6] The presence of the adverb *morally* is noteworthy. Utilitarian and Kantian theories do not have an exclusive purchase on the notion of the moral. Taylor concludes, "The ethical is not a homogeneous domain, with a single kind of good, based on a single kind of consideration."

Taylor's insistence on an irreducible diversity of ethical discourses reflects his own practice as a philosopher. Over a long career, he has examined the varied and conflicting "sources" of the modern self, the varieties of religious belief and even of styles of secularism. He has also written explicitly on multiculturalism.[7] In all these areas he has resisted reductionist accounts, of ethical languages, of modernity, of religion, and of secularism. In "The Politics of Recognition," Taylor makes a case for diversity, for a balanced approached to multiculturalism and the expansion of the canon in university curricula. The task is to develop "new vocabularies of comparison" that enable us to reach "judgments through transforming our standards."⁸ Of course, the celebration of new vocabularies and of the "strange and unfamiliar" is all the rage in certain academic fields and in academic culture generally. A number of important philosophical questions typically get suppressed in the midst of the cheerleading for otherness. There seems to be a normative assumption, at least in the manner in which the injunction to cultivate diversity is delivered, that the strange, unfamiliar, and the new is of necessity better or at least that its presence imposes some sort of moral obligation on us.

There are serious problems with any radical postmodern conception of otherness. Commenting on Derrida's phrase *every other is wholly other*, Denys Turner observes that the

> Otherness of another person . . . cannot be an absolute heterogeneity; an incorrigible and incommunicable 'thisness' which is not a this something or other; it cannot be an inaccessible singularity, not unless some ethic of the other is to be founded upon the otherness of the other as some blank, anonymous referent point of a semantically empty demonstrative pronoun.⁹

Richard Kearney expands on this point. He categorizes the fascination with radical otherness as a form of "postmodern sublime," which—in the field of continental philosophy of religion—is purportedly a way of avoiding an idolatrous philosophy of presence. But what it invites is a new and different sort of "idolatry: that of the immemorial, ineffable Other." Kearney worries that the absolute alterity of the divine deprives us of any basis upon which to distinguish God from a "sublime monster," the love of God from madness. It is less likely to generate "praxis than paralysis." He explains, "If the saturated phenomenon is really . . . bedazzling . . . , how can we tell the difference between the divine and its opposite? How are we to distinguish between enabling and disabling revelations?" As Kearney writes in *Strangers, Gods and Monsters*, the obsession with the radical other courts regression to a pre-Hebraic sublime, to mythic monsters beyond good and evil. If the "Other surpasses all our categories of interpretation and representation, we are left with a problem—the problem of discernment. How can we tell the difference between benign and malign others?"¹⁰ The celebration of radical alterity, of that which transgresses "the limits of representation," ends up "negating any notion of the ethical."¹¹ Whatever function the jarring experience of unanticipated otherness might have, it cannot by itself constitute an ethic. If we cannot even meaningfully describe the other—a point on which Turner and Kearney concur—then how could we begin to know how we ought to comport ourselves with respect to the other?

The promotion of difference for its own sake is not just naive; it risks inviting unintelligibility and nihilism. The transformation of standards in light of an encounter with the unfamiliar occurs in part by making the unfamiliar familiar, by enabling us, at least through sympathetic imagination, to bridge the gap between what is known to the inquirer and what is unknown. The completely or simply other could not only make no claim on me; indeed, it would remain utterly unintelligible to me.[12]

If we set aside epistemologically and ethically problematic conceptions of radical otherness, we are left with the more mundane but quite difficult problem of translation. It is a mark of how shallow so much of our talk in academic circles about diversity is that it is rarely accompanied by advocacy of the study of the history of other cultures or the languages in which the cultures are expressed. Often enough this is because the interest in diverse cultures is nothing more than superficial. Sometimes, however, it is rooted in theories that would undermine the very possibility of translation. Indeed, in contemporary philosophy, theses regarding untranslatability compete with claims that there is no text: every work is appropriately subject to indefinitely many possible translations. On either of these views, it is hard to see how the other could ever be encountered. As Alasdair MacIntyre argues in *Whose Justice? Which Rationality?*, the latter claim is a natural result of the uprooting of texts from contexts, living traditions of inquiry and reflection, in which the texts are intelligible.[13] Without access to the ways of life in which a language makes sense, the likely result of the interpretation of a text is "distortion by translation out of context."[14] Meanwhile, the former asserts more than is warranted. To say that something is untranslatable, we must know what it is that resists translation. Coming to terms with an alternative tradition requires painstaking attention to the language of the other tradition, progress in which occurs only when one begins to inhabit the other tradition and to deploy its language as a second first language. That is the first stage in progress toward identifying what is untranslatable. Only when we can occupy both communities of discourse are we able to see what is translatable and what is not—the second stage.[15]

Before one can intelligently encounter alternative views, one must have some sense of one's own tradition. Now, MacIntyre is wary of the assumption underlying some curricula focused on reading the "Great Books," precisely because they assume the easy accessibility of texts quite foreign to our own linguistic context; they also tend to assume that each author in the canon is engaging in an ongoing conversation with every other author. But this is to ignore the distances and the disagreements between various authors in the canon. Thus, we need not move to non-Western texts to encounter conflicting "vocabularies of comparison." Any serious study of the so-called Western canon of authors must begin with the assumption that these authors are also in crucial respects "strange and unfamiliar" to us, that they embody diverse and incompatible positions on justice, rationality, and the human good.

For MacIntyre, the obligation to expand our "vocabularies of comparison" by studying diverse views falls under the obligation to pursue the truth. Hence, MacIntyre does the sort of work most postmodernists who talk of encountering the other utterly fail to do. He works out an account of tradition and of the necessity of, and conditions for, debate between rival traditions of inquiry.[16] It is important from the outset that we see that MacIntyre's account of tradition is at variance with Burkean conception, according to which tradition is "wisdom without reflection."[17] An alternative theory of tradition-constituted practice can be had in the final chapters of *Whose Justice? Which Rationality?* He describes the initial development of such a tradition in three stages.

A first in which the relevant beliefs, texts, and authorities have not yet been put in question; a second in which inadequacies of various types have been identified, but not yet remedied; and a third in which response to those inadequacies has resulted in a set of reformulations, reevaluations, and new formulations and evaluations, designed to remedy inadequacies and overcome limitations.[18]

Elsewhere, for example, in his essay "Politics, Philosophy and the Common Good," MacIntyre distinguishes between a *Volk* and a *polis*, the latter of which is "always potentially or actually a society of rational inquiry and self-scrutiny." MacIntyre's depiction of the particular or local aspiration for the universal good cuts across the contemporary divide between particularists or communitarians, on the one hand, and universalists, on the other. Political reflection is at first, and to some extent always, local. Debates and issues are framed in local terms, but even here the answers given have universal import and, if followed to their logical term, engender questions about the human good, not just about the good for me as an individual or about the good of my community and about the good as such.[19] In the movement from particular to universal, we encounter other particular accounts of justice and the human good. Engaging these rival traditions is an indispensable exercise in the pursuit of truth, in the testing of one's tradition. Toleration for MacIntyre matters because everyone is a potential teacher of everyone else.

If MacIntyre is skeptical of conservative Great Books curricula, he is equally skeptical of the dominant liberal manner of fostering toleration, through what contemporary literary and culture critic Michael Berube calls "critical cosmopolitanism." In his book, *What's* Liberal *About the* Liberal Arts?: *Classroom Politics and "Bias" in Higher Education*, Berube laments the absence of "historically informed readings of literary works" by conservatives.[20] But then he offers only a caricature of what conservative reading of literary texts would look like: "opening great books and reciting key passages" without the analytical and dialogical engagement of texts with which he associates liberal approaches. The abstractionist tendencies of which he here accuses conservatives afflict academic liberalism as well, particularly in the superficial approach to multiculturalism, which, as we have noted, is often pursued and promoted in the absence of detailed historical knowledge or competence in foreign languages—multiculturalism lite in the service of political fads.

Moreover, academic liberalism overlooks the way in which a certain strain of academic postmodernism facilitates in students the conformity to popular, consumer capitalism. As David Brooks has astutely observed, the indeterminacy of truth, the sense of language itself as an endless series of provisional constructs, is

> perfectly suited to the ethos of the achievement-oriented capitalist. After all, why should the achiever want to make enemies or waste time in angry conflict? Why should the time-maximizer struggle to find that thing called Absolute Truth when it is more efficient to settle for perception? Why should one get involved in the problematic rigor of judging? Easy-going tolerance is energy-efficient.[21]

Berube's identification of liberal arts education with "critical cosmopolitanism" looks awfully superficial.[22] And he never really makes an argument for it; instead, he simply lists the alternative as a right-wing celebration of self-esteem and cultural triumphalism. But it is not at all clear that these are the only alternatives. The danger with Berube's approach is that it can create rootless cosmopolitans who end up identifying diversity with an opportunity to choose from a smorgasbord of ethnic restaurants.

Moreover, one wonders what impact such an educational vision will have on today's students, many of whom are bright and interested in learning but who are woefully ignorant of their own heritage, the heritage that has made possible the very institutions in which they study. The point of assuring that they have a mastery of certain portions of Western civilization is not parochial self-esteem, but an intellectual appropriation of the richness, complexity, and the internal debates of Western civilization. Only with some mastery of their own heritage and its internal debates can they even begin to recognize another culture as in some sense other.

JUSTICE AND THE RECOGNITION OF OTHERS

A debate both ancient and ever new in Western philosophy has to do with the nature of justice and our duties toward others. As we have noted, one of the attractions of modern ethical theories is that they focus on strict obligations and proffer decision-procedures for the determination of what one is obliged to do. They also tend to focus on discrete acts of choice, isolated from other acts, indeed from the ongoing ethical life of the agent. In his book *Character*, Joel Kupperman provides a telling critique of decision-procedure models of ethics: "Ethics in this view is at work only at those discrete moments when an input is registered and the moral decision-procedure is applied." But "before we can implement a decision-procedure we must notice that a situation is problematic and then reflect on it. Thus, priority must be given to the moral agent's sensitivity."[23] The decision-procedure is parasitic on an antecedent capacity to recognize what is morally salient in the circumstances of an action.

In her famous essay "Modern Moral Philosophy," Anscombe castigates the exclusive modern preoccupation with the moral ought. The "morally ought" has "no reasonable sense outside a law conception of ethics," and the latter is inconceivable apart from the notion of divine lawgiver, something modern ethical theories eschew at the very outset of their investigations. As an alternative, Anscombe proposes that it would be a great improvement if, instead of "morally wrong," one always named a genus such as "untruthful," "unchaste," "unjust." We should no longer ask whether doing something was "wrong," passing directly from some description of an action to this notion; we should ask whether, e.g., it was unjust; and the answer would sometimes be clear at once.[24]

As David Solomon has urged, the origins of what is now called virtue ethics can be traced to this passage in Anscombe's short essay.[25] Its appeal has at least in part to do with the diversity of assessments the virtues afford as well as their greater proximity to concrete instances of human action. The virtues are thus seen to be superior on precisely the point at which they appeared most vulnerable at the outset of modernity: epistemology. The virtues help us to understand what differentiates different kinds of acts in their concreteness and complexity.

If the varied descriptions of virtuous action can better account for what Taylor calls the diversity of goods, virtue ethics has in turn come under fire for its inability to account for diversity of a different sort; namely, social or political diversity. Indeed, the very strength of Kantian and utilitarian theories is that they aid us in operating in complex, diverse political settings in which disagreement is common and there is no shared ethos regarding the virtues. As Jerome Schneewind puts it, in modern society, "the central difficulties of life" come from "disagreement—disagreement involving nations, religious sects, parties to legal disputes, and ordinary people trying to make a living in busy commercial societies." In modern, Western social settings, "classical virtue theory is of little or no use."[26] Rather than to Aristotle or Aquinas, Schneewind thinks we would be better off looking to early modern legal theorists like Grotius and Pufendorf, who attend not to the intentions or character of the agent but to their acts: "to be just is simply to have the habit of following right reason with respect to the rights of others."[27] Schneewind goes so far as to say, "The man who regularly carries out all his perfect duties is a just man even if he dislikes acting justly."[28] Justice specifies perfect duties whose performance is not optional, but obligatory. Their fulfillment is necessary for the preservation of a society of free individuals. Set aside for the moment the question of how agents can have the habit of acting in accord with right reason without the development of character or some attention being given to inculcating appropriate intentions in the character of individuals. Set aside also the astonishing naivete in supposing that a healthy society could rest upon mere external obedience to a set of rules. Schneewind's account ignores a host of communitarian and feminist critiques of modern legalism. It also ignores the sort of critique that gave rise to the revival of virtue ethics in the first place.

Another way to put Schneewind's objection is to say that virtue ethics comes up short when it comes to the question of justice. This is in part because the cultivation of virtue is thought to require a thick, shared account of the good, something that is increasingly and inevitably attenuated in the modern world. It is also because virtue ethics attends primarily to the cultivation of character traits of the agent, not to others. And justice has to do, as Schneewind points out, with how I treat others. Now there are certainly responses to these criticisms. In "Internal Objections to Virtue Ethics,"[29] David Solomon addresses the agent-centered objection. He acknowledges that the cultivation of virtue involves the moral agent keeping "his or her own character at the center of attention." But that is only one dimension of the life of virtue. In another dimension, there is the "set of virtues the agent aims to embody"; here the virtues and the attention they require of the agent can be as "other regarding as one might wish."[30] Indeed, justice would seem to be precisely the sort of virtue according to which the agent is required to be fully other-regarding.

That is precisely how Thomas Aquinas sees it. Justice is the "perpetual and constant will to give another what is due" (ST, II-II, 58, 1). Justice is, Aquinas concurs with Schneewind, a realm of perfect duties, focusing on the good of others, rather than on the perfection and flourishing of the agent. Unlike the due or mean of the virtues of courage and temperance, which have to do with a right ordering in the subjective passions of the agent, the mean of justice consists in "operations or things" in relation to what is due to another (ST, II-II, 58, 10). Justice is defined as the "good of another." Indeed, Aquinas embraces Cicero's claim that "men are chiefly called good from justice" and that "the splendor of virtue is greatest in justice" (ST, II-II, 53, 3). And yet, unlike Schneewind, he does not dismiss the significance of the intention of the agent. For Thomas, we might call someone just who merely fulfilled what was externally required. But we would call someone more just or more admirable in the order of justice if she intends, and delights in, giving to others what is due. Thomas would resist Schneewind's tendency to collapse a set of distinctions we commonly make in the ordinary appraisal of the actions of ourselves and others. For example, we distinguish between someone who does what is right because of a concern for others or because of a commitment to rectitude in his or her behavior and someone who does what is right because he realizes in the long run this is what is most likely to bring him profit or because he has a craven desire to be thought well of by others or because he thinks it will advance his career and so forth. Moreover, the virtue of justice has a common or unifying formality that has to do with giving what it due to another, but Thomas insists that what is due varies widely: "Something is due to an equal in one way, to a superior in another, to an inferior, in yet another, and a debt varies as it arises from a contract, a promise, or a benefit received" (ST, I-II, 60, 3). Thus Thomas's account of justice is more differentiated and more capacious than the accounts prominent in modernity. We might say it recognizes a diversity of goods within justice. But this is precisely what we should expect of a virtue, rather than a decision-procedure model of ethics.

Indeed, Aquinas has a broad and deep conception of the virtues that need to be cultivated if we are to be just in the full sense of the term. He is skeptical that, without the cultivation of other, related virtues, a society will be able to maintain any reliable commitment even to the legally just, the minimum respect for others that makes public order possible. Furthermore, justice toward others will often require something like solidarity or hospitality, whose cultivation involves much more than the habit of performing minimal, external acts of legal justice. These involve capacities to identify and respond appropriately to the sufferings, deprivations, and disabilities of those who seem quite other than and distant from oneself. To use the words of Paul Ricoeur, they involve seeing "oneself as another."[31]

Before turning to Thomas's treatment of these virtues, it is important to see that his reliance on a broad and deep account of the virtues allied to justice does not entail a reversion to the sort of ethic that modern justice is designed to combat. The danger, it might seem, is that of the submersion of justice under a set of allied virtues. We turn to a focus on the dispositions of the agent and away from the needs of others and the obligations we have toward them. But this is manifestly not the case. Thomas continues to uphold the demands of justice as consisting in the use of external things in a way that gives to each other person his or her due. Indeed, Thomas holds that law does not enforce all the requirements of ethical behavior; in fact, it can coerce only external conformity in action, not the internal disposition toward virtue. In his discussion of the "utility" of human law, he speaks principally of the negative function of law, its checking of "audacity" through "fear," its providing safety for the innocent in the "midst of wickedness" through the "dread of punishment" (ST, I-II, 95, 1). Human law forbids only the most grievous vices, especially those that are harmful to others, such as murder and theft (ST, I-II, 96, 2). Law leads indirectly to virtue. In circumstances in which the people are not virtuous, the goal is to move the people to virtue, "not suddenly but gradually" (ST, I-II, 96, 2, ad 2).

Any attempt to reform the character of a people by the enactment of law must take its cue from the existing customs of the society. Custom itself, Aquinas writes, has the force of law, abolishes law, and is the interpreter of law (ST, I-II, 97, 3). In situations in which the people are free to make their own law, custom "has greater authority than the sovereign" (ST, I-II, 97, 3, ad 3). Aquinas certainly has an account of shared human nature and the common goods of political life; yet the way in which these goods are realized in any given community will vary depending on the customs of that society.

Aquinas himself responds in pedagogical terms to the question whether it is useful for human beings to frame laws (ST, I-II, 95, 1). Human beings, he states, attain the "perfection of virtue by training," and law supplies a crucial part of that training. For example, whenever Aquinas addresses the issue of private property, he justifies it not in terms of rights antecedent to civil government, but in light of the common good. The role of laws regarding property is to "accustom men to give of their own readily" (ST, I-II, 105, 2). Aquinas's sense of the indispensable but circumscribed role of law complements his sense of the indispensable but limited role of the customs or mores of a community. The realm of mores, in which we find the cultivation of virtues and vices, will do much to determine how effectively the prohibition of heinous acts is realized. Moreover, it is precisely in Thomas's treatment of virtue and vice that we find the basis for a) the practice of solidarity and hospitality toward the other and b) a critique of corrupt social and political practices that undermine the just treatment of others.

JUSTICE AS SOLIDARITY WITH OTHERS

Among a host of other senses of the obligatory, Thomas includes contractual agreements. By contrast, in modernity there is a tendency to construe the contractual model, which imagines a kind of clean slate onto which we can enter debits and credits by entering into contractual agreements with others, as normative. Yet Thomas presupposes that we are born indebted, that some of our debts arise independently of, and prior to, our conscious consent, and that some of them can never be fully repaid. Such is the case with our duties to God, country, parents, and virtuous individuals who have exercised heroic virtue on our behalf.

Aquinas associates justice with a host of other virtues: gratitude, liberality, affability, and mercy. Liberality, which is a mean between covetousness and prodigality, concerns the virtuous use of excess riches (ST, II-II, 17, 1). The inordinate desire to possess, covetousness, has a host of daughters: treachery, fraud, falsehood, perjury, violence, restlessness, and insensibility to mercy, the last of which erodes our capacity to respond to, or even appropriately sympathize with, others in need. The account of *misericordia* takes aim at a false notion of self-sufficiency. Misericordia is hard to render in English; literally, it indicates a suffering of the heart at the misfortune of another. It involves both being affected by the misery of others and responding to that condition (ST, II-II, 30, 1). As a virtue, it is related both to justice, what we owe to others, and charity, the love in us for others inspired by the love that God has for us. Imitating God's own ordering of justice to mercy, misericordia is the supreme virtue governing our disposition and actions toward fellow human beings (ST, II-II, 30, 4).

Misericordia, thus, underscores the universally shared human condition, a condition in which no one possesses the good in an independent, autonomous manner and in which everyone is dependent and vulnerable in various ways.[32] Thus Aquinas's account of justice contains a critique of certain pagan, philosophical understandings of virtue, which repose upon strong divisions between the few and the many, citizens and barbarians, free and slaves. If it is a weakness of certain contemporary accounts of virtue ethics that they have no room for justice understood as fulfillment of external obligations regardless of internal dispositions, it is a weakness of certain accounts of the good life that they treat invulnerability to things outside of one's control, to harm or even to passion, as a paramount value. Noting that a passion itself cannot be a virtue, Aquinas nonetheless argues that the feeling of sorrow, which is part of mercy, is not a vice or a defect (ST, II-II, 30, 3). MacIntyre lays out the dimensions of the virtue of misericordia, which he translates as "just generosity": "they are communal relationships that engage our affections, they extend beyond the long-term relationships of the members of a community to each other to relationships of hospitality to passing strangers, and, they include those whose urgent needs confronts the members of such a community."³³

If virtue requires that we be generous toward others, the disposition called forth by what one has received from others is gratitude. As matters of justice, religion specifies what we owe to God, piety what we owe to our country and our parents, and observance to those who excel in dignity. Included within these virtues is a duty to be grateful. But gratitude also surfaces as a distinct virtue, as a proper response to benefactors. Gratitude fulfills a moral debt that is distinct from the legal debt, a matter of commutative justice, fulfilling what we owe those with whom we have made contractual arrangements. There is a certain paradox in calling gratitude a debt, one which we are obliged to fulfill spontaneously and where possible in a manner that exceeds the original gift. The accent is not, however, on a quantitative calculus. Whereas justice looks to the quantity received and seeks an equality of things, gratitude looks to the motive and seeks an equality of wills. It is akin to friendship rather than to the legal due; a sign of this is that while we should immediately acknowledge the gift of the benefactor, we should not be hasty in repaying it, for alacrity here can indicate an unseemly urge to pay up and be free from a debt. It also underscores the crucial role of gratitude. His account of justice includes reference to the contingency of our possession of whatever goods we possess, even as it counsels gratitude for those goods. As Josef Pieper comments: "The just man who . . . realizes that his very being is a gift, and that he is heavily indebted before God and man, is also the man willing to give where there is no strict obligation. He will be willing to give another man something no one can compel him to give."³⁴

For Aristotle, the vice opposed to justice is "graspingness," the desire to have more than what one is due. For Aquinas, the possession of wealth breeds the illusion of self-sufficiency (ST, I-II, 84, 3); wealth denotes the possession of things over which we have "absolute mastery" (ST, II-II, 118, 2). It is, Aquinas says, rooted in a kind of pride, since "the avaricious takes pleasure in the consideration of himself as the possessor of riches"

(ST, II-II, 118, 6). This is an unjust and false esteeming of self as superior to others because one is rich. Countering this injustice is liberality, the disposition that renders us "ready to give with pleasure, when and where we ought" (ST, II-II, 118, 1–2). Gratitude is another virtue that informs Thomas's treatment of justice, a virtue that forms us in appropriately responding to what we receive from others, whether these be God, our parents, or a range of benefactors.

Of course in the modern world where graspingness is touted, if not as an intrinsic good, then at least as an indispensable instrumental good, we need to be concerned about the systematic subversion of the Thomist understanding of virtue. There is a danger, as John Paul II notes in *The Gospel of Life*, that the good life comes to be construed in terms of "material well being," while "quality of life" comes to be identified with "economic efficiency, functionality, and usefulness."[35] The attitude affects not only our relations to external things but also our disposition toward human persons. The result is the instrumentalization and commodification of human persons, with potentially devastating consequences for the unproductive members of society, the unborn, the poor, the weak, the disabled, and the elderly. Injustices mild and severe ensue. The counter to these tendencies in our culture is only partly achieved by legal protection. It needs as well the cultivation of the virtue of *misericordia*. MacIntyre comments: "The care that we ourselves need from others and the care that they need from us require a commitment . . . that is not conditional upon the contingencies of injury, disease, and other afflictions." MacIntyre notes that my relationships with others can be destroyed by what the other does in the form of vicious actions, but it should not be "diminished or abolished by what happens to the other, by her or his afflictions."[36] We might wonder, what are the motivations of those who practice misericordia? Is it grounded in Kantian universalization? In long-term calculative self-interest, in the fear that if I do not help others suffering deprivation, they will not help me when I am afflicted? Or in the hope that if I do, they may reciprocate? Or that if such care is provided, the result will be to the benefit of the greatest good of the greatest number? There is no question that elements of each could figure, in varying measures, in the deliberation of those who practice "just generosity." But it is hard to see how any of these alone or in combination could effectively form individuals with the capacity to identify and be appropriately affected by those who are afflicted or to respond in a virtuous manner.[37]

Each of these motivations leaves out of the picture the deep bond, akin to friendship, that Thomas associates with misericordia, which flourishes, as MacIntyre notes, in communities where networks of giving and receiving take priority over the individual pursuit of profit or the bureaucratized management of human affairs. In the very act of showing misericordia, moreover, there is equality and reciprocity, not just dependence of the receiver on the giver. For, as Ricoeur astutely observes, those whose suffering and deprivation puts them in need of others give to those others an opportunity for a shared recognition of "fragility and mortality."[38]

The question of what sort of practices, what sort of communities, what sort of institutions foster the practice of misericordia is a crucial one for societies that would seek to practice justice beyond the requirements of the legally due. For Aquinas, misericordia supposes a universally shared human condition in which each person no matter how afflicted shares in human dignity and each counts as one. Thus does Thomas's account not only encompass both desiderata (the legally due and solidarity with the afflicted) of justice, but it also salvages the moral insights at the core of Kantianism and utilitarianism. Because it is a virtue theory, it is more attuned than either of these schools of ethics to the diversity of goods operative in human life and especially in the communal human pursuit of justice, according to which individuals aim, as Ricoeur puts it, "at the good life with and for others in just institutions."[39]

NOTES

1. Charles Taylor, "The Diversity of Goods," in David Lewis, *Philosophical Papers: Volume 2, Philosophy and the Human Sciences* (Cambridge: Cambridge University Press, 1985), 230–47.

2. Elizabeth Anscombe, "Modern Moral Philosophy," in *Virtue Ethics*, ed. Roger Crisp and Michael Slote (Oxford, UK: Oxford University Press, 1997).

3. "The Diversity of Goods," 234.

4. "The Diversity of Goods," 232.

5. "The Diversity of Goods," 244.

6. "The Diversity of Goods," 234.

7. Amy Gutmann, "Introduction," in *Multiculturalism: Examining the Politics of Recognition*, edited and introduced by Amy Gutmann (Princeton: Prince-

ton University Press, 1994), 16–19. In making the case for expanding the canon to include African American authors, Gutmann asks, "Is Aristotle's understanding of slavery more enlightening than Frederick Douglass's? Is Aquinas's argument about civil disobedience more defensible than Martin Luther King's?" (15).

8. Charles Taylor, "The Politics of Recognition," in *Multiculturalism: Examining the Politics of Recognition*, 67.

9. Denys Turner, *Faith, Reason, and the Existence of God* (Cambridge: Cambridge University Press, 2005), 167.

10. Richard Kearney, *Strangers, Gods and Monsters: Ideas of Otherness* (New York: Routledge, 2002), 67.

11. Kearney, *Strangers, Gods, and Monsters: Ideas of Otherness*, 101.

12. Paul Ricoeur does not go quite so far in his criticisms of Levinas's notion of the obligation to encounter the face of the other, but he does worry that in the encounter the face remains external and anonymous to the ethical agent, thus depriving the agent of the possibility of any sort of reciprocal relationship with the other. See *Oneself as Another* (Chicago: University of Chicago Press, 1991), 1881–89.

13. Alasdair MacIntyre, *Whose Justice? Which Rationality?* (Notre Dame, IN: University of Notre Dame Press, 1989).

14. MacIntyre, *Whose Justice? Which Rationality?*, 385.

15. MacIntyre, *Whose Justice? Which Rationality?*, 386.

16. See, for example, *Whose Justice? Which Rationality?*, 349–69. For a response to the charge that MacIntyre is a political conservative, see Kelvin Knight's "Revolutionary Aristotelianism," in *Contemporary Political Studies 1996*, vol. 2, ed. I. Hampsher-Monk and J. Stanyer (Belfast: Queen's University, 1996).

17. MacIntyre, *Whose Justice? Which Rationality?*, 353.

18. MacIntyre, *Whose Justice? Which Rationality?*, 355.

19. Alasdair MacIntyre, "Politics, Philosophy, and the Common Good," in *The MacIntyre Reader*, ed. Kelvin Knight (Notre Dame, IN: University of Notre Dame Press, 1998), 249.

20. Michael Berube, *What's Liberal About the Liberal Arts?: Classroom Politics and "Bias" in Higher Education* (New York: W. W. Norton & Company, 2007). Inexplicably, Berube speaks of the "intractable postmodern conflict" between reason and faith (288). A pupil of Rorty, he seems not to realize that postmodernism means reason itself is ungrounded and thus rests on a kind of faith.

21. David Brooks, *On Paradise Drive* (New York: Simon and Schuster, 2004), 161.

22. Berube, *What's Liberal About the Liberal Arts?*, 56 and throughout.

23. Joel Kupperman, *Character* (Oxford: Oxford University Press, 1991), 72.

24. Anscombe, "Modern Moral Philosophy," 22.

25. David Solomon, "Virtue Ethics: Radical or Routine?," in *Intellectual Virtue: Perspectives from Ethics and Epistemology*, ed. Michael DePaul and Linda Zagzebski (Oxford, UK: Oxford University Press, 2003), 57–80. Solomon observes that "Kurt Baier's attack on her paper—delivered a quarter of a century after it was written—characterized her views as an instance of 'Radical Virtue Ethics.'"

26. J. B. Schneewind, "The Misfortunes of Virtue," in *Virtue Ethics*, 199–200.

27. Schneewind, "The Misfortunes of Virtue," 183.

28. Schneewind, "The Misfortunes of Virtue," 186.

29. David Solomon, "Internal Objections to Virtue Ethics," *Midwest Studies in Philosophy* 13 (1988): 428–41. Solomon describes three standard types of objection: (a) The action-guiding objection that claims that a virtue theory fails to give adequate guidance in situations of practical perplexity. The rules and principles characteristic of deontological and consequentialist theories are alleged to guide action more effectively and more determinately. (b) The self-centeredness objection that claims that an ethics of virtue is insufficiently other-regarding. It alleges that virtue theories in their classical form ground the need for virtue on the part of agents in the desire of agents for their own fulfillment or satisfaction, and that this seems to turn ethics upside down. Instead of my needing to be good in order to benefit others, I am required to be the sort of person who benefits others in order to be fulfilled myself. Virtue seems to be itself compromised by a kind of vanity or prissiness. (c) The conscientiousness objection that claims that an ethics of virtue fails to do justice to the special kind of motivation peculiar to the moral. Genuine goodness, according to this objection, must involve acting under a certain kind of constraint. The perfectly virtuous person apparently finds it easy to do what he or she ought, but this seems to fly in the face of any realistic moral phenomenology.

30. Solomon, "Internal Objections to Virtue Ethics," 432 and 434.

31. Paul Ricoeur, *Oneself as Another* (Chicago: University of Chicago Press, 1992).

32. Misericordia involves both being affected by the suffering of others and responding to that condition. As a virtue, it is related both to justice, what we owe to others, and charity, the love in us for others inspired by the love God has for us. Imitating God's own ordering of justice to mercy, misericordia is the supreme virtue governing our dispositions and actions toward others. For an examination of compassion in Jewish and early Christian texts and practice and its relationship to the teaching of Aristotle and other pagan philosophers as well as its relation to pagan philosophy, see Christoph Markschies, "Compassion:

Some Remarks on Concepts of Divine and Human Compassions in Antiquity," *Proceedings of the Israel Academy of Sciences and Humanities* VIII. 5, 91–104.

33. Alasdair McIntyre, *Dependent Rational Animals* (Chicago: Open Court, 1999), 126.

34. Josef Pieper, *The Four Cardinal Virtues* (Notre Dame, IN: University of Notre Dame Press, 1966), 111.

35. Pope John Paul II, *The Gospel of Life* (New York: Random House, 1995), 40.

36. MacIntyre, *Dependent Rational Animals*, 128.

37. Martha Nussbaum has devoted a number of essays to the role of pity in the moral and political life of a just society. See, for example, "Pity and Mercy: Nietzsche's Stoicism," in *Nietzsche, Genealogy, Morality: Essays on Nietzsche's* On the Genealogy of Morals, ed. Richard Schacht (Berkeley: University of California Press, 1994); "Tragedy and Self-Sufficiency: Plato and Aristotle on Fear and Pity," *Oxford Studies in Ancient Philosophy*, Vol. 10 (1992): 107–59; "Compassion: The Basic Social Emotion," *Social Philosophy and Policy*, Vol. 13 (1996): 27–58; "Compassion: Human and Animal," in *Ethics and Humanity: Themes from the Philosophy of Jonathan Glover*, ed. N. Ann Davis, Richard Keshen, and Jeff McMahan (Oxford: Oxford University Press, 2010), 202–26. Yet Nussbaum seems to think that literary education could do the job of forming democratic citizens in the appropriate virtues. Also she assumes that the pity tradition arises in Greece and then disappears until the modern period. For a corrective to these and other errors, see John O'Callaghan, "*Misericordia* in Aquinas: A Test Case for Theological and Natural Virtues," forthcoming in the *Jaarboek Thomas Instituut te Utrecht*.

38. Ricoeur, *Oneself as Another*, 191–92.

39. Ricoeur, *Oneself as Another*, 180.

3

ON DEONTOLOGY

Is Diversity for Real?

Aaron Szymkowiak, Xavier University

> The purpose of secular morality is to allow each student to be free, because the starting point of secularism is the absolute respect for freedom of conscience. To provide freedom of choice, we must be able to remove the student from all determinisms, family, ethnic, social, intellectual. . . .
> The possibility of building one's own autonomy, that is to say the ability to give oneself the rule, means being able to take some distance from all heritages. This does not mean that we abandon these legacies, but simply that one is able to choose for oneself.
> —Vincent Benoît Camille Peillon, French Minister of Education, March 2013[1]

Perhaps no history of philosophical ethics can better illustrate the difficulties of human difference than one limning the trajectory of deontology. The loose tradition of "duty ethics" can be read, at least in its initial and high stages, as a project to wrestle with the significance of human particularity, treating problems of culture, religion, or ethnic character by adverting to universal principles. The most obvious figures of importance in any such reading are Kant and (early) Rawls. For these thinkers and others who follow them, duty is bound to the concept of autonomy. The fundamental difficulty at the core of duty ethics is the fact of its having progressively diminished—in the name of enlightenment universalism—the moral salience of the very phenomenon it set forth to address. Contemporary thinkers have attempted to rectify this problem, but have not, and cannot, succeed on the terms of discussion as they stand.

Present-day writers on diversity work almost fully within concepts of self-rule inaugurated by Kant, while simultaneously endeavoring in late-Rawlsian fashion to give cultural identity its due. Still, in this literature direct speculation on the nature of diversity itself, let alone its place in the scheme of things, is conspicuous by its near-total absence. In view of this fact—which I will maintain is a crippling deficiency—it behooves us to trace some (admittedly brief) history of deontology with an eye to this question. A full view of the attempt at "re-culturing" deontology must start with the roots of the tradition in that particular division of nature and convention inaugurated with the modern natural lawyers. Deontological ethics has historically treated the issue of diversity; the question is whether this treatment amounts to a dehumanizing reduction.

NATURAL LAW AND PRODUCTIVE CULTURAL DIVERSITY: GROTIUS AND THE *IUS GENTIUM*

In asking this question, it is helpful to begin with Hugo Grotius, and the distinction he drew between the law of Nature and the law of Nations. Though it would be incorrect to call Grotius a duty ethicist in any contemporary sense of the term, in his work we find the basic elements from which such a tradition would later emerge: obligation as a function of agency, an elevation of right over good, and a concern with the status of adventitious or constructed principles. Though, in Grotius's scheme these elements cohere rather differently than in contemporary deontology. For one thing, those aspects of human obligation amenable to logical analysis lie strictly under the Law of Nature. They originate in "ideas which are so certain that nobody can deny them without doing violence to their fundamental being."[2] These ideas are philosophically accessible apart from history or culture. Grotius concludes the prolegomena to the first edition of *The Rights of War and Peace* with a claim that he is proceeding mathematically, conceiving (natural) law "in the absence of all particular circumstances."[3] His analysis involves conditions of sociality as such, rather than manifestations of social life that may happen to exhibit some commonality of a less-than-necessary sort. Grotius considers these latter elements of human life "chosen," and places them under a different heading from (logically) natural ones. They are associated with tradition, classified under the law of nations, and understood to be a matter for empirical-historical investigation. The *ius gentium* is for Grotius a record of common consent by civilized societies. This general agreement of civilized mankind serves as a working assumption for handling the diversity of human cultures. In *The Rights of War and Peace*, we accordingly see the language of choice being applied to questions at the casuistic end of jurisprudence; issues of cultural difference may be studied by way of testimony. This manner of analysis affords some admirable flexibility with difficult moral issues. What constitutes inhumanly brutal treatment of subjects, for instance, might admit of some latitude, and rests with the history of commentary by civilized peoples. This might further inform our sense of legitimate pretexts for forceful intervention on behalf of the victims.[4]

Against the backdrop of Roman precedents, Grotius argued that some common principles came from nature directly through reason, while others rather indirectly arose through common feeling. In the process he addressed directly many of the very issues troubling contemporary deontologists. But this achievement was not without a heavy price in terms of argumentative consistency. From his own time to ours, a persistent line of criticism of Grotius's thinking has been that he could never quite make up his mind on the question of moral motivation.[5] The consent of convention (the stuff of the *ius gentium*) attached to matters felt and subsequently chosen. It remained unclear just what force, by contrast, brought adherence to natural law, particularly since Grotius hinted that natural obligations held without the direct application of God's will. And if this occurred in purely intellectual fashion, then such natural obligations would seem to bear little relation to the adventitious duties of the *ius gentium*. These ambiguities permit historians to describe Grotius with some justification as the modern font of empiricist as well as deontological moral thought.[6] Subsequent natural law thinkers within the Protestant tradition—particularly Cumberland and Pufendorf—sought to render Grotius's scheme immune to Hobbes's scathing critique of the half-formed intellectualism at the heart of this ambiguity. They did so by assimilating the will to the intellect in some fashion, paving the way for Kant's later outright identification of the will with practical reason.

By virtue of these developments, the role of diversity was significantly attenuated. By the time Grotius's translator Beyberac edited what would become the definitive edition of *The Rights of War and Peace*, he would dismiss rather perfunctorily the whole notion of a separate *ius gentium*. Citing Pufendorf in a footnote, Beyberac claimed, "This Positive Law of Nations, distinct from the Law of Nature, is a mere Chimera."[7] By subsuming the *ius gentium* into a more fully "voluntarized" *ius naturae*, these subsequent thinkers gained consistency on the question of obligation at the price of teleological clarity with respect to difference. Grotius had, by contrast, a compelling explanation in moral-religious terms for human diversity: it existed to facilitate our participation in a sphere of active, living contention. Commerce brings us together to improve our condition both morally and materially, and diversity is the engine of commerce. Thus, in *The Free Sea*:

> God himself speaketh this in nature, seeing he will not have all those things, whereof the life of man standeth in need, to be sufficiently ministered by nature in all places and also vouchsafeth some nations to excel others in arts. To what end are these things but that he would maintain human friendship by their mutual wants and plenty, lest everyone thinking themselves sufficient for themselves for this only thing should be made insociable? Now it cometh to pass that one nation should supply the want of another by the appointment of divine justice, that thereby (as Pliny saith) that which is brought forth anywhere might seem to be bred with all.[8]

Under these conditions, we can see why for Grotius, the *ius gentium* would always exhibit some imprecision, and would need to remain separate from the natural law. Certain features of our being were, by design, flexible and differentiated from place to place; fruitful contention rested on this providential dispensation. Accordingly, Grotius resisted a cosmopolitan juridical order of any positive variety. Peace among peoples was equated with commerce, not with administration or positive arbitration. On these terms, it was never to be expected that human difference would be counted a "determinism" to be overcome in the name of morality. Natural law comprised the rules by which difference might profitably be leveraged for the good of all; this was its "necessity," at least on an intellectual level. But without the assumption of a more or less permanent diversity, this law loses much of its salience. Meanwhile, the Grotian legislator was not in the business of deciding just who was truly "free" or which arrangements had come about without compulsion. "Choice" played out in history, and not at the level of radically indeterminate individuals.

The idea of diverse peoples in ordered, commercial relations for a time withered in the face of the post-Hobbesian and, even more, the post-Westphalian predicaments. "Productive contention" would take on a new meaning and, with it, a more rigorist universalism would emerge.

KANT: DIVERSITY AS CONTENTION, HISTORY, AND RIGHT

In Kant's work, it is easy to see the beginnings of the radically formalized agency characteristic of later, post-Rawlsian deontology. The comparison holds rather well if one sticks to the basic formulae of the *Groundwork*, arguably the text from which deontology gets it start. The famous categorical imperative takes the Grotian flight from the particular and extends it to the whole of morals. Or perhaps, we should say that for Kant, the particular has its value in the calculus of moral knowledge only insofar as it can be articulated as part of a universalizable principle. Reason is reason; the will is either consistent or not. Under such a description there remain no "contingencies" like national origin, gender, or even religious tradition. These facets of human life go beyond the logic of willing as such, and can therefore demarcate nothing of right and wrong; an autonomous agent is one not determined by psychological or historical circumstance. It would seem that from this orientation, it is but a small jump to Rawls's "original position," or to the pronouncements of our opening epigrams.

Diversity in Kant, however, is not so fully negative in its moral significance as these first appearances suggest. This much is evident from the speculative theodicy appearing in the political essays, and also from comments going directly to the question of national characters in other works. On the one hand, it is likely that various cultural and religious commitments would for Kant come under the heading of "self-incurred immaturity."[9] Nonetheless, these qualities, like more basic and "unsociable" desires, appear in history as occasions of *antagonism*, which as we shall see, is a significant force in Kant's scheme of things. Quarrels among peoples are the brutal manifold from which a condition of right might conceivably emerge. And yet, as with Grotius, Kant gives us reason to think that national difference is not a condition to be superseded; it is not a mere historical artifact in the moral scheme of things.

This is clearest in Kant's treatment of national characters in *Anthropology from a Pragmatic Point of View*. There, he touches briefly upon the question of the origin of national characters, rejecting both the Montesquiean account in terms of climate and soil, and also the roughly Humean approach[10] where such things might be attributable to moral or political institutions. This leaves open the possibility of some biological explanation, although Kant appears not too concerned to establish the point, seeing the attempt as "risky" and having more to do with empirical geography than philosophy.[11] He sketches characterizations of the various European nations, focusing in each case upon their flaws, "because criticism leads to improvement."[12] Kant's descriptions stand as moral critiques, not as "neutral" ethnographic studies of the sort later anthropologists would find respectable. Human diversity means, first, a scattering of vices and virtues, and not quite, as Grotius had emphasized, a divergence in talents and productive capacities. Still, the fact of difference would seem to be intended by nature:

> We can judge with probability that the intermixture of races (caused by large-scale conquests), which gradually extinguishes their characteristics, does not seem beneficial to the human race—all pretended philanthropy notwithstanding.
>
> Instead of assimilation, which was intended by the melting together of various races, Nature has here made a law of just the opposite. In a nation of the same race (for example, of the white race), instead of allowing the characters to develop constantly and progressively toward resembling one another . . . Nature has preferred to diversify infinitely the characters of the same stock, and even of the same family as to physical and spiritual characteristics.[13]

If this establishes the permanence of diversity, it is important not to misinterpret what for Kant was its moral significance. Contra Grotius, national characters do not exist for the sake of a commercial process of material improvement, or trading of deeds. Nor, however, are they self-subsisting centers of value, proverbial tiles in God's mosaic. The latter point is evident when we consider Kant's reaction to the work of his erstwhile student Johann Gottfried Herder. Herder argued, in a proto-Romantic manner, that each individual and each nation had his (or its) moral essence in a traditional-spiritual center. These might be read empirically through the study of history. On the matter of individuals, the point extended to a doctrine of immortality. Herder argued that the inherent worth of nations was demarcated by unique constellations of historical forces. Both cases—individuals and nations—stood as differentiated manifestations of a divinely appointed organic force. For Herder, the meaning of human life was to be revealed by investigating cultural history.

From Kant's standpoint, much of this appeared fanciful, speculative, and "wholly outside the field of scientific observation."[14] Still, it is important to consider that from Herder's side of the question, Kant was the more guilty party in the question of indulging in "metaphysics." Herder objected especially to what he viewed as Kant's denial of the particular, and the attendant claim of a "freedom" entirely separated from nature. For Herder, the particular person or nation appears in the progression of history; the value of that place, however, is not reducible to a function in a grand process.[15] Freedom here is the product of deeper forces manifested organically, and is not an irreducible absolute.[16] These positions help to illuminate Kant's by way of contrast. We know from Kant's treatment of the issue in *Groundwork* II, for instance, that humanity in its moral aspect is coextensive with rational freedom; in this capacity we have unconditioned worth.[17] When it comes to reckoning the historical and political manifestations of this value, Kant departs quite radically from Herder. Our worth comes from *actions*, Kant tells us, and not from obscure spiritual essences or their concrete manifestations. The dismissal of empirical particulars follows closely from their impermanence and contingency: "Here, all nature reveals to us is that it abandons individuals to total destruction and preserves only the species."[18]

As such, the brute facts of human particularity retain no significance in and of themselves. They are, however, consequential insofar as they serve some function for the species as a whole. Kant discusses the historical destiny of the human race throughout several works, especially *Idea for a Universal History with a Cosmopolitan Purpose* and *Perpetual Peace: A Philosophical Sketch*. In the first, Kant suggests that since reason entails an unbounded "range of projects," its improvement cannot be corralled or defined by instinct, natural guidelines, or a finite human life. Instead, our various antagonisms aim at something larger: moral improvement within a rightful condition. In emphasizing antagonism, Kant enlarges the Grotian idea of "unsocial sociability" to suggest contention of a more violent sort. We have not quite arrived with Kant at the Hegelian idea of history as a "slaughter bench," but no longer can we discern a process of reciprocation in productive good deeds. History "aims" at a rightful condition because self-interest demands an end to the infelicities magnified by commerce.

Though in Herder's mind, this would constitute a most unfortunate reduction, diversity has for Kant a fully political significance. Here, in the realm of intractable differences and their attendant political conflicts, we find the proper task of empirical-historical speculation: to render conceivable the possibility of continual moral improvement under a lawful external condition. Movement toward this condition, Kant argued, was the ultimate aim of the species. In the "guarantee" section of *Perpetual Peace*, he set about to sketch an account of how this might occur. Through observable natural forces, men would be *forced*, perhaps in some cases against their wills, into an arrangement in which moral relations might actually flourish. Particular differences *compel* us, typically through some combination of commerce and subsequent quarrel, to accommodate ourselves lawfully to one another. Achieving this peaceful condition in progressively larger spheres, we might thenceforth dedicate ourselves more fully to the cultivation of our characters. This, to Kant, was not factual history, but a realistic possibility. The diversification of nations, races, talents, and even families is a constant force for irritation or stirring-up. That we differ in virtues, vices, and a host of other proclivities is inevitable; from the standpoint of meaningful freedom, diversity is a motivating force. Morality itself takes no indications from nature, since the consistent will of the autonomous individual is our standard. Nonetheless, it may be said that as a matter of historical process, nature furnishes some bracing shocks to awaken us to our deeper reflective vocation. That Kant never accepted a total political "solution" to such developmental pains (say, a world-state) bespoke his view of their intractability. In Kant's deontology, diversity was thus very real, serving a function through its generation of conflict. It was not a phenomenon to be obviated entirely by correct moral judgment, or even by good laws. For Kant, our relation to the historical end of the species would be asymptotic, and never materially final. We may hope for perpetual peace, but perpetual diversity is, alas, well assured.

RAWLS AND CONTEMPORARY DEONTOLOGY: IS THERE AN *IUS GENTIUM* AFTER ALL?

Little remains of such teleological speculation in late-twentieth-century deontology. Rawls's famous *A Theory of Justice* advances Kant's emphasis on rational agency, positing a separation from empirical particulars as the core of moral judgment. From Rawls's early to late work, there is a shift of *emphasis* on this point, if not quite of substance, and diversity is arguably the occasion for this shift. In *A Theory of Justice*, Rawls tells us that he is updating the project of Locke, Rousseau, and Kant, albeit at a higher level of abstraction.[19] The "original position" is the standard for rules of justice, involving an assumption of equivalent liberty for each agent in the social contract. In deliberating about rules, each person stands behind a "veil of ignorance," removing the inequalities of empirical particulars; no one could know whether he stood to benefit from such qualities, therefore it would behoove him to choose those rules going to the criteria of freedom and equality alone, and not much else besides.[20] This, Rawls argues, is "fairness"; it reconciles freedom and equality—at least in a polity dedicated to such ideals—by demonstrating that the latter can be seen as the essential condition of the former in deliberation about public rules. From these considerations there arise a panoply of rights and duties on matters ranging from religious tolerance to welfare. We shall not be concerned with the particulars here; instead, let us note that Rawls exhibits some important ambivalences on the classic Grotian question of justifying reasons. These ambiguities apply not at the level of individual psychology (on which Rawls is either sufficiently detailed or justifiedly reticent), but instead at the level of adoption for the framework itself. This problem goes rather directly to the matter of what one is to make of diversity.

On the one hand, Rawls takes for granted a working civilized order, where reasons of a certain sort are given as justifications. This much is assumed by his concept of "reflective equilibrium," in which an actor strives for consistency among particular applications of general principles and past accounts or justifications for them. Rawls explains reflective equilibrium as a movement toward considered judgments. Deliberation itself has a role in constituting an ideal; this permits Rawls to sidestep any charges of excessive rationalism or intuitionism. At the same time, though, it leaves his account rather slippery on the question of formal structure, particularly where great changes are introduced in the point of reflective equilibrium by incongruent descriptions. How great should we expect the differences between these descriptions to be, particularly before we rule some of them "unreasonable" in light of the original position? If the answer is "never," then it is difficult to see what work the contractualist elements of Rawls's theory are doing; induction from moral experience would need to come under *some* criterion of judgment. Rawls's answer to this question in *A Theory of Justice* seems to be a splitting of the difference. A finite tradition of inquiry is inescapable, and forms the material of which we judge, and hence also theorize;[21] still, the justification for seeing something like an original position as dispositive is broadly Kantian.[22] If not quite our motives, then at least the material of our judgments, will be bounded somewhat by traditions of discussion. And yet, justifications must go beyond these constraints to ideals not entirely circumscribed by them.

Rawls's reluctance to advance comprehensively—or even to stipulate tentatively—the boundaries of such ideals[23] led naturally to political questions on the significance of diversity and pluralist societies. What should we make of those social groups who seem to reject this mode of late-liberal reasoning about the public sphere? Is a decent form of politics, or even mere comity, possible where groups begin with radically differing conceptions? Such questions are given greater emphasis in Rawls's later work *Political Liberalism*. In terms of the ambiguities just sketched, we can say that in this work and in his later essay "The Law of Peoples," Rawls tilted to the conventional or "pluralist" elements of his philosophy, further sidelining any aspirations to develop a comprehensive theory of agency as a justificatory framework. With "political liberalism" the justifying mechanism for rules is minimal; "public reason" rests with "overlapping consensus," those external principles and institutions to which each group can accede. Further efforts to explain or justify these arrangements "comprehensively" are at best superfluous, at worst corrosive of the arrangements themselves. It is to be expected that each faction will have its own justifying reasons, that there are many reasonable alternatives, and that they will never be the same. The legitimacy of the liberal state, Rawls seems to be arguing, rests with liberal logic being applied to the question of the liberal state itself. This clears the way for a return to a more Grotian conception of the *ius gentium*, or at least it would, if Rawls were to freight empirical investigations with some normative significance. He comes closest to this possibility, appropriately enough, in "The Law of Peoples," where he is willing to speak of "decent" peoples and nations.[24] Foreign policy aside, however, subsequent deontological theorizing on diversity has been framed instead by the recursive quality of Rawls's domestic version of "political liberalism." Does this formulation reduce liberal theory to mere sociology or concept analysis? Is it an unwitting cover for a more invidious forms of Western paternalism? Or instead, a tactical retreat from the enlightenment project altogether?

For a certain strain of European thinkers and statesmen, Rawls's late shift comes dangerously close to the last possibility. This suspicion likely motivates our opening quotation, and the pronouncements of other advocates for a more "muscular" liberalism or assimilationism. This political orientation finds theoretical support among post-Frankfurt "transcendental-pragmatic" thinkers like Jürgen Habermas and Karl-Otto Apel. Apel's 1997 essay "Plurality of the Good? The Problem of Affirmative Tolerance in a Multicultural Society from an Ethical Point of View" is a paradigm instance of this continental approach to diversity from a Kant-informed deontological perspective. For Apel, "discourse ethics" stands against the "empirical pragmatics" of the late-Rawlsian position. That is to say, Apel focuses on the problem of justifying actual points of factual consensus, taking up the task that Rawls had, even in his early writings, deemed "beyond our reach."[25] The promise of a theory like Apel's is that the agent-centered arguments for autonomy and the moral law in Kant might be replaced by "transcendental pragmatics" and "transcendental hermeneutics." In plainer language, this is the claim that discourse itself, both in action and meaning, exerts normative constraints upon our politics and its mechanisms of justification. This grounds what Apel calls an "affirmative" view of tolerance, where respect for judgments on the good made by others is a precondition of meaningful political discourse. At the same time, discursive restraints forbid actions from certain conceptions of the good on the ground that they would not be publicly intelligible in principle to everyone. This is Kant's categorical imperative given a linguistic turn. Apel contends, for instance, that the constraints of discourse speak against slavery, where the Roman *ius gentium* could not.[26]

On the matter of presently existing forms of diversity, however, Apel's account obscures rather than illuminates. Though eschewing Rawls's "mere empiricism," it is not apparent that "discourse ethics" differs significantly from empirical pluralism at the level of practice. This is because, when push comes to shove, Apel, like Rawls, contends that we must defer to actual discourse. The only change seems to be that we say it is an a priori demand of reason that this should be the case:

> It is actually demanded a priori by the principles of discourse ethics that concrete solutions have to be sought again and again through practical discourse between the representatives of the constitutional states and those of the various ethno-religious communities. This holds good, although—as I emphasized already—discourse-ethical mediation cannot content itself by reaching compromises, along the lines of the factual common denominators, between the different communities or their pressure groups.[27]

To any reader not thoroughly immersed in liberal-deontological thinking, this must appear a distinction without a difference. Apel seems to be saying that agreement must have justification beyond itself. But is it not typical of most political agreements that the parties involved would tend to see their assent in terms of universal validity? How are we to judge the difference between "mere" assent and assent oriented, as it were, to universality?[28] A recursion to "working ideals," themselves hardly uncontroversial (e.g., "the idea of human rights"), would seem to be doing much of the work here in Apel's system, and in others like his.[29] Once we grant such working ideals, and also the pragmatic-constructivist assumptions surrounding them, it is notable just how little remains to be said of diversity. We enter not upon a commonsense realm of concretized or less metaphysical categorical imperatives, but instead a hyper-Kantian *Traumwelt*, where language alone leads the way through purgation of insufficiently "self-aware" attachments. Supposing the truth of this vision, human difference exists as a moral obstacle, but little more. As Mssr. Peillon would put it, we achieve moral goodness through our "maintaining some distance from all heritages."

Less ornately conceived statements of post-Rawlsian deontology pervade the Anglo-American literature. T. M. Scanlon's essays are some of the most prominent among these. Scanlon argues, particularly in *The Difficulty of Tolerance*, that though typical accounts of tolerance take a "negative" view of said quality, there is a positive case also to be made. This argument tracks closely in some respects with Apel's, inasmuch as human difference serves as the context for deliberative reasoning, and hence the field on which equality is to be presumed as a norm. Scanlon, though, makes less of transcendental forms of logic and focuses instead upon the meaning of existing commitments. He considers that part of being a citizen involves an attempt to influence the society of which one is a part, according to a conception of good. This is unavoidable and even desirable. However, "What is objectionable about the 'legal enforcement of morals' is the attempt to restrict individuals' personal lives as a way of controlling the evolution of mores."[30] Hence, there is talk of the good, but its permissible bounds are procedural ones, taking their cue from maximal *individual* liberty. Actions upon views of the good not going to the "evolution of mores" through public discourse are to be eschewed. Here "alienation from one's fellow citizens" comes from intolerance. So what would count as intolerance? For Scanlon, this could be something as simple as attempting to block NEA or NEH funding, or as apparently innocuous or anodyne as a politician's proclaiming, "America is a Christian nation."[31]

Scanlon allows that there might be a kind of "partisan zeal" also operating in those (namely himself) pressing for a secular order. But this is to miss the point in which the broader question of tolerance and diversity is concerned. It frames the question in familiar liberal fashion (zeal versus detachment, fanaticism versus universal standards) while leaving untouched the question of why positions not viewing the good exclusively in terms of individual liberty are invalid, or at least unfit as examples of "public" standing. In short, why should "shared" only mean "process"? Scanlon's argument seems to be that as soon as any other kind of sharing appears, respect for those who disagree as fellow citizens is impossible. The unavoidable irony in this position, though, is that the liberal view cannot see itself as a view. The moment it does, it courts a self-referential hypocrisy on the matter of tolerance. This holds especially when the view at issue is a "positive" one, conferring legitimacy on the basis of a highly abstracted account of sharing.[32] If our "positive" duty is to preclude inhibitions on the evolution of mores, then we can't quite get around the absurdity posed by the fact of our precluding being itself inhibitive. It is equivalent to telling groups both domestic and foreign, "Yes, that is what you say, but what you really *mean* is that the good is a process of seeking the good." All views must be contingent, except the view that to articulate is to constitute. For the post-Rawlsian liberal, this claim is not transcendental in the strictly Kantian sense, where one might advert to a noumenal realm. It must instead be true of language or politics themselves. Hence we have, to paraphrase Mandeville, a vast inlet for dogma.

In practice, this circle is squared through the adoption of ironic detachment, or cultural self-abasement. Contemporary deontology must perforce adopt an essentially gnostic position on the fact of diversity: as a moral phenomenon, diversity would be unreal *but for* stubborn backwardness, political-historical accidents, or other temporary impediments in need of rooting out. This stance is the price paid for elevating tolerance to the status of a first-order virtue. Liberal duty thinkers treat diversity repeatedly without touching on one strictly forbidden alternative: that it has some genuine ontological status, not entirely subject to the modifications of agency or discourse. That some groups might not be compatible, or could live peaceably together only with great pain or authoritarian compulsion, is not an eventuality to be countenanced.[33] These "Kants" care not to acknowledge Herder.

Or perhaps it should be said that they care not even to consider what Kant, Mill, or other earlier liberals treated of their own accord; namely, that diversity might have some status as relating to the development of morals. This would presumably involve deductions on the nature of feeling or agency beyond the "nonmetaphysical" scope of contemporary thought. Deduction or no, wittingly or not, such reticence serves a function: it leaves undisturbed a perseverating circle of abstraction that looks askance at the world. For a tradition so ostensibly attached to "discourse," it is notable that discussions rarely break the protective cocoon of late-Rawlsian assumptions. Contemporary duty thinkers on politics will tend to believe such things, for instance, as that events like the Danish cartoon controversy would have been obviated were it not for a deficit of respect generated by inadequate conceptions of autonomy.[34] They look with seriousness not upon groups and cultures themselves, but instead upon the phenomenon of dissent, no matter how miniscule; the former must be assimilated to the latter to advance the claim that foreign cultures are works in progress and, hence, incipiently liberal.[35] Post-Rawlsian theory is thereby dedicated to a curious moral ontology: dissent is prior to those groups from which its departure would make it "dissent" in the first place. The first is real, the second ephemeral.

Of course, no respectable moral theory treating the reality of groups has placed before itself such high Cartesian empirical hurdles. We make do, as Aristotle would say, with what is usually the case, and the absence of unanimity does not render a human phenomenon illusory. But as the last work of Rawls attests, it would seem that deontology cannot get on without something like a *ius gentium*. This development would require, however, a point that cannot be granted under present "discursive restraints": groups as nonvoluntarized realities, subjects for moral investigation. Grotius had such an investigation in mind as he searched for patterns in the testament of civilized history; "chosen" did not yet mean willed freedom of a categorical, formalized variety. An approach like this demands some confidence regarding "civilization," a thing of which contemporary Western thinkers and political figures are largely bereft. In light of this fact, the appeal of political liberalism, discourse ethics, tolerance as a positive virtue, or other late-deontological formulations is obvious: they unburden us of some necessary but unpleasant political judgments; they allow us to remain within the comfortable circle of universal negation.

As mass migration, terrorism, religious conflict, and other cultural clashes intensify, the appeal of the post-Kantian deontological position will strengthen in the short term for precisely this reason. More people will be inclined, with Mssr. Peillon, to argue that the solution to our ills resides in a further distancing from "all heritages." Such "muscular liberalism," however, will exacerbate tensions among groups, not quell them, since it fails on the very grounds of recognition it promises. By positing a conception of human life so alien to the way that most of humanity understands itself, we are doomed to oscillate between self-abnegation and haughty imperiousness.[36] David Hume saw this clearly, two-and-a-half centuries ago, as he addressed social contract theory and the insistence of its partisans that by the logic of consent, monarchy and civility were obviously incompatible:

> What authority any moral reasoning can have, which leads into opinions so wide of the general practice of mankind, in every place but this single kingdom, it is easy to determine.[37]

Are we far from this predicament when we suggest, for instance, that in availing themselves of Western religious freedoms and asking to be respected, Muslims "presuppose a Kantian form of autonomy?"[38] Whether we like the fact or not, the period in which such reveries will seem plausible is coming to a close. The circle of comfortable detachment can remain only where late-Western society enjoys a position of unquestioned hegemony. In the meantime, we would do well to consider stepping beyond commitment to the idea that the morally significant elements of our being always reduce to choice. Mssr. Peillon, it's ok to be French.

NOTES

1. "Peillon: 'Je veux qu'on enseigne la morale laïque,'" leJDD.fr, September 1, 2012, http://www.lejdd.fr/Societe/Education/Actualite/Vincent-Peillon-veut-enseigner-la-morale-a-l-ecole-550018 and Assemblée nationale XIVe legislature Session ordinaire de 2012–2013, http://www.assemblee-nationale.fr/14/cri/2012-2013/20130175.asp.
2. See Hugo Grotius and Richard Tuck, *The Rights of War and Peace*, Vol. 3 (Indianapolis, IN: Liberty Fund, 2005), 1762. (Hereafter Grotius *RWP*.)
3. Grotius *RWP*, 1762.
4. Grotius's position—rather contrary to the emphasis of much present-day policy—was that intervention on behalf of a severely brutalized people might in some rare cases be permitted, whereas interventions for the sake of their liberty would not. This illustrates rather succinctly his disinclination—unlike many later deontologists—to adopt concepts like liberty or self-determination as positive metrics.
5. For a well-stated précis of this issue, see pages 73–75 in J. B. Schneewind, *The Invention of Autonomy: A History of Modern Moral Philosophy* (Cambridge; New York: Cambridge University Press, 1998).
6. Grotius's place within any history of modern voluntarism is well assured, but the empiricist element in his thought is underappreciated. Grotius himself has little reticence in highlighting the importance of historical investigation in his theory, citing it as the occasion for a proper understanding of the difference between the law of nature and the law of nations, and crediting his predecessor Alberico Gentili in particular for taking this historical turn. See Grotius *RWP*, 1755.
7. Grotius *RWP*, 163, fn. 3.
8. See page 18 in Hugo Grotius, Richard Hakluyt, William Welwood, and David Armitage, *The Free Sea* (Indianapolis: Liberty Fund, 2004).
9. In *An Answer to the Question: "What Is Enlightenment?"* Kant argues that enlightenment is properly understood as the human emergence from reliance upon others for understanding; the essay is Kant's strongest polemic on the modern trope of "thinking for oneself." Its open exhortations are mitigated somewhat by more cautious or skeptical tones in much of the rest of Kant's political writing. But it nonetheless presents enlightenment boldly as an ongoing process in which freedom breaks habitual bonds and traditional authority, and is among

Kant's writings probably the closest in spirit to a manifesto. See pages 54–60 in Immanuel Kant, H. S. Reiss, and H. B. Nisbet, *Kant: Political Writings* (Cambridge, UK: Cambridge University Press, 1991). [Hereafter Kant *PW*.]

10. In *Of National Characters*, Hume attributes the diversity of national types to "moral causes." For him this meant habitual motivations too complex to be traceable to climate, soil, or brute biology. This is not to link human diversity to government alone (the position Kant is most directly rejecting here) but instead to suggest that the same inscrutable forces might operate on culture and government. For reasons obvious from the whole of his moral theory, Kant was loath to attach direct normative significance to imprecise and irreducible anthropological forces. See pages 197–215 in David Hume and Eugene F. Miller, *Essays, Moral, Political, and Literary* (Indianapolis: Liberty Classics, 1987).

11. See pages 225–28 in Immanuel Kant, *Anthropology from a Pragmatic Point of View* (Carbondale: Southern Illinois University Press, 1978).

12. Kant, *Anthropology from a Pragmatic Point of View*, 228.

13. Kant, *Anthropology from a Pragmatic Point of View*, 236–37.

14. See Kant's review of Herder's *Ideas on the Philosophy of the History of Mankind*, 210, in Kant *PW*.

15. "In a certain sense all human perfection is therefore *national, secular*, and examined most closely, *individual*. One does not develop anything but that for which *time, climate, need, world, fortune* gives occasion . . . ," page 26 in Johann Gottfried von Herder and Ioannis D. Evrigenis, *Another Philosophy of History and Selected Political Writings* (Indianapolis; Cambridge: Hackett Publishing Company, 2004).

16. Herder claimed, for one instance, that rationality was traceable to the physical development of walking erect. Though ultimately, spiritual forces were first causes, physical events were the more accessible phenomena, and proper subjects of investigation for questions moral and cultural.

17. I refer here to the well-known "formula of humanity," the idea that rational nature exists as an end in itself, the only end with absolute worth. See pages 78–80 in Immanuel Kant and Mary J. Gregor, *Practical Philosophy* (Cambridge; New York: Cambridge University Press, 1999).

18. Kant *PW*, 209.

19. See page 11 in John Rawls, *A Theory of Justice* (Cambridge, MA: Belknap Press of Harvard University Press, 1971). (Hereafter Rawls *ATJ*.)

20. The "besides" here is best articulated by Rawls's "difference principle," the idea that where inequalities appear, they must work in some way to the advantage of those least powerful or influential in order to be justifiable from the original position, and thus have the sanction of law.

21. Rawls states that it is reflective equilibrium among highly divergent positions and descriptions (and not the kind where an actor makes smaller adjust-

ments) that concerns moral philosophy. Yet "it is doubtful whether we can ever reach this state." Therefore, "the most we can do is to study the conceptions known to us through the tradition of moral philosophy and any further ones that occur to us, and then consider these . . . justice as fairness moves us closer to the philosophical ideal; it does not, of course, achieve it" (see Rawls *ATJ*, 49–50). Interestingly, Rawls follows with a footnote (*ATJ*, 51) comparing his approach to Aristotle's, and to "British writers through Sidgwick." From a purely methodological standpoint, this makes clear sense, but philosophically speaking, the analogy is inapt, since these thinkers would have varied but considered reasons for seeing principles as arising in some stronger constitutive fashion from character traits, natural function, emotions, or pleasure, and not merely from the elements of reflection.

22. Rawls, *AJT*, 251–57.

23. "This explanation of reflective equilibrium suggests straightaway a number of further questions. For example, does a reflective equilibrium (in the sense of the philosophical ideal) exist? If so, is it unique? Even if it is unique, can it be reached? Perhaps the judgments from which we begin, or the course of reflection itself (or both), affect the resting point, if any, that we eventually achieve. It would be useless, however, to speculate about these matters here. They are far beyond our reach" (Rawls *ATJ*, 50).

24. See page 57 and following in John Rawls, "The Law of Peoples," *Critical Inquiry* 20, no. 1 (1993).

25. See page 207 in Karl-Otto Apel, "Plurality of the Good? The Problem of Affirmative Tolerance in a Multicultural Society from an Ethical Point of View," *Ratio Juris: An International Journal of Jurisprudence and Philosophy of Law* 10, no. 2 (June 1, 1997): 199–212. On Rawls, see previous footnote.

26. Apel, "Plurality of the Good?," 208.

27. Apel, "Plurality of the Good?," 210.

28. Apel refers to Kohlberg's famous distinction between "conventional" and "post-conventional" standards of morality in explaining an intervention on behalf of a hypothetical Turkish woman being violently repressed by her family. Surely, he argues, we intervene not simply on the basis that German law says such violence is bad, but because we believe the intervention to be right in a universal sense. This may be the case, but the more difficult questions are whether opposition to convention is the sine qua non of an act's moral status, and whether we can meaningfully sort "conventional" from "post-conventional" morality. See Apel, "Plurality of the Good?," 209.

29. One comes to suspect, ruefully, that much of contemporary deontology consists in just this: presenting what is inherently controversial as actually settled, "respectable" opinion. Thus one encounters too frequently the first-person plural pronoun where (rather ironically) further discussion would be warranted.

Even Apel appeals, for instance, to mystifications like the "tacit agreement among predominant collective groups" (208–9).

30. See page 192 of "The Difficulty of Tolerance," in Thomas Scanlon, *The Difficulty of Tolerance: Essays in Political Philosophy* (Cambridge; New York: Cambridge University Press, 2003).

31. Scanlon, *The Difficulty of Tolerance*, 195.

32. A recent and partial exception to these highly formalized and hermetic approaches can be found in Erik Christensen, Revisiting Multiculturalism and Its Critics, *Monist* 95, no. 1 (January 1, 2012): 33–48. Christensen takes seriously some of the recent work done among social scientists and communitarian thinkers on the question of diversity and civil engagement. He is willing to see cultures in a positive light, but ultimately subsumes their value into the same criterion of development-as-autonomy ("we should focus on developing rich contexts of choice").

33. Apel walks right up to the idea in citing the "facticity" and "historicity" of Heidegger and Gadamer, but subsequently folds this hint at human limitation back into the larger process of discourse. He argues that Kant did not see that human beings need contexts for the development of norms; we, by contrast, should support "all the value-traditions that make up the cultural identity of the members of a multicultural society" (see Apel, "Plurality of the Good?," 206–7). The argument here is much the same as the one later advanced by Christensen (cf. 32). More importantly, though, this is a conveniently incomplete reading of Kant. In shifting the issue of limitation to the sphere of history, anthropology, and international politics, Kant exhibited an awareness of the difficulty and took a position, however we might ultimately shrink from his conclusions. One suspects Apel is shrinking from Kant's default assumption to single-nation states, and from the suggestion that international rapprochement could not be materially final. It is easier to say that Kant did not "get" finitude than to make a more difficult (but necessary) argument to the effect that he misplaced it.

34. See Christian F. Rostbøll, "Autonomy, Respect, and Arrogance in the Danish Cartoon Controversy," *Political Theory: An International Journal of Political Philosophy* 37, no. 5 (October 1, 2009): 623–48.

35. See especially pages 192–95 in Scanlon, *The Difficulty of Tolerance*, who, like many other liberal thinkers, seldom goes far in speaking about culture or groups without spilling a cascade of quotation marks. For an even more explicit argument to the effect that groups are far less than what they appear, see Richard Thompson Ford, "Cultural Rights Versus Civic Virtue?," *Monist* 95, no. 1 (January 2012): 151–71. Ford maintains that most disagreements in multicultural society are not really cultural, but the product of overemphasizing both rights and culture, to the detriment of civic virtue. The latter turns out, somewhat unsurprisingly, to be a matter of dialogue.

36. See Geoffrey Brahm Levey, "Liberal Autonomy as a Pluralistic Value," *Monist* 95, no. 1 (January 2012): 103–26. Levey counsels minorities to "speak the language of autonomy," parsing various descriptions of the term to be employed as political criteria, so-called autonomy credentials.

37. See David Hume, "Of the Original Contract," page 487 in *Essays, Moral, Political, and Literary*.

38. Rostbøll, "Autonomy, Respect, and Arrogance in the Danish Cartoon Controversy," 640.

4

UTILITARIANISM ON JUSTICE (AND DIVERSITY)

Raymond Hain, Providence University

> It is expedient for you that one man should die for the people, and that the whole nation perish not.
> —John 11:50

When Jeremy Bentham (1748–1832) introduced the word *utilitarian* into English in 1781,[1] it was already the case that "utilitarians" were both praised and vilified for their account of justice. Utilitarians have at all times counted among their ranks passionate and successful social reformers: John Stuart Mill (1806–1873) on behalf of women's rights,[2] for example, and Peter Singer (b. 1946) today on behalf of the poor.[3] But utilitarianism has likewise never wanted for critics who believe that the utilitarian conception of the moral life leads inevitably to gross violations of justice. William Godwin (1756–1836), husband of the feminist social reformer Mary Wollstonecraft, scandalized readers by claiming, among other things, that a man "has no right to his life, when duty calls him to resign it. Other men are bound . . . to deprive him of life or liberty, if that should appear in any case to be indispensably necessary to prevent a greater evil."[4] This twofold tendency in the development and reception of utilitarianism is a direct result of its central theoretical claims and highlights both the power and controversial nature of utilitarian ethics.

The origins of utilitarianism stretch back beyond the late eighteenth century (J. S. Mill even famously claimed Socrates as an early adherent[5]) and include, besides figures like Godwin, Francis Hutcheson

(1694–1746) and David Hume (1711–1776).[6] But utilitarianism as a clearly delineated moral theory owes most to the systematizing and proselytizing work of Bentham. In turn, Bentham and his friend James Mill (1773–1836) together designed a strictly utilitarian upbringing for James's son, John Stuart, who became and remains utilitarianism's most well-known apologist. Though there are today many rival strands of utilitarian thought, the most popular introduction to utilitarianism is still J. S. Mill's *Utilitarianism*, first published serially in 1861 in London's *Fraser's Magazine* (a revue aimed at the generally educated public, and a reminder that the early utilitarians, like their descendants, desired much more than merely academic converts).

According to Mill, "The creed which accepts as the foundation of morals 'utility' or the 'greatest happiness principle' holds that actions are right in proportion as they tend to promote happiness; wrong as they tend to produce the reverse of happiness."[7] For Mill, as for Bentham before him, the only thing valuable in itself and worth pursuing for its own sake is happiness, and happiness consists in "pleasure and the absence of pain."[8] Mill's understanding of "pleasure" is capacious, for he means to include the full range of enjoyment that we take in things as diverse as a peaceful afternoon walk, a lasting friendship, Bach's cello suites, and scratching an itch. But unlike Bentham (who compared pleasures only quantitatively, in terms of "greater or less"[9]), Mill organizes these pleasures according to their quality (either higher or lower) as well as their quantity (determined by their intensity and duration). Quality matters more than mere quantity, and intellectual pleasures in particular satisfy us in a higher-quality sense than mere physical delight. Because of this, says Mill, "It is better to be a human being dissatisfied than a pig satisfied; better to be Socrates dissatisfied than a fool satisfied. And if the fool, or the pig, are of a different opinion, it is because they only know their own side of the question. The other party to the comparison knows both sides."[10] You act well, therefore, when you promote happiness, and to promote happiness in the fullest sense is to promote the greatest number of highest quality pleasures possible: "According to the greatest happiness principle, . . . the ultimate end, with reference to and for the sake of which all other things are desirable—whether we are considering our own good or that of other people—is an existence exempt as far as possible from pain, and as rich as possible in enjoyments, both in point of quantity and quality."[11]

Later utilitarians have for the most part rejected the classical focus on pleasure and Mill's addition of the distinction between "higher" and "lower" pleasures. "Pleasure" has generally been replaced by "preference" or "interest" satisfaction, which might or might not be connected to pleasure and pain, and which can be measured only in quantitative terms (by "degrees" or "strengths"). Although one necessarily possesses preferences if one possesses the ability to feel pleasure and pain, it is not necessarily the case that all preferences are reducible to pleasure and pain. After all, one might prefer a life of freedom joined to great suffering over a life of completely controlled, drug-induced pleasure. Likewise, "happiness" (which is, in connotation if not in actual meaning, too closely connected to pleasure) is more often "well-being" or "maximal preference satisfaction" instead. And more serious critics have rejected the claim that the only intrinsically valuable goods are the satisfactions of sentient beings. There are strong reasons for including other goods as well: given two worlds, identical in their satisfaction of the preferences of their sentient inhabitants, but differing with respect to their relative beauty, would we not think the more beautiful world a better place, absolutely speaking, and therefore more choiceworthy?[12] On the other hand, although Mill's distinction between higher- and lower-quality pleasures has been discarded in the form in which he developed it, the motivation for that distinction has remained and given rise to arguments over whether or not equally strong preferences have equal moral weight: assuming two persons with equally strong preferences, one of whom prefers friendship, knowledge, love, and so on while the other prefers counting blades of grass, is it reasonable to consider them equally well off if their equally strong preferences are equally satisfied?[13] Despite these difficulties, the formal structure of Mill's utilitarianism remains: the moral life aims at the production of the most good possible, and while that good might include more than sentient satisfactions, it cannot exclude their fundamental importance.

Given that happiness (or, more generally, intrinsic value) should be the end of human action, Mill emphasizes that the "greatest happiness principle" is in no way a selfish principle. It is not my happiness, or your happiness, the pursuit of which determines the moral life; it is instead the total happiness of the whole, for the utilitarian standard "is not the agent's own greatest happiness, but the greatest amount of happiness altogether."[14] My own personal happiness is not the primary goal, and as is clear in the passage from Godwin above, my personal happiness might indeed need to be sacrificed for the sake of the greater happiness of the whole. This is already implicit in the "greatest happiness principle" itself, for you act well by promoting happiness; this will require you to sacrifice some pleasures in your own life for the sake of your own overall greater happiness, and it might likewise require you to sacrifice the pleasure of your own life for the sake of the greater pleasure of the larger community of lives.

Though later utilitarians have disagreed with Bentham and Mill about the precise nature of the good that is to be maximized, there has been no real disagreement over this universal and impartial nature of utilitarian morality. Nevertheless, because of disagreements over the good to be universally maximized, as well as other differences, Mill's descendants typically take to themselves the title *consequentialist* rather than *utilitarian*, and though there are some wrangles over the meaning and application of the term *consequentialist*, it generally names those whose moral theories are descendants of the utilitarianism of Bentham and Mill.[15]

Mill's single utilitarian principle is clearly both plausible and powerful. After all, surely it makes intuitive sense that *what matters* is that things go well for people, that they flourish, that they make and realize serious and lasting projects, enjoy the fruits of the earth and the comforts of one another's company. In short, that people *be happy*, that they achieve as much as they can the real satisfactions possible for human life. And it likewise seems eminently reasonable that it is better for more people to be happy than for fewer, better that the world be full of the genuinely happy rather than the miserable or even only the moderately happy. And naturally if I can through some small sacrifice make possible the much greater happiness of many of my fellows, I should certainly without hesitation make such a sacrifice. This principle in turn yields immediate practical results with obvious implications for the reformation of social practices, and once I know how my various possible actions will influence the happiness of myself and others, I will know how to act. Mill makes clear on the opening page of *Utilitarianism* that he is looking for a first principle of ethics that will do precisely this, a first principle analogous to the first principles of the other sciences—a principle, that is, from which, in combination with scientific knowledge of the causal interactions around us, it is possible to conclude to the practical demands morality places upon us.[16]

I turn now to utilitarianism's account of justice, beginning with Mill and the final chapter of *Utilitarianism*, comprising one-third of its total length, titled "On the Connection between Justice and Utility." "In all ages of speculation," begins Mill, "one of the strongest obstacles to the reception of the doctrine that utility or happiness is the criterion of right and wrong has been drawn from the idea of justice."[17] This is true partly because justice seems a superior, and different, criterion of right and wrong, and so Mill must argue that while justice does possess a special moral status, it is nevertheless, as a criterion of right action, reducible to the greatest happiness principle. He does this by arguing that justice is only a part, though the most important part, of utilitarian morality. What separates it from the rest of morality is that it "implies something which it is not only right to do, and wrong not to do, but which some individual person can claim from us as his moral right."[18] Generosity does not fall under justice, since while I should be generous, I need not be generous to *this* particular person rather than *that*, even though it is true that I should be generous. But justice requires that I keep my promise to a particular individual, that I not steal from my neighbor, and that I judge correctly between these two claimants. In these cases some one individual can claim that I have wronged him or her, and likewise seek remuneration or punishment. We act justly, therefore, when we fulfill our moral obligations that we bear toward particular namable individuals.

It might seem that at least the "wronging" of some definite person must be grounded not on the principle of utility, but instead on some independent principle of absolute rights. But the vocabulary of absolute rights is merely clothing cast upon the figure of utility, a convenience justified by the particularly important place that rules of justice play within society: "To have a right, then, is, I conceive, to have something which society ought to defend me in the possession of. If the objector goes on to ask why it ought, I can give him no other reason than general utility."[19] Even Kant can save the content of his formal system only by drawing on the justificatory force of utilitarianism, for when he

> propounds as the fundamental principle of morals, "So act that thy rule of conduct might be adopted as a law by all rational beings," he virtually acknowledges that the interest of mankind collectively, or at least of mankind indiscriminately, must be in the mind of the agent when conscientiously deciding on the morality of the act. Otherwise he uses words without meaning; for that a rule even of utter selfishness could

not *possibly* be adopted by all rational beings—that there is any insuperable obstacle in the nature of things to its adoption—cannot be even plausibly maintained. To give any meaning to Kant's principle, the sense put upon it must be that we ought to shape our conduct by a rule which all rational beings might adopt *with benefit to their collective interest.*[20]

The ultimate justification of any demand of justice must therefore be its contribution to the general happiness of all, and in this way Mill fits justice directly into the utilitarian system: "I account the justice which is grounded on utility to be the chief part, and incomparably the most sacred and binding part, of all morality. Justice is a name for certain classes of moral rules which concern the essentials of human well-being more nearly, and are therefore of more absolute obligation, than any other rules for the guidance of life."[21]

Given this account of justice, it is now possible that what utilitarianism considers just will appear, at least in some cases, manifestly unjust. As Godwin argued, it might be the duty of the innocent man to sacrifice his life for the general happiness, and our duty to take it from him if he refuses. Here is Mill in the penultimate paragraph of *Utilitarianism*:

> It appears from what has been said that justice is a name for certain moral requirements which, regarded collectively, stand higher in the scale of social utility, and are therefore of more paramount obligation, than any others, though particular cases may occur in which some other social duty is so important as to overrule any one of the general maxims of justice. Thus, to save a life, it may not only be allowable, but a duty, to steal or take by force the necessary food or medicine, or to kidnap and compel to officiate the only qualified medical practitioner. In such cases, as we do not call anything justice which is not a virtue, we usually say, not that justice must give way to some other moral principle, but that what is just in ordinary cases is, by reason of that other principle, not just in the particular case. By this useful accommodation of language, the character of indefeasibility attributed to justice is kept up, and we are saved from the necessity of maintaining that there can be laudable injustice.[22]

Mill is helped here by his choice of examples; few would argue that one may not "steal" when faced with bounty and the prospect of starvation. But the principle ("any one of the general maxims of justice" may be overruled by circumstances) implies cases that are far from compelling and have led some to conclude that something is amiss in utilitarian ethics.

Although this is a significant objection (and one to which I will return below), it is undeniably true that utilitarianism has provided the inspiration for significant social reform; according to Henry Sidgwick (1838–1900), the greatest systematic defender of utilitarianism, a "sincere utilitarian" would most likely be "an eager politician,"[23] and the utilitarian tradition has repeatedly confirmed this. On July 7, 1974, *New York Times* magazine published a short essay titled "Philosophers Are Back On the Job." Its author was Peter Singer, the most visible contemporary example of utilitarian activism, and he meant by his title, among other things, that although academic moral philosophy had, for most of the twentieth century, abandoned practical ethical problems to nonphilosophers in favor of abstract theoretical work, moral philosophers were eminently qualified to help solve them, and indeed were well on their way back to the kind of engagement with politics encouraged by moral philosophers like Sidgwick. Singer was speaking from personal experience, for he had already published in the previous two years both "Famine, Affluence, and Morality,"[24] a powerful and influential argument in favor of aid to the poor, and "Animal Liberation,"[25] a review essay in the *New York Review of Books* (later expanded into a book of the same name[26]) that provided the philosophical foundation of the animal rights movement.

The central argument of "Famine, Affluence, and Morality" has been developed and repeated by Singer in many places since 1972.[27] It consists of very few premises, and in its first incarnation only two:

1. Suffering and death from lack of food, shelter, and medical care are bad.
2. If it is in our power to prevent something bad from happening, without thereby sacrificing anything of comparable moral importance, we ought, morally, to do it.[28]

As long as we assume that it is indeed in our power to prevent some of this suffering without sacrificing anything of comparable moral importance, then we are required to do so. The persuasive power of Singer's argument comes from his central example: "If I am walking past a shallow pond and see a child drowning in it, I ought to wade in and pull the child out. This will mean getting my clothes muddy, but this is insignificant, while the death of the child would presumably be a very bad thing."[29] If you are convinced by this example, Singer argues, then there is no relevant difference between this case and sending a significant portion of your income (which you spend on things of little or no moral relevance) to aid agencies that will help save the lives of those dying of hunger. After all, the mere fact that the famine is *far away* is not morally significant (and instant communication and swift transportation have lessened the *practical* significance of distance). Nor does it matter that others are doing nothing (surely you would not be excused from saving the child even if there were others watching him or her drown who did nothing).

Though Mill argued that justice is only a part of utilitarian morality, it is not clear that utilitarianism ultimately includes any moral demands distinct from justice (at least with regard to our duties toward others). Mill explicitly claimed that generosity, for example, is no part of justice. But Singer concludes that his argument implies a drastic revision to our common understanding of the distinction between justice and charity, for whereas we might think that sending a percentage of our income to help the poor is an act of charity, if this action is instead comparable to saving the drowning child, then duty demands it of us.[30] Singer claims that the strongest interpretation of his argument (and the one he himself accepts) requires that we reduce ourselves to the level of marginal utility; we have fulfilled the demands of justice only when giving up more of our goods will make us equally as poor, or more so, than those to whom we would give, as long as doing so does not require us to sacrifice something of comparable moral significance.[31] Despite Mill's insistence that generosity is distinct from justice, it seems that here he would have agreed with Singer: "The equal claim of everybody to happiness . . . involves an equal claim to all the means of happiness except in so far as the inevitable conditions of human life and the general interest in which that of every individual is included set limits to the maxim." This is a "dictate of justice."[32] Unless my possession of an excess of goods contributes to the "general interest" (the greatest happiness of the greatest number), or is a result of the "inevitable conditions of human life" (such as the practical problems created by distance or the inability to communicate), I owe aid to my fellows as a matter of justice. Utilitarianism, therefore, moves with great and constant energy toward a fully just society; but it quickly overtakes the traditional places of charity and generosity and all those actions that we sometimes refer to as "supererogatory"—morally good, but not morally required.³³ To say that it is morally good to help relieve the suffering of the poor is to say that such relief is justly deserved and therefore that it is morally required.

Whereas "Famine, Affluence, and Morality" argues that we must work to prevent the suffering of our fellow human beings, "Animal Liberation" argues that we must extend the scope of our concern beyond the merely human to all sentient beings as such. Having proposed to the *New York Review of Books* that he discuss in its pages the recently published *Animals, Men, and Morals*,³⁴ Singer used the occasion to call for a transformation in our treatment of animals and to develop the philosophical foundations of such a transformation. "Jeremy Bentham," says Singer, "expressed the essential basis of equality in his famous formula: 'Each to count for one and none for more than one.' In other words, the interests of every being that has interests are to be taken into account and treated equally with the like interests of any other being."³⁵ One possesses interests so long as one is sentient and so can feel pleasure or pain. Singer here quotes Bentham:

> The day *may* come, when the rest of the animal creation may acquire those rights which never could have been withholden from them but by the hand of tyranny. The French have already discovered that the blackness of the skin is no reason why a human being should be abandoned without redress to the caprice of a tormentor. It may one day come to be recognized, that the number of the legs, the villosity of the skin, or the termination of the *os sacrum*, are reasons equally insufficient for abandoning a sensitive being to the same fate. What else is it that should trace the insuperable line? Is it the faculty of reason, or, perhaps, the faculty of discourse? But a full-grown horse or dog is beyond comparison a more rational, as well as a more conversable animal, than an infant of a day, or a week, or even a month, old. But suppose the case were otherwise, what would it avail? The question is not, Can they *reason*? Nor, Can they *talk*? but, Can they *suffer*?³⁶

For Bentham, Singer, and the utilitarian tradition in general,³⁷ the ability to feel pleasure and pain has intrinsic moral significance always and everywhere, such that "if a being suffers, there can be no moral justification for refusing to take that suffering into consideration, and, indeed, to count it equally with the like suffering (if tough comparisons can be made) of any other being."[38] While perhaps human beings are capable of more acute, or even "deeper" or "higher quality" pleasures and pains, the suffering or satisfaction of animals weighs equally in the scales with an equal measure of human suffering or satisfaction. If we grant more importance to the pleasures or pains of human beings *merely* because they are human, we are guilty of speciesism, which, like racism, favors one particular class of beings over another for no morally justifiable reason.

As with "Famine, Affluence, and Morality," the consequences of this line of thinking are radical. The enormous number of animal experiments that occur each year for little or no significant human gain (for the sake of the cosmetics industry, for example) are morally reprehensible and must be abandoned. Factory farming, which demands that millions of animals be raised in deplorable conditions so that we have cheap and readily available meat, is likewise a complete disgrace. To ignore animals in our moral calculations is to ignore those who, like you reading this chapter, possess moral weight, for what matters is bringing about the greatest happiness of the greatest number, and those "numbered" are those who can experience "happiness," even in its most basic forms. As long as one can be a voluntary and responsible cause of the pleasure or pain of animals, one can likewise be a just benefactor, or an unjust moral monster.

Singer is powerfully persuasive with respect to famine relief and animal cruelty partly because a great deal of this human and animal suffering can be prevented without the loss of much that is morally problematic. Living with fewer material goods so that one can contribute to famine relief, or becoming a vegetarian so that one does not support factory farming, are not immediately problematic choices (though there are of course counterarguments even here), but if we continue this line of thinking, we get the challenge implied by Mill at the end of *Utilitarianism*. If I could prevent the suffering and death of five people by sacrificing myself and donating my organs to them, am I (other things being equal) required to do so? If the suffering of a deformed human infant is of less moral importance than the suffering of five mature pigs (as Singer himself believes is perfectly possible[39]), should our scarce medical resources be transferred from the human child to the pigs? It seems that such difficult things will sometimes be required of us, and this is just and acceptable, for the greater good demands it.

Some utilitarians, like Godwin, have been willing to accept these extreme conclusions and to call for the required revisions to our ordinary moral intuitions. But many utilitarians believe that some other kind of response is necessary. Consider first the response of Singer's Oxford mentor, R. M. Hare (1919–2002): were we to possess perfect knowledge of the relevant circumstances of a problematic case, we would find that utilitarianism does not after all require that we violate our deeply held moral convictions concerning justice. He argues for this in the following way. Moral reasoning occurs on two levels; there is first an intuitive level, a level that includes general factual knowledge, moral assumptions, habits of judgment, claims regarding one's duties, and spontaneous moral responses to difficult situations. Much of our thinking at the intuitive level turns out to be correct, but it is perfectly possible (and in some circumstances very likely) that we will make mistakes at the intuitive level, that our factual knowledge will be significantly misleading, that the demands of our duties will conflict, that our emotions will confuse us, and so on. Critical moral thinking, on the other hand, is reflective, taking all the various circumstances of a situation into account, and balances potentially competing duties against one another so as to arrive at a final correct judgment in light of all the relevant facts. What might seem an objection to utilitarian justice at the intuitive level will evaporate under the steady light of the critical level. Here is Hare's example: "There are in a hospital two patients, one needing for survival a new heart and the other new kidneys; a down-and-out who is known to nobody and who happens to have the same tissue-type as both the patients strays in out of the cold. Ought they not to kill him, give his heart and kidneys to the patients, and thus save two lives at the expense of the one?"[40] It seems clear that the utilitarian must say yes, while it seems equally clear that this would be unjust. Therefore, something must be wrong with utilitarianism. But if we respond by thinking critically about this case, our view will change:

> Have the doctors checked on the down-and-out's connexions or lack of them? (How? By consulting the police records, perhaps! But a colleague of my psychiatrist sister once wrote in his notes, about a disheveled individual brought in off the streets very late at night by the police, "Has delusion that he is a high-ranking civil servant," and it turned out that he was in fact a *very* high-ranking civil servant.) Have they absolute confidence in the discretion and support of all the nurses, porters, mortuarists, etc., who will know what has happened? Add to

this the extreme unlikelihood of there being no other way of saving these patients, if they can be saved at all, and it will be evident that your opponent is not going to get much help out of this example once it is insisted that it has to be fleshed out and given verisimilitude.[41]

Examples meant to show that utilitarianism requires gross violations of justice are disingenuously constructed precisely so that they will do so. But for any example of this sort to succeed, it must be realistic enough to have the possibility of occurring in the real world, and once we "flesh out" all the relevant details, we will find that utilitarianism harmonizes after all with what we want to say about justice—it will not contribute to the greater overall good to sacrifice the vagrant for the sake of the other two patients. Hare does admit that it is at least theoretically possible to construct a realistic case, but that so far this has not been done, and given that we will need to think critically about any presumptive candidate, it is entirely likely that any putative example will fail to survive close scrutiny.[42]

For Hare, utilitarianism allows the abstract possibility that we must sacrifice the innocent for the sake of the greater good, but practically speaking this is never or almost never actually demanded of us and therefore the putative counterexamples to utilitarianism's account of justice are misleading. A second response to the objection that utilitarianism requires violations of justice, however, rejects Hare's optimistic view of everyday circumstances, admits that the sacrifice of the innocent will be required more often than many people would like, and concludes that therefore this aspect of utilitarianism must be kept secret. Sidgwick explains this in the following way:

> On Utilitarian principles, it may be right to do and privately recommend, under certain circumstances, what it would not be right to advocate openly; it may be right to teach openly to one set of persons what it would be wrong to teach to others; it may be conceivably right to do, if it can be done with comparative secrecy, what it would be wrong to do in the face of the world; and even, if perfect secrecy can be reasonably expected, what it would be wrong to recommend by private advice or example.[43]

In the case of the doctor and his three patients, whether or not he should sacrifice the innocent man for the sake of the other two depends on, among other things, the relatively public nature of his action and his reasons for doing it. That is, perhaps the kind of example described by Hare will not justify killing the one for the sake of the others, but if the doctor can act in complete secrecy, and if the fact that he believes complete secrecy will justify this sort of act can itself be kept secret, then it is perfectly plausible that it is indeed the morally right action. Even more, this theoretical aspect of utilitarianism should *itself* be kept secret. Here again is Sidgwick:

> The Utilitarian conclusion, carefully stated, would seem to be this; that the opinion that secrecy may render an action right which would not otherwise be so should itself be kept comparatively secret; and similarly it seems expedient that the doctrine that esoteric morality is expedient should itself be kept esoteric. Or if this concealment be difficult to maintain, it may be desirable that Common Sense should repudiate the doctrines which it is expedient to confine to an enlightened few. And thus a Utilitarian may reasonably desire, on Utilitarian principles, that some of his conclusions should be rejected by mankind generally; or even that the vulgar should keep aloof from his system as a whole, in so far as the inevitable indefiniteness and complexity of its calculations render it likely to lead to bad results in their hands.[44]

We should admit that in some cases utilitarianism will demand the sacrifice of the innocent for the sake of the greater good, but we will promote the most good possible if this aspect of utilitarianism is not well known, not only because most people are mistakenly prejudiced against such actions but also because the delicate nature of the judgments involved in such difficult cases requires that they be reserved to a very small and well-educated elite. One utilitarian advocate of this response is Singer himself, who claimed recently that "esoteric morality is a necessary part of a consequentialist theory."[45] After describing a case similar in structure to Hare's, though here the doctor can save four patients rather than two and her action will remain perfectly secret, Singer claims that

> the consequentialist must accept that, in these circumstances, the right thing for the surgeon to do would be to kill the one to save the four, but we do not agree that this means that consequentialism should be rejected. We think, on the contrary, that the appearance of unacceptability here comes from the fact that this is one of those rare cases in

which the action is right only if perfect secrecy can be expected. Moreover, it is not an action that should be recommended to others.[46]

For good utilitarian reasons, it is right that most people believe that the doctor in this case acts badly, and indeed we must, as a society, encourage people to believe this, but nevertheless it remains true that sometimes the greatest good can be brought about by this sort of action, and therefore here and in other equally rare cases such actions are morally good and just. The proper response to these difficult extreme cases is then twofold: the educated elite must recognize that their natural revulsion is an expected and proper response, but that nevertheless this intuitive reaction is misleading, whereas the majority should be encouraged to believe that their immediate response is indeed morally correct (and as a consequence that utilitarianism does not require the sacrifice of the innocent, or that utilitarian conclusions are mistaken, at least in these cases).

I have so far left to one side an important distinction within utilitarian ethics, a distinction that is necessary in order to explain a third response, different in kind from those of Hare and Singer. Does one act well if one performs the particular *act* here and now that will (or can be expected to) bring about the greatest good, or instead does one act well if one follows the *rule* that will (or can be expected to) bring about the greatest good? "Act-utilitarianism" (or today, more typically, "act-consequentialism") requires that your actions be evaluated according to their individual contribution to the good, but "rule-utilitarianism" (or "rule-consequentialism") instead requires that your actions be evaluated according to whether or not they conform to the rules that will bring about the greatest good.[47] The utilitiarian's basic commitment is to the greatest good, but the rule-utilitarian honors this commitment in terms of the rules, and *not* in terms of individual actions. Therefore, a particular action might indeed bring about less good (perhaps even a great deal less good) than an alternative action, and yet if it accords with the best rules then it is the right action to perform. Brad Hooker (b. 1957), the best recent defender of rule-consequentialism, explains this as follows:

> Whatever act-consequentialism says about day-to-day moral thinking, act-consequentialism's criterion of moral rightness implies that *whenever* killing an innocent person, or taking or harming the possessions of others, or breaking a promise, and so on, would maximize the good, such acts would be morally right. Rule-consequentialism denies this. It

claims instead that individual acts of murder, torture, breaking promises, and so on can be wrong even when they result in somewhat more good than not doing them would. Morality, according to rule-consequentialism, is not a matter of the (expected) consequences of individual acts, but rather a matter of the expected value resulting from the general internalization of codes of rules. And general internalization of a code prohibiting physical injury (except when necessary for defense of the innocent or as part of competitive games played voluntarily), prohibiting stealing and vandalizing property, and prohibiting promise-breaking and lying would clearly result in more good than general internalization of a code with no prohibition on such acts.[48]

In this way Hooker can avoid the implications of Singer's example. Even if it is true that the doctor can act in perfect secrecy and that sacrificing the innocent patient will bring about more good than otherwise, because the doctor would in doing so violate the code of rules whose "general internalization" would bring about the greatest "expected value," the doctor must refrain from the murder. This strategy makes rule-consequentialism align much more easily with typical intuitions about justice.

Hooker nevertheless acknowledges that it is still possible, in extremely rare cases, that violating a particular rule will be necessary to avoid disaster, and in these special cases we should accept that perhaps an innocent person must die for the sake of the greater good. In this way the central utilitarian insight that what matters most is that things go best for the greatest number retains it central role. Here is Hooker's example, which is importantly much more extreme than Singer's:

> Suppose that, because of some bizarre twist of fate, torturing to death a child who happens to be on a different planet is the only way to save the rest of *the entire human species* (and every other species) from excruciating suffering followed by painful death. . . . Now in this case, refusing to save the world at the cost of one innocent child would, I believe, be morally worse than sacrificing the child. After all, this really is the only way to save *billions* of others, and indeed the very future of humanity. . . . Think carefully about cases such as [this one]. . . . Don't you agree that, when so much is at stake, torturing and killing the innocent must be the "lesser evil"? If so, you admit that normal prohibitions on harming others should be overridden in the most extreme (and unlikely) cases.[49]

Hooker therefore disagrees with Singer with respect to the case of the doctor (and similar examples), since foregoing the increase in overall good in such cases would not constitute a disaster. Rule-consequentialism in this sense does not violate our ordinary intuitions about justice. But in disaster situations, we should violate the particular rule in question in order to avoid extreme losses, as in his example above. But Hooker thinks that here our intuitions are not necessarily against him, for if we "think carefully," we will find that, even if we do not embrace his conclusion, we likely are at least unsure what is right, and therefore such examples constitute no objection to rule-consequentialism.

I have focused above on the structural features of utilitarianism, and on the way these give rise to the utilitarian account of justice, without yet saying anything about diversity. And yet all the elements are now in place to allow me to say what should be said, for the value of diversity, like justice, is reducible to the greatest happiness principle and implies a particular set of human behaviors that promote the greatest good of the greatest number. The most important example here is again that of Mill, whose *On Liberty*, published in 1859, two years before *Utilitarianism*, remains one of the most persuasive and powerful defenses of autonomy and diversity.

Citizens, he claims, should be left to themselves to live out their lives as they see fit, as long as doing so does not harm others against their will, because autonomy and diversity are necessary for the general happiness and future social progress. We should, for example, allow others the freedom to think and speak as they wish, as long as they do not harm others against their will, because (1) their opinions might turn out to be true, (2) or if erroneous they might contain at least a portion of truth, (3) and even if completely false we maintain clear understanding of our own opinions only through genuine debate with those who disagree with us, (4) and likewise our own opinions have no emotional force in our lives if we are not forced to defend them against those who disagree with us.[50] The freedom of all to think and speak is important, therefore, because it allows us to achieve the truth with certainty and passion, and in this way contributes to our overall good and the good of society. Freedom of action, Mill's primary concern, is important for similar reasons:

> If [the individual] refrains from molesting others in what concerns them, and merely acts according to his own inclination and judgment

in things which concern himself, the same reasons which show that opinion should be free prove also that he should be allowed, without molestation, to carry his opinions into practice at his own cost. That mankind are not infallible; that their truths, for the most part, are only half-truths; that unity of opinion, unless resulting from the fullest and freest comparison of opposite opinions, is not desirable, and diversity not an evil, but a good, until mankind are much more capable than at present of recognizing all sides of the truth, are principles applicable to men's modes of action not less than to their opinions.[51]

We must allow freedom of action because we achieve "progress" through "experiments of living,"[52] most obviously in the case of the rare, gifted genius who pushes against the customs of society and in doing so expands our conceptions of the greatest and best that human life can offer. Freedom is necessary for more average citizens as well, for only by developing according to the tendency of our own inward forces that constitute us as individuals do we have the best chance at a full and happy life, and even the "experiments of living" of the average are valuable to society as a whole. Individual autonomy therefore significantly promotes the greatest happiness of the greatest number as does its proper fruit, the rich diversity that parallels the diversity of a vast experimenting scientific community that over time yields great and lasting scientific progress. As with the utilitarian conception of justice, this account of autonomy and diversity is grounded on the greatest happiness principle: "It is proper to state that I forego any advantage which could be derived to my argument from the idea of abstract right as a thing independent of utility. I regard utility as the ultimate appeal on all ethical questions; but it must be utility in the largest sense, grounded on the permanent interests of man as a progressive being."[53]

As in the case of justice, utilitarianism provides a powerful defense of liberty and diversity, and history counts many utilitarians among the most vocal defenders of individual autonomy and social diversity. *On Liberty* ends with, among other examples, criticisms of legal restrictions on so-called private vices and arguments in favor of no-fault divorce,[54] and Peter Singer has been and remains a strong advocate of the permissibility of physician-assisted suicide.[55] But unlike those who defend autonomy and diversity in terms of absolute rights, the utilitarian's defense depends on whether or not the greatest happiness is genuinely promoted by these means; it is no surprise, therefore, that Sidgwick would later criticize Mill in precisely these terms:

> To attempt the required division [between individual freedom and social control] by means of any such general formula as "the individual is not responsible to society for that part of his conduct which concerns himself alone and others only with their free and undeceived consent" seems to me practically futile: since, owing to the complex enlacements of interest and sympathy that connect the members of a civilized community, almost any material loss of happiness by any one individual is likely to affect some others without their consent to some not inconsiderable extent. And I do not see how it is from a utilitarian point of view justifiable to say broadly with J. S. Mill that such secondary injury to others . . . is to be disregarded in view of the advantages of allowing free development to individuality; for if the injury feared is great, and the presumption that it will occur is shown by experience to be strong, the definite risk of evil from the withdrawal of the moral sanction must, I conceive, outweigh the indefinite possibility of loss through the repression of individuality in one particular direction.[56]

Diversity is necessary if it promotes the overall greatest good, but if it frustrates that good, it must be suppressed. How often and when this will occur is a matter of circumstance. If we recoil at certain cases, we have available the responses above with respect to justice. Perhaps such cases are practically speaking nonexistent (Hare), or their possibility should be kept secret (Singer), or the best rules available to us require the promotion of autonomy and diversity and we act well by following those rules, even if by certain individual acts we could promote more good by acting against autonomy and diversity (Hooker). Regardless, utilitarianism's judgments with respect to autonomy and diversity are generally much less controversial than those with respect to justice, for everyone agrees that one's autonomy must have at least some limits, and that diversity is not so valuable as to trump all other social goods. Precisely where we mark those limits merely depends, as it does in all other situations, on what will promote the greatest good for the greatest number.

NOTES

1. In a letter from Bentham to George Wilson; see *The Works of Jeremy Bentham*, 11 vols. (Edinburgh: William Tate, 1838–1843), vol. 10, 92.

2. This is evidenced throughout Mill's writings, but most especially in his essay *The Subjection of Women*, originally published in 1869 and still widely reprinted. Elected to Parliament in 1865, Mill also became, in 1868, the first person to introduce into Parliament a bill for women's suffrage.

3. Beginning with "Famine, Affluence, and Morality," this has been a special focus of Singer's professional life. See below for references and a discussion of his central argument.

4. William Godwin, *Enquiry Concerning Political Justice* (London: Oxford University Press, 1971), 89. This reproduces the third and final edition, originally published in 1798 (the first edition was published in 1793 and the second in 1796).

5. John Stuart Mill, *Utilitarianism* (Indianapolis, IN: Hackett, 2001), 1 (chapter 1, §1).

6. For an excellent discussion of these early roots, see Geoffrey Scarre, *Utilitarianism* (New York: Routledge, 1996), chapter 3. Chapter 2 is a discussion of even more ancient progenitors, including Jesus and Aristotle, though the connections here are more tenuous.

7. Mill, *Utilitarianism*, 7 (chapter 2, §2).

8. Mill, *Utilitarianism*. For Bentham, see his *The Principles of Morals and Legislation* (1781), chapter 1, §§1–3, in *The Works of Jeremy Bentham*, vol. 1, 1–2.

9. Jeremy Bentham, "The Principles of Morals and Legislation," in *The Works of Jeremy Bentham*, vol. 1, 29-32.

10. Mill, *Utilitarianism*, 10 (chapter 2, §6).

11. Mill, *Utilitarianism*, 12 (chapter 2, §10).

12. Utilitarian arguments on behalf of goods independent of pleasure or preference satisfaction began especially with G. E. Moore (1873–1958) and the publication in 1903 of his *Principia Ethica* (esp. §§55, 57, and 112–35). G. E. Moore, *Principia Ethica: Revised Edition* (Cambridge: Cambridge University Press, 1993), 144–47 and 236–73. His version of utilitarianism came to be known as "ideal utilitarianism."

13. For a brief and insightful discussion of the difficulties involved in giving a satisfying utilitarian account of what counts as valuable, see Brad Hooker, *Ideal Code, Real World: A Rule-Consequentialist Theory of Morality* (Oxford: Clarendon Press, 2000), 37–43. Scarre goes so far as to say that "production of a satisfactory theory of value is probably the hardest, yet at the same time the most vital, task facing utilitarians today" (Mill, *Utilitarianism*, 151).

14. Mill, *Utilitarianism*, 11 (chapter 2, §9).

15. For a clear, general overview of these terminological difficulties as well as an introduction to contemporary consequentialism, see Walter Sinnott-Armstrong, "Consequentialism," in *Stanford Encyclopedia of Philosophy* (Palo Alto, CA: Stanford University Press, 2011), available at http://plato.stanford.edu/entries/consequentialism/.

16. Mill is clearer about this in his *Logic* (first published in 1843 and revised seven times with the eighth and final edition appearing in 1872), Book VI, chapter 7, §2: "The relation in which rules of art [sc. Ethics] stand to doctrines of science may be thus characterized. The art proposes to itself an end to be attained, defines the end, and hands it over to the science. The science receives it, considers it as a phenomenon or effect to be studied, and having investigated its causes and conditions, sends it back to art with a theorem of the combinations of circumstances by which it could be produced. Art then examines these combinations of circumstances, and according as any of them are or are not in human power, pronounces the end attainable or not. The only one of the premises, therefore, which Art supplies, is the original major premise, which asserts that the attainment of the given end is desirable. Science then lends to Art the proposition (obtained by a series of inductions or of deductions) that the performance of certain actions will attain the end. From these premises Art concludes that the performance of these actions is desirable, and finding it also practicable, converts the theorem into a rule or precept." *A System of Logic*, vol. 2 (Toronto: University of Toronto Press, 1974), 944–45.

17. Mill, *Utilitarianism*, 42 (chapter 5, §1). The situation has not changed in the ensuing century and a half.

18. Mill, *Utilitarianism*, 50 (chapter 5, §15).

19. Mill, *Utilitarianism*, 54 (chapter 5, §25).

20. Mill, *Utilitarianism*, 52–53 (chapter 5, §22).

21. Mill, *Utilitarianism*, 59 (chapter 5, §32).

22. Mill, *Utilitarianism*, 63–64 (chapter 5, §37). Again, Mill is somewhat clearer in the *Logic*: "By a wise practitioner . . . rules of conduct will only be considered as provisional. Being made for the most numerous cases, or for those of most ordinary occurrence, they point out the manner in which it will be least perilous to act, where time or means do not exist for analysing the actual circumstances of the case, or where we cannot trust our judgment in estimating them. But they do not at all supersede the propriety of going through (when circumstances permit) the scientific process requisite for framing a rule from the data of the particular case before us." *A System of Logic*, 946.

23. Henry Sidgwick, *The Methods of Ethics* (first published in 1874 with its seventh and last edition published in 1907), seventh ed. (Indianapolis: Hackett, 1981), 495 (Book 4, chapter 5, §4).

24. Peter Singer, "Famine, Affluence, and Morality," *Philosophy and Public Affairs* 1, no. 3 (Spring 1972): 229–43.

25. April 5, 1973.

26. Peter Singer, *Animal Liberation* (New York: Avon Books, 1975). *Animal Liberation* has been reprinted several times since then, most recently in 2009 with a new preface by Singer (New York: Harper Perennial).

27. The argument (and forthcoming pond example) appears in each of the three editions of *Practical Ethics*, most recently in 2011 (New York: Cambridge University Press, 2011), 199ff. See also *One World: The Ethics of Globalization* (New Haven: Yale University Press, 2002), 156ff., and *The Life You Can Save* (New York: Random House, 2009), 3ff. Singer has also inspired other philosophers, the best example of which is Peter Unger, *Living High and Letting Die: Our Illusion of Innocence* (Oxford: Oxford University Press, 1996).

28. Singer, "Famine, Affluence, and Morality," 231.

29. Singer, "Famine, Affluence, and Morality."

30. Singer, "Famine, Affluence, and Morality," 235–36.

31. Singer, "Famine, Affluence, and Morality," 240–42.

32. Mill, *Utilitarianism*, 62–63 (chapter 5, §36).

33. For an interesting utilitarian discussion of superogatory actions, see R. M. Hare, *Moral Thinking* (Oxford: Clarendon Press, 1981), 198–203. Hare defends supererogatory language (we should praise those moral heroes who go above and beyond what the rest of us achieve as doing what the rest of us cannot be required to do), but argues that those heroes, because they are able to act as they do, are required to do so, and so for Hare there is no deep distinction between what is morally required and what is supererogatory.

34. *Animals, Men, and Morals: An Enquiry into the Maltreatment of Non-Humans*, ed. Stanley Godlovitch, Rosalind Godlovitch, and John Harris (New York: Taplinger, 1971).

35. Singer, *Animal Liberation*, 17.

36. Jeremy Bentham, *The Principles of Morals and Legislation*, chapter 17, fn. to §4, in *The Works of Jeremy Bentham*, vol. 1, 311 (quoted by Singer on page 17).

37. Consider, for example, Henry Sidgwick's *The Methods of Ethics*, Book 4, chapter 1, §2 (414): "We have next to consider who the 'all' are, whose happiness is to be taken into account. Are we to extend our concern to all the beings capable of pleasure and pain whose feelings are affected by our conduct? or are we to confine our view to human happiness? The former view is the one adopted by Bentham and Mill, and (I believe) by the Utilitarian school generally: and is obviously most in accordance with the universality that is characteristic of their principle. It is the Good *Universal*, interpreted and defined as 'happiness' or 'pleasure,' at which a Utilitarian considers it his duty to aim: and it seems

arbitrary and unreasonable to exclude from the end, as so conceived, any pleasure of any sentient being."

38. Singer, *Animal Liberation*," 17.

39. Singer wrote in the first edition of *Practical Ethics* that "the life of a newborn [human] is of less value than the life of a pig, a dog, or a chimpanzee." (Cambridge: Cambridge University Press, 1979), 123. Subsequent editions of *Practical Ethics* have moderated the tone of this claim somewhat, but the fundamental view has remained the same. Because a newborn human's capacities are so extraordinarily underdeveloped (including not only characteristically human capacities but even capacities for general awareness, fear, pleasure, etc.) in comparison to the mature pig, dog, or chimpanzee, that the nonhuman animals' interests are of greater moral significance than the human infant's. This would change, of course, once the infant reached a sufficient level of maturity.

40. Hare, *Moral Thinking*, 132.

41. Hare, *Moral Thinking*, 133–34.

42. Hare, *Moral Thinking*, 135.

43. Sidgwick, *The Methods of Ethics*, Book 4, chapter 5, §3 (489).

44. Sidgwick, *The Methods of Ethics*, 490.

45. Katarzyna de Lazari-Radek and Peter Singer, "Secrecy in Consequentialism: A Defense of Esoteric Morality," *Ratio* 23, no. 1 (March 2010): 34–58, 36.

46. de Lazari-Radek and Singer, "Secrecy in Consequentialism," 40.

47. The theoretical relationship between act-utilitarianism and rule-utilitarianism became programmatic in the utilitarian tradition only in the twentieth century. There is debate, therefore, about where Mill should be placed. For a good introduction to the interpretive problem as well as the general issue, see Roger Crisp, *Mill on Utilitarianism* (London: Routledge, 1997), 102–33.

48. Hooker, *Ideal Code, Real World*, 145.

49. Hooker, *Ideal Code, Real World*, 129–31.

50. Hooker, *Ideal Code, Real World*, 50 (chapter 2, §§39–42).

51. Hooker, *Ideal Code, Real World*, 53–54 (chapter 3, §1).

52. Hooker, *Ideal Code, Real World*.

53. Hooker, *Ideal Code, Real World*, 10 (chapter 1, §11).

54. Hooker, *Ideal Code, Real World*, 96–97, 102–3 (chapter 5, §§5, 9).

55. For a recent example, see the third edition of *Practical Ethics* (Cambridge: Cambridge University Press, 2011), 169–76.

56. Sidgwick, *The Methods of Ethics*, Book 4, chapter 5, §1 (477–78).

5

SYSTEMS OF JUSTICE AND ROLE OF THE MORAL PROPHET

James Campbell, University of Toledo

This chapter considers a pair of related themes. On the one hand, what is a system of justice? How do these systems develop and flourish, and why do they decline? On the other hand, what role does the moral prophet play in this process? My intention is not to offer a new system of justice or a new prophet. It is, rather, to explore an approach to understanding our historical systems of justice, and the role of moral prophets, that arises out of the broad American Pragmatic tradition. Readers may find that the ideas that I present will uproot their current ways of thinking; more likely, these ideas will leaven their thinking with some novel themes that may cause them to reexamine what they now believe.

SYSTEMS OF JUSTICE

My source for much of this first part will be the thought of John Dewey and his colleague James Hayden Tufts, who largely codified this approach in their coauthored volume, *Ethics* (1908, rev. ed. 1932).[1] Because of the importance of the ancient and central social value of justice to human well-being, some definition of the term as they understand it is necessary. Tufts writes that justice is "[w]hat is right or due or fair." He continues that the standard for justice "is found either in those formulated customs and statutes of a people which are enforced by public authority as in legal justice, or in those *mores* and ideals which are rather a matter of feeling, or reason, or conscience in the broad use of the term."[2] Moreover, Tufts further maintains that justice has a kind of primacy among our social goods. He notes that "[i]t may be doubted whether any of the words since framed to express human values takes so strong a hold as 'justice.'" He sees it as embodying "the claim of personality, of the aspirations and expanding life of the human spirit." Because justice presents "the rights of each as the concern of all," it forces us to recognize "the essentially social nature of man's higher development." Similarly, we feel the sting of injustice because it is "virtually a denial of humanity. He who has no rights is not a person but a thing." When we consider justice historically—or as they sometimes write, genetically—we encounter "the history of the emerging one by one of higher and more social powers—life, property, liberty of thought and speech, education—and of the recognition and protection of these by society." The history of justice is further "the history of various standards or balances for measuring these claims—custom, the decrees of rulers and assemblies, the will of God, the rule of reason."[3] Moreover, when we approach systems of justice Pragmatically, we recognize that notions of justice grow in the course of social practice, beginning as the solution to a particular problem, developing into a useful law, and frequently becoming irrelevant or even counterproductive over time.

We can begin our exploration with a 1908 passage from Tufts that, while not without its problems, offers a clear presentation of the Pragmatic understanding of justice. He writes:

> Our conceptions of honesty and justice, of rights and duties, got their present shaping largely in an industrial and business order when mine and thine could be easily distinguished; when it was easy to tell how much a man produced; when the producer sold to his neighbors, and an employer had also the relations of neighbor to his workmen; when responsibility could be personally located, and conversely a man could control the business he owned or make individual contracts; when each man had his own means of lighting, heating, water supply, and frequently of transportation, giving no opportunity or necessity for public service corporations. Such conceptions are inadequate for the present order.[4]

Please try to overlook the problematic themes, particularly those of class and gender, that this excerpt contains—issues that demonstrate exactly the transiency of notions of justice to which Tufts is pointing—and consider his main theme. What seems just to us is largely a social inheritance that developed slowly over time and became sacralized, but must ever be held up to the light of contemporary criticism. Our task as moral beings is to attempt to bring the customary into agreement with what seems to us rational.

For Tufts, any current system of justice is a mixture of both higher and lower. "Our justice is in part the divine principles, but it is also in part the work of barbarous times and selfish men," he writes. "It embodies class interests and vested wrongs, as well as fairness and hard-won rights." The great difficulty that confronts us as moral beings is that "[t]he sacredness that belongs only to the one is sometimes invoked for the other,"[5] making the defense of the ways of the past our moral obligation. However you decide the intent of his term *divine*—another theme for the sort of reflective consideration that the Pragmatists advocated[6]—Tufts maintains that our current problems with finding and enacting justice are to a great extent "the carrying-over of the methods—and even the virtues—of one age into the changed conditions of another."[7]

Speaking broadly, Tufts maintains that justice has two interpretations. "The one emphasizes order and established rights," he notes, "the other, progress and new claims." With regard to "the inequalities between strong and weak," the former holds that "the strong are entitled to retain all or most of the advantages to which superior natural ability or existing institutions have given them 'rights.'" Moreover, the interpretation of justice that defends the present arrangement also holds that "the advance of civilization" is primarily the result of the efforts of "the strong," and it "considers it just to uphold them in all their gains." The latter, progressive interpretation of justice "sees as desirable and just a larger measure of equality than has already been embodied in past law," and he points to such issues as "equality in educational opportunity, in bargaining power, in the distribution of the goods of advancing civilization." This view "holds that the good of society is furthered by lifting the weak."[8]

Tufts maintains that there are aspects of any system of justice that we will find defensible, and others that we will not, parts that seem quite rational as they are and parts that we believe need to be reconstructed. The reason for this, he continues, is that, while at any time our sense of "[j]ustice, together with its allied conceptions of what is fair, or equitable, or reasonable, may plausibly claim to be a conception reached by rational analysis," it is impossible for us "to disclaim any sociological, or economic, or political warping." He notes further, as we have just seen, that when we examine the history of the concept of justice as it appears in law and morals, two strands must be distinguished. On the one hand, justice "magnifies permanence and fixity . . . it is the decree of authority" that works to preserve "vested interests or existing status"; on the other hand, justice is "the ideal of reason" that "seeks equality through its principle of equality before the law" and "leans toward giving some place for change." Further, the task of distinguishing what is defensible from what is not is made more complicated—and our analysis more realistic—when we include the realization that citizens do not universally agree on which aspects of our system of justice should be defended and which should not. We thus find ourselves in what Tufts sees as "[a] head-on collision between conceptions of justice." Through the eyes of the property-owning class, "rights of property seem fundamental to the established order and good of society." From this perspective, he notes, "the alleged right of a workman to his job seems a fantastic and fully unjustifiable claim." He continues that when the employer believes that "he has built up a business largely through his own organizing ability," any claims of justice from a worker "beyond the close of the day or week or month for which he is hired" are invalid. "There may be a place for kindness to the workman who is ill, but there is no requirement of justice."[9] To the working classes, however, this grudging allowance for charity toward the unfortunate, devoid of any sense of entitlement, fails to satisfy justice.

As we move into the future, moreover, we need to realize that no system of justice that we devise can be presumed to be permanent. Often—perhaps always—a system of justice is presented as eternal; claims of timelessness are part of its perceived warrant. Another challenge to this temporalized interpretation of justice is, as we have seen, that inherited values have the advantage of inertia and are generally strong enough to take care of themselves. The emerging values of the present and of the future, however, are in a much weaker position. It is here that our efforts at rational reconstruction are most necessary. "A justice that looks merely to existing status will not give lasting peace," Tufts continues. "Peoples change in needs as truly as they differ in needs." In such a context, a system of justice that would preserve vested interests and the status quo must be subjected to the "constructive spirit" that is able both to recognize the "expanding interests" that are present in the current situation, and to revisit the entire question in future situations.[10]

Switching now from Tufts's contribution to Dewey's, we find parallel concerns. For most of human history, particularly in relatively stable situations, Dewey notes that the method of custom has guided impulses into socially acceptable pathways. This system of channeling conduct has not been without its costs, of course, because to some extent those individuals whose errant impulses were diverted into socially approved channels were sacrificed in any such system. He reminds us that historically tradition establishes moral standards. "In customary society, it does not occur to any one that there is a difference between what he ought to do, i.e., the moral, and what those about him customarily do, i.e., the social." In such a society, "[t]he socially established *is* the moral."[11] This customary morality, integrated as it usually is into the society's religious practices, is a strong force in maintaining a static society. He continues that in relatively stable societies people "take their social relations for granted; they are what they are, and, in being that, are what they *should* be." In such societies, moral problems "have to do with the adjustments which individuals make to the institutions in which they live, rather than with the moral quality of the institutions themselves." When there is a moral problem, "it is due to the failure of individuals to do what social customs tell them to do."[12]

In times of relatively great change, however, when "social life is in a state of flux," Dewey maintains that moral issues do not focus on "personal conformity and deviation." Rather, their central interest is in "the value of the social arrangements, of laws, of inherited traditions that have crystalized into institutions, in changes that are desirable."[13] In a changing world, we must adapt how we think about justice, and our rules must be reconstructed as well. Old habits and customs must be evaluated and modified to fit new situations. We cannot continue reliance "upon precedent, upon institutions created in the past, especially in law, upon rules of morals that have come to us through unexamined customs, upon uncriticized traditions."[14] We cannot expect eternally correct arrangements to arise out of situational responses. When circumstances have changed, the old rules lose their value and new ones must be developed, or we will be hampered in our attempts to face the evolving world. In particular, when customs have persisted beyond their advantageous applicability, when they have become "merely" customary or "merely" traditional, they no longer function successfully in our social lives. For example, a system of justice that has petrified into the blind defense of current property arrangements or national borders, or that attempts to decide social policy based upon the sacralization of the perceived intentions of the Founding Fathers, finds itself in need of further legitimacy.

Dewey thought that we had—or soon would—overcome such customary society. He thought that it had become possible to use our intelligence "to effect continuous reconstruction," rather than waiting until "an accumulation of stresses suddenly breaks through the dikes of custom." If this ongoing rational reconstruction is possible, however, why is it that customs usually do persist, and we continue to hear calls to return to the "proper" ways of the past? Doctrinal considerations—theological, economic, racial, gendered, and others—have had a strong influence toward stability, as do the powerful positions of those who benefit from the inherited system; but these factors are able to succeed only because the status quo has grounded itself upon our fundamentally habitual human nature. Dewey tells us that "[h]abit is energy organized in certain channels"; and he continues that to assert that habit "will be obeyed, that custom makes law, that *nomos* is lord of all, is after all only to say that habit is habit."[15] It is in this way that our inherited system of justice continues to function. He writes:

> There are today multitudes of men and women who take their aims from what they observe to be going on around them. They accept the aims provided by religious teachers, by political authorities, by persons in the community who have prestige. Failure to adopt such a course would seem to many persons to be a kind of moral rebellion or anarchy. Many other persons find their ends practically forced upon them. Because of lack of education and because of economic stress they for the most part do just what they have to do. In the absence of the possibility of real choice, such a thing as reflection upon purposes and the attempt to frame a general theory of ends and of the good would seem to be idle luxuries.

Being habitual creatures, we normally maintain our systems of justice until they buckle under us. Because we defend them with such tenacity, often in spite of the facts, we give some evidence to those who see such codes to be established in "human nature." When these traditional moral systems have broken down and are no longer able to process our impulses adequately, Dewey indicates that we have a *problem*. The existence of such a problem can lead to emotional excitement, nonproductive activity, and even violence; but it can also lead to reflective thought. "If habit fails," he writes, "the sole alternative to caprice and random action is reflection,"[16] with the hope of advancing a more critical morality. Tradition that no longer functions must give way to a reflective approach.

We can thus examine what might be called the "career" of a system of justice as it develops, flourishes, and declines relative to specific problematic situations. The Pragmatic perspective suggests that any such system of justice is an institutionalization of habits that has developed within the flow of social conduct. This is an insight, not a criticism. "The genetic standpoint makes us aware that the systems of the past are neither fraudulent impostures nor absolute revelations," Dewey writes, "but are the products of political, economic and scientific conditions whose change carries with it change of theoretical formulations."[17] The great problem with the habitual approach is that there are times when, as he continues, "[r]ules formed accidentally or under the pressure of conditions long past, are protected from criticism and thus perpetuated."[18]

The genetic method thus has a dual value for our understanding of systems of justice. First of all, it enables us to evaluate past systems as they provided more-or-less adequate solutions to the social perplexities dominant when they were adopted. Capitalism, for example, arose as an economic system that more justly rewarded the contributors to social advance than its predecessor had done; similarly, socialism arose in the context of the excesses of capitalism and defended a new system of justice that gave more weight to the contributions of the working classes. The second and chief "impact of the evolutionary method is upon the present."[19] The genetic method requires us to continue to evaluate our systems of justice in relation to their helpfulness with the problems we are facing now and the issues with which we will have to deal as we continue into the future. Critical rather than customary morality and the genetic method emphasize "the dynamic, progressive character of morality,"[20] and thereby undercut any timeless or absolute stance.

We have been examining the Pragmatic position of Tufts and Dewey on the development, flourishing, and decline of systems of justice. Each new understanding of justice arises out of a context that finds the inherited system inadequate to current issues, flourishes when it is able to replace that system and represent a new interpretation of justice, and declines when it no longer solves the problems of its present day. We have not considered, however, the role that the individual plays, for good or ill, for advancing or retarding the well-being of society in this process. In particular, what is the place of the moral prophet in challenging and replacing systems of social justice? Whether that prophet be Franklin Delano Roosevelt or Ronald Reagan, John XXIII or Paul VI, Hugh Hefner or Gloria Steinem, or Booker T. Washington or W. E. B. Du Bois, what role does the moral prophet play?

THE ROLE OF THE MORAL PROPHET

Turning to a consideration of William James's approach to Pragmatism, and how it will advance our understanding of systems of justice and the role of the moral prophet, we must note initially that he tended to a strongly negative evaluation of institutions. For him, institutions play the same role in society as habitual social responses do in Tufts's and Dewey's understanding. James's emphasis, however, is on the negative influence of institutions and how they tend to stymie individuals' ability to flourish. He writes, for example, that, when the satisfaction of human wants is formalized into institutions, the institutions themselves tend to hamper "the natural gratification" of those wants. Whether the institution be legal or religious, educational or medical, he believes that too often these institutions "frustrate the spiritual purpose to which they were appointed to minister."[21] Rather than advancing justice or holiness, learning or health, such institutions tend rather to advance institutional values like stability and conformity. "*Every* great institution is perforce a means of corruption—whatever good it may also do," he writes. "Only in the free personal relation is full ideality to be found."[22] He was a strong individualist who remained ever suspicious of social organizations, cooperation, and interaction as means to advance justice.

In a related fashion, James maintains that ethics is not a science with deductive rules, whether those rules be theological or economic or political in nature. He writes that in deciding moral questions we "must wait on facts." The moral philosopher must be a cautious and open-minded person who is able to learn from others. He or she must recognize that individuals' moral ideals come from sources that no philosopher can completely trace, that "their sensibilities are evolved" in ways that no philosopher can fully understand, and that the resolution of conflicting ideals as to "the best universe then and there" can be reached by the philosopher "only through the aid of the experience of other men." Myopic philosophers, with their desire to enact premade systems of value, thus cannot lead the search for justice. In consequence, he views "ethical science" in the same way that he views physical science: rather than trying to deduce a system of justice "all at once from abstract principles," ethics must "bide its time, and be ready to revise its conclusions from day to day." Most of the time, of course, we can rely upon "the vulgarly accepted opinions" in both cases. As he notes, "It would be folly quite as great, in most of us, to strike out independently and to aim at originality in ethics as in physics." James does admit that occasionally, however, society meets with a moral prophet, someone who is "born with the right to be original, and his revolutionary thought or action may bear prosperous fruit." Like the person who revises our thinking in physics, the moral prophet may, "by breaking old moral rules in a certain place, bring in a total condition of things more ideal than would have followed had the rules been kept."[23]

Even if we are comfortable with all that Dewey and Tufts wrote about the processive nature of systems of justice, they do not have much to offer us about the origin of moral ideas like these conceptions of justice. For James, the answer is to be found in the individual consciousness of the moral thinker. He begins in good empiricist fashion by noting that "[a]ssociation with many remote pleasures will unquestionably make a thing significant of goodness in our minds." At the same time, he continues, it is impossible to account for "all our sentiments and preferences in this simple way." The empiricists' "associations of coexistence and succession" cannot fully explain how our "secondary affections" arrange our impulses and the environmental influences to produce the directions of our lives. He urges us to consider a vast array of human behaviors. "Take the love of drunkenness; take bashfulness, the terror of high places, the tendency to sea-sickness, to faint at the sight of blood, the susceptibility to musical sounds; take the emotion of the comical, the passion for poetry, for mathematics, or for metaphysics." Attributing these diverse behaviors to "incidental complications to our cerebral structure," James further suggests that "a vast number of our moral perceptions also are certainly of this secondary and brain-born kind."[24] As examples, we can add here the strong personal insights, driven by a hunger and thirst for greater justice, of the early Abolitionists and of the current advocates for the homeless. "Rightness is not *mere* usualness, wrongness not *mere* oddity," he notes. When it comes to what he calls "[t]he most characteristically and peculiarly moral judgments that a man is ever called on to make," he writes that they represent "unprecedented cases and lonely emergencies, where no popular rhetorical maxims can avail, and the hidden oracle can alone speak."[25]

In line with this individualism, James notes that, "[i]nstinctively, one judges everything differently, according as it pertains to one's self or to someone else," and "[e]mpirically one notices that everybody else does the same." In spite of this handicap, we find ourselves drawn by the power of justice, and we eventually come to realize that "'nothing can be right for me which would not be right for another similarly placed'; or 'the fulfillment of my desires is intrinsically no more imperative than that of anyone else's'; or 'what it is reasonable that another should do for me, it is also reasonable that I should do for him.'" As a result of such considerations, habits—and even social customs—can be called into question. The customs are at first "overturned only in a few fanatical heads," others follow later; and the "overturning is due to a back-door and not to a front-door process,"[26] by which he means that the origin of the reevaluation is not to be found in social experience but deep within the recesses of the individual.

James urges the importance of this recognition of personal moral insight for a fuller appreciation of the centrality of individualism. Because these moral perceptions depend upon individually "felt fitnesses between things," they often oppose values that are more habitual and utilitarian. For example, he writes that "[t]he sense for abstract justice which some persons have is as eccentric a variation, from the natural-history point of view, as is the passion for music or for the higher philosophical consistencies which consumes the soul of others."[27] Not surprisingly, often we cannot successfully articulate why our understanding of justice is as it is. He notes that "[i]n ethical, psychological, and aesthetic matters, to give a clear reason for one's judgment is universally recognized as a mark of rare genius,"[28] and both educated and uneducated people frequently find themselves virtually unable to account for their likes and dislikes. As a result of this ineffability, we are not able to agree on instances, or even on systems, of justice. We can thus understand why we seldom attain the sort of social agreement that Tufts and Dewey pursue by means of community education. We can also understand how for some—but not for all—a certain social response represents a solution to a particular problem of injustice. Similarly, we can understand how for others the matter in question does not even represent an instance of injustice.

At one point, James turns to a consideration of Walt Whitman, who he notes is "accounted by many of us a contemporary prophet." He notes that Whitman undermines many familiar distinctions and "brings all conventionalisms into solution." Further, because the poet celebrates the vibrant simplicities of life, "he becomes a sort of ideal tramp, a rider on omnibus-tops and ferry-boats, and, considered either practically or academically, a worthless unproductive being." James admits that, for many, even Whitman's poems do not work hard enough: "His verses are but ejaculations—things mostly without subject or verb, a succession of interjections on an immense scale"; and he continues, Whitman's lifestyle is thought to represent "a futile way of passing the time," a way of living that is "not altogether creditable to a grown-up man." James, however, urges us to consider the following question: "from the deepest point of view, who knows the more of truth, and who knows the less—Whitman on his omnibus-top, full of the inner joy with which the spectacle inspires him, or you, full of the disdain which the futility of his occupation excites?"[29] In a similar fashion, who knows more about particular instances of injustice, those who are oblivious to the problem or the prophet who would awaken us to its impact?

Dewey and Tufts were fundamentally interested in the process of social change, and, Darwinians that they were, they saw adaptability to change as the basis of our natural existence. James, although he did not reject this processive view, was far less interested in change considered in this global fashion. For him, the important question with regard to change was the role played by individuals. This is especially true in his discussions of the role of moral prophets in the process of social change. He rejects what he sees as the Spencerian view that social changes are "irrespective of persons, and independent of individual control," that they are "due to the environment, to the circumstances, the physical geography, the ancestral conditions, the increasing experience of outer relations." He maintains, on the contrary, that social changes over generations are the result of "the accumulated influences of individuals, of their examples, their initiatives, and their decisions." James continues that "the relation of the visible environment to the great man is in the main exactly what it is to the 'variation' in the Darwinian philosophy." As he sees it, the environment "adopts or rejects, preserves or destroys" individuals, but it cannot make them what they are. The individual remains a mystery. To the extent that the environment adopts the perspective of Vladimir Lenin or Martin Luther or Mother Teresa on justice, it is in turn "modified by his [or her] influence in an entirely original and peculiar way."[30] To the extent that it neglects the perspective of George Lincoln Rockwell or Rachel Carson or Dorothy Day, no such modification occurs.

For James, the moral prophet is the determining factor in social change; it is the individual who modifies, to a greater or lesser extent, the future of the society. He continues:

> The mutations of societies, then, from generation to generation, are in the main due directly or indirectly to the acts or the example of individuals whose genius was so adapted to the receptivities of the moment, or whose accidental position of authority was so critical that they became ferments, initiators of movements, setters of precedent or fashion, centres of corruption, or destroyers of other persons, whose gifts, had they had free play, would have led society in another direction.

In any instance of social change, James reminds us of the importance of both factors. On the one side, there is the individual who derives "his peculiar gifts from the play of physiological and infra-social forces, but bearing all the power of initiative and origination in his hands." On the other side, there is "the social environment, with its power of adopting or rejecting both him and his gifts." Without the operation of both factors change will not occur. "The community stagnates without the impulse of the individual. The impulse dies away without the sympathy of the community."[31] While he thus shares with Tufts and Dewey recognition of the power of both factors, his focus is different from theirs. James wants to foster the variety of individual insights, while Tufts and Dewey want to advance social reconstruction through educational and other communal means. James continues that when individuals respond to particular problems of injustice, it is their uniqueness that makes the difference. "Individuals of genius show the way, and set the patterns, which common people then adopt and follow."[32] The moral prophet recognizes and exposes the problematic nature of the system of racial justice under Jim Crow, or of our disparate systems of unequal education and health care, and calls for a solution. The larger society then adopts this insight or ignores it. The solution to any problem, James writes, will initially appear in "one brain, and no other, because the instability of that brain is such as to tip and upset itself in just that particular direction." Here he is pointing to "the personal tone of each mind, which makes it more alive to certain classes of experience than others, more attentive to certain impressions, more open to certain reasons"; and he emphasizes that this personal uniqueness is the result of the unknown forces within the nervous system that make each brain function one way rather than another. This unique contribution, and the contributions of others, then enters into the process of social selection. The individual who is troubled by the racial and economic inequalities of our current system of justice presents his or her complaint to the rest of us. If we are able to transcend our customary understanding of the issue, we will respond positively; if not, we will continue to look on blindly, or simply look away. In the long run, the attitude that triumphs will function as "a ferment in the community," and help to shape its future direction, for good or ill.[33]

Before this consideration of James comes to a close, let me mention three more points. The first is that, for him, the moral prophet is the one who is able to stand up to the problems of communal life, the individual who, although he or she may have "drunk more deeply than anyone of the cup of bitterness," remains committed to the task at hand. He maintains further that the outcome in many cases of human concern depends upon the contribution that we are willing to make. "*Will you or won't you have it so?*," he writes, "is the most probing question we are ever asked."[34] Thus, James suggests that we should attempt to draw our inspiration from those prophets who are operating within our communities and attempt, without guarantees, to believe in and act toward a more just world.

A second point is that part of the faithfulness of the moral prophet, and of our faithfulness if we choose to follow, is the belief that we have the power to bring about the proposed changes. "If we survey the field of history," he writes, "and ask what feature all great periods of revival, of expansion of the human mind, display in common, we shall find, I think, simply this: that each and all of them have said to the human being, 'The inmost nature of the reality is congenial to *powers* which you possess.'" He interprets our prophets such as Wesley, Rousseau, and Goethe to be offering such a sense of possible revival. His interpretation of Emerson is similar: "Emerson's creed that everything that ever was or will be is here in the enveloping now; that man has but to obey himself—'He who will rest in what he *is*, is a part of Destiny'—is in like manner nothing but an exorcism of all scepticism as to the pertinency of one's natural faculties."[35] When we find ourselves fired with a sense of injustice, we must believe that a resolution is possible.

Third, James cautions us not to rely blindly upon moral prophets. In particular, because we are all partisans of our own moral visions, no one should be accepted as moral dictator over the lives of others. Not all prophets would lead us into the light; and he notes that even our recognized moral saints "must not only be insensible, but be ludicrously and peculiarly insensible, to many goods." As philosophers, fighting to prevent values that they recognize from being "submerged and lost from out of life," these individuals perform a vital social function; but, "as schoolmasters deciding what all must think," and attempting "to substitute the content of their clean-shaven systems" for broader visions, these purifying moralists too often attempt to determine "which good shall be butchered and which shall be suffered to survive." From his point of view, it would be better to live in the midst of moral chaos rather than in "an order based on any closet-philosopher's rule, even though he were the most enlightened possible member of his tribe."[36] Clearly, the system of economic justice imposed by Stalin, or of theological justice imposed by the Puritan Divines in New England, represents seriously misguided versions of justice; but so do many others.

Proposed systems of justice of whatever sort must be able to defend themselves in the court of public opinion. This democratic process of proposal and defense is more central to Tufts and Dewey's approach than to James's. For them, it is essential that we advance ongoing attempts to move from systems of justice that have become—or are just becoming—primarily traditional to others that are more current and rationally defensible. James's emphasis is different. For him, what matters is the role of the prophets in advancing the new perspectives. As we have considered these two poles of Pragmatic thinking on systems of justice and the role of the moral prophet, I hope that readers will be left with—if not some answers—at least some questions that will help them to advance their own thinking on the ancient and central social value of justice.[37]

NOTES

1. Although Tufts and Dewey wrote distinct portions of the two editions of *Ethics*, each "contributed suggestions and criticisms to the work of the other in sufficient degree to make the book throughout a joint work" (*Ethics* [1908], *Middle Works of John Dewey*, volume 5 (Carbondale: Southern Illinois University Press, 1978), 6; *Ethics* [1932], *Later Works*, volume 7 (Carbondale: Southern Illinois University Press, 1985), 7.

2. Tufts, "Justice," *A Dictionary of Religion and Ethics*, ed. Shailer Matthews and Gerald Birney Smith (New York: Macmillan, 1923), 241.

3. Tufts, "The University and the Advance of Justice," *University of Chicago Magazine* 6 (April 1913): 186 (*Selected Writings*, ed. James Campbell (Carbondale: Southern Illinois University Press, 1992), 146.

4. Tufts, *Ethics*, 443–44.

5. Tufts, "The Test of Religion," *University of Chicago Sermons by Members of the University Faculty*, ed. Theodore Gerald Soares (Chicago: University of Chicago Press, 1915), 101 [*Selected Writings*, 184].

6. See, for example, John Dewey, *A Common Faith* (1934), *Later Works of John Dewey*, volume 9 (Carbondale: Southern Illinois University Press, 1986).

7. Tufts, "The Adjustment of the Church to the Psychological Conditions of the Present," *American Journal of Theology* XII/2 (April 1908): 184 [*Selected Writings*, 85]. Cf. Jane Addams, "To attain individual morality in an age demanding social morality, to pride one's self on the results of personal effort when the time demands social adjustment is utterly to fail to apprehend the situation" (*Democracy and Social Ethics* [New York: Macmillan, 1905], 2–3). Dewey misquotes this passage in *Ethics* (1932), 315.

8. Tufts, "Liberal Movements in the United States: Their Methods and Aims," *International Journal of Ethics* XLVI/3 (April 1936): 254–55; cf. Tufts, "A Social Philosopher's Idea of Good Government," *Annals of the American Academy of Political and Social Science* CLXIX (September 1933): 194 [*Selected Writings*, 307].

9. Tufts, "What I Believe," *Contemporary American Philosophy*, ed. George Plimpton Adams and William Pepperell Montague (New York: Macmillan, 1930), 2:343–44 [*Selected Writings*, 10–11].

10. Tufts, *The Ethics of Cooperation* (Boston: Houghton Mifflin, 1918), 57 [*Selected Writings*, 224].

11. Dewey, *Ethics*, 387.

12. Dewey, *Ethics*, 314.

13. Dewey, *Ethics*, 314–15.

14. Dewey, *The Quest for Certainty: A Study of the Relation of Knowledge and Action* (1929), *Later Works*, volume 4 (Carbondale: Southern Illinois University Press, 1984), 217.

15. Dewey, *Human Nature and Conduct: An Introduction to Social Psychology* (1922), *Middle Works*, volume 14 (Carbondale: Southern Illinois University Press, 1983), 73, 54.

16. Dewey, *Ethics*, 184–85.

17. Dewey, "Intelligence and Morals" (1908), *Middle Works*, volume 4 (Carbondale: Southern Illinois University Press, 1977), 44.

18. Dewey, *Human Nature and Conduct*, 167.

19. Dewey, "Intelligence and Morals," 44.

20. Dewey, *Ethics*, 12.

21. James, Human Immortality (1898), in *Essays in Religion and Morality* (Cambridge: Harvard University Press, 1982), 77.

22. James, *The Correspondence of William James*, ed. Ignaz K. Skrupskelis and Elizabeth M. Berkeley (Charlottesville: University Press of Virginia, 1992–2004), Vol. 12, 9:41.

23. James, *The Will to Believe, and Other Essays in Popular Philosophy* (1897), (Cambridge: Harvard University Press, 1979), 157–58.

24. James, *The Will to Believe*, 143.

25. James, *The Principles of Psychology* (1890) (Cambridge: Harvard University Press, 1981), three volumes, 2:1265; cf. 1235; *The Varieties of Religious Experience: A Study in Human Nature* (1902) (Cambridge: Harvard University Press, 1985), 211–15; *Essays in Radical Experience* (1912) (Cambridge: Harvard University Press, 1976), 136; *The Will to Believe*, 144.

26. James, *The Principles of Psychology*, 2:1266.

27. James, *The Will to Believe*, 143–44.

28. James, *The Principles of Psychology*, 2:988.

29. James, *Talks to Teachers on Psychology and to Students on Some of Life's Ideals* (1899) (Cambridge: Harvard University Press, 1983), 141, 144.

30. James, *The Will to Believe*, 164, 170. For clear statements of the importance of individuals by Tufts and Dewey, see: Tufts, "The Adjustment of the Church to the Psychological Conditions of the Present," 182–84 [*Selected Writings*, 83–85]; Dewey, "Time and Individuality" (1940), *Later Works*, volume 14 (Carbondale: Southern Illinois University Press, 98–114).

31. James, *The Will to Believe*, 170, 174.

32. James, "The Social Value of the College-Bred" (1907), in *Essays, Comments and Reviews* (Cambridge: Harvard University Press, 1987), 109.

33. James, *The Will to Believe*, 186–87.

34. James, *The Principles of Psychology*, 2:1182.

35. James, *The Will to Believe*, 73-74. In the essay "Greatness," Emerson writes: "He who rests on what he is, has a destiny above destiny." (*Letters and Social Aims*, the Concord Edition of *The Complete Works of Ralph Waldo Emerson* [Boston: Houghton, Mifflin, 1904], twelve volumes, 8:303).

36. James, *The Will to Believe*, 154–55.

37. For some consideration of James's contributions as a social reformer, see my volume: *The Community Reconstructs: The Meaning of Pragmatic Social Thought* (Urbana: University of Illinois Press, 1992), 10–22.

6

JUSTICE THROUGH DIVERSITY FROM AN ANALYTICAL PERSPECTIVE

Paul Weithman, University of Notre Dame

There are a number of challenges to writing about "justice through diversity from an analytic perspective." Recent decades have seen a great deal of work on justice and related topics in Anglophone political philosophy. We might be inclined to describe many of the thinkers who have produced this work as "analytic," including Brian Barry, John Rawls, Robert Nozick, Bruce Ackerman, Ronald Dworkin, T. M. Scanlon, Thomas Nagel, Amartya Sen, Charles Larmore, Joshua Cohen, and Gerald Gaus. Yet it is far from clear whether their work is united by any substantive or methodological commitments that justify grouping that work together or categorizing it as work done from an "analytic perspective." Even if we can justify the claim that there is a distinctively analytic approach to questions of justice, it is far from clear that that approach leads to a distinctive set of conclusions about diversity. For it is far from clear that thinkers who adopt this approach would conceptualize or respond to the challenges of diversity in the same way. Finally, the title of this volume, "Justice *through* Diversity"—and the cognate title of this chapter—suggests that diversity presents an opportunity for achieving justice, rather than a challenge that must be overcome. Not all of the thinkers whom we might initially be inclined to describe as analytic think of diversity that way.

With the qualified exception of Brian Barry, one of whose books antedated Rawls's *Theory of Justice*,[1] Rawls is the earliest of the thinkers whom I characterized as analytic. Many of the others wrote under his influence or developed their own views in response to his. I shall assume, for reasons I shall state later, that if the adjective *analytic* can aptly be applied to Rawls's own work on justice, it can be applied to the work of these other thinkers as well.

In this chapter, I shall first consider whether the Rawlsian approach to justice constitutes an analytic one and, if so, why. I willl then say something about how diversity is thought of within the various approaches to justice that can be described as "analytic" because of their relationship to his. Finally, I willl consider the ability of various analytic approaches to help us realize justice both through and in the face of diversity.

I

What counts as analytic philosophy is now quite unclear. We might think of *analytic* as a term that is best grasped contrastively—that is, as a term whose meaning can be grasped by seeing clearly what philosophical approaches and commitments it excludes. The traditional contrast has been with Continental philosophy, but that contrast does not seem serviceable since the denotation of "Continental philosophy" is no clearer than that of its supposed opposite. This volume juxtaposes analytic moral and political philosophy with virtue-theoretic, deontological, and natural-legal accounts of justice. But these juxtapositions should not be mistaken for contrasts that are intended to clarify the meaning of "analytic." For asserting such contrasts would imply that virtue theorists and natural lawyers cannot simultaneously be analytic philosophers. That seems clearly to be false. Asserting a contrast between analytic and deontological views about justice would be an especially infelicitous way to see what makes Rawls an analytic philosopher, since the contrast would imply that his view cannot be a deontological one, but its Kantianism undoubtedly qualifies it as such.

It might seem more promising to define *analytic philosophy* by a metaphilosophical commitment to solving philosophical problems with the tools of logic and linguistic analysis. Thus, Richard Rorty defines it as "the view that philosophical problems are problems that may be solved (or dissolved) either by reforming language or by understanding more about the language we presently use."[2] Understood this way, "analytic" picks out a line of work in moral philosophy that runs at least from G. E.

Moore's *Principia Ethica*³ through R. M. Hare's *The Language of Morals*.⁴

The problem, for present purposes, of characterizing analytic philosophy as Rorty does is that the line it plots seems not to run through Rawls. Early in *Theory of Justice*, Rawls says rather peremptorily that "definitions and analyses of meaning do not have a special place" in the theory.⁵ This methodological remark, his distinction between the concept and the conception of justice,⁶ his later equation of concept with meaning,⁷ and his insistence that substantive conceptions are what is really of interest, all signaled that Rawls's own metaphilosophical commitments are quite different from those of Moore and Hare.⁸

If Rawls's way of doing philosophy distinguishes his work from the analytic moral philosophy of the last century, there are other features of his work in virtue of which the description as "analytic" is natural. While it would be tendentious simply to identify analytic philosophy as philosophy which prizes exactness of language and argumentation, Rawls's concerns with clarity and rigor help to give *Theory of Justice* the feel of a classic work in analytic philosophy. So too do Rawls's evident knowledge of mathematical economics and rational choice theory, his attempt to address the practitioners of these disciplines,⁹ and his stated aspiration eventually to offer arguments in the original position which satisfy game-theoretic and geometric standards of proof.¹⁰

Most important but considerably less obvious is that Rawls entered directly into the debates roiling analytic moral philosophy when he began writing. To see this, it is useful to recall the task Rawls set himself. That task was not just to show what principles an enduringly just society would satisfy, but also to show that such a society is possible in light of psychological facts about human nature. To show that it is possible, Rawls needed to show that it would be stable for the right reasons. To show that, he needed to show that members of a just society would develop a sense of justice. And to show *that*, Rawls needed to say something about what a sense of justice is and how it moves those who have it. This need brought Rawls to questions about the nature of moral motivation. These questions were central to analytic moral philosophy at mid-century. Rawls's task, therefore, demanded that he consider the answers to these questions that were offered by the best of contemporaneous moral theory. Rawls argued that the answers offered by intuitionists such as Moore and utilitarians such as Hare were badly flawed, and that a desire to be just is instead to be identified with a desire to act from principles that would be accepted by free and equal persons in a hypothetical contract that is fair.[11]

For the moment I am less concerned with Rawls's answer to the question than with the fact that he addressed it. An important part of what qualifies Rawls as an analytic philosopher, I suggest, is that he brought an argumentative precision characteristic of the exact social sciences and of analytic moral philosophy to bear on that question. Rawls may have transformed analytic moral philosophy by rejecting the metaphilosophical commitments that had previously defined it. But he also advanced it from within by engaging its canonical texts and central problems.

If we grant that Rawls falls into the succession of analytic moral philosophers at least in part by virtue of the relationship his work bears to the work of those who preceded him in the succession, then it seems plausible to count those whose work bears a similar relationship to Rawls's as following him in the succession and, therefore, as employing an analytic approach to moral and political philosophy as well. The standard is not a necessary condition of employing such an approach, since thinkers such as Joseph Raz and John Finnis, whose work certainly seems to be analytic, do not satisfy it. But taken as a sufficient condition, the standard yields some desirable results. For by this standard—to cite examples which could be multiplied—Nozick's defense of libertarianism,[12] Scanlon's work on moral motivation,[13] work by Dworkin[14] and Larmore on the moral foundations of liberalism,[15] work by Ackerman on dialogue,[16] Nagel's work on political legitimacy,[17] Sen's work on justice,[18] Cohen's work on deliberative democracy,[19] and Gaus's attempt to draw out the implications of his own version of hypothetical agreement,[20] all qualify their authors as analytic political philosophers. All, we might say, view central questions of political philosophy from an analytic perspective.

II

There is no one way that philosophers who I have said theorize about justice analytically treat diversity. I shall focus on the different ways Rawls treated it and, along the way, say something briefly about some other analytic theorists whose views resemble Rawls's in an important respect. It will help to begin by saying something about what diversity is.

It may be tempting to equate diversity with difference. To equate it with individual difference would make for so much diversity within a society as to render the term *diversity* meaningless. It might seem more plausible to equate diversity with categorical difference, with differences due to the fact that people fall into or can be grouped into different categories. The problem, of course, is that of identifying the relevant categories. While natural kinds may initially seem promising, some natural differences, such as differences in eye color or month of birth, are treated as trivial and as irrelevant to theorizing about justice, while other natural differences—or differences that are natural—are taken to be of great significance. Moreover, many of the categories that are of greatest interest are not natural but are constructed. Rather than trying to offer a general account of diversity that overcomes the difficulties of equating diversity with differences among natural kinds, I shall argue that analytic accounts of justice are framed to deal with some kinds of diversity, and ask whether—as has been alleged—they have difficulty coping with others.

Rawls identifies one kind of diversity in his account of the circumstances of justice in *Theory of Justice*: "a diversity of religious and philosophical belief and of political and social doctrines."[21] This fact about our circumstances is what Rawls would later call "the fact of pluralism." In *Theory* he ventures an explanation of it, which he amplified in later work and to which I shall return: he implies that the fact of pluralism ultimately springs from "men's natural situation."

Rawls does not say a great deal about this kind of diversity in *Theory of Justice*, but in retrospect it seems clear that justice as fairness was developed to accommodate it. Rawls's aim in *Theory* was to develop a conception of justice that could be "public"—a conception that members of society could all "acknowledge" as "a common point of view from which their claims may be adjudicated."[22] I take it what he has in mind in requiring that the conception be common is that its principles are to be those which each person treats as the ultimate grounds[23] for settling questions of justice, conditional on everyone else's also so treating them. When everyone treats the principles this way, and is known to do so, those principles are treated or mutually acknowledged as morally authoritative.

Rawls thinks we need principles that can be so acknowledged if society is to be just and known to be just. He also thinks people will not acknowledge principles as morally authoritative that are at odds with their moral and religious views, or that are founded on claims that they think fail to account for the principles' authority. And so he thinks his goal of defending principles that can be mutually acknowledged constrains the bases on which those principles can be identified and defended. They cannot be identified and defended solely on the basis of moral and religious views, which some people quite reasonably reject. Because the modern societies for which the principles are intended are characterized by a diversity of such views, the needed principles are best identified and defended without appeal to any of them.

Rawls therefore identifies and defends his principles using the device of the original position. The conditions of the original position are themselves defended without appeal to the moral or religious views on which reasonable people are divided. They simply enable us to "make vivid to ourselves the restrictions that it seems reasonable to impose on arguments for principles of justice."[24] Moreover, those conditions include the veil of ignorance, which keeps parties from relying on the purported truth of any one of the religious and moral views people actually hold. So by incorporating into the original position only "conditions . . . that we do in fact accept"[25] and by maintaining that one of those conditions implies that parties in the original position should not adopt fundamental principles on the basis of contested moral and religious views, the Rawls of *Theory of Justice* accommodates a kind of diversity that he assumes is morally significant—namely, moral and religious diversity—using what Peter de Marneffe has called "neutrality of grounds."[26]

It is hard to deny that moral and religious diversity is one important kind of diversity, though as we shall see some thinkers who approach questions of justice analytically deny that the appropriate response to diversity of this kind is to retreat to neutral grounds that are commonly accepted. As we shall also see, other thinkers have identified morally significant kinds of diversity that they think cannot be handled by that tactic. But a number of analytic political theorists writing in the decade or so after the publication of *Theory of Justice* concurred with Rawls in maintaining that fundamental political principles should be based on grounds that are neutral among diverse moral and religious views. Two of the most prominent members of that group of thinkers were Bruce Ackerman[27] and Ronald Dworkin.[28]

Even those who endorsed Rawls's strategy for identifying and defending fundamental political principles did not follow *Theory*'s treatment of diversity completely. The task Rawls set himself in *Theory of Justice* was not just that of identifying and defending principles of justice for societies in circumstances of moral and religious pluralism. That was the task of part I of that book. In part III, Rawls argued that the principles, if institutionalized and publicized, would be freely adhered to over time, so that his well-ordered society would be stably just.

The argument for stability falls into two parts. In the first, found in *Theory of Justice*, chapter 8, Rawls argues that those who grow up under just institutions would normally acquire a sense of justice. In the second, found in chapter 9, Rawls argues that they would find that having and maintaining a sense of justice belongs to their good, and so would commit themselves to preserving it. This latter argument, for what Rawls calls the "congruence" of justice and goodness,[29] is complex and weaves together a number of strands. In one thread of that argument—spun out in *Theory of Justice* section 79 on "A Social Union of Social Unions"—Rawls argues that members of a well-ordered society would prize its rich diversity of developed talents, interests, and ways of life. He concludes that they would value their sense of justice because that quality of character moves them to uphold the free institutions that make such diversity possible. Insofar as he thought that diversity contributes to the stability of justice, the Rawls of *Theory of Justice* part III thought that justice can be achieved *through* diversity and not just, as in part I, *in the face of* one important kind of diversity.

Rawls's concern with the stability of principles of justice was not widely shared. The arguments of part I, with their reliance on neutrality of grounds, received considerably more attention and, as I have already noted, elicited considerable agreement. To see who disagreed with this strategy and why, it will be helpful to see how Rawls's own thought about diversity deepened in the years after he wrote *Theory of Justice* and how his reflection on diversity motivated his turn to what he called "political liberalism."

As we have seen, the Rawls of *Theory of Justice* numbered moral and religious diversity among the circumstances of justice—the circumstances in which the need for principles of justice arises. He treated such diversity as a premise or a starting point of his attempt to identify those principles. His appeal to the broader diversity characteristic of a society that satisfies principles of justice, in his discussion of social unions, suggests that even in *Theory of Justice*, Rawls also thought of diversity as the product of justice society. It suggests that he thought of a just society as one that *fostered* or *encouraged* diversity. The suggestion is correct, and a growing appreciation of the thought the suggestion imputes to Rawls is what led him to reformulate justice as fairness. To see that, we need to consider his arguments for congruence more closely.

The congruence arguments are supposed to show that members of a just society would all value their sense of justice and try to preserve it. They would all value it, Rawls argued, because having and acting from a sense of justice made certain goods available to them—goods including, but not limited to, the richness of a social union of social unions. Let us call these "the moral goods of congruence." Rawls's congruence arguments require that, despite the moral and religious diversity of a just society, members of that society would converge in attaching considerable value to these moral goods.

The problem Rawls came to see is that the institutions of a just society would protect individual freedom, and in conditions of freedom, members of that society might well embrace conceptions of the good life that would not converge in the way the congruence arguments required. Exactly why this might occur is itself an interesting question. In *Political Liberalism*, Rawls accounts for moral and religious diversity in part by what he calls "the burdens of judgment." That account hearkens back to and amplifies his discussion of diversity in the section of *Theory of Justice* devoted to the circumstances of justice. In *Political Liberalism* as in *Theory of Justice*, Rawls thinks that diversity arises because of limitations of ability and perspective that are part of "men's natural situation." Under free institutions, he thinks, it is a diversity of conceptions of the good, rather than a rational consensus on the best human life, that is natural to us.

My own reading of Rawls is that the explanation of diversity draws on deep facts in moral psychology. The just institutions of a Rawlsian society are to be publicly justified by a view of human beings as free. This publicly announced view would encourage members of that society to think of themselves as free to explore and revise conceptions of what is good in life. It is when we freely explore and revise those conceptions that the limitations of our nature become apparent. Thus, though Rawls does not say so, I believe he thinks the burdens of judgment lead to diversity when we act under an idea of freedom. Be that as it may, what matters for present purposes is this: Rawls came to believe that the picture of a stably just society that he had offered in *Theory of Justice* was "unrealistic"[30] because of the convergence that it required. The fact that the congruence arguments of part III required a convergence that would be undermined by institutionalizing the principles defended in part I meant that part III's stability argument was "not consistent with the view as a whole."[31]

In short, Rawls came to realize that while justice requires liberty, liberty would encourage diversity, and diversity would pose a challenge for his accounts of congruence and stability. To meet this challenge, Rawls recast justice as fairness as a political liberalism, famously giving definitive expression to his reformulated view in a book of that title. He continued to maintain that the original position incorporated only "conditions . . . that we do in fact accept,"[32] though he stressed that acceptance of those conditions follows from our accepting certain "basic intuitive ideas"[33] found in our common political culture. More important for present purposes, he argued that adherence to his principles of justice could be stabilized without congruence.[34] Instead, stability was to be achieved by an overlapping consensus of diverse—but reasonable—moral and religious views, each of which could endorse justice as fairness for reasons internal to itself.[35] When the diverse moral and religious *views* in a society all support justice as fairness, their *adherents* all find reason to value taking part in the life of a just society and therefore find reason to value being just persons.

Did Rawls's reliance on an overlapping consensus to secure stability mean that he had abandoned his previous attempt to find neutral grounds for principles of justice? The answer is "no." I noted just above that in his later work, Rawls says the conditions on the original position follow from ideas that are latent in the political culture of democratic societies. In fact, from his essay "Political not Metaphysical" onward, he presents the whole of justice as fairness as founded on such ideas. The shared fund of political ideas, worked out through centuries of liberal democratic theorizing, provide grounds for an account of justice that are neutral among citizens because they are common to all of them.

Moreover, though Rawls is not always as clear about this as he might be, he seems to have thought that when an overlapping consensus obtains, reasonable comprehensive doctrines do not just endorse his principles of justice. They also all endorse a set of political values that are central to justice as fairness. These values include political equality and political autonomy. They are neutral among citizens of a just society because all endorse them. The fact that these values are realized when the principles of justice are satisfied provide at least prima facie reason for affirming justice as fairness, and therefore provide neutral grounds for it—grounds that might themselves find deeper support from values that are peculiar to diverse moral and religious views. The values of justice as fairness differ importantly from what I called the "moral values of congruence" in that they are political values, drawn from political culture and realizable largely in political life rather than in life as a whole.[36] Thus Rawls recast justice as fairness as a political rather than a moral liberalism in hopes of finding neutral grounds for it amid the moral and religious diversity that he thought would be encouraged by just institutions.

At about the same time that Rawls made his political turn, Charles Larmore independently attempted to present liberalism as a political rather than a moral view.[37] Unlike Rawls, he did not do so because he was troubled by liberalism's inability to solve a stability problem. Rather, his own deep study of Romantic reactions to the Enlightenment led him to conclude, with Rawls, that moral and religious diversity is natural to reasonable persons under free institutions. Since, like Rawls, he thought that fundamental political arrangements had to command the principled assent of those who live under them,[38] he also thought that no one moral view could provide the basis of such arrangements. He concluded that such arrangements can be neutrally grounded only if they are grounded in political values.

Since the pioneering work of Rawls and Larmore, other thinkers—most notably Martha Nussbaum—have tried to find neutral grounds amid diversity by presenting their own liberalisms as political rather than ethical.[39]

I remarked earlier that the Rawls of *Theory of Justice* might be said to have achieved "justice through diversity" because he argued that a just society would be a social union of social unions and that the rich diversity of the encompassing social union would be among the moral values of congruence. He came to think that the congruence arguments of *Theory of*

Justice were unrealistic in part because he began to think it unrealistic that members of a just society would converge in valuing diversity.[40] The political values of political liberalism do not include it.

One of the functions of political values in Rawls's later work is to provide grounds on which all members of a well-ordered society can affirm justice as fairness and the good of their sense of justice. But those values enable Rawls to extend neutrality of grounds beyond the basic framework of justice as fairness to legislation and public policy through his account of "public reason." Rawls does not say why he developed the idea of public reason in *Political Liberalism* and later work,[41] but he devoted a great deal of attention to elaborating and refining the idea over the last ten years of his working life. I conjecture that Rawls offered the account because, as he came to appreciate the diverse grounds members of a just society would have for affirming justice as fairness, he also came to appreciate the diversity of moral considerations they would bring to bear on questions of justice. For the possibility that stability can be secured by an overlapping consensus of diverse moral and religious views presupposes that those views have diverse intellectual and moral resources that have implications for those questions. And so Rawls thought that adherents of these views might naturally want to argue about them in, for example, religious terms. This thought seemed to be borne out by the copious use of religious language in American political debate about abortion and other matters.

Appeal to what Rawls called "comprehensive doctrines" in public political argument raises two concerns. Those concerns are best explained by reference to a society well ordered by justice as fairness, though the explanation can be generalized to other cases.

To see the first, recall that Rawls's goal in developing justice as fairness was to frame a conception of justice that members of society could all "acknowledge" as "a common point of view from which their claims may be adjudicated."[42] A society in which claims are adjudicated from a common and mutually acknowledged point of view is a society in which everyone's claims are justly adjudicated and in which the fact that they are is public knowledge. The need for just and public adjudication is especially acute when the claims at stake are fundamental—when the concern is, for example, basic rights and liberties, or access to the means of subsistence. Adjudication of these claims is by political institutions and officeholders rather than by ordinary citizens. When officeholders reason in public about fundamental questions using terms drawn from comprehensive doctrines rather than from justice as fairness, they suggest a willingness to settle those questions on a basis that not all can acknowledge. Even if they do not actually settle questions that way, their apparent willingness to do so threatens public knowledge of just adjudication.

Second, if some citizens in that society were to rely on comprehensive doctrines to debate fundamental political questions, their doing so could easily lead others to wonder whether they really are committed to adjudicating questions on the basis of justice as fairness. If those in the second group think they are not, they might withdraw their own support for justice as fairness, thus undermining stability. To put this concern another way, the stability of justice as fairness requires that each citizen have some assurance that others accept it. The use of comprehensive doctrine to debate political questions raises an assurance problem.

Rawls's account of public reason addresses both of these concerns. Rawls modified the account considerably from its initial introduction, particularly as it applies to ordinary citizens.[43] To simplify, his mature view was that when what he called "constitutional essentials and matters of basic justice" are at issue, officeholders and candidates for office should explain their support for political positions by reference to the principles and values of a political conception of justice.[44] Ordinary citizens, and not just candidates and public officials, are also subject to what Rawls famously called "the proviso." The proviso says that reasonable comprehensive doctrines may be introduced into public political argument at any time "provided that in due course public reasons, given by [the principles and values of] a reasonable political conception, are presented sufficient to support whatever the comprehensive doctrines are introduced to support."[45] The principles and values of political liberalism thus provide fundamental laws and policies with grounds that are, like the grounds of the principles themselves, neutral among citizens. Rawls's account of public reason therefore extends his idea of neutral grounds from the principles of justice to the laws and policies that implement them.

Perhaps because of the prominence of religion in American politics, and the implications of Rawls's account of public reason for it, that account has attracted a great deal of scholarly attention. Many liberals who adopt an analytic approach to political philosophy have concurred with Rawls in thinking that moral and religious diversity requires that laws be based on grounds that are in some way neutral. Thus Ronald Dworkin,[46] Bruce Ackerman,[47] and Joshua Cohen[48] all seem to endorse the requirement in some form. Robert Audi has long argued that citizens must have and be willing to offer one another—not Rawlsian public reasons—"secular reasons" for the laws and policies they advocate.[49]

Some of the attention devoted to Rawls's and other accounts of public reason has been critical. Charles Larmore, for example, has argued that Rawls's proviso is too permissive because it allows citizens to introduce their religious and moral views into public argument at all. Such views, Larmore says, cannot but be "out of place" in arguments about law and policy.[50] Other critics, such as Christopher Eberle,[51] Nicholas Wolterstorff,[52] and Gerald Gaus and Kevin Vallier,[53] have argued that Rawls's proviso and Audi's norms are too restrictive because they require citizens who offer religious political arguments to make good their arguments by appeal to public or secular reasons. More generally, these critics argue that the right account of public reasoning would be maximally or almost maximally inclusive: it should allow citizens to argue for or against laws and policies for any, or almost any, reasons at all.[54]

My own opinion about these criticisms is that they misfire in both directions. Rawls's proviso is neither too permissive nor too demanding, and this is apparent once we recall the second of the problems that his account of public reason was introduced to solve. That problem is an assurance problem. If citizens of a Rawlsian well-ordered society are to commit themselves to adjudicating political questions on the basis of justice as fairness, they need some assurance that others are willing to do the same. Perhaps others' willingness can generally be taken for granted. But if it cannot—if the introduction of comprehensive doctrines into public political argument raises questions about someone's or some group's commitment to justice as fairness—then, on my reading, the proviso is triggered. Those whose conduct raises the questions have to provide the requisite assurance by providing public reasons "sufficient to support whatever the comprehensive doctrines are introduced to support." Rawls could have defended a stronger requirement that would have preempted assurance problems by forbidding the appeal to comprehensive doctrines in the first place. Instead, he allowed the kind of discourse that threatens assurance, and then defended the weakest requirement needed to provide it.

What of societies that are not well ordered? Here I think some variant to the Rawlsian proviso—one that results from substituting something like "legitimating principles and values" for "public reasons, given by [the principles and values of] a reasonable political conception"—is correct. For if political life in nonideal societies is not to be a mere modus vivendi, then citizens should seek solutions to political questions that are and can be seen to be legitimate even if not perfectly just. But if we are to commit ourselves to seeking such solutions, we have to have some assurance that others are similarly committed. Assurance problems therefore arise in societies that are not well ordered, just as they do in well-ordered ones. Rawls's proviso assumes that citizens of just societies have common knowledge of what reasons are public and requires that citizens be ready to provide those reasons should their conduct raise questions about their acknowledgement of justice as fairness. I assume that citizens of nonideal societies have common knowledge of what kinds of considerations legitimate the enactment and enforcement of law and policy and what do not. I believe that reasoning like that that supports Rawls's proviso supports the requirement that we who live in nonideal societies be willing to provide such reasons for the political outcomes we favor.

Amartya Sen's recent treatment of justice gives a central place to public reasoning. His inclusive view of such reasoning is reminiscent of the views of Wolterstorff, Eberle, and Gaus, but his inclusiveness has a quite different motivation than theirs and requires independent consideration.

Sen criticizes what he calls Rawls's "transcendental institutionalism," by which he means Rawls's focus on providing an ideal theory of basic social institutions. The proper focus of a theory of justice, Sen argues, is a problem of social choice facing us in the actual world. That problem is posed by the fact that we live in a world that is rife with injustices, not all of which are amenable to institutional remedy.[55] We must choose which of those injustices are most urgently in need of correction and which among various superior and feasible social states we wish to realize.

One question is what information we need about those states—including the status quo—if we are to make a responsible choice. Kenneth Arrow showed that knowledge of everyone's ordinal preferences among those states is not enough.[56] Sen argues that we need to know what kind of lives people could actually live in the various alternatives, as determined in large part by looking at the capabilities they actually enjoy and would enjoy under feasible alternatives.[57] He thinks that that information will be available only if public deliberation about alternatives is broadly inclusive. Thus, though Sen's view of public deliberation is similar to that of other inclusivists, his argument for inclusivism is not that it is required to do justice to the participants. It is that inclusivism is necessary to enrich the information basis of social choice.

Sen does not address the question of what procedures we are to use to move from information about alternatives to choice among them. His use of the phrase *government by discussion*[58] suggests that he thinks it less important to work out the details of governing institutions than it is to emphasize the inclusiveness of public deliberation. Sen does not argue that government by discussion will help us realize or more closely approximate an ideal of justice, since he thinks we have no such ideal at which to aim. Rather, he thinks that at least some identifiable injustices can be ameliorated if we govern ourselves that way, and that they can best be ameliorated if discussion includes information from and contributions by a variety of perspectives. Because of the inclusiveness of public discussion as Sen understands it, he might be said to intend "meliorism"—rather than justice—"through diversity."

III

Sen's criticisms of transcendental institutionalism and his own treatment of justice have been subject to searching critique. I shall evaluate Sen's view, briefly, along with other views that are relevantly similar. To see what these views have in common, note that while the bulk of this chapter has discussed how a group of analytic political philosophers have sought to accommodate moral and religious diversity, I have not said what "moral" and "religious" mean. It is easy enough to point to examples of moral and religious differences that generate some such diversity, but the boundaries of these terms—and hence the kind or kinds of diversity under discussion—are so hard to specify with any precision that we may think any human diversity at all qualifies as an instance of the diversity that is of concern to these philosophers. To show that it does not, and to see what Sen's view has in common with those I shall now consider, note a few points about the moral and religious diversity that Rawls includes among the circumstances of justice. Such diversity is encouraged by institutions which allow freedom of thought, communication, conscience, and association. Because just institutions would be free in these ways, moral and religious diversity would be present in a just society. Moreover, its presence would be a salient feature of a just society in at least this sense—some members of such a society would attach considerable importance to living in accord with their moral or religious views. It is because of this importance that moral and religious diversity poses two related justificatory challenges. First, if an account of justice such as Rawls's is to be justified to adherents of all reasonable moral and religious views, it cannot be premised on claims which divide those views. Second, some reasonable moral and religious views have implications for the demands of justice. If an account of justice is to be justified, then adherents of diverse views will have to see its demands as consistent with the demands of their views.

Rawls's insistence that fundamental principles, laws, and policies all be defended on grounds that are neutral among moral and religious views is an attempt to meet these justificatory challenges. When the challenges are met and society is just, no moral or religious view is favored. Adherence to one or another moral or religious view is not the source of advantage or disadvantage that it historically has been. As we have seen, the grounds Rawls identifies as neutral are basic ideas about freedom, equality, and fairness found in liberal democratic culture. One of Rawls's real advances is to show that those shared grounds not only support equal rights and liberties but also have implications for economic justice.[59] More specifically, he argues that they support the difference principle, which implies that differences of native ability and class of origin—like moral and religious differences—will not be to anyone's disadvantage.

Thus Rawls uses the requirement of neutral grounds, first for principles of justice and later—via his account of public reason—for debate over laws and policies, to fill out his picture of an ideally just society. The requirement shows Rawls's appreciation of an important truth. His recognition—now widespread—that political philosophy must take as given the reasonable disagreement that is an enduring feature of free and just societies undoubtedly marks an important advance in the subject.

Sen has argued that Rawls's ideal of just institutions cannot guide the social choices of we who live in societies that are not fully just. Here I will focus on just one line of thought that is alleged to support this conclusion, since it is a line that ties Sen to the other critics with whom I am presently concerned.

If an account of justice is to guide social choice in the actual world, it must enable us to identify injustices in prevailing circumstances and to say enough about what makes them injustices that we can weigh the status quo against the alternative social states among which we are to choose. Sen and other critics grant that Rawls's theory may do well enough at making us sensitive to unjustifiable disadvantages of liberty, income, or opportunity that are due to someone's religious or moral view or to her class of origin. And they grant that Rawls's theory may provide us the conceptual tools she needs to decry the injustice and to argue for its improvement. But, they imply, Rawls's theory provides much less help in identifying and criticizing disadvantages that are due to disability, age, gender, race, and sexual orientation. These disadvantages take the form of stigma, exclusion, shaming, fear, or evident social discomfort. They are pervasive and obvious features of actual societies, but not—it is said—features to which Rawls's theory of justice is appropriately sensitive. And so critics conclude that Rawls's theory provides insufficient help in identifying and conceptualizing injustices that we intuitively recognize as such and that plague the world as we know it.

The alleged insufficiency of Rawls's theory can be traced to the facts that (i) it measures disadvantage using primary goods and (ii) what makes a disadvantage unjustifiable can be described by its offense against the values and principles of public reason. I shall leave aside the critiques of (i), since debate about the appropriateness of using resources as an index of advantage has gone on for some time and the topic has been extensively explored.[60] Instead I shall focus on (ii), which is not unique to Rawls's own theory. As I indicated earlier, a number of thinkers have agreed with Rawls in endorsing some account of public reason and in holding—at minimum—that citizens must be able to provide public reasons in defense of laws and policies they favor when those laws and policies touch on the most fundamental questions of justice. And so these thinkers are said to share Rawls's problem.

I said that the problem is insensitivity to certain forms of injustice that pervade the actual world. But how, exactly, does a commitment to public reason cause that problem?

I believe the idea is this. If citizens favor legislative, executive, or judicial remedy for discrimination or exclusion, they must be able to defend those remedies by public reasons. Since such a defense would presumably involve a comparison between the status quo and the state of affairs that would result were the remedy adopted, those who argue for change would—it is implied—have to describe the deficiencies and injustices of the status quo using public reasons. The values and principles of public reason play a special justificatory role because they are neutral in the face of certain forms of diversity—moral and religious diversity. Theories of public reason were not framed to accommodate the other forms of diversity that are the bases of the kinds of discrimination now in view, and so are inadequate to describe them. Moreover, if those kinds of discrimination are to be addressed rather than merely described and criticized, political coalitions will have to be assembled behind the remedies. Assembling coalitions to abolish injustice requires the use of language that can arouse sustained anger at injustice and inspire people to a commitment to do better. But, it is said, the language of public reason is inadequate to those tasks.[61] More than one critic of Rawls has implied that the language and requirements of public reason are better suited for the seminar room or the courtroom than for the streets or the hustings.[62]

My own opinion is that these criticisms may be based on an unduly narrow understanding of what reasons count as public. They may well be based on an underestimation of what can be accomplished politically by eloquent appeal to values that are undoubtedly public, such as freedom, equality, and the common good. Finally, they are based on misunderstanding of what compliance with the norms of public reason is supposed to accomplish. As I indicated earlier, I take Rawls's view of public reason to be correct. According to that view, compliance with the norms that apply to ordinary citizens are supposed to solve assurance problems. They require that citizens be ready to demonstrate their allegiance to a liberal democratic constitution or to a reasonable political conception of justice,[63] should their allegiance ever be in doubt. Provided they are ready and willing to do that, they may offer whatever political arguments they wish, rallying supporters and building coalitions as they like. If the identification and description of injustice, and the struggle against it, require the use of nonpublic reasons—or nonargumentative public action—theorists of public reason need not disapprove, so long as those who engage in them satisfy a very weak proviso.

IV

Liberalism began as an attempt to accommodate a specific kind of diversity—the religious diversity brought about by the Protestant Reformation in Europe. In recent years, liberals of an analytical bent have explicitly attempted to accommodate the diversity of ways of life and conceptions of the good that free institutions encourage. Rawls, the paradigmatic such liberal, includes moral and religious diversity among the circumstances that make justice necessary. He attempts to accommodate that circumstance, and the diversity of natural talents, in a single unified framework that ensures that diversity of the latter kind works to everyone's advantage.

As we saw in the previous section, a recurrent challenge to many analytical liberals, pressed by theorists otherwise as different as Amartya Sen and the proponents of a "politics of difference," is that it lacks the conceptual resources to describe and criticize many forms of discrimination and exclusion that beset the world as we know it. I suggested that liberals committed to a suitably weak account of public reasoning about political problems could answer the charge. My suggestion was premised on the claim that public reasoning of the sort favored by Rawls, Larmore, and others is best understood as concerned with an assurance problem, a problem that arises because parties to political contests are assumed to want assurance that other parties all accept the essentials of liberal democratic constitutionalism. This assumption reflects an important fact about how liberals who adopt an analytic approach try to achieve justice in the face of diversity.

Justice requires that citizens enjoy political liberties. The enjoyment of those liberties requires a liberal democratic constitution. Liberal democratic theories of what constitutions should include assume the kind of diversity with which all political theories are designed to cope: diversity of political opinion. The electoral and political institutions endorsed by liberal democratic theory, and the politics to which it gives liberty and scope, allow for the expression of opposing points of view—including points of view that oppose the status quo and the interests of the socially and politically powerful. Liberalism traces its origins in a time in which diversity threatened warfare. It therefore recognizes the need for stable "forms, structures and processes that can house and frame"[64] the diversity they allow. The stability of these forms, structures, and processes for political decision making requires that political opponents be committed—and assured that others are committed—to sustaining a common political life. The analytic political philosophy of recent years has tried to say just what commitments they should hold in common.

NOTES

1. Brian Barry, *Political Argument* (1965).
2. Richard Rorty, *The Linguistic Turn*, 2. The quote describes what Rorty calls "linguistic philosophy" rather than "analytic philosophy," but he seems to equate the two at page 24.
3. Which Moore virtually begins by saying "But our question 'What is good?' may still have another meaning. We may . . . mean to ask . . . how good is to be defined. This is an enquiry which belongs only to Ethics, not to Casuistry; and this is the enquiry which will occupy us first." G. E. Moore, *Principia Ethica*, Second edition (Cambridge University Press, 1993), 57.
4. Where Hare writes: "Ethics, as I conceive it, is the logical study of the language of morals." See R. M. Hare, *The Language of Morals* (Oxford University Press, 1952), iii.
5. John Rawls, *A Theory of Justice* (Harvard University Press, 1999), 44.
6. Rawls, *Theory of Justice*, 5.
7. John Rawls, *Political Liberalism* (Columbia University Press, 1996), 14, note 15.
8. A fact not lost on Hare; see his review "Rawls' Theory of Justice - I," *The Philosophical Quarterly* 23, no. 91 (1973): 144–55, especially 47ff.
9. See, for example, Rawls, *Theory of Justice*, 16.
10. Rawls, *Theory of Justice*, 104–5.
11. See Rawls, *Theory of Justice*, 501.
12. Robert Nozick, *Anarchy, State and Utopia* (Basic Books, 1973).
13. T. M. Scanlon, "Contractualism and Utilitarianism," in *Utilitarianism and Beyond*, ed. Amarta Sen and Bernard Williams (Cambridge University Press, 1982), 103–28.
14. Ronald Dworkin, "Liberalism," in his *A Matter of Principle* (Harvard University Press, 1985), 181–204.
15. Charles Larmore, "The Moral Basis of Political Liberalism," *Journal of Philosophy* 96 (1999): 599–625.
16. Bruce Ackerman, "Why Dialogue," *Journal of Philosophy* 86 (1989): 5–22.

17. Thomas Nagel, "Moral Conflict and Political Legitimacy," *Philosophy and Public Affairs* 16 (1987): 215–40.

18. Amarya Sen, *The Idea of Justice* (Harvard University Press, 2011).

19. Joshua Cohen, "Deliberation and Democratic Legitimacy," in *The Good Polity*, ed. Alan Hamlin and Philip Pettit (Blackwell, 1989).

20. Gerald Gaus, *The Order of Public Reason* (Cambridge University Press, 2010).

21. Rawls, *Theory of Justice*, 110.

22. Rawls, *Theory of Justice*, 4.

23. For the ultimacy condition, see Rawls, *Theory of Justice*, 116–17.

24. Rawls, *Theory of Justice*, 16.

25. Rawls, *Theory of Justice*, 514.

26. Peter de Marneffe, "Liberalism, Liberty, and Neutrality," *Philosophy & Public Affairs* 19 (1990): 253–74.

27. Bruce Ackerman, *Social Justice in the Liberal State* (Yale University Press, 1980), 10ff.

28. See, for example, Dworkin, *Matter of Principle*, 191; also his review of Ackerman, "What Liberalism Isn't," *New York Review of Books*, January 20, 1983, available online at: http://www.nybooks.com/articles/archives/1983/jan/20/what-liberalism-isnt/?pagination=false (accessed March 16, 2013).

29. Rawls, *Theory of Justice*, 350.

30. Rawls, *Political Liberalism*, xviii.

31. Rawls, *Political Liberalism*, xvi.

32. Rawls, *Theory of Justice*, 514.

33. Rawls, "Political not Metaphysical," 223.

34. Rawls, *Political Liberalism*, 169.

35. Rawls, *Political Liberalism*, 134.

36. Rawls, *Political Liberalism*, 77.

37. Charles Larmore, "Political Liberalism," *Political Theory* 18 (1990): 339–60.

38. See Larmore, "Moral Basis of Political Liberalism."

39. See, for example, Martha Nussbaum, "Perfectionist Liberalism and Political Liberalism," *Philosophy and Public Affairs* 39 (2011): 3–45.

40. Rawls, *Political Liberalism*, 388, note 21.

41. The idea is anticipated in *Theory of Justice*, 187–88.

42. Rawls, *Theory of Justice*, 4.

43. See John Rawls, "The Idea of Public Reason," *in Political Liberalism*, 212–54; "Preface to the Paperback Edition," in *Political Liberalism*, especially l–lvi, and "Idea of Public Reason Revisited," in John Rawls, *Law of Peoples* (Harvard University Press, 1999), 129–80.

44. See Rawls, "Public Reason Revisited," 135.

45. Rawls, *Political Liberalism*, li–lii.

46. Dworkin, *Matter of Principle*, 191.

47. Bruce Ackerman, "Why Dialogue?," *Journal of Philosophy* 86, no. 1 (1989): 5–22, especially 16ff.

48. Cohen, "Deliberation and Democratic Legitimacy."

49. The *locus classicus* of Audi's view remains his "The Separation of Church and State and the Obligations of Citizenship," *Philosophy and Public Affairs* 18 (1989): 259–96.

50. Charles Larmore, "Public Reason," in *The Cambridge Companion to Rawls* (Cambridge University Press, 2003), 368–93, especially 386.

51. See Christopher Eberle, *Religious Convictions in Liberal Politics* (Cambridge University Press, 2002).

52. See Nicholas Wolterstorff, "Why We Should Reject What Liberalism Tells Us about Speaking and Acting in Public for Religious Reasons," in *Religion and Contemporary Liberalism*, ed. Paul J. Weithman (University of Notre Dame Press, 1997), 162–81. See also Nicholas Wolterstorff and Robert Audi, *Religion in the Public Square: The Place of Religious Convictions in Political Debate* (Rowman & Littlefield, 1996).

53. Gerald F. Gaus and Kevin Vallier, "The Roles of Religious Conviction in a Publicly Justified Polity," *Philosophy and Social Criticism* 35 (2009): 51–76.

54. I include the word *almost* in deference to some nuances of Gaus's account.

55. Sen, *Idea of Justice*, 1–22.

56. See Kenneth Arrow, "A Difficulty in the Concept of Social Welfare," *Journal of Political Economy* 58, no. 4 (1950): 328–46.

57. Sen, *Idea of Justice*, 231ff.

58. Sen, *Idea of Justice*, xiii.

59. See Rawls, *Theory of Justice*, 20; also Joshua Cohen, "Democratic Equality," *Ethics* 99 (1889): 727–31.

60. For a useful early guide to the debate, see Norman Daniels, "Equality of What: Welfare, Resources or Capabilities?," *Philosophy and Phenomenological Research* 50 (1990): 273–96.

61. See Iris Marion Young, "Activist Challenges to Deliberative Democracy," *Political Theory* 29 (2001): 685–87.

62. I take this charge to be one piece of the larger critique that Rawls "judicializes" politics or reduces it to administration. For a concise statement of this larger critique, see Bonnie Honig, *Political Theory and the Displacement of Politics* (Cornell University Press, 1993), 126–61.

63. By modifying the statement of the assurance problem so that it concerns allegiance to the constitution in liberal democracies that are not well ordered, I hope to meet objections of the sort found in Marc Stears and Mathew Humphrey,

"Public Reason and Political Action: Justifying Citizen Behavior in Actually Existing Democracies," *The Review of Politics* 74 (2012): 285–306.

64. Jeremy Waldron, "Representative Law-Making," *Boston University Law Review* 89 (2009): 353.

7

THE DILEMMA OF DIVERSITY

Rawls, Derrida, and Political Justice

Fred Evans, Duquesne University

ABSTRACT

The ideas of unity and diversity, one and many, in society logically oppose one another. This "dilemma of diversity" requires that we develop a conception of a unity *composed of* rather than *imposed upon* difference. John Rawls and Jacques Derrida provide concrete but disparate interpretations of this abstract idea. Rawls views a just democracy as possible, a "realistic utopia" based on the deliberations of "free" and "equal" individuals or peoples under hypothetical conditions of fairness (the "original position" and "veil of ignorance"). More specifically, these conditions allow citizens with different "comprehensive doctrines of the good" to arrive at a unifying "political conception of justice" for society. In contrast, Derrida sees democracy as involving a "quasi-transcendental" or "unconditional injunction" that renders such a polity "only possible as impossible" and protected from its worse tendencies because of its "indecidability" as a concept; that is, its status as an ineffaceable "democracy to come." On his view, moreover, justice *is* a radical form of diversity or "alterity." I argue that we can resolve the dilemma of diversity and do justice to heterogeneity by accepting Derrida's notions of indecidability and justice as alterity but reinterpreting them as generated by—as conditional upon—what I call free and equal "voices" that contest one another unendingly over the meaning of justice and democracy. Indecidability and alterity are then immanent rather than transcendent forces within a multivoiced or dialogic society.

The "age of diversity" is one of the names we can use to designate the second half of the twentieth century and the beginnings of the twenty-first. Ethnic, gender, religious, moral, political, and other differences have always been a fact; now they increasingly are considered to be a value as well. Those of us in the United States often justify affirmative action because it increases the variety of citizens who can participate in our institutions. Similarly, our neighbors to the north have provided special legal provisions to ensure the cultural and linguistic flourishing of its French-speaking minority. To the south, Mayan and other indigenous groups are struggling to have the majority mestizo population of Mexico grant greater national recognition to their languages, cultures, and territorial legacy. These efforts join the emphasis placed on heterogeneity in many other parts of the world.

But this new value faces two problems. The first is ethnic cleansing, terrorism, racial profiling, attacks on immigrants, and other tendencies that resist diversity. The second is related to the first but is conceptual in nature and concerns the difficulty of reconciling the idea of diversity with that of social unity. This "dilemma of diversity," like all such quandaries, has two horns.[1] The first is our tendency to think of social unity as requiring a homogenous totality and a univocal notion of the good. But this type of solidarity eliminates or devalues heterogeneity. The second horn of the dilemma negates the first in the name of pluralism. But this tends to reduce society to a conglomeration of groups held together by material necessities, mutual fear, or some other type of pure expediency. If this is the only bond among these groups, then none of them will feel prohibited from dominating and exploiting the others when a clear opportunity arises.

This dilemma has been recognized and addressed by two important contemporary philosophers, John Rawls and Jacques Derrida. Rawls captures the dilemma by asking "[h]ow is it possible for there to exist over time a just and stable society of free and equal citizens, who remain profoundly divided by reasonable religious, philosophical, and moral doctrines?"[2] Similarly, Derrida acknowledges that European cultural identity should not be "dispersed into a myriad of provinces, into a multiplicity of self-enclosed idioms or petty little nationalities." Yet he recognizes with equal force that Europe "cannot and must not accept the capital of a centralizing authority that, by means of its trans-European mechanisms . . . would control and standardize."[3]

These articulations of the dilemma of diversity suggest that we should escape its two horns by conceptualizing society as a unity *composed of* rather than *imposed on* difference. Such a form of unity must somehow be generated by the creative interplay among the voices of society instead of by a centralized authority. If this notion can be clarified and found compelling by those who oppose diversity, it could contribute to countering the violence that often follows in the wake of such reaction. At the very least, it could provide a basis for a just policy toward those who would continue to reject diversity nationally or internationally. But for the idea of a form of unity that is composed of difference to be attractive, we must find a concrete meaning with which to replace its abstract formulation.

Rawls's notion of "political liberalism" and Derrida's idea of "democracy to come" contribute two very distinct ways for providing the concreteness we seek. Rawls demands that any satisfactory political conception of justice, including domestic liberalism and a more global "law of peoples," must be based on an "overlapping consensus" among the doctrines that constitute a "reasonable pluralism" in society. Derrida stretches farther than Rawls in bequeathing us with a workable version of a unity composed of difference: his paradoxical or "aporetic" notion of "democracy to come" treats justice *as* diversity or "alterity." Indeed, we could say that Rawls valorizes plurality for the sake of unity and Derrida for the sake of undoing *any* form of sovereignty. Our task, then, will be to examine these two disparate views of democracy and justice and see if they can help us pass between the horns of the dilemma posed by diversity and still remain on the right side of justice. Because either the valorization or the rejection of a group implies a notion of the good in whose name such a response is given (no matter how negatively this notion is defined), I will let "diversity" stand for "heterogeneous ideas of the good" rather than continually presenting a list of racial, gender, and other differences followed by "etcetera."

RAWLS: THE LEGACY AND TEMPORALITY OF POLITICAL LIBERALISM

For Rawls and Derrida, the age of diversity is simply the most recent moment in the history of Western civilization. They see this longer heritage as involving the latent meaning of democracy and thus as a necessary component for understanding and evaluating what can be said today of that political idea. But the two thinkers draw radically different notions of democracy from this legacy: the Anglo-American philosopher sees democracy as a "possible" attainment, indeed a "realistic utopia," whereas the French-Algerian philosopher claims that it is paradoxically "only possible as impossible."[4] This difference, moreover, has to do largely with the very distinct ways they understand time.

To clarify this difference and to see what difference it makes for confronting the dilemma of diversity, we can begin with Rawls. He places his ideas of "political liberalism" and "justice as fairness" in the tradition of Western democratic "social contract theory." More specifically, he believes that translating the proverbial "state of nature" into his idea of the "original position" will lead to principles—to a social contract—that captures an "alternative conception of justice . . . implicit in the contract tradition." This contract also "best approximates our considered judgments of justice" and "constitutes the most appropriate moral basis for a democratic society."[5] In his hypothetical original position, we are to ask what principles of justice "free and equal" members of society would choose if they were operating behind a "veil of ignorance"; that is, without prior knowledge of the social position, idea of the good, generational status, or any other circumstance they might have under the social contract. The resulting principles would therefore presumably be fair, hence *just*, and could be used for evaluating the rules that currently guide our societies.[6]

Rawls considers citizens as "equal" when they have the two "moral powers" he feels are necessary for justice as fairness—the capacity for a "sense of justice" and for a "conception of the good"—as well as the additional "capacities and abilities to be normal and cooperating members of society over a complete life."[7] Such citizens must also be "free," by which Rawls means those who "conceive of themselves and one another as having the moral power to have a conception of the good" and are capable of "revising . . . this conception on reasonable and rational grounds [when] they so desire." As free, they also see themselves as "self-authenticating sources of valid claims" and thus as entitled "to make claims on their institutions so as to advance [and take responsibility for] their conceptions of the good."[8]

Although Rawls does not use the term *hermeneutics*, he approximates its meaning when he says that the principles of justice chosen and revealed in the original position are already "implicit" in the tradition of democracy. But his additional comment that determining these principles would also provide us with "the most appropriate moral basis for a democratic society" indicates that he thinks he is also elaborating and improving upon that tradition. He therefore says that choosing the principles involves achieving "reflective equilibrium" between our "considered judgments of justice" (the meaning of justice implicit in the tradition) and the versions of them at which we arrive through our deliberations in the original position. If the two are not in complete equilibrium, the principles not sufficiently "reflecting" the considered judgments, then we must achieve congruence either by clarifying further the considered judgments or by revising the neutralizing conditions of the original position and the principles derived on their basis.[9] Rawls emphasizes that this adjudicating process is a method of "practical reason," one that constructs principles explicitly related to "reasonable" or moral political aims and not based on a theoretical concept of truth or intuition into an order of values that exist independently of the original position and its process of reflective equilibrium.[10]

Rawls believes that strict adherence to practical reason in the context of the original position and its veil of ignorance will lead to political liberalism and justice as fairness as opposed to utilitarianism or perfectionist views of democracy and justice. More specifically, this observance will construct two principles of justice. The first, the *principle of liberty*, states that all citizens have "an equal claim" on freedom or liberty of thought, conscience, association, and the rest of a "scheme of equal basic rights" adequate to ensure the "social conditions" for citizens to exercise the two moral powers defined above. The second or *social-economic principle* stipulates that all citizens have equal opportunity to gain "offices and positions" and also to abide by the "difference principle" that any social and economic inequalities are acceptable only if they are "to the greatest benefit of the least advantaged members of society."[11] The first principle has priority over the second in that the liberties it specifies cannot be overridden by the concerns of the second; they can "be limited or denied solely for the sake of one or more other basic liberties."[12]

The primary focus of these two principles of justice is "the basic structure of society." This structure concerns the distribution of "fundamental rights and duties" and determination of the "division of advantages from social cooperation"; that is, the dispensing of what Rawls's calls "social primary goods."[13] The two principles also dictate two other regulative ideas at the heart of Rawls's notion of social cooperation. The first of these ideas is "reasonableness." This notion holds when "citizens, viewing one another as free and equal in a system of social cooperation over generations, are prepared to offer one another fair terms of cooperation according to what they consider the most reasonable conception of social justice; and when they agree to act on those terms, *even at the cost of their own interests in particular situations, provided that other citizens also accept those terms*." The second of these two regulative ideas, the "criterion of reciprocity," adds that those proposing these terms of cooperation "*must think it at least reasonable for others to accept them*, as free and equal citizens, and not dominated or manipulated, or under pressure of an inferior political or social position."[14] Rawls's emphasizes that the reasonable is different from the rational: the former requires that citizens agree to act on fair terms of social cooperation as a *moral* commitment whereas the rational is only a matter of an individual calculating how to achieve his or her individual ends.[15]

This distinction between the reasonable and the rational should not surprise us—Rawls takes justice and hence his notion of political liberalism to be intrinsically moral.[16] This moral status also allows him to claim that political liberalism escapes the status of a *modus vivendi* arrangement or a mere expedient strategy to achieve social stability.[17] We can note that it additionally permits Rawls to avoid the negative results of ending up on the second horn of the dilemma of diversity. Moreover, Rawls feels that such a moral bond among members of liberal society helps his view constitute the "realistic utopia" to which we referred earlier.[18]

In a later section, we shall see how Rawls feels he must change his theory of justice in order to accommodate the diversity of societies more effectively and thus avoid the homogenizing unity of the first horn of the dilemma of diversity. But we must first understand how time figures into Rawls's idea of society—for it sets up a vital difference between his liberalism and Derrida's paradoxical view of democracy and justice.

Rawls takes for granted a notion of time that supports his idea of political liberalism and its related principles as "regulative" ideas. No entry designates "time" in the index to Rawls's *Political Liberalism*. A few do exist for this term in the earlier *A Theory of Justice*. However, these limit time to the traditional idea of a "temporal sequence" of moments in which past, present, or future have equal standing. Each sequence is occupied by an activity that is part of a plan and "carried on for a certain length of time."[19] According to Rawls, the principles of justice constitute the ultimate and regulative aim or idea of these plans in liberal society. Indeed, the principles are *morally right* or fair insofar as they are derived from within the original position and *rationally good* insofar as compliance with them allows "human beings" individually and collectively "to express their nature as free and equal moral persons."[20] On this view, then, democracy and justice as fairness are regulative ideas or maxims that at least in principle can be fulfilled in a future moment or complied with in the present. They concern, in short, democracy that is considered to be, at least in principle, possible.

DERRIDA: THE LEGACY AND TEMPORALITY OF DEMOCRACY TO COME

Derrida agrees with Rawls that the ideas of democracy and justice are implicit in the Western tradition and contract theory. But he experiences these tacit ideas as a solicitation or "call" to reveal and consent to them. More specifically, Derrida refers to a "hermeneutic circle" and says that if "we did not already have some *idea* of democracy . . . we would never seek to elucidate its meaning or, indeed, call for its advent."[21] This idea calls to us, and we respond by calling for its coming to be. Moreover, this voice from the past, from our "European legacy," is not conservative, not a mere repetition of what has already been said or instituted. Instead, it "gestures toward the past of an inheritance only by remaining to come."[22]

One can also construe Rawls's idea of the "latent" meaning of democracy as a call for its refinement via the process of reflective equilibrium. This dialogue between the call of the past and our response to it, our refining of it, results in the formal principles that Rawls derives from his hypothetical original position. But Derrida provides the "call" with an even more pronounced role when, following and revising Plato, he speaks of what we can consider to be the event of all events, *khora*. Khora is an all-encompassing event because it "comes before everything" and designates the "place" of the legacy of Europe as well as what is intrinsically linked to the latter, "the call for a thinking of the event *to come*, of the democracy *to come*." Though first to arrive, the khora only makes a place for its progeny. It does not determine their content and thus ensures the unfinalizable character, the always "to come" status, of democracy and justice.[23]

To see how radical this idea is, we must examine the notion of "to come" further and grasp how different its temporality is from Rawls's idea of sequences of acts aimed at conforming to moral political principles that also serve as a regulative idea of the good. We can begin by noting that khora and democracy to come have the universal structure that Derrida calls "spacing." This notion is equivalent to his well-known idea of *différance* and constitutes both the spatiality and temporality of democracy to come.[24] According to Derrida (and phenomenology), our experience of the present moment must paradoxically include an absence—the "past" and the "future"—without which it would lose its thickness, its duration, and disappear into nothing. Differing from itself in this way, as both a presence and an absence, the spacing of the present is simultaneously the "becoming-space of time" and the "becoming-time of space." It is the becoming-*space* of time because the temporal interior of the present and thus of our experience necessarily opens onto an "outside," their past and future. It is the becoming-*time* of space because it also *defers* the future of the present moment and our experience. That is, the present moment, and thus our experience (and the presumptive "identity" of what takes place within it), always remains still to come, always deferred, never finalizable. Furthermore, the event or present moment accomplishes this deferral and thus its own possibility of existence by carrying with it a "trace" of itself as it disappears into the past and opens onto its future. The event, so to speak, sacrifices its being (an impossible pure sameness or univocal identity) in order to be what the event primarily is, a "to come" that intrinsically defers its arrival and thus is always differing from itself.[25]

Because the legacy of democracy can be recalled by us only within the spacing of the present moment, within its interminable differentiation or *différance*, it too, and thus the closing of the hermeneutic circle we spoke of earlier, is always only to come. More precisely, Derrida says that due to this temporality the "essence" of democracy is inherently "undecidable." As undecidable, the concept of democracy is "interminable in its incompletion beyond all determinate forms of incompletion."[26] As a meaningful term, *democracy* must be repeatable, interminable (this is a condition for any meaning),[27] but what will come can always be different from what it was, can be at most a "determinate form" (this or that possible democracy) of "incompletion" (of the "to come") and hence not what is to come.[28] Thus democracy has no fixed essence and is always ahead of we who speak of it despite its status as also our past, our inheritance. Our legacy, paradoxically, is always to come.

But Derrida does not intend to leave the concepts of democracy and justice as simply things to be put aside because of their indecidability. He thinks that democracy to come is also an "unconditional injunction" and a "promise"—a "quasi-transcendental" force—that makes democracy possible (albeit as impossible) and whose indecidability can protect domestic and international democracies from their worse inclinations.[29] As an injunction, democracy to come is a demand for its fulfillment: we can ignore this call but it still asserts itself as an obligation for those sharing its legacy and the structure of spacing.[30] As unconditional and always to come, this obligation is "*im-possible*" to fulfill and "must remain" outside of the realm of "the theoretical, the descriptive, the constative, and the performative"—of anything that we could possibly achieve in theory or in practice, of anything that could be a condition for finalizing it as this or that democracy, *as any possible* democracy.[31] In other words, democracy to come is conceptually formal or pure form, "indifferent to any content," and must not present us with a description of any possible democracy.[32]

Although it is an injunction, democracy to come also has "the structure of a promise—*and thus the memory of that which carries the future, the to-come, here and now*."[33] This memory opens onto or "carries" the future here and now, but like no other promise; for what it promises, pure democracy, is in principle "unpresentable," even as a finalized concept. Therefore, "to come" does not mean "a future democracy that one day will be 'present,'" nor the memory of a past democracy that was once here; instead, "to come" means "exposure" to a demand that "opens itself, that opens us to time, to what comes upon us . . . to the event" or "unforeseeable [and impossible] coming [of pure democracy]."[34] This demand, therefore, "does not wait for," is even "beyond," the future.[35] In other words, the very impossibility of fulfilling the promise of democracy's "to come" ensures that the unconditional demand for this pure polity is "ineffaceable" and transcends the possible.[36]

Democracy to come's status as a summons and a promise means that it is "real" and "sensible." Derrida captures this quality by describing what he takes to be our experience of democracy to come's status as an unconditional demand. For example, he says that it is "an unforeseeable coming of the other," of a law, responsibility, and decision of the other, of "an other in me, an other greater and older than I am." Moreover, this injunction or "other" is unrelenting: it "never leaves me in peace and never lets me put it off until later," it "comes upon me from on high," "swoops down upon me and seizes me *here and now* in a nonvirtualizable way, in actuality and not potentiality."[37]

If Derrida is right about the character of time as to come, about time and its content as an event rather than as a sequence of moments, then Rawls's regulative ideas and free and equal participants must be the secondary and misinterpreted effects of spacing and the unconditional injunction of democracy to come. More specifically, democracy to come is not the same as an *idealized* "regulative idea." It is not idealized because it is real and sensible, an "urgent" demand. This might also be said of the obligatory quality of Rawls's moral conception of justice for members of his liberal democracy. But Derrida adds that the temporality of democracy to come differentiates it from any type of regulative idea. A regulative and in principle definitive idea like that of Rawls's (his goal of "equilibrium" between the implicit meaning of democracy and his refined principles of justice) is in the realm of the *possible*; that is, within the theoretical power of someone, of some *ipseity* or "I can," to realize it, to think it as accomplishable, even in the case where we could never actually reach the end of an infinite duration.[38] But the always "to come" of democracy denies that any idea, regulative or otherwise, can have decidable content or a univocal sense; it allows that the idea of democracy might diverge from rather than converge upon what is taken or could be taken as its meaning at any time.[39] It therefore could never be self-consistently thought of as reachable even at infinity.

Regulative ideas like the presumably possible ones of Rawls are also principles or rules that one can follow. But Derrida points out that it is not possible for an unconditional injunction, all form and no specific content, to obey preset rules. Such a condition would mean that decision making is akin to a computer piloted by software and therefore would not really be a true choice or responsibility.[40] These two considerations show that Derrida's notion of time as an event gives his idea of khora and democracy to come priority over Rawls's political liberalism as a possible democracy and its status as a regulative idea. Indeed, it constitutes the form that any democracy must have (including its temporality) and therefore is the *transcendental condition* of the former's existence as a thought or a reality. But if this informs us of the temporality of democracy, it has not yet made clear how Rawls's and Derrida's conception of democracy and justice link up to real societies; that is, ones that are characterized by specific conditions, including a plurality of ideas of the good. In particular, it has not yet shown us its implications for resolving the dilemma of diversity.

DIVERSITY: RAWLS'S "REASONABLE PLURALISM"

By the time Rawls refers to political liberalism as a realistic utopia, he has already made one radical change in his theory of justice. He sees that his theory cannot adequately ensure a place for diversity and stability unless he is willing to make room for the plurality of ideas of the good that are at play in every society and the world as a whole. But the cost of securing such a guarantee requires him to relinquish the traditional notion of "autonomy" ("human freedom") as the ruling idea of the good of society. Yet autonomy still must continue playing its role in relation to the "free" and "just" participants in the original position and in the general political life of liberal society. Because of this necessity, Rawls will call his new version of freedom "full autonomy" and claim that it is "realized by citizens when they act from [the moral] principles of justice"—rather than from a comprehensive doctrine of the good—and "enjoy" protection by these same principles.[41]

To accommodate these new innovations, Rawls distinguishes between "comprehensive doctrines of the good" and a "reasonable political conception of justice." The former consist of moral, political, or religious ideas of the good that extend to aspects of life that go beyond the strictly political realm. In contrast, reasonable political conceptions (and "full autonomy") concern only what Rawls's designates as the political realm.[42] In this realm, public reason is restricted to debates, issues, the legislation of laws, and other matters typical of governmental venues.

The actors involved in these venues are government officials, candidates for public office, and the other citizens of the polity. The latter are to think of themselves "as if they were legislators" and to exercise their civic duty by voting and ensuring that public officials are acting in accordance with reasonableness and the criterion of reciprocity: "the idea of political legitimacy [is] based on the criterion of reciprocity" and "[reasonable] political conceptions must justify only constitutions that satisfy this principle."[43] Because public reason involves the intrinsically moral notions of reasonableness and reciprocity, this activity, like the "freestanding" political conception of justice itself, is intrinsically a moral as well as a civic duty.[44] Indeed, Rawls says that these two notions are the basis of public citizenship or "civic friendship" as well as of public reason.[45]

More concretely, Rawls holds that public reason and the reasonableness associated with it are necessary for excluding *unreasonable* comprehensive doctrines and also for achieving an "overlapping consensus" among *reasonable* comprehensive doctrines; that is, doctrines which can initially affirm the political conception of justice from within their own views of the good.[46] In both the reasonable and unreasonable cases, and despite the compatibility of reasonable doctrines with the political conception, we can (and must) put aside the ideas of the good dictated by our different comprehensive doctrines and only then interpret the principles and liberties that constitute the basis for a constitutional democracy.[47] Rawls proclaims that we must "contain" unreasonable comprehensive doctrines, some of which are even "mad," so that "they do not undermine the unity and justice of society."[48] These doctrines are neither "well-ordered" nor, with respect to the criterion of reciprocity, "politically moral."[49] Indeed, Rawls says unreasonable comprehensive doctrines embody two different types of "political relations," each of which rejects the criterion of reciprocity and are "incompatible with an idea of public reason that belongs with democratic citizenship." The first type consists of those who divide society into "friends and foes"—into people belonging to a "particular religious or secular society" and those outside of them. The second type of political relation involves those with "the zeal to embody the whole truth in politics," to "[relentlessly] struggle to win the world for the whole truth."[50] Derrida would agree with the antipathy Rawls feels toward both these ways of hegemonizing society.

In contrast to unreasonable comprehensive doctrines, reasonable ones subordinate their ideas of the good to political liberalism when they conflict with the latter in the political domain.[51] For example, political liberalism supports the separation of church (religious comprehensive doctrines) and state. Political parties would therefore have to refrain from imposing their religious values on society if they were elected to power and still wished to comply with the tenets of political liberalism.[52] Moreover, religious or other groups could not prohibit apostasy, heresy, proselytization, or gender equality even in the private sphere.[53] When reasonable comprehensive doctrines are taken to be the basis of legislation compatible with political liberalism, it is only because a reasonable political conception can provide them with *independent* support. Thus, Martin Luther King's religious justifications for civil rights are admissible because, in principle, one could reinterpret them in terms of its principles of liberty and difference and the criterion of reciprocity.[54] Moreover, adherence to the criterion of reciprocity prohibits citizens from invoking "the grounding reasons of their comprehensive views" even when there is a "stand-off" between different positions within the framework of political liberalism. In the case of such an irresolvable disagreement, Rawls thinks that citizens should not attempt to win each other over to their "doctrines," but must simply vote their best estimate of the situation in accordance with the idea of public reason and the criterion of reciprocity.[55] In general, then, Rawls distinguishes the public forum from "background culture" or "civil society" and its many comprehensive doctrines, where "the idea of public reason does not apply."[56]

In his *Law of Peoples*, Rawls extends his notion of overlapping consensus to global politics and what he calls "the Society of Peoples."[57] The representatives of "peoples" are to regard one another as free and equal participants in a hypothetical "society of peoples" and seek consensus on how to apply the principles of justice in their interactions with one another. Furthermore, peoples that are liberal domestically must treat all their members as free and equal and respect the basic human rights of all individuals. A second type, those that Rawls calls "decent hierarchical peoples," have to respect human rights, but they do not nor are required to treat all their own individual members or groups as socially or politically equal to one another.[58] Because both liberal and decent peoples respect basic human rights, they are not expected to tolerate and can even intervene militarily in states that violate the basic human rights of their own individual citizens. Rawls claims that this two-tiered ontology of individuals and peoples extends a "political (moral) force" to all societies, including outlaw states, and thereby provides his law of peoples (and hence the political liberalism on which it is based) with a "universality of reach."[59]

Relative to his earlier theory of justice, Rawls's idea of reasonable pluralism and overlapping consensus is more sensitive to group diversity. But it still seems truncated when we recall that various comprehensive doctrines of the good, both domestically and globally, must subordinate themselves to his political version of autonomy in the political sphere and to some degree in their own private spheres. This suspicion is increased when we take into account that the "universal reach" of political liberalism, of freedom and equality, does not apply to individual members of decent hierarchical peoples and appears to makes no commitment to dialogical interaction with the states deemed "outlaws." The thought that an exclusionary form of unity trumps diversity in Rawls's view of justice is augmented still further when we realize that the split between the political conception of justice and the comprehensive doctrines of the good is itself the product of a comprehensive doctrine of the good. The very idea of splitting the two and considering the result more than a *modus vivendi* requires the idea that autonomy in the political sphere is more valuable or moral than a religious, perfectionist, or other basis for justice and social and political order. The idea of political autonomy may in fact be better in the opinion of many of us (though we may not agree with Rawls's acceptance of inequality in decent hierarchical societies[60]). But unless Rawls is willing to accept what we have seen him eschew, a basis for justice independent of constructionism, he can found the primacy of the "original position," the "free and equal" decision makers in that position, the principles of justice, and the claim that his political liberalism is a realistic utopia (in either its domestic or international form) only on his hermeneutic reading of the historical tradition of democracy and the reflective equilibrium method for refining it. That is, and contrary to Rawls's own opinion, political liberalism is only another comprehensive doctrine of the good. Thus, his view of the good supports a homogenizing unity imposed on diversity (by procedural vote or otherwise) rather than a unity composed of diversity. His revised justice as fairness doctrine does not give equal emphasis to diversity, let alone provide what is much stronger, a sense in which justice is diversity.

DIVERSITY: DERRIDA'S "JUSTICE AS ALTERITY"

In contrast to Rawls's political liberalism and the traditional notion of time to which it marches, Derrida's idea of the temporal event and democracy to come does support justice as diversity. But his notion of diversity is "alterity" or otherness. Because of his claim that "spacing" (*différance*) is the structure of all experience and thought, alterity is the character of democracy to come and justice as well as of subjects and voices. To see what this means exactly and at what price, we must understand the linkage Derrida establishes between his transcendental notion of unconditional democracy to come (which includes justice) and the conditional realm of possible democracies. We must, that is, grasp what makes his unconditional notions *quasi*-transcendentals. This will also reveal how he goes beyond basing indecidability and democracy as only possible as impossible on the temporality of "to come" alone and instead links it directly to the more specific notion of "autoimmunity."

The characterization of democracy to come we have given thus far might appear to manufacture two separate realms, one unconditional and impossible, the other conditional and possible. However, Derrida links these two realms, ensuring that democracy to come must always be descending from the heaven of the unconditional to the earth of the conditional, from the impossible to the possible. In particular, these two realms are "absolutely heterogeneous" and yet "indissociable" from each other. On the one hand, the democracy of the United States and other possible democracies require the unconditional idea of democracy to come for their "guidance" and "inspiration."[61] Indeed, it is as if Derrida agrees with his paraphrase of Rousseau: even if democracy "in the strict sense" could never exist because of its "amorphousness" or "polymorphousness," "one must, one ought, one cannot not strive toward it with all one's force."[62] On the other hand, pure democracy needs to engage in "conditions of all kinds" in order to "arrive" in its interruptive manner and be other than merely utopian thought, other than "nothing at all." Only in the gap between these two irreconcilable and indissociable poles, only between a benign oracle and earthly voices, are "decisions and responsibilities" to be taken.[63] Because Derrida combines the unconditioned with the conditioned in this indissociable manner, the transcendental status of the unconditional is more properly referred to as "quasi-transcendental" or "infrastructural."[64] It makes possible the conditional, but would be only an undecidable thought without the latter, would lack anything to affect or "interrupt."

We must now examine some of these quasi-transcendentals to see how their indissociable relation with the earthly conditions for possible democracies brings about autoimmunity and the effects we have indicated. Derrida includes a number of quasi-transcendentals within the "form" of democracy to come.[65] For brevity's sake, we will examine only three of them: unconditional criticism including self-critique, unconditional freedom that renounces the sovereignty it otherwise implies, and unconditional hospitality or equality. Derrida introduces the first of these by saying that democracy is the only "constitutional paradigm" in which one has "in principle . . . the right to criticize everything publically, including the idea of democracy." He adds that this right of unlimited criticism and questioning makes democracy "the only [constitutional] paradigm that is universalizable."[66]

The full extent of what Derrida means by "unlimited" or "universalizable" becomes clear when we consider these terms in relation to the two other quasi-transcendentals we are considering. He equates the second quasi-transcendental, unconditional freedom, with "a freedom of play" and also the "interminable self-criticizability" of the first quasi-transcendental. He adds that this "indetermination" and "essential historicity" is "at the very center of the concept of democracy" and is presupposed by any freedom of the more common sort that involves the "I can" or individual initiative of liberty and license.[67] In other words, Rawls's "free and equal" status required for the participants in the original position—his political idea of autonomy—is possible only if the quasi-transcendental form of freedom is in play. But there is more—this unconditional freedom renounces sovereignty absolutely in order both to save itself from the limit such control would place on its own universality and to prevent sovereignty's intrinsic "abuse of power."[68] As we saw earlier, such sovereignty would nullify the responsibility required for democracy by laying down a "determinative knowledge" of a norm or law, including the sort professed by Rawls's political liberalism. Decision making would have to follow these rules in advance and would therefore not amount to a true choice or responsibility.[69]

The unconditional questioning of the first quasi-transcendental is complemented by the limitlessness of the number of those who can pose questions and thus by the third quasi-transcendental, unconditional hospitality. This quasi-transcendental is particularly important because Derrida thinks ethics is constituted by hospitality to others.[70] These foreign voices include those that are absolutely unlike us; the injunction must be an expression of a "pure ethics" that recognizes the "respectable dignity" of the "unrecognizable" and "exposes itself without limit to the coming of the others, beyond rights and laws." This unconditionality, then, implies "a universal beyond all relativism, culturalism, ethnocentrism, and especially nationalism," beyond all sovereignty.[71] To capture further the idea of these foreign others and the universality of unconditional hospitality, Derrida uses the term *vertical*. The verticality of the other refers not to one who is "simply a worker, or a citizen, or someone easily identifiable," but to "that which in the other . . . exceeds precisely the horizontality of expectation."[72]

As these comments make clear, Derrida takes the unconditional form of democracy to come as including the absolute universality or, in his terms, "verticality" of hospitality. This verticality encompasses the otherness or alterity not only of persons but also democracy to come, justice, and all other quasi-transcendentals that exceed "the horizontality of expectation"—in short, everything that is characterized by "spacing." Thus his valorization of heterogeneity, in contrast to Rawls's idea of overlapping consensus, is equivalent to justice as diversity or alterity: "the coming of the other, the absolute and unpredictable singularity of the *arrivant as justice*."[73] To do justice to the other is to recognize the indecidability of the identity we might want to assign to the other, to acknowledge its always being open to and calling for decisions that cannot claim any form of absolute knowledge as their justification.

The notion of "autoimmunity" comes into play when these three quasi-transcendentals are linked to possible democracies by way of the procedure of voting. Because democracy to come involves unconditional hospitality, freedom, and self-critique, it is an invitation even to those who would argue against democracy and vote it out of existence. The only way to immunize democracy against this possibility is to restrict it to those who uphold it. But such a restriction, Derrida believes, would destroy democracy's call for universal inclusivity and equality and thus immunize democracy against itself, making it suffer a fatal and latent "autoimmunity."[74] Despite this autoimmunity, we must still follow the injunction of democracy and, in its name, never mistake any of our possible democracies and their degree of hospitality, freedom, and self-critique for what we, impossibly, can claim as final and truly democratic.[75]

Before raising some questions about Derrida's idea of autoimmunity, we should note the latter's full effect. Derrida sees it as the basis for politics, ethics, and "reasonableness" as well as for democracy. Autoimmunity makes these possible because it produces the indecidability and the urgency that ensures there always must be ethico-political "negotiations" that are endless and irresolvable in principle.[76] Indeed, the indecidability created by autoimmunology—by the tension between democracy as an unconditional injunction and as a conditional or possible polity—means that we must go beyond "rationality" (as the calculation of the best laws and policy judgments) to what exceeds this form of thought and is "preferable" to it: "reasonableness." More specifically, Derrida defines *reasonableness* as "rationality that takes account of the incalculable so as to give an account of it, there where this appears impossible, so as to account for or reckon *with* it, that is to say, with the event of *what* or *who* comes."[77] In other words, reasonableness takes into account the incalculable when deciding upon a course of action. In taking account of the incalculable or unconditional, it strives (impossibly but urgently) toward democracy to come in the midst of all the conditions that demand endless negotiation and the invention (rather than the following) of "maxims of transaction."[78]

Derrida's articulation of reasonableness has two implications pertinent to the concerns of this chapter. It stands up to nation-states, to the "homogenizing hegemonies" of capitalist globalization, and all other limiting sovereignties except that which is (impossibly) "at once indivisible and yet able to be shared"; that is, the antisovereignty, democracy to come itself.[79] The second implication is related to this first one. We have seen that Rawls's description of reasonableness is not unconditional: it is contingent upon a possible democracy, one based on the sort of justice that can be derived from deliberations of free and equal persons in the original position. In other words, it does not involve taking into account the incalculable or unconditional form of democracy to come or of justice to come, each of which would interrupt the claims vouchsafed by political liberalism and Rawls's notion of reasonableness.[80] Indeed, Derrida's idea of reasonableness is a quasi-transcendental injunction that makes possible Rawls's or any other definition of reasonableness (and subject to critique, to the charge of autoimmunity insofar as reasonableness is part of a possible democracy). In other words, the quasi-transcendental relation between unconditional reasonableness and its conditional offspring is the same as the connection between impossible democracy to come and possible democracies, pure freedom, and that of the "I can" form (including all types of possible sovereignty), and absolute hospitality or heterogeneity and the restrictions placed on the reach of reasonable comprehensive doctrines of the good.

IMPOSSIBLE VERSUS POSSIBLE DEMOCRACY

Which of these two approaches to democratic justice, the possible or the possible only as impossible, allows us to escape the dilemma of diversity? We have already seen that Rawls's political liberalism valorizes a form of unity that subordinates heterogeneous ideas of the good to one that privileges "full autonomy" and a bifurcation of society into political and social spheres. Before looking critically at Derrida's idea of diversity, we can note three more possible deficiencies in Rawls's political liberalism. First, we can add an argument by Will Kymlicka to bolster our claim that Rawls's position is itself a comprehensive doctrine of the good. Kymlicka points out that Rawls's notion of political autonomy includes the right to form and revise one's conception of the good and is therefore tantamount to comprehensive autonomy: the revisability that political liberalism takes as a political right for *all* members of society means that a "responsible" communitarian group has to surrender, in effect if not by proclamation, the inviolability of its constitutive ends. The right of "revisions" or autonomy ends up trumping these communitarian conceptions of the self and their notions of the ultimate good. Kymlicka adds that in this case the communitarian group would be better off in a millet-system (within which a group can maintain internal restrictions on rights—or not—and still be an accepted part of the nation) than under political liberalism.[81] Second, Kymlicka argues compellingly that Rawls's political liberalism either stipulates universal rights or, as we have suggested, follows a particular traditional comprehensive notion of the good. If the former, then the relative abstractness of these rights (the first principle of justice) makes it difficult for people to be motivated by them. But if the latter, the historical-cultural context of these rights curtails diversity by excluding the notions of the good that are not congruent with political liberalism.[82]

Johan van der Walt levels a third criticism against Rawls's claim for the freestanding status of political liberalism. Walt argues that Rawls's conception of public reason fails when two opposing parties each "have claims that can be reasonably defended before the other as fully considerate of everyone as free and equal."[83] When this happens, one of the parties must be coerced to accept the other contender's version of public reason. This coercion, however, can only be justified by appealing "to considerations external to public reason"; that is, "*for the sake of* Rawls's principles of justice but not *in terms* of them." Walt points out that Rawls recognizes this situation and also the necessity of "urging" the losing party (and all other losing parties in the same bind) to continue with public reason even though it doesn't help that party in this particular case.[84] But this "motivational" move is not the same as justification—not the same as appealing to the criterion of reciprocity—and thus, on Rawls's own terms, does not treat the losing party as "free and equal."[85] This means that political liberalism must ultimately act as a comprehensive doctrine rather than as Rawls's idea of a "freestanding" political conception of justice. Walt even thinks that this amounts to "the worst political cynicism possible, namely, the cynicism of justifying political expedience in the name of a sincere respect for everyone as free and equal."[86]

The following example will help illustrate Walt's point. Imagine a group of workers who try to litigate in favor of collective ownership of the means of production. But they lose the case to the opposing private owners. Yet both positions are consonant with public reason, assuming that Rawls's principle of difference can include collective ownership and still remain consistent with the criterion of reciprocity. Presumably the jury and the voters have opted for "private property rights" and the market value or "commodification" of labor over the workers' appeal to labor as the expression of human nature (labor power as one's essence) and thus collective ownership as necessary for their and everyone else's freedom. But insofar as both outcomes—collective or private ownership of the means of production, democratic communism or liberalism—are consistent with Rawls's principles of justice and hence public reason, the workers are nonetheless "urged" for *external reasons* to accept the verdict and political liberalism. That is, they are not being treated as "just and equal." Instead, a comprehensive doctrine such as utilitarianism, libertarianism, or market fundamentalism, one that is not their own, is being used covertly or overtly to justify their remaining in and complying with a polity characterized misleadingly as a pure political conception of justice.[87]

The inability of political liberalism to adjudicate on its own terms between two comprehensive doctrines in a practical and common case (the abortion or pro-choice versus pro-life debate could serve as another) suggests that the *agon*—the political contestation among comprehensive doctrines of the good—is the more realistic and perhaps preferable ethico-political situation of society. The call to articulate the implicit idea of democracy embedded in Western civilization is better answered by an open and ongoing political struggle among advocates of heterogeneous ideas of the good than from a group sharing the same historical tradition and deliberating behind the veil of ignorance in the original position.[88] Moreover, Rawls's political liberalism emphasizes an overlapping *consensus* as the primary goal of public reason; but others see consensus as a threat to heterogeneity and as better thought of as an always temporary stage in policymaking, one intended to allow the productive continuation of *dissensus*—difference and the ongoing production of new voices—as the primary meaning of democracy.

Despite the limitations of Rawls's political liberalism and its failure to allow us to escape the horns of the dilemma of diversity, Derrida's appeal to autoimmunity as a basis for democracy as "only possible as impossible" also raises a question: Is democracy really autoimmune? Derrida indicates that the procedure of voting links the quasi-transcendentals to the conditional world of possible democracies. He holds that this procedure is democratic and that it remains so even when used by Islamists in Algeria, fascist and Nazi regimes in Europe, and other antidemocratic groups. Thus, as we noted earlier, one is antidemocratic if one doesn't recognize the democratic legitimacy of the antidemocratic results brought about by voting and a numerical majority:

> There is something paradigmatic in this autoimmune suicide: fascist and Nazi totalitarianisms came into power or ascended to power through formally normal and formally democratic electoral processes. . . . [T]he aporia in its general form has to do with freedom itself: must a democracy leave free and in a position to exercise power those who risk mounting an assault on democratic freedoms and putting an end to democratic freedom in the name of democracy and of the majority that might actually be able to rally around to their cause? . . . When

assured of a numerical majority, the worst enemies of democratic freedom can, by a plausible rhetorical simulacrum . . . present themselves as staunch democrats. That is one of the perverse and autoimmune effects of the axiomatic developed already in Plato and Aristotle.[89]

But this claim seems to contradict the force of the quasi-transcendental that concerns unlimited questioning and self-critique. If democracy to come has unlimited criticism at its center, as Derrida says, then any democratic process must be done in the name of such endless critique. This means that the results of any electoral process must preserve what we can call an "open space" for *always further* critical commentary in order to qualify as democratic. In other words, when a "numerical majority" votes out democracy and eliminates the polity's dialogic space, we cannot legitimately say that it is acting democratically. Instead, it is achieving its results only by a formal or expedient procedure. It is a mistake to call such a procedure democratic when its aim is antidemocratic, done in the name of some political order other than democracy. More exactly, the procedure is *internal* to democracy only if it is coupled with unlimited questioning and the condition the latter implies: the commitment to maintain a space for rejoinders. When it is not accompanied by this commitment, such a procedure is nondemocratic and *external* to democracy. Even if the idea of "open space" is itself characterized by spacing, the questioning of its meaning always requires that it remain open for a rejoinder to any of its proposed translations: the open space mandate always reinserts itself. Democracy, therefore, is susceptible to (not immune to) a possible procedural overthrow from fascist and other nondemocratic forces or tendencies; but it is not autoimmune, not destructible by its own hand or in its own name.

If these reflections have weight, then our idea of democracy would be conditional rather than unconditional—conditional on the commitment to maintaining the open space necessary for unlimited questioning, even when it consists in criticism of democracy itself. This would mean that democracy is a conditional rather than an unconditional injunction. This criticism coheres with the comments of those who find Derrida's unconditional notion of democracy to come and its variants too abstract or empty.[90] A similar criticism of autoimmunity might arise in the case of spacing (*différance*) itself. If the self-differentiation of the present is life, then one does not necessarily die in the name of life as advocates of autoimmunity might think. If to live is to vocalize one's ideas, feelings, and other dispositions to oneself and others, then there is nothing intrinsically suicidal in that; we will all die, but not necessarily because we speak.

Derrida would appear to agree that life is more than just biological existence when he states that there is no "strict opposition" between *zoe* (biological life) and *bios* (cultured life).[91] But this link between life and speech is made even more reasonable when we recall Derrida's emphasis upon characterizing khora, deconstruction, and democracy to come as "calls" and when we further note that he often describes himself as not just one but many voices and as the dialogic interplay among them. A brief excursus of this idea may provide a response acceptable to those who see his appeal to quasi-transcendentals, to unconditional injunctions indifferent to content, as too abstract, and may constitute a basis in place of autoimmunity for guaranteeing the unfinalizability of the idea of democracy. In other words, we may secure a political view of justice and democracy that combines the immanency of Rawls's free and equal actors with Derrida's indecidability and generous approach to hospitality, to justice as alterity.

THE PRIMACY OF VOICES AND POLITICAL JUSTICE

Some of Derrida's more direct and innovative uses of "voices" are contained in his response to a question from the French feminist Hélène Cixous. Derrida says that for himself "a monologism, univocity, a single voice . . . is impossible, and plurivocity is a non-fictional necessity." He adds that in writing a text he often has "to change voices . . . to make several persons speak . . . and that the essential thing comes from another voice in some manner, from another voice in [him] . . . which is the same and not the same."[92] In another text, he says that what inspired him to start writing was "the adolescent dream of keeping a trace of all the voices which were traversing [him]," and that "deep down this is still [his] most naïve desire."[93] Part of this "tracing" takes place when he alludes to his roots in French Algeria and refers to himself as an "overcolonized European hybrid."[94]

Derrida reinforces his allegiance to this idea of hybrid voices in his remarks on Husserl and European memory. His work on Husserl provides compelling arguments for the impossibility of the very idea of a univocal voice, of one that is not immediately open to its other.[95] In his claim, against Husserl, that a pure voice *is* open to its other, the latter term can be interpreted as "other voices."[96] Similarly, Derrida says we have a "*duty* to respond to the call of European memory," to recall "what has been promised under the name Europe." He is, however, very careful to claim that this Europe is shot through with "other headings" or non-European voices.[97] More specifically, Derrida says that we must "make ourselves the guardians of an idea of Europe, of a difference of Europe, *but* of a Europe that consists precisely in not closing itself off in its identity and . . . assign[s itself] identity from alterity, from the other heading and the other of the heading, from a completely other shore."[98] In other words, the lead voice of Europe, its heritage, is so shot through with other voices that we cannot assign it a teleological or other form of strict identity, cannot legitimately make of Europe any of the oracles that have historically claimed or would claim to speak for it. The heritage of Europe, therefore, has built into itself a principle of self-critique and recognition of the alterity that helps to constitute its social body.

We can imagine that each of these voices is always already responding to the rest and that the vocal interplay among them holds them together at the same time as it keeps them separate, forming a dialogic body. This body would be the *agon* we spoke of earlier as a replacement for Rawls's original situation and the overlapping consensus among its constituent comprehensive ideas of the good. We might go further and consider again Derrida's remark that each "heading" or voice "assign[s itself] identity from alterity"—we might take it as meaning that each voice is part of the identity and, at the same time, the other of the rest, that each is what it is through its difference from the rest. Because of this "identity from alterity," the affirmation of one's own voice would be immediately the valorization of the others and hence of our unity composed of and by difference. It would also be the simultaneous affirmation of solidarity and heterogeneity, of an identity shared with those who are at the same time our other, and thus would amount to the resolution of the dilemma of diversity with which we started this chapter.[99]

Concretely, this affirmation of the voices resounding within our own implies hearing the other voices. In its most profound meaning it signifies a hearing that is more than mere reception or recording—it signifies a willingness to court changes in one's own discourse on the basis of what the others say, to "really" hear.[100] In other words, it would reach beyond any national or ethnic boundaries as well as the boundary between human and nonhuman voices. It would be hospitality to all "ears" and therefore democratic and also a multivoiced form of socialism or communism, one opposed to the "homo-homogeneity" that Derrida repudiates, resisting market fundamentalism and all other material and spiritual barriers to equal audibility.

The affirmation of this dialogic society, of this mutual hearing of and responding to one another, also ensures the unfinalizability or indecidability of this social body and its "to come." The interplay among these heterogeneous voices would continually produce new ones. Because each voice is established by its difference from the rest, the creation of each of these new voices would immediately be a change in all the rest, in the same way that a new gender would change the meaning of female and male or a new color the identity of the rest. This implies that the dialogic or multivoiced body would continually undergo metamorphosis, would be the same body as always different. The becoming-space of time would mean the differences between the voices, each the outside of the other that it also inhabits, their mutual external-internality; and the becoming-time of space would be the continual interplay among them and the metamorphosis of the society this brings about. This "spacing" or transformative interplay of voices, then, would generate the dialogic body's temporality of "to come." It would mean that this temporality is the immanent rather than transcendental form of the voices and their productive contestations. It would also imply that the very meaning of society as a multivoiced body is unfinalizable, always intrinsically open to the articulations of the voices, even "unexpected" ones, to come—that democracy *is* the unending dialogue about itself, and justice the guarantee of this dynamic alterity.

Despite the indecidability of this voice-based social body to come, it poses conditions. Hearing one another is what determines the dialogic body's production of new voices and hence its indecidability. This implies that all voices must be heard but also that only certain voices could legitimately make governmental policy for the polity at any given time. These policymaking voices would be those whose proposals included an affirmation of the "open space" we discussed above. The democracy expressing this dialogic or multivoiced society would be conditional on committing itself to keeping that space permanent, to hearing other voices. This fecund hearing of other voices might require limits on hate speech. But the democratic open space would guarantee that the idea of what counts as illegitimate policymaking voices or hate speech remains continually open to debate and thus to changes in the laws. It would also allow the possibility that white supremacists, patriarchic groups, and others hostile to universal dialogic exchange might rethink their positions and come to affirm society as a multivoiced body.

This view, then, is itself a hybrid voice. It takes Rawls's immanent or conditional "free and equal citizens or peoples" and transforms them into the voices of the comprehensive ideas of the good for which he sought an overlapping consensus. It courts Derrida's "indecidability" and reinterprets it as the preordained and constant metamorphosis produced by the creative interplay among the voices of society. In other words, it brings down to earth the unconditional or transcendental injunction of a democracy to come. But this earthly descent, this ongoing interplay among voices and constant metamorphosis, does just what Derrida wanted from the indecidability guaranteed by the temporality of "to come": it interrupts all those who would claim the final word about democracy and justice. And it keeps "diversity"—"alterity"—as the primary meaning of identity and justice.

NOTES

1. See Fred Evans, *The Multivoiced Body: Society and Communication in the Age of Diversity* (New York: Columbia University Press, 2008; 2011), chapter 1 and *passim*.

2. John Rawls, *Political Liberalism*, expanded edition (New York: Columbia University Press, 2005), 4.

3. Jacques Derrida, *The Other Heading: Reflections on Today's Europe*, trans. Pascale-Ann Brault and Michael Nass (Bloomington, IN: Indiana University Press, 1992), 38–39; cited in Giovanna Borradori, *Philosophy in a Time of Terror: Dialogues with Jürgen Habermas and Jacques Derrida* (Chicago, IL: Chicago University Press, 2003), 170–71.

4. John Rawls, *The Law of Peoples* (Cambridge, MA: Harvard University Press, 1999), 5–7, 11, 17–18, 126–28; Jacques Derrida, *Negotiations: Interventions and Interviews, 1971–2001*, ed. and trans. Elizabeth Rottenberg (Stanford, CA: Stanford University Press, 2002), 344, 374; and Jacques Derrida, "A Certain Impossible Possibility of Saying the Event," in *The Late Derrida*, ed. W. J. T.

Mitchell and Arnold I. Davidson (Chicago, IL: Chicago University Press, 2007), 235–36.

5. John Rawls, *A Theory of Justice*, revised edition (Cambridge, MA: Harvard University Press, 1999), xviii, 10. See also, *Political Liberalism*, 14, 22–28, 292.

6. Rawls, *Theory of Justice*, 9, 11–12, 16–17, 118–19.

7. Rawls, *Political Liberalism*, 81.

8. Rawls, *Political Liberalism*, 30, 32, 33.

9. Rawls, *Theory of Justice*, 17–18, 41–43, 78, 380–81. Rawls adds that our "considered (moral) judgments" are those "in which our normal moral capacities are most likely to be displayed without distortion," for example, judgments about which we are not hesitant or uncertain about and do not make under conditions of greed or fear (*Political Liberalism*, 42).

10. *Political Liberalism*, 93–98. Rawls calls this method "political constructivism" and acknowledges its relation to, and differences from, Kant's moral philosophy and method as well as Kant's notion of the "kingdom of ends." His use of "reasonable" in this context is a theme to which we shall later return.

11. Rawls, *Political Liberalism*, 291–92, 332.

12. Rawls, *Political Liberalism*, 294–95.

13. Rawls, *Theory of Justice*, 6, 54–55.

14. Rawls, *Law of Peoples*, 136–37. These are my italics, used in order to emphasize the slight difference between these two regulative ideas (cf. ibid., xlii, xliv, 446).

15. Rawls, *Political Liberalism*, 50–51.

16. Rawls, *Political Liberalism*, 11 and 11n11, 147. Rawls also calls "intrinsically moral" his notions of reasonableness and the criterion of reciprocity (ibid., xlii, xlv, 50).

17. Rawls, *Political Liberalism*, xli, xliii, 11, 147–48, 168, 392.

18. Rawls, *Law of Peoples*, 5–7, 11, 17–18, 126–28: "realistic utopia" applies to the "Society of Peoples" (see below) as well as to politically liberal societies.

19. Rawls, *Theory of Justice*, 360.

20. Rawls, *Theory of Justice*, 462–63; for the linkage of regulative role of the principles as "right" and "good" with the "Aristotelian Principle" of the "good life," see 364, 374; with the idea of "a rational plan of life," 380, 392–94, 450–51; with a "moral person" and his or her capacity to have a conception of "their good as expressed by a rational plan of life" plus a "sense of justice," 415, 418–19, 442–43; and with our "social nature," 458–59.

21. Jacques Derrida, *Rogues: Two Essays on Reason*, trans. Pascale-Anne Brault and Michael Naas (Stanford, CA: Stanford University, 2005), 9, 18; see also Jacques Derrida, *The Other Heading: Reflections on Today's Europe*, trans. Pascale-Anne Brault and Michael B. Nass (Bloomington, IN: Indiana University

Press, 1992), 77–78, and Derrida, "Saying the Event," 238. I have documented and elaborated upon Derrida's extensive use of the notion of "call" and "voice" in another paper, "Cosmopolitanism to Come: Derrida's Response to Globalization," in *A Companion to Derrida*, eds. Zeynep Direk and Leonard Lawlor (London: Wiley-Blackwell, forthcoming).

22. Derrida, *Rogues*, 9.

23. Derrida, *Rogues*, xiv, xv, 135, 144, 148, 152.

24. Jacques Derrida, "Khora," in *On the Name*, trans. and ed. Thomas Dutoit (Stanford, CA: Stanford University Press, 1995), 124–25.

25. Derrida, *Rogues*, 35–36; see also Jacques Derrida, *Positions*, trans. Alan Bass (Chicago: University of Chicago Press, 1981), 28–29, 33; Jacques Derrida, *Speech and Phenomena: And Other Essays on Husserl's Theory of Signs*, trans. David B. Allison (Evanston: Northwestern University Press, 1973), 85–86.

26. Derrida, *Rogues*, 38–39.

27. Derrida, "Saying the Event," 234.

28. Indeed, Derrida says that we have the possibility of abandoning the name or heritage of democracy, but "always in the name of the name, thereby betraying the heritage *in the name of* the heritage" (*Rogues*, 89; Derrida's italics).

29. *Rogues*, 86. In particular, Derrida takes this indecidability to be virtuous because it delegitimizes the "roguery" that he feels the United States, in the name of its democratic values as well as its unfounded fears, perpetrated on Iraq after September 11, 2001 (ibid., xiv, 40, 96). I will explain later the reason why democracy to come is only a "quasi" transcendental force.

30. Jacques Derrida, *The Politics of Friendship*, trans. Georges Collins (London: Verso, 2005), 105–6; Derrida, *Rogues*, 91–92.

31. Derrida, *Rogues*, 84, 144; see also Derrida, "Saying the Event," 239.

32. Jacques Derrida, *Specters of Marx*, trans. Peggy Kamuf (New York: Routledge, 1994), 59, 73.

33. Derrida, *Rogues*, 85–86; Derrida, *Specters of Marx*, 73; Derrida, "Saying the Event," 240–42.

34. Jacques Derrida, "Autoimmunity: Real and Symbolic Suicides—A Dialogue with Jacques Derrida," trans. Pascale-Anne Brault and Michael Naas, in *Philosophy in a Time of Terror*, ed. Giovanna Borradori (Chicago: Chicago University Press, 2003), 120. See also Derrida, "Saying the Event," 240–42.

35. Derrida, *Rogues*, 87.

36. Derrida, *Rogues*, 86.

37. Derrida, *Rogues*, 84; see also 90, 149, Derrida, *Specters of Marx*, 73, and Derrida, "Saying the Event," 238, 242.

38. Derrida, *Rogues*, 83–84.

39. See above and Martin Hägglund, *Radical Atheism: Derrida and the Time of Life* (Stanford, CA: Stanford University Press, 2008), 211n9.

40. Derrida, *Rogues*, 84–85, 158; see also Derrida, *Negotiations*, 298.

41. For the points in this paragraph, see Rawls, *Theory of Justice*, 226, and Rawls, *Political Liberalism*, xlin8, xlv, 7–79, 199–200, 375n3. He expresses the importance of the social stability that he hopes to achieve in the following manner: "[T]he problem of stability [surprisingly] has played very little role in the history of moral philosophy . . . yet [it] is fundamental to political philosophy" (ibid., xvii; see xvii–xix).

42. Rawls, *Political Liberalism*, 38.

43. Rawls, *Political Liberalism*, 445–46, 446–47. Ultimately, neither Rawls's political liberalism nor utilitarianism or any other particular political conception of justice can specify public reason: it, in conjunction with reflective equilibrium (ibid., 28), is used to determine which of the family of reasonable political conceptions of justice is the most adequate (ibid., l–li). Rawls thinks that political liberalism will ultimately win.

44. Rawls, *Political Liberalism*, xlii, xlv, 40, 441–46. As these cited pages attest, the political conception of justice is freestanding in that its moral status is independent of any comprehensive doctrine of the good.

45. Rawls, *Political Liberalism*, 446–47. He prefaces this comment with: "This fundamental political relation of citizenship has two special features: first, it is a relation of citizens within the basic structure of society, a structure we enter only by birth and exit only by death; and second, it is a relation of free and equal citizens who exercise ultimate political power as a collective body" (ibid., 445).

46. Rawls, *Political Liberalism*, 147.

47. "[T]he idea of the reasonable makes an overlapping consensus of reasonable doctrines possible in ways the concept of truth cannot" (Rawls, *Political Liberalism*, 94; see also xlv, 39–40, 144–50). Moreover, the moral status of an overlapping consensus is assured because its *object*, "the political conception of justice, is itself a moral conception," and because the principles of justice and other *grounds* upon which the consensus is affirmed are seen as moral from within people's comprehensive moral view as well as from within the original position (ibid., 147–48). Rawls also thinks his notions of "reasonable pluralism" and "overlapping consensus" require that he eschew the more unitary concept of "community" because it is always based on one or another comprehensive doctrine of the good (ibid., 146, 201).

48. Rawls, *Political Liberalism*, xvi–xvii.

49. Rawls, *Political Liberalism*, 35.

50. Rawls, *Political Liberalism*, 441–42.

51. Rawls, *Political Liberalism*, 138, 145–46, 155–58, 243–44, 392–94, 460–620.

52. Rawls, *Political Liberalism*, 477–78.

53. Rawls, *Political Liberalism*, 468–69, cf. Will Kymlicka, *Contemporary Political Philosophy: An Introduction*, 2nd ed. (New York: Oxford University Press, 2002), 236–41, 243–44. This criterion of reasonableness would also exclude theocratic democracies; that is, ones that respect their citizens' human rights, have regular elections, but on religious grounds restrict who can hold at least high political office.

54. Rawls, *Political Liberalism*, xlviii–l.

55. Rawls, *Political Liberalism*, li–liv.

56. Rawls, *Political Liberalism*, 443.

57. For Rawls's declaration that the law of peoples is an extension of political liberalism, see his *Law of Peoples*, 9–10, 18, 23, 55, 128.

58. More specifically, Rawls's "law of peoples" can include nonliberal though "decent" groups; for example, theocracies that respect their citizens' human rights and consult regularly with the subcommunities of their society but restrict who can hold high political office, so long as these groups agree to a liberal political conception of justice in international forums. Peoples rather than individuals become the primary citizens on this global political arrangement—see Rawls, *Law of Peoples*, 17–19, 62–68, 75–76, 83.

59. Rawls, *Law of Peoples*, 6, 80–81. For the use of the term *ontology* in connection to Rawls's distinction between peoples and individuals, see Philip Pettit, "Rawls's Political Ontology," *Politics, Philosophy, and Economics* 4, no. 2 (2005–2006): 157–74.

60. See Thomas Pogge, *Realizing Rawls* (Ithaca, NY: Cornell University Press, 1990).

61. Jacques Derrida and Anne Duformantelle, *Of Hospitality*, trans. Rachel Bowlby (Stanford, CA: Stanford University Press, 2000), 79; Derrida, *Politics of Friendship*, 104, 106, 134.

62. Derrida, *Rogues*, 74.

63. Jacques Derrida, *On Cosmopolitanism and Forgiveness*, trans. Mark Dooley and Michael Hughes (London: Routledge, 2001), 44–45; "Autoimmunity," 130; *Rogues*, 91–92; Derrida and Duformantelle, *Hospitality*, 79.

64. Jacques Derrida, "Marx & Sons," in *Ghostly Demarcations: A Symposium on Jacques Derrida's* Specters of Marx, ed. Michael Sprinker (London: Verso, 1999), 254; cf. Rodolphe Gasché, *The Tain of the Mirror: Derrida and the Philosophy of Reflection* (Cambridge, MA: Cambridge University Press, 1986), 217; and Vincent B. Leitch, "Late Derrida: The Politics of Sovereignty," in *The Later Derrida*, ed. W. J. T. Mitchell and Arnold I. Davidson (Chicago, IL: Chicago University Press, 2007), 19. As stated earlier but worth repeating, democracy (and justice) to come are transcendental for Derrida in that they, respectively, make democracies and law possible and yet are themselves unconditional injunctions, demands about what is intrinsically to come and thus never them-

THE DILEMMA OF DIVERSITY

selves determined (conditioned) by what goes on in the world of presence (see *Negotiations*, 366–67). We shall see, however, that they exert a crucial effect on that world.

65. Derrida, *Rogues*, 86–92, 149–50.
66. Derrida, *Rogues*, 87; see also 72, 90, and "Autoimmunity," 121.
67. Derrida, *Rogues*, 24, 25.
68. Derrida, *Rogues*, xiv, 102.
69. Derrida, *Rogues*, 84–85, 158; *Negotiations*, 298.
70. Derrida, *Cosmopolitanism*, 16–17; "Autoimmunity," 129–30.
71. Derrida, *Rogues*, 60, 149; see also, 86.
72. Derrida, "Saying the Event," 243; see also *Hospitality*, 53, 54, 57, 65, 79–81, 124–25, 147–48, 149, and "Sons of Marx," 65.
73. Derrida, *Specters*, 28. See also Jacques Derrida, "Force of Law: The Mystical Foundation of Authority," trans. Mary Quaintance, in *Acts of Religion*, ed. Gil Anidjar (London: Routledge, 2002), 244, 245, 248, 254, 256.
74. Derrida, *Rogues*, 40–41, 63, 86–87, 101–2; "Autoimmunity," 128–29.
75. Derrida, *Rogues*, 86.
76. Derrida, *Negotiations*, 298–99, 304–6; *Rogues*, xii, 29. "Urgency" involves the refusal of rules that would destroy responsibility for making one's own decision.
77. Derrida, *Rogues*, 158–59.
78. Derrida, *Rogues*, 150–51, 158–59.
79. Derrida, *Negotiations*, 372–74; *Rogues*, 158; see also 101, 109, 143, 151.
80. Just as democracy to come is an unconditional injunction that interrupts confidence in the purity of any possible democracy, so (unconditional) justice does the same to any possible laws. For this same reason, we can consider Derrida's idea of justice to be part of the form of democracy to come and vice versa (see Derrida, *Rogues*, 88, 150; also, justice is a "trace" of itself and "every trace is a trace of democracy," ibid., 39).
81. Kymlicka, *Political Philosophy*, 236–41.
82. For the pros and cons of each of these alternatives in general and in relation to Rawls specifically, and also in relation to such topics as justice, citizenship, communitarianism, and nationalism, see Kymlicka, *Political Philosophy*, 136–37, 209–10, 212, 252–61, 268–70, 299, 310–12. For the claim that Rawls's political liberalism is basically a form of liberal communitarianism, see Charles Taylor, "The Politics of Recognition," in *Multiculturalism: Examining the Politics of Recognition*, ed. Amy Gutmann (Princeton, NJ: Princeton University Press, 1994), 58–59 and *passim*, and, in the same volume, Michael Waltzer's "Comment," 99. Onora O'Neil, in her article "Constructivism in Rawls and Kant," in *The Cambridge Companion to Rawls*, ed. Samuel Freeman (Cambridge, UK: Cambridge University Press, 2003), suggests as much when she

states that the Rawlsian as opposed to the Kantian notion of "reasonableness" is "identified . . . with the public reason of fellow citizens in a given, bounded, democratic society" (362). William Rehg, in his *Insight and Solidarity: The Discourse Ethics of Jürgen Habermas* (Berkeley, CA: University of California Press, 1994), goes in the opposite direction and says that Rawls should recognize political liberalism as a universal principle and provide a moral intuition as its foundation (123–24). For a critical treatment of the various ways Rawls's political liberalism appears at times communitarian and at others universal, see also Stephen Mulhall and Adam Swift, "Rawls and Communitarianism," in *The Cambridge Companion to Rawls* (Cambridge, UK: Cambridge University Press, 2003).

83. Johan van der Walt, "Rawls and Derrida on the Historicity of Constitutional Democracy and International Justice," *Constellations* 16, no. 1 (2009): 27. Michael Sandel makes a similar argument and provides illustrative examples. See his *Justice: What's the Right Thing to Do?* (New York: Farrar, Straus and Giroux, 2009), 251–60.

84. See Rawls, *Political Liberalism*, liii–lv.

85. Walt, "Rawls and Derrida," 27. Cf. Rawls, *Political Liberalism*, liii.

86. Walt, "Rawls and Derrida," 28. Walt argues that this sort of discrepancy shows up in cases of attempting to determine punishments that are commensurate with the crime committed (28–29).

87. This example is a free rendering of one offered by Jean-François Lyotard, though he does not use it in the context of an explicit criticism of Rawls's political liberalism. See his *The Differend: Phrases in Dispute*, trans. Georges Van Den Abbeele (Minneapolis: University of Minnesota Press, 1988), 9–10.

88. Amartya Sen advocates this alternative to Rawls's "transcendent" idea of consensus produced by noumenal subjects in the original position. See his *The Idea of Justice* (Boston, MA: Harvard University Press, 2011), xiii, 129–30, 144–45, 148, 197–99, 321, 402–3. I feel that this position is akin in spirit to the Derridean alternative—"experimental moment of deferral"—offered by Walt in the name of remaining forever open to new ideas of the meaning of justice (Walt, "Rawls and Derrida," 30–31). Walt also cites Derrida as stating "[t]he only life worth living is an im-possible life beyond the economy of the possible" (ibid., 31), which we can contrast with Rawls's admonition that life is worth living because justice and democracy are possible (Rawls, *Law of Peoples*, 128n7).

89. Derrida, *Rogues*, 33–34; see also 30, 30–31.

90. See Walter Mignolo, *Local Histories/Global Designs: Coloniality, Subaltern Knowledges, and Border Thinking* (Princeton, NJ: Princeton University Press, 2000), and the articles by Aijaz Ahmad, Terry Eagleton, Antonio Negri, and others in *Ghostly Demarcations: A Symposium on Jacques Derrida's Specters of Marx*, ed. Michael Sprinker (London: Verso, 1999).

91. Derrida, *Rogues*, 24.

92. Hélène Cixous, "Jacques Derrida as Proteus Unbound," in *The Later Derrida*, ed. W. J. T. Mitchell and Arnold I. Davidson (Chicago, IL: Chicago University Press, 2007), 50.

93. Jacques Derrida, *Acts of Literature*, ed. D. Attridge (London: Routledge, 1992), 35.

94. Derrida, *Other Heading*, 7.

95. Derrida, *Positions*, 85–89.

96. See Evans, *Multivoiced Body*, 123 and *passim*, and Leonard Lawlor, *Derrida and Husserl: The Basic Problem of Phenomenology* (Bloomington, IN: Indiana University Press, 2002), chapter 7.

97. Derrida, *Other Heading*, 10, 15, 77–78; cf. Rodolphe Gasché, *Europe, or the Infinite Task: A Study of a Philosophical Concept* (Stanford, CA: Stanford University Press, 2009), esp. 265–70, 284–86, 298, 299–300, and 301.

98. Derrida, *Negotiations*, 27–30.

99. I have treated these notions extensively in Evans, *Multivoiced Body*.

100. Thus Derrida exhorts us "to hear each other [*nous devons nous entendre*]" in "[each others'] languages" (Derrida, *Other Heading*, 60–61).

II

Particular Issues in Justice and Diversity: Philosophy

8

DIVERSITY

How Far?

Rémi Brague, University of Paris

The notion of "diversity" has come to dominate much of American academic life, from the curriculum to admissions and hiring. The claim for diversity is harped upon in Europe, too. Respect for diversity should be a basic concern for justice. Yet the meaning and purport of this idea is seldom analyzed and debated, so that it more often than not boils down to a very narrow interpretation—the "differences" that are most important and relevant to justice are limited to race, gender, and sexual orientation. The aim of the present chapter is to enlarge our outlook.

THE PRESENT-DAY DIVERSITY FAD

Diversity has become a catchword, together with other phrases expressing the positive valuation of the manifold. Words describing a fact like *plurality* yield to words that express the same idea, but with a positive shade of meaning, like *pluralism*. Symmetrically, words that summarize a historical narrative, like *colonization*, are more and more pushed out by negative words like *colonialism*. On the other hand, present-day parlance abounds in derogatory adjectives qualifying what is one, like *monolithic*.

Diversity is hardly more than the last among many catchwords that form a continuous stream. In the early twentieth century, William James gave the word *pluralism* the value of a general principle.[1] More recently, others, like the German philosopher Odo Marquard, in the wake of Max Weber's metaphor for the values, which he called "gods," used "polytheism" as a symbol for a state of affairs in which the individual may freely choose what he or she will adore.[2]

Such words may have been coined as early as the eighteenth century. "Pluralism" is in Kant as the contrary of "egoism"; that is, as the consciousness of being a citizen of the world.[3] But their present-day use is relatively recent, for it harks back to hardly more than some dozens of years. Yet the idea that they express can be traced back at least to the American Revolution. For instance, we read under the pen of James Madison: "When men exercise their reason coolly and freely on a variety of distinct questions, they inevitably fall into different opinions on some of them. When they are governed by a common passion, their opinions, if they are so to be called, will be the same."[4] This sounds paradoxical, for we would expect the very contrary: when men "sit down in a cool hour" and hold their passions in check, they should be able to come to the same conclusions. Here, passions are seen as what blindly sweeps a mob toward a common goal, reason as what opens a broad spectrum of possible, all equivalent options.

The earliest evidence of such a positive view on diversity might be the description Plato gave of the democratic city. He compared it with a shop in which everything is to be sold (*pantopōleion*), we would say, a supermarket of sorts.[5] Plato was far from condoning democracy as the best possible regime. On the contrary, democracy was in the whole ancient world, albeit not a boo-word properly speaking, yet rather looked down at. As for Aristotle, he considered democracy to be the worst of the good regimes or the best one among the bad ones.[6] The best regime was currently thought to be "aristocracy," which judgment, this being the very meaning of the word ("government of the best people"), was some sort of tautology. The first writer to use the word *democracy* with a positive shade of meaning, as a regime that respects traditional values, in contradistinction to the limitless whims of the mob (*okhlokratia*), may have been the historian Polybius, in the second century BC.[7]

Be that as it may, our present-day cities resemble more and more the state of affairs that Plato ironically characterized as a motley patchwork of pursuits and characters. But this is supposed to be a positive feature. Diversity is not to be avoided. It can't be. And perhaps it should not be. For diversity is supposed to be a richness, or at least the way leading to it.

The respect for diversity stretches even to the subhuman realm. Thus, "biodiversity" is supposed to be something that should be kept at all costs. The disappearance of a living species is felt as a catastrophe, and as a crime when it is the (real or alleged) consequence of technology.

THE NOBLE DREAM OF DEMOCRACY

Our democracies are guided by a view of things that originates in Greece and again in Plato. In his dialogue, *Protagoras*, the sophist who plays the lead and gave the work his name, sketches the functioning of the Athenian assembly of the people. Whenever a technical matter is at stake—for example, how ships should be built—the Athenians won't listen to anybody who does not possess the necessary competence. On the other hand, when the discussion shifts to whether the fleet is to be sent abroad for it to wage war against some enemy, competent people lose their privileged position and are not paid attention to more than other people. In fact, no regard whatsoever is paid to any particular feature of the speakers. Technical expertise, but also birth (for example, noble ancestors), age, and more are discarded. What counts is the worth of the arguments and nothing more.[8]

This ideal situation, to be sure, never was fully realized. In particular, it was not in Greek "democracy," which excluded women and foreign residents, and rested on an infrastructure of slave labor.[9] Nevertheless, it furnishes some contemporary political thinkers with a model of what a full-fledged democracy should be. The German philosopher Jürgen Habermas is among those people.

Democratic space should be devoid of any preexisting hierarchy. In it, everybody should be listened to and followed exclusively on the basis of the arguments that he or she puts forward. Any legitimate superiority should be the result of the discussion, not its point of departure.

Anyway, in order to get this happy state of affairs, it is better to have in front of us a large panoply of possible opinions and, first of all, of people susceptible to stand for them. Democracy tolerates, and even enhances, diversity because it redounds to its interest.

HISTORICAL ROOTS

Diversity and its neighboring words are not only the dream of well-meaning abstract thinkers who outsoar our petty matter-of-fact problems. It is the result of most concrete historical events. It tries to answer problems that arose in societies at definite points in time, and that did so because of unpleasant circumstances.

This is the case with "tolerance," the virtue with the help of which we expect to face the challenge of diversity. The idea has its roots in the late sixteenth and mid-seventeenth centuries. It arose in the context of what came to be called, probably inadequately, the European "religious wars"—in fact a stage in the development of the modern nation-state under its first form as absolute monarchy in France and Britain. Attempts at either converting or even simply doing away with one's opponents failed. The upshot was that people who considered each other as holding false or even perverse opinions, hence as good candidates to eternal damnation, had to accept each other's existence for want of anything better.

The principle according to which the subjects were supposed to have the religion of the reigning family (*cuius regio, eius religio*), first formulated in 1646, was hardly more than an awkward compromise and a rule of thumb, but it put a stop on bloodshed. People who lived under a prince who belonged to another denomination either chose to leave or to accept being only "tolerated" by the local authorities.

Even mutual tolerance in the United States, as is well known, arose from a desire to escape the religious persecution that was rampant in Europe, especially in Britain, which did not prevent some contagion, like the Battle of the Severn and the burning down of Catholic churches in Maryland by the Puritans.

Generally, whereas "to accept" is neutral and "to authorize" has positive connotations, the shade of meaning of "to tolerate" definitely is a derogatory one. It is a highly ironical fact that it came to designate some sort of virtue, and finally one of our most highly praised virtues, not to say the only virtue that is left for us to preach and boast about; in any case, it is the only virtue whose mention does not trigger a sneer among the people who hear it named.

TWO POWERFUL SUPPORTERS OF DIVERSITY

What speaks on behalf of diversity is a naïve idea, expressed in the proverb: "the more, the merrier." For plurality permits a choice. The more possibilities there are, the broader is the spectrum of possible choices. This is all very well, but this supposes two things.

First, the subject must be really able to choose. This supposes that all the identities or roles between which he or she has to choose are weak enough, so that he or she will have free reins. The identities must constitute some sort of catalogue in which articles to be sold are all on the same footing. The underlying model is commercial in nature. The basic image is the market: a great deal of shops, offering various commodities. Pluralism might be an indirect way for the market to assert itself as the ultimate master, thereby fostering the very contrary of pluralism—that is, monism as its sovereign and exclusive domination. If the market were a conscious being, it would wish as much diversity as possible, so that each element would be weakened and less susceptible to resist its appeal and thwart its development. *Divide et impera* is a motto that the market would willingly make its own.

The second requirement is the existence of a strong instance that wields the power to judge between different elements of identity that all claim to the same authority. This instance must be endowed with the power, in extreme cases, to exclude a participant from the social dialogue. This instance is the State. The State, too, wishes as much diversity as possible, in order to counteract the possible resistance of intermediary bodies. In the United States, the coexistence of a great deal of individuals and groups of all ilk is made possible only by a common allegiance to the Constitution. Tolerance is a virtue of the individual. But the State simply *cannot* tolerate what contradicts its basic tenets, not because of any intrinsic malignity, but because it does not possess the necessary power and can't afford to put its very existence at stake. No State has ever received the promise of eternal life.

Hence, the question is to know which kind of diversity will be welcomed, and which, on the contrary, will be acted against.

An elegant way to solve the problem, not to say an easy cop-out, consists in choosing among the points on which diversity should be tolerated, and even promoted—characteristics of the individual as, for example, race, gender, and sexual orientation. Thus, homosexuality is commonly taken as representing a paradigmatic case of diversity. This is not without some irony, for a homosexual couple consists of two persons who are *not* diverse, but on the contrary similar not only in their bodies but also in their sensibility, and more.

In any case, discrimination will be carefully avoided, and even, when it occurs, punished in a more or less heavy-handed way. On the other hand, differences that concern large groups will be looked at with mistrust. Whatever can be done in order to bring to heel possible communities, to deprive them of any relevance or even to dissolve them, will be welcome. Big chunks melt away less easily than small pieces. Therefore, the State will prefer to mince up things as much as possible.

WHAT IF SOME PEOPLE DON'T WANT DIVERSITY?

The problem with diversity is that the diverse elements that enter the melting pot must at least be compatible. In other words, the possibility of the one should not exclude the possibility of the other ones; they must be, to quote a word coined by Leibniz in another, metaphysical context, *compossible*.

Now, if some element in the mixture considers itself as excluding the other ones, what is to be done? This is especially the case if this element claims to possess an identity that is divine in origin, so that the other ones would necessarily be ungodly in nature—an adjective that, in this case, must mean not neutral toward the different claimants, but plainly against God. Modern political philosophy is grounded on the assumption according to which no voice in the concert can claim an exclusive divine authority. This leads to the different devices contrived by Western democracies: from the American "wall of separation" to the happily untranslatable French *laïcité* through widely different nuances—for example, the British and Scandinavian State-Church, various concordats, and more.

Religions are especially prone to resist submission to a system that intends to put them on exactly the same footing as anything else; for example, another religion or even a secular view of life. Religions, by definition, have a reference point that is external and, in their eyes, superior to the public realm. But they draw different consequences out of this basic principle. Let us have a look at the three religions that claim a share in Abraham's heritage.

Judaism has been distinguishing since the Talmudic age between religious commands and civil laws, so that the civil law of the country is considered as binding for the Jews who live there (*dina de-malkhuta dina*).[10]

Says Saint Peter before the Sanhedrin, "It is better to obey God rather than men" (Acts 5:29). In Christendom, Thomas Hobbes secured a foundation for modern political philosophy by taking as the implicit target of his critique the very utterance of Saint Peter that I have just quoted and that he, as a matter of course, never quotes.[11] According to him, obedience to God boils down to obeying civil authorities, supposed to have received their legitimacy directly from the Overlord. As a matter of fact, obedience to God in Christianity never implied a direct intervention of God as foisting specific rules upon the community of the believers.

There is an Islamic formula, a sentence put into the mouth of the Prophet (*hadith*), that very much resembles the sentence of s. Peter just quoted: "No obedience which would entail disobeying God" (*lā tā'ata fi ma'siyati Allah*), or "No obedience to who disobeys God" (*lā tā'ata li-man 'asā Allah*).[12] The trouble is that, whereas some Islamic rules of conduct have to be painstakingly deduced from the Book and first of all from the Hadith, some commands are clearly and unambiguously uttered in the Quran, which pious Muslims believe to have been dictated by God to Muhammad. This is the case, for instance, of the veil that should cover Muslim women and that the French state recently made quite a fuss about—rightly or wrongly, I have not decided.

THE INTRINSIC DIVERSITY OF WESTERN CULTURE

The problem of diversity is a feature of present-day Western culture. Other cultures in the past and in the present as well contained or still contain diverse elements. Ancient Persia, for instance, invented the empire as a political form that was later to be adopted by the Greek heirs of Alexander the Great, the Romans, and other ones until the British in India. Furthermore, the Persians built an empire that was the first multicultural state, a thin cobweb, merely juridical in nature, cast over a patchwork of different races, languages, and religions that were allowed to keep their mores and beliefs. In South America, Brazil always was and remains a multiethnic country in which Africans, local Indians, and the

Asiatic rub their shoulders with whites of Portuguese, German, and other origins.

Nevertheless, Western culture constitutes a particular case, for diversity was its constitutive principle from the outset. It even made it possible as such. Therefore, it can furnish us with a model of the way in which diversity can be handled in order to yield positive results.

Western culture is in itself already a certain way for a culture to handle diversity. It did that first by admitting it in itself by the process that I called "inclusion."[13] A "normal" culture assimilates foreign elements by digestion, so that they lose their original identity and become part and parcel of the culture that receives them. Each and every culture brings this method to bear on whatever exerts an influence on it from the outside, and Western culture is no exception. Nevertheless, something singularizes this culture; to wit, the presence in it of another way to deal with otherness, the one I called "inclusion." Digestion applies to cultural things, a process that belongs emphatically to the realm of the natural, and even that makes life possible; that is, exchanges with the surrounding milieu (metabolism). On the other hand, inclusion is a highly artificial process. It sort of elevates culture to its square. Culture no longer imitates natural phenomena, but to some extent cultivates itself.

Western civilization is basically a synthesis. This doesn't constitute an exception. Athens was founded when different small communities decided to join their forces and launch into a common adventure. Hence the plural form of the name of the city, Athen*ai*, which survives in the "s" of the English Athen*s*. Ironically, the name of the other paradigmatic city, Jerusalem, Yerūšala*yim*, grammatically speaking, is a plural, too, although it is anybody's guess to explain why. In Athens, this difficult and in no way self-evident step toward union (*synoikismos*) was said to have been taken under the influence of a hero, Theseus. Left to their own resources, men probably would not have been equal to the task of negotiating such a sea change. But after all, the citizens of the villages that were to constitute Athens had in common the same variety of the Ionian dialect and the cult of the goddess Athena.

What is remarkable and surprising in Western culture is that it actually realizes the synthesis of forces that are diametrically opposed, and even at loggerheads to one another. A common image of this tension is furnished by the phrase *Athens and Jerusalem*, which has become hackneyed since the title of the book that the Russian philosopher Lev Šestov published in

1937, first in his own French translation, then in the original Russian in 1953.[14] The first apparition of the idea of a conflict between the two cities is the well-known passage in which Tertullian asks the rhetorical question about what Athens and Jerusalem have in common, obviously expecting a negative answer.[15] Yet, as a matter of fact, the idea of an irreconcilable opposition between two poles of sorts between which Western culture was stretched and that could tear it asunder were it not for some beneficent force to compel them to accept each other is hardly older than Šestov.

ROME AS SYNTHESIS AND TENSION

A third city, equally endowed with a great symbolic weight, Rome, has to come to the fore here, not as the historical reality of this town in Latium that succeeded in submitting the whole Mediterranean area, but as the symbol of a definite cultural policy, as a "way."[16] Rome is sometimes considered as being the unifying force that produced or at least fostered the synthesis between the two elements represented by the other two cities. There is some truth in that, but we should go further.

First, it should be noted that this synthesis did not happen in a peaceful and harmonious way. On the contrary, Rome as a historical power had first to vanquish the Greeks on the battlefield. Some three centuries later, it had to crush the revolts of the Jewish people, the latter leading to a tremendous bloodshed and to the destruction of the Temple. The Romans hardly pampered whosoever revolted against them.

Interestingly, however, both the Greeks and the Jews vanquished their former conquerors on another, deeper level. A line of Horace became almost a proverb: "Greece, vanquished, vanquished its rude conqueror" (*Graecia capta ferum victorem cepit*). Seneca, in a work that we know only thanks to a quotation by Saint Augustine, says something like that about the Jews, although the keynote is far less positive, for he calls them a "most criminal people" (*sceleratissima gens*): "the vanquished gave their laws to the victorious" (*victi victoribus leges dederunt*).[17]

Furthermore, the synthesis itself never was a peaceful blend, either. It never could force "Athens" and "Jerusalem" to speak with the same voice. One may even ask whether there was such a thing as a synthesis. On the contrary, Rome sort of kept open the tension between them, thereby compelling both poles to an extreme and unswerving affirmation of its own originality. The conflict that thus came to a head proved more fruitful than a too-easy conciliation.

Greek philosophy developed into a science of nature that does not require any reference to things divine, let alone the personal God of the Bible.

Christianity became a religion. This ceases to be a platitude when one considers that no other religion is just that—a religion, full stop. Greek or Roman religion was a religion, plus a city. Judaism is a religion, plus a people with its history. Islam is a religion, plus a system of law. Buddhism is a religion, plus wisdom. Shinto is a religion, plus a nation, and so on. Christianity is the only religion that claims to be *only* a religion. It leaves alone, at least in principle, the other realms of human endeavor and interest.

In particular, it leaves alone science. The conflicts that arose with the new Copernican worldview, like the Galileo affair, or the present-day so-called creationism of the Bible Belt, are mere misunderstandings. There is no Christian cosmography, in the sense of a descriptive account of the structure of the material universe.[18] There were, for instance, quite elaborated Gnostic and Manichean cosmographies, and Augustine could poke fun at the latter, with which he was acquainted firsthand.

THE CHRISTIAN CONCEPTION OF DIVINE LAW[19]

Among the realms that Christianity leaves aside as not germane to its purpose, law deserves pride of place. Christianity, said in the nineteenth century by the French historian Fustel de Coulanges, is "the first religion that did not pretend that law depended upon it."[20] On the contrary, Christianity contented itself with keeping traditional morality, what C. S. Lewis called the "great platitudes," what I should call the basic survival kit of humanity, such as it was formulated in the Decalogue.

"Do good, avoid evil" (Psalm 34:15, quoted in 1 Peter 3:11, paraphrased in Romans 11:9) is a formula that often drives us to smile because of its emptiness. We are not told *what kind* of good is to be pursued and *what kind* of evil is to be left alone, so that we are tempted to ask for some more specific recipe. Being called a "do-gooder" is not exactly a compliment. Nevertheless, this opens up a space of freedom. The emptiness of the formula is the flipside of the trust that God puts into man. Man is in principle capable of finding the best ways for him to act, on the basis of the abilities that were bestowed upon him by the Creator. God has endowed us with the capacity to tell the good from the evil, be this power called "practical reason," "conscience," or whatever else. God doesn't have to tell us what we should do, but rather to help us to do it by giving His grace. Saint Augustine says that in a wonderfully concise formula: "give us what you command, and then command what you want" (*da quod jubes et jube quod vis*).[21]

All this supposes further a definite conception of the divine that does not manifest itself, or doesn't do that primarily, as legislator, as He does in Islam. The famous bugbear of "applying the *šarī'a*," which has just regained some actuality, may not be the worst. For, and this argument is often put forward, the *šarī'a* as a human endeavor is manifold, and, since it has always been that way, it is still susceptible to many interpretations, including more friendly ones than those defended by radical Islamists. There is some truth in this. Yet behind any concrete system of law, behind any attempt on the side of human beings to build one, there subsists the very core idea of a divine legislation (*šar'*); that is, that God is believed to be, through his Book and through the example and sayings of His prophet, the only legitimate legislator, the only one who can tell people what they will have to do and call to absolute obedience.[22]

In Western culture, to be precise, the divine is still there, but it doesn't manifest itself as setting an external law but as acting through conscience. Paul explains how decent pagans who have no inkling of Moses's law can behave in a laudable way. In order to do that, he borrows from Stoic philosophy the notion of conscience (*syneidesis*) and gives it a moral twist (Romans 2:14–15). He thereby opens the possibility of a direct access to what God revealed to Israel, hence introducing the idea of a "divine voice" or a "divine instinct," a phrase by Rousseau that we should take literally, probably more than Rousseau himself intended.[23] By this token, the ultimate instance that prompts us to act in an ethical way and judges whether we complied to its demands is divine in nature, so that we Westerners, too, live under a theocracy of sorts.[24]

THE IDEA OF A CULTURAL REALM[25]

What we mean with "culture" is something that did not exist as such in the ancient world. What we would have called by this name was a part of a whole that included religious elements. For instance, dramatic performances were an element in the cult rendered to the god Dionysus. Sportive competitions took place in the framework of games dedicated to gods like Zeus in Olympia or Apollo in Delphi. Philosophers associated in guilds were placed under the patronage of a god or a hero, and others.

Something like profane culture was made possible by Pauline Christianity. This doesn't mean, to be sure, that people who never underwent the Pauline revolution are devoid of culture. This absurdity would mean, by the way, that they are not human beings in the full meaning of this term. What I mean is that culture as such, culture that is only culture, and nothing more, in particular a culture that leaves aside the religious dimension, was made possible by the severance of the Greek *paideia* from its religious elements.

Pauline Christianity put Mosaic law at rest (*katargein*), thereby producing a momentous ebb that left bare the whole realm of norms. Precisely for this reason, it had to fill itself with a content that it had to borrow from the outside. Christianity has to suck into itself what was already available on the market of civilizations. This is what it did, first with Roman culture—the Roman system of law and of administration, together with what the Roman world already had borrowed from the Greek scientific, literary, and philosophic achievements.

There is something like Greek culture since the Pauline revolution only. What undoubtedly existed previously was the Greek *paideia*. It was a global way of life. To be sure, *paideia* included what we call "culture"—that is, literature and art, and even culture of the body. It was inseparably, in Plato's words, gymnastic and music. But the package included at the same time what we call "religion," a cult of the gods that was not palatable for Jews and, for that matter, not for Christians either.

Pagan culture underwent a process of neutralization. Whatever could claim to an absolute value independently of its ground on God had to be pruned away. In particular, "pagan" religious claims were put into brackets. Whatever claimed to be sacred had to submit to the ultimate revelation. This revelation had its peak in Christ; the Word became "flesh"—a human creature. As such—as dead and risen to a new mode of being through his resurrection—he couldn't possibly become sacred. But his was another mode of sacredness; that is, holiness.

As a consequence of this neutralization, European elites, including Christian clerics, were trained for centuries to understand and translate the "classical"—that is, pagan—writers. The Latin Middle Ages could keep Homer and Virgil (or the precious little knowledge they had of them) without the Greek and Roman gods. Dante is a wonderful example of this stance. The Renaissance, begun in Italy and spread into the whole of Europe, could even afford to keep the pagan gods; it even gave them a new lease on life, but without their claim to have an influence on human affairs, as mere aesthetic beings in painting, sculpture, and music.

ARE ALL WAYS OF LIFE EQUALLY LIFE ENHANCING?

This double model, classical Rome and Christianity, teach us the same lesson: there is no diversity without a principle that must be higher than the market and the state. Now, this principle might be no less than life itself.

In his famous *On Liberty*, John Stuart Mill coined the formula "experiments of living."[26] It quickly became immensely popular and furnished some legitimacy to many people who were eager to leave the trodden path and to venture into new ways of life. Now, scientific experiments can fail. What could prevent their analogous counterparts in real life from failing? The most secular minds somehow keep a naïve faith in Providence that is expected to hand us a parachute when we practice bungee jumping without an elastic.

Ironically, Mill wrote his provocative essay in the same year as Darwin's path-breaking *Origin of Species*. Now, there is a natural selection in social phenomena, too. Choosing a way of life is something; choosing life itself is a preliminary step that we can't skip. Now, it so happens that "choosing life" is not a self-evident attitude. This might be the reason why the God of the Bible has to command it (Deuteronomy 30:19).

Each and every human group has to face a set of eternal problems linked to something like human nature: how should we relate to what is above us (the divine), underneath us (nature), around us (enemies), among us (the other sex), after us (death, offspring, afterlife), and more. They all set forward some answers that they formulate in myth or philosophy and enact in various forms of cult, political, and social life. But not all ways of life are fit for survival in the long run. Some solutions given to those big problems menace the survival of the group that adopt them and bring about its disappearance if they are not checked in time. Such blind alleys can be criticized by clear-sighted people, be they philosophers or prophets. But at the end of the day, they need not: bad answers eliminate themselves together with the societies that chose them, as a tree brings the parasite that preys upon it into its own death.

For instance, a city like Sparta required from her citizens so tremendous an amount of restraint and self-mastery, together with a complete militarization of life and a hardly humane harshness against enslaved peoples, that it could not survive more than some centuries. Models of family life that bring about that the birthrate plummets may be tolerable and even pleasant for people who live in them. But they inevitably tend to the disappearance of the human groups that adopt them and to their replacement by other ones in which family life may be more old-fashioned and perhaps less fair, especially toward the female, but better ensure the continuance of the species. A telling North American example is the fate of French-speaking Canadians. Their communities could survive in a linguistically and religiously hostile surrounding because of their higher fertility rate, made possible by the crushing social pressure exerted by the Catholic Church, the only elite left after the treason of nobility, which embarked back to France in the eighteenth century. The possibility for women to get out of the kitchen and of the nursery in order to access higher education and birth control is undoubtedly a good thing. Yet it contributes to the shrinking of the number of children and irresistibly brings about the demise of the whole group.

CONCLUSION

Can we push the logics of diversity to its last consequences and put on the same footing what conduces to life and what conduces to death? As philosophers sitting in our studies, we can and must discriminate and try to argue in favor of life over death, thereby taking a stance for optimism against pessimism—an issue that G. E. Moore, for example, still considered to be an open one.[27] It is the duty of public intellectuals to expose what endangers the city. As private citizens, we may choose what behavior looks the best for us. But responsible leaders are hard put to find an adequate policy, and even scarcely likely to look for one. First, because what really endangers the survival of the society in which they are supposed to play the lead develops at a very slow tempo, much slower than the longest stretch of time during which they can hope to wield power and influence it. Second, because (in our democratic countries at least) they have to get elected; now, few voters would be willing to sacrifice their own present advantages on behalf of future generations. Third, because the modern political compromise has it that all questions involving judgments on ultimate values be excluded from the public space and relegated into the private. Questions about the good life, and even about the very goodness of life, are outside the ken of democratic politics.

In order to discriminate between different projects of life in a society in which diversity rules, we have to shift to a higher gear, which is metaphysical in nature.[28]

NOTES

1. William James, *A Pluralistic Universe* (1909).
2. Odo Marquard, *Lob des Polytheismus. Über Monomythie und Polymythie* [1978], in *Zukunft braucht Herkunft. Philosophische Essays* (Stuttgart 2003), 46–71.
3. Kant, *Anthropologie in pragmatischer Hinsicht*, §2, in *Werke*, ed. Wilhelm Weischedel (Darmstadt: Wissenschaftliche Buchgesellschaft, 1962), t. 6, 411.
4. James Madison, *The Federalist*, n. 50 [February 5, 1788], ed. Isaac Kramnick (London: Penguin, 1988), 317.
5. Plato, *Republic*, VIII, 557d8.
6. Plato, *Statesman*, 302e; see Aristotle, *Politics*, IV, 2, 1289b7–9.
7. Polybius, *History*, VI, 4, 4–5.
8. Plato, *Protagoras*, 319bd.
9. See Henri Bergson, *Les deux sources de la morale et de la religion* [1932], chapter 4 (Paris: P.U.F., 1962), 300.
10. See *Talmudic Encyclopedia. A Digest of Halachic Literature and Jewish Law from the Tannaitic Period to the Present Time Alphabetically Arranged* [Hebrew], Jerusalem, t. VII, 1968, col. 295–308 (S. Shilo).
11. Hobbes, *Leviathan*, III, chapter 39, ed. M. Oakeshott (Oxford: Blackwell, 1960), 306; chapter 42, 378.

12. See Arent Jan Wensinck et al., *Concordance et indices de la Tradition Musulmane*, vol. 4 (Leyden: Brill,1962), col. 43a.

13. See my "Inclusion and Digestion: Two Models of Cultural Appropriation," in *The Legend of the Middle Ages: Philosophical Explorations of Medieval Christianity, Judaism, and Islam* (Chicago: University of Chicago Press, 2009), 145–58.

14. See the commodious trilingual edition (French, Russian, Italian): Lev Šestov, *Atene e Gerusalemme*, ed. Alessandro Paris (Milan: Bompiani, 2005).

15. Tertullian, *De Praescriptione ad Haereticorom*, chapter 7, PL, 2, 23a. See my "Is European Culture 'A Tale of Two Cities'?," in *Historical, Cultural, Socio-Political and Economic Perspectives on Europe*, eds. Suzanne Stern-Gillet and M. T. Lunati (The Edwin Mellen Press, 2000), 33–50.

16. See my *Eccentric Culture: A Theory of Western Civilization*, tr. Samuel H. Lester (South Bend, IN: Saint Augustine's Press, 2000).

17. Horace, *Epistles*, II, I, 156–57; Augustine, *City of God*, VI, 11.

18. See my *The Wisdom of the World: History of the Human Experience of the Universe*, tr. T. Fagan (Chicago: University of Chicago Press, 2003), Introduction.

19. See my *The Law of God: The Philosophical History of an Idea*, tr. L. Cochrane (Chicago: University of Chicago Press, 2007).

20. Numa Denis Fustel de Coulanges, *La Cité antique: Etude sur le culte, le droit, les institutions de la Grèce et de Rome* [1864], vol. 3 (Paris: Flammarion, 1984), 453.

21. Augustine, *Confessions*, X, XXIX, 40.

22. See Wilfred Cantwell Smith, "The Concept of Shari'a Among Some Mutakallimun" in *Arabic and Islamic Studies in Honor of H. A. R. Gibb*, ed. G. Makdisi (Cambridge, MA: Harvard University Press, 1965), 581–602.

23. Jean-Jacques Rousseau, *Emile*, IV, in *Œuvres complètes*, vol. 4, ed. B. Gagnebin and M. Raymond (Paris: Gallimard, 1969), 600.

24. See my "Are Non-Theocratic Regimes Possible?," in *The Intercollegiate Review* 41, no. 1 (2005): 3–12.

25. See my "Jew, Greek and Christian: Some Reflections on the Pauline Revolution," *Expositions. Interdisciplinary Studies in the Humanities*, I, 1 (2007): 15–28.

26. John Stuart Mill, *On Liberty* [1859], chapter 3, ed. A. D. Lindsay (London: Dent, 1968), 115.

27. George Edward Moore, *Principia Ethica* [1903], chapter V, §95, ed. Thomas Baldwin (Cambridge: Cambridge University Press, 1993), 206.

28. See my recent *Les Ancres dans le ciel* (Paris: Seuil, 2011).

9

INTOLERANCE AND DIVERSITY IN THREE CITIES

Ancient Babylon, Renaissance Venice, and Nineteenth-Century Philadelphia

Camille Paglia

Tolerance and diversity emerged as ideal principles of campus discourse and governance forty years ago at the rise of identity politics, which empowered formerly marginalized groups such as women, gays, African Americans, Latinos, Native Americans, and Asians. Once used relatively neutrally by historians and sociologists, these two terms now carry a distinct value judgment and even a punitive moralism. Insofar as both tolerance and diversity are usually the products of slow social forces in the wider culture, it is debatable to what degree they can be imposed from above by campus administrations or inculcated by professors. As a libertarian, I remain very concerned about the speech codes that, whether codified or ad hoc, have become a tool of enforcement of tolerance in American academe and which from my point of view threaten constitutionally guaranteed free expression.

An uneasy tension persists between identity politics and tolerance; that is, the more forcefully group identity is affirmed, the more likely that rivalry or conflict with other groups will be perpetuated. Conditions of true tolerance eventually lead to assimilation, through which a tremendous amount of cultural heritage may be lost, as is happening to my own generation of Italian Americans and perhaps also to secular American Jews. What I want to show in this chapter about three cities separated by hundreds of years is how intolerance, with all its persecutions and rampant injustice, has sometimes led to the consolidation of group identity through fierce external pressures. In my three choices—ancient Babylon, Renaissance Venice, and nineteenth-century Philadelphia—geographical and economic factors played a crucial role in the achievement or suppression of diversity. In contrast to the Marxist assumptions of the 1930s-based Frankfurt School that currently pervade the humanities, I would submit that commerce has often played a *liberalizing* role, breaking up the static traditionalism of agrarian societies and reducing provincialism and xenophobia through the introduction of new ideas. Furthermore, religion, which is often treated with indifference or hostility on today's elite campuses, has been a defining force in ethnic history. (I am speaking here as an atheist.) At the end of this chapter, I will offer some personal reflections about tolerance and diversity in contemporary academe.

My first example is Babylon in ancient Mesopotamia, whose territory was roughly congruent with modern-day Iraq. Although it was a center of immense learning, especially in mathematics, astronomy, and medicine, Babylon as a symbol of sin and decadence has become imprinted on Western culture via the Bible, which records the highly intolerant eyewitness accounts of Hebrews deported to that city after the conquest of the kingdom of Judah and the destruction of Jersualem in the sixth century BC. The handicraft skills of thousands of Hebrews were needed and exploited by King Nebuchadnezzar in his systematic reconstruction of Babylon. The Babylonian Captivity of the Hebrews would last fifty-nine years (not seventy years as prophesied by the Book of Jeremiah), until they were freed after the invasion of Babylon by Persia. What the Book of Genesis attacks as the Tower of Babel was the sacred ziggurat of the god Marduk-Bel, a triumph of ancient engineering that soared over 270 feet high and was sheathed in shiny copper. Babylon is excoriated even in the last book of the New Testament, the Book of Revelations, where imperial Rome is portrayed as the bejeweled Whore of Babylon, the "Mother of Harlots" arrayed in purple and scarlet as she rides a seven-headed beast and holds a golden cup brimming with "the filthiness of her fornication."

It is hard to believe that the nondescript piles of melted mud brick spread across a desert fifty miles south of contemporary Baghdad were once a spectacular, palm-ringed metropolis whose hanging gardens were a wonder of the ancient world. Elite Babylonians were highly sophisticated in dress and manner: both sexes evidently wore cosmetics such as kohl eyeliner and anointed themselves with heavily perfumed oils. While it is probably not true, as the Greek historian Herodotus reported, that every Babylonian woman had to prostitute herself once in her lifetime in the Temple of Ishtar, it does seem as if prostitutes operated openly in the Temple grounds. Furthermore, the festivals of the war goddess Ishtar may have involved ritual public sex acts of some kind, perhaps even involving transsexuals. There can be no doubt that Judeo-Christian values, with their strict regulation of sexuality and hatred of idolatry, were partly formed in opposition to Babylonian paganism, which was organized around elaborate rituals for the dressing, feeding, and daily transfer of massive golden idols, in which the gods were thought literally to reside.

The culture shock of the Hebrews in big city Babylon was partly due to their own pastoralist roots: they had been shepherds, herdsmen like the Arab Bedouin, who dressed modestly and followed a conservative code of stoicism, frugality, and sexual discipline. What the exiled Hebrews recorded as a babel of voices inflicted as a punishment by God was actually the immense ethnic diversity of Babylon, which was a fabulously wealthy trading center perfectly situated between the Mediterranean and the Persian Gulf. A huge variety of people and languages were always represented in the mixed population of Babylon, with its masses of immigrants, fugitives, deported laborers, and itinerant merchants.

Babylon's diversity began with its physical location in the five-hundred-mile-long alluvial plain of the flood-prone Tigris and Euphrates rivers, which stream down from the snowy mountain ranges of Armenia. Babylonia was mythically fertile, a true Garden of Eden, but its sedimentary landscape lacked stone, timber, and metals. (Indeed, it was precisely its lack of stone that would reduce Babylon to ruins by the time of imperial Rome. Babylon's clay bricks did not have the sturdiness of Egypt's abundant stone.) Babylon's tolerant outward orientation toward other peoples began in its economic need to exchange its surplus of crops for other basic resources. In other words, commerce was the basis of that industrious but open and pleasure-loving civilization. Furthermore, merchants, with their adventurous mobility, shrewd alertness, and pragmatic flexibility, provided a liberating counterpoint to the ponderous fixities of the bureaucrats and pedagogues whose obsessive list making constitutes the bulk of the cuneiform tablets yet discovered in Mesopotamia. A massive system of canals, created and maintained by a sometimes dictatorial hierarchical government, provided reliable irrigation and efficient transport of goods. Babylon collapsed when its government weakened and could no longer effectively maintain the canals as they silted up. Furthermore, the soil became irretrievably salinized due to poor drainage on the flat plain, leading to abandonment of the land.

The Hebrews' experience in Babylon helped to consolidate their sense of cultural identity as well as their theology. In the Babylonian destruction of the Temple in Jerusalem, the Hebrews lost their hallowed place of worship but as a consequence developed in their exile a more refined concept of divinity that would eventually be absorbed by Christianity. Yahweh, a symbol of Hebrew nationalism, ceased to be the resident or patron of a building but became a spirit suffusing the universe, a living flame carried in all hearts.

As a coda to the story of Babylon, I would cite the 1916 silent film *Intolerance*, a three-and-a-half-hour epic conceived and directed by the controversial D. W. Griffith. With its giant set of the walls of Babylon, it was the most ambitious and expensive film yet made, featuring thousands of costumed extras. However, the film was a commercial failure, partly due to Griffith's stipulation that showings be accompanied by a symphony orchestra. *Intolerance* was Griffith's attempt at self-justification after the bitter national backlash over his prior film, *The Birth of a Nation* (1915), which remains infamous for its racist caricatures of African Americans as well as its glorification of the Ku Klux Klan. *Intolerance* daringly or dizzyingly crosscuts among four story lines, each dealing with some aspect of historical bigotry, including the St. Bartholomew's Day massacre of 1572, when thousands of Protestant Huguenots were slaughtered by Roman Catholics in France. Griffith's ancient story focuses on the fall of Babylon to the Persians. Prince Belshazzar (whose ominous vision of a hand writing on the wall was interpreted by Daniel in the Bible) is presented as a devotee of Ishtar and a defender of religious tolerance, but he is fatally conspired against by the intolerant high priest of Bel, whose betrayal of Babylon leads to its destruction in flames.

My second example is Renaissance Venice, which because of its position at the north end of the Adriatic Sea had been a major trading center since the Middle Ages. Built for defensive purposes on a chain of marshy islands, Venice was physically separated from the mainland and was psychologically oriented less toward Italy than toward Constantinople, the great gateway between East and West. Venice consequently became one of the most culturally diverse cities in world history. Its central church, St. Mark's Basilica, is Byzantine in style, as was Venetian taste in general, with its luxurious ornateness. The Venetian instinct for pleasure, as embodied in its sensual art, would become increasingly sybaritic over time, especially as compared to the austere sensibility of the more intellectual Florentine Renaissance.

The constant presence of foreign (and often Levantine) merchants in Venice gave it a cosmopolitan character. At times, the Venetians tried to safeguard their ethnic identity by limiting itinerant merchants' stay to a fixed period of months or years and by banning them from bringing their families to the city, but such rules were often flouted. Ethnic tensions became blatant in Venice's official establishment of the Ghetto, in which Jews were compelled to reside after 1516. Jews had created and controlled the money-lending industry in the region of Venetia since the twelfth century. It was the religious tolerance of Venice that drew them and that eventually produced the largest population of Jews in Europe. Jews were usually permitted to practice their religion in Venice without state interference. In contrast, England had expelled the Jews in 1290; France had expelled them in 1306; Spain did the same in 1492, followed by Portugal in 1497. Lingering anti-Semitism in England was illustrated by Shakespeare's play *The Merchant of Venice*, where the fictitious Shylock makes cruel and arbitrary loan demands that would never have actually been permitted under Venetian law.

The word *ghetto*, which was revived in the twentieth century for the Nazi sequestration of Jews in Warsaw and for the urban blight of African American neighborhoods, was derived from *geto*, the Italian word for "foundry": an abandoned fourteenth-century cannon factory had once occupied the Venetian island to which Jewish merchants and bankers were restricted. The high walls of the Ghetto were designed as much for the protection of the Jews as for their confinement. Resident Jews were responsible for paying four Christian sentries to keep watch at night, when the two gates were shut. No Jews except for doctors were allowed on the streets of Venice until the morning bell rang at St. Mark's. While Jews were originally required to wear a yellow badge in Venice, that was modified to yellow and then red headgear for most of the Renaissance. Jews were not permitted to own property, and they could not become Venetian citizens until the early nineteenth century. Overcrowding in the two districts of the Ghetto caused higher and higher buildings to be built (resembling modern apartment buildings), leading to occasional collapses on the spongy soil.

The Ghetto population itself was highly diverse, with a multiplicity of ethnicities and languages—Hebrew, Spanish, French, German, Polish, Greek, Turkish, and Judeo-Arabic, as well as many Italian dialects. There were eight splendidly designed and furnished synagogues in that limited space, each devoted to a single ethnicity; five have survived, restored but intact. The wealth of the Venetian Jews, as signaled by the lavish jewelry worn by strikingly beautiful women attending synagogue, was reported by a British traveler, Thomas Coryat, in a 1611 memoir published in London. That their own diversity presented a challenge to Venetian Jews was demonstrated by the energy and attention they continually devoted to adjusting the ethnic representation of the internal governing committees of the Ghetto.

Venetian power and glory would fade after the Portuguese discovery of the Cape of Good Hope in South Africa, which allowed merchant ships from northern Europe to travel directly to Asia without passing through the Mediterranean and transferring cargo to slow overland caravans. Now supplanted by Lisbon as a rich commercial capital, Venice began its decline, which would turn into the eighteenth-century decadent hedonism of Casanova and then the city's humiliating dependence on tourism, captured in Thomas Mann's portrayal of the rotting, plague-filled resort during the Belle Epoque in *Death in Venice*.

My third example is nineteenth-century Philadelphia. The "city of brotherly love" began as a Quaker refuge founded in 1682 by William Penn, who was escaping persecution of the Quakers in Britain. The city was laid out in mathematical squares between two great rivers, with north-south streets assigned numbers and east-west streets given tree names, reflecting the Quaker interest in botany as a symbol of harmonious nature. The Quaker ideal of tolerance drew immigrants to Philadelphia throughout the eighteenth century, but Quakers lost power within the city when their code of antimilitarism led them to abstain from any involvement with the American Revolution, so much of which occurred around Philadelphia. It was the Quaker commitment to social justice that led to Philadelphia becoming a center for abolitionism, which had begun among English Quakers. America's first antislavery society was formed in Philadelphia in 1833. The Quakers themselves were not immune to dissension: a major schism between Orthodox and Hicksite Quakers in the Northeastern United States led to the "Great Separation" of 1827 that was not healed until 1955.

Women had always been active and prominent in the Religious Society of Friends. Indeed, it was in Quaker meetinghouses, with their absence of a hierarchical clergy, that women were first permitted and encouraged to gain experience in public speaking, which was considered improper and unfeminine for respectable ladies well into World War I. A New England–born Quaker resident of Philadelphia, Lucretia Coffin Mott, founded an antislavery society for women but was denied delegate status because of her gender at the World's Anti-Slavery Convention held in London in 1840. Mott's indignation led her to collaborate with Susan B. Anthony and Elizabeth Cady Stanton to organize a convention on women's rights, held at Seneca Falls, New York, in 1848 that produced the woman suffrage movement and marked the birth of modern feminism.

But there were contrary forces at work in nineteenth-century Philadelphia. In 1838, three days after the opening of Pennsylvania Hall, erected by the Pennsylvania Anti-Slavery Society as a headquarters for abolitionism, a mob attacked the building and burned it to the ground. A black church (Bethel AME) and the Quaker Shelter for Colored Orphans were burned the same night. There had already been race riots in the city several years earlier between Irish immigrants and African Americans competing for the same jobs in manual labor. Hostility to working-class immigrants was building in the United States. The Native American Party was founded in 1837 in Germantown, a historic seventeenth-century village outside Philadelphia that is now part of the city. The Nativist campaign against immigration would take rabidly anti-Catholic form. Samuel F. B. Morse, the Massachusetts-born inventor of the telegraph, ran unsuccessfully for mayor of New York on the Nativist ticket and published an incendiary 1835 tract (*Imminent Dangers to the Free Institutions of the United States Through Foreign Immigration*) denouncing the Jesuits as "a *secret* society" bent on subduing American democracy to the monarchical tyranny of "Popery," with newly formed Catholic schools as their diabolical wedge. Condemning Roman Catholicism as "intolerant and illiberal," Morse called for stringent naturalization reform to stop the incursion of "the priest-ridden slaves of Ireland and Germany."

Back in Philadelphia, there was a tremendous surge of hostility to Irish Catholics, who began arriving in the city even before the Great Potato Famine of 1845 to 1849. Some of the animus came from Scots-Irish

Protestants (mainly Presbyterians) from Northern Ireland. For much of the nineteenth century in Boston and New York as well as Philadelphia, the Irish were stereotyped and vilified as violent, dirty, coarse, clannish drunks. In 1842, the militant American Protestant Association was formed in Philadelphia. Two years later, there were anti-Catholic riots in the city that resulted in twenty deaths, one hundred injuries, and the burning to the ground of St. Michael's Church, St. Augustine's Church, and the Seminary of the Sisters of Charity. Mobs invaded Irish neighborhoods and burned a dozen homes. The militia was called out to restore order, and martial law was declared for a week. These civil disturbances would lead to the creation of a professionalized police force and to the 1854 consolidation of the city, which officially incorporated all districts, boroughs, and outlying towns in Philadelphia County.

Anti-Irish sentiment would linger into the early twentieth century, when the Philadelphia social elite snubbed wealthy John B. Kelly, the self-made son of an immigrant from County Mayo, because he had begun his meteoric business career as an apprentice bricklayer. Although he had won six U.S. National Championships in rowing, the super-athletic Kelly was rejected from competing in the Diamond Sculls on the Thames at the Henley Royal Regatta in England because it was a written rule that no one could compete in the regatta "who is or has been by trade or employment for wages a mechanic, artisan, or labourer." In other words, Kelly was not a gentleman. But he became a hero to the Irish everywhere when, later that same year, he won a gold medal by beating the British sculling champion in the 1920 Summer Olympics in Antwerp, Belgium. A bronze statue of Kelly at his oars stands today in Philadelphia on the banks of the Schuylkill River where he trained. His daughter, Grace Kelly, who was excluded from the city's debutante balls because she was Irish Catholic, would have her revenge not only by marrying a prince of Monaco but by acidly playing the supercilious socialite role of Tracy Lord in *High Society*, a 1956 musical version of the 1940 classic MGM comedy, *The Philadelphia Story*.

Industrialization in the mid-nineteenth century led to the rapid transformation of Philadelphia, which physically expanded with the erection of factories for consumer goods and the construction of vast new neighborhoods of inexpensive two-story brick row houses for workers. Starting in the 1880s, a flood of job-seeking immigrants poured into the United States from Italy and Eastern Europe. Most of them were unskilled workers from a lower social level than the craftsmen and small merchants who had emigrated earlier from Northern Europe. Tensions rose even within the Jewish community because of ethnic differences. Earlier Jewish immigrants, like the Swiss-born Meyer Guggenheim, whose first job after his arrival in Philadelphia in 1847 was selling metal polish in the streets, were Sephardic or German Jews, while the new immigrants came from the rough farmlands of Poland and Russia. Guggenheim would go on to accumulate one of the greatest fortunes of the century by buying mining and smelting operations here and abroad and bequeathing them to his numerous, productive, and philanthropic children and grandchildren.

In the early nineteenth century, the genteel Protestant establishment of Philadelphia had been concentrated in banking and finance, but huge fortunes were now being made in railroads, coal, and manufacturing. This local aristocracy adopted a defensive posture toward the non-English-speaking immigrant hordes who were changing the character of the city, increasingly afflicted with noise and soot. Gilded Age families in Philadelphia began to migrate themselves, moving from their mansions in fashionable Rittenhouse Square in Center City to estates in the rolling countryside along the Main Line of the Pennsylvania Railroad heading west toward Pittsburgh and Chicago. There they built lavish country houses in the British manner, ironically often employing virtuoso Italian stonecutters, woodworkers, and gardeners. Many of those houses, which represented some of the most beautifully designed and situated domestic architecture in U.S. history, were demolished to make way for suburban developments following World War II.

The aggressive Anglophilia of the Main Line elite was a calculated strategy against diversity, as was also the invention of country clubs in the Northeastern United States in the late nineteenth and early twentieth centuries. The country club, ostensibly devoted to golf and tennis, was a sanctuary for the preservation of WASP (white Anglo-Saxon Protestant) hegemony. A related development was the creation of associations tracing lineage to the colonial period, such as Sons of the American Revolution, founded in 1889; the Colonial Dames of America and the Daughters of the American Revolution, both founded in 1890; and the General Society of Mayflower Descendants, founded in 1897. These organizations, which were clearly a reaction to the rising tide of immigration, undertook to proclaim who the *real* Americans were, now under assault by grubby ethnic invaders.

Publication of the Social Register, starting in 1886 with the volume for New York, catalogued the important individuals and families in polite society in every major city, virtually all of whom were Protestants. Metropolitan men's clubs also arose in this period, allowing the leaders of finance, industry, and law to meet in leisurely, privileged access behind closed doors. Discrimination could be overt: it is reported that the original University Club in Cincinnati, founded in 1879, was dissolved seven years later during a controversy over the admission of a Jewish member. New England boarding schools and Ivy League universities became arenas for inter-city reinforcement of the WASP cultural code. The initial lack of diversity at those institutions is demonstrated by the fact that no Ivy League humanities department appointed a Jewish tenured professor until after World War II.

Indeed, I can recall even upon my arrival at the Yale Graduate School in 1968 how charged the atmosphere was in the Yale English Department over faculty appointments, who remained mostly Protestant. Jewish professors still felt like an embattled minority, and there had just been a rumored purge of gay male teachers, who had all gone off to Smith College. I was questioned about the pronunciation of my Italian surname by the chairman of the English Department in what I felt to be an offensively condescending manner. When Yale named its first Italian American president in 1978, it is no coincidence that he had always called himself A. Bartlett Giamatti—Bart for short—when his real first name was Angelo.

I could detail here incidents of overt discrimination or insulting treatment experienced by my immigrant family (all four of my grandparents and my mother were born in Italy) when they were transplanted to old Protestant upstate New York, the location of the Endicott-Johnson shoe factories where my grandfather and many other relatives were employed. Given this background, it might be assumed that I would welcome all campus initiatives to achieve tolerance and diversity, but I have certain reservations. Surely tolerance and diversity in regard to race, ethnicity, gender, and sexual orientation must also be extended toward ideological diversity, if colleges and universities are to succeed in their mission of fostering the free exchange of ideas. But from my own observation, as well as my participation in the long-running culture wars, little deviation is permitted from approved political positions, which are usually predicated on a utopian, big-government liberalism that bears little resemblance to the fiery, freedom-oriented liberalism of my student days in the 1960s. I for one am not entirely comfortable with a national environment in the humanities where I am surrounded by fellow Democrats who vote exactly the way I do (although in the last national election I rebelled by casting a protest vote for the Green Party).

Elite American colleges and universities have undermined their credibility and authority by their intolerance to conservative views, particularly in regard to ethical issues such as the debate over abortion, which has divided the nation for nearly a half century. My militant prochoice position, based on my libertarian principles, does not blind me to the great moral weight on the prolife side, whose arguments should be honestly presented without prejudice to students. Furthermore, despite their claims of seeking and nurturing diversity among the student body, the elite universities still end up homogenizing everyone to the same bland, genteel Protestant style that I found so limiting and prejudicial when I arrived at Yale in the late 1960s. The costliness of the uniformity of thought imposed at elite universities over the past three decades—some have called it a "monoculture"—is now becoming manifest in the failure of major new intellectuals or culture critics to emerge among the young.

To create an atmosphere of tolerance on college campuses, the spectrum of permissible ideological opinion must be broadened, a reform that must begin at the classroom level. Second, it must be shown through a study of history that no group has ever had a monopoly on the truth and that virtually every political or social movement has been subject to factionalism and eventually fanaticism. Third, efforts must be made to undo, wherever they occur, power concentrations that impede free thought and free speech. Currently, those reside in the bureaucratic sprawl of campus administrations, which have eaten up budgets and slowly usurped faculty prerogatives. For it is ultimately well-meaning administrators, in their zeal to comply with sometimes intrusive government regulations, who have diverted tolerance and diversity from noble goals into dictates of social engineering that turn institutions from the organically dynamic to the soullessly mechanical.

10

ESSENTIALIZING THE CLASSED OTHER

Gayatri Chakravorty Spivak, Columbia University

Professor Michael Sweeney gave me my title three years ago: "Feminism and Postmodernism." "We have a particular interest in your understanding of the relationship between postmodernism and diversity." He continued, "For example, the debate between feminist 'essentialism' and postmodernism."

My response to the generosity of my brother Michael Sweeney is a refusal. I refuse to be interpellated as a single-issue visible minority feminist deconstructivist. It is not just feminists who are essentialists. Everybody is. We cannot live, act, or think without essentializing. If for the moment I accept my friend Craig Owens's definition of *postmodernism* as "the death of self-mastery," the question is: What do you choose to essentialize? Craig died in 1990, but I believe he directed us to these and similar questions. He died of AIDS and knew the import of such questions. How are you obliged to essentialize yourself as master of your destiny, or others, knowing the methodological and practical need to essentialize is a grounding error, that it is a mistake to essentialize? But alas, without essentializing—this is the Kantian tradition—we cannot think or act, so we choose a good grounding error. What do you essentialize? "I, I, I, master of my destiny, pursuit of happiness"? or do you essentialize others? That is the real difference, because, postmodernism, Craig was correct, is the death of self-mastery; he did not have the time to add "unquestioned self-mastery."

The debate is not between feminist essentialism and postmodernism; the debate is between essentialism and one version of postmodernism.

The most self-righteous form of that version of postmodernism can be summed up as follows, an addition to the signature section of the message section of the email of Jean Enriquez, executive director, Coalition Against Trafficking in Women, Asia Pacific: "No intellectual movement of recent memory has so beggared the truth as poststructuralism, denied the oppressed the truth and they are left with nothing." As if the oppressed are sitting there reading poststructuralism. The problem is that it questions the mastery of the unoppressed top-down philanthropists, especially when picked by international civil society from among the talented tenth of the global South, as Marx described the Church picking from the peasantry. On the email it is credited to somebody called Sanbonmatsu. Professor Kira Sanbonmatsu, who is herself a feminist, kindly directed me to her brother, who responded as follows: "The actual quote is: 'No intellectual movement of recent memory has so beggared the truth as poststructuralism has.' Full stop. Here is the citation: 'Postmodernism and the Corruption of the Academic Intelligentsia,' *Telling the Truth: Socialist Register 2006* (London: Merlin Press, 2005), 196–227." It is obvious that our truth-teller for the oppressed is not above bending the truth some when it will allow her to practice criticism by hearsay.

John Sanbonmatsu's version of postmodernism is what positivist academics oppose, often in the name of activism. I was giving a talk in Bengali as it happens, my mother tongue, in Calcutta, on deconstruction (they had asked me to speak on deconstruction) when another Bengali woman, living in Canada, stood up and delivered a diatribe to the effect that "poststructuralism has destroyed all our activism," and I asked her if postmodernism was worse than capitalism. "Focus where the real enemy lies," said I, somewhat solemnly, as my wont, alas. This denial of truth—a hearsay version—is the version against which there is a so-called debate.

I set aside the question of cleaning up the terms *postmodernism* and *poststructuralism* and especially their substitutability and continue with Mike's lovely invitation. It was, he said, to "give a lecture in the series on the relationship between justice, tolerance, and diversity as part of Xavier University's Ethics, Religion, and Society Program." The basic diversity that we tend to ignore is that of class. The demands for diversity as such, the other side of voting block identitarianism, are class located. I believe this is why the African National Congress repudiated J. M. Coetzee's novel *Disgrace*. Here I will show a series of pictures to bring my point home. Figure 10.1 is my female teachers among the rural landless, enjoying the sun at a housewarming.[1]

It can even be argued that the claim to diversity can only be made if one comes up to a certain class position. Diversity, for me, then, is an object of passive revolution rather than tolerance. From the subaltern—the female teachers among them—removed from the agency of the abstract welfare structures of the State, I learn. I do not tolerate them. In a moment I will give examples; in fact, my entire talk is an example of what I have learned. "What are the limits to a just tolerance of diversity?" Mike asked in his letter. "Unconditional ethics," say I, as I would then and now. Unconditional ethics is what is called an aporia; that is to say, it is not porous, in the sense of something through which nothing can pass. In my language, unconditional ethics is called *ahaituki prem*. Unconditional ethics, in that sense, is a heterotautology; if it is ethical, it is unconditional though conditioned necessarily by time, place, person(s), event.

The peculiarity of an aporia is that it is always crossed. You have already crossed it. You always have to, and in the passing you make it

Figure 10.1. My teachers.

Figure 10.2. Author winning the Kyoto Prize. I am being given a solid gold medal. It is not just me who is differentiated by class from the female teachers, it is also the Japanese women. All of us are in "traditional" clothes. The difference is class.

conditional, for you cannot save everybody in the world. You have already crossed it. This acknowledgement is the double bind of life, and here I offer the fact that we must rearrange our desires at this limit to perform epistemologically—in other words, to change the way in which we construct things for knowing. The mother constructs the same thing as honor as the daughter constructs it as reproductive rights. It is the same thing that they "know" but they construct it as objects of knowledge in two different ways. I have no husband, no children. My mother taught me well enough that I seriously and solidly am able to construct this as freedom, whereas in much of the world it would be constructed as misfortune. This is what epistemological performance is. You construct objects differently for knowing.

In other words, we must ask ourselves the question of the subject. Who is the subject of the debate between feminist "essentialism" and postmodernism? Kant had suggested that the subject of enlightened practice (in his little newspaper essay) was the *Gelehrt* or formally educated.[2] We have not moved too far because, this particular debate, whatever is

ESSENTIALIZING THE CLASSED OTHER

Figure 10.3. An ex-slave woman, pictured in the 1920s.

said about the oppressed suffering and more, is in fact lodged among and between the formally educated. Near the end of the last book that he published in his lifetime, *Voyous*, translated as *Rogues*, Jacques Derrida, in the name of New Enlightenment, assigned a task to the formally educated. "It remains to be known," wrote Derrida, "to save the honor of

Reason," thus incidentally proving that this postmodernism is not against reason—"how to translate." This is diversity. "For example," Derrida wrote, "the word reasonable and how to greet (*saluer*) beyond its Latinity and in more than one language the fragile difference between the rational and the reasonable." To think that this difference exists only in this Latinate language is a mistake. Unless you can begin to do that "translation-work" that requires intimacy, you are not going anywhere with mere top-down slogans of recognition and tolerance. You have to acknowledge the limit to this self-declared task.

What do I want to translate in this way? I want to translate the difference, in all of the languages beyond Latinity, between male and female. The difference as it is understood in the language—not like, ooh they're so backwards, therefore they think gender differences differently—nope, I'm talking about the language. When I go to my mother tongue, and there were a few people in that room who knew Bengali, it's one of the major North Indian languages, and I go below in class—not focusing on

FISK JUBILEE SINGERS.
Who for seven years gave concerts in this country and in Europe, and secured funds sufficient to erect Jubilee Hall.

Figure 10.4. In 1871 the Jubilee Singers raised $153,000 for Fisk University. They sang for kings and queens of Europe.

the top-level words that share more or less the same kind of difference as "male" and "female," though not exactly—I move on to *byatachhele* and *meyechhele* because the word *chhele* is in both of them. *Chhele* is a generic word for a "son," or even "a male person." Or you can look at *purusmanush, meyemanus. Manus* is the word for "human being," and between the two preceding adjectives *purush* is the big Sanskrit word on which even I could play a philosophical riff, and *meye* just a colloquial word for "female." I would begin to think about these differences and know that other languages will bring other baggage. I rather then go with the Platform of Action of Beijing+20, which can talk cultural difference but walks sameness. It is hard to understand that equality is not sameness.

I would also want to look at the difference between Democracy, the abstract structure of the State, and democracy, that is to say, the intuitions of democracy without which one can neither mourn nor judge. How to translate this difference in the many languages of the world beyond the Hellenic character of the word *democracy*? The public good, and the good in terms of the intuitions of democracy, has been my work, not just at the bottom, but also at the top. I was just asking the artist Nalini Malani to think about the fact that perhaps the subaltern, oppressed people that she is celebrating in her work also have law. What they see in terms of the abstract structure, the law of the land, is a complete negation of the law within which they live. We should do something more than to recognize them as illiterate, unlettered victims. I mentioned two words, one of them is *bidhi*, and this is something that I got from an illiterate person in the villages where I have my schools. He, being illiterate, is the one who still sings, and he sings to me when nobody else is around because being illiterate is not so nice. I quoted this song when I was talking about world literature at Brown. I will quote just one line, *mon karey uribar torey, bidhi dey na pakha*. This is a little different from straight Bengali; it's Bengali creole, but it could in fact just be "poetic" Bengali: "the mind makes as if to fly but *bidhi*"—which is not just God, not just custom, not just law, but all of those put together; judgment is *bidhan*; *bidhi* is a big word"—*Bidhi* does not give wings." This description I gave to the people who think that they can metonymically create a world literature, because, as the song sums it up: "the mind wants to fly," but "*bidhi* does not give wings." *Bidhi* there is not fatalistic; it is a word for not just "law," but something more than the law.

I gave Ms. Malani another word, *niyama*, which is not just "rule." In the hills of Odisha in India, the Supreme Court asked a mining conglomerate, ironically called "Vedanta" after the name of the most philosophical discourse of Hinduism, that was encroaching upon tribal land called *niyamagiri*, and the Supreme Court suggested that the tribal *gramshavas*, the local self-government units among the tribals, be heard. They spoke very strongly, and they won. On the other hand, their winning means nothing. They are being decimated by the police and the forces of capital. When we turned the World Bank back from Bangladesh in 1992, the World Bank found other ways of establishing themselves there. Nonetheless, the victory meant something. What did I learn from this? *Niyamagiri*, the Mountain of Rule, the Mountain of Law, is where their divine sovereign lived. We say divine because we are speaking in English. It isn't a god as the language goes, it is *niyamaraja*, King Law, King Rule, his rule being: "Don't ruin the forests, don't ruin the waters, don't ruin the rivers, don't ruin the mountains." If you want to think of this in a contemptuously tolerant way, you think, ooh, yes, this is how tribals think, but you will never think that in fact this is, uncontested though it may be by voting citizens of what CNN calls "the world's largest democracy," a critique of the anthropocene. Here one might do well to follow Derrida's exhortation, "one must learn how to translate" to save the honor of Reason, not just reasonableness. Reasonableness is sustainable underdevelopment, which is what makes the world go round in the name of development, but the rational is posthumanism social justice as a critique of the anthropocene. These kinds of translations, the translation of these laws, limits of ambition, limits of the anthropocene, and so on—*bidhi, niyam, niyamraja*—we do not know how to translate these into an idiom that will teach us something about who inhabits that other space. So essentialize, not romanticize, the other rather than our own self-mastery, because they are history, they are not actually lodging a critique of what can be called anthropocene—so knowing that to essentialize thus is a methodological necessity in the face of the racist pride of either the helpers or the destroyers, same difference. That's what I learn from the situation in *niyamgiri*. The approach to equal rights is identical with the struggle in the larger polity. To approach internalized gendering, surviving in spite of full involvement in the struggle here described, we have to achieve critical intimacy. Last year, I did not risk being shot at by the police.

What I tell the students and teachers at my own rural schools is that I have not been able to learn how to teach them in thirty years. I see how they are teaching—I teach them how to teach—and they say, "Oh yes, we taught this," and when the students are not able to give the answer, I say, "Well, if you taught it, then the student would have known." And I say, "Look, it's the same rule that applies to me. I'm trying to teach you intellectual labor, *matha khatano*, but that can't be taught because you've been destroyed for thousands of years by people of my caste, my class, and so you were not given the right to intellectual labor and it's very hard to undo that. You see, this is why I'm failing." We talk about this, and I say, "I'm trying to repay my ancestral debt," you know people will come in and they will fly off saying they're doing good, don't believe them, they don't care for you, they won't wait and listen and learn.

When I was invited by the University of Utrecht to celebrate the three-hundredth anniversary of the so-called Peace of Utrecht to give a keynote, I said to my students and teachers, landless near-illiterate, this is what I'm going to say to these people in this place—they now can look at the map, here is Europe—in this place they were the kings, they won, and I praise Europe, I talk about James Watt watching the lid dance on the saucepan and planning the steam engine.[3] So, I say to them that I'm going to say to the Europeans what I have learned from you. I explain this business of the right to intellectual labor, then I read that sentence out in English and I say, "This is the same sentence." And then again, when I was invited to give a Golden Jubilee lecture at the Center for the Study of Developing Societies in Delhi, which to them is like an unbelievable metropolis, I said the same sentence and I am saying it again here and I said to them again—this in another time—"Look, this is the only lesson I have learned and this is therefore the only thing that I say and you know what I'm saying."[4] Here is the sentence: The will to social justice builds itself and nests in all children's and therefore all people's capacity to use the right to intellectual labor, not just ease and speed of learning. The right to intellectual labor, the right to abstraction, which is completely not allowed and to women even less, among these illiterate groups, the right to theorize rather than just apply theory, which is all that the feminism debate is about, and also the right to feel that intellectual labor is important in the face of poor education; these are to me more crucial than the struggle of dominant feminism against postmodernism by hearsay. This problem of detachment from intellectual labor is true also at the top now because of digital idealism. And yet, the subject of social media is a fool unless it's been taught in the slow way, how to perform intellectual labor, epistemological performance, change how you know objects, otherwise it's just venting. So, I continue when I am keynoting on the Peace of Utrecht or Developing Societies:

> All accountable and quantifiable efforts at social justice are no more and no less than the way in which we can access justice as such, if there is such a thing. However impractical and unsustainable it may sound, nurturing translation as practice rather than convenience, necessarily confronting the political implications and the resulting competitive winning of consent outlined by Gramsci, will only happen if this kind of effort is sustained. To translate how ethics and politics are differentiated in the common sense of the subaltern in many of the languages of the world would be another task. Activism cannot be sustained if this kind of question is not asked. Let us take some of the money feeding the dumb greed of the many elite Translation Studies institutes that regularly send me invitations and put it to use this way.

Translation studies are really there for a sort of publicity for the big languages of the world that rob those who speak them as mother tongues from the experience of what Derrida is exhorting you to do, from the experience of knowing that translation is only a convenience, not a substitute. This is an unfortunate thing.

Most subaltern groups think in terms of prenational communities, mobilizable into violence. This I have learned as a humanities-style reader through thirty years of language-based "reading," critical intimacy, in my home state and about ten years of English- and French-based "reading," critical intimacy as far as possible, in Ghana, Kenya, Nigeria, Senegal, and South Africa. I had made an effort based on imperfectly learned Peace Corps Arabic to establish critical intimacy with socialist women in Algeria until the Front Islamique du Salut (the Islamic Salvation Front) came in. Twelve years at mud schools near the Laos border of China with elementary Chinese, the idea of supplementing vanguardism supported by humanities-style reading, the attempt to establish critical intimacy with past political classics, has helped me through what you would call postmodernism, essentializing the other as grounding error. This is where I began: what do you essentialize, you *have to essentialize*. What do you essentialize, yourself as master of your destiny—this is also the basic double bind of democracy, even Aristotle knew this, this is why Plato didn't like democracy all that much, that it is the double bind between ipseity, autonomy, me and alterity, others: liberty and equality. This is a real tug of war; this is what democracy is. You have to teach participating in this tug of war even to the subaltern, to the disenfranchised. Otherwise the oppressed become suboppressors. This is a quote from Paolo Freire. The ones who do human rights are morally outraged, no self-interest, helping others, but what do they teach? Justified self-interest, resulting in interest groups, voting blocs undermining democracy. One must consult Du Bois writing about the formation of Negro unions after Emancipation because of the hostility of white labor, saying that the democracy of unified labor is being undermined.[5] This is what you have to think about. It is not something that you begin after you have become financially independent; no, it begins right as education begins, and it is not leadership. How do you do this? How do you claim this? That is a very long story and I'm not going to talk about this at all because I have been moving further and further away, then, from feminism and essentialism.

Among these subaltern children, these children of the landless illiterate, the polarization between top and bottom comes undone. Children's minds are like wet cement; we are inscribing contradictory habits into them. No competition, yet unconditional pursuit of excellence. Pleasure in schoolwork, yet training to enter the mainstream. Discourage in situ leadership, yet encourage questioning authority. Nothing through sermons, everything through classroom moves, both for the teacher and for students. The students are smarter than the teachers obviously, because they've not yet been ruined by the cruelty of socializing. The students are getting bad socializing at home, but still, they are very small. We start from two to three years old, even if they cannot learn anything yet; I say, sit them down, give them a meal, let them hold the slate, do something with the pencil, feel that school is a good place. In the so-called government schools, primary schools, free compulsory education, no one pays mind to them at all. In the so-called play schools, behavior appropriate to middle-class children with educated parents and a book culture at home is taught, largely by untrained housewives who follow a toolkit. Therefore, that whole thing is just a saying, that India has compulsory free primary education. It is true on the register of exactitude, but not on the register of "truth." "Postmodernism," whatever it is, allows me to see this, also in the case of gender empowerment statistics.[6]

Gender balance, yet gender preference to undermine established gendering. I follow Kant, I find, when I write about it. Freedom as human, equality as subject, independence as citizen. Yet remember that human meaning, as modern informatics demonstrates, may be produced from meaningless bits in inaccessible psychic mechanisms—that's pomo, that's Lacan—tremendously difficult to devise as habit formation, not blind obedience in child subjects and teacher subjects that are equal but not the same. Equal—I am a citizen of India, I have one vote, so arithmetically I am equal to them, one person, one vote—but of course we are not the same. I am a rich upper-caste person who was brought up by supereducated, wonderful parents, house full of books, now lives in the United States, teaches also at the top. No, I am not the same as they, but I am equal, because I have one vote, if you believe in that arithmetical reduction of democracy.

Now, ground-level law enforcers, the rural police, often belong to these subaltern social groups. These law enforcers, because of class apartheid in education, which exists in the whole world, are not really corrupt but have internalized rape and bribe culture as normal. Because, under a certain line, people can't even recognize that what I'm doing is education, because they'll fail exams if they read this way. I was told this by a high school principal. To say rape in India is only a gender problem is inadequate. Of course, it is always a gender problem, but it is also a problem of class apartheid in education. Why do the people at the top do it? Well, that is a much bigger gender problem than the ones at the bottom because the ones at the bottom internalize rape culture and bribe culture. At the top it is capitalist greed feeding alpha maleship. There is nobody to move the muscles of their mind into something that will allow them to essentialize the other. And indeed, female CEOs going on about how their families do not suffer although they are CEOs is the other side of the same coin. What might work as an intuition of democracy may be an exhortation to essentialize other people's children as real. In a place where there is hardly any social security, and therefore your children are your social security, this slogan can work toward an intuition of democracy: not just your own children, but other people's children.

In order to change passionate self-interest, even if it is a group interest—nationalism, class struggle, gender struggle—to a steady will to social justice—something that is empirically impossible to sustain—we need training in the reflexes of unconditional ethics. This is where a humanities education—to philosophize, to read—comes in handy. It is not a question of tolerance. I will certainly theoretically insist on that. Reasonable self-interest cannot bring about a developing society, except in a statistical, existentially impoverished description. This is why revolutions and national liberations, which are not revolutions of course, do not last. Let us restore the autocritical moment. We must change, we must rearrange our desires, we must construct objects differently from "we good ones giving back and helping and those bad ones, poor ones, sad ones, are being helped by us, from the top." Let us realize that we cannot escape the subject-shaping part of the norm as we agentially rewrite it in various ways, as task or event, that we may be providing an alibi for sustainable underdevelopment. I am going to take a moment to explain the difference between subject and agent à la pomo, à la postmodernism.

The subject-agent distinction is acknowledged by most of us who are intellectual activists inspired by what you folks call pomo/postmodernism, or poststructuralism (that ugly word was invented by me and has entered the stream of language). The subject is "I," and the agent is also "I." The agent is limited, confined to self-consciousness, what we call the intending subject, and with that we have to save the honor of Reason. The agent, the part with which we do right or wrong, is thus a small but important thing; it is our black box in the head. The way we are formed as subjects is much broader, *not fully* accessible to us; it is history, it is psychology, it is all of the hormones working inside. I am talking here, you all are sitting here; you think you are understanding me, it is a language we all know. On the other hand, to each of you I am giving a curve ball, because if I ask each and all of you to tell me what I was saying, the versions will be different. The subject is inaccessible to us in its breadth. Its flexible outlines vanish indefinitely. The agent, on the other hand, we must take responsibility for, never thinking that doing the right thing by our rational judgment is unconditional ethics, never making that mistake, but realizing that that is all we can do. Postmodernism teaches us this. It does not take everything away; it just undermines the pride of self-mastery in doing good, feminist or masculist.

I want to go to Lacan for a moment. Arguably, Lacan's most wonderful piece is called "The Subversion of the Subject and the Dialectics of Desire."[7] Early Lacan. We all know that rape is to treat the borders of the female body as permeable, and that permeability can also be a source of pleasure. This is the incalculable mystery of gendering. Even violence can be desired. If Freud was an ethical, body-mind philosopher, Lacan was much more like a poet. When we read him, we who are not actually trained in the practice of whatever kind of psychoanalysis he did, we read him as poetry. In my book, poetry is not a bad word. I have been living with poetry as the main thing in my life for a long time. So when I say Lacan was a poet, I am not dispraising him. He imagines the construction of the possibility for a self-conscious socio-genetic abstraction, which is gender. Gender is the first instrument of abstraction; that is why it is so strange when the gendered folks of a certain elite class want to be only concrete. *Concrete* is an abstract word. Lacan imagines the construction of the possibility of the self-conscious socio-genetic abstraction in gendering in the presubjective drive. Drive, which is translated into English in the standard edition as "instinct," is thus unfortunately put inside the psychology of the person. Freud's understanding of what he called the "meta-psychological"—when little babies learn their first language, they are not yet sentient, and they learn the language—meta-psychological circuits are getting activated and, even before that, when the subject is coming into existence, the presubjective drives operate the emergence. It is a mechanical intuition, as it is in Kant. Kant's English translators have psychologized him and turned him into a Christian gentleman. And Freud is also psychologized at random. Lacan is talking about the presubjective drives.

The drive inside the human being that is constructing the psyche falls upon the "anatomical trace." A trace is not a sign, it offers itself for meaning-making, sign-ification, dependent upon contingencies; whereas signs operate together on a (false) promise of coded meaning, me talking to you here depends on that promise. I quote now the English translation, modified: "Anatomical trace of a margin or border. Lips, enclosure of the teeth, rim of the anus, penile fissure, vagina, fissure of eyelid, indeed hollow of the ear, respiratory erogeneity comes into play through spasms." [8] Border-thinking, then, is an undecided and primary constituent of our perception of reality itself, where reason is fashioned out of a certain kind of instinct toward war or peace, borders. That is where the roots of the unconditional ethical begin to take shape, as the subject is being made, not the agent. If you read postmodernism carefully, this is the kind of thing that you look at. The translation is not very good, but look at the debate itself, as reflected for example by Toril Moi's *Sexual/Textual Politics*, or Irene Diamond and Lee Quinby's *Feminism and Fou-*

cault, or yet Paul Patton's *Nietzsche, Feminism, and Political Theory*.[9] When they are praising Foucault or Nietzsche, they are actually looking at what they said, "Foucault said power, Foucault said body" or "Foucault's idea of body was not so good, Nietzsche's idea was better." In my estimation, that is not the way to go. I teach theory, and poets have been my best theory students because their imaginations are conflagrated with theorizing. That is what I try to teach, theorizing. When you read the theory, you read it as if it is a primary text, not an instrument for you to apply, so that feminism becomes an example of the good Foucault or the good Nietzsche, feminism becomes an example of postmodernism, and the subject of that debate is the learned woman who thinks that she is the best example of womanship. You read theory carefully, without any thought of instrumentalizing—this applies even to Marx, not just pomo—with sympathy going toward the other, essentializing that other in the text, the theory that you are reading, so that it begins to become part of your mental furniture. When you theorize, then you begin to use all of that stuff, if you have read with enough critical intimacy; you begin to use that stuff as you theorize. What you do with it is not imitate what Foucault thought about the body and what Nietzsche thought about the body and what Derrida thought about the body. That particular lesson, what is it to theorize, is the question of pomo, or any theory. So for me, the feminist debate disappears.

I was giving a talk in Japan at a very fine university where two of my friends teach, Hitotsubashi, and it was rather a large audience. There was a fantastic translator, Ted Motohashi, sitting beside me; I was giving a sentence, he was translating. We were having a great time, but in the middle of it my sister called, but that story does not belong to this story. I say at some point, taunting the "male" model of knowledge: "Kant corrected Descartes, Hegel corrected Kant, Marx corrected Hegel, Nietzsche corrected Marx, Freud corrected Nietzsche, Habermas corrected Freud, Habermas is my master. This is a male model exam topic type approach to the idea of knowledge being knowledge about knowledge." It was an ad lib sentence, this was exactly what I was saying one shouldn't do, and unfortunately the debate about feminism and postmodernism is vested in this kind of "who wins" logic. When I uttered this impromptu sentence, poor Motohashi begins "*Kanta, Marxa*" in Japanese, and then he puts up his hands and says, "I cannot go any further with that one, Gayatri." So, let's not do the debate that way, the alpha-male approach to "who wins?"

is untranslatable, that is not what postmodernism teaches us. It is the death of self-interest. Remember that? Craig Owens is dead, but he has given us that. Derrida is gone too. But he left us the request to be careful enough to be able to translate.

Let us look at the first sentence of Michael's letter to me: "I'm a professor of philosophy at Xavier University, a Jesuit institution in Cincinnati." My family, for four generations now, has been involved with what was closest to the *Jesuit*, the Society of Jesus, the early Ramakrishna mission. When I was invited by their university to give them a talk about Ramakrishna, I was shaking. I went. It is a fine, autonomous college, something like a university. The vice chancellor was sitting in front among two rows of monks, very learned, one with a Berkeley PhD, one doing epistemology, and others, smart people, but monks in saffron. Ramakrishna was different; he was an ecstatic, much more like William Blake; the mission came out of a challenge to colonial organized religious orders. They are wonderful. I gave my talk. In conclusion, I point out that I am the first half of *kamini kancana*—the desiring woman and gold—that a monk must avoid. "I can explain it away," said I—they themselves do now—"but will not, even as I know the absurdity of the will"—agent, not subject. I had brought a prop, a skull cap, which I wear in winter. I used to live at that time just at the border of Harlem. I am pretty tall, and in the dark, if I am wearing an overcoat, short haircut, people quite often cannot tell if I am male or female. If I put that hat on, people think I am Muslim and they cross the street, they are afraid. In the heat of summer in Calcutta, I put on this hat to tell this to the monks. I told them, I say to myself, if others are afraid of me, I need not fear. I said to the monks, "I feel the same way about your *kamini kancana*. If as a sexed instrument of desire, I am an object of fear, I don't need to be afraid." That's where I ended.

That is where I will take this Catholic example, and read a comment on a passage from James Joyce. The piece is by Mary Lydon, who is a feminist, to be found in *Feminism and Foucault*. Joyce's Molly Bloom says: "I hate that confession when I used to go to Father Corrigan he touched me father and what harm if he did where and I said on the canal bank like a fool but whereabouts on your person my child." "This vignette," writes Mary Lydon, a piece of flotsam surfacing on the flux of Molly Bloom's reminiscences, puts the question of sexuality as raised in *La volonté de savoir* in a nutshell. The lover's tact yields to the confessor's probing, spuriously tactful ("and what harm if he did"), shockingly pointed ("where"). Molly artlessly or artfully parries the thrust but only gains a reprieve. The inquisitorial gaze, fleetingly deflected onto the grassy borders of the canal, swivels immediately back to its favorite object of scrutiny, the woman's body, or as Father Corrigan more circumspectly puts it, "person."[10]

Speaking from within the complicity of being folded together as I was doing when I was speaking to the Ramakrishna monks—I am one of you, I know how to make *kamini-kancana* palliative and more, but I will not be interpellated for the excusing, because I will not accuse. So, I would say to Mary Lydon from Wisconsin that here again epistemological performance is required from the person who is creating the us and them. Feminism should not just be mastery of my body, that does not work anymore; we know our body is scripted beyond our ken. It is now just opposition in a book of theory-fighting. If you oppose through acknowledgment of complicity, which is what I was doing with that last story, it is an epistemological performance, it is not mere tolerance. Literature is not evidence. Is James Joyce a good guy or a bad guy?

John Rawls's point in *Political Liberalism* is made in such a complicit way. In a volume necessarily committed to the Cold War liberal logic of containment, this smart man picks up "neutrality," as postmodernism does reason, as the best grounding error: "The term *neutrality* is unfortunate; some of its connotations are highly misleading, others suggest altogether impracticable principles. For this reason I have not used it before in these lectures. But with due precautions taken, and *using it only as a stage piece, as it were*, we may clarify how the priority of rights connects with the above two ideas of the good."[11] It is almost as if Rawls is acknowledging the need to acknowledge complicity.

I want to close with a remark on the change that is brought about in judgment if complicity is acknowledged, by way of a long quote from Adrienne Rich:

> To write directly and overtly as a woman, out of a woman's body and experience, to take women's existence seriously as theme and source for art, was something I had been hungering to do, needing to do, all my writing life. . . . But we were—and are—living and writing not only within a women's community. We are trying to build a political and cultural movement in the heart of capitalism, in a country where racism assumes every form of physical, institutional, and psychic vio-

lence, and in which more than one person in seven lives below the poverty line. The United States feminist movement is rooted in the United States, a nation with a particular history of hostility both to art and to socialism, where art has been encapsulated as a commodity, a salable artifact, something to be taught in MFA programs, that requires a special staff of "arts administrators"; something you "gotta have" without exactly knowing why. As a lesbian-feminist poet and writer, I need to understand how this *location* affects me, along with the realities of blood and bread within this nation.[12]

Today we would have to revise "the United States feminist movement is rooted in the United States," and write "dominant single-issue feminism is rooted in elite globality." With the onset of globality, there is a North in the South. Virginia Woolf's remark, which Rich quotes—"As a woman my country is the whole world"—has been travestied by the top-down philanthropy of the gender section of the international civil society, largely U.S. women, who need few visas—"my country is the whole world." At this point, I cite another powerful passage from Adrienne Rich, a passage that I often cite, reminding us of the need for "calling up the voices we need to hear within ourselves."[13]

The best of postmodernism—and not by hearsay—asks you to be open for other voices. I have cited almost nothing here. Check it out.

NOTES

1. Spivak, private communication.
2. Immanuel Kant, "An Answer to the Question: 'What Is Enlightenment?,'" in *Political Writings*, trans. H. B. Nisbet (Cambridge: Cambridge University Press, 1991), 54-60.
3. Spivak, "A Borderless World," forthcoming in colection edited by Rosi Braidotti.
4. Spival, "What Good Are the Humanities for the Study of Development?," unpublished keynote, Golden Jubiless Lecture Series, Center for the Study of Developing Slocieties, New Delhi, August 5, 2013.
5. W. E. B. Du Bois, *Black Reconstruction* (New York: The Free Press, 1998), 356.
6. Spivak, "Empowerment?: A Keynote," unpublished presentation. Conference on Women's Empowerment, Teachers College, Columbia University, April 12, 2014.

7. Jacques Lacan, *Écrits*, trans. Bruce Fink (New York: Norton, 2002), 671–702.

8. Jacques Lacan, "The Subversion of the Subject and the Dialectic of Desire in the Freudian Unconscious," in Bruce Fink, trans., *Écrits: The First Complete Edition in English* (New York: Norton, 2007), 692.

9. Toril Moi, *Sexual/Textual Politics* (London and New York: Routledge, 2002); Irene Diamond and Lee Quinby, *Feminism and Foucault* (Boston: Northeastern University Press, 1988); Paul Patton, *Nietzsche, Feminism, and Political Theory* (London and New York: Routledge, 1993).

10. Diamond and Quinby, *Feminism and Foucault*, 135-36.

11. John Rawls, *Political Liberalism* (New York: Columbia University Press, 1996), 19; emphasis added; "neutrality" emphasized by author.

12. Adrienne Rich, "Blood, Bread, and Poetry: The Location of the Poet," in *Blood, Bread, and Poetry: Selected Prose 1979–1985* (New York: Norton, 1994), 182–83.

13. Rich, "What Does a Woman Need to Know?," in *Blood, Bread, and Poetry*, 10.

11

RACIST DISRESPECT IN MORAL THEORY
Dialogue with Glasgow

Jorge Garcia, Boston College

This material was originally prepared for presentation at the 2008 Rutgers Summer Institute for Diversity in Philosophy, and later presented at Xavier University in 2012, the 2013 Minnesota Philosophy Society's meeting at the University of St. Thomas, and a 2014 ANCO Seminar at the University of Paris. I am grateful to those events' audiences, and to Professors Lawrence Blum, Sally Haslanger, Lionel McPherson, Ifeanyi Menkiti, and Tommie Shelby for continued discussion of these topics and several of the texts here treated. I am especially indebted to Professors Joshua Glasgow and Thomas Carson for sharing with me their ideas and unpublished writings, and appreciative of research assistance from Boston College by Ms. Teresa Fenichel, Mr. Kevin Marren, and Mr. Matthew Ray.

In the late 1990s and early 2000s, I published a series of articles sketching what I call a volitional account of racism (VAR), according to which racism, in its basic phenomenon and at its heart, consists in an attitude of insensitive indifference toward, or insufficient concern for, or ill will to, another, on the basis of the race we impute to her. Other things—including an individual's beliefs, a society's accepted doctrines, social habits, informal customs, institutionalized practices and norms, and so on—are racist only by being informed (infected) by such noncognitive racist attitudes. In my version of a VAR, moreover, these attitudes are morally vicious, because they are opposed to moral virtues of goodwill and justice. In that way, VAR not only helps explain what racism most fundamentally consists in but also why, how, and when it is immoral.

Here, I develop this account so as to respond to criticisms recently leveled by Joshua Glasgow (and by the late John Arthur), who charge such an understanding of racism scants what they take to be the centrality of disrespect. In the first section, I sketch Glasgow's principal criticisms of my VAR and offer preliminary responses, sometimes rebutting his charges, sometimes clarifying his apparent misunderstandings, and sometimes making concessions. In the second and third sections, I take the opportunity that replying to Glasgow affords me to offer a somewhat deeper exposition of VAR, grounding it more deeply in recent work on virtues, and therein making good on a promissory note I issued early in my writing on racism. I show that and how VAR can find ethical theoretic support, sketching a distinctive approach to moral theory that treats the virtues as foundational, sees our moral features (virtues, vices, duties, and rights) as pervasively relative to and centered in some role-relationships, focuses on what those to someone to whom we are relevantly related needs from us or benefits by, and regards the motivation from which our behavior emerges—what we can call its input—as decisive to its ethical status, including whether it is morally permitted, prohibited, or required. I indicate some of what such an ethical theory involves. Building on this virtues-based, role-centered, patient-focused, and input-driven ethical theory, my fourth section summarizes, and exposes inadequacies in, Glasgow's own account of "racism as disrespect."

GLASGOW'S AND ARTHUR'S CRITIQUE OF MY VOLITIONAL ACCOUNT OF RACISM (VAR)

First among his criticisms, I treat Glasgow's complaint that VAR gives no adequate account of the scope of institutional racism. Against VAR's contention that institutional racism is always institutionalized personal racism, he holds that there can be "pure institutional racism," which is "pure" in that the institution is not made racist by its origin in some persons' racist attitudes. Rather, in his view, what matters to an institution's racism is whether it perpetuates interracial disparities.[1]

Racism, however, can infect an institution in its operation or continuation today, not just at its origin in the past. If we now maintain an institution from our racist insensitivity, that taints it with our racism, even if it was free from racism in its origin or operation. So it is misleading for Glasgow to say there is a "genetic thesis" internal to VAR's account of institutional racism's derivation from more fundamental forms of racism in individual minds.[2] According to VAR, an institution is racist, at least in a minimal and technical sense, to the extent that it is informed by racism, whether, in a *weak*, technical, and vestigial sense, in its design and original setup, or in a *strong*, operative, and more substantial sense, in its later functioning, and current maintenance.

I accept Glasgow's claim that VAR analyzes institutional racism as institutionalized attitudinal racism.[3] That is, VAR identifies the former with the latter. Nevertheless, contrary to Glasgow, I deny that the fact that institutional racism involves institutionalizing some persons' racist attitudes, as VAR holds, entails that the institutionalization must be "intentional" in the sense of being intended.[4] In fairness to Glasgow, we should admit that Glasgow may have been misled here by terminology. VAR holds racism fundamentally to be a matter of noncognitive mental states, including what someone likes and does not like, wants and does not want, dislikes and does not dislike, is averse to and is not thus averse, and what she does and does not intend. So, though the term *volitional* in its name may suggest otherwise, VAR is not committed to seeing all racism as requiring intended harm to members of a racial group.

Still, I must admit that Glasgow is correct that what I assert in "The Heart of Racism"—that an institution must operate from racism at Time t1 for it to be racist at t1—is in some conflict with something I say in "Current Conceptions of Racism"; that is, that vestigial racism within an institution is a "rather marginal and insignificant" phenomenon.[5] To avoid such apparent inconsistency, I here distinguish between, on one hand, a *strong* and substantial institutional and, on the other, *weak*, merely technical and vestigial institutional(ized) racism, where the substantial kind requires current operation, execution, implementation, or direction from racist attitudes (especially for the sake of racist objectives), and the merely technical form is what I earlier called "marginal and insignificant."

Second, Glasgow charges my VAR with "reductionism" in its analysis of institutional racism and raises what he calls the "location problem" of where racism fundamentally (that is, in its fundamental forms) resides.[6] Against this, I note that deriving some forms of racism from other, more fundamental ones is not an ontic reduction of the former to the latter. The derivative forms—here including racist behavior and belief in individuals, institutionalized procedures, and more—are real, neither illusory nor fictive, and they exist as separate entities. VAR's analysis of institutional racism is not at all eliminativist. Thus, even if Glasgow is correct to say that "on this kind of theory, all institutional racism [of a robust sort] derives from agent-based . . . racism [i.e., individual racism] operative at that time," that is not to "reduc[e]" the institutional to the individual, so Glasgow's classification of the view as "reductionist" is misleading.[7] VAR as such simply claims that what is institutionally racist ultimately derives (i.e., inherits, contracts, is infected with) its racism from instances of racism in individuals. So, it remains open to (not, *pace* Glasgow, required of) VAR to restrict these instances of individual racism to ones concurrent with the racism-infected institutional operations. Likewise, according to VAR, actions, beliefs, and institutions are racist only in a somewhat different and derivative sense of the term from that in which persons and their noncognitive attitudes are themselves racist. That shows only that "racist," like "healthy," is something of a polysemous (in older nomenclature, an analogous) term, used to predicate slightly different but related features in different contexts. Thus, in the end, neither an institution's "reduction" nor "gene[sis]" is crucial here, despite what Glasgow says. Rather, it is what is tainted, infected, polluted, contaminated by racist inputs that matters for institutional (and other derived forms of) racism.

Third, while ultimately himself choosing to strive for what he calls a "monistic analysis" of racism rather than to accept an irreducible plurality of "racisms," Glasgow objects to my argument that if there is nothing in common across the various forms of racism, then we can have little reason to think that "racism as such, i.e., every [instance of] racism is morally objectionable." He reasons that, to the contrary, "otherwise disparate forms of racism might have distinctive morally objectionable features."[8] I concede that Glasgow correctly observes that what I earlier asserted is too weak.[9] Every instance of racism could be immoral, in VAR, even if there were nothing common to all instances of racism. Glasgow is correct that each type, even instance, of racism might be immoral for its own reasons. However, what remains true is my larger point that racism cannot be essentially immoral—that is, immoral by its nature—if it has no nature, no essence. For then it would be no one thing.[10]

Fourth, Glasgow criticizes VAR for inadequately accommodating "the possibility of benevolent racism." He maintains that this "possibility" shows that "not all [racism is] . . . malicious," and that we know this is genuinely possible because "we can at least imagine a paternalist[ic racist] who does not intend to infantilize or stunt" her victims.[11] However, we need to be more careful here. VAR does not require that whatever is racist be "malicious," only that whatever is racist in one of the fundamental ways relevantly stem from (i.e., be informed by) ill will, callous indifference, or insufficient goodwill. What VAR requires of a paternalistic racist is that she be deeply amiss in her will, even if also somehow well intentioned.

Is VAR's claim plausible? I think so. The paternalist, if we take the term seriously, is someone who treats an adult as if her (taking the metaphor more literally, his) nonadult child. Glasgow does not explain how the supposedly benevolent, paternalistic racist avoids instrumentally willing the eradication of such fundamental goods of the human person as self-direction. That she acts with the goal of avoiding such stunting of victims does not show that she avoids it in her chosen means. Even if some racism is at some level well meaning, that is consistent with my claim that all racism also viciously deviates from the virtues of goodwill and justice. Of course, the paternalistic racist, like other racists, need not *do* anything racist at all. If she does nothing racist (i.e., from her racism), then she will not, of course, act with instrumentally vicious intentions. However, she must nonetheless be disposed to adopt such intentions, and that disposition properly counts as a relevant form of ill will.[12]

Fifth, Glasgow follows a line of reasoning by John Arthur in holding there are, or may be, instances of morally justified racism (or of nonracist racial hatred). They offer two scenarios; I will present, and argue against the conclusion they draw from, each.

Blackmail Scenario. "If a very powerful alien reliably told you he would kill all [Rs] unless you daily refer to all [Rs] by using a racist slur, or unless you successfully internalize an attitude of hatred of [Rs], perhaps it would be obligatory, all things considered, to [comply by becoming racist]. . . . Cases like this one suggest that it overstates the immorality of racism to say that it is always conclusively immoral."[13]

This "suggest[ion]," however, merely presuppose the dubious and discredited doctrine of consequentialism in Anscombe's original sense of that now misused term, which applies to any doctrine that allows the goal of avoiding various undesirable consequences to justify doing anything to anybody.[14] No such strong assumptions are warranted in social theory. After all, to the extent a moral approach treats an action's actual or probable results as affecting its moral licitness, it therein distances the action's (im)morality from the action's origins in human agency, from the action's human meaning as an expression of the agent (distinct from its status as a mere event), and from those virtues in relation to which we specify the respect in which any wrong action is immoral (i.e., as dishonest, cruel, an infidelity, etc.); holds moral right and wrong hostage to chance; and treats agents as mere causes rather than as persons in relation.

Such cases are better accommodated by allowing that repudiating racism can sometimes have undesirable and regrettable side effects (here, genocide) than by claiming such effects suffice to justify embracing racism. Moreover, even if someone accepts a moral theory according to which such bad effects meant repudiating racism is here wrong, she needs further theory to rule out such scenarios being "moral dilemmas" (in the philosophical sense of cases in which the agent acts immorally no matter what she does). Otherwise, it could be that racism remains immoral even if there are cases where repudiating it is also immoral. My treating *R*s with racist disregard (i.e., malice, contempt, etc.) is worse of me (to them), more racist in me, than is my declining to dishonor them at the cost (to them) that a villain kills them. That is really all that matters in morally considering (deliberating over, weighing) my options. Though it will be said that the agent's deliberately making herself racist may nevertheless be morally justified as the lesser evil, it needs to be explained that and why it is a lesser evil in the relevant sense of being a less vicious (bad-making) choice. Such a claim is quite implausible. It may be true that she would act in a less racist way in instrumentally embracing racism than would the alien in intentionally murdering all the *R*s. However, a controvertible theory is then needed to explain why that fact about the alien determines the morality of the human agent's choice.

Even then, I think embracing racism would still be ineligible because it would be the *worse* option in that the racist agent treats her victims more viciously (more disrespectfully, unjustly, and maliciously) than she treats anyone who suffers as an indirect result of her eschewing racism.

Racism would thus remain the graver breach of interpersonal relationship, which is all that would be needed to be shown in a properly relation-centered ethical theory. In fact, this strategy of serial comparison of the way each person is mistreated is the best way to assess the agent's options. So, even if we reject "moral dilemmas," as I think we should, it doesn't follow that such instances of racism are licit.

Best understood, the respect in which the alien's murdering all the Rs is a morally objectionable action is that it is egregiously vicious, and the sense in which the Rs' deaths is an undesirable result is that it is an immoral (vicious) occurrence for anyone to favor. So conceived, it is hard to see how avoiding these warrants doing or be(com)ing what analyzing this very atrocity shows to be vicious. How is it better (desirable, more virtuous of anyone to want) that some person actually become racist to avoid a possible outcome it would be vicious of anyone to want? (In relation) To whom is that person more virtuous?

Trading off trying to harm this person in order to benefit that one, or showing contempt for this one now and in these ways in order to spare her or another being shown contempt later and in that way treats the person and her claims as mere means, like a fungible commodity rather than as a ground for the reverence, respect, deference, and even awe, that is suitably expressed in "honoring" her as above (immune to) any licit violation. To see why aggregation is nondispositive and even irrelevant in the philosopher's nightmare-dilemma scenarios, we need to remember that justice, like other moral virtues, is patient focused, which captures individualism, in its revolving around not some group's interest, nor the overall welfare, but that of each person.

We turn, then, to Glasgow's second scenario from Arthur, with which we can deal more expeditiously, building on what has already been said: scenario of antiracist racial hostility and contempt. "Suppose, in the manner of *Star Trek*, that a race of people arrives on Earth whose members enjoy nothing more than torturing and oppressing other races—a trait that (I will assume) is inherent in the race itself. . . . [I]t is part of their nature, as members of that race, to hate and oppress others. Hostility toward those persons seems [epistemically] justified, but it is also clear, I think, that such hostility is not what we think of as racism. Justified racial contempt directed at all members of a race, were it ever to exist, would not constitute racism."[15]

We should immediately note that this case is underdescribed. We need to know: Can the aliens control their supposedly natural impulse? If not, as is generally recognized even by compatibilists, they are not culpable and no hostility is warranted. If so, the racist group's "race" is irrelevant to whether such hostility is warranted. Anyway, whichever is the case, contempt for rational persons is always illicit; as Kant saw, a violation of their dignity. While we should criticize and oppose such people, holding them in contempt is unjustifiable, because patently incompatible with the honor and favor that suit and are virtuous toward each rational being. In my view, devising and concentrating on situations where racism—or rape, torture, murder, and more—appears attractive (better, tempting) tends to corrupt rather than refine our moral sensibility and replace moral reasoning with the mere toting up of goods and evils. I think it corruption because moral sensibility and reasoning are chiefly about cultivating, enhancing, and preserving, rather than breaching and deforming, our interpersonal relationships.[16]

GROUNDING VAR IN VIRTUES-BASED MORAL THEORY

This chapter affords me opportunity to clarify and develop my earlier claim that VAR illuminates racism by showing how it is explicable from within what is often called "virtue ethics." I think VAR, reciprocally, is best expressed within, illustrates, and lends support to virtues-based ethical theory.

Adapting and extending a promising (though problematic[17]) suggestion from R. M. Adams's *A Theory of Virtue* and T. Hurka's *Virtue, Vice, and Value* illuminates for us how and that it can help us systematize vice's varieties and forms if we treat virtue as a good-making (i.e., self-improving) intentional/psychological response to what is valuable. Someone's psychological response may go wrong (i.e., fail in helping make its subject a good *F*) by being *absent* (as when someone cares nothing for some human being's welfare); or inappropriate in its *valence* (i.e., favoring what it to be disfavored, or disfavoring what is to be favored, as when someone aims to make miserable some innocent); or in its *type* (as when someone strives merely to maximize occurrences/bearers of beauty, which is rather to be appreciated, or tries to maximize the number of her friendships, *each* of which should rather be intensified). Additionally, her psychological response may be defective; that is, tend to make her a bad R rather than good as an R, in its degree/*intensity* (e.g., being excessively or insufficiently opposed to something only moderately bad, as when somebody finds her intimate's suffering only mildly sad); or in its actual *psychological ground*, which should correspond to its normative justification in what makes its object/content/target (dis)valuable (e.g., insufficiently prioritizing those goods distinctive of persons in responding to a person by treating her as if she were, like an animal, merely the subject of pains and pleasures, instead of a rational subject); and in its *orientation to practice* (as when someone merely feels bad about someone's suffering, which she should seek to alleviate by her actions).

VAR allows for all the corresponding types of racism—the racism of callous indifference (a vice of absence), that of ill will (vice of valence), that of insufficient goodwill (vice of degree), that of merely affectively enjoying (e.g., perhaps being titillated by the looks or company of) those of the targeted race(s) without (even the disposition to) willing what is good for them (vices of type and of inappropriate grounding). With respect to racism, then, it is vicious, opposed to virtue, in that the racist responds to some individual or group with hostility or contempt, opposed in its valence to the respectful benevolence appropriate to persons (or with a callous indifference with no such valence), or in being too tepid and limited in her goodwill (a response of the wrong degree/intensity), or in being too little disposed to act (having formed volitional attitudes that are not condign) against racism, or in treating some persons (because of their race) like children or other incompetents (a response).

Given this sketch, how can disrespect be understood within VAR? Moral respect is for individuals, since they alone are persons, having the unique status and dignity that its links to reason bestow on personhood. A group can be said to be treated with disrespect only in that its members are, perhaps because of their membership in the group. Moral disrespect is at the core of the moral vice of injustice, since respect is the heart of the moral virtue of justice. For someone to possess human dignity, as its etymological origin in Latin's *dignitas* (worth) suggests, is for her to (a) hold a special kind of *worthiness* (merit/desert) that is distinctive in being (b) grounded in, and justified by, *facts* about persons and in the (rational) capacities characteristic and definitive of them, and (c) in its exceptional ethical *stringency* (so that claims grounded in one's human dignity are often indefeasible).

Recent work on respect distinguishes what we can call its "cognitive, affective, and conative [better, volitional] dimensions."[18] Accordingly, within VAR, the racist typically refuses fully to acknowledge/admit the racial victims' status and dignity as a person (cognitive) and, necessarily, neither cares appropriately and adequately about them (affective) nor is properly committed to their welfare (volitional). Respect and disrespect are always matters of (appropriate or inappropriate) response *of* a person, *in* her heart and will, *to* a person, *in response to* the latter's dignity, *as* honoring her (*qua* person). As we just noted, we can talk of treating groups with disrespect only when we mean their members are so treated because they belong to the groups. As disrespect is at the core of the moral vice injustice, so respect is at the center of the moral virtue of justice.

Institutional conduct, social customs, traditions, informally shared practices, and more can only be disrespectful to the extent they are "filled" with (that is, tainted, contaminated, infected, or polluted by) disrespect, normally that of the relevant agents. They are so filled when they show contempt, disdain, scorn, or condescension, all of which are modes of being disrespectful. Treating someone with disrespect offends against justice by violating that person in her status and dignity as a person; that is, her worthiness of honor and favor.

Moral respect is inherently tied to the moral virtue of justice, disrespect to the moral vice of injustice. Still, contra Kant, that does not mean they have little to do with the virtue of benevolence and the vices of callousness and hatred. Kant famously claimed that love brings us closer to one another, while justice makes us keep a distance.[19] We can see his point, since the infant's parents normally feel intimately connected to the child they protect, while the adolescent's parents sometimes have difficulty keeping a respectful distance, not interfering in things their young one must decide for herself. For all that, justice is not greatly opposed to benevolence, though it is contrary to utilitarianism's aggregative consequentialism. The moral virtue of benevolence toward each human person requires justice. Thus, any grave offense against benevolence offends also against justice because anyone is entitled to a certain degree of concern, goodwill. Similarly, any offense against the virtue of justice also violates that of benevolence, a vicious failure to will someone some good. However, someone can treat another justly in certain ways without therein being fully benevolent to her, as Kant correctly noted in his *Groundwork*'s discussion of the shopkeeper.[20]

Better to comprehend racism within moral philosophy, I should sketch some key elements of a somewhat distinctive approach I take to normative ethical theory. It involves structural concepts that I call virtues basing, role-relativity and -centering, patient focus, and, in its account of actions' deontological features, input-drive. I briefly treat each of these in turn.

Ethical theory is virtues-based (V-B) when it takes concepts of virtues and derivative vices, such as benevolence to this person, justice toward that one, honesty and truthfulness in relation to each of these, and loyalty to each of those, and so on, as more foundational than are either concepts of the impersonally desirable or undesirable (and the similarly good or bad, the valuable and disvaluable), on one hand, or deontic concepts (including moral obligation and forbiddenness, what someone ought to or mustn't do) on the other. Very promising accounts of both deontic discourse and also talk of what is impersonally valuable reformulate them in terms of virtue/vice.[21] Thus conceived, what it is for something to be impersonally good or bad must be nonreciprocally understood and analyzed in terms of what is virtuous or vicious. Likewise, that in which moral duty and more consist will be somehow constituted by, and needs to be analyzed in terms of, what is virtuous or vicious.

There is also great promise and appeal in ethical theory that views the moral realm as relative to and even centered in certain important roles. Since virtues are what make something (and its work) to be good, in Aristotle's most general definition of virtue, and vices that make it bad, there is a natural connection between virtues and roles, relationships. For nothing is simply good or bad, but only a good this, a bad that; in general, a good or bad thing of type of K or K^*. The human kinds to which we intuitively link the moral virtues and vices are such relationships as friend, neighbor, wife or husband, brother or sister, mother or father, even fellow in the very broad sense and scope to which Christians follow their founder in adapting the term *neighbor*. If we only (and, it can be argued, at least implicitly, always and necessarily) think of our moral virtues as thus internal to our relationships, and if the same is true of duties—which can, arguably, be understood in terms of vicious actions—and also of rights (rights-talk being a kind of duty-talk), we can say that various role-relationships determine anyone's moral features and therein constitute her moral life.²² This role-centering (R-C) helps explain why, as J. J. Thomson says, for our traits, actions, and us to be morally virtuous—as we say, good—is for them to be (somehow) just or benevolent (including being honest, truthful, faithful, etc., and, I should add, also helps explain the importance of such derivative, regulative virtues as courage and temperance). It is in being an *R* who is just, considerate, and so on that we fulfill certain roles, which constitute our moral lives in that it is in her being just, and more that S1 gives S2 what S2 needs or benefits S2 in having an *R*. Thus, role-centering points toward and supports a further structural metatheoretic feature that I call patient focus.

We can call an ethical theory patient focused (P-F) when the needs and welfare of person S2 are what determine what counts as role-virtue (and, thence, role-duty) in someone S1, when S1 is *R* to S2, in where *R* is one of the role-relationships that constitute S2's moral life and are internal to S2's human flourishing. Role-centering supports patient focus as R-C's theoretically most sensible, and also most intuitive, interpretation.²³

Finally, virtues-basing, especially in union with our other structural concepts of role-centering and patient focus, persuasively leads us to a further structural concept that I call input-drive (I-D).²⁴ With this term, I mean to refer to ethical theories in which the factor that ultimately fixes what it is permissible, forbidden, or obligatory to do (or to omit) lies in the motivational input to an action (or omission), in why the agent acts or doesn't. Virtues-basing, wherein we interpret wrongful action as acting viciously, highlights an important fact that is little noticed: the deep moral question about our conduct is not, *contra* Kant, *what* (i.e., which action) someone ought to *do*, but rather, *how* she is to behave (if, that is, she is to avoid behaving viciously).²⁵

An input-driven, virtues-based moral theory accords great moral significance to an action's *intended* effects, what she intends for the patient with whom she stands in a morally critical role, and more limited significance to foreseen and even foreseeable consequences of what we do (individually, jointly, etc.), all in a way compatible and of a piece with enlightened moral theory; that is, personalist- and relationship-centered. Of course, even if we reject what we might call consequentialism's strict output-drive, that doesn't by itself force us to accept an understanding of wrongdoing as being (no less narrowly?) entirely input-driven.²⁶

IMPLICATIONS OF VIRTUES-BASED MORAL THEORY (V-BMT) FOR THE STUDY OF RACISM

V-B makes it easier for us to understand why racism is inherently wrong and how it is wrong. R-C helpfully keeps the theorist of racism duly focused on how people are regarded and treated by others with social structures, institutions, culture, and more, at best secondary. P-F reminds us that the racist wrongs people, which is more important than setting back a race or perpetuating inequalities. (In fact, inequalities chiefly matter morally only insofar as some people are being vicious, callous in the ways that they cause or tolerate them.) I-D is closely connected to, follows closely on, V-B, R-C, and P-F, since (a) virtues are internal states, (b) the relevant role-relationships are shaped, even defined, by internal states, and (c) what we (as patients) most need from those who fill those crucial roles in our lives are various types and levels of commitment, devotion. Virtues-basing, *pace* Thomson, lends support to an input-driven account of racist actions' viciousness, and thus justifies the theorist's concentrating on what motivates a supposedly racist action or policy rather than on its effects.[27] This feature helps explain where and why their overattention to disparate racial impact (effects) leads such thinkers as Glasgow astray.

Though I have argued that VAR can effectively draw on virtues-based ethical theory to illuminate the nature and varieties of racism's immorality, some will complain that so-called virtue ethics cannot do the job of comprehending racism on the grounds that it is, like Aristotle himself, too conservative in its view of society. I think this critic paints with too broad a brush. It is notable that P. Taylor displays a nascent form of virtue ethics that is radical, aesthetic, and epistemically revisionist. Approaches that take the virtues seriously, and perhaps even as basic, then, need not be apolitical, let alone conservative.[28]

More important, there are theoretic advantages to an account of racism that, while not conservative, is free of Left ideological blinders and "radical," activist commitments, presuppositions, and agenda. We find those faults in the work of L. McWhorter, who has recently drawn attention to Foucault's late expansive conception of racism. Foucault contrasted "traditional, historical . . . 'ethnic racism,'" which he identified with "the prejudice or defense of one group against another," with what he called "racism against the abnormal" that scrutinizes and restricts through "disciplinary normalization" those deemed defective lest they transmit the contamination imputed to them.²⁹

McWhorter approvingly interprets Foucault as "choos[ing] to equate racism and . . . 'homophobia' as well as other bigotries aimed at people considered deviant in many other ways" and with "discourses and institutions," "networks of power," and "systems of oppression" that "aim to eliminate, contain, manage or exploit abnormality . . . in ways that very often threaten, harm, and oppress individuals who are classified as abnormal."³⁰

Any such exceptionally broad account of racism is problematic. McWhorter herself asks, "What sense does it make to call prejudice and discrimination against those deemed abnormal racism? Isn't stretching the term to cover such disparate social phenomena a needless dilution of an important category?" She worries such usage "violate[s] conventional definitions," is "overstatement," and appears to be "just another example of a white person appropriating or colonizing critical territory that doesn't belong to him."³¹ I judge the worries she here expresses more insightful than her positive account of racism, and her Foucauldian proposal that "racism is a biopolitical *dispositif* bound up with discourses of development and practices of disciplinary normalization" should be rejected as obscure, unhelpful, conceptually confusing, and confused. I return to the political question, briefly, at this chapter's conclusion.

A person's racist disrespect, like racist ill will or callousness, can infect her actions in ways that should be obvious to us, when those actions manifest/express such attitudes in her. Thus, my racist attitudes may move me contemptuously to mistreat a job applicant, or somebody I happen upon in a casual encounter of the sort to which modern urban life lends itself (e.g., in elevators, buses, and so on). In that way, rac*ial* discrimination, formal or more informal discrimination against someone on the basis of her race, is often rac*ist* discrimination; that is, discrimination not just based on race but rooted in a racist mentality. VAR can also accommodate what we can call "deferential racism," wherein an agent who may not be racist in her own personal attitudes defers to others' racism. A personnel officer, for example, may defer to her bosses' insistence that no Black candidates be hired; a retail owner may refuse to employ Black workers, lest they offend and put off her racist clientele; a homeowner may urge (even pressure) her neighbor not to sell to a Black family because she fears local racists will avoid the neighborhood (fleeing it, or refusing to move there), driving down property values to her financial detriment. VAR shows how we can responsibly accommodate the intuition many have that these agents' actions are racially discriminatory, and in an invidious way, though the agents themselves are *ex hypothesi* not racists.

We should also consider a kind of case that perhaps removes racist action even further from any racism in the agent herself. Thomas Carson interprets Abraham Lincoln, though personally only minimally tainted by the racism of his social environment growing up in (the slave state of) Kentucky and sometimes living in central Illinois, sometimes stooped to anti-Black slurs, stereotypes, stories, and proposals, especially when campaigning for office.[32] Lincoln seems to have wanted to portray himself as an appealing moderate, someone opposed to slavery on grounds of political and moral principle but, for all that, still someone with whom his prospective constituents could feel comfortable, because he is someone who shared their own negative feelings about Black people. In Carson's view, Lincoln was here speaking disrespectfully about the Africans and their descendants, for reasons of political strategy, though he personally didn't feel disrespect for them. Can VAR accommodate that phenomenon? I think so. We can say that Lincoln was there showing and expressing disrespect for Black people, but not his own racial disrespect. Rather, he deliberately deferred to his constituents' racist attitudes in order to curry favor with them. In this deference, he infected his behavior with their racism. Since, in VAR, actions become racist by such contamination, it allows us to classify actions like Lincoln's as racist while allowing that he may not have been a racist himself. Notice, however, that this account does not concede Bonilla-Silva's category of "racism without racists," since the racism of Lincoln's actions was still informed by the racism of real racists, racist individuals. There is no racism merely in things—"structures," "systems," "cultures," "social imaginaries," and more—as many today would have it, that has not gotten there from a deeper, more fundamental kind of racism in individuals' attitudes—as we say, in their hearts.[33]

PROBLEM IN GLASGOW'S ALTERNATIVE ACCOUNT OF RACISM

To Glasgow, "[Something] is racist if and only if [it] is disrespectful towards members of racialized group R as Rs."[34] This claim is multiply problematic. It is, for example, quite vague, since Glasgow offers no detail on disrespect's nature or criteria: "I have left open what does, and what does not count as disrespectful."[35] Likewise, he neither specifies nor defends any account of *why* or *how* something so counts.

More important, *contra* Glasgow, there is no real alternative to conceiving disrespect as fundamentally "attitudinal," because its contrasting concept is respect (just as the word *disrespect*'s root term is *respect*), and whatever the details, respect must be a complex of mental attitudes (including recognition, appreciation, and deference). Likewise, disrespect's modes—including disdain, contempt, scorn, dishonor, condescension—are all fundamentally attitudes. Thus, the individual and collective actions, social practices and customs, institutional operations, beliefs, and more that we correctly designate as disrespectful are properly so called in that they are informed by (show, express, manifest) someone's attitude of disrespect. This latter is alone the "ground-floor" instance of racism, what Glasgow would call its primary and central "location." Glasgow's discussion crucially fails to distinguish something's being disrespect from its being disrespectful. His article's very title implies that he thinks racism is (identical with a certain kind of) disrespect. However, he then continually fails to distinguish this foundational instance of racism, which is an attitude, from the behaviors, institutions, and more that we call "disrespectful" because they are relevantly informed by (i.e., "ful[l]" of) that attitiude.

Glasgow's claims notwithstanding, disrespect *is* an internal, mental, personal attitude. It is a vice and, moreover, the vice that underlies all injustice. Thus, any program of "deattitudinalizing" respect is incoherent.[36] This is easily shown by considering respect's necessary similarity to honor and reverence (the nouns for which are near synonyms for "respect"), both of which are plainly mental states, and virtuous ones. We reach the same conclusion by considering contrast terms such as *disdain, contempt,* and *disgust*, which are, again, terms for (vicious) mental states. While honor, reverence, disdain, condescension, scorn, and contempt, and, with them, respect and disrespect, are all themselves mental states, nonetheless, actions, omissions, practices, projects, and so on (individual, joint, or collective) can be honoring, reverent, disdainful, condescsending, scornful, and contemptuous, in virtue of their various connections to, derivations from, those underlying and focal mental states.[37]

Thus, Glasgow's (odd) rejection of and supposed "location-neutral" alternative to what we might call ordinary, "layered" accounts of racism (in which, often, something, X, is racist only because of its relevant relation to something else, Y, which is fundamentally racist) is misconceived. He has no plausible alternative conception of how to organize racism's multiple occurrences. Leveling them all as instances of disrespect is contrary to what we know of respect's nature. Either actions, beliefs, institutions, and more are racist because they are informed by racist noncognitive attitudes (as VAR holds), or the noncognitive attitudes are racist because they are derived from beliefs, which are then taken as fundamentally racist, or any person (or personal feature) is racist because supporting an institution that is fundamentally racist, or something similar, must be true. Glasgow's own account requires him to say that it is only failing to respect a *person* that is racist. Thus, he has no basis for his claim that someone *S1* (or her behavior, or her attitude) is racist simply because *S1* fails to respect "individual differences" between or among *S2*, *S3*, *S4*, et al.[38] Besides that, not all cases of *S1*'s failing to respect (e.g., ignoring) *S2*'s differences from *S3* are cases of failing to respect *S2* herself (nor *S3*). Plainly, any two people are alike in many ways. The issue becomes morally fraught only when *S1* implicitly (or explicitly) fails to appreciate the unique personhood of some individual(s).

In addition to these problems, Glasgow offers no consistent account of racist disrespect's objects, sometimes discussing disrespect for (or failure to respect) "individual differences," sometimes for persons, sometimes for a person's "right[s]," sometimes for "their equal moral and political standing."[39] That racism is always disrespectful, even if true, would not entail that whatever is racist is racist (only) because it is disrespectful. Racial disrespect is one of the vicious racial attitudes VAR counts as a central form of racism and is a moral offense against the virtues of both justice and benevolence, since justice involves a volitional disposition to defer to persons' rights because of their inherent status and dignity.

This brings us to what he says about institutional racism. Glasgow insists on the possibility of "pure institutional racism," as stated above, comprising "cases where the racism bottoms out at the institutional level."[40] He means that sometimes an institution's racism does not derive from racist attitudes in individual minds.[41] Glasgow seems to think some social arrangements are racist simply by their actually working to the detriment of certain racial groups. At least, they are racist if this occurs against a historical background of those groups' racist mistreatment. Yet what merely happens to operate so as to perpetuate racial (or, e.g., wealth) disadvantage is, for all that, racist (or otherwise unjust) only insofar as some people therein manifest their racist callousness in failing to mend it. (I suspect it is the lingering suspicion that, given the history of racism, such callousness must be present, even in cases where it is claimed to be absent, that grounds whatever inclination some have to classify such cases as institutional racism.) This includes the case where they do not care enough about the victims of potential injustice even to find out whether the institution is operating to leave some people so badly off that the more powerful would treat the victims disrespectfully and unjustly if they failed to amend it.[42]

It is a problem for his position that Glasgow offers no explicit reason in his initial discussion why what he classifies as "pure institutional racism" is really racist even on his own account. He gives an example in which an initial disadvantage of the $R1$s relative to the $R2$s, a disadvantage perhaps caused by a natural disaster erasing the former's wealth or even by ineptitude of $R1$'s leadership at a crucial historical juncture, is perpetuated by the way an institution subsequently operates.[43] However, this classification seems to enshrine moral luck in the worst way, allowing something to become immoral (here, racism, which Glasgow allows is at least presumptively immoral) just because of what results. The result is presented as predictable, discernable, and observed. But this seems to involve immorality only in people's (perhaps callously) failing to take action to avert the $R1$'s suffering. (I leave it open whether the moral objection is to the suffering itself, perhaps in the context, or explicitly to the comparison between the $R1$s and $R2$s.)

Glasgow seems to find justification for a broad account of institutional racism in his effort to accommodate some people's "legitimate" applications of the term *institutional racism*.[44] Yet this may move too fast. While philosophical analysis should accommodate claims made in ordinary discourse, this is less true of charges of racism lodged for strategic reasons by involved partisans eager to elicit emotions and change both attitudes and behavior. The predications internal to such accusations may not be judicious reflections of their makers' conceptual and linguistic mastery, advanced by speakers careful to ensure their claims' content is accurate. Glasgow also needs to contend with counterintuitive implications of views of institutional racism (more or less) similar to his. Those who deem its disproportionally harmful impact on Black people enough to make a practice an instance of institutional racism seem committed to saying that cases of Black-on-Black neighborhood crime—muggings, burglary, coercion by street gangs, drug dealing, and drug pushing—constitute institutional racism (albeit of an informal sort). Suppose further that the frequency of such crime helps perpetuate negative stereotypes, even stigmatization, of Black people. While there may be good reason to call the perpetrators of such crimes racial "sell-outs" for willingly harming Black people for personal gain, to add that they are also racist (or participating in racism) seems to me to go too far.[45]

Now imagine that a program of large-scale deincarceration, undertaken for antiracist reasons of the sort recently advanced by Angela Davis and Glenn Loury (among many others), turned out to hurt Black people on the whole, or most Black people, or the worst-off Black people, and to do so in ways that could have been anticipated.[46] Note that, like Glasgow's first "Real Estate" scenario,[47] the program's implementation depends on the occurrence of past racism, which partially accounts for the disproportionally large number of Black inmates. Does this combination of racially disparate impact with racially tainted history suffice to make the decarceration program institutional anti-Black racism? Intuitively, we think not. Indeed, just the opposite: it is an antiracist initiative, even if an unsuccessful, even counterproductive, one. However, we need some explanation from Glasgow of how he avoids commitment to such classification.

Keeping track of the race of job, student, housing, and other potential candidates may have started as a way of keeping Black people out of certain jobs, schools, professions, marriages, offices, and so on. Today, however, its continuation is defended chiefly by dedicated antiracist advocates, who insist on continued racial record-keeping as a way of monitoring progress (or its lack) in integration. Suppose now that some political conservatives are right (or, if that is too difficult for readers, imagine a faraway world in which they were right) that this works to the overall detriment of Black people (or of most Black people, or of the worst-off

Black people) in various ways: feeding anti-Black resentment among some Whites, fueling suspicion of Black achievers who are seen as succeeding for reasons independent of their competence, making successful Black candidates insecure about their achievements' basis and filling them with self-doubt, convincing some Black candidates they do not need hard work to succeed and discouraging others from exerting themselves because they think the numbers too low, and so on. (I have seen all these criticisms of racial record-keeping and racial preference, and still more besides them, in the literature.) Since this racial record-keeping had its origins in anti-Black racism and now, in our imagined scenario, operates counterproductively to harm Black people, shouldn't that suffice to render it institutional racism, on Glasgow's account? Yet remember that it is maintained today precisely as an antiracist measure. Again, the implied classification is unacceptable—both outlandish and unfair. Still, it remains unclear how Glasgow means to avoid it.

In any case, what Glasgow says throughout his essay seems to require him to maintain that, since it is racist, the institution imagined must show disrespect.[48] But therein it is marked by vicious racial disregard, and thus fits my account. How is Glasgow's account superior to VAR here, or even different from it? Moreover, that an institution or other phenomenon is racist because disrespectful still ties its racism to people and their attitudes. That is because something's being disrespectful can only be understood by its relation to the *personal attitude* of respecting someone. (There are two stages to this argument. First, any action, remark, institution, etc., is disrespectful to some persons only because of its relation to some person being disrespectful to them. Second, we understand disrespect and its wrongness only in its contrast with, and as an offense against, respect. [And therein as an offense against the virtue of justice.])

It follows that Glasgow is mistaken to think his "disrespect analysis of racism"[49] has "location-neutrality"—in contrast with VAR, doxastic, behavioral, or institutional accounts of racism—with no one type of bearer of racism "where . . . racism is fundamentally located"; that is, "its sole fundamental site."[50] Although things of many and radically different kinds can all be disrespectful, only a certain mental stance is disrespect itself. Further, the disrespectful things can only be disrespectful because of their relation to that mental stance of respect. In fact, relation to the fundamental mental stance of respect for persons is what racism would require if Glasgow is correct that racism must be "disrespectful towards members of racial group R as Rs." Contrary to what he may think, his own view does not allow an institution to be racist simply because of its effect of perpetuating racial disparities. As noted above, the real issue is not about "location," but whether all cases of racism are at the same level, as he thinks, or, as in VAR, the racism of some kinds of things necessarily derived from that of certain more central instances? Glasgow thinks his view is "location-neutral" and "anti-reductionist" because it holds that everything racist is at the same level and racist only in that it is "racially disrespectful." What we have just shown is that Glasgow cannot sustain this claim. Some things are (constitute) disrespect, which is a complex of personal attitudes in mental subjects. Things of other kinds—that is, such as individual or joint actions, customs and practices, social institutions—can only be informed and tainted by such attitudes (and thus be disrespectful). Glasgow may have masked this fact from himself by his willingness to use the term *disrespect* in a nonstandard manner, as a verb that can take institutions, and more, as subject. This use is substandard, however, and such things can themselves only show and be filled with the mental stance of disrespect.

There is more. Glasgow needs to tell us, when an action, custom, or institution is disrespectful, *whence comes* and *where resides* the original disrespect that now "fills" it? I say it must be in the people who perform the action, practice the custom, and who implement the institutions' operations (or, in a weaker sense of "institutional racism," who once designed and adopted it).

Glasgow seems to think that disparate racial impact alone is insufficient to make an institutional racist, but can nevertheless do the trick when it also had racist origins. I agree that this makes the institution racist in a weak, technical sense that it is a vestige of racism, but Glasgow wants more.[51] Yet if its original racist taint (O) now works with its disparate impact (I) to make it racist, despite what are *ex hypothesi* now racially neutral procedures (P), we need some explanation of how this original racist sin is now duly catalyzed so as to have this implication. Glasgow gives no account of this, and I doubt any plausible one is available. Rather, the tainted origins (O) seem not to interact at all with either the current untainted operations (P) or the latter's unfortunate effects (I).[52] The most sensible thing to say is that what people have to contend with in Glasgow's Real Estate scenarios are the lingering effects of past racism, not any kind of contemporaneous racism. While it is incorrect to characterize "color-conscious" attempted remedies as "reverse (i.e., anti-White) racism," as some do, neither are race-blind approaches, even slow-acting ones, *eo ipso* (a new form of) anti-Black racism.

Even Arthur says that the contempt he sees as central to racism takes the form of either hostility or indifference.[53] It is hard to see how Glasgow's "disrespect" can occur without a similar disposition to racial hostility (ill will) or indifference (better, insufficient goodwill). Nor can I see how someone can respond to another person with vicious ill will or indifference without therein failing to accord them the respect appropriate to persons. So, Glasgow's disrespect analysis, once shorn of its specious "location-neutrality," seems to coincide with VAR. No substantive difference is so far discernible.

Can VAR make adequate room for the contempt, disdain, and other forms of disrespect that are plausibly seen as close to racism's heart? Bell quotes Schopenhauer's aphorism, "Hatred is a thing of the heart, contempt a thing of the head," and mentions his argument for the conclusion that the two attitudes are "decidedly antagonistic."[54] She rightly says neither excludes the other, but she does not see what is in fact their close connection. Whatever Schopenhauer may have thought, hatred always includes ill will, not mere averse feeling. Hatred proper is malice (better, malevolence), a willing of ills for another which willing is itself evil. Disrespect for any person similarly involves breach of a virtuous resolve to defer to her authority in certain matters and thus a failure to will that person the personal good of (limited) self-direction. (More strongly, contempt often involves the will that she not enjoy that good.) Thus, disrespect, including contempt, is, like hatred, a matter of what someone does, and does not, will for a person.

We can conclude our critique of Glasgow's positive, supposedly alternative, view of racism with some final observations. What Glasgow imagines to be his position's "location-neutrality" may generate a homologicality problem for him. Racist contempt—which Arthur, for one, sees as central to racism—is itself called disrespectful only constitutively, not predicatively. But Glasgow's account needs anything racist to be called racist predicatively—he needs it to bear the feature of being disrespect(ful). This is a problem for him. Glasgow also worries that we should not say that propositions, or signs, or symbols are themselves racist, but only that using them is racist.[55] He is correct to deny, and Blum wrong to propose, that there are or could be "racist propositions." VAR shows how attribution of such vices as racism's to a proposition, an abstract object, is absurd. Still, contrary to Glasgow's tentative suggestions, a swastika is plainly called a racist symbol in that it is a symbol *of* the Nazis' racist program, malice, and propaganda. So too, *mutatis mutandis*, for the KKK's hoods and initials, burning crosses, for the Stars & Bars battleflag, and more. Note that sometimes a Star of David is a sign of Judaism or Jews, but sometimes more a symbol of anti-Jewish hate. It is never a mark itself, but only its salient uses, which may not all be relevantly similar, that can be racist by bearing, expressing, signifying racist attitudes. Uses however, are not all relevantly similar. We should acknowledge that any of these signs may also (or instead?) symbolize other things, and one of those latter meanings may be foremost in a given individual's thinking about, plans for, and use of, them. When that is racist—and it can be—note that it is because of the user's egregious racial insensitivity and callousness.

Perhaps a more interesting type of case comprises racial slurs and epithets, which we might even call "racist words." Here we seem to have words whose use tends be racially offensive because they have historically been parts (or concomitants) of, and still contribute to, viciously inconsiderate and insulting ways of addressing or referring to people. Again, though, it is always someone's *using* such words, and sometimes even just mentioning them, that is racist because it is informed by some form of racial disregard, never the words by or in themselves.

MOVING FORWARD

The appropriate objective of conceptual inquiry into racism is to explicate its nature.[56] VAR is an ontic claim about racism's reality, its essence and nature, undertaken through examining our discourse to identify the assumptions and insights behind it. It is not a mere proposed definition of a word, a question of whether "racism is morally wrong by definition."[57] Rather, the issue is whether, given what we find racism to be, it can sometimes be other than immoral. Such an account must answer to common sense but also, contrary to what Glasgow suggests, can and should be used to correct ("revis[e]") minor inconsistencies in usage and clarify cases where we are unsure what to say. It is "useful" chiefly in illuminating reality and extending our understanding. Its chief goal is not to advance a political agenda (as in Haslanger), nor to guide social change (as in Blum), nor to help craft public policy (as in Corlett). Nor, contrary to Glasgow's insouciance, is it legitimate for people deliberately to extend words beyond their proper and recognized application simply to advance.[58] That is an offense similar to what C. L. Stevenson used to call "persuasive definition," only here it is persuasive (or, better, sneaky) application.

Another important and characteristic objective of philosophical analysis is to explicate something's normative aspects, components, and structure. VAR does that especially well when grounded in, and articulated through, ethical theory that is virtues-based, role-centered, patient-focused, and input-driven. Some will object that any form of virtue ethics (VE) is inherently conservative. This is not so. There are even "radical" strands of virtues-based thinking as shown in P. Taylor's suggestion, mentioned above, of a virtue epistemology for undoing racist cognitive distortions, and in L. Tessman's *Burdened Virtues*, with its consideration of traits that cannot achieve human fulfillment because of social conditions. Still, VAR and its close companion, Slote's agent-based virtue ethics (A-BVE), may be most consistent and continuous with personalist applied/practical (and theoretical) ethics. Rhetoric, though little substance, of the sanctity or sacredness of life is found in R. Dworkin's *Life's Dominion*. Antihumanist radicals such as S. Pinker and P. Singer reject any special dignity and elevated status of persons in pursuing their low-minded, mechanical consequentialism.[59] However, the mid-2000's President's Council on Bioethics has helpfully explored some practical implications of a personalist ethics that stresses human dignity.[60] Perhaps VAR may best be theorized as extension of such an ethics. In that way, VAR can draw on wide resources of ancient, medieval, Enlightenment, and current forms of what is called "virtue ethics." Thus it can pose an important alternative to familiar efforts at theorizing racism by forcing it into dull categories of Marxist mythology and its recent intellectual offspring (droppings?), including ideology, strong social constructionism, identity politics, critical race theory, and so on, and so on, *ad nauseam*.

To make progress, we will need a different sort of social theory. It should be a personalist social theory, centered on the status and dignity of the person and the attitudinal (and other) responses appropriate thereto.[61] Similarly, we shall have to recover and develop a virtues-based normative political theory, highlighting the attitudes that constitute excellence within certain central person-to-person role-relationships, and focusing on the Other's needs and welfare/interest in such a way that motivational inputs drive the account of obligatory, forbidden, and permissible institutional operation.

NOTES

1. Joshua Glasgow, "Racism as Disrespect," *Ethics* 120 (October 2009): 72–74.
2. Glasgow, 74.
3. It is important to note that "institution" is used quite loosely and broadly throughout, since not only formal and established structures (institutions) but also informal customs, habits, and practices can all count.
4. Glasgow, 72.
5. J. L. A. Garcia, "The Heart of Racism," in *Racism,* ed. Leonard Harris (Amherst: Prometheus/Humanity Books, 1999), 404; J. L. A. Garcia, "Current Conceptions of Racism," *Journal of Social Philosophy* 28 (1997): 27.
6. Glasgow, 72ff.
7. Glasgow, 72.
8. Glasgow, 71.
9. J. L. A. Garcia, "Racism and Racial Discourse," *Philosophical Forum* 32 (2001): 129; J. L. A. Garcia, "Philosophical Analysis and the Moral Concept of Racism," *Philosophy and Social Criticism* 25 (1999): 21.
10. There is a complication here. If racism were essentially a disjunction (as Blum once held), with each disjunct something necessarily immoral, then would it be essentially immoral? Perhaps so, but it would not really be immoral by its nature, insofar as a genuine nature cannot be thus a hodgepodge of disparate elements. (Contrast Blum's disjunctive view of racism as presented in *"I'm Not a Racist, But . . . "*, chapter 1, with his later skepticism about any analysis of racism in "What Do Accounts of Racism Do?"). Lawrence Blum, *"I'm Not a Racist, But . . . .: The Moral Quandary of Race* (Ithaca, NY: Cornell University Press, 2002), chapter 1; Lawrence Blum, "What Do Accounts of 'Racism' Do?," in *Racism in Mind,* eds. Michael Levine and Tamas Pataki (Ithaca, NY: Cornell University Press, 2004), 56–77.
11. Glasgow, 69.
12. It is worth noting that the human goods the paternalist denies her victims are constitutive aspects of human welfare, not mere causes about which one might easily make a mistake.
13. Glasgow, 78 at note 35.

14. See G. E. M. Anscombe, "Modern Moral Philosophy," in *Ethics, Religion and Politics* (Minneapolis: University of Minnesota Press, 1981), 36.

15. Anscombe, 36.

16. Consider this insightful episode, which should put our modern moral philosophers to shame. "[Douglas, a childish monster, speaking:] 'I mean, we shouldn't eat heads, and that makes sense. But what if we find ourselves in a situation where we really *want* to eat someone's head or maybe arm?' [As young Max, exasperated, tries to explain his rules against cannibalism,] Alexander [another monster] interrupted. 'But what if someone's head *falls* off? That sometimes happens. Can we eat it then?' he asked, eliciting a chorus of approving murmurs [from the assembled monsters]." Dave Eggers, *The Wild Things* (San Francisco: McSweeney's Books, 2009), 127, 128.

17. Contrary to what Adams and Hurka may think, I do not think we can *analyze* (metaphysically or conceptually) virtues as proper affective responses to value—nor can we *reduce* virtue to such value-response—because it is the concept of impersonal value that itself needs to be understood in terms of that of virtue. Nevertheless, many virtues are good-making responses to what is valuable, and this fact can be exploited for theoretical purposes in line with Adams's and Hurka's work.

18. Robin Dillon, "Respect," *Stanford Encyclopedia of Philosophy* (Spring 2014 edition), Edward N. Zalta (ed.), http://plato.stanford.edu/archives/spr2014/entries/respect/.

19. "According to the principle of mutual love they [i.e., rational beings] are directed constantly to approach one another; by the principle of respect which they owe to one another they are directed to keep themselves at a distance." Immanuel Kant, *Metaphysical Principles of Virtue*, trans. James Ellington (Indianapolis, IN: Bobbs-Merrill, 1964), *Ak.*, 449; Ellington's translation, 113.

20. Kant, *Grounding for the Metaphysics of Morals*, *Ak.*, 397; Ellington's translation, 10. The centrality of benevolence and justice in understanding racism and its immorality points to what below we call "virtues-basing." For those who cannot accept a theoretical claim unless they find it first in the writings of one of the Great Dead Philosophers, note that M. Rhonheimer interprets Aquinas as similarly holding that "every act injurious to [the moral virtue of] justice also transgresses [the moral virtue of] love for one's fellows." Martin Rhonheimer, "Sins Against Justice [S.T.] 2a–2ae, qq. 59–78," in *Ethics of Aquinas*, ed. S. Pope (Washington, DC: Georgetown University Press, 2002), 287–303 at 288. Quoted in Brian Feltham, "Introduction," in *Partiality and Impartiality*, ed. B. Feltham and J. Cottingham. (Oxford: Oxford University Press, 2010), 12, note 42. Immanuel Kant, *Grounding for the Metaphysics of Morals,* in *Ethical Philosophy: Grounding for the Metaphysics of Morals, and, Metaphysical Principles*

of Virtue, with, "On a Supposed Right to Lie Because of Philanthropic Concerns," 2nd. edition, trans. James Ellington (Indianapolis, IN: Hackett, 1995).

21. Linda Zagzebski, *Virtues of the Mind* (Cambridge: Cambridge University Press, 1996); Michael Slote, *Morals from Motives* (Oxford: Oxford University Press, 2001); Rosalind Hursthouse, *On Virtue Ethics* (Oxford: Oxford University Press, 2001).

22. This role-centering suggests some theoretical departure from Aristotle's classical understanding of moral virtue in terms of being good (*qua*) men. Still, the substantive difference may not be so great as might first appear. That is because it can be argued that, since we are essentially social animals, much of being a good (*qua*) human being consists in being good in (i.e., as occupant of) certain important person-to-person role-relationships. So conceived, the Aristotelian idea of being a good (*qua*) human being becomes transparent, a bridge to the deeper matter, which we here indicate, of being good within these relationships. In fact, a role-centered virtues-based moral theory is quite close to Aristotle's, and more distant from such recent innovations as M. Slote's understanding of moral virtues as "inner traits" that are "fundamentally admirable," T. Hurka's "recursive account" of virtues as intrinsically good responses to what has intrinsic value, or R. M. Adams's identification of moral virtue with "excellence in being for the good." See Thomas Hurka, *Virtue, Vice, and Value* (Oxford: Oxford University Press, 2001); Slote, *Morals from Motives,* 37; Robert Adams, *A Theory of Virtue* (Oxford: Oxford University Press, 2009).

23. Patient-focus thus helps normative ethical theory avoid the worry raised by Thomson lest her theory ultimately reduce to aggregative consequentialism. Likewise, it alleviates M. Slote's worry that appeal to Martineau's virtue of "universal benevolence" threatens to collapse "virtue ethics" into aggregative consquentialism. A role-centered, virtues-based moral theory need not flirt with consequentialism because, in it, it is not what is good or bad for the world, nor for all humanity, that matters morally, but what is good or bad for this or that person (or sometimes, for some special group), in making the agent a good or bad R in some morally determinative role-relationship she occupies in the other's life.

24. Note that what Slote calls "agent-basing," and the related feature that Zagzebski calls "motivation-basing," both of them quite similar to my "virtue-basing," in their theories lead directly to something like "input-drive," even though they accept neither what I call role-centering nor patient-focus.

25. We can justifiably reject J. J. Thomson's insistence on the supposed "objectiv[ity]"—that is, nondependence on their agents' mental states—of acting virtuously or viciously. Her view, implausibly and with excessive complication, sunders actions' virtue and vice from those of agents and their attitudes. We should also reject Gelfand's and Hursthouse's reliance on hypothetical agents,

since what matters to whether someone acts virtuously, viciously, or neither is what does feed into her action, not what would inform that of an imaginary agent.

26. Might a mixed, pluralistic account of the factors that make wrong acts wrong do better, even be best? The question is too far afield from our concern here to permit us to explore in any depth. Still, I will say that I think such a mixed approach to wrongdoing—allowing both an action's input and output to matter morally—is not best. For to the extent that a putative moral theory accords wrong-making force to actual or merely probable effects, it exaggerates significance afforded to mere luck in results, depreciates the Other by regarding her as a mere producer of beneficial and harmful effects, strips actions of their chief significance as exercises of agency and expressions of personal attitudes, severs actions' rightness from their meaning (in the lives of and relationship between agent and patient), detaches actions' morality from the agents' personhood and identity (as related in these ways to these other persons), divorces actions' moral status from their agents' (inter)personal relationships and roles, and threatens so to sunder the right from virtue (and from being a good person) that morality loses its unity and coherence. Judith Thomson, *Goodness and Advice* (Princeton, NJ: Princeton University Press, 2001).

27. Contrast the claim in Thomson, 60–65, that, in application to actions, virtue-talk is "objective," by which she means that whether what you did for me was, for example, generous is independent of your reasons, motivations, intentions, and so on, in acting, and of other aspects of your mind.

28. See also Lisa Tessman, *Burdened Virtues: Virtue Ethics for Liberatory Struggles* (Oxford: Oxford University Press, 2005).

29. Michel Foucault, *Abnormal* (2003), 316–17, as quoted in Ladelle McWhorter, *Racism and Sexual Oppression in Anglo-America* (Bloomington: Indiana University Press, 2009), 32.

30. McWhorter, 34.

31. McWhorter, 32, 33.

32. Thomas Carson, *Lincoln's Ethics: A Philosophical Approach* (New York: Cambridge University Press, 2015), chapter 10.

33. See Eduardo Bonilla-Silva, *Racism without Racists* (Lanham, MD: Rowman & Littlefield, 2006); Albert Atkin, *Philosophy of Race* (Durham, NC: Acumen, 2012).

34. Glasgow, 81.

35. Glasgow, 85.

36. Glasgow, 83, at note 44.

37. Bell says, "Disgust is contempt's closest neighbor" (Bell, 52), but it seems contempt and disdain are the principal forms disrespect takes in its opposition to virtuous respect. In any case, our point holds there too, for disgust itself is an

internal attitude, while actions, and others, are disgusted insofar as the attitude of disgust informs them. Macalester Bell, *Hard Feelings: The Moral Psychology of Contempt* (New York: Oxford University Press, 2013). Perhaps some have taken this rejection of disrespect too far. "[H]e who feels contempt/For any living thing, hath faculties/Which he has never used; . . . Thought within him is in its infancy." William Wordsworth, "Thoughts Left Upon a Seat in a Yew Tree" (composed 1795, published 1798). It is persons who must always be respected, though sometimes their behavior, decisions, tastes, and more are contemptible. Does any "living thing" merit contempt? I, for one, am not sure Wordsworth is wrong though, contrariwise, I doubt everything therefore merits the kind of respect that human persons do.

38. See his proposition "DA" at Glasgow, 81; contrast Glasgow, 83.
39. Glasgow, 83, 84.
40. Glasgow, 72.
41. Glasgow, 72ff.
42. See his "Accident" scenario at Glasgow, 75.
43. Glasgow, 74.
44. Glasgow, 73 at note 29.
45. See Randall Kennedy, *Sellout: The Politics of Racial Betrayal* (New York: Pantheon/Random House, 2008).
46. See Angela Davis, *Are Prisons Obsolete?* (New York: Seven Stories Press, 2003); Glenn Loury, *Race, Incarceration, and American Values* (Cambridge: MIT/Boston Review, 2008).
47. Glasgow, 72–73. His "Real Estate" scenario goes like this. "For centuries members of [racial group] *R1* have systematically targeted the economic structures of *R2* for unjust suppression, first through a state-supported system of segregation. Eventually, there was a racial rapprochement, where all state-supported means of *R2*'s economic repression (including criminal laws, voting rights, and tax-and-transfer schemes) were abolished. However, the rapprochement was not complete in the sense that no reparations were made to members of *R2*, and therefore the postrapprochement era begins with *R1*s uniformly having more wealth than *R2*s. Two hundred years later, there are no longer any attitudes, behaviors, or beliefs, among either *R1*s or *R2*s, which we would ordinarily identify as racist. However, there also is no change in mortgage policies, which ensures that more, and more beneficial, mortgages go to those with better credit ratings, and better credit ratings are assigned to those with greater assets. As a direct result of this state of affairs, *R2*s still have fewer good homes, less wealth, and a weaker sense of economic security than *R2*s have" (Glasgow, 72–73).
48. Glasgow, and *passim*.
49. Glasgow, 82ff.
50. Glasgow, 69, 80, 81.

51. Glasgow, 72ff.

52. I think that, in a properly virtues-based account, wrong-making must be driven by an action's or operation's vicious input, so as to exclude any such catalyzing by bad side effects.

53. Arthur, 14–15.

54. Bell, 55.

55. Glasgow, 84.

56. Glasgow, 64–65, 71, 92–93.

57. Glasgow, 16.

58. Glasgow, 91–92.

59. See Stephen Pinker, "The Stupidity of Dignity," *New Republic,* May 28, 2008; Peter Singer, "A Convenient Truth," *New York Times* (Op-Ed), January 26, 2007, http://www.nytimes.com/2007/01/26/opinion/26singer.html?_r=2&oref=slogin&.

60. See the President's Council on Bioethics, *Human Dignity and Bioethics: Essays Commissioned by the President's Council on Bioethics*, Washington, D.C., March 2008.

61. It should be noted that Martin Luther King Jr., apparently following his Boston University teachers or influenced by that intellectual ambience, sometimes classified his ethical position as "personalist." See his *Where Do We Go From Here?*, chapter 6, and his essays collected and edited by James Washington in King, *Testament of Hope*. (I owe this observation about Rev. King, and these citations, to a July 2014 conversation with Prof. Judith Green.) Martin Luther King, Jr., *Where Do We Go From Here?* (Boston: Beacon, 2010); Martin Luther King, Jr., *A Testament of Hope: The Essential Writings of Martin Luther King, Jr.*, ed. James Washington (San Francisco: Harper & Row, 1986). King, however, is said (by Green) to have meant his personalism to include both the thesis that "ultimate reality is of a personal character" and that individual persons have supreme value. My concern here is only with the latter thesis.

12

A FEMINIST DEFENSE OF THE COMPLEMENTARITY BETWEEN MEN AND WOMEN

Laura L. Garcia, Boston College

I wish to thank the audience at Xavier University in Cincinnati for their comments on an earlier version of this chapter, and Jorge Garcia and Sara Ellenbogen for helpful discussions of the themes of the chapter.

My thesis is that feminists should acknowledge and even celebrate the fact that there are inherent, natural differences between males and females and that these differences harmonize in such a way as to further the common good. I have argued previously that the fundamental value of human persons is grounded solely and completely in their nature or essence.[1] No properties, accidents, or characteristics can make someone more or less a human being, so every human being has the same intrinsic value and the same fundamental rights. This entails, of course, that men and women have the same value and the same human rights. For the purposes of this discussion, I will simply assume that men and women are equal in this sense.

The complementarity thesis I propose here consists of three claims: (1) there are significant, innate, gender-based differences between human males and females; (2) these differences complement each other so as to make collaboration between the sexes advantageous to both; and (3) promoting and celebrating women's distinctive strengths is essential to an authentic feminism. Appreciation for the gifts and insights of women offers the most compelling reason to encourage women's contributions to every sphere of society—education, medicine, law, politics, industry, finance, social services, and the entire range of human activities.

I divide my goal of defending complementarian feminism into four parts. The first part attempts to construct an adequate definition of feminism. I then offer a short history of feminism from the early twentieth century to the present, ending with a movement I call "fourth-wave feminism" or "personalist feminism." In the third section I argue in favor of the three claims above. Finally, I respond to some criticisms of complementarianism and end with the question of whether there is a distinctive vocation for women.

DEFINING FEMINISM

Feminism is famously difficult to define, since most definitions tend to be too wide or too narrow—either everyone is a feminist or no one is. It might be more helpful to speak of "feminisms" or different understandings of feminism, since feminism is a historical phenomenon that has taken many forms. My definition is more a general rubric that is specified by particular forms of feminism. I understand feminism (or a feminism) as having three parts: a view about the nature of women, moral and social implications of that view, and a program of action for enhancing the status of women and promoting their interests.

A broader definition of feminism is offered by Rosalind Delmar in an essay titled "What Is Feminism?" Delmar proposes a definition that captures virtually every form of feminism: it is "a concern with issues affecting women and a concern to advance women's interests."[2] This definition allows men to count as feminists, so some members of the feminist movement will reject it on those grounds alone. A deeper problem is that it lacks a view about the nature of women, making it difficult to describe women's interests. Are they different from men's interests, perhaps even in competition with them? Are women's interests mainly political, or do they include cultural attitudes about women? Delmar's definition includes the second two aspects of feminism but fails to explain their theoretical basis, so it's hard to see how a particular form of feminism arrives at definitions of "concern for women" and "the interests of women."

On the other hand, more detailed definitions of feminism are liable to result in endless controversy over what counts as true or authentic feminism. As Delmar notes, differing conceptions of feminism "have manifested themselves as a sort of sclerosis of the movement."[3] Significant numbers of women may conclude that they are not feminists, making it difficult for the movement to claim that it speaks for women and their interests. For an example of a narrow concept of feminism, we can look to bell hooks's (as she styles herself) definition in her book *Feminist Theory: From Margin to Center*.[4] She begins with a rather expansive definition: "Feminism is a movement to end sexist oppression."[5] That definition lacks a theoretical component, but hooks believes that a clear statement of the political agenda will enable feminists to develop the relevant theoretical context for it.

The claim that advancing the cause of women can only be served by overcoming (male) oppression, however, simply presupposes that male domination and subjugation of women is the primary obstacle to their flourishing. hooks does not consider her brand of feminism to be antimale, but her descriptions of male privilege and domination belie a hostility to men, especially white men, that puts them in the crosshairs of her revolutionary movement. In fact, hooks cites with approval philosopher John Hodge's contention that the nuclear family is the prime locus of male domination:

> It is in this form of the family where most children first learn the meaning and practice of hierarchical, authoritarian rule. Here is where they learn to accept group oppression against themselves as non-adults, and where they learn to accept male supremacy and the group oppression of women. . . . Here is where the relationship of superordination-subordination, of superior-inferior, or master-slave is first learned and accepted as "natural."[6]

The inflated rhetoric of this passage bears little resemblance to most American women's experience of family life, however. I suspect the use of hyperbole is one strategy for justifying the radical solution proposed by hooks: "Feminist movement to end sexist oppression can be successful only if we are committed to revolution, to the establishment of a new social order."[7] One conceptual difficulty with this view is that "we need to explicate further what it means to be oppressed 'because you are a woman.' E.g., is the idea that there is a particular form of oppression that is specific to women? Is to be oppressed 'as a woman' to be oppressed in a particular way? Or can we be pluralists about what sexist oppression consists in without fragmenting the notion beyond usefulness?"[8]

Setting that problem aside, we turn to the practical agenda that is common to most secular forms of feminism whatever their ideological commitments. For example, hooks folds certain moral and political commitments into her original definition of feminism as resisting sexism:

> Losing ground on the issue of legal, safe, inexpensive abortion means that women lose ground on all reproductive issues. The antichoice movement is fundamentally antifeminist. While it is possible for women to individually choose never to have an abortion, allegiance to feminist politics means that they still are prochoice, that they support the right of females who need abortions to choose whether or not to have them.[9] Apparently, prolife women need not apply—they are assumed to be on the side of the oppressors.

hooks's emphatic insistence on women's access to abortion is puzzling on three counts. First, the gains made by liberal and radical feminists in the 1980s and 1990s gave women the opportunity to have both a family and a job outside the home and to combine childrearing with graduate school. The original feminist rationale for promoting contraception and abortion was that it would enable women to compete with men in the workplace, and the silent assumption was that women could gain respect and equality with men only if they excelled in ways men value, approaching their work with the same motivations and priorities. Since that project was both ill conceived and unsuccessful, the continuing drumbeat for universal access to abortion is perplexing. The benefits of abortion for black women have always been a little obscure in a nation where over 50 percent of black pregnancies end in abortion. It is hard to see this as a gain for black women.

A further problem for hooks is that abortion "rights" have become virtually the sole focus of established national women's groups like the National Organization of Women. That organization lists its number one priority as "reproductive rights and justice": "NOW affirms that reproductive rights are issues of life and death for women, not mere matters of choice. NOW fully supports access to safe and legal abortion, to effective birth control and emergency contraception, to reproductive health services and education for all women."[10] hooks does not have a flattering opinion of the kind of feminist agenda embraced by NOW, which is one of reform within the current system rather than revolutionary transformation. In describing its six main priorities, NOW uses terms such as *affirms*, *supports*, *advocates*, *condemns*, and the like—hardly a call for revolution. In fact, NOW's mission statement reflects the genre of feminist literature hooks condemns, one produced by autonomy-obsessed, comfortably wealthy white women who offer at best a golf clap for the causes hooks holds dear.

Women outside academia and the upper middle class, says hooks, always "recognized the possibility that feminism defined as social equality with men might easily become a movement that would primarily affect the social standing of white women in middle and upper class groups while affecting only in a very marginal way the social status of working class and poor women."[11] Her analysis of the shortcomings of this feminist agenda is spot-on:

> Reformist feminism became their route to class mobility. They could break free of male domination in the workforce and be more self-determining in their lifestyles. While sexism did not end, they could maximize their freedom within the existing system. And they could count on there being a lower class of exploited subordinated women to do the dirty work they were refusing to do. . . . They give themselves the right to lead a double life, one where they are the equals of men in the workforce and at home when they want to be.[12]

Secondly, hooks repeatedly insists that contemporary feminism must be as inclusive as possible, taking into consideration women of every race, culture, and social class, and even recruiting men to the cause. In eliminating women who are prolife, however, she excludes with one stroke more than half the women and men in the country. The majority of women in the United States and a majority of Americans generally are against universal access to abortion.[13] Worse still, hooks wishes specifically to include black women in the struggle against sexism, resulting in a fusion of antisexism and antiracism. But her proabortion requirement ends up excluding more black women than it includes.[14]

It should be obvious at this point that defining feminism is almost as fraught as defending it. The definition I proposed above is intended to enable us to compare the forms that feminism has taken since its inception and to shed light on contemporary feminist theories, especially those that take their inspiration from past movements.

A BRIEF HISTORY OF FEMINISM

First-Wave Feminism

The women's movement of the early twentieth century focused primarily on the right to vote, but there were other important battles as well, such as the right to gain custody of one's children in a divorce. In 1920 the suffragists won a great victory when the Nineteenth Amendment to the Constitution was ratified, giving women in all fifty states the right to vote. It may not be coincidental that this recognition of women's rights passed into law shortly after the end of World War I, which had forced thousands of women into the workforce and into positions of responsibility previously unheard of for members of the "fairer sex."

Feminists of this era defended the equality of women by appealing to fundamental human rights. Many suffragists had participated in the abolitionist movement, which was animated especially by the efforts of women.[15] Early feminists argued that equality of the sexes is grounded on the same principle as racial equality—a shared human nature. The right to participate in forming the laws and policies of the state could not be withheld from some persons without contradicting one of the founding principles of the nation, that "all men are created equal" (where "men" in this context refers to all members of the human race). Denying women the vote would require showing that women were somehow "less human" than men. But it is clearly impossible to possess human nature (or any other nature) by degrees. One's nature is not a property of some kind that one *possesses*; it is *what one is*. Membership in a species is an all-or-nothing affair.

In 1998, on the 150th anniversary of the first women's rights convention in the United States, Rosemary Oelrich Bottcher offered this succinct description of the early feminist agenda:

> Elizabeth Cady Stanton and Lucretia Mott, who had met in London at the World AntiSlavery Convention in 1840, decided to organize a similar convention to discuss the issue of rights for women. In 1848, they and three other women met to plan such a convention at Seneca Falls, N.Y. They decided to develop a list of resolutions demanding that the rights of women be recognized. Stanton used the American Declaration of Independence as her guide in creating the Declaration of Sentiments to be presented to the convention delegates for approval.

> The resolutions in the Declaration of Sentiments denounced laws that discriminated against women and demanded that women be recognized as the full equals of men, having equal rights and equal responsibilities.[16]

During World War II, the economy began to recover from the Great Depression and the demand for women's labor reappeared. Rosie the Riveter became a symbol for the modern woman who rose to the challenge of keeping farms, factories, and mills running during the war. When the war ended, soldiers returned home to fill many of these positions. Some women continued to work, of course, whether out of desire or necessity, since countless husbands and fathers did not return. There is little evidence that postwar working women felt empowered by their role in the workplace, however. Perhaps this is because many had no other option, or because the jobs they held in factories and textile mills afforded little job satisfaction.

The 1950s marked the beginning of the baby boom, and men and women settled into the relative normalcy of family life following decades of social upheaval. Traditional roles for husbands and wives were the norm. Housing developments sprang up in outlying areas of the cities in order to accommodate these families, so the 1950s woman with children often found herself in the suburbs devoting most of her time tending to the home and the children. These wives and mothers did not spend all their time in the house, of course. Many found outlets for their talents in civic and educational organizations—churches, PTA, 4-H, and Junior League, among others. They formed networks of friendship within the neighborhood, looked out for one another's children, and got together over cards or coffee or developing plans for the next fund-raiser. Many volunteered at schools, hospitals, cultural events, and community centers, providing invaluable support and expertise in those community-building roles.

Suburban life suffered from certain drawbacks, however. It separated husbands and wives for a major part of each day and so contributed to the assumption that men and women were destined, by God or nature, to fit into narrowly prescribed roles. Women were to take care of the home and see to the children while men were to find a well-paying job to meet the family's financial needs. Women who pursued higher education or sought a job outside the home were frequently frowned upon, even by other women, on the assumption that they were probably neglecting their proper domestic responsibilities.

By the 1960s women began to chafe against societal expectations they perceived as restrictive and unfulfilling. While men reaped the benefits and rewards of paid work, women wore themselves out in domestic work that was unremunerated and underappreciated. Both in the home and the workplace, male attitudes toward women were often dismissive or condescending. Jokes about women and what we now call sexual harassment were the order of the day for women in public life. Cultural perceptions were based on the empirical fact that most women worked in the private sphere, which could easily be interpreted to mean that they weren't suited for anything else. Women were too vulnerable and emotional to survive in a man's world, on this view, and likely to be underqualified as well. Finally, the ideal of femininity inherited from previous generations dictated a certain mode of dress that included clothing and shoes that would make some jobs impossible for women to perform.

Second-Wave Feminism

Indignation about such perceptions and a desire for a wider range of opportunities fueled the women's movement of the 1960s and 1970s. This time, however, the argument for the equality of the sexes did not appeal to a shared human nature. Perhaps some felt this point had already been established in principle but was not being honored in practice. In spite of the gains in legal rights, women continued to receive fewer opportunities than men for pursuing education, careers, and political posts. As Christina Hoff Sommers explains in her 1994 book *Who Stole Feminism?*, "It is now commonplace for feminist philosophers to reject the Enlightenment ideals of the old feminism. According to the University of Colorado feminist theorist Alison Jaggar, 'Radical and socialist feminists have shown that the old ideals of freedom, equality and democracy are insufficient.'"[17]

The second-wave feminist movement organized women primarily to press for further legal and political reforms that would close the gap between women and men. Equality of the sexes would be demonstrated not by theoretical arguments but by showing that women could do whatever men could do just as well or better. Any woman who came of age during this era felt pressured to contribute to that mission. The fate of womankind seemed to rest on the ability and drive of younger women to enter traditionally male professions and excel in them. When asked about their plans after college, women felt uncomfortable saying they hoped to marry and have a family. Instead, they talked of graduate school, a challenging career, or joining the Peace Corps.

A parallel strategy attacked the traditional concept of femininity that had generated norms for clothing, behavior, and daily pursuits. These expectations tended to benefit men and hinder women, feminists argued, by keeping women in traditional roles so men could monopolize the world of work with its accompanying wealth, prestige, and power. This reaction triggered a major shift in women's fashions. Pantsuits appeared, then slacks, and finally jeans and overalls—formerly icons of masculinity. With jeans came sneakers, T-shirts, denim jackets, and hiking boots. While reports of bra-burning ceremonies are probably exaggerated, younger women often opted to forego uncomfortable, China-doll clothing and confining bras, girdles, nylons, and spiked heels.

Such theoretical underpinnings as there were for second-wave feminism resembled Marxist social theory. The egalitarian goals of communism, with its determination to undermine distinctions among workers, appealed to many. Angela Davis, writing in 1981, envisioned a world in which no woman would be burdened with domestic tasks like cleaning, cooking, and caring for children: "What is needed, of course, are new social institutions to assume a good portion of the housewife's old duties. This is the challenge emanating from the swelling ranks of women in the working class. The demand for universal and subsidized child care is a direct consequence of the rising number of working mothers."[18]

Women taking on the challenges of graduate degrees and demanding careers could view themselves as contributing to this vision. Instead of feeling guilty about hiring others for domestic tasks and care of the children, women should perhaps embrace that arrangement as necessary for their self-fulfillment and for equality with men. Even women without this socialist agenda could tell themselves that pursuit of a career or significant periods of absence from the home was actually in the interest of their children. After all, they reasoned, children will not be happy if their mother is unhappy. While Davis's vision of specialized cadres of supercleaners moving from house to house was unrealistic, it had a certain appeal for women burdened with demanding jobs as well as a long list of household responsibilities.

Second-wave feminism and its agenda dominated the academy, the press, and the entertainment world for many years. It became famous for consciousness-raising sessions for suburban housewives who might not realize how oppressed and miserable they were, and for bumper sticker slogans like "A woman without a man is like a fish without a bicycle." Women's desires and abilities had been suppressed for far too long, the movement claimed, while society acquiesced in a pervasive patriarchy in the family and the public realm alike.

While it does not follow from the existence of male/female inequalities that men are responsible for them, second-wave feminists perceived male attitudes of superiority toward women as the main factor preventing women from achieving the kind of success men have attained. Sommers notes that "feminist ideology [of this kind] has taken a decisive, gynocentric turn, and the emphasis now is on women as a political class whose interests are at odds with the interests of men."[19] Resentment of men sometimes reached a fever pitch, as when University of Michigan law professor Catherine MacKinnon opined that "perhaps the wrong of rape has proven so difficult to articulate because the unquestionable starting point has been that rape is definable as distinct from intercourse, when for women it is difficult to distinguish them under conditions of male dominance."[20]

Second-wave feminism won many important victories for women, opening doors that had long been closed to them, but it ultimately came to grief over several issues. First, leaders of the movement claimed to speak for women in general, characterizing them as an oppressed group of persons who must overthrow their oppressors; that is, men in general, by revolutionary means if necessary. This hostility toward men failed to resonate with many women, so rallying phrases like "sisterhood is powerful" rang hollow for them. Not all women shared the same political or personal agenda, so the radical feminist program for advancing the cause of women appeared to some to be irrelevant or even counterproductive.

Second, founders of second-wave feminism pressed for equal treatment on the grounds that women are identical with men in every important respect. Some insisted that the very meanings of "woman" and "man" are culturally constructed, based on deep-seated prejudices, assumptions, and stereotypes rather than on reality. This social construction theory of gender gained credibility from sexist attitudes and practices that persisted even after legal and political victories for women made them illicit.[21] Second-wave feminists feared, with some justification, that acknowledging objective differences between the sexes would open the door to continued discrimination against women.

Social constructionism continues to have its defenders, mainly in the academy. Some wish to eliminate "woman" and "man" from the language in the hope that this will lead to a more flexible conception of sex differences. Another strategy is to substitute the term *gender* for *sex*, since there are only two sexes but one might imagine several gender types that would accommodate homosexual and bisexual persons. This strategy has largely succeeded, so that the term *gender* no longer refers to one's sex—an objective, inherent, fixed feature of individual persons.[22] Rather, it is used to capture any set of sexual inclinations, preferences, and practices in various combinations. We might call this the silly-putty definition of gender since, at last count, Facebook listed fifty-six different genders.[23] Overlap or even identity between two genders is not problematic in the new parlance, since genders are fluid, subjective, and generally thought of as chosen self-descriptions. In my view, this outcome qualifies as a *reductio ad absurdum* of the new concept of gender. Of course, not every second-wave feminist supports the shift from a clear definition of women, since without such a definition it is impossible to determine which set of persons is suffering from discrimination.

Third, the strategy of urging women into male-dominated professions in order to prove themselves men's equals began to backfire. Under the guise of equal treatment of workers, some employers removed whatever they had in place to accommodate women. The young women who bought into the feminist agenda found when they married and had children that the dual obligations of work and family were too much to handle. In order to address this problem, feminists argued that husbands should be lobbied into a 50/50 division of housework and child-rearing duties. But not every woman saw this goal as desirable, and almost none achieved it. In spite of its almost self-evident reasonability, the 50/50 goal simply presupposes that men and women are essentially interchangeable, so that this arrangement will mean that the interests, values, and desires of each spouse are equally accommodated. Since women and men are not interchangeable in this way, however, parsing the division of labor in a home in purely numerical terms came to seem both overly simplistic and completely unworkable.

The fourth and most serious blow to second-wave feminism was its tendency to press for ever more radical reforms that fewer and fewer women identified with. Feminists determined to keep women competitive with men in the workplace lobbied for universal access to contraception and abortion so pregnancy and children would not interfere with women's productivity. To be fair, many men voiced similar reservations about women's ability to perform on the same level as men, since pregnancy and a greater burden of child care are likely to diminish their availability and productivity. A recent *non sequitur* cartoon depicts a man behind a large desk, obviously a high-level company executive, interviewing a woman for a job. The caption underneath reads: "The Antonym of Progress in Action," since the boss is saying, "OK, first things first. Before I look at your resume, we need to talk about contraception." The sad fact is that second-wave feminists simply accepted this attitude rather than challenging it as inherently sexist and insulting to women.

The 1960s feminist movement fought tirelessly and tenaciously for the rights of women to enter the workplace, receive the same wages as men, take legal action against sexual harassment, and so on. Liberating women to pursue activities and employment outside the home is an important goal—indeed a requirement of justice—but feminist rhetoric of this era also tended to heap scorn on housekeeping and child care as unworthy of women's intelligence and talents. Work at home was portrayed as pure drudgery, a form of indentured servitude perpetuated by men in order to keep women "in their place."

For women who were unaware of their own subjugation, feminists made use of television, magazines, and pamphlets, and launched consciousness-raising groups to educate women about the perils of patriarchy and the need to overthrow it. The goal was to make women angry enough about their victimization at the hands of men to support the feminist cause. However, many joined the movement without having a clear understanding of what the feminist cause amounted to. As spokeswomen for the movement became ever more radical, they attracted fewer and fewer ordinary women to their cause. Most centrally, feminists' hostility toward men, marriage, and motherhood alienated the vast majority of women who (perhaps secretly) actually liked men and might even want to marry one of them.

Some women were offended by feminist attitudes of contempt for women who devoted their lives to home and children; that is, women like their mothers and grandmothers. Second-wave feminists accurately described the culture's lack of respect for so-called women's work. Unfortunately, in trying to free women to pursue an education or a practice a profession, they also bought into the widespread (mostly male) assumption that staying at home was a waste of women's time. As early as 1949, in an interview with Betty Friedan, feminist Simone de Beauvoir declared, "No, we don't believe that any woman should have this choice. No woman should be authorized to stay at home to bring up her children. Society should be totally different. Women should not have that choice, precisely because if there is such a choice, too many women will make that one. It is a way of forcing women in a certain direction."

Taking her cue from de Beauvoir, 1970s feminist wild card Shulamith Firestone suggested that women create a female-only society using the new reproductive technologies and so eliminate the need for men altogether.[24] By the 1990s, Rutgers University law professor Drusilla Cornell was arguing that children should be brought up by groups of women in a kind of mothering co-op and men should be limited to sending their paychecks, since that is their only useful role.[25] Philosopher Jeffner Allen trumped these proposals by advising women to take a twenty-year moratorium on bearing children in order to devote themselves to the pursuit of economic and political power.[26]

As feminist rhetoric grew more radical, it lost its appeal for many women, even among those who thought of themselves as feminists. Elizabeth Fox-Genovese, a social scientist, historian, and women's studies professor, published a groundbreaking book in 1996 titled *Feminism Is Not the Story of My Life*. Her research showed that most contemporary women place a high value on marriage and children and want to spend significant time at home with their children, and they see these goals as incompatible with the feminist agenda as they understand it.[27]

Finally, women who had entered the workforce, especially in professions that are not "on the clock," found the dual demands of work and family life both exhausting and demoralizing. Many wondered why they could not find a livable balance between employment and attention to their husbands, children, and the environment of their homes. The latter concerns, contrary to radical feminism, are not necessarily forced on wives and mothers; rather, women already care about these things and want to do justice to each of them. Unfortunately, employers and institutions had done little to adapt to the influx of women into their ranks, and their expectations were guided by their experience of what men could accomplish, not taking into account the fact that men usually had wives to handle everything on the home front. This situation led to a common refrain among working moms: "What I need is a wife."

THIRD-WAVE FEMINISM

In the 1980s and 1990s, a third form of feminism began to take shape. Instead of insisting on identity between women and men, this approach pointed to differences between the two that tended to favor the distinctive traits of women over those of men. Several influential academic publications in the social sciences reported on research indicating significant differences between the sexes with respect to conversation styles and moral problem solving. Educational psychologist Carol Gilligan's *In a Different Voice*[28] summarized several studies showing that females resolve moral dilemmas by means that are virtually never used by males, such as trying to alter the situation by talking to the parties involved or looking for a third alternative. Her conclusion was that women operate from an ethics of care while men tend to apply moral rules in order to achieve a rational and just solution.

Linguistics professor Deborah Tannen authored two best sellers on the different conversational styles of men and women, along with some speculation about the psychological traits underlying these distinctive ways of communicating.[29] The psychological difference Tannen invokes most frequently is the male orientation toward rank and competition versus the female world of connection and understanding.

Even as they spoke, however, it was clear that difference feminists are reluctant to give up their credentials as second-wave feminists with an added curlicue. In *You Just Don't Understand!* Tannen spends three hundred pages detailing the differences between men and women with no suggestion that either sex is likely to change—rather, women can understand men's conversational style (and vice versa) once they are aware of the attitudes and beliefs behind what men say. Yet in the final section of the book, Tannen claims that "these differing understandings of independence grow out of the distinct kinds of relations women and men learn and practice as boys and girls growing up."[30] It is hard to imagine that parents and other adults have the power to instill such fixed and fundamentally different attitudes and values in the first few years of a child's life. More to the point, unless sex differences are deeply ingrained and nearly universal, Tannen would not be able to track the effects of those differences on everything from sex to minivans.

Philosopher Sara Ruddick's book *Maternal Thinking*[31] celebrated the cognitive skills and moral virtues required for effective mothering, showing that these are just as rigorous and demanding as skill at logic or abstract reasoning. By making motherhood respectable again, Ruddick enabled thousands of academic and professional women to prioritize their families over their careers. Rather than denigrating the work of women in raising children and nurturing relationships, Ruddick celebrated such work and insisted on its importance. Women gradually began to grow bolder in stressing the value of raising healthy, loving adults.

Ruddick makes a beautiful and compelling case for the importance of the kind of thinking mothers do in order to keep their children safe and help them mature. She might have gone on to celebrate the sex-specific traits that make women good mothers and enable them more generally to attend to individual persons who need understanding and empathy. This would underline the fact that women bring certain strengths and capacities to the table that, by and large, men do not.

Sadly, Ruddick undermines her own thesis by claiming that maternal thinking can be done just as well by men. This is a puzzling remark, since all her examples of maternal thinking are about (female) mothers and describe struggles and dilemmas that women solve in their own way— consulting other mothers, listening to anecdotes and comparing them to one's own situation, and trusting their own instincts. These are not problem-solving strategies typical of men. In her defense, suggesting that women have capacities and sensitivities that differ from those of men might have been academic suicide in 1985. But by 1995, in the preface for her book's second printing, Ruddick seems to have given up on sex differences altogether, taking pains to insist that "it is not difficult to imagine men taking up mothering as easily and successfully as women— or conversely, women as easily declining to mother as men."[32] Perhaps this is not difficult to imagine but it is surely difficult to believe.

When Ruddick turns in the second half of her book to considerations of justice and peace, she contends that if women were in positions of power there would be fewer wars. This is because, as she puts it, women know the value of the human body. A pregnant woman's body is intimately bound up with that of another, and she brings that body into the world with much labor and suffering. For a mother, an injured body is a violation of something sacred.[33] But it cannot be true both that women operate from different insights, sensitivities, and priorities than men and that there are no significant differences between the sexes. If the latter is true, war is just as likely to happen with women in charge as it is with men.

A PARENTHESIS: FLAUNT-IT FEMINISM

A peculiar form of feminism emerged in the late 1980s, personified by Madonna with her "Boy Toy" T-shirts and hypersexualized dance routines. This woman-as-seductress feminism might be described as the bastard child of radical feminism and difference feminism. It takes the radical feminist claim that women are exactly like men and applies it to sex. Women are just as interested in superficial sexual liaisons as are men, the story goes, and just as eager to experiment or "play the field" without making any commitments. In keeping with difference feminism, however, there is also an affirmation of feminine distinctiveness.

The second-wave feminist notes in Madonna's attitude included radical independence in dress and behavior, though her style was the polar opposite of 1960s feminists' commitment to eschewing makeup and sexy outfits as a way of showing their contempt for male expectations. Feminists of that era deplored standards of femininity designed to sexualize women, since they presented women primarily as objects of male desire or as accessories of successful men ("trophy wives"). Madonna, in celebrating individuality and women's' hold on male desires, dressed as provocatively as legally possible and encouraged other women to do the same, using their influence over men to get what they wanted—especially money, status, and expensive clothes. As Madonna sings it, "We're living in a material world and I am a material girl."[34]

Flaunt-it feminism freed women from the deliberate sexlessness of earlier feminist fashion and encouraged them to dress in ways calculated to appeal to (gasp!) men. But there is a mean streak in this form of feminism. It takes the goal of women to be power, especially power over men, by taking advantage of their more active libido to manipulate and dominate them, in effect turning them into sugar daddies. For Madonna, boys are toys too. Flaunt-it feminists promote their agenda largely through music and their charismatic public personae rather than through political speeches or academic books.

It is clearly a young woman's feminism with its emphasis on sexiness, flirtation, and free-spiritedness, and this limits its appeal. It is as shallow and ephemeral as the baubles and glamor it glorifies. But the greatest flaw in flaunt-it feminism is neither its limited appeal nor its shallow consumerism. It is the cynical message that there can be no genuine, trusting relationships between women and men. Instead, women must allow men to treat them as objects so they can treat men as objects. This hardly seems like a winning strategy for advancing the cause of women.

FOURTH-WAVE FEMINISM

The new millennium ushered in a different form of feminism, one that acknowledges the significant empirical and social differences between men and women and celebrates the strengths of each—especially focusing on those of women. Authentic feminism can only flourish in the real world. This does not mean that cultural changes in the treatment of women are impossible, but it acknowledges the empirical facts and includes them in its understanding of the nature of women and of the strategies that will best serve their interests. Here I refer to this view either as fourth-wave feminism or personalist feminism. Some refer to it as the new feminism, but of course it will not always be new.

The first pillar of personalist feminism is that acknowledging differences between the sexes does not justify denying basic human rights to anyone. It may be true that, in practice, some will appeal to the characteristics more common to women as a pretext for restricting them to a narrow sphere of activity. This must be resisted by arguments and political action alike. On the other hand, a "thicker" understanding of the qualities, concerns, and priorities of women and men can reveal the ways in which they complement one another, making for fruitful collaborations both in the home and in the workplace.

Wikipedia describes fourth-wave feminism as follows:

> New feminism, as a form of difference feminism, supports the idea that men and women have different strengths, perspectives, and roles,

while advocating for the equal worth and dignity of both sexes. Among its basic concepts are that the most important differences are those that are biological rather than cultural. new Feminism holds that women should be valued in their role as child bearers, both culturally and economically. . . . Its main aim is to promote the idea that women are individuals with equal worth as men; and that in social, economic and legal senses they should be equal, while accepting the natural differences between the sexes.[35]

Personalist feminism, which includes complementarianism, also celebrates the achievements of women in the traditional roles that radical feminism tended to despise—wife, mother, child-care worker, community volunteer, and so on. In fact, women's recognition of the priority of persons over things embodies a fundamental moral outlook that should inform the entire culture. My choice of the term *personalist feminism* is meant to capture this movement's commitment to the immeasurable value of human beings. This may seem like an obvious truth, but many of our social policies conflict with it.

An extended philosophical case for the priority of persons can be found in the personalist philosophy of Karol Wojtyła (Pope John Paul II). In a series of university lectures, later published as *Love and Responsibility*,[36] Wojtyła argues that the self-determining nature of human beings entails that they are essentially irreplaceable or nonsubstitutable. One person's will can never become the will of another, as each is inviolable in his or her inner agency. "The point here is not that a person is a unique and unrepeatable entity," Wojtyła explains, "for this can be said just as well of any entity. . . . The incommunicable, the inalienable, in a person is intrinsic to that person's inner self, to the power of self-determination, free will. No one else can want for me."[37]

Wojtyła adds that these facts about the nature of persons present us with an absolute moral obligation to respect their dignity and to respond to them as beings like ourselves, subjects of their own acts. This echoes Immanuel Kant's second formulation of the categorical imperative, the fundamental law of morality: act in such a way that you always treat humanity, whether in your own person or in the person of any other, never simply as a means, but always at the same time as an end. Wojtyła takes Kant a step further, arguing that what we owe to persons includes not only refraining from treating them as objects or instrumental goods, but also a positive concern for their well-being. On this view, the fundamental moral norm is: "The person is a good towards which the only proper and adequate attitude is love."[38] We ought to care about persons, since this is what we most deeply want from them. Even if there is nothing they can do to benefit us, we want them to wish us well—we want to matter to them.

This view of persons shapes personalist feminism in its commitment to the flourishing of every human, male or female. It is a commitment to one's own flourishing as well, since one is also a person deserving of love. Fourth-wave feminists do not see men (or other people generally) as potential enemies of their happiness. Rather, since humans require loving relationships in order to flourish, the goal is to foster relationships of love and respect among those within one's sphere of influence.

Personalist feminism thus incorporates the concern for justice and equal opportunity characteristic of second-wave feminism. While justice is not all that we owe to others, it is certainly the bare minimum. But their program for advancing justice for women distances itself from 1960s-style feminism's major ideological commitments and their gender-neutralizing strategy for overcoming sexism. We might describe personalist feminism as a marriage between difference feminism (interpreted a certain way) and complementarianism. It values women and the things women value while also appreciating men and their distinctive qualities.

Personalist feminism celebrates the invaluable contributions women have made in the demanding traditional roles that radical feminists viewed as demeaning and merely servile—wife, mother, homemaker, educator of children, community volunteer, and so on. Since women place the good of persons above other goods, it is to be expected that they will give special importance to tasks that further human formation and flourishing. Further, these tasks cannot be done well without intelligence, thoughtfulness, commitment, attentiveness, and a life worthy of being a role model for one's children (and their friends). The 1960s feminists fought to increase the number of opportunities available to women, and there is nothing wrong with that goal. But it need not entail a denigration of the work women have done for centuries. Since the next generation will shape the world of the future, helping children grow into thoughtful, well-adjusted adults is arguably the most important social task there is.

Personalist feminists and their opponents agree, however, that women should not be disadvantaged in the workplace when they take time away from it to focus on their children. On this point, most new feminists agree with St. John Paul II that there is no justice for women without the freedom to create a workable relationship between public and private roles. I cite him at length here since he eloquently summarizes both the principles and the practical agenda of personalist feminism, including giving women penalty-free time with their children:

> It is a fact that in many societies women work in nearly every sector of life. But it is fitting that they should be able to fulfill their tasks in accordance with their own nature, without being discriminated against and without being excluded from jobs for which they are capable, but also without lack of respect for their family aspirations and for their specific role in contributing, together with men, to the good of society. The true advancement of women requires that labor should be structured in such a way that women do not have to pay for their advancement by abandoning what is specific to them and at the expense of the family, in which women as mothers have an irreplaceable role.[39]

Operating on this principle would not prevent single women, wives, and mothers from holding jobs. In fact, as we will see, there are strong reasons to include women in every sphere of society.

Second-wave feminists have continued to lose ground in today's culture, ironically because women want more choices than they envisaged. The majority of women want to marry and have children, and many want it more than they want to have the respect, authority, and salary that count as success in public life. But these are not the only two options. Younger women assume that if the marketplace undervalues or penalizes women for devoting time to their children, it is the marketplace that needs to change. If male attitudes toward caring for children and making the home a pleasant environment are dismissive, it is those attitudes that need to change. These women wonder why they are expected to choose between having a family and getting an education or having children and pursuing a career. True freedom for women, it seems, would allow them to harmonize these goals.

In 1963 the federal government passed the Equal Pay Act, which required employers to compensate women and men equally for doing the same job. This was a major step forward, since women had often been paid much less than men even when working at the same job for the same employer. Some women pressed for even more radical reforms, such as paying women for the work they do in the home. For a time, this proposal was up for serious consideration, but many politicians were skeptical that it could be adequately funded and properly implemented. Eventually, second-wave feminism turned from supporting women in the home to "liberating" them from it, reversing whatever momentum the proposal had at the time.

Given this background, it raised some eyebrows when Pope John Paul II revived the idea in a discussion of women's labor:

> Just remuneration for the work of an adult who is responsible for a family means remuneration which will suffice for establishing and properly maintaining a family and for providing security for its future. Such remuneration can be given either through what is called a family wage—that is, a single salary given to the head of the family for his work, sufficient for the needs of the family without the other spouse having to take up gainful employment outside the home—or through other social measures such *as family allowances or grants to mothers devoting themselves exclusively to their families. These grants should correspond to the actual needs, that is, to the number of dependents for as long as they are not in a position to assume proper responsibility for their own lives.*[40]

Proposals to require a living wage for heads of households or to remunerate women for their work in giving formation to their children have met with strong opposition from free market advocates. But since the market lacks a conscience, interventions are necessary at various points to prevent injustices to workers, monopolies, price fixing, and the like. While there is more than one way to reward the work of women in the home, failing to offer financial support effectively penalizes them for engaging in work that the society desperately needs them to do, and to do well.

Finally, personalist feminists insist that women be valued for their own sake, not as instrumental to the advancement of men or to other ends outside themselves. Similarly, men must be valued for their own sake, not as instrumental to obtaining money, prestige, or power. All human persons are called to work, to the privilege of contributing to the common good. When men and women are aware of and grateful for the contributions of each gender to that task, the so-called war between the sexes can transform into a productive partnership.

COMPLEMENTARIANISM

In what follows, we examine the three key components of the thesis laid out in the beginning: (1) there are inherent and ineradicable differences between women and men; (2) these differences complement one another so as to foster fruitful collaboration between the sexes in both private and public spheres; and (3) authentic feminism requires a recognition of (1) and (2). First, though, we need a clearer definition of complementarianism.

What Is Complementarianism?

Defining complementarianism is almost as difficult as defining feminism. Some interpretations prescribe limited social roles for women and emphasize the authority of men in family and public life. Others are so eager to emphasize differences between the sexes that they portray women and men as coming from different species—maybe even different planets.[41]

Philosopher Prudence Allen, in her comprehensive two-volume history of the concept of woman, defines complementarianism by way of contrast with two (main) competing views. Allen's proposed categories for theories about men and women have become standard among new feminists. According to Allen, the *sex identity* position views men and women as identical in most respects and declares that they are equals—morally, intellectually, and socially. *Sex polarity* theories accept important differences between the sexes and see these as leading to tension and hostility between the two so that one is considered superior to the other. She defines *sex complementarity* as "a belief in the equal dignity and worth of women and men that at the same time recognizes significant differences between the two sexes."[42]

While this captures virtually every form of complementarianism, it says nothing about which differences between the sexes are significant. On the other hand, as Allen rightly points out, "there has been very little attempt to develop a systematic foundation for a theory of sex complementarity."[43] In fact, she is among the first in this generation to undertake that project.[44]

While she is sympathetic with Allen's theory, lawyer and author Erika Bachiochi suggests abandoning the term *complementarity* in favor of *sexual asymmetry*, since that terminology "allows us to talk about sexual difference, and women's disproportionate burden in reproduction, without drawing ultimate conclusions about women's roles in their families or in society."[45] Bachiochi is probably right that talk of sex complementarity has the potential to scare off feminists who are leery of any view that might imply rigid social roles for women. But limiting the discussion to biological asymmetries, especially those that result in "the disproportionate burden women have in reproduction," could be seen as supporting the radical feminist agenda of erasing such asymmetries through contraception and abortion.

This is the polar opposite of the position Bachiochi defends in the rest of her paper, of course, and she does a masterful job of how to equalize the playing field without resorting to the war on female fertility. My concern is not with her conclusions but with the strategy, though of course the test of any strategy is whether it works, and Bachiochi is absolutely right in noting that so far it has not even been tried.

While no definition will satisfy everyone, I offer the following description: complementarianism is the view that there are significant psychological, physiological, and other differences between men and women and that these differences are conducive to productive collaborations between women and men in both private and public life. In what follows, I will sketch some of these differences and offer some reasons to think that they mesh in positive ways.

Sex Differences

Beyond the obvious biological differences between the sexes, empirical evidence for sex-specific traits is overwhelming. It comes from many different sciences and includes controls for differences of age, race, social class, nationality, and so on. There are two important factors to bear in mind with respect to these findings. First, some evidence of features typical of men or women finds differences that are statistically significant but not necessarily free from exceptions. This allows for the possibility that the distribution of a particular trait might in principle be explained differently; for example, by environmental factors of some kind. It is also one reason that research in this area often focuses on newborns or very young children.

Second, even when a trait is exhibited exclusively by women or men and tracks differences in hormones or brain structures, it is possible to devise a competing theoretical explanation of those facts. Some scientists working in this field are not convinced that being genetically male or female is the key to explaining the behavioral and psychological differences between the sexes.

Physical and Social Differences

The most obvious reason to suspect that there are important differences between the sexes is that their bodies are different, and not just in the way every human body is different from every other. Human beings exist only as male or female. Clearly, women and men make different contributions to procreation. A woman carries a child in her womb for nine months and can provide all the nourishment he or she needs for many months after birth. It is hardly surprising, then, that women are especially attuned to the needs of persons and have greater capacities than men for recognizing those needs. Fathers are outside the intimate events of pregnancy, childbirth, and breast feeding, but they focus on the task of protecting the mother and child, especially when they are most vulnerable. This is a natural, hence traditional, role for men, and one consistent with their greater physical strength and their typical focus on the big picture.

Second-wave feminists denied the significance of these biological differences and claimed that even mentioning them smacked of sexism. After all, Western culture has associated women with the "dark side" of the ancient dichotomies: women are emotional/men are rational, women are the body/men are the mind, women are passive/men are active, and more. The concern is that focusing on biological differences will play into these stereotypes. The 1960s feminists fought these stereotypes by insisting that bodily differences play no role in explaining behavioral or social differences; these are simply products of social conditioning. But as Sara Ruddick points out, an adequate feminism must acknowledge the very different relationships women and men have to human birth.

Brain Differences

The most compelling evidence for differences between the sexes comes from neurological research on brain structures and activity, as well as studies of the influence of hormones on women's health, including their risk factors for depression and heart disease. Brain research made a giant leap forward with the advent of MRIs (Magnetic Resonance Imaging), which allow for noninvasive observations of brain activity when subjects are performing various tasks. Evidence of gender differences in the brain is striking, and it is beginning to change the practice of medicine. Scientists now agree that there are innate differences between males and females and that these differences affect their favored activities, primary interests, emotional states, and approaches to work and relationships.[46]

Males have smaller brains than females but greater facility with spatial perception. Men are able to focus on a task with one side of the brain alone, and tend to compartmentalize different kinds of activity. In a study of how men and women view works of art, researchers found that "while both sexes use parts of the brain associated with spatial awareness to process beauty, men use an area associated with big-picture thinking, while women also use a region linked to local details."[47] Men do better than women on tasks involving mechanical reasoning and spatial visualization.

In females, the language center of the brain is larger and more complex than in males. Women have better hearing and are better at distinguishing different tones of voice. Both sides of a woman's brain are active at all times, and there is much more interaction between different areas of the brain. Women do better than men on such tasks as language skills, spelling, and perceptual speed. They have much greater facility in reading emotions than men do. This is humorously illustrated in a cartoon that depicts a wife standing in the kitchen when her husband walks in. She is holding a large sign that reads, "I'M ANGRY," and he says, "Something's wrong. I can tell by that sign you're holding."

With respect to social characteristics, boys tend to play alone or side by side rather than with others, and they are much more action-oriented than girls. Males usually speak only about basic facts when recounting a past event, so their descriptions are briefer than those of females. Men value physical strength, athletic ability, ambition, competitiveness, and dominance much more than females do, and more of their brain cells are devoted to these pursuits. On average, men think about sex a hundred times a day, and male hormones make pleasurable sex independent of psychological states like feelings of closeness.

Unlike boys, girls tend to play in groups with other girls, and females are much more relationship-oriented than males. Women have better recall of emotionally charged situations and tend to provide more context and detail in recounting past events. On average, women think about sex once a day, and female hormones and emotional sensitivities make pleasurable sex heavily dependent on positive psychological states like feeling safe, cherished, attractive, and so on.

This is just a brief overview of the extensive research on gender differences. Findings from the social sciences are naturally more general than those deriving from studies of body chemistry or the brain. Some sex-specific traits are common to most women or men, but a particular woman may have some of the characteristics more typical of men and vice versa. Some exceptions to the rule might be explained by physiological factors (e.g., hormone levels) that are atypical for persons of that sex, but it is safe to say that not every departure from the norm can be accounted for in this way. Still, the day has passed when sex-based differences could be dismissed as idle speculation.

Occupational Differences

So far we have looked at biological differences between males and females and some of the differences in the way they interact with others, solve problems, talk, play, and think. This research casts doubt on second-wave feminists' implicit belief that men's and women's desires and preferences are more or less the same. If there is a paucity of women in a given line of work, radical feminists reasoned, the obvious culprit is discrimination against women. This assumption missed the possibility that in choosing an occupation, women might use a set of criteria different from that of men.

Complementarianism offers an alternative explanation for vocational differences between men and women. In some cases at least, it may be that few women or men want to do a particular kind of work. While discrimination might also play a role, it is not especially mysterious if men's and women's strengths, foci, and priorities draw them in the direction of different kinds of work. To take one example, in comparison with men, women are both better equipped for and more interested in caring for children and creating a positive home environment. A 2012 *New York Times* article cited a study that concluded: "Men have more than doubled the time they spend on child care since 1985. Yet women still spend twice as much time with the kids as men."[48] This might be due to male oppression, of course, but it might also be due to a mother's greater interest in being available to her children.

In fact, evidence suggests that women's career choices often differ from those of men. We have noted that women tend toward person-oriented activities and pursuits where their ability to articulate emotional content and to identify the needs of individuals is especially important. Men gravitate toward activities that are oriented toward things, where physical strength, mechanical ingenuity, self-reliance, and competitiveness are key. These facts are hardly reason to exclude a man or woman from a particular occupation, of course, or to force them into jobs in which they have no interest.

Here the relevant differences between the sexes pertain to general characteristics and typical pursuits, aptitudes, priorities, values, and so on. Unlike intellectual abilities or skill sets, they are operative in a person's every activity, since they stem from being a male or a female. They influence desires, evaluations, interests, and even perceptions, but they do not dictate a particular role or arrangement of tasks in public or private life. In these matters, it seems, we are condemned to be free.

The Dutch research company Statistics Netherland published a study in 2005 on occupational differences between men and women across Europe. They found that the top ten women-dominated positions (those with the greatest percentage of women over men), from highest to lowest, were student nurse, day care worker, nurse, home nurse, secretary, executive secretary, medical receptionist, pharmaceutical assistant, and medical secretary. The top ten male-dominated occupations were welder, HVAC technician (heating, ventilation, and air conditioning), auto mechanic, carpenter, electrician, bus driver, bricklayer, road paver, construction mechanic, and landscaper. All of the women-dominated occupations had at least some men in them, but there were no women in the top three male-dominated occupations.

For occupations that are probably equally attractive to both sexes, the percentages of men and women were the same. Such occupations include academic, lawyer, judge, retail manager, and designer. Statistics lend themselves to more than one interpretation, of course, but gender differences offer a plausible explanation of discrepancies between women and men in choosing an occupation. Since each occupation makes an important contribution to the common good, it seems that encouraging men and women to choose an occupation in line with their desires and interests will both serve the needs of the society and honor personal preferences. The Dutch study also suggests that the 1960s feminist agenda of engineering a 50/50 split between men and women in every occupation would actually undermine women's freedom in the name of advancing it.

Male/Female Collaboration

We focus next on fourth-wave feminists' claim that differences between men and women make collaboration between the two fruitful and even necessary for human flourishing. Prudence Allen points to what is perhaps the best reason to take complementarianism seriously. "[*Sex complementarity*] seems to me," she says, "to be the only theory that presents an integrated view of the place of materiality [i.e., the body] in human identity and for this reason it also seems to offer the greatest possibility for fertile and creative relations between men and women."[49]

Her point is not that humans should be reduced to their biology, but that humans are by their very nature embodied, and this has significance for the human vocation. Male and female bodies are themselves different and make different contributions to procreation, so the species cannot survive unless men and women cooperate voluntarily in welcoming children and caring for them. A child belongs equally to both parties—not as a possession but as a gift and a responsibility. Since human children take many years to reach maturity, a child's mother and father are joined in a shared project that will occupy them, in many ways, for the rest of their lives. Even from an evolutionary point of view, it makes sense that differences between women and men would make them a good team for these purposes.

Since the qualities of both sexes contribute something unique to this task, there is a natural incentive for couples to stay together—each recognizing the importance of the other's perspective and sensitivities. In spite of the high incidence of divorce, most people view the dissolution of a marriage as a tragedy, not a triumph—especially when children are involved. Everyone recognizes that the harm to a child cannot be undone simply by adding another person to the home, as if the main thing were to have two caregivers instead of one. It is the loss of a father or a mother, of mothering or fathering, that breaks a child's heart, and in spite of what many feminists claim, these are not the same thing.

Given the numerous and important physiological and psychological differences between women and men, it should simply be admitted that women are better equipped than men for some (certainly not all) home-related tasks. In particular, a woman's greater facility in reading the emotional states of others through their facial expression, tones of voice, and body language gives her greater insight into individual persons and their needs. In family life, women (generally speaking) see their primary role as caring for the others and helping them to develop physically, emotionally, spiritually, and socially. They are the guardians of relationships, and they work to maintain strong and healthy relationships both within the family and between the family and those outside it.

As reams of studies show, children also need their fathers. But men bring a different toolbox to the job—not better or more important, just different. Even looking at the short list above of male and female characteristics, the obvious conclusion is that men and women complement each other. A father sees his primary responsibility within the family as providing for their material needs and protecting them from harm. Most men measure their success as husbands and fathers by their ability to do these tasks well. For the most part, a man's greater strength and protective instincts better equip him to fend off dangers to the family from forces outside it.

Some feminists are as suspicious of protecting as providing, however. Deborah Tannen is especially hostile to the male instinct to keep women safe. In her view, to be protected is to be cast in the role of a child. "Along with the privilege of being protected comes the loss of rights, and not being respected and treated like a full-fledged person. Being the protector frames someone as competent, capable, and deserving of respect. Being protected frames one as incompetent, incapable, and deserving of indulgence."[50] These are puzzling claims, since at first blush it seems that protecting is neutral about the status of the protected.

To protect means to defend or guard from attack, invasion, or loss; to cover or shield from injury or danger. Secret service agents who protect the president are not by that fact superior to him. It is true that the president can protect himself if the need arises, and wives and mothers can do the same, but they may not be as well equipped. The secret service agent has a gun and many other agents to assist her, and a man who opens a door for a woman is, generally speaking, stronger than she is. Allowing a person to enter before oneself can also be a sign of respect or honor, as it is in the deference given to royalty.

Most men believe they should protect their wives and children, the weak, the elderly, and those in danger, and be willing to risk their lives to defend home and country. It seems to most people, I think, that receiving such protection does not entail having less authority, value, or independence. Perhaps there is some psychological relationship between protecting a person and feeling superior to them, but surely the connection is not inevitable and there is no empirical evidence of its frequency.

Tannen finds a myriad of similar day-to-day male/female interactions that, in her view, reinforce the conception of women as childlike vis-à-vis men. But her defensiveness and suspicion toward men gets in the way of appreciating their strengths and positive characteristics. If a woman who lays her head on her husband's shoulder is selling out, it is hard to believe we will ever arrive at Tannen's utopian dream, where both men and women are comfortable with their natural way of communicating and "are inclined to accept difference without blaming themselves, their partners, or their relationships."[51]

Complementarianism will always face challenges. Many attempts to discredit it warn of dire consequences if it becomes generally accepted. Sometimes the link is said to be causal—endorsing complementarianism will reinforce earlier beliefs (still alive in the culture) that women's proper place is in the home and so reverse the gains made by second-wave feminism. Other attacks portray the connection as a logical one—differences between men and women entail that they are better suited for some social roles than others, and it would make sense to discourage them from operating outside those roles.

A tighter logical argument points out that acknowledging important and ineradicable differences between the sexes makes it possible to rank them as superior or inferior according to some standard of value. This cannot be denied. Many observers of the women's movement believe that, in view of the long history of misogyny and discrimination against women, men will seize the opening provided by complementarianism to justify women's subordination. This argument combines a logical inference with a causal prediction that has some plausibility. Complementarians need to respond to these criticisms.

REPLIES TO OBJECTIONS

Complementarianism is frequently misunderstood. Objections usually take the form of a *reductio ad absurdum* argument along the following lines: If complementarianism is true, it is acceptable to restrict women to a narrow set of social roles; it is not acceptable to restrict women to a narrow set of social roles; therefore, complementarianism is false. Responding to the following versions of this argument will enable us to deepen our understanding of personalist feminism and its commitments.

Objection 1. *Complementarians believe that characteristics typical of women are universally held and exclusive to women.*

Rather, complementarians believe that gender differences are a matter of natural propensities, priorities, focus, and capacities, not traits common to every woman or every man. These differences do not determine an individual's personality, intelligence, or social role. There are stay-at-home dads and women in the military, male nurses and female boxers, and these arrangements are perfectly compatible with complementarianism.

Further, complementarians endorse the obvious truth that many differences between men and women are not mutually exclusive. Some people have qualities that are more typical of the other gender, though in most instances they will not possess them to the same degree. Many of the brain and hormone-based differences are mutually exclusive, but preferences about work and play are not.

Objection 2. *Complementarians claim that mothers should stay home with their children or at least minimize commitments outside the home.*

To be fair, this objection finds justification in the work of some scholars claiming to defend complementarianism but giving it a rigorist interpretation that implies completely distinct and nonoverlapping social roles for men and women. One of the most influential Catholic theologians of the twentieth century, Hans Urs von Balthasar, seems to endorse a very strong version of that view. In a discussion on women and the priesthood, he remarks: "The Church stresses the equal dignity of man and woman, so that the extreme oppositeness of their functions may guarantee the spiritual and physical fruitfulness of human nature. Every encroachment of one sex into the role of the other narrows the range and dynamics of humanly possible love, even when this range transcends the sphere of sexuality, birth and death."⁵²

Von Balthasar's prominence and impressive theological work on many other themes could lead some to conclude that the teachings of the Catholic Church support a rigid conception of gender roles. Nothing could be further from the truth. The actual implications of Catholic teaching on the nature and vocation of women are clearly articulated in recent papal documents (especially St. John Paul II's *On the Dignity and Vocation of Women*) and by faithful Catholic women in the professions and the academy. They include Mary Ann Glendon, Helen Alvare, Lisa Schiltz, Sara Butler, and Erika Bachiochi, among many others. Bachiochi's book *Women, Sex, and the Church*⁵³ brings together essays by several of these women on topics of special concern to feminists. In spite of their commitment to complementarianism, not one of them supports a position like that of von Balthasar. Certainly it is incompatible with the personalist feminism defended in this chapter.

As we have already seen, it is undeniable that differences between the sexes make some activities and professions more attractive to women. But this in no way justifies constraining the choices of women with regard to their roles in private or public life. Women rightly resent the assumption that since they tend to be more skilled in caring for the home and children they are morally required to make domestic tasks their only sphere of activity. Rather, even in family life husbands and wives must devise a workable plan for meeting the responsibilities they have in common, which include providing, protecting, and nurturing the children as well as caring for the environment of the home, the school, and the neighborhood.

Of course, each of us is personally and individually responsible for the needs of those entrusted to us, regardless of our gender. Feminist theory naturally tends to focus on women—how to expand their opportunities and enhance their value within the culture. But no woman is an island, and women see themselves as the primary guardians of persons and positive relationships among them. Given their natural desire to care for others, there is something counterintuitive about defining women's interests as consisting primarily in achieving their own happiness or in securing things men characteristically value—status, power, wealth, and public achievement.

Many a woman has decided that following her heart means finding a way to balance her personal needs (including the desire for salaried work) with the needs of those entrusted to her care. True freedom for women in this regard would require the kind of family-friendly policies recommended by John Paul II in his reflections on human work, including maximum flexibility with respect to employment and perhaps even financial compensation for those not in the paid workforce. Society has already come some distance toward that ideal, though it is a still a long way from being realized. To the extent that authentic feminists have a political agenda, it would be to press for greater flexibility in allowing both women and men to fulfill their personal and professional responsibilities and aspirations in ways that benefit everyone.[54]

Objection 3. *Complementarians see women's distinctive qualities as less valuable than those of men.*

It may be true that society views men as the winners in traditional divisions of labor, but complementarians emphatically reject that assumption. In fact, since women and men are equally necessary for the survival of the human race, there is at least *prima facie* evidence to believe that differences between the two make equal contributions to the common good. It is also important to note that social and behavioral sex differences are merely qualities or potentialities, and these are irrelevant to the equality between men and women, which is based on their common nature as persons. Since capacities and qualities can wax and wane, and may acquire different social significance over time, any calculations of their relative value will be both arbitrary and unstable.

Objection 4. *Given the qualities and capacities characteristic of women, complementarians believe women have little to contribute to the public sphere.*

Complementarians actually believe that differences between the sexes make it advisable for public institutions to attract capable women and profit from their perspective. A recent column in *The Boston Globe* reports that "there are a mountain of studies showing that companies with women executives and board members have healthier bottom lines and happier workplaces."[55] One such study was conducted by McKinsey & Company, an international management consulting firm. In a series called *Women Matter*, McKinsey collected data over a seven-year span on the impact of women in leadership positions in the corporate world. They found that "companies with a 'critical mass' of female executives perform better than those with no women in top management positions. . . . One reason for this outperformance lies in the leadership behaviors that women leaders tend to exhibit more often than their male counterparts."[56] This confirms what complementarians have been saying all along, that women make a positive contribution in the workplace precisely because their skill set is not identical with that of men.

A VOCATION FOR WOMEN

Still, differences between women and men seem to point toward some differences in their vocations. Today the term *vocation* is normally used to refer to one's occupation. Here I use it in a much more general sense, as a call to develop fully the potential that belongs to each person—adding one's gifts, labor, time, and commitment to building a civilization worthy of human persons. A vocation can be understood either as a calling from God or simply as an imperative arising from one's nature, based on the talents, experiences, and dreams that no one else brings to the table.

Philosopher Edith Stein describes a vocation as having three levels, beginning with the most general. Every person's first or primary vocation is to become fully human—to acquire the virtues and the wisdom that enable one both to give and receive genuine love. Second, since every human being is either male or female, one's vocation also includes realizing the potential inherent in being a man or a woman. We might see this as a specification of the human vocation, a particular way of living it out.[57] The traits more characteristic of one's own sex are needed in order to effectively realize the human vocation, and women and men should draw on them consciously and proudly.

Finally, there is a vocation unique to oneself, to become the person one is meant to be. This vocation is only revealed over time, as it involves finding and developing one's interests and abilities and having the courage to make them a gift, bringing to the human enterprise what no one else can offer. I believe that an authentic feminism is one that recognizes the common human vocation of men and women, celebrates their complementary vocations, and encourages each one to place his or her talents at the service of others.

NOTES

1. Laura L. Garcia, "Natural Kinds, Persons, and Abortion," *National Catholic Bioethics Quarterly* 8, no. 2 (2008): 265–73.
2. Rosalind Delmar, "What Is Feminism?," in *Theorizing Feminism: Parallel Trends in the Humanities and Social Sciences*, ed. Anne C. Harmann and Abigail J. Stewart (San Francisco: Westview, 1994), 8.
3. Delmar, "What Is Feminism?," 9.
4. bell hooks, *Feminist Theory: From Margin to Center* (Boston: South End Press, 1984).
5. hooks, *Feminist Theory*, 31.
6. John Hodge, *The Cultural Basis of Racism and Group Oppression* (Berkeley: Time Readers Press, 1975), 233.
7. hooks, *Feminist Theory*, 159.
8. Sally Haslanger, Nancy Tuana, and Peg O'Connor, "Topics in Feminism," *The Stanford Encyclopedia of Philosophy* (Spring 2014 edition), ed. Edward N. Zalta, http://plato.stanford.edu/archives/spr2014/entries/feminism-topics/.
9. bell hooks, *Feminism Is for Everybody: Passionate Politics* (Cambridge, MA: South End Press, 2000), 29.
10. National Organization for Women, Our Issues, http://now.org/about/our-issues/.
11. hooks, *Feminism Is for Everybody*, 4.
12. hooks, *Feminism Is for Everybody*, 5.
13. A 2013 Gallup poll found that "58 percent of adults say abortion should be illegal in all circumstances, or only permitted in 'a few.' Just 39 percent say the practice should be legal in 'all' or 'most' circumstances. On that same question, 57 percent of women adopt a pro-life view; 40 percent adopt the more doctrinaire 'pro-choice' position, which is supposed to be the official stance of their entire gender." Guy Benson, "Gallup: 58 Percent of Americans Oppose All or Most Abortions," Townhall.com, May 10, 2013, accessible at http://townhall.com/tipsheet/guybenson/2013/05/10/gallup-58-percent-of-americans-oppose-all-or-most-abortions-n1592505.
14. A 2009 Pew poll on abortion found that "several groups that were previously divided in their views on abortion now come down clearly on the pro-life side. Among Hispanics . . . abortion opponents now outnumber supporters of abortion rights." Among African Americans, 51 percent favored the prolife position and 42 percent opposed it. Pew Research Center for the People and the Press, October 1, 2009, accessible at http://www.people-press.org/2009/10/01/support-for-abortion-slips/.

15. See a publication of the National Women's History Museum entitled "The Abolition Movement and Women's Suffrage" (1970), accessible at https://www.nwhm.org/online-exhibits/rightsforwomen/abolitionandsuffrage.html: "In the 1830s, thousands of women were involved in the movement to abolish slavery. Women wrote articles for abolitionist papers, circulated abolitionist pamphlets, and circulated, signed, and delivered petitions to Congress calling for abolition. Some women became prominent leaders in the abolition movement. Angelina Grimke and Sarah Moore Grimke became famous for making speeches to mixed (male and female) audiences about slavery." NWHM is an organization dedicated to building a world-class National Women's History Museum on the National Mall in Washington, D.C.

16. Rosemary Oelrich Bottcher, "A Seneca Falls Revolution," *The American Feminist* (Spring 1998): 18.

17. Christina Hoff Sommers, *Who Stole Feminism? How Women Have Betrayed Women* (New York: Simon and Schuster, 1994), 23–24. Sommers cites Alison Jagger, *Feminist Politics and Human Nature* (Totowa, NJ: Rowman & Littlefield, 1988), 148.

18. Angela Y. Davis, *Women, Race and Class* (New York: Random House, 1981), 243.

19. Sommers, *Who Stole Feminism?*, 24.

20. Catherine A. MacKinnon, "Feminism, Marxism, Method, and the State: Toward Feminist Jurisprudence," *Signs* 8, no. 4 (1983): 647.

21. For an example of this kind of social construction theory, see MIT philosopher Sally Haslanger's *Resisting Reality: Social Construction and Social Critique* (New York: Oxford University Press, 2012) and her earlier collection of essays, *Theorizing Feminisms: A Reader*, ed. Elizabeth Hackett and Sally Haslanger (New York: Oxford University Press, 2005).

22. This is true even for those who undergo sex-change operations, since they are genetically (and so permanently) either male or female, regardless of appearance or balance of hormones. Similarly, so-called intersex babies are genetically either male or female (with XX or XY chromosomes). While their genitals and hormone sensitivities may appear closer to those of the opposite sex, it seems to me that medical interventions to correct this condition should be based on one's sex as determined at conception rather than on such accidental features as the body's shape. Regardless of what decision is made here, it is worth noting that the Intersex Society of North America opposes assigning intersex children to a third gender category: "We are trying to make the world a safe place for intersexed kids, and we don't think labeling them with a gender category that in essence doesn't exist would help them." See http://www.isna.org/faq/ten_myths/third_gender.

23. For a list and explanation of each of these, see Peter Weber, "Confused by All the New Facebook Genders? Here's What They Mean," *Slate*, February 21, 2014, accessible at http://www.slate.com/blogs/lexicon_valley/2014/02/21/gender_facebook_now_has_56_categories_to_choose_from_including_cisgender.html.

24. In her memorial of Shulamith Firestone, Susan Faludi recounts that in her 1970 book, *Notes from the Second Year*, authored with Anne Koedt, Firestone "envisioned a world in which women might be liberated by artificial reproduction outside the womb; in which collectives took the place of families; and in which children were granted 'the right of immediate transfer' from abusive adults." "Death of a Revolutionary," *New Yorker*, April 15, 2013, 54.

25. Drusilla Cornell, Comments in a Panel Discussion held at Rutgers University on *The Crisis of Fatherlessness*. Her opinion was that the crisis is not about children needing fathers but about mothers needing economic support from fathers. In her view it seems that "deadbeat dads" are the only real problem.

26. Jeffner Allen, "Motherhood: The Annihilation of Women," in *Mothering: Essays in Feminist Theory*, ed. Joyce Trebilcot (Totowa, NJ: Rowman & Allenheld, 1984).

27. Elizabeth Fox-Genovese, *Feminism Is Not the Story of My Life: How Today's Feminist Elite Has Lost Touch with the Real Concerns of Women* (New York: Talese, 1996).

28. Carol Gilligan, *In a Different Voice: Psychological Theory and Women's Development* (Cambridge: Harvard University Press, 1982).

29. Deborah Tannen, *That's Not What I Meant!: How Conversational Style Makes or Breaks Relationships* (New York: Morrow, 1986), and *You Just Don't Understand! Women and Men in Conversation* (New York: Random House, 1990).

30. Tannen, *You Just Don't Understand!*, 292.

31. Sara Ruddick, *Maternal Thinking: Toward a Politics of Peace* (Boston: Beacon, 1989, 1995).

32. Ruddick, *Maternal Thinking*, xii.

33. Ruddick, *Maternal Thinking*, 206. Ruddick says, "In material practice there is a real, unromantic, material basis for a revisionist history of the body.... In this history, a body is a testament to hope. Every body, and therefore every death, counts; the promise of birth includes a dying well tended and a death well mourned."

34. From Madonna, "Material Girl," released on November 30, 1984, by Sire Records, as the second single from her album *Like a Virgin*.

35. See http://en.wikipedia.org/wiki/New_feminism. The article offers a lengthy description of new feminism that is largely accurate, though it incorporates some elements that would be rejected by most self-described new feminists.

36. Karol Wojtyła, *Love and Responsibility* (San Francisco: Ignatius, 1993). There is a more recent translation by Grzegorz Ignatik published by Pauline Books & Media in 2013. However, all of my references are to the 1993 edition. Wojtyła's book was published in Polish in 1960.

37. Wojtyła, *Love and Responsibility*, 24.

38. Wojtyła, *Love and Responsibility*, 41.

39. Pope John Paul II, *Laborem Exercens* (On Human Work), September 14, 1981, 19.

40. John Paul II, *Laborem Exercens*, 19, emphasis mine.

41. See the series of books by John Gray following his initial best seller *Men Are from Mars, Women Are from Venus* (New York: HarperCollins, 1992).

42. Prudence Allen, *The Concept of Woman: The Aristotelian Revolution, 750 BC–AD 1250* (Montreal: Eden Press, 1985), 5.

43. Allen, *Concept of Woman*, 5.

44. See a relatively recent contribution to this project in Prudence Allen, "Man-Woman Complementarity: The Catholic Vision," *Logos* 9 (2006): 85–97.

45. Erika Bachiochi, "Engaging Women: Finding a New Translation for Catholic Sexual Teaching," forthcoming in a collection of essays to be published by *Our Sunday Visitor*.

46. I draw the majority of these claims from Louann Brizendine, MD, *The Female Brain* (New York: Three Rivers, 2006). The book became a *New York Times* best seller. A helpful chart of male/female differences can be found on pages xviii–xix. Additional sources include Alan Feingold, "Gender Differences in Personality: A Meta-Analysis," *Psychological Bulletin* 116 (1994): 429–56; Steven E. Rhoads, *Taking Sex Differences Seriously* (San Francisco: Encounter Books, 2004); and Douglas D. Burman, Tali Bitan, and James R. Booth, "Sex Differences in Neural Processing of Language among Children," *Neuropsychologia* 46 (2008): 1349–62.

47. Men and women react to beauty differently.

48. Tara Parker-Pope, "Do Women Like Child Care More Than Men?," The Well Column, *New York Times*, March 22, 2012, accessible at http://well.blogs.nytimes.com/2012/03/22/do-women-like-child-care-more-than-men/?_php=true&_type=blogs&_r=0.

49. Allen, *Concept of Woman*, 5.

50. Tannen, *You Just Don't Understand!*, 287.

51. Tannen, *You Just Don't Understand!*, 297.

52. Hans Urs von Balthasar, *New Elucidations*, trans. Sr. Mary Theresilde Skerry (San Francisco: Ignatius, 1986), 195–96.

53. Erika Bachiochi, ed. *Women, Sex, and the Church: A Case for Catholic Teaching* (Boston: Pauline Books and Media, 2010).

54. This position is comprehensively articulated by law professor Elizabeth R. Schiltz in her article "A Contemporary Catholic Theory of Complementarity," in *Feminism, Law and Religion*, eds. Marie A. Failinger, Elizabeth R. Schiltz, and Susan J. Stabile (Burlington, VT: Ashgate, 2013), 3–24.

55. Yvonne Abraham, "For Men Only. Still," *The Boston Globe*, January 26, 2014, Metro Section, accessible online at http://www.bostonglobe.com/metro/2014/01/26/for-men-only-still/ZRC7d0MTjKvi7NtIB7qCZO/story.html.

56. Sandrine Devillard, Sandra Sancier, et al. *Women Matter 2013: Gender Diversity in Top Management—Moving Corporate Culture, Moving Boundaries* (McKinsey & Company, 2013), available online at http://www.mckinsey.com/features/women_matter.

57. This point is amplified at length by Edith Stein in her *Essays on Woman* (Washington, DC: ICS Publications, 1986), translated from the German by Romaeus Leuven and Freda Mary Oben.

13

IMMIGRATION AND AMERICAN EXCEPTIONALISM

Robert P. George, Princeton University

That the United States of America is an exceptional nation seems to me to be a proposition whose truth is too obvious to debate. Our nation was, as our greatest president said, "conceived in liberty and dedicated to the proposition that all men are created equal." And not only was our nation "so conceived, and so dedicated," we as a nation have proven to the world that "a nation so conceived and so dedicated can [indeed] long endure." The history of our nation is the story of "We the people"—the American people—struggling (sometimes struggling against each other) to protect, honor, and live up to the exceptional principles around which we have integrated ourselves and constituted ourselves as a people. And while our record is far from unblemished, we have not been left unblessed with success.

No one needs me to remind him that part of what is unique about the United States is that our common bonds are not in blood or even soil, but are in a shared moral-political creed. "We hold these truths to be self-evident, that all men are created equal, that they are endowed by their Creator with certain unalienable rights, and among these are life, liberty, and the pursuit of happiness." This is clearest in the fact that people really can, in the richest and fullest possible sense, *become* Americans. And millions upon millions of people have done so. Of course, one can become a *citizen of* Greece or France or China, but can one really become a *Greek*, or a *Frenchman*, or *Chinese*? An immigrant who becomes a citizen of the United States becomes, or at least can become, not merely an

American citizen, but an American. He is as American as the fellow whose ancestors arrived on the *Mayflower*.

Now, how do immigrants become Americans? In practice, it goes beyond becoming an American citizen, and even formally signing on with the American creed. The additional key ingredient, I believe, is something I know intimately from my own family's experience; namely, *gratitude*. It is, typically, an immigrant's feelings of gratitude to America for the liberty, security, and opportunity our nation affords him and his family that leads to his appreciation of the ideals and institutions of American cultural, economic, and civic life. From this appreciation comes his belief in the goodness of American ideals, as articulated above all in the Declaration of Independence, and the value of the constitutional structures and institutions by which they are effectuated. And from this belief arises his aspiration to become an American citizen together with his willingness to shoulder the responsibilities of citizenship and even to make great sacrifices for the nation, should it come to that.

My own immigrant grandfathers came to the United States a little over a hundred years ago. Like most immigrants then and now, they were not drawn here by any abstract belief in the superiority of the American political system. My father's father came from Syria fleeing oppression visited upon him and his family as members of a relatively small ethnic and religious minority group in that troubled country. My mother's father came to escape the poverty of southern Italy. They both worked on the railroads and in the mines. My maternal grandfather settled in West Virginia, where there was a small Italian immigrant community in Clarksburg, Fairmont, and Morgantown—a trio of cities along the Monongahela River a little south of the Pennsylvania border. He was able to save enough money to start a little grocery store, which soon became a flourishing business. My paternal grandfather spent his entire life as a laborer. He died of emphysema, no doubt as a result of the pulmonary health hazards of coal mining in those days. Both men were exceedingly grateful for what America made possible for them and their families. Their gratitude was not diminished when times got hard—as they did for all Americans—in the Great Depression. Although both my grandfathers encountered ethnic prejudice, they viewed this as an aberration—a failure of some Americans to live up to the nation's ideals. It did not dawn on them to blame the bad behavior of some Americans on America itself. On the contrary, America in their eyes was a land of unsurpassed blessing. It was a nation of which they were proud and happy to become citizens. And even before they became citizens they had become patriots—men who deeply appreciated what America is and what she stands for.

Like so many other immigrants, my immigrant grandparents particularly appreciated the opportunities that America made available to their children. My father's father had a sister—she too an immigrant—who had a son named John Solomon who wanted to be a lawyer. He finished college and then completed law school at West Virginia University. The law school in those days was located on University Avenue in Morgantown near the center of the campus. It was a grand building that one entered by walking up a broad set of stairs. When my cousin John's mother—we knew her as Halte Gemile—came to attend her son's graduation ceremony, she stopped to kiss each step as she ascended those stairs. Such was her gratitude. Of course, her son was thoroughly embarrassed by this display. My father, who was there, tells me that his cousin John turned to his mother at about the fourth step and pleaded: "Please mom, you're acting like an immigrant." Indeed, she was.

I talked a moment ago about how gratitude for liberty, security, and opportunity leads immigrants to an appreciation of American ideals and institutions, and in turn gives rise to an aspiration to American citizenship and a willingness to bear its responsibilities and even to make great sacrifices. Four of my paternal grandparents' five sons were drafted into the U.S. military to serve in World War II. My maternal grandparents' only son was also drafted. All of these men served in combat and returned with decorations. Their immigrant parents were immensely proud of them—proud of them precisely because they fought for America and for what America stands for. They considered that their sons were fighting for *their* country—not for a country in which they were resident aliens or guests. They were fighting for a country that was not only great, but good. A country whose ideals were noble. A country to whom they were immensely grateful—and not merely because it provided a haven from poverty and oppression. *A country whose principles they believed in.*

When their boys were fighting, they knew that it was entirely possible—all too possible—that ultimately they would be called upon to give what Lincoln at Gettysburg described as the "last full measure of devotion." You can imagine the anxiety this would cause in an Italian family whose one and only son had been sent into the brutal combat of the Pacific theater. But however much sleep was lost as a result of fear and even dread, they remained proud that their son was fighting for his country, for their country, for America. Nor did the fact that Italy under fascist rule was on the other side of the conflict give them so much as a moment's pause. The gratitude leading to appreciation leading to the conviction and commitment at the heart of true American patriotism left them in no doubt as to their loyalty.

I have the sense that my uncles' service to the nation at a time of peril was not only an expression of their Americanism, and the Americanism of their immigrant parents, it was a profound confirmation and ratification of it. If they had any doubts in their own minds about whether they were truly and fully Americans—as American as their fellow citizens whose ancestors really had arrived here on the *Mayflower*—military service erased those doubts. I dare say that the same was true, as has always been true, just in case any native-born citizens had any doubts about whether their immigrant neighbors really were Americans. The willingness of immigrants and their children to take the risks, and in many, many cases to be counted among the fallen, leaves the question of allegiance and American identity in no doubt.

Of course, some Protestant Americans wondered whether non-Protestants—and especially Catholics—could truly become Americans. They were concerned that hierarchical and nondemocratic forms of church governance would hinder the ability of non-Protestant immigrants to appreciate and fully give their allegiance to democratic institutions and principles of civic life. Some even believed that Catholic immigrants would have to be de-Catholicized by the public school system and other mechanisms in order to become patriotic Americans. The natural and understandable Catholic reaction to this—the establishment of Catholic parochial schools across the country—only heightened Protestant worries. But part of what eventually made these worries go away was the record of service and heroism of Catholic and other non-Protestant soldiers (including countless products of parochial schools) fighting for democracy and against authoritarian regimes and totalitarian ideologies in the First and especially the Second World War. Catholics saw no contradiction between their faith and their allegiance to the United States of America. On the contrary, religious commitment tended to support patriotic conviction. Faithful Catholics wanted to be, and not merely to be seen to be—though that, too—the very best of good American citizens.

And as they saw and see it, that doesn't require the slightest dilution of their Catholic faith.

Now, I have been talking about how gratitude launches immigrants on the path to becoming Americans. It has happened to millions. There are countless permutations of the story, but they are permutations of the same story. I suspect that as you hear me tell the stories of my grandparents, many of you are thinking of stories, not at all dissimilar, of your grandparents, or great-grandparents, or great-great-grandparents, and how they became Americans. The amazing and wonderful thing is that a family story like mine of immigrant ancestors becoming Americans, sharing in the blessings of American life, and taking upon themselves their share of the nation's burdens, is not the exception; it is the norm. (Of course, the story of Africans brought to America as slaves and then subjected to segregation and discrimination even after slavery was abolished is a radically different one—a story of injustice and a stain upon our nation's history. Yet the great efforts to right these wrongs and live up to our national ideals of liberty and justice for all are also part of our American heritage.)

I believe that immigration has been a great strength for America and that it will continue to be so. I certainly hope that immigrants to our land will continue to want to be Americans. Does this mean that I reject what has come to be known as "multiculturalism"? Well, it depends on what one means by that term. I certainly see no need to encourage immigrants to abandon their customs, traditions, and ethnic or religious identities; on the contrary, I think it is good for families, and good for America, for immigrants to honor their ethnic customs and identities and pass them along to the next generation. Immigrants have always done this, and it is fine and good—a source of strength. Of course, this is to be distinguished from an ideology that promotes the rejection of a primary and central political allegiance to the United States and its ideals and institutions. And it is certainly to be distinguished from any ideology that denies the fundamental goodness of America's principles of political and civil liberty.

Now, where a culture of *opportunity* flourishes, immigrants will feel, as my grandparents felt, *gratitude* for the opportunities they are afforded to lift themselves up and make a better life for their children, by dint of hard work and determination to succeed. However, it appears to be a brute fact of human psychology that where a culture of *entitlement* prevails, gratitude even for charitable assistance will not emerge. In part, of course, this is to be explained by the fact that upward social mobility is dampened in circumstances of a culture of entitlement. This is the phenomenon known as welfare dependency. I observed its soul-destroying effects on many *nonimmigrant* families in West Virginia as I was growing up. You see, dependency is an equal opportunity soul destroyer. And this, in turn, leads to resentment as people persuade themselves that the reason they are not getting ahead is that those who are already better off are cheating or manipulating the system to hold down people at the bottom of the ladder (who are dependent on entitlements). So the culture of entitlement ends up reinforcing an *attitude* that impedes the *gratitude* that enables immigrants to become Americans.

As I said, I *want* immigrants to become Americans. I want them to believe in American ideals and institutions. I want them to "hold these truths to be self-evident, that all men are created equal, that they are endowed by their Creator with certain unalienable rights, and among these are life, liberty, and the pursuit of happiness." I want them to believe, as I believe, in the dignity of the human being, in all stages and conditions of life; in limited government, republican democracy, equality of opportunity, morally ordered liberty, private property, economic freedom, and the rule of law. I want them to believe in these ideals and principles not because they are *ours*, but because they are *noble and good and true*. They honor the profound, inherent, and equal dignity of all members of the human family. They call forth from us the best that we are capable of. They ennoble us. Our efforts to live up to them, despite our failures and imperfections, have made us a great people, a force for freedom and justice in the world, and, of course, an astonishingly prosperous nation. It is little wonder that America is, as it always has been, a magnet for people from every land who seek a better life.

But the transmission of American ideals to immigrants and, indeed, to anyone, including new generations of native-born Americans, depends on the maintenance of a culture in which these ideals flourish. The maintenance of such a culture is a complicated business—one with many dimensions. But in this nation of immigrants, this democratic nation of immigrants in which "We the People" have the privilege and responsibility of governing ourselves, it is every citizen's business. And it is certainly the special business of institutions of higher learning. For such institutions, civic education—education that advances the understanding of our nation's constitutional principles and institutions—is a high calling and a solemn obligation. If, as James Madison said, "only a well-educated people can be permanently a free people," then civic education is vital to the success of the grand experiment in ordered liberty that Madison and the other Founding Fathers bequeathed to us and our posterity.

14

WHAT MARRIAGE CAN BE

John Corvino, Wayne State University

The marriage debate is over, and the gays won. At least, this is the view of many observers, in light of the dramatic recent shift in both public opinion and the U.S. legal landscape. Even steadfast opponents concede the point in a limited sense. As National Organization for Marriage co-founder Maggie Gallagher put it in a *Huffington Post* interview, "We are now in the 'gay marriage in all 50 states' phase whether we like it or not."[1] She made these remarks even prior to the U.S. Supreme Court's *Obergefell* decision, which legalized same-sex marriage across the United States in June 2015.[2]

Against this backdrop, an academic debate about same-sex marriage may seem like a quaint parlor game. Worse, it may unwittingly hurt people. Debates are not mere intellectual exercises; they have social consequences, and one consequence of the same-sex marriage debate—however unintentional—is to signal to LGBT people that their equal citizenship remains an open question.

Yet polls show that over a third of Americans continue to oppose same-sex marriage.[3] Many of these people would argue that equality is not what's at issue; what's at issue is the very meaning of marriage. Among them are reasonable, thoughtful, decent people, including contributors to this volume such as my friend Sherif Girgis. It remains important to engage their arguments vigorously, which is what I aim to do here.

The most sophisticated opposition to same-sex marriage comes from the natural law tradition, specifically the "new" natural lawyers, who will therefore be my main focus. Their position is stated most thoroughly by

Girgis, Ryan T. Anderson, and Robert P. George in their book *What Is Marriage? Man and Woman: A Defense*.[4] They argue that a proper understanding of marriage—what they call the conjugal view—makes clear that same-sex "marriage" is in fact impossible. It is therefore no violation of justice to deny civil marriage to same-sex couples, because same-sex couples cannot achieve real marriage, and the state should not distort the true meaning of marriage by extending the label to counterfeit versions.

I will proceed as follows. In the first section, I'll argue that Girgis, Anderson, and George contrast the conjugal view with a straw man. In the second section, I will critically examine their key concepts of comprehensive union, bodily union, and "reproductive-type" acts. In the third section, I will make a *reductio ad absurdum* argument against their view in order to undermine the claim that it captures widespread intuitions about what marriage is. In the fourth section, I'll respond to objections, especially the contention that alternatives to the conjugal view can't explain how marriage differs from ordinary companionship. I conclude in the final section by considering a thought experiment from Girgis, Anderson, and George.

TWO VIEWS OF MARRIAGE?

Girgis, Anderson, and George contrast two visions of marriage as follows:

Conjugal View: "[Marriage is] a *comprehensive* union: Joining spouses in body as well as mind, it is begun by consent and sealed by sexual intercourse. So completed by acts of bodily union by which new life is made, it is essentially apt for and deepened by procreation, and calls for that broad sharing of domestic life uniquely fit for family life. Uniting spouses in these all-encompassing ways, it also objectively calls for all-encompassing commitment: permanent and exclusive. Comprehensive union is valuable in itself, but its link to children's welfare makes marriage a public good that the state should recognize and support" (WIM 3).

Revisionist View: "[Marriage is] the union of two people who commit to romantic partnership and domestic life: essentially an emotional union, merely enhanced by whatever sexual activity the partners find agreeable. Such committed romantic unions are seen as valuable while the emotion lasts. The state recognizes them because it has an interest in their stability, and in the needs of spouses and any children they choose to rear" (WIM 4).

According to Girgis, Anderson, and George, to embrace same-sex marriage is to reject the conjugal view in favor of the revisionist view. But, they claim, the revisionist view cannot capture widespread and important intuitions about marriage: intuitions related to its permanence, exclusivity, connection to childrearing, and suitability for state regulation.

One might suspect at the outset that Girgis, Anderson, and George are setting up a false dilemma, and one would be correct. Put aside the tendentious labeling of the pro-same-sex-marriage view as "revisionist." My main concern is with their description of marriage as "essentially an emotional union . . . valuable while the emotion lasts." Among the best advocates for same-sex marriage (Dale Carpenter, Andrew Koppelman, Martha Nussbaum, Jonathan Rauch, Andrew Sullivan, Evan Wolfson, and others), none hold such a view; quite the contrary, many reject it explicitly. As I explain in *Debating Same-Sex Marriage*, "even more important [than romantic love] is *love as commitment*—an ongoing activity, not an ephemeral feeling. Marital love is not just something people *feel*, it's something they *do*."[5]

Indeed, it is precisely the romantic origin of marriage that makes social support for it both apt and important: even as romantic passion waxes and wanes, as romantic passion tends to do, our family and friends remind us of our commitment to stand by our spouses "for better or for worse."

COMPREHENSIVE UNIONS, BODILY UNIONS, AND REPRODUCTIVE-TYPE ACTS

Girgis, George, and Anderson's misconstrual of the revisionist view is noteworthy, because the emphasis on ephemeral emotions allows them to connect same-sex marriage with widespread divorce, promiscuity, spousal neglect, deadbeat dads, and other social ills. Girgis unfortunately continues this trend in this volume; for example, when he imagines the case of a young boy who is taught by the revisionist view that it's "inauthentic" to stick with a marriage once desire has wandered and is thus less likely to stay with his spouse for the sake of their children, or to give his children "lasting attention."[6] And yet, research suggests that these problems are less prevalent in states where a higher percentage of citizens favor same-sex marriage.[7]

They contrast this "mere emotional union" with what they describe as the conjugal's view's of *comprehensive* union. A key part of that is bodily union:

> [U]nlike ordinary friendship, marriage unites people in all their basic dimensions. It involves a union of minds and wills that unfolds in a sharing of lives and resources. But marriage also includes bodily union. This is because your body is an essential part of *you*, not a vehicle driven by the "real" you, your mind, nor a mere costume you must don. . . . Because of that embodiedness, any union of two people *must include bodily union* to be comprehensive. If it did not, it would leave out—it would fail to be extended along—a basic part of each person's being.

This argument not only fails to establish its intended conclusion; it actually undermines it. From the fact that our bodies are essential to us, it follows that *any* union we form (and not just the comprehensive ones) must in some sense be bodily: disembodied human minds don't form friendships, sing in choirs, collaborate on scholarly projects, and so on. Moreover, marriage's being comprehensive clearly doesn't require that the spouses unite in every way possible: they need not sing together or coauthor books, for example. So this argument gets us no closer to understanding why marital unions (qua *comprehensive* unions) must be more bodily than other unions, as opposed to being, say, more intellectual.

Girgis, Anderson, and George mean something very specific by "bodily union." Such union occurs whenever bodies "coordinate toward a common biological end of the whole that they form together" (WIM 25). This, they say, happens only in coitus—that is, penis-in-vagina sex:

> [I]t is a remarkable fact that there is one respect in which this highest kind of bodily unity *is* possible between two individuals, one function for which a mate really does *complete* us: sexual reproduction. In coitus, and there alone, a man and a woman's bodies participate by virtue of their sexual complementarity in a coordination that has the

biological purpose of reproduction—a function that neither can perform alone. (WIM 26)

But what about infertile couples? They cannot achieve the "biological purpose of reproduction." Consider a woman whose cancerous uterus has been removed. Her sex with her future husband can never result in reproduction, and they both know it. Yet no one (including the new natural lawyers) would deny that they are capable of marriage.

Girgis, Anderson, and George claim that even though the infertile couple cannot *achieve* reproduction, their sex is still *coordinated toward* it. As they explain in their *Harvard Journal of Law and Public Policy* article,

> When Einstein and Bohr discussed a physics problem, they coordinated intellectually for an intellectual good, truth. And the intellectual union they enjoyed was real, whether or not its ultimate target (in this case, a theoretical solution) was reached—assuming, as we safely can, that both Einstein and Bohr were honestly seeking truth and not merely pretending while engaging in deception or other acts which would make their apparent intellectual union only an illusion.
>
> By extension, bodily union involves mutual coordination toward a bodily good—which is realized only through coitus. And this union occurs even when conception, the bodily good toward which sexual intercourse as a biological function is oriented, does not occur.[8]

But there seems to be an important moral difference between a goal which "does not occur" even though people are "honestly seeking" it, and a goal which *cannot* occur, and which thus cannot be honestly sought by anyone aware of its impossibility. Girgis, Anderson, and George regularly elide this difference.

Elsewhere George claims, "Acts that fulfill the behavioral conditions of procreation are reproductive in type even where the non-behavioral conditions of procreation do not happen to obtain."[9] But this claim construes "behavioral conditions" in a question-begging way. When a man chooses *coitus with a woman who lacks a uterus*, he chooses behavior which, given that description, *never* results in procreation. The same is true when such a woman chooses coitus with any man. In response to a similar objection from Andrew Koppelman,[10] George replies that "every aspect of the behavior the heterosexual couple (in a marital act) chooses to perform may be the same on two different occasions, and yet one may result in procreation but the other not. This fully establishes that the difference is a difference extrinsic to *what they do*."[11] But now George seems to have abandoned the holism that helped make the new natural law view attractive in the first place. Having previously emphasized that humans are integrated bodies and minds, he now casts "what they do" reductively as the physical act of coitus, divorced from what partners know and intend. Only by selective myopia can we regard such coitus as having "reproductive-type" significance.[12]

Girgis exhibits the same myopia in this volume, when he notes that "*biological* processes, unlike intentional or artifactual ones, have their end not by our intentions but by nature."[13] That's true as far as it goes. But the same nature that requires a male and female for human reproduction also requires that the female have a functioning uterus. More to the point, when a biological process is known to be permanently missing essential components, what value is there in intentionally assembling the remaining ones?

Additional cases will make clear the disconnect between the new natural lawyers' "reproductive-type" and actual reproduction. Consider:

a. Adam ejaculates into Eve, who conceives. A child is born.
b. Adam ejaculates into Eve, who is capable of conceiving but does not.
c. Adam ejaculates into Eve, who lacks a uterus.
d. During contracepted coitus with Eve, Adam ejaculates into a condom, which is then thrown away.
e. During contracepted coitus with Eve, Adam ejaculates into a condom. In a Petri dish, he combines sperm from that condom with an ovum from Eve, in whose uterus he implants the resulting zygote. A child is born.
f. With manual assistance from Eve, Adam ejaculates into a plastic cup, which is then thrown away.
g. With manual assistance from Eve, Adam ejaculates into a plastic cup. In a Petri dish, he combines sperm from that cup with an ovum from Eve, in whose uterus he implants the resulting zygote. A child is born.

George claims that "Where one has deliberately frustrated the possibility of conception, it is not clear to me how one can say that an act of sexual intercourse is reproductive in type."[14] Fair enough. So on his view, Adam and Eve engage in reproductive-type acts and fulfill the "behavioral conditions of procreation" in a, b, and c, but not in d, e, f, or g. But this result is odd, not only because procreation *cannot* occur in c but also because it *actually occurs* in e and g.

It is difficult to escape the conclusion that what Girgis, Anderson, and George are aiming at is not really *coordination toward procreation*, as long as we take "coordination" to include human knowledge and intentions (as we should). What they're aiming at is uncontracepted coitus. After all, even in g—the IVF case—Adam's and Eve's bodies "participate by virtue of their sexual complementarity in a coordination that has the biological purpose of reproduction—a function that neither can perform alone." They just do so via a more complicated route than coitus.

More important, it is difficult to see how such coitus retains special moral value relative to other sexual acts. Most people regard coitus as morally special because it can lead to the creation of new life, but that explanation is unavailable here. The goodness of an end redounds to its means or constituents only if the end is possible. If a good end is impossible, the "means" or "constituents" may still be valuable, but their value must stem from some other source.[15]

Consider some illustrations. The parts of a watch are coordinated for telling time, and they are good insofar as they serve that good end. But if the watch is permanently broken, whatever goodness the parts retain must come from elsewhere: revealing the watchmaker's skill, perhaps, or providing scrap metal. Similarly, to borrow Girgis, Anderson, and George's example: the goodness of Einstein and Bohr's collaboration stems largely from the value of the solution that they might reach (and are "honestly seeking"). But if the problem is unsolvable, *that* goodness disappears, and any residual goodness must come from the collegiality they experience, or from the mental exercise achieved.

Elsewhere (in a case that similarly involves biological processes), George appears to concede that ends cannot confer their goodness on means once the ends become impossible. In a paper with Patrick Lee, he considers the example of Smith, who cannot digest his meals. Digestion is oriented toward nourishment, and ultimately the basic good of health. When Smith eats, nourishment is neither possible nor intended. Yet Lee and George argue that his eating "would still be a nourishing-type act if his disorder got worse, his stomach was closed, and he obtained his nourishment intravenously. In that case, he might eat in order to exercise that part of his digestive system still functioning, or to share a meal with a friend."[16] Notice the explanation for what makes Smith's eating reasonable (and thus good) in this case: exercising bodily parts, and fellowship. The goodness of nourishment falls away.

In a similar way, the goodness of procreation falls away in the case of the permanently infertile couple. They are not intending procreation. They are not even intending *coordination toward* procreation, except in a rather stilted sense. They are intending coitus—an act that, *under other circumstances*, might be one step toward the goal of procreation. On the other hand, as I've argued, so might Eve's masturbation of Adam.

DOES MARRIAGE REQUIRE COITUS?

To sum up the last section: Girgis, Anderson, and George do not explain why so-called comprehensive unions must be more bodily than other kinds of union, much less why they must include coitus. While it is of course true that humans reproduce sexually, coitus is neither necessary nor sufficient for reproduction, as various cases demonstrate. When new natural lawyers refer to "reproductive-type" acts, they are really just referring to uncontracepted coitus. But in cases where reproduction is known to be impossible, the goodness of coitus can't flow from procreation's goodness. So coitus's special moral value, as well as its special connection to marriage, remains mysterious.

Girgis answers that the value is "personal union" and mistakenly claims that I assume that he treats sex as having purely instrumental value: the value of procreation. But he misses the force of the objection. If the partners are "coordinated" toward some good that they know to be impossible, what is the value *of that coordination*? How does it create a genuine, and morally special, union, without the end that gives it shape— the one that answers the question "Coordination toward *what*?"[17]

The claim that coitus is necessary for marriage is essential to Girgis, Anderson, and George's argument against same-sex marriage: same-sex couples cannot engage in coitus, which is necessary for bodily union, which is necessary for comprehensive union, which is what marriage is.

But the claim exposes them to a powerful counterexample, one that undermines their contention that the conjugal view fits better with people's intuitions about marriage than the alternatives.

Consider a hypothetical couple I'll call Bob and Jane. Bob and Jane were high school sweethearts. Eventually, Bob proposed marriage, and Jane accepted. But prior to their wedding, tragedy struck: Bob was in a terrible car accident that paralyzed him from the waist down. As a result, he would never be capable of coitus. Bob offered to cancel the engagement, but Jane would have none of it: "You are the same person I have always loved," she declared. "We will make this work." So Bob and Jane legally wed, spent many years together, and eventually raised several adopted children. Although coitus was impossible, they engaged in other acts of sexual affection, which enhanced the special intimacy between them. For decades, until parted by death, they enjoyed each other and the happy family they jointly created.

Were Bob and Jane married? They were certainly *legally* married, and also according to virtually everyone's commonsense understanding of marriage. But not according to Girgis, Anderson, and George. The problem is that they were unable ever to achieve bodily union—to "coordinate toward a common biological end of the whole that they form together" (WIM 25). The conjugal view thus entails that Bob and Jane's so-called marriage was in fact a sham, and that (at least in principle) it should never have been legally recognized by the state.

Girgis, Anderson, and George concede that Bob and Jane were never really married given the "strong" version of their view, in which marriage requires the intention (and thus the expected ability) to perform coitus. They also attempt a "softer" version, on which a couple's union can be marital so long as coitus "is possible *in principle*."[18] It is not clear how this softer version gets off the ground, however. Any random male-female pair could *in principle* engage in coitus, just as they could in principle do any number of other things that the conjugal view requires. But marriage does not consist in things that people *might* do if the world were different; it consists in what they actually do. Suppose Bob were kidnapped before the wedding and never returned to Jane. In that case, they would (sadly) never marry, even though they could marry *in principle* and even though their failure to do so is entirely outside their own control. So if marriage requires "bodily union," and Bob and Jane are incapable of that union, then they are incapable of marriage: the strong conjugal view.

On the legal point, Girgis, Anderson, and George backpedal: they respond that the state should still permit such marriages because it would be too "invasive" to inquire about such matters and because the hidden nature of Bob's incapacity means that recognition of his marriage would not undermine the proper public understanding.[19] But there are several problems with this response. First, the question "Do you intend to perform coitus?" written discreetly on an application form is far less invasive than, say, a blood test (which several states require for a marriage license). Second, the case could be modified so that Bob's incapacity is as obvious to any court clerk as his sex/gender: imagine, for example, that his horrible accident severed him at the waist but that he somehow survived.

Third, and most significantly, the response does not cure the view of its counterintuitive implication: Girgis, Anderson, and George still concede (with the strong conjugal view) that Bob and Jane were never really married; they simply "slipped by" the state's and the public's notice and are essentially engaging in an act of deception or fraud.

Why do we recognize Bob and Jane's union as a marriage? Salient factors include their public lifelong commitment, romantic love, mutual care and concern, sexual intimacy, and joint raising of a family. Viewed holistically, this union looks like a marriage, even if it lacks one feature (coitus) commonly associated with marriages. Yet once one concedes that marriage is possible without coitus—once one recognizes Bob and Jane as married—one removes the new natural lawyers' bar to same-sex marriage.

As an aside: some have told me that Bob and Jane's case is "exceptional," and we do not define marriage by the exceptions. But this response, aside from being vague, essentially gives up the argument: once we allow room for "exceptions" to the rule that marriage must include coitus, we can simply include same-sex marriages among the so-called exceptions.

Beyond providing a powerful counterexample to Girgis, Anderson, and George's argument, the Bob and Jane case teaches us something about the definition of marriage. As a complex and evolving social institution, marriage does not lend itself to tidy definition. It cannot easily be captured in terms of necessary and sufficient conditions, at least not without hedge words such as *typically*. As Nussbaum explains, marriage "is plural in both content and meaning"—involving a diverse cluster of goods and defining elements.[20] For most of those elements, there will be numerous exceptions, as well as "gray areas." Notice, however, that loose edges are typical of social institutions. (Does secular humanism count as a religion? Do tribal councils count as governments?)

Girgis and other opponents of same-sex marriage sometimes complain that I don't offer enough of a definition of marriage to provide a clear point of contrast with the conjugal view, so let me do so here. Instead of "revisionist," let's call it "inclusivist," to avoid begging the question against those who believe that embracing same-sex marriage involves an expansion of who may marry, not a redefinition of what marriage is.

> Inclusivist view: Marriages are committed adult unions which are presumptively sexual, exclusive, and lifelong; and which typically involve shared domestic life, mutual care and concern, and the begetting and rearing of children.[21]

Girgis charges that this definition is "parasitic on the conjugal view," which is the only way to justify combining these features into one bond. On the contrary, what justifies this definition is actual human behavior: This is how most competent English speakers now use the term *marriage*, and the features it picks out form a cluster of activities that many (gay and straight) couples strive for, and some happily achieve.

SOME OBJECTIONS

I turn now to some possible objections. After all, while the Bob and Jane case exposes a counterintuitive implication of the conjugal view, perhaps the alternatives are worse. Girgis, George, Anderson, and others have questioned whether the revisionist view (and by implication, the inclusivist view) can explain how marriage differs from ordinary companionship, why it is closely associated with procreation and childrearing, why the state should be involved in it, and why it should be monogamous rather than polygamous; I shall touch upon each of these points in what follows.

Girgis writes that his "main objection to the revisionist view is that it has no cogent way of distinguishing marriage from companionship *simpliciter*":

> [Most revisionists would] stipulate that sex is uniquely relevant to marriage. They can certainly *stipulate* as much, but they cannot *explain* it. They may say sex generally fosters and expresses the emotional intimacy that *really* makes a marriage, but they cannot maintain that sex is in that respect unique. Two celibate monks can share deep conversation, cooperation amid hardship, custody of an orphaned child, or a passion for art, and feel themselves to be twin souls. That does not give their bond the distinctive value and norms of a marriage.[22]

He goes on to argue that only *coital* sex can "accomplish something so different from other activities that it can set a whole class of bonds apart (in terms of the basic good they realize and the commitment they require) from the spectrum of friendships sealed by non-sexual activities and compatible with a variety of commitments."[23] That's because only coital sex can constitute bodily union.

One way to undercut this objection is to challenge Girgis's denial that noncoital sex can set apart a class of relationships from ordinary friendships. Sex, including noncoital sex, has a pervasive character: it tends to affect how people relate to each other even when they're not in the act. In the context of a relationship, it is more like a spice, which permeates the entire dish, than a garnish. "Deep conversation, cooperation amid hardship, custody of an orphaned child, [and] a passion for art" are no substitutes.

The more general problem, however, is Girgis's insistence that there must be a single aim (in his view, aptness for procreation and family life) that distinguishes marriage from other goods. I argue that this insistence is wrong: marriage, like friendship, may be distinguished by a set of overlapping aims and practices, rather than a single shared one.

It is Girgis's inability to grasp this point that lies behind his repeated complaint that I cannot distinguish marriage from other forms of companionship. One might just as well charge that I cannot distinguish baseball from other games, for baseball, like marriage, is distinguished by a cluster of features that arose historically, rather than one simple unifying principle. Moreover, although baseball is governed by rules, those rules allow some alteration without changing the game's fundamental nature. Whether or not we observe the designated hitter rule, for example, the game is still baseball, notwithstanding the objections of some National League purists. If we were to slightly alter the size of the bat, the game would still be baseball. But if we were to replace the bat with a tennis racket, the game would not be baseball (even though it might well be a game worth playing).

Now Girgis might retort that I do not offer any reason—"Not a mediocre reason, not a bad one, but none"—to accept this understanding of baseball. He might write:

> What is special, either in itself or for policy, about a game that combines a bat and four bases? Or four bases and two teams of nine players each? . . . What makes this list anything more than an arbitrary assemblage of characteristics?[24]

To be sure, there are important disanalogies between marriage and baseball, but none of them affect my point here: human social practices are often distinguished by a cluster of features—the assembly of which may seem arbitrary from the outside—rather than by a single unifying essence. It's also worth noting that "comprehensive union" is just slippery enough of a principle to allow quite a bit of gerrymandering in the features it comprises (union of bodies and minds, exclusivity for some aspects of the union but not others, and so on).

Nor am I suggesting (as Girgis implausibly claims) that we can "wrench thick judgments about basic justice from the barest data about our language."[25] Here, as elsewhere, Girgis is conflating two questions: first, whether a relationship is a marriage, and second, how should a just society treat that relationship vis-à-vis others. Justice demands that similar relationships be treated similarly, and conceptual analysis—which Girgis here dismisses as "our attitudes and linguistic habits"—is a useful if imperfect tool for identifying similarities. But justice does not demand that particular legal incidents be granted to all and only marriages. After all, even things that are similar *qua* marriages may be dissimilar in other morally relevant ways.[26]

Girgis, Anderson, and George ask why the state ought to be involved in marriage thus understood. In their view, the state regulates marriage because it is concerned with children's welfare, and only conjugal marriage explains the inherent link between marriage and procreation. Notice, however, that a concern with children's welfare does not automatically entail the state's interest in *conjugal marriage*. Instead, it entails the state's interest in relationships that *might produce children or do include childrearing*—a class that is both narrower and broader than conjugal marriages.

In response to the point that the class is narrower than conjugal marriages (because not all conjugal marriages are fertile), Girgis, Anderson, and George might note that fertility tests for marriage would be intrusive and infeasible; the law is a rough instrument.[27] I agree. But is restricting civil marriage to *male-female* unions the best rough way for the state to ensure children's welfare? I argue that it is not.

Some contend that the state should restrict marriage to male-female unions because research demonstrates that children do best with a mother and father. This is the worst kind of argument: it proceeds from what is not true to what does not follow.

It is not true that research demonstrates that children do best with a mother and father. Take, for example, the New Family Structures Study by sociologist Mark Regnerus, widely touted by marriage-equality opponents as debunking the claim that children raised in same-sex households show no disadvantages compared to those raised by their own biological mother and father.[28] Regnerus collected data on a random sample of nearly three thousand adult children between the ages of eighteen and thirty-nine, including 175 who reported that their mother had a same-sex romantic relationship and seventy-three who reported the same about their father. It found that adults in these two groups fared significantly less well on various measures of well-being than those who reported being raised by their "intact biological families."

The problem stems from how Regnerus set up his categories. He asked respondents, "From when you were born until when you were eighteen, did either of your parents ever have a relationship with someone of the same sex?" If they answered yes, he put them in the "Lesbian Mother" or "Gay Father" category—regardless of the length of the relationship and regardless of any other transitions. Only 23 percent of the so-called Lesbian Mother respondents lived with their mother and her partner for at least three years. Less than 2 percent of the "Gay Father" respondents did so. And in the entire study, only two children lived with a same-sex couple for their entire childhood. This is not a study of same-sex parenting at all: it's a study of heterosexual families that fell apart. It confirms what social scientists have known for a long time: divorce, abandonment, and other such disruptions negatively impact child welfare. It tells us nothing about the *planned* children of same-sex couples, much less about whether such couples should be allowed to marry.

Regnerus's study has been widely criticized by mainstream social scientists and professional organizations. As the American Sociological Association explains,

> Numerous nationally representative, credible, and methodologically sound social science studies . . . reveal that children raised by same-sex parents fare just as well as children raised by opposite-sex couples across a wide spectrum of child-wellbeing measures: academic performance, cognitive development, social development, psychological health, early sexual activity, and substance abuse.[29]

Similar conclusions have been reached by the American Academy of Pediatrics, the American Psychological Association, the Child Welfare League of America, the National Association of Social Workers, the American Academy of Child and Adolescent Psychiatry—indeed, every mainstream health and welfare organization that has examined the data.[30]

But suppose, notwithstanding this dramatic consensus, that mainstream social science is simply wrong. Even in that case, the conclusion about marriage would not follow. Restricting marriage to male-female unions does not ensure that more children would be raised by their own intact biological families; it only ensures that the thousands of existing children being raised by same-sex couples will not get the benefit of marriage. They will not enjoy the stability and security that would stem from extending civil marriage recognition to the parents raising them. As Judge Bernard Friedman explained in his ruling in the Michigan marriage case:

> [C]ontrary to the state defendants' contentions, the [Michigan Marriage Amendment, which prohibits same-sex marriage or similar unions] actually fosters the potential for childhood destabilization. For instance, in this particular case should either of the plaintiffs die or become incapacitated, the surviving non-legal parent would have no authority under Michigan law to make legal decisions on behalf of the surviving children without resorting to a prolonged and complicated guardianship proceeding. And in the event that a state court were to award guardianship of the surviving children to the non-legal parent,

the guardianship would have to be renewed annually and would remain susceptible to the challenge of an interested party at any time. This . . . places such children in a legally precarious situation and deprives them of "social capital."[31]

In the world as we know it, the state's interest in child welfare is not an argument *against* same-sex marriage; it is an argument for it.

The public benefits of marriage go beyond its benefits to children, which is why the state recognizes the marriages of couples (gay and straight) who do not have, cannot have, or never intend to have children. Marriage benefits spouses in creating for them a legally recognized zone of familial privacy. It announces their transition from being children in their family of origin to being adults in their family of choice. As such, it has a fundamentally expressive aspect, one to which the state currently holds the keys.[32] And marriage benefits society at large in promoting stable households: when there's someone whose lifelong "job" it is to take care of you and vice versa, that means less burden on the state.

Of course, reasonable people may differ on whether the state ought to be involved in marriage as deeply as it is.[33] They may also differ on whether it makes sense to limit state recognition to presumptively romantic relationships, given that (as Girgis rightly notes) these are not the only relationships that involve voluntary adult mutual caregiving—although they do tend to be the only ones that involve a presumptively permanent sharing of life and property without arising from families of origin. My point here is not to make the case for a particular legal regime, however, but to argue that there's no reason to think that conjugal marriage is uniquely able to explain our intuitions about state involvement. Again, there are state-relevant features of marriage that apply to childless adults, and the class of relationships that might produce children or do involve childrearing is both broader and narrower than conjugal marriages.

What about polygamy? Polygamy is very common historically, and there are areas of the United States where it is still practiced among fundamentalist Mormons and other ultraconservative religious communities. I am personally agnostic on the question of whether the state ought to recognize multiple-partner relationships (although I do believe such relationships should be decriminalized[34]). The point I want to make here is twofold: first, the inclusivist view does not entail a particular position on polygamy, and second, the conjugal view itself offers no cogent argument against polygamy.

On the first point: for public-policy reasons, many inclusivists are wary of polygamy. Polygamous societies are almost always polygynous, where one husband has multiple wives. (Polyandry—one wife with multiple husbands—is quite rare.) The usual result is a sexist and classist society where high-status males acquire multiple wives while low-status males become virtually unmarriageable. This result is bad for social stability, and the state may properly take that fact into account in setting marriage policy.[35] (As for Girgis's "harder" case of polyamory: the state may properly take into account that legalizing polyamory would have the practical result of legalizing—and perhaps fostering—traditional polygamy.)[36]

The new natural lawyers would doubtless object that this response does not rule out polygamy *in principle*. They are correct; it does not. But that brings me to the second and more important point: despite their claims to the contrary, the conjugal view does not convincingly rule out polygamy in principle either. Here's Girgis, Anderson, and George's core argument against polygamy:

> Marriage is possible between only two because no act can organically unite three or more, or thus seal a comprehensive union of three or more lives. If bodily union is essential to marriage, we can understand why marriage, like the union of organs into one healthy whole, should be total and lasting for the life of the parts ("till death do us part"). Being organically united—as "one flesh"—spouses should have, by commitment, the exclusive and lifelong unity that the parts of a healthy organic body have by nature. (WIM 33)

This is a rather peculiar argument. Put aside the fact (explained in section II above) that Girgis, Anderson, and George fail to show why marital unions, qua comprehensive unions, must be more bodily than other unions—as opposed to, say, more intellectual. Put aside as well our earlier argument (via the case of Bob and Jane) that marriage does not in fact require "organic bodily union" in coitus—although either of these two asides would be sufficient to sink the argument at hand. What's odd is the use of analogy. Girgis, Anderson, and George appear to be arguing that, because bodily union in coitus is like the union of bodily organs (heart, stomach, lungs), which is naturally permanent and exclusive, marriage too should be permanent and exclusive. One might just as well argue that bodily union should be constant (perpetual coitus!) and also pinkish in color. The fact that coitus shares *some* features with the union of organs in a single human body does not entail that is shares *all* features, including exclusivity.

In a footnote, Girgis, Anderson, and George claim that they "are not inferring that x is a property of marriage, from the fact that something like x is a property of bodily union" (WIM 114 n11). Rather, they are pointing to "parallels and harmonies" among the ways in which marriage is comprehensive. But comprehensiveness and exclusivity are two distinct things, and the latter is not deducible from the former. After all, Girgis, Anderson, and George can presumably enjoy intellectual union with each other, and with other scholars, without undermining the so-called comprehensive unions (marriages) that they have with their wives. Why does comprehensiveness entail exclusivity for bodies but not for minds?

To be clear, I am not denying that exclusivity and permanence are valuable features of marriage. But the argument for them will need to come from somewhere other than the nature of "organic bodily union." While it is true that human biological reproduction requires two and only two people,[37] one male and one female, it is equally true that individuals can form reproductive pairs with multiple others. In that sense, they are quite unlike the heart and the lungs, which (aside from transplants) are pretty much stuck where they are. Yet if the argument for permanence and exclusivity comes from somewhere other than organic bodily union, it will likely be just as available to inclusivists. The conjugal view has no advantage with respect to the challenge of polygamy.

CONCLUSION: LOVE AND MARRIAGE

Girgis, Anderson, and George claim that same-sex couples are not capable of real marriage, and that the state should not distort the meaning of real marriage by extending civil marriage to them. I have argued that their conjugal view of marriage depends on selective myopia, has seriously counterintuitive implications, and fares no better than the alternative in accounting for important intuitions about marriage and its goods. The alleged problems with the alternative stem largely from their straw-man characterization of it, which portrays marriage as a mere "emotional union . . . valuable while the emotion lasts," rather than as an active commitment.

WHAT MARRIAGE CAN BE

Girgis, Anderson, and George conclude their book with a thought experiment, which they say crystallizes their central argument:

> Almost every culture in every time and place has had some institution that resembles what we know as marriage. But imagine that human beings reproduced asexually and that human offspring were born self-sufficient. In that case, would any culture have developed an institution anything like what we know as marriage? It is clear that the answer is no. (WIM 96)

What appears clear to Girgis, Anderson, and George is by no means clear to me.

The point of this thought experiment is to show that the biological facts of procreation—and specifically, organic bodily union in coitus—are essential to marriage. Notice that its force rests on the genetic fallacy (no pun intended): the erroneous belief that a thing's current nature depends on its origin. After all, it might well be the case that marriage arose because of certain biological facts without it following that marriage only makes sense given those facts. Similar to how ears arose for hearing, but are also useful for keeping one's eyeglasses for sliding off one's nose, it's quite possible that marriage arose (in large part) because of the realities of procreation, but is also useful for other purposes sufficient in themselves: promoting social stability, for example, or expressing a distinctive kind of adult commitment.

In any case, Girgis, Anderson, and George aim to show that marriage makes no sense without organic bodily union. In order for their thought experiment to establish this conclusion, we must take organic bodily union out of the picture—as they do by positing asexual human reproduction—while leaving other elements as untouched as possible. (This is a thought experiment, not a biology test.) So let's try that: imagine that human beings reproduced asexually and that their offspring were born self-sufficient, but that they still had the tendency to fall passionately in love with each other. Imagine that when they did so, they often sought to form household units, so that they could come home to their beloved partners each evening and wake up together each morning and share life's daily joys and sorrows. Imagine, further, that such relationships were difficult to maintain, given the vagaries of human passion, but that people nevertheless strived to make them work, recognizing the profound mutual security and comfort that long-term intimate companionship would bring.

Indeed, suppose they felt so strongly about doing so that they were willing to make public commitments, in the presence of family and friends, "to have and to hold, for better or for worse, until death do they part." And suppose that their family and friends encouraged such commitments, because they understood their tendency to provide unparalleled security and comfort and intimacy and joy.

Now return to the actual world, where all of these things do in fact happen for people who don't want or can't have children—*and also for people who don't want or can't have the kind of sex that typically makes children*. Is it really so far-fetched that they, too, want to make these kinds of commitments? Or that their family and friends would encourage them to do so? Or that they would seek social and legal recognition for the families that they form? Whether or not you see marriage here, it's hard to deny—as Girgis does explicitly—that it's "anything like what we know as marriage," or that it might make sense even if biological reproduction happened differently.

It's worth noting that as public opinion has shifted dramatically on same-sex marriage in recent years, many credit their evolution at least in part to personal experience. (Think, for example, of statements from public former opponents such as David Blankenhorn, Charles Murray, or Senator Rob Portman.) They observe their gay and lesbian neighbors, colleagues, and family members falling in love, making commitments, settling down, and trying to make a go of it. They see them engaged in this awesome, familiar human project of trying to weave together romantic passion with quotidian reality. In other words, they see marriage. Girgis accuses me of seeing in monochrome, while claiming that his view countenances "the more sprawling and splendid diversity."[38] But his inability to recognize the distinctive joys and challenges of same-sex couples' committed *romantic* relationships—the differences between them and those of bachelor brothers, or cohabitating monks, or comrades—betrays a stubborn moral blind spot. [39]

NOTES

1. Lila Shapiro, "Leading Gay Marriage Opponent on Losing the Battle: 'I Have a Lot More Freedom Now,'" February 2, 2016, http://www.huffingtonpost.com/2014/03/20/maggie-gallagher_n_5001848.html, accessed May 20, 2014.

2. *Obergefell v. Hodges*, 576 U.S. ___ (2015).

3. Justin McCarthy, Gallup.com, "Record-High 60% of Americans Support Same-Sex Marriage," http://www.gallup.com/poll/183272/record-high-americans-support-sex-marriage.aspx, accessed March 1, 2016.

4. Sherif Girgis, Ryan T. Anderson, and Robert P. George, *What Is Marriage? Man and Woman: A Defense* (New York: Encounter Books, 2012), hereafter cited in the text as WIM; based on Sherif Girgis, Robert P. George, and Ryan T. Anderson, "What Is Marriage?," *Harvard Journal of Law and Public Policy* 34, no. 1 (Winter 2010): 245–87.

5. John Corvino and Maggie Gallagher, *Debating Same-Sex Marriage* (New York: Oxford University Press), 203.

6. Girgis, this volume.

7. See Naomi Cahn and June Carbone, *Red Families v. Blue Families: Legal Polarization and the Creation of Culture* (New York: Oxford University Press, 2010).

8. Girgis, George, and Anderson, "What Is Marriage?," 254.

9. Robert P. George, "What's Sex Got to Do with It? Marriage, Morality, and Rationality," in Robert P. George and Jean Bethke Elshtain, eds., *The Meaning of Marriage: Family, State, Market, and Morals* (Dallas: Spence Publishing Company, 2006), 160.

10. Andrew Koppelman, *The Gay Rights Question in Contemporary American Law* (Chicago: University of Chicago Press, 2002), 86–88.

11. George, "What's Sex Got to Do With It?," 164 (emphasis in original).

12. Jason Lee Steorts has made a similar point. See "Two Views of Marriage, and the Falsity of the Choice Between Them," http://www.nationalreview.com/article/263672/two-views-marriage-and-falsity-choice-between-them-jason-lee-steorts, accessed July 1, 2014.

13. Girgis, this volume.

14. George, "What's Sex Got to Do with It?," 160 n59.

15. Indeed, I'm inclined to make some stronger claims here: the goodness of an end redounds to its means or constituents only if the end *occurs*; the goodness of a merely possible end redounds to the *subjective intention* to achieve it—"A for effort!"—and the goodness of an end that is known to be impossible redounds to nothing. But the stronger claims are unnecessary for my argument.

16. Patrick Lee and Robert P. George, "What Sex Can Be: Self-Alienation, Illusion, or One-Flesh Union," *American Journal of Jurisprudence* 42 (1997): 175; as reprinted in Robert P. George, *In Defense of Natural Law* (New York: Oxford University Press, 1999).

17. He writes, "Marital acts are valuable as a form of *coordination between two people toward* a single bodily end, and hence as a form of *bodily union*, and

hence as part of a *comprehensive union*." But the single bodily end is precisely what's unavailable in this case. (Girgis, this volume.)

18. WIM 127 n5.

19. WIM 127 n5.

20. Martha Nussbaum, *From Disgust to Humanity: Sexual Orientation and Constitutional Law* (New York: Oxford University Press, 2010), 128.

21. I first offered this definition in "What's Wrong with Gay Marriage?," *The Philosophers' Magazine* 62 (3rd Quarter 2013): 33–39.

22. Sherif Girgis, "Making Sense of Marriage," in *Contemporary Debates in Applied Ethics*, 2nd ed., eds. Andrew I. Cohen and Christopher Heath Wellman (New York: Wiley-Blackwell, 2014), 293.

23. Girgis, "Making Sense of Marriage," 293.

24. Modified from Girgis, this volume.

25. See Girgis, this volume.

26. For example, some married couples may be eligible for certain tax breaks in virtue of their income, while others fail to meet the relevant threshold.

27. Of course, the law does not currently restrict legal marriage to conjugal unions, for it could not practically enquire as to whether couples intend the sort of *comprehensive* union that the conjugal view demands. It could, however, achieve a better approximation than it does currently; for example, by prohibiting remarriage after divorce.

28. Mark Regnerus, "How Different Are the Adult Children of Parents Who Have Same-Sex Relationships? Findings from the New Family Structures Study," *Social Science Research* 41, no. 4 (July 2012): 752–70.

29. "Brief of *Amicus Curiae* American Sociological Association in Support of Respondent Kristin M. Perry and Respondent Edith Schlain Windsor," available at http://www.asanet.org/documents/ASA/pdfs/12-144_307_Amicus_%28C_Gottlieb%29_ASA_Same-Sex_Marriage.pdf, accessed July 1, 2014, 6.

30. For a handy summary of these statements, see chapter 3 of Leslie Cooper and Paul Cates, *Too High a Price: The Case Against Restricting Gay Parenting* (New York: American Civil Liberties Union Foundation, 2006), at http://www.aclu.org/lgbt-rights_hiv-aids/too-high-price-case-against-restricting-gay-parenting, accessed July 1, 2014.

31. *DeBoer v. Snyder*, Civil Action No. 12-CV-10285.

32. On this point, see Nussbaum, *From Disgust to Humanity*, 126ff.

33. As does Nussbaum, *From Disgust to Humanity*.

34. What I mean is that the state should not criminalize the activity of multiple partners *living together as spouses*; I am not here addressing bigamy, where people have fraudulently sought marriage licenses while currently married.

35. One recent paper observes that "In suppressing intrasexual competition and reducing the size of the pool of unmarried men, normative monogamy re-

duces crime rates, including rape, murder, assault, robbery and fraud, as well as decreasing personal abuses." See Joseph Henrich, Robert Boyd, and Peter J. Richerson, "The Puzzle of Monogamous Marriage," *Philosophical Transactions of the Royal Society B* (2012): 367, 657–69.

36. Yes, these are empirical claims, and difficult ones. And that's why I remain agnostic about polygamy: I don't know if they're correct, and I leave it to the polygamists and polyamorists to make their case.

37. True, given current technology.

38. Girgis, this volume.

39. My thoughts on new natural law and marriage have benefitted from dialogue with various friends and colleagues over the years. For comments on various drafts of this chapter, I would like to thank Matthew Lee Anderson, Chris Arroyo, Andrew Koppelman, Lawrence B. Lombard, Bruce Russell, Sean Stidd, Jonah Wacholder, Robert J. Yanal, and, of course, Sherif Girgis. I am grateful for this opportunity to continue the conversation with him.

15

MARRIAGE

Whose Justice? Which Diversity?

Sherif Girgis, Princeton University

Rare is the diversity-based argument for same-sex civil marriage. Advocates usually appeal to *equality*—sameness in some respect—because marriage law makes disparate things alike in legal status. And this presupposes that they have the same basic link to the common good. If same-sex sexual partnerships introduce significant diversity—difference—that might tell *against* assimilating them to marriages, as some queer theorists contend.

Still, one can imagine an argument appealing to the diversity of sexual identities. Maybe this case would rest on Anthony Appiah's nondiscrimination principle that we mustn't disadvantage people because of their social identity: as Zoroastrians, Asians, or—as with marriage, the argument would go—as gay people.[1]

Then again, we shouldn't simply avoid unjust discrimination. Perhaps pluralism requires us to offer identity groups the resources needed to pursue their life plans on an equal basis[2]—including, on this view, marriage recognition for their primary (sexual) partnerships.

One way or another, then, sexual-relationship diversity might seem to require same-sex civil marriage.

It does not. There is no logical bridge from diverse patterns of sexual desire to the conclusion that we should recognize same-sex relationships as marriages. So it's fitting that the debate hasn't centered on diversity.

The real questions, lurking behind the arguments above, concern what marriage is and why it matters socially.

In particular, the nondiscrimination argument, that traditional marriage laws are premised on devaluing people identified as gay or lesbian, assumes that there aren't meaningful differences relevant to the common good between same- and opposite-sex bonds. The second argument, about positive duties to equip everyone with basic resources, assumes that the social need (properly) filled by marriage law is to recognize publicly your most personally fulfilling bond—that this is what makes marriage different from other bonds.

Yet both assumptions are false. They get marriage wrong and mistake its public relevance. To show how, I take as a counterpoint my friend John Corvino's chapter in this volume. His defense of what I will call the revisionist view of marriage is, like its author, sophisticated, civil, and well informed. But as I show, it suffers from several flaws.

Contradicting virtually every philosophical and legal tradition until yesterday, it nonetheless offers no positive case for its thesis. (This allows it to focus entirely on objections to my view—which still miss their mark.) Proposing an ideal of marriage, it can't even explain how marriage differs from nonmarital companionship. Prescribing major changes to a social institution, it takes a flatfooted view of how social norms work. Corvino's view narrows our opportunities for the emotional intimacy it tries to champion, and steals what plausibility it has from the more traditional, conjugal view, on which, I will show, it is parasitic. And it would wrench normative conclusions from bare statistics about romantic behavior and linguistic usage, in this way relying on moves that neither Corvino nor his readers would (or should!) accept from intellectual opponents.

I frame the issues in sections 1 and 2 below, and discuss the revisionist view's weaknesses in 3 and the harms of enshrining it in 4. I defend the conjugal view in 5, answer objections in 6, and revisit in 7 the topic of diversity, to show that embracing the conjugal view better serves that value.

CONSIDER FIRST TWO COMPETING UNDERSTANDINGS OF MARRIAGE.

In the *conjugal view*, marriage is a comprehensive union. Joining spouses in body and mind, it is begun by consent and sealed by sexual intercourse. So completed in acts of bodily union by which new life is made, marriage itself is deepened by procreation, and calls for that broad sharing of domestic life uniquely fit for family life. Uniting spouses in these all-encompassing ways, it calls for all-encompassing commitment: permanent and exclusive. Comprehensive (*conjugal*) union is valuable in itself, but its link to children's welfare makes marriage a public good that the state should recognize and support.[3]

The revisionist view, rejects the criteria for comprehensiveness just proposed. What sets marriage apart from other bonds, on this view, is an affective, emotional union of special intensity, lived out in home life and enhanced by any agreeable sexual activity. There is special personal value in such (romantic) unions as such, and public value in their stability.

Corvino charges that I'm unfair to the latter view; in saying that revisionists distinguish marriage by romantic-emotional union, I overlook their interest in upholding commitment. That is nearly an empty response. The question is what marriage is a commitment *to*. The *only* available revisionist reply is: maintaining romantic-emotional union. If a relationship has indefinitely lost its romantic hue, it has lost any revisionist basis for being a marriage, as opposed to some other companionship.[4]

Consider what Corvino himself says must survive life's oscillations: love. Though the slogan that love makes a marriage is a familiar one, no one has ever believed it as stated—not even today, not even Corvino. The love of mother for daughter, of teacher for pupil, of pastor for flock; the love of brothers or best friends is true love. No one thinks these forms of love can make a marriage. The question is what is distinctive of *marital* love. How will the revisionist reply, if not along the lines I've sketched?

Now on the conjugal view, only one man and one woman can form the bodily union required for truly marital (comprehensive) union. Two men or two women cannot. It is equally clear that any two people can enjoy the affective union central to the revisionist view. So this debate is not about whether to expand marriage, but whether to replace one view of it with a new one, finishing (I will explain) what policy changes like no-fault divorce began.

Here I defend the conjugal view as an account of marriage and principle for our policy. My argument requires no particular view about the moral status of same-sex sexual acts, and it rests nothing on the fallacious "perverted faculty" argument (which considers it wrong to use organs against their natural purposes). I infer nothing about how marriage *must* be from how it *has* been. And I require no theology. Indeed, ancient thinkers who never saw a Hebrew parchment or heard a Christian preacher—including Aristotle, Plato, Socrates, Musonius Rufus, Xenophanes, and Plutarch—reached views of marriage in line with the one I defend.

Nor can animus have produced this view, which was implemented long before the nineteenth-century medicalization of homosexuality and subsequent rise of gay cultural identity, let alone the Stonewall Riots. Some cultures, as in ancient Greece, took the conjugal view for granted while *celebrating* certain same-sex relations.

Finally, pure appeals to equality can't refute my argument. Theories (or laws) of any type that distinguish marriage will *always* leave something out, yet they don't all violate equality. To know when it is a true marriage that goes unrecognized, arbitrarily, and when what is excluded is something else entirely, one must first grasp what marriage is and why we recognize it. The conjugal and revisionist views are two answers: both morally charged and controversial among citizens and religious bodies, neither neutral.

Which, then, is right? What is marriage?

MANY JURISDICTIONS NOW HAVE SAME-SEX CIVIL MARRIAGE. SO HOW CAN I ARGUE THAT SAME-SEX MARRIAGE IS IMPOSSIBLE?

Marriage is not just a legal category; it's also an inherently valuable form of association, just as *ordinary* friendship is. And both sides of the debate agree that the law can get that category right or wrong. So marriage itself must have certain features, *whatever* the law says. These give a bond the distinctive personal and social value of marriage; any marriage law should capture them as best it can.

Today we disagree on what defines marriage, so understood, but most share certain intuitions: marriage is inherently sexual, it is uniquely enriched by family life, and it uniquely requires permanent and exclusive commitment to begin at all.

What best explains this combination? I contend that these are characteristics of a basic human bond that only a man and woman can realize together. The movement to redefine marriage in the law, should it succeed, will culturally entrench a profound error about this human good, which will affect people's choices and behavior in ways that harm the public good.

THE REVISIONIST VIEW'S CENTRAL FLAW IS THIS: IT CAN'T DISTINGUISH MARRIAGE FROM OTHER BONDS— ESPECIALLY OTHER FORMS OF COMPANIONSHIP— WHICH IS THE MOST BASIC JOB OF ANY ACCOUNT OF MARRIAGE.

So revisionists *effectively eliminate* the very category (i.e., marriage) that they set out to describe. This objection, if sound, is fatal. But there is no good reply. Corvino's answers in this volume, where they aren't simply parasitic on the conjugal view, are easily exposed for fallacies if only we imagine the parallel points being made in defense of more traditional laws. They can support Corvino's view only on overly generous readings from sympathetic audiences.

Let me explain. Say two men share a home and domestic duties. Their mutual trust makes each want the other to manage his care if he is ill and inherit his assets if he dies. Each offers the other ready counsel in distress, security amid hardship, company in defeat, and in every personal victory. They face the world together.

On the revisionist view, they should have every right to a marriage license. But what if they are bachelor brothers in a platonic bond? Here revisionism's clear consequences conflict with near-universal judgments. This relationship may be worthy of great respect, but it is not a marriage, because marriage centrally involves a sexual component.

Most revisionists would agree, but could they explain the connection? They may say that sex fosters the emotional intimacy that *really* distinguishes marriage, but in that way sex is not unique. Celibate monks can share deep conversation, cooperation in hardship, custody of an orphaned child, or a passion for art, and feel like twin souls. That does not give their bond the value or norms of marriage.

Corvino just says that marriages are presumptively sexual. But so what? In the same sense, marriages are presumptively opposite-sex, yet Corvino would never see this bare statistical fact as a reason to exclude same-sex bonds from marriage. Why then exclude platonic bonds?

So, again: What about sex, *apart* from its emotional and attachment effects, makes it critical to marriage? I argue in section 5 that only *coitus* accomplishes something different in kind and central to marriage: it constitutes a *bodily union* as nonsexual acts (even noncoital sex) cannot.

Now consider a romantic triad (like a "throuple" profiled in *New York Magazine*). If one dies, the others are coheirs. If one is ill, either can visit. They advise and console each other and share major experiences. Why can't they form a marriage?

The revisionist could *stipulate* that the emotional union setting marriage apart should include only two people. But why? Or why should marriage be pledged to permanence?

Corvino addresses the social costs of polygamy (actually polygyny: one man, several wives), but offers no good argument about what is for him the much harder case of polyamory—a romantically involved group, of any combination, forming a single marriage. (Yes, as Corvino points out, a law recognizing polyamory would also, incidentally, cover some cases of polygyny, with its social costs. But does that justify denying what polyamorists will consider their marriage equality? Every marriage law is overinclusive in *some* way.)

As for linking permanence and romance, Corvino says little indeed: there's value in supporting people's *lifelong* support of each other, which occurs most often in *romantic* bonds.

Set aside the empirical assumptions packed into these claims, which many same-sex marriage advocates reject. (Isn't it better, they ask, to have different partners at different life stages, so that interest and passion stay strong? Don't multiple-partner bonds offer more fulfilling variety and freedom from suspicion and deceit?) The fact that desire for permanence "typically" happens in romance (between just two, we can add) isn't a reason—not even a little one—to keep marriage restricted to romance, or dyads. After all, again, the fact that romance typically involves the opposite sex is no good argument against same-sex marriage. If catering to the majority is unjust in the second case, it is in the first.

Here again, Corvino's logic leaves the courthouse door open to any form of consensual companionship. And to stop these clear implications, he offers the sort of hand waving that he would rightly reject from a defender of male-female marriage.

Corvino says the conjugal view does no better at grounding these stabilizing marital norms. I respond in section 5c. For now, consider this striking historical point. Roughly coincident with the many centuries in which the conjugal view prevailed in Western (though not just Western) law and culture, norms like permanence and exclusivity were taken for granted as integral to marriage. Then, roughly coincident with the seventeen years between the federal Defense of Marriage Act's passage and its judicial gutting, almost every marital norm has been questioned or opposed by serious people in serious outlets: we've seen growing calls for legally recognizing or promoting multiple-partner, deliberately temporary (e.g., five-year-renewable), sexually open, even nonsexual and multiple-household bonds—all premised on the idea that love and commitment, in all their polymorphous splendor, are what make a family. Just a coincidence?[5] As I'll show, it isn't.

Finally, the revisionist can't explain marriage's unique relation to children. Traditional jokes and modern sociology alike show that childrearing can take an emotional toll. The conjugal view can acknowledge this and still explain (see section 5b) how family life enriches marriage *as such*, even as compared with other stable bonds—say, our monks raising an orphan. Revisionists can't explain this, or, again, any systematic difference between marriage and companionship.

In reply, Corvino offers this view of marriage:

> Marriages are committed adult unions which are presumptively sexual, exclusive, and lifelong; and which typically involve shared domestic life, mutual care and concern, and the begetting and rearing of children.

This list is plausible as far as it goes, *but only because it is parasitic on the conjugal view*. It's that view, and no alternative of Corvino's, that makes sense of combining these features.

What *else* could justify using a public institution to single out relationships with this particular bundle of traits? What is special, in itself or for policy, about a bond that combines sex and exclusivity? Or sex and lifelong commitment? Why care more about cases where sexual partnership and domestic sharing overlap than cases where they don't? What makes this list more than an arbitrary assemblage of characteristics?

Corvino would evade these objections with qualifiers like "presumptively" and "typically," but these are entirely beside the point. The problem is not that marriage for Corvino has fuzzy edges, but that its basic shape (fuzzy borders or not) is arbitrary. Even if marriage is marked by presumptions, the question remains: What makes *this combination* of presumptions fit together more tightly, or deserve more public recognition, than others?

Maybe the answer is that two people sharing a home are especially close. They're (presumptively!) sharing each other's ups and downs, their deepest worries and goals.

If that is the answer, the bond may well have value. But is it necessarily a marriage? Why must it have (even presumptively) other features of marriage, or be legally regulated?

Corvino will answer that falling in love and making a home is just what people do. This perfectly true sentence misses the objection. The whole point is that people form (romantic) relationships of all kinds; the whole task is figuring out which of the many companionate relationships that people do form are, and should be recognized as, marriages.

But if the point is that sex can lead to children, who deserve to know their own parents in a stable home; or that sex and its fulfillment in family life can so fully unite two people that total commitment is called for; *then* picking out bonds with this combination of features does make sense. But that supports the conjugal view (see section 5). Insofar as Corvino's definition seems plausible, it's just a bare abstraction of that view. Its elements can't be unified by the idea of companionship or emotional union, or statistical patterns in romantic behavior.

So what? asks Corvino: "One might as well charge that I cannot distinguish baseball from other games." Baseball's rules have developed over time. We can change some, but not others, without effectively ending baseball, but there's no principle telling us which are which.

Corvino says marriage is in these ways like baseball. But here he gives away the argument.

What makes bats essential to baseball, but not the designated hitter rule? That enough people would still think of it as "baseball" if the rule were thrown out, but not the bats. Are our attitudes and linguistic habits all that fix the essential features of marriage? Then traditional marriage laws are perfectly just wherever people are disposed to think of marriage as heterosexual. If there are no principled boundaries to which relationships are marriages, then majorities violate no principle in voting to exclude same-sex ones.[6]

This suggests that Corvino would wrench thick judgments about basic justice from the barest data about our language. In his argument, ultimately, justice requires recognizing same-sex bonds but not, say, platonic bonds because (in his words) "most competent English speakers" use the word *marriage* to include the first but not the second.[7] This is an absurd result.

So I've argued for my view of marriage, which entails that it is a male-female bond. Corvino, by contrast, hasn't offered *a single affirmative reason* to accept his view of marriage generally, or of same-sex partnerships in particular. Not a mediocre reason, nor a bad one, but none. He relies on stipulation, perhaps counting on his audience to be disposed to sympathize with him. Whatever this is, it is not an argument.

But an argument is precisely what Corvino needs, and what he owes open-minded readers, given the contrary consensus of virtually every culture and philosopher in history, and his view's logical implication that it's just as arbitrary, unjust, and discriminatory to expect twoness or sexuality or sexual exclusivity in marriage, as to require complementarity.

THIS LAST POINT HIGHLIGHTS THE SOCIAL HARMS AT STAKE.

A revisionist redefinition of marriage law would teach people to internalize a view that makes marriage's stabilizing norms seem optional. That would erode them in practice, which would undermine stability for children—and as Corvino says, "Social scientists have known for a long time [that] divorce, abandonment, and other such disruptions negatively impact child welfare." (Besides, there's independent value, for both parents and children, to keeping children with their biological parents where reasonably possible.[8]) So these effects would harm the next generation and thus every aspect of the common good. If the policy status quo (including no-fault divorce) already erodes key marital norms, as the conjugal view's defenders contend, then resisting the redefinition of marriage is for us not an end, but one step toward strengthening marriage.

Corvino answers that the public definition of marriage won't affect how many children grow up with their own, committed mother and father. (Can what happens with same-sex couples affect anyone else, he asks?) This reply reveals an extraordinarily flatfooted view of social institutions—which Corvino elsewhere gets beyond, as anyone concerned about this institution must.

To make this vivid: imagine two boys in different societies. One comes of age learning revisionism. He's taught by law—and, not unrelatedly, by school and popular culture—that marriage is set apart by emotional union for adult satisfaction. That it's therefore inauthentic to stay married once romantic desire has faded for good, or wandered. That mothers and fathers are interchangeable.

The other grows up leaning from law, school, and popular culture that marriage isn't just your number one bond. It requires a man and woman because their uniquely all-encompassing union requires total commitment; because they tend to have different parenting gifts; because it takes both to make children, who do best when reared by their own mother and father.

Once grown, each falls in love with a woman. Now: Which will be likelier to marry her before having children? To stay with her, for their children, however he feels? Whose children will more likely have the lasting attention of both their father and mother? These questions answer themselves and highlight the argument Corvino entirely misses.

Moreover, promoting same-sex marriage as a right means perforce promoting same-sex parenting as a right. And it would be a surprise if that did not lead to more same-sex partners artificially creating children deprived (deliberately) of their own father or mother.

So social institutions affect people's behavior, with consequences for third parties. Why else should Corvino, or anyone, care about the shape of this one? And yet his prescribed changes for it would entrench changes to the social meaning of marriage that undermine children's good, and thus the common good.

These revisionist harms would apply even if same- and opposite-sex adoptive parenting had all the same measurable outcomes. But I should take a moment to note that Corvino overstates the evidence for the "no differences" thesis and downplays incipient contrary evidence.

No same-sex parenting study meets the standard to which top-quality social science aspires: large, random, and representative samples observed longitudinally. Most compare same-sex parenting with single-, step-, or other-parenting arrangements known to be suboptimal. Using convenience samples, they tend to compare middle-class, white, same-sex couples to more representative opposite-sex couple populations.

Corvino cites the American Psychological Association's statement on same-sex parenting. But even revisionists William Meezan and Jonathan Rauch concede in a literature review that "methodological difficulties" prevent us from knowing whether outcomes studied so far are "representative of the general population of children raised by gay and lesbian couples."[9] Corvino criticizes a contrary study that *was* based on a large, random, and representative sample. But in a review acknowledging its limits, Penn State's Paul Amato said its methodological advantages still made it "probably the best that we can hope for, at least [for now]."

Note, meanwhile, that every thoroughly studied alternative to married biological parenting has been shown less effective, including single and step parenting as well as parenting by cohabiting couples. As Princeton and Wisconsin sociologists Sara McLanahan and Gary Sandefur found, based on several longitudinal studies of nationally representative samples including twenty thousand subjects, "Children [reared] in a household with only one biological parent are worse off, on average" than those reared "in a household with both of their biological parents . . . *regardless of whether the resident parent remarries*." This reinforces the state's primary interest in upholding marital norms *to keep biological parents together*, not simply in promoting two-parent households. In light of this, and the arguments about the nature of marriage in section 5, this argument doesn't turn on comparisons of same- and opposite-sex adoptive parenting outcomes—though that's no reason to exaggerate the current state of that science.

HOW THEN SHOULD WE UNDERSTAND MARRIAGE?

Let's start with a general vocabulary and set of concepts for all voluntary relationships. People form a voluntary bond by committing to do certain things—to engage in certain characteristic *activities*—that aim at shared *goods*. They also commit to protect and facilitate their pursuit of those goods. This commitment is specified by certain *norms* governing their behavior throughout the relationship. When people commit to pursue certain goods through certain activities under the restraint of certain norms, the result is relationship, community.

Here's an example. Wanting to acquire knowledge, three women form a scholarly community; they commit to cooperate in research and other activities ordered to learning. These distinctly build up their kind of bond; they make it most present and real. And for all these reasons, their bond demands a commitment shaped by norms that specially serve the truth—for example, high standards of accuracy even at the cost of embarrassment or economic loss.

So these three features make a union: unifying activities, unifying goods (the objects of those activities), and unifying commitments (to pursuing together those activities and goods). What defines the union of marriage, in these respects, is its *comprehensiveness*:

a. in the basic dimensions in which it unites two people (body *and* mind);
b. in the goods with respect to which it unites them (with respect to procreation, and hence the broad domestic sharing of family life);
c. in the kind of commitment that it calls for (permanent and exclusive).

Comprehensive Unifying Acts: Body and Mind

Marriage requires unity of mind and will, begun by consent. But it also includes bodily union. This is because your body is a real part of *you*, not a vehicle driven by the "real" you, your mind. This point is of pervasive ethical importance. Ruin my car and you vandalize my property; slicing my leg injures *me*. More positively (to inch closer to our subject), spouses find it fitting when their legal children are also a genetic mixture of their two bodies. These points underscore that our bodies are part of *us as persons,* not mere instruments. So any union of two people must include bodily union to be comprehensive, to avoid leaving out a basic aspect of each person.[10]

Most will agree and say that this is where sex comes in. It is what satisfies the criterion of bodily union, which makes two people one flesh. The contested question is why.

Consider, again, a more general point.[11] Why do disparate things ever form a unity? How, for example, do your many organs form one body? If the key were spatial proximity, a house of cards would be a unity in the same sense, and your coffee cup would be part of you for as long as you held it. Nor is the critical factor genetics, which you and an identical twin might share.

So what makes for unity is, rather, activity toward common ends. Two things are parts of a whole—*are one*—if they *act as one*; and they act as one if they coordinate *toward one end encompassing them both*. Your organs form one body because they are coordinated for the single biological purpose of sustaining your life.

Here's the critical point. Even separate beings—a man and woman—can achieve, in a limited but real sense, the kind of union enjoyed by parts of a single body, in that their bodies can coordinate toward a common biological end. This happens in just one mutual, voluntary act: sexual intercourse, coitus.

As with other forms of bodily union, that is, coitus involves coordination toward a single bodily end (reproduction) of the whole (the couple). Their achieving that end would crown and extend their union, but the coordination is enough to create it.

Corvino answers that the category of acts I've identified is gerrymandered since it includes the coitus of infertile couples. After all, if we both know that a math problem is unsolvable, we can't really have a conversation oriented to solving it. So if a man and woman know they're infertile, how can they engage in a sexual act oriented to procreation? Or what's the point of assembling the parts of a broken watch? On the other hand, Corvino presses, why not include in this category couples producing children artificially?

Every one of these points can be answered in one fell swoop, because they all betray the same mistake. Corvino writes as if I think the point of marital acts is simply procreation. It is not. The point is comprehensive (including bodily) *union*. You get that when you have (among other things) coordination toward a single bodily end of the pair (here, toward reproduction), *whether or not* children later arrive. You don't get it by producing children in a lab. That's the bottom line, and it makes things fall into place: it justifies the boundaries of the marital act.

His counterexamples—the unsolvable math problem and the broken watch—are meant to show that infertile coitus isn't even *coordinated* toward a single end. But this overlooks a key difference between biological, and many nonbiological (e.g., mechanical), processes.

Intentional processes (conversations) and artifacts (watches) have their purposes (solving a problem, telling time) from our *intentions* about how to use them. So they can have those functions only if we *keep* the relevant intentions, which requires us to think them achievable. For a conversation about math even to *have* an intellectual end—and so, potentially, realize personal (intellectual) union—the partners must intend for it to have a certain effect (e.g., producing a solution), which they must therefore think possible.

But biological processes have their end by their nature. The behavioral stage of the reproductive process is oriented to reproduction even when later stages don't cooperate to lead to conception—just as a stomach remains oriented to breaking down food, even when nutrients aren't ultimately absorbed. So coitus can involve a bodily end—and hence bodily coordination, and comprehensive personal (including bodily) union—when we know children won't result.[12]

That *personal union* is what has basic value. (And as a partly organic-bodily union, its value is distinct from that of unions coordinated toward purely intellectual ends.) By assuming that marital acts could have value only as a means, Corvino takes aim at a view *directly at odds* with the conjugal view. This is presumably because his own view can only see sex as instrumental (whether to offspring or feelings of intimacy and attachment). But it dooms his critique to misfire altogether. Marital acts are valuable as a form of *coordination between two people toward a single bodily end, and hence as a form of bodily union*, and hence as part of a *comprehensive union*—the last category being what has value in itself.[13]

In short, coitus, which achieves biological coordination, can add value—by contributing to a distinct type of interpersonal union. It does so whether or not it leads to children since union toward biological ends doesn't depend on beliefs as other forms do. And like all loving personal unions, marital union has value in itself, not just as a means.

So there is no arbitrariness in saying that the marital act involves distinctively marital behavior (bodily union in coitus), chosen for distinctively marital reasons: to make spousal love concrete (literally to *embody* it), to unite as spouses do, to extend their union of hearts and minds onto the bodily plane.

But the same point explains why marriage, unlike many other enriching bonds, is only possible for biologically complementary couples. If marital love seeks (if marriage achieves) comprehensiveness, we need bodily union, and for that—coordination toward a single bodily end of the whole—there is no substitute for mating: coitus.[14]

Comprehensive Unifying Goods: Procreation and Domestic Life

We have seen that marriage unites spouses in mind and in body, and is in that sense uniquely encompassing or comprehensive. Because it is oriented to children and family life, marriage also uniquely requires spouses to be open to the whole range of human goods.

The connection between marriage and parenthood is intuitive, but easily misstated. Children are not necessary to create a marriage. Marriage is not a *means* to procreation, but it is *oriented* to procreation—inherently enriched by it and shaped by its demands. And procreation so fulfills and extends a marriage by fulfilling and extending the act that embodies the *commitment* of marriage: sexual intercourse. The embodying act of coitus, by its nature (i.e., even apart from partners' expectations), has procreation as its biological end. Marriage is ordered to family life because the kind of act that makes marital love is also the kind that makes new life.

And this orientation is unique to male-female couples. Partners in other bonds may regard sex as uniquely sealing their commitment, but neither the bonds nor their activity will have an inherent orientation to procreation. (If simply choosing to rear children together gave a bond this feature of marriage, then childrearing would have no more fittingness for married couples than for two committed cohabiting sisters who think childrearing would enhance their bond.)

Finally, the life sharing that most forms of community call for is limited, because the common values that define them are limited. (Sports may call for regular weekly or monthly cooperation, but there is no loss in not *living* with your bowling partner.) But marriage unites spouses in mind and body, and is oriented to producing not just one or another human value but whole new persons, new centers of value. So it calls for the broad sharing of life that would be needed for helping new human beings develop their capacities for pursuing *every* basic kind of value.

Spouses benefit as spouses from *some* cooperation intellectually, in recreation, and so on. Thus, again, the conjugal view makes sense of marriage's links to family and domestic sharing.

Comprehensive Commitment: Norms of Permanence and Exclusivity

We have seen that marriage is comprehensive insofar as it (i) unites spouse comprehensively (i.e., in mind and body) and (ii) unites them in pursuit of a comprehensive range of goods, the range of goods proper to childrearing and family life. But a union comprehensive in these two senses also calls for comprehensive commitment:[15] through time (vowed permanence) and at each time (vowed exclusivity). Revisionists can't offer this, or any good basis for requiring permanent and exclusive commitment in marriage.

Marriage is possible between only two persons because no act can organically unite three or more, or thus seal a comprehensive union of three or more lives. If bodily union is essential to marriage, we can understand why marriage, like the union of organs into one healthy whole, should be total and lasting for the life of the parts ("till death us do part"). Being organically united—as "one flesh"—spouses should have, by *commitment*, the exclusive and lifelong unity that the parts of a healthy organic whole have by nature.[16]

Moreover, their mind-body union is ordered to the comprehensive good of rearing whole new people—an open-ended task calling for the coordination of their whole lives, and thus undivided commitment. Such comprehensive commitment doesn't just fit a concept of marriage-as-comprehensive; it also creates the stability needed for what enriches that union: family life. This harmony between conceptual elegance and practical wisdom is fitting and bolsters the conjugal view's plausibility.

But for the revisionist, organic bodily union (impossible for three people as a unit) and a natural orientation to family life (had only by relationships embodied in the generative act) aren't integral to marriage. So permanence and exclusivity are at best optional. The above explanations of the total commitment required for marriage are simply unavailable to the revisionist.

Indeed, despite Corvino's contrary argument, it is the conjugal view that has a better explanation of what spouses should be exclusive *about*.

For revisionists, what distinguishes marriage is its degree of felt intimacy. Grant for a moment that they can explain why such a union should be exclusive; they cannot show why it should be exclusive about sex. What if a couple feels their emotional intimacy is better served by sexual openness?

But the conjugal view distinguishes marriage not by degree but by type of cooperation: bodily union and the natural fulfillment in family life integrated with it. Since these features are what is intrinsic to marriage, they are what spouses must be exclusive about: that is, sexual union,[17] and the widely committed domestic life built around it, involving the commitments to coordination of all life pursuits, and to *some* active cooperation in every basic dimension of personal development, that would be apt for developing together whole new persons.

To answer Corvino's particular objection, then, the scholarly union my coauthors and I enjoy doesn't undermine the comprehensive union of our separate marriages, because coauthoring books is not, as such, intrinsic to marriage—even if it and other activities can contribute to the wide-range sharing of family life that does partly characterize marriage.

Accept it or reject it, my judgment about the nature of marriage is nothing new, obscure, or discredited. The three great philosophers of antiquity—Socrates, Plato, and Aristotle—as well as Xenophanes and Stoics such as Musonius Rufus, defended something quite like it, sometimes amid homoerotic cultures. Especially clear is Plutarch's statement in *Erotikos* that marriage as a class of friendship is uniquely embodied in coitus, which he calls a *renewal* of marriage. Plutarch also says, in his *Life of Solon*, that intercourse with an infertile spouse realizes the good of marriage—even as he and the others denied that other sexual acts could do the same.[18]

Then there is the history of the common law, an important guide to the community's enduring moral understandings. For centuries, infertility was no ground for declaring a marriage void, and only coitus was recognized as completing one. Draw the reasonable inferences: If marriage is purely instrumental to the good of the children, why not let the clearly infertile dissolve their marriages? If the law aimed at stigmatizing a sexual minority, why not permit all heterosexual acts to consummate a marriage? There is no puzzle at all here if we assume the law reflected this rational judgment: the uniquely comprehensive unions embodied by coitus are valuable in themselves, and different in kind from other bonds; that is, the conjugal view.

WHAT ABOUT CORVINO'S CASE OF A MALE PARAPLEGIC AND HIS FEMALE PARTNER? DOES IT REBUT THE FORGOING DEFENSE OF THE CONJUGAL VIEW AND OVERCOME THE SEVERAL OBJECTIONS TO THE REVISIONIST?

Granted that on the conjugal view, consummation is needed to *complete* a marriage, can a paraplegic's commitment be marital at all? There are two possible responses consistent with the argument so far.

On what I would call *the strong view*, you cannot commit to marriage unless you intend coitus, which you can't do unless you think it feasible. This would mean that someone prevented by physical defect from consummating could not form a true marriage. But good policy would go on recognizing such bonds since excluding them would have social costs but no social benefits: recognition would not undermine the public understanding of marriage as conjugal union while a stricter policy would require asking questions about deeply private issues.

On *the softer view*, marriage only requires the intent to perform coitus when reasonably feasible, which requires only that coitus be possible *in principle*.[19] Maybe the paraplegic's bond is on a spectrum with other opposite-sex unions: each could consummate given normal conditions (sufficient time and health, etc.), which the paraplegic will go on lacking for contingent reasons.

The strong view, applied here, sits ill with many people's intuitions. But even if reflection eventually commits all supporters of the conjugal view to the strong view (we're currently a house divided on the issue), the position overall will remain much stronger.

First, what we want as philosophers or thoughtful citizens is not a theory that justifies the exact constellation of intuitions dominating our society here and now, shaped as these are by all sorts of factors. They are where we start our reasoning, but rarely where we end. What we need is a line of *best* fit with our practices and judgments about how human beings are constituted, as mind-body unities, and how clearly distinct goods like general companionship are structured.

That the revisionist view has no basis in principle—*none at all*—for distinguishing marriage from companionship is, unlike the current objection to the conjugal view, disqualifying. Add to that the burden of proof facing the revisionist—given the near-consensus of cultural, intellectual, and legal traditions—and the circularity of even sophisticated arguments like Corvino's, and the conclusion is clear. The paraplegic case does not rebut the conjugal view—either immediately or on reflection and comparison with the revisionist.

Second, if you have even a minimally plausible view of marriage, it will leave out some relationships whose partners seek recognition. It would be surprising if the conjugal view—with its volitional and bodily criteria—entailed that only same-sex bonds aren't marriages. And it's no worse that a paraplegic can't marry than it is that, on *anyone's* view, someone unable to find a mate cannot marry, or an only child busy caring for her ailing mother can't marry. These are all people of equal dignity who didn't choose what impedes them from marriage.

At the same time, no one should equate "nonmarital" with "trivial." Everyone can form loving, sustaining relationships of various kinds—and only the revisionist will mistake this for a mere consolation prize. For revisionists, marriage is simply the deepest and hence most valuable bond. To have something else is to have something less. On the conjugal view, to have something else is just to have *something else* (a certain form of companionship), excellent in its incommensurable way. So the unmarried are not denied the pinnacle of social fulfillment.

Let me end this excursus on the criteria of bodily union by reminding us why we should care about it at all. For sometimes in investigating even the most straightforward topic, we find ourselves as it were in a dark forest, cutting our way through vines, and losing heart. But that is no discredit to the topic. For example, consent is clearly critical to the value of sex, but if we spent hours considering what it required (there are very hard cases), we might get lost in the weeds. It is then that we must look up to remember our destination, the point of our inquiry. I have belabored the importance of bodily union not because it is all that makes a marriage but because it is essential and has lately been neglected.

Keeping this all in mind, one can indeed—as for centuries, almost every culture did—see something morally distinctive, even awe-inspiring, and crucial for marriage, in the sort of act that unites generation to generation as one blood, and man to woman as one flesh.

CORVINO ENTERTAINS A THOUGHT EXPERIMENT MY COAUTHORS AND I OFFER: IF PEOPLE REPRODUCED ASEXUALLY AND OUR OFFSPRING EMERGED SELF-SUFFICIENT, WOULD ANYTHING LIKE MARRIAGE EXIST?[20]

He says yes, if people still wanted to make a life together for the sake of "unparalleled security and comfort and intimacy and joy." Of course. But to equate this with marriage would be drearily narrow-minded. That description is obviously true of a healthy marriage; it is just as obviously *not* true of marriage *alone*. So it doesn't fix the relationship in question as marital, rather than companionate in another way.

And this brings me to my final point. Not only this last axiom of Corvino's but his arguments generally presuppose the fairly desiccated social landscape that our culture has been trudging toward for decades, in which your social options are effectively reduced to two: spouse (fulfilling, intimate, deep) or comrade (diverting, reserved, superficial), with little in between.[21] His arguments evade my objection—that he collapses marriage and companionship—by assuming so narrow a view of companionship that the objection seems obscure or of uncertain effect. Companionship is thus confined to marriage, and the unmarried consigned to loneliness.

So Corvino's view, for all its analytic sophistication, boils down to the slogan that "love makes a marriage." His replies to my main objection—that he collapses the difference between marriage and companionship—for all their variety, boil down to the insistence that there's no difference to collapse. And so his view, for all its focus on love, disserves that ultimate human ideal. To see in monochrome isn't just to miss out on all colors but one; it is to lose all contrast, and hence, in a sense, even the only shade you had. Equating marriage with love doesn't just mean downgrading or entirely missing other forms of love; it means distorting or entirely missing the shining contrasts, and defining features, of the marital form.

Revisionists at their best want us all to have an answer to loneliness. Can anyone blame them? "We have all known the long loneliness," wrote Dorothy Day, "and we have learned that the only solution is love." But even at their best, revisionists miss what Day also saw: "and that love comes with *community*."[22] If only love makes a marriage, then only marriage offers love, and our opportunities for real community are reduced to just one type, now likelier to disappoint.

The conjugal view, giving marriage specific shape, envisages a more crowded landscape of forms of community—of oases to slake our loneliness in different ways. Refusing simply to equate closeness with marriage, it frees us for more and more varied companionship. Of the two views, then, it is the more capacious; it contains, after all, the richer humanism, the more sprawling and splendid diversity.[23]

NOTES

1. See Kwame Anthony Appiah. *The Ethics of Identity* (Princeton, NJ: Princeton University Press, 2005), 88.

2. See John Rawls's discussion of primary goods on pages 58 to 59 of *Justice as Fairness: A Restatement*, ed. E. Kelly (Cambridge, MA: Harvard University Press, 2001).

3. For a more complete defense of the view I sketch here, see Sherif Girgis, Ryan T. Anderson, and Robert P. George, *What Is Marriage? Man and Woman: A Defense* (New York: Encounter Books, 2012), on which I draw at various points here.

4. On the other hand, if revisionists really *would* recognize any significant sharing of life, romantic or not, then it's even *clearer* that, as I will show, they can draw no principled distinction between marriage and the wider class of companionship. So the primary objection that I develop below to the view holds, even if Corvino is right (irrelevantly, in this case) that my exposition on the way to establishing that objection is inaccurate.

5. Thus, since the rise of same-sex marriage advocacy, prominent gay writers (like Andrew Sullivan, Dan Savage, and Michelangelo Signorile) have argued—even in mainstream venues like the *New York Times*—that redefining marriage could and should encourage sexually "open" marriages throughout society. Temporary renewable marriage licenses have been advocated in venues like the *Washington Post*—and considered by lawmakers, as in Mexico City. "Throuples," or committed three-person bonds, have been sympathetically profiled in magazines, promoted in school curricula, and even granted a civil union. More than three hundred LGBT and allied activists and scholars have advocated legally recognizing multiple-partner, sexually open, multiple-household, and expressly temporary bonds. A respected philosopher has argued for a "minimal marriage" policy allowing any number and mix of partners to determine their

own preferred set of rights and duties. For citations and details on this and other developments, see page 20 and chapter 4 of Girgis et al., *What Is Marriage?*

6. Unless the conjugal view could only originate in spite—which I showed in section 2 is disproved by history.

7. Corvino says that our linguistic usage is just indicative of the qualitative differences that really do distinguish the bonds we should recognize from those we needn't. But the rest of my argument in section 3 belies this reply.

8. For example, New York University philosopher David Velleman has argued that children have powerful interests in being reared by their biological parents—a conclusion that he has cited as motivating his opposition to anonymous gamete donation. J. David Velleman, "Family History," 34 *Philosophical Papers* 357 (2005).

9. Likewise, in a review of all fifty-nine studies on which the APA relied, published in the first-rate mainstream journal *Social Science Research*, LSU's Loren Marks observes, "The available data, which are drawn primarily from small convenience samples, are insufficient to support a strong generalizable claim either way.... Such a statement would not be grounded in science. [For that] representative, large sample studies are needed—many of them."

10. Corvino objects that if we are essentially body-mind composites, all our unions are in some sense bodily unions. I agree that any personal union involves two embodied beings. But the type of union they enjoy will depend on the type of end uniting them. Silently consenting to an agreement unites people; a marital act unites people. But the latter uniquely involves bodily union because *only it involves coordination toward a single biological end*. Only marriage characteristically involves coordination toward both biological and other types of ends.

11. The following discussion owes much to philosophical parts of the work of Germain Grisez, "Why Is Every Marriage a Permanent and Exclusive Union?," in *Way of the Lord Jesus*, vol. 2 (San Jose, CA: Franciscan Press, 1993); Alexander Pruss, *One Body* (South Bend, IN: University of Notre Dame Press).

12. To summarize the response to Corvino's counterexamples: Digestion, though a biological process, is not a coordination involving two people. So it isn't even potentially an interpersonal union of any distinct sort. So it doesn't even potentially have the value of an interpersonal union in addition to the value of its (nutritive) effects. The functioning of a watch is neither a biological process nor one that involves two people. So it is even farther from being the ground of (a) an interpersonal (b) bodily union that (c) has its end even apart from the intentions or beliefs of the persons united. (Likewise, artificially producing children doesn't unite persons bodily.) So Corvino's examples fail. We needn't expect or intend coitus to produce a child in order for it to contribute to the distinctive value of comprehensive union, because coitus (like all biological processes) retains its end—which is a *bodily* end, and of *two* people.

13. Corvino shows awareness of this distinction at some points but loses sight of it where recalling it would obviate his own objections.

14. Some might be tempted to say the pursuit or enjoyment of sexual pleasure unites spouses, but it cannot. Pleasure adds value only when taken in some independent good. Even if it were inherently valuable, it would benefit the partners as individuals, not as a whole. Pleasure, after all, is private like other mental states. This point suggests the last reason—pleasure is a feature of experience, and is so not really bodily in the relevant sense.

15. Why comprehensive in *these* three respects? Because these are the three dimensions that make a community, and give it its distinctive character and value. So, no, comprehensive cannot mean "comprehensive in *every* dimension." But the same holds of most revisionists' master principle: a spouse cannot be your "number one partner" or "soul mate" in *every* activity and domain.

16. Corvino asks why this analogy wouldn't imply that conjugal union should, like our organs, also involve pinkishness and constant activity ("perpetual coitus!"). Pinkishness is an accidental characteristic of some organs. Constancy of active characteristic functioning, too, is a feature of some organs (e.g., of hearts but not limbs). None of these traits pertains to what's proper for the parts of organic wholes as such. Permanence and exclusivity do. And this analogy between bodily and marital union, besides holding up in this case, can plausibly be extended. Thus, there are close and informative analogies between how one should regard and prioritize one's own body and physical health and those of one's spouse, as compared with those of others. Another piece of evidence for this rational link is that moral as well as legal traditions that have most explicitly conceptualized marriage as one-flesh union have also been the clearest on seeing it as requiring permanent and exclusive commitment.

17. If it is wrong to engage in sex with others, it is by that token also wrong to engage with them in other stimulating acts aimed at fostering the characteristic desires or pleasures of sex.

18. See the essays on sex and marriage in J. Finnis, *Collected Essays of John Finnis*, vol. III (Oxford & New York: Oxford University Press, 2011).

19. Corvino replies that marriage isn't simply about what's possible in principle. But here the couple's marriage (like any other) would only get started when the couple actually exchanged consent and committed to each other; and without more cooperation, it would never get far past the starting line. It's just that, on this view, their consent could be marital even if they foresaw practical obstacles to ever completing it by consummation.

20. Corvino says we commit the genetic fallacy, of assuming that a thing's current nature depends on its origin. He can sustain that charge only by omitting key language from our argument, where we clarify just what we think reflection

shows; namely, that marriage wouldn't arise for asexual beings because "there would be no human need that only marriage could fill."

21. For more on this set of issues and concerns, see the section on friendship in chapter 4 of Gergis et al., *What Is Marriage?*

22. Dorothy Day, *The Long Loneliness* (New York: HarperOne, 1980), 286 (emphasis added).

23. Special thanks to John Corvino for comments on this piece, and for a fruitful discussion over several years.

III

Justice and Diversity from Diverse Theological Perspectives

16

DIGNUM ET IUSTUM

Justice, Diversity, and the Mystery of Catholicity

Peter A. Huff, University of Mary

At first, our title *Dignum et Iustum* sounds like a long-lost Roman-themed counterpart to *Tristan und Isolde* or *Porgy and Bess*. On closer inspection, we realize it is not a title in the repertoire of grand opera or even the playlist of contemporary opera, source of such dubitable masterpieces as *Nixon in China* and *Einstein on the Beach*. In fact, after just a few moments of reflection, it becomes quite evident that *Dignum et Iustum* is not related to the world of opera at all.[1]

In making that judgment, however, we are in a sense only half right. For *Dignum et Iustum*, while not an artifact from the stage of classical opera, is indeed closely related to the world of an *opus*, a very distinctive *opus* or "work" whose significance on the stage of history could arguably be measured in proportions not too far from the Wagnerian. This short Latin phrase (or rather clause, because of the implied *est*) should be recognizable to anyone familiar with the traditional text of the Roman Catholic Mass. And the *opus* in question is what the ancient Fathers of the Christian tradition called the *Opus Dei*.

In what follows, we shall play on this complex and half-intuitive connection as we seek to offer a sketch of the meaning of justice and diversity in the Catholic worldview. Rooting the outline of these great values in the technical language of the Mass is no accident or arbitrary choice. Justice pervades the entire biblical heritage and the expansive experience and mental framework, which from the early second century have borne the title *katholike*. In his now classic study, biblical scholar Norman H. Snaith identified justice—stemming from the Hebrew *tsadaq* and *mishpat*, and variously rendered "justice," "judgment," and "righteousness"— as one of the six "distinctive ideas" of the Old Testament.[2] Justice also plays a crucial role in the New Testament. From the "just man" Joseph (Matthew 1:19) to the "just and true" ways of the Alpha and Omega (Revelation 15:3),[3] it runs through the "memoirs of the apostles" like a scarlet thread.[4] Justice served as a great conceptual bridge linking the early Christian *kergyma* to the wisdom of the ancient Mediterranean world. No one acquainted with the verve and fervor of the Reformation debate can deny the impact that Saint Paul's "righteousness (*dikaiosune*) of God" (Romans 1:17ff.) has had on the course and character of the modern Christian experience.[5]

All too often, however, justice is confined to a single, isolated dimension of Christianity—either an abstract question of soteriology (justification) or a technical question of forensics or casuistry. Modern academic theology's penchant for *social* justice, which is typically fueled by post-Enlightenment assumptions, only accentuates the temporal and temperamental distance separating contemporary Christian moral reflection from the comprehensive *sacra doctrina* that compelled Saint Thomas Aquinas and others to see an integral relationship between justice and the virtue called *religio*.[6] An exclusive emphasis on social justice, usually promoted as enlargement of moral consciousness, levies a heavy toll on the Christian theological project, narrowing the range of its vision and aggravating the "loss of the Catholic historical memory."[7] What is too frequently missing in contemporary treatments of justice (and companion categories such as diversity and tolerance) is the remarkably organic context of premodern Christianity, which insisted on the inseparability of ethics and the realities, or better mysteries, of corporate church and corporeal rite. Paul's admonition to "take every thought captive to obey Christ" (2 Corinthians 10:5) allows for no truly Catholic principle of moral existence outside the circumference of devotion and wonder.

The Second Vatican Council's *Sacrosanctum Concilium*, the landmark Constitution on the Sacred Liturgy that marked its fiftieth anniversary in 2013, spoke of the Church's public worship, echoing Saint Thomas and his predecessors, as "the summit toward which the activity of the church is directed" and "the source from which all its power flows."[8] In *The Spirit of the Liturgy*, Joseph Ratzinger, *peritus* at Vatican II and the last of the conciliar popes, reaffirmed this same insight in his thesis: "Worship . . . is essential for the right kind of human existence in the world."[9] This chapter calls for a renewal of this conciliar perspective as it seeks to shed light on the distinctively Catholic idea of justice and moral commitment. In Catholicism's sacramental view of reality, what Avery Cardinal Dulles called the "Catholic cast of mind,"[10] justice entails both horizontal and vertical dimensions that only the Church's rich liturgical life can fully reveal and elucidate. What could be construed as merely an instrumental principle for the practical negotiation and adjudication of rights and responsibilities in secular society, when set against the backdrop of the *Opus Dei*, appears to be nothing less than another witness to the One before whom "every knee should bow" and "every tongue confess" (Philippians 2:10–11).

AT THE HEART OF THE MASS

To this day, the life of prayer and worship at the heart of Christian experience—manifested broadly speaking in the Divine Office, the hours of monastic contemplative practice, and the Eucharistic sacrifice celebrated by members of the world's largest priesthood fellowship on consecrated altars around the globe "from the rising of the sun to its setting" (Malachi 1:11), is rightly called liturgy, the "work of the people" (from the Greek *leitourgia*, "public service"). A more accurate term, though, is *Opus Dei*, the "work of God." Properly understood, liturgy is God's work, divinely initiated and executed action in which humans participate by invitation and grace and a certain degree of natural inclination and desire. In the sacramental economy, liturgy has an unexpected dual character. The *Catechism of the Catholic Church* recognizes the priority of divine action in human worship: "Through the liturgy Christ, our redeemer and high priest, continues the work of our redemption in, with, and through his Church" (CCC, 1069).

The statement, or better declaration, *Dignum et iustum est*, appears on the spine of the Church's ultimate expression of prayer: the Eucharistic liturgy. It also plays a major role in the *Exsultet* of the Easter Vigil, the ninety-line hymn sung by the deacon during the blessing of the paschal candle, best known for its reference to the *felix culpa* of Adam: "O happy fault, O necessary sin of Adam."[11] In the Eucharistic ceremony, the declaration *Dignum et iustum est* occurs as the great cathedral door of the rite turns on its ancient hinges and we are ushered across the threshold that serves as the boundary between the liturgy of the Word and the liturgy of the Eucharist in the strict sense. This transition, noticeable to even the most somnolent Mass-goer, has been part of the natural cadence of Catholic life for centuries. As Planet Catholicism orbits the "sun of justice" (Malachi 4:2, DR), it rotates on its axis, alternating between acts of proclamation and acts of adoration—the two hemispheres of Catholic reality. *Dignum et iustum* is the signal marking the halfway point in that rotation. It is high noon in the universe of Catholic liturgical time.

This passage from liturgical AM to PM takes place in the section of the Mass called the *Sursum Corda*, a rhythmic call-and-response construction that functions as a prologue or introductory dialogue to the Eucharistic Prayer—according to the eminent Jesuit liturgical scholar Joseph A. Jungmann, "*the* prayer of the Church, her Great Prayer."[12] The clause *Dignum et iustum est* is the exclamation point that brings that interchange to a climatic conclusion.

The priest, extending his hands according to the liturgical rubrics, begins the dialogue with the traditional greeting *Dominus vobiscum*, and the people follow with replies deeply rooted in Jewish and pagan antiquity. Again, the dialogue, rendered in the English of the current third edition of the *Roman Missal*, should be familiar to anyone even minimally acquainted with the literary content of the Mass:

Priest: The Lord be with you (*Dominus vobiscum*).

All: And with your spirit (*Et cum spiritu tuo*).

Priest: Lift up your hearts (*Sursum corda*).

All: We lift them up to the Lord (*Habemus ad Dominum*).

Priest: Let us give thanks to the Lord our God (*Gratias agamus Domino Deo nostro*).

All: It is right and just (*Dignum et iustum est*).[13]

At last, we can place our unusual title in its natural setting of the *Opus Dei*. Fed by the Word of God, we turn to the altar of God, the point where time and eternity meet face to face, the "most sacred thing on earth."[14]

The priest, acting *in persona Christi*, the "one mediator between God and men" (1 Timothy 2:5), sets in motion a whole series of vibrations in the Abrahamic cosmos, calling to mind especially the enthronement of the ark of the covenant in the Jerusalem temple's Holy of Holies. In the priest's call to worship, we can hear echoes of ancient Israel's majestic twenty-fourth Psalm:

> Lift up your heads, O gates!
> and be lifted up, O ancient doors!
> that the King of glory may come in. (Psalm 24:7)

Next, the priest's cohortative admonition "Let us give thanks," again accompanied by the *Missal*'s prescribed hand gestures, reminds us that the essential act of sacramental worship is thanksgiving. In fact, the supreme rite of Catholic worship, the Eucharistic feast of consecrated bread and wine, receives its name from the Greek word for thanksgiving: *eucharistia*. In our first records of the institution of the Lord's Supper, Saint Paul uses two key terms that will lay the foundations for the highly specialized language of Christian civilization: communion (from *koinonia*) and *eucharistia* (see 1 Corinthians 10:16, 11:23–24, and 14:16). The apostle even envisions the full sweep of the Christian life as one enormous Eucharist, one great "sacrifice of praise" (Hebrews 13:15), "overflowing in many acts of thanksgiving to God" (2 Corinthians 9:12, NAB).

The people's response to all of this is the simple and direct proclamation: "It is right and just." The compact sentence carries a burden of meaning that approximates the sort of short text or email responses that we send all the time today in our personal and professional communications: "Good," "Great," "Excellent," "Yes." Only the weight of its significance requires something evoking greater gravity and grace. "Amen," perhaps the world's best known and most frequently used Hebrew word, would be a not-too-rough equivalent.

But *Dignum et iustum*, of course, is not an ending point. It is the pivot point marking the true liturgical entrance into the full mystery of "Christ our passover . . . sacrificed for us" (1 Corinthians 5:7, KJV). Again, as Father Jungmann so eloquently put it, "Our eyes aglow with wonder and awe before such munificence, what else can we do but give thanks? *Vere dignum et justum est . . . semper et ubique gratias agree.* A sense of gratitude must be the basic sentiment of every true Christian."[15]

THE UNITY OF TRUTH

The formula *Dignum et iustum* itself, a "most ancient Christian tradition," according to Jungmann,[16] actually originated in the context of pagan Rome's political and social life. As the German theologian and historian Erik Peterson has demonstrated, the clause was used routinely as a "doxological acclamation" to articulate popular approbation of or submission to an election or legislative decision or even praise for a superior athletic achievement. A new senator takes office or a new law is promulgated, and the people proclaim: "It is right and just."[17]

Here we see one of the most recognizable traits of the historic Catholic tradition: the appropriation and effective "baptism" of ideas, images, institutions, practices, even places from pre- and non-Christian sources and their incorporation into Catholic creed, code, and cult. In this case, we observe the integration of political and social custom into sacred liturgical conduct. Some observers might identify this tendency as a sign of the genius of the Catholic vision of things. From Protestant and post-Protestant points of view, however, it is perhaps the single most disconcerting feature of the Catholic phenomenon or "Thing," as G. K. Chesterton used to say.[18] Its scriptural types are the "spoliation of the Egyptians" mentioned three times in the Book of Exodus (3:21–22, 11:2–3, 12:35–36) and the New Testament description of Moses as learned in "all the wisdom of the Egyptians" (Acts 7:22), themes nearly ubiquitous in patristic literature and, arguably, catalytic for modern creative works such as Freud's *Moses and Monotheism* (1937) and Philip Glass's opera *Akhnaten* (1983). For early Church Fathers such as Clement of Alexandria, the marriage of Christian gospel and *paideia* (non-Christian culture, broadly conceived) was a match made in heaven.[19]

In more philosophical language, the basic principle at work in this supremely Catholic pattern of behavior is the concept of *unitas veritatis* (the unity of truth), the axiom on which Catholicism as a worldview stands or falls. What we mean by the unity of truth can be put simply this way: that (1) truth is reality in itself, transcending all historical periods, cultural perspectives, and personal limitations, and that (2) the things we affirm to be true in religious traditions, philosophical systems, academic disciplines, and aesthetic and personal experiences ultimately correspond to or harmonize with this reality or they are not in the final sense true.[20] For the contemporary Catholic, this means that the truth or data of, say, the natural sciences cannot ultimately be in conflict with the truth or data of divine revelation—most fully seen in Jesus Christ, who is "the Way, the Truth and the Life" (John 14:6, JB) and the true light "who enlightens every soul born into the world" (John 1:9, Knox). Long before Saint Thomas Aquinas enshrined this concept in his magisterial theo-philosophical synthesis, Saint Augustine, arguing for the legitimacy of pagan classical literature in Christian education, expressed it this way: "Every good and true Christian should understand that wherever he may find truth, it is his Lord's."[21]

We should also recognize this principle as the cardinal insight that makes the university work. In the hard-wiring of the university, itself a distinctive product of Catholic civilization,[22] we discover the fundamental conviction that truth and reason, broadly understood, do not change as we move from classroom to classroom or major to major. All talk of a "multiversity" undercuts the one thing the university has been trying to foster for nearly a millennium: liberating and meaningful human engagement with the universe created by the God who is Reason itself. Harvard's shift in motto from *Veritas Christo et Ecclesiae* to simply *Veritas* may be empirical evidence of secularization, what historian George Marsden called the transition from "Protestant establishment to established nonbelief" in the United States.[23] But a secularized Christian institution or culture still retains some of the features of its earlier Christian incarnation. "The modern world," as Chesterton once observed, "is full of the old Christian virtues gone mad."[24] It is "living on its Catholic capital."[25] The complete elimination of *Veritas*, on the other hand, would spell the unmaking of the university itself.

In both the pagan political and the Christian liturgical contexts, then, the declaration *Dignum et iustum* is not the expression of individual interest or private judgment. It is not the ancient form of "liking" that we know so well in the age of Facebook. Nor is it the ovation of devotees celebrating their candidate's or their party's victory in an electoral or ecclesiastical contest. Rather, it is the collective, nonpartisan, impersonal, and almost universally instinctive conviction that an event or deed in the finite realm of space and time corresponds directly to and coheres meaningfully with an objective standard or criterion exterior to and independent of subjective tastes and personal preferences. It is the unprejudiced and disinterested recognition of an excellence that transcends parochial loyalties and contingent understandings and demands universal and unconditional respect.

THE SENSE OF WHAT IS FITTING

We have translated *Dignum et iustum* as "It is right and just." Other renderings, found in the liturgical books of a wide range of churches and ecclesial communities, include: "It is proper and right," "It is worthy and right," and "It is fit and right."[26] This last version is particularly intriguing, mainly because such a use of "fit" or "fitting" no longer enjoys significant currency in our everyday language and experience. We still talk about someone "pitching a fit" or being "fit to be tied" (although many might think these sound a bit old-fashioned). We definitely talk about "being fit" in the sense of enjoying good health or athletic bearing; on our university campuses, in our workplaces and hotels, and throughout our suburban sprawl "fitness" centers abound. Sometimes, we talk about being properly "outfitted" for a trip or adventure, and, though our clothes come in standardized sizes and "fit" seems to have been reduced to questions of physical comfort and the conditions necessary for the expression of what is called personal style, we still tend to try on new clothes in enclosures called "fitting rooms." Most of us would agree, though, that we rarely speak of some act or thought or occurrence as "fitting." This sense of "fit" does seem to have slipped from the center of our language and our outlook.

We do find such usage in Shakespeare. In *Hamlet*, for example, after the stabbing of Polonius, King Claudius says to Gertrude, "O heavy deed! . . . We would not understand what was most fit" (*Hamlet* IV.i). Likewise, "fit" and related words permeate the Anglican King James Bible and the Catholic Douay-Rheims Bible, both tremendously important products of the seventeenth century. Here are some examples from the King James Version (1611):

"And of the Gadites there separated themselves unto David . . . men *fit for the battle*" (1 Chronicles 12:8). "Is it *fit to say* to a king, Thou art wicked?" (Job 34:18). "A word *fitly spoken* is like apples of gold in pictures of silver" (Proverbs 25:11).

Our Lord's call to discipleship is summed up in this verse: "No man, having put his hand to the plough, and looking back, is *fit for the kingdom of God*" (Luke 9:62). And Saint Paul used the same sort of language in what is today quite possibly his most controversial instruction: "Wives, submit yourselves unto your own husbands, as it is *fit in the Lord*" (Colossians 3:18).[27]

This cluster of terms is also found in more recent translations of the Bible, even the National Council of Churches' New Revised Standard Version, which first appeared in 1989 and is best known for its sensitivity to what the chair of the translation committee called the "danger of linguistic sexism."[28] The continued use of "fitting" and other borderline archaic words in English-language Bibles is at least partly due to the fairly well-established principle of Bible translation that seeks to preserve a certain antique patina (for public liturgical or private devotional reading) while maximizing nonthreatening rapport with contemporary readers. In other words, we want a Bible to sound like a Bible but read like a popular newspaper, magazine, or blog. Anyone who enters the world of Bible translation—or the translation of any ancient text—will soon see that the allegedly ivory tower domain of classical literary scholarship is fraught with questions of justice and diversity. The great historian of Christian dogma Adolf Harnack observed that "every historical study is an ethical task."[29] The same can be said of Englishing ancient books. But we should be very frank about this point: the main reason we continue to use old-fashioned words like *fit* and *fitting* in our otherwise up-to-date versions of scripture is because holy writ has a habit of saying things that cannot be fully captured by the linguistic net of the modern or postmodern mind. They represent bits or bites of an alien worldview that resist digestion into a post-Enlightenment system of thought and articulation in a present-day vocabulary. To express some of the Bible's most characteristic ideas, we have two choices: (1) retrieve outdated words or (2) force foreign concepts into the ill-fitting categories of what Huston Smith has called the "tunnel vision of modernity."[30] Even so, as Bible translator J. B. Phillips once noted, "There is no escape or insulation from the throbbing insistence of the voice of God."[31]

Examples from the New Revised Standard Version include:

"Praise the Lord! How good it is to sing praises to our God; for he is gracious, and *a song of praise is fitting*" (Psalm 147:1). "*It is not fitting for a fool to live in luxury*" (Proverbs 19:10).

And speaking of the Risen Christ: "*For it was fitting* that we should have such a high priest, holy, blameless, undefiled, separated from sinners, and exalted above the heavens" (Hebrews 7:26).[32]

What these verses (and the others that use similar language) have in common is the sense that a canon or standard of value, separate from and prior to the individual, defines what is proper, appropriate, or suitable for certain courses of action, social situations, and states of being. A Gadite man "fit for battle," for instance, is not simply a soldier in good condition or effectively trained and equipped. Nor, by any stretch of the imagination, is he a professional serviceman in the modern sense. Rather, he is a native member of a traditional agrarian honor society whose psyche as well as physique corresponds to a preexisting idea of what an authentic warrior is and ought to be. Yes, these are men who can "use both the right hand and the left" and "handle shield and buckler," but more importantly, these are men whose faces are "like the faces of lions" (1 Chronicles 12:2, 8, KJV). This last qualifying feature clearly transports us from the utilitarian to the ideal, the archetypal, even the mythic. The true measure of the "mighty man of valor" (Judges 6:12) is none other than the Lord God of Israel, who is himself a "man of war" (Exodus 15:3). Likewise, when we consider proper speech to a monarch, the behavior of spouses "in the Lord," or a would-be disciple's eligibility to share in the kingdom of God, the biblical writers keep suggesting that a fixed point of judgment, separate from pragmatic considerations and individual choice, is or at least ought to be the determining factor in such cases.

THE ANCIENT UNITY OF WORK AND WORSHIP

It is in places like these that we see very plainly the distance between ourselves and the people of premodern eras, and admittedly some of us feel the throb of an existential ache when we contemplate the full extent of the separation. Many others, no doubt, feel profound relief. Most will be guilty of what was dubbed "chronological snobbery" by C. S. Lewis, "temporal parochialism" by Dietrich von Hildebrand, and "chronolatry" by Jacques Maritain—for all three thinkers, the uncritical assumption that the ideas and values of one's historical epoch are superior to the ideas and values of all previous periods and virtually if not actually infallible.[33] According to Lewis, the only palliative for this unwarranted conviction, a form of "blindness," he says, is the reading of old books, so as to "keep the clean sea breeze of the centuries blowing through our minds."[34]

For the ancient Israelite and the early Christian, sources of some of our best old books, what was of supreme concern was doing the thing, saying the thing, indeed, being the person that was fitting—not, as we might insist, exercising personal freedom, expressing personal selfhood, or maximizing personal enjoyment. Saint Augustine's well-known distinction between using (*uti*) and enjoying (*frui*) powerfully exposes the immense chasm stretching between ancient and modern sensibilities. The only thing truly to be enjoyed, the Bishop of Hippo says, is the Trinitarian God, "if," he continues, "it is a thing and not rather the cause of all things."[35]

None of this is appreciably unique to either the Bible or the classical Christianity of ambo and altar. In *The Abolition of Man*, whose seventieth anniversary we celebrated in 2013, C. S. Lewis attempts to show that every major ancient civilization—from China to Rome—understood human experience as played out within the context of an overarching and comprehensible pattern of meaning that makes the ordinary experience of men and women an odyssey or divine comedy. Considering East Asian, Vedic, Platonic, Aristotelian, Stoic, and Christian systems of thought, Lewis argues that "what is common to them all is something we cannot neglect. It is the doctrine of objective value, the belief that certain attitudes are really true, and others really false, to the kind of thing the universe is and the kind of things we are."[36]

What is particularly striking about these ancient systems is the way in which they not only included what we call religion but also insisted on the centrality and necessity of ritual in human life. Confucius saw ritual observance or *li* as an indispensable element in the formation of the genuinely humane or noble person (*junzi*). Careful and reverent attention to the rites of court and temple, especially their poetic and musical dimensions, he said, would contribute to the harmony of society and foster the much-needed "rectification of names," making the parent a true parent, the child a true child, the teacher a true teacher, the ruler a true ruler.[37] Krishna's vision of life in tune with the eternal *dharma*, communicated to the prince-warrior Arjuna on the eve of a great battle and immortalized in India's beloved *Bhagavad Gita*, also emphasized the significance of both "holy work" and worship.[38] In our haste to turn the Greeks into proto-moderns, we sometimes forget that they, too, found it hard to dislodge ceremony from love of *sophia*. The Grove of Academus in Athens, the location of Plato's famous school, was a cult site dedicated to the city's best-known goddess, and Plato's great dialogue on justice, *The Republic*, begins with Socrates' unremarkable pilgrimage to a new religious shrine. Roughly four centuries later, Saint Paul effectively combined scholarship and sacrifice into what he called our "reasonable service" (Romans 12:1, DR): work and worship in accordance with the *Logos*, God's creative reason—or as Ronald Knox rendered the passage, "the worship due from you as rational creatures" (Knox). Freud's hunch about the genesis of civilization in primal rite may not have been too far off the mark.[39]

A EUCHARISTIC ETHIC

All of which brings us back to *Dignum et iustum est*. This Latin clause, anciently borrowed from pagan polity and artfully woven into the seamless garment of Christian piety, is more than an invitation to the *Opus Dei*. It is also more than a reminder of every human's most basic obligation to acknowledge God as God, "the Creator and Savior, the Lord and Master of everything that exists" (CCC, 2095). As a witness to the unity and universality of truth, a transcendent scheme within which human acts and attitudes attain meaning and value to the degree that they adhere fittingly to a divinely established pattern preceding all creaturely experience, the clause testifies to the fundamental relationship between liturgy and the perennial quest for human excellence. The Eucharist's celebrated call to prayer, *Dignum et iustum*, is also an introduction to Catholic moral consciousness and Catholic moral life. At the midpoint of the Mass, *cultus* and *ethos* are revealed to be twin responses to the unnecessary gift of creation and the unmerited grace of redemption.

There is nothing new in this recognition of the link between worship and work, veneration and virtue, rites and rights. The patristic maxim *Lex orandi, lex credendi* ("The law of prayer is the law of belief") reminds us that the way we worship has a profound impact on what and how we believe. Much the same could be said of the link between the way we worship—if we worship at all—and the way we conceive of and reckon with the moral challenges of justice, tolerance, diversity, and the common good. Even the language of liturgy bleeds into the moral order. Just as justice and righteousness form a conceptual partnership in the ancient Hebrew mind, terms such as *sacrifice* and *service* enjoy a kind of dual citizenship in our experience, highlighting the deep affinities between the profane public square and the sacred sanctuary.[40]

Many examples of this principle can be found in early Christian literature. Saint Paul mixed devotional directives and disciplinary advice as he exhorted his charges to present their bodies as a "living sacrifice" (Romans 12:1), to pray for "kings and all who are in high positions" (1 Timothy 2:2), in fact to "pray without ceasing" (1 Thessalonians 5:17, NAB), and to render "respect to whom respect is due, honor to whom honor is due" (Romans 13:7). During the period of Roman persecution, the first apologists argued that Christian prayer itself was a major contribution to the health and welfare of Caesar and his empire. As Tertullian explained in his *Apology*, "We pray . . . for the emperors, for their ministers and those in power, for a stable world, for universal peace, and for the delay of the coming end of the world."[41] The Church Father Origen envisioned the entire life of the Christian a "great synthesis of prayer." "What we normally call prayer," he said, "is only a small part of praying."[42] From that point on, a distinctively Eucharistic ethic became the hallmark of the Catholic moral imagination.

THE COVENANT OF CULT AND CODE

Historically seven core themes in the Catholic worldview have worked together to effect this uncommon communion or covenant of cult and code. Today, they function as key principles or ingredients for responsible and resourceful Catholic discipleship in a pluralistic society. First and foremost, there is the doctrine of creation in the *imago dei*. Humankind as male-and-female, made in the image and likeness of God (Genesis 1:26–27) through the agency of the *Logos* or Reason of God (John 1:3), enjoys an inherently unique relationship with the God who is not only good but also the Good itself. In many ways, the entire Catholic moral project and the Church's enormous investment in prayer and devotion stem directly from this single and seemingly simple affirmation of longer" (2 Corinthians 5:16, Knox). He was, however, supremely interested in the cosmic Christ, the exalted Lord who is "far above all rule and authority and power and dominion" (Ephesians 1:21), who is "all in all" (Ephesians 1:23), and in whom "all things hold together" (Colossians 1:17). The Second Vatican Council's hymn to this expansive vision of the universal Christ reminds us of how often our highly speculative (and at times, self-serving) portraits of Jesus of Nazareth trivialize the Incarnation and its breathtaking grandeur:

> The Word of God, through whom all things were made, was made flesh, so that as a perfect man he could save all women and men and sum up all things in himself. The Lord is the goal of human history, the focal point of the desires of history and civilization, the center of humanity, the joy of all hearts, and the fulfillment of all aspirations.[51]

The seventh and final theme actually constitutes the extension of the Incarnation throughout space and time: the catholicity of the Catholic Church. Catholicity is one of the four traditional marks or "notes" of the Church. According to the Nicene Creed, the Church is one—holy, catholic, and apostolic. In the early second century, Saint Ignatius of Antioch put *katholike* and *ekklesia* together for the first time—on his way to martyrdom no less.[52] For him, "catholic church" meant something like the "real" church, the "full" church, or the "authoritative" church.[53] Since then, the adjective-noun combination has been part of what Peter Maurin called the "dynamite of the Church."[54] It has served as the ever-expanding horizon for the Church's vision of a redeemed human race: "one new man" in Paul's unforgettable words (Ephesians 2:15).

The Church is universal in space, embracing all nations, languages, ethnicities, and cultures. A stunning variety of orders, rites, vocations, charisms, apostolates, ministries, institutions, offices, devotional styles, personality types, holy places, local customs, and local costumes make the Catholic Church arguably the world's most diverse religious organization (it is already the world's largest) and perhaps the world's most diverse organization of any kind. It is the Church of crusader and pacifist, monarchist and democrat, prince and peasant, venerable saint and vile sinner. It has always recognized the value of multiple schools of philosophy, the presence of numerous senses in sacred scripture, the necessity of many paths for the spiritual life, and "diversities of graces" (1 Corinthians 12:4, DR). Attempts to make the Church the domain of one or another of these always end in the sacrifice of the Church's full catholicity. According to *The Imitation of Christ*, "All cannot use the same kind of spiritual exercises, but one suits this person, and another that."[55] At the highest levels of authority, the Church's official teaching condemns all forms of racism, defends the sanctity of every human life, and supports religious freedom for all people.[56] The Second Vatican Council lauded the "wonderful diversity" of the People of God and commended "unity in what is necessary, freedom in what is doubtful, and charity in everything."[57] Magisterial teaching also makes ecumenical dialogue and interreligious outreach mandatory components of Catholic mission in the contemporary world.[58]

The Church's catholicity in time enables it to count among its own all the saints and martyrs and faithful departed from ages past, including matriarchs and patriarchs, prophets and seekers of a "better country" (Hebrews 11:16) from pre-Christian eras. The Church is the only organization, Chesterton once quipped, that increases its rolls as its members die.[59] And some have speculated on the presence of angels in its ranks—at least, in the Church Triumphant. Membership, then, is not even limited to one species or "race" of intelligent life. Commenting on the thought of the "Angelic Doctor" Thomas Aquinas, Karl Rahner suggested that premodern angelology reminds the individual Catholic Christian that she "stands in the midst of a wider than human society of salvation and damnation."[60] From this vantage point, we begin to catch a glimpse of what the anonymous author of the second-century Epistle to Diognetus meant by his haunting description of the Christian community: "the new breed of men."[61] If Chesterton's "Thing" were an opera, it would truly stage a cast of thousands and truly last an eternity.

Here we draw near to the supernatural quality of the all-too-often all-too-human Church. As Vatican II's *Lumen Gentium* declares, the Church transcends all limits of time and space.[62] Jesuit saint Robert Bellarmine and others have always been inclined to call the Church a "perfect society"—only to be mocked by modern cynics (many of them inside the Church) who miss the centrality of the call to perfection in evangelical discipleship (see Matthew 5:48, 19:21; John 17:23; and especially 1 John 4:12) and the *scala perfectionis* in the literature and practice of Catholic mysticism.[63] Paul linked the Church, "without spot or wrinkle . . . holy and without blemish," to the sacred institution of marriage and saw in both realities the contours of "a great mystery" (Ephesians 5:27, 32, NAB).

An overly sociological approach to the Church (part of a far-reaching loss of theological voice) has hampered the theological discipline of ecclesiology for the half century since Vatican II, through no fault of the Council itself. By its very nature, the methodology of the social sciences can only barely touch the "anthropological catholicity" of the empirical Church; it is completely incapable of penetrating to the mystery of the Church's true mission and identity—its "Christological Catholicity," in the words of Hans Urs von Balthasar.[64] The Church understands itself only by contemplating Christ. Ultimately, the catholicity of the Church is the catholicity of the Body of Christ—perhaps the greatest of Saint Paul's world-changing metaphors, based of course on Christ's own words (see Romans 12:4–5; 1 Corinthians 12:12–31; Ephesians 4:4–16; Colossians 3:15). The Church's most audacious teaching is this: We become responsible moral agents not by obeying Christ, not even by imitating Christ. We become fully human and fully humane when we become Christ.

Pope Pius XII's landmark encyclical *Mystici Corporis Christi*, which also celebrated its seventieth anniversary in 2013, pictures for us this full-scale "christening" of the human race in the Mystical Body of Christ. This selection shows us the sort of perfection to be found in the Church:

> [The] communication of the Spirit of Christ is the channel through which all the gifts, powers, and extra-ordinary graces found superabundantly in the Head as in their source flow into all the members of the Church, and are perfected daily in them according to the place they hold in the Mystical Body of Jesus Christ. Thus the Church becomes, as it were, the filling out and the complement of the Redeemer, while Christ in a sense attains through the Church a fullness in all things. Herein we find the reason why . . . the mystical Head, which is Christ, and the Church, which here below as another Christ shows forth His person, constitute one new man, in whom heaven and earth are joined together in perpetuating the saving work of the Cross: Christ we mean, the Head and the Body, the whole Christ.[65]

CONCLUSION

Perhaps the best example of a Catholic vision of the moral vocation, shaped by the Church's career through history and enriched by the treasures of its liturgical life, is another papal encyclical that marked an anniversary in 2013. *Veritatis Splendor*, released in 1993, was "one of the major intellectual and cultural events" of Saint John Paul II's phenomenal pontificate.[66] Today, the document stands as a masterful application of classical Christian moral thought to the challenges of post-Christian culture. In this passage, John Paul takes as his point of departure the language of the Mass that had been part of his priestly heartbeat since ordination in 1946:

> It is right and just, always and for everyone, to serve God, to render him the worship which is his due and to honor one's parents as they deserve. Positive precepts such as these, which order us to perform certain actions and to cultivate certain dispositions, are universally binding; they are unchanging. They unite in the same common good all people of every period of history, created for the same divine calling and destiny. These universal and permanent laws correspond to things known by the practical reason and are applied to particular acts through the judgment of conscience. The acting subject personally assimilates the truth contained in the law. He appropriates this truth of his being and makes it his own by his acts and the corresponding virtues.[67]

When Pope John Paul II wrote these words, he was convinced that Western culture was on a collision course with a "crisis of truth," a pancivilizational debate over the most basic of issues: the nature of humanity and the nature of God.[68] During the pontificate of his successor, the severity of the mounting crisis became all too clear. Critique of a "dictatorship of relativism" emerged as one of the signature themes of Benedict XVI's papacy. In a historic homily preached in Saint Peter's on April 18, 2005, ten days after the funeral of John Paul II, then Cardinal Ratzinger articulated his most forceful assessment of the contemporary intellectual and moral climate:

> Having a clear faith, based on the Creed of the Church, is often labeled today as a fundamentalism. Whereas relativism, which is letting oneself be tossed and "swept along by every wind of teaching," looks like

the only attitude (acceptable) to today's standards. We are moving toward a dictatorship of relativism, which does not recognize anything as certain and which has as its highest goal one's own ego and one's own desires.[69]

Two years before his historic retirement in 2013, Pope Benedict XVI pinpointed the exact nature of the crisis with chilling precision. It is not a contest among rival claims to truth, he said, but a debate over, or revolt against, the very notion of truth: "It is obvious that the concept of truth has become suspect."[70]

This may be something radically new in the history of the world: an entire society seemingly stumped by the question of truth. Pilate's infamous foray into philosophical inquiry—"What is truth?" (John 18:38)—has now become the epigraph hanging over virtually the whole of the Western intellectual enterprise. In light of such an unprecedented development, the Catholic community may be forced in the coming years to embrace more fully its status as a cognitive minority and rediscover its primordial vocation of nonconformity.[71] Still, Malachi's ancient prophecy remains. And with it the Catholic certainty, born of the Church's age-old pilgrimage and shared by billions of believers in other faiths, that the urge to worship is unquenchable—and fundamentally inseparable from the longing to do good, to be good, and to know the Good. Bow the head, bend the knee, and it is not unreasonable to believe that the "sun of justice shall rise, with healing in its wings" (Malachi 4:2, DR).

NOTES

1. Martin E. Marty's advice to "opera composers and dramatists" in his foreword to David J. O'Brien's biography of Isaac Hecker inspired this operatic introduction. See O'Brien, *Isaac Hecker: An American Catholic* (New York: Paulist Press, 1992), vii.

2. Norman H. Snaith, *The Distinctive Ideas of the Old Testament* (New York: Schocken Books, 1975). The other distinctive ideas are holiness (*qodesh*), salvation, covenant-love (*chesed*), election love (*'aheb*), and the spirit (*ruach*) of God.

3. Unless otherwise noted, scripture quotations are taken from the Revised Standard Version Catholic Edition (RSV-CE). Other versions used include the Douay-Rheims Bible (DR), the Jerusalem Bible (JB), the King James Version

(KJV), Ronald Knox's translation (Knox), the New American Bible (NAB), and the New Revised Standard Version (NRSV).

4. Saint Justin Martyr, *First Apology*, 67. Cyril C. Richardson, ed., *Early Christian Fathers* (New York: Collier Books, 1970).

5. See Alister E. McGrath, *Iustitia Dei: A History of the Christian Doctrine of Justification*, 3rd ed. (Cambridge: Cambridge University Press, 2005).

6. Thomas Aquinas, *Summa Theologica*, 2a2ae, 81ff. See Robert Jared Staudt, "Religion as a Virtue: Thomas Aquinas on Worship through Justice, Law, and Charity," ThD diss., Ave Maria University, 2008.

7. Thomas Storck, "Social Justice According to Pius XI," *Homiletic and Pastoral Review* (December 2012), http://www.hprweb.com/2012/12/social-justice-according-to-pius-xi/.

8. *Sacrosanctum Concilium*, 10. Quotation from the documents of the Second Vatican Council are taken from Austin Flannery, ed., *Vatican Council II: Constitutions, Decrees, Declarations* (Northport, NY: Costello, 1996). See Aquinas, *Summa Theologica*, 3a, 63 and 73.

9. Joseph Ratzinger, *The Spirit of the Liturgy*, trans. John Saward (San Francisco: Ignatius Press, 2000), 21.

10. Avery Dulles, *The Catholicity of the Church* (Oxford: Clarendon Press, 1987), 180.

11. For the full text of the *Exsultet*, see International Commission on English in the Liturgy, http://www.icelweb.org/musicfolder/openpdf.php?file=ExsultetLong.pdf.

12. Joseph A. Jungmann, *The Mass of the Roman Rite: Its Origins and Development*, trans. Francis A. Brunner, revised ed. (New York: Benziger Brothers, 1959), 371.

13. *The Roman Missal*, trans. International Commission on English in the Liturgy, 3rd ed. (Washington, DC: United States Conference of Catholic Bishops, 2011), 531.

14. Martin J. Scott, *The Holy Sacrifice of the Mass* (New York: P. J. Kenedy and Sons, 1928), 43.

15. Josef A. Jungmann, *The Early Liturgy: To the Time of Gregory the Great*, trans. Francis A. Brunner (Notre Dame, IN: University of Notre Dame Press, 1959), 47.

16. Jungmann, *Mass of the Roman Rite*, 369.

17. Erik Peterson, *Heis Theos: Epigraphische, formgeschichtliche und religionsgeschichtliche Untersuchungen* (Göttingen: Vandenhoeck und Ruprecht, 1926). See Giorgio Agamben, *The Kingdom and the Glory: For a Theological Genealogy of Economy and Government*, trans. Lorenzo Chiesa and Matteo Mandarini (Stanford, CA: Stanford University Press, 2011), 168–71.

18. See G. K. Chesterton, *The Thing: Why I Am a Catholic* (New York: Dodd, Mead, 1930).

19. See Werner Jaeger, *Early Christianity and Greek Paideia* (Cambridge, MA: Belknap Press of Harvard University Press, 1985). The providential nature of Christianity's encounter with Hellenism is the true burden, often overlooked, of Pope Benedict XVI's controversial 2006 Regensburg Lecture, "Faith, Reason and the University." See James V. Schall, *The Regensburg Lecture* (South Bend, IN: St. Augustine's Press, 2007).

20. The literature on the unity of truth is rich and vast. See Mortimer J. Adler, "The Unity of Man and the Unity of Truth," in *Truth in Religion: The Plurality of Religions and the Unity of Truth* (New York: Macmillan, 1990), 113–28.

21. Saint Augustine, *On Christian Doctrine*, trans. D. W. Robertson Jr. (New York: Macmillan, 1958), II, 28.

22. See Thomas E. Woods Jr., *How the Catholic Church Built Western Civilization* (Washington, DC: Regnery Publishing, 2005).

23. See George M. Marsden, *The Soul of the American University* (New York: Oxford University Press, 1996). See also George M. Marsden, *The Outrageous Idea of Christian Scholarship* (New York: Oxford University Press, 1998), and George M. Marsden and Bradley J. Longfield, *The Secularization of the Academy* (New York: Oxford University Press, 1992).

24. G. K. Chesterton, *Orthodoxy: The Romance of Faith* (New York: Image, 1990), 30.

25. Chesterton, *The Thing*, 13.

26. See Bard Thompson, ed., *Liturgies of the Western Church* (Philadelphia: Fortress Press, 1980).

27. Italics added for emphasis.

28. Bruce M. Metzger, "NRSV: To the Reader," National Council of the Churches of Christ in the USA, http://www.ncccusa.org/newbtu/reader.html.

29. Adolf Harnack, *History of Dogma*, trans. Neil Buchanan (Boston: Little, Brown, and Company, 1902), I, viii.

30. Huston Smith, *Why Religion Matters: The Fate of the Human Spirit in an Age of Disbelief* (San Francisco: HarperSanFrancisco, 2001), xiv.

31. J. B. Phillips, *The Price of Success: An Autobiography* (Wheaton, IL: Harold Shaw, 1984), 148.

32. Italics added for emphasis.

33. C. S. Lewis, *Surprised by Joy* (New York: Harcourt, Brace and World, 1955), 207. Dietrich von Hildebrand, *Trojan Horse in the City of God* (Chicago: Franciscan Herald Press, 1967), 119–23. Jacques Maritain, *The Peasant of the Garonne: An Old Layman Questions Himself about the Present Time*, trans. Michael Cuddihy and Elizabeth Hughes (New York: Holt, Rinehart and Winston, 1966), 13. Cardinal Joseph Ratzinger (later Pope Benedict XVI) aimed at

something similar in his critique of "banal, uncritical assent to the convictions of the present time." See Joseph Cardinal Ratzinger with Vittorio Messori, *The Ratzinger Report* (San Francisco: Ignatius Press, 1985), 144.

34. C. S. Lewis, Introduction to St. Athanasius, *On the Incarnation*, trans. and ed. *A Religious of C.S.M.V.* (Crestwood, NY: St. Vladimir's Seminary Press, 1993), 5.

35. Augustine, *On Christian Doctrine*, I, 5.

36. C. S. Lewis, *The Abolition of Man* (New York: HarperCollins, 2001), 18.

37. Confucius, *The Analects*, trans. D. C. Lau (London: Penguin Books, 1979), XIII, 3.

38. Juan Mascaro, trans., *The Bhagavad Gita* (London: Penguin Books, 1971), 5, 2.

39. See Sigmund Freud, *Totem and Taboo*, trans. James Strachey (New York: W. W. Norton, 1950).

40. See W. Norman Pittenger, *Life as Eucharist* (Grand Rapids, MI: William B. Eerdmans, 1973), and William Willimon, *The Service of God: How Worship and Ethics Are Related* (Nashville: Abingdon Press, 1983).

41. Tertullian, *Apology*, chapter 39. Robert D. Sider, ed., *Christian and Pagan in the Roman Empire: The Witness of Tertullian* (Washington, DC: Catholic University of America Press, 2001).

42. Origen, *On Prayer*, 12.2. Quoted in Boniface Ramsey, *Beginning to Read the Fathers* (New York: Paulist Press, 1985), 168.

43. *The Spiritual Exercises of Saint Ignatius*, trans. Anthony Mottola (New York: Image, 1989), 47.

44. Saint Augustine, *Confessions*, trans. F. J. Sheed, ed. Michael J. Foley, 2nd ed. (Indianapolis, IN: Hackett, 2006), 3.

45. Chesterton, *Orthodoxy*, 15.

46. Aldous Huxley, Introduction to *Bhagavad-Gita: The Song of God*, trans. Swami Prabhavananda and Christopher Isherwood (New York: Signet Classic, 2002), 15.

47. See Roderick Strange, *The Catholic Faith* (Oxford: Oxford University Press, 1989), 171.

48. John Henry Newman, *An Essay on the Development of Christian Doctrine* (Notre Dame, IN: University of Notre Dame Press, 1989), 40.

49. Alasdair MacIntyre, *After Virtue*, 2nd ed. (Notre Dame, IN: University of Notre Dame Press, 1984), 263.

50. From Alfred Noyes's poem "The Book of Earth" in his *The Unknown God* (London: Sheed and Ward, 1937), 7.

51. *Gaudium et Spes*, 45. For a model of a Christological synthesis emphasizing the unity of the "Jesus of history" and the "Christ of faith," see Pope Benedict XVI's trilogy: *Jesus of Nazareth* (New York: Doubleday, 2007), *Jesus of*

Nazareth: Holy Week (San Francisco: Ignatius Press, 2011), *Jesus of Nazareth: The Infancy Narratives* (New York: Image, 2012).

52. See Ignatius of Antioch, Letter to the Smyrneans, 8:2 in Kenneth J. Howell, trans., *Ignatius of Antioch and Polycarp of Smyrna*, rev. ed. (Zanesville, OH: CHResources, 2009).

53. See Dulles, *Catholicity*, 13–29, 185.

54. Peter Maurin, *Easy Essays* (Chicago: Franciscan Herald Press, 1977), 3.

55. Thomas a' Kempis, *The Imitation of Christ*, trans. Leo Sherley-Price (London: Penguin Books, 1975), 49.

56. See Pontifical Council for Justice and Peace, *Compendium of the Social Doctrine of the Church* (Washington, DC: USCCB Publications, 2005).

57. *Lumen Gentium*, 32. *Gaudium et Spes*, 92.

58. See Vatican II's Decree on Ecumenism, *Unitatis Redintegratio*, and its Declaration on the Relation of the Church to Non-Christian Religions, *Nostra Aetate*.

59. See Ian Ker, *Mere Catholicism* (Steubenville, OH: Emmaus Road Publishing, 2006), 99.

60. Karl Rahner and Herbert Vorgrimler, *Concise Theological Dictionary*, ed. Cornelius Ernst, trans. Richard Strachan (London: Burns and Oates, 1965), 21.

61. Epistle to Diognetus, 1, in *Early Christian Writings*, trans. Maxwell Staniforth, rev. Andrew Louth (London: Penguin Books, 1987).

62. See *Lumen Gentium*, 9.

63. See Avery Dulles, *Models of the Church* (New York: Image, 2002).

64. Hans Urs von Balthasar, "The Catholicity of the Church," in Hans Urs von Balthasar and Joseph Ratzinger, *Mary: The Church at the Source*, trans. Adrian Walker (San Francisco: Ignatius Press, 2005), 157–76.

65. Pope Pius XII, *Mystici Corporis Christi*, 77. The full texts of papal encyclicals may be found on the Vatican website: http://www.vatican.va/holy_father/index.htm.

66. George Weigel, *Witness to Hope: The Biography of Pope John Paul II* (New York: HarperCollins, 2001), 686.

67. Pope John Paul II, *Veritatis Splendor*, 52.

68. John Paul, *Veritatis Splendor*, 32.

69. John F. Thornton and Susan B. Varenne, eds., *The Essential Pope Benedict XVI: His Central Writings and Speeches* (San Francisco: HarperSanFrancisco, 2007), 22.

70. Pope Benedict XVI and Peter Seewald, *Light of the World: The Pope, the Church, and the Signs of the Times*, trans. Michael J. Miller and Adrian J. Walker (San Francisco: Ignatius Press, 2010), 50.

71. See Ratzinger, *The Ratzinger Report*, 35–37, 114–17.

17

DIVERSITY IN EASTERN CHRISTIANITY
Historical Traumas and Cultural Dislocations

Dr. Paul L. Gavrilyuk, University of St. Thomas

I'd like to begin with a true story. Ashurbel Pirayou was an undergraduate student at one of California's private universities. While taking his religion course, he told the instructor that he was an Assyrian Christian. His instructor replied that this was impossible, since the Assyrians were wiped out thousands of years ago. The student protested that the Assyrian Christians, the members of the Assyrian Church of the East, most certainly existed, that they spoke the language of Jesus—Aramaic—and that there were colonies of them in North America. The tragic irony of the situation is that the Assyrians, while they survived until the twenty-first century, are indeed in danger of being wiped out as we speak. At one point Ashurbel had the idea of trying to increase his financial aid from his university by appealing to his status as the member of a minority, which, by any rational definition, he certainly was (ethnic and religious both). The response he got was essentially this: "You can't be a minority; there aren't enough of you." By which the university bureaucracy was telling him that minorities had to be registered and recognized as such in order to qualify for assistance, and that entailed having the numbers and political muscle to demand and to receive the attention—nothing so obvious and rational as just *being* a minority, and a very tiny and disrespected one at that.[1]

By extension, Eastern Christians, and this includes not only the Assyrian Church of the East but also the Eastern and Oriental Orthodox in the

United States, also cannot be a minority, because there are not enough of us. The subject of this chapter is Eastern Orthodoxy, which is the best-kept secret in America.

I will approach my subject on three levels.

First, we need to have some preliminary grasp of who are Orthodox Christians. In what countries do they live? What does Eastern Orthodoxy look like as a worldwide communion? In other words, I will first address diversity on the global level.

Second, I will speak about Orthodox Christianity in the United States. What forms of Orthodox Christianity do we find in the United States? In what ways is the American situation unique? This part of my chapter will address diversity on the local level.

Third, I will speak about the changing attitudes toward Orthodox theology in the West, especially in the United States. How does Orthodox theology define itself vis-à-vis its Western counterparts? In turn, how do contemporary Western theologians deploy the resources of the Orthodox tradition? In this final part of my chapter, I will consider four transformations of Orthodox theology in the West in the twentieth century.

DIVERSITY ON A GLOBAL LEVEL

Let me begin with a bit of history. Orthodoxy derives its qualifier *Eastern* from its association with the eastern half of the Roman Empire. In the first millennium, its centers included Jerusalem, Antioch, Alexandria, Constantinople, and other major cities of Asia Minor. Strictly speaking, the division of Christians into the Roman Catholics, populating the Western Roman Empire, and the Eastern Orthodox, populating the Eastern Roman Empire, does not apply to the first five hundred years of Christian history. Thus, the question, whether the first Christians living in Antioch were Roman Catholics or Eastern Orthodox, has very little historical meaning. On the one hand, they were *both* Catholics and Orthodox, if one uses these terms loosely, to refer to the mainline Christians. On the other hand, they were *neither* Roman Catholic *nor* Eastern Orthodox, as these churches came to be differentiated from each other in the second millennium. The second half of the first millennium is characterized by the gradual political, cultural, and linguistic drifting apart of the western and the eastern parts of the Roman Empire. Politically, the western part of the empire became divided as a result of the barbarian invasions of the fifth and later centuries. Linguistically, the problem was exacerbated by the fact that the predominantly Latin-speaking West could no longer understand the predominantly Greek-speaking East, and vice versa.

The second millennium began with the so-called Great Schism of 1054, when the envoys of the pope and the patriarch of Constantinople exchanged mutual excommunications in Hagia Sophia. Most historians today recognize that a more decisive break between the Christian West and the Christian East came later, in the beginning of the thirteenth century, when Crusaders sacked Constantinople. The subsequent attempts to reconcile the Western and the Eastern churches using political pressure, such as the Council of Ferrara-Florence (1438–1445), proved futile. The ecumenical movement of the twentieth century made the problem of the division more salient in the minds of Christians, although it had not reached the goal of reunion. The healing of divisions will continue to occupy the attention of the Church leaders in the twenty-first century.

The political history of the Orthodox Church may be divided into five periods, the chronological boundaries of which overlap, depending upon the geographic region: the Eastern Church began its existence as an association of small faith communities scattered around the Roman Empire. During the first three hundred years, the Church was a persecuted minority. The situation changed in the fourth century CE, when the emperor Constantine granted Christians freedom of worship by the Edict of Milan. Toward the end of the fourth century, under the emperor Theodosius, Orthodox Christianity became an established religion of the Roman Empire. This arrangement continued in the Eastern Roman Empire until the Muslim conquest of Syria, Palestine, and Egypt in the seventh century. This new political arrangement did not end the existence of the Church in these areas of the former Roman Empire but reduced Eastern Christians to the status of religious minorities, or millets within the Islamic civilization. The only area of the Eastern Roman Empire that retained a majority Christian population was Byzantium. In the last centuries of the first millennium, Byzantine missionaries evangelized the Eastern Slavs. When Constantinople fell into the hands of the Ottomans in the fifteenth century, the only Orthodox empire that remained was Russia. The nineteenth and early twentieth centuries saw the formation of the national Orthodox churches of Greece, Serbia, Bulgaria, Romania, and so on. The Russian Revolution brought to power a political regime that was intent on destroying the Church. Militant atheism became an official policy of the totalitarian government. As a result, tens of thousands of Church leaders and hundreds of thousands of believers suffered for their faith in Russia, Ukraine, Belarus, and the countries that became a part of the Socialist Bloc, such as Bulgaria and Romania. It could be said that the Bolshevik Revolution of 1917 put an end to the imperial period of global Orthodox Church history.

Presently, many Orthodox churches in the historically Orthodox countries are recovering from the trauma of religious and political oppression. The situation of the Church of Greece could be described as post-Ottoman, and the Church in the Slavic countries—Russia, Ukraine, Belarus, Bulgaria, and Serbia—as post-Communist or posttotalitarian. As one Moscow priest put it to me in a personal conversation in the early 1990s: "The Church is like a man that has been hit by a bus. He is lying on the ground, nursing his injuries, hardly able to breathe, but the bystanders shout: 'Stand up and run; stand up and run.'"

The Orthodox churches in Greece and several Slavic countries presently enjoy the status of a privileged majority. These churches are gradually learning to live with their newly found freedom. Since the transition from a persecuted minority to a privileged majority occurred rapidly, the learning curve was rather steep. In Russia, for example, the Church that was formerly persecuted by the government was now prepared to use the hand of the same government in order to limit the influence of religious minorities, especially the activity of Western missionaries. In some cases, this was a result of the post-Communist xenophobia. In other cases, however, it was a real fear to lose national and historical identity as a result of seismic political changes that shook the post-Communist countries in the last two decades.

The political situation of the traditionally Christian communities in the Middle East is quite different. The Eastern Christian populations of Egypt, Syria, and Iraq are declining for different political, social, and economic reasons. Generally, in the aftermath of the wars and revolutions, in the absence of a stable government, these communities often remained defenseless against religious extremists, terrorists, and other criminals. The situation of Christians in the Middle East requires more international and media attention.[2]

How does the worldwide Orthodox communion look today? The historically Orthodox countries include Russia, Ukraine, Romania, Greece, Serbia, Bulgaria, Belarus, and Georgia.

What is the basis of *unity* in the worldwide Orthodox communion? The churches are united in faith. It is common to refer to the Orthodox Church as the Church of the Seven Ecumenical Councils. This means that the adherence to the dogmatic definitions and decrees of the ecumenical councils is of paramount importance in the Orthodox Church. From the standpoint of Orthodox Christians, there could be no true unity among Christians without common faith in the trinity and in the incarnation. The Nicene Creed expresses the substance of faith in the trinity, and the Chalcedonian definition establishes the truth of Christ's two natures, human and divine.

The Orthodox Christians are also united by a common liturgical tradition. The liturgy of St. John Chrysostom plays a central role in the sacramental life of the Orthodox Church. With some regional variations, Orthodox churches also share a common rhythm of the liturgical week and a common liturgical calendar. In public worship and private devotion, the veneration of religious images or icons plays a major role. The Orthodox Christians view icons as a portal into the kingdom of God, just as the icons on your touch screens are portals into the world of the Internet.

All Orthodox churches accept the threefold ministerial orders of bishops, presbyters, and deacons. However, there is no exact equivalent of a pope in the Orthodox communion. Some Church leaders may be elevated to the status of archbishops, metropolitans, and patriarchs. The patriarchs (and in some cases the metropolitans) function as the heads of self-governing (autocephalous) churches. While there is a historical seniority among the patriarchs, the most senior hierarch, patriarch Bartholomew of Constantinople, enjoys the status of the first among equals. The patriarch of Constantinople is not an Orthodox equivalent to the pope. Supreme authority rests with the whole Church, gathered for a worldwide council. On a national level, conciliarity is realized through the Holy Synod of bishops. On a worldwide level, conciliarity exists largely in theory, since the Orthodox Church has not had an ecumenical council for more than one thousand years. To conclude, the unity of the worldwide Orthodox communion is secured by the episcopal oversight, the common confession of faith, common sacramental life, a common liturgical calendar, common veneration of icons, saints, and the Church Fathers.

Many of the aspects of the faith that I mentioned—the creed, the sacraments, and so on—are shared by Roman Catholics and other Christian communions. But what are the characteristic features of Orthodoxy? To provide for a more focused discussion, I will concentrate on the characteristic emphases of Orthodox *theology*.[3]

First, Orthodox theologians of the twentieth century, especially Alexander Schmemann, have emphasized the bond between theology, spirituality, and worship. According to Schmemann, all theology must be grounded in liturgical experience. The Church's worship, in turn, has profound theological significance. Theology, spirituality, and worship must mutually inform each other.

Second, Orthodox theology emphasizes the mysterious character of God. The God who makes himself known in revelation is also a God whose essence remains an unfathomable mystery. For example, we know that God is triune, but we do not know how God is triune. We know that the divine Logos assumed human nature, but the exact character of that union is defined in the negative adjectives of the Chalcedonian definition: without division, without separation, without confusion, and without change. Orthodox theology emphasizes that the assertions about what God is must be counterbalanced by the negations of what God is not.

Third, Orthodox theology is characterized by its sacramental vision of the world. The world is not an end in itself, but it is a vehicle through which we come to know God. To seek knowledge about humanity and the world—something to which you are dedicating much time in your college education—is to study creation in order to glorify the creator. The sacramental vision of the world rejects a permanent separation of the sacred and the profane, of the religious and the secular. To view the world as a sacrament is to receive it from God and offer it back to God.

Fourth, Orthodox theology views salvation as deification, as participation in the life of God. Orthodox theology emphasizes ontological and therapeutic, rather than juridical and transactional, aspects of salvation. While divine grace or divine energies are the primary agent of deification, salvation is impossible without human cooperation. This notion of cooperation of the creaturely will with that of the creator is pivotal for Orthodox soteriology.

The fifth principle of Orthodox theology is *sobornost'*, sometimes translated as *catholicity* of *conciliarity*. *Sobornost'*, as Orthodox understand the term, is free unity-in-diversity. Let me unpack this concept a bit further. The freedom that is at stake here is the freedom of discipleship, the freedom of adherence to Christ and the gospel, the freedom from external authority accompanied by the acceptance of the authority of the Church, as the body of Christ. The unity-in-diversity is the unity of faith and life, which allows for the exercise of diverse gifts within the Church. The diversity at stake here is the diversity of the gifts of the Holy Spirit. Genuine charismatic diversity does not undermine the hierarchical structure of the Church's ministry, but serves to enrich it.

Diversity in the Church cannot exist for diversity's sake. Diversity that undermines unity is harmful to the life of the Church. The diversity that builds up the Church is impossible without unity. At the same time, unity that excludes diversity may generate a juridical mindset, conformity to a rigid set of rules that the Orthodox decry in the Western churches.

Let me give you one historical example. With the emergence of the nation-states in Central and Eastern Europe in the nineteenth century, some Orthodox churches that were previously administratively united under the jurisdiction of the patriarch of Constantinople separated and organized self-governing national churches. In this way, the churches of Greece (declared autocephalous in 1833, recognized in 1850) and Romania (declared autocephalous in 1872, recognized in 1885), which were previously governed from Constantinople, became national churches. On the one hand, autocephaly provided the conditions for the revival of national religious traditions. The leadership of the autocephalous churches came to play a role in the rebuilding of the nation-states and, in principle at least, became closer to the faithful. This was a positive change. But on the other hand, the creation of national churches led to the alienation of the ethnic churches from their mother churches and to an increasing sense of separation from the worldwide Orthodox communion. As a result, the ties between the national churches weakened and a sense of the universality of Orthodoxy decreased. Religiously fueled nationalism became a strong political force. Positively understood, nationalism could be regarded as a revival of culture and political consciousness in a suppressed nation. Negatively understood, nationalism is a love for one's nation at the expense of other nations. When the love of one's nation is placed above the love of God, nationalism becomes a form of idolatry. The nationalist agenda locked the self-governing churches in the web of their ethnic concerns. As a result, the universal and cosmic vision of salvation, while in theory accepted by the Orthodox Church, was in practice abandoned.

Presently, there are reassuring signs that the alienation that I have just described is being recognized as a problem. The twenty-first century will be characterized by an increased cooperation between the national churches. Remarkably, the American situation may provide some helpful paradigms.

ORTHODOXY IN THE UNITED STATES

The history of the Orthodox Church in the United States begins in the eighteenth century, when Russian missionaries converted the native population and built churches in Alaska, which at the time was a part of the Russian Empire. (The U.S. Senate purchased Alaska from Russia in 1867). The approach of the Russian missionaries, as opposed to Russian frontier men and explorers, was characterized by respect for the cultural uniqueness of the Alaskan people. The missionaries translated the Bible and the liturgy into Aleutian and ran schools for the natives. The Orthodox communities in Alaska have survived into the present day.

In the nineteenth century, the *missionary* church became an *immigrant* church, as the immigrants from Greece, Galicia (a region in the former Austro-Hungarian Empire), and the Russian Empire began to settle in the United States. Russian-speaking immigrants settled in California, whereas the Greek-speaking communities came to Florida. The two world wars, the Communist revolutions in Eastern European countries, and the civil war in Greece caused new waves of immigration. The immigrant communities divided along national and political lines. For example, the faithful of the Russian Church who immigrated to the West after the revolution divided into those who were in communion with the Moscow Patriarchate and those who joined other jurisdictions, such as the Patriarchate of Constantinople or the Russian Orthodox Church Abroad. Similar political divisions also occurred in the Serbian and Ukrainian communities. The result was multiple jurisdictions, some sharing, but others not sharing, communion with each other. Presently, some of these divisions have been healed. Here, in Cincinnati, you have a microcosm of the world Orthodox community. A similar situation obtains in other major cities in the United States, such as New York, Chicago, Minneapolis, San Francisco, and so on. Perhaps nowhere else in the world is the Orthodox Church more ethnically diverse than it is in the United States. Just for this reason alone, the Orthodox churches in the United States deserve a closer study.

In the last fifty years, the Orthodox Church has become increasingly open to converts. In the absence of potent new waves of immigration and given a rapid rate of assimilation of the immigrant population, especially of the Slavs, in fifty years the Orthodox Church may become predominantly a convert church, while also remaining the church of the first-, second-, and so on generation immigrants. As an immigrant whose family has included Orthodox clergymen for several generations, I welcome this development. As the first-century church opened its doors to the Gentiles, the twenty-first-century Orthodox Church in America must open its doors to all inquirers, irrespectively of their ethnic background. As one of the parishioners put it to me: "I became a member here, because finally I did not feel like I had to become Greek, or Russian, or whatever, before I become Orthodox." At the same time, the converts must have patience and tact if they find out that ethnic Orthodox Christians do not wish to assimilate and become culturally American.

What place does the Orthodox Church occupy on the map of American Christianity? There are about 1.9 million Orthodox Christians in the United States, roughly about 0.6 percent of the population. While the Orthodox in the United States are numerically small, "there are not enough of us in the U.S. to be a minority," there are signs that Orthodoxy, while remaining the best kept secret in the United States, is becoming more known.

Presently, in the second decade of the twenty-first century, the landscape of Orthodox academic theology in the West is changing in some fundamental ways. For the past hundred years, four interconnected transformations of Orthodox theology have taken place in the West. The first is:

From an Unknown Commodity to a Respectable Minority Theology

In the beginning of the twentieth century, Catholic and Protestant theologians tended to treat Orthodox theology, if they noticed its existence at all, in a dismissive and cursory manner. With the exception of a few Anglican theologians, Orthodox theology inspired little sympathy or even interest in the West. Writing in the 1930s, Georges Florovsky described the situation vividly: "In the West one has become accustomed to regard Orthodoxy as a sort of exhumed Christianity, retrograde and stagnant, to think that the Christian East, at best, is in a state of historic coma. Historic separation and estrangement account for this deceptive interpretation."[4] Presently the situation has changed dramatically. Many major universities in the United States pride themselves on having at least one Orthodox faculty member in their departments of religion, theology, or philosophy. Remarkably, the theology departments of Fordham, Marquette, and Duquesne Universities each have *two* full-time Orthodox faculty members. I am particularly enthusiastic about the Program in Orthodox Christian Studies that professors Georges Demacopoulos and Aristotle Papanikolaou have established at Fordham. Such a program, hardly possible thirty years ago, is something worth replicating at other non-Orthodox schools. Irrespective of the denominational alignment of a given school, we as a rule enjoy considerable intellectual freedom and no ideological pressure at the non-Orthodox schools that employ us. Our Catholic hosts accept us as potentially offering a corrective to what they perceive as limitations of "Latin" theology. Our Protestant colleagues see the representatives of Orthodoxy as offering the goods of Catholic Christianity without the historical traumas of the Reformation. There are a growing number of Catholics and Protestants to whom the "book version" of Orthodoxy looks quite attractive. As a minority, we enjoy a unique, politically nonthreatening status and are respected for who we are. From these observations, the second shift, to which we now turn, follows naturally:

From the Primary Institutional Location at Orthodox Seminaries to Teaching Posts at Non-Orthodox Schools

A century ago, the majority of Orthodox theologians who relocated to Europe either held posts at the established Orthodox schools, such as the theology departments at the University of Belgrade and the University of Sofia, or had to create new Orthodox institutions, such as the famous St. Sergius Theological Institute in Paris and St. Vladimir's Orthodox Theological Seminary in the United States. After the war, in the United States, most Orthodox theologians taught at the recently established Orthodox schools. Today the situation is quite different. The total number of full-time faculty at the Holy Cross Greek Orthodox School of Theology, St.

Vladimir's Orthodox Theological Seminary, and St. Tikhon's Orthodox Theological Seminary is around fifty. The number of Orthodox scholars who are teaching religion-related subjects at non-Orthodox institutions and seminaries is at least twice more. Due to the financial challenges and relatively slow church growth in the United States, it is unlikely that the number of full-time faculty at the Orthodox schools is going to increase considerably in the near future. Naturally, those working at mainstream academic institutions, unlike those teaching at Orthodox schools, interact on a regular basis with their non-Orthodox peers as well as the non-Orthodox student population. In such circumstances, our thinking, teaching, and writing turn into an implicit dialogue with the non-Orthodox "Other." Any act of accountable and serious scholarship becomes in some sense an "ecumenical" act, whether we meet for highly ritualized ecumenical discussions or not. The third shift, then, is:

From Ecumenical Dialogue to Postdenominational Condition

In the beginning of the twentieth century, the ecumenical dialogue was predicated on the assumption of clear and rigid denominational boundaries. Those outside of one's own group were typically regarded as heretics or schismatics. Orthodox theology was too often "Orientalized" by being presented as a mere antithesis to Western theology. To simplify the frequently invoked dichotomies to the point verging on caricature, the individualistic, legalistic, rationalistic, and anthropocentric "West" is contrasted with the supposedly communitarian, holistic, mystical, and theocentric "East." Such dichotomies convey more about internal tensions within various expressions of Western theological thought than they do about the alleged contrast between the "East" and the "West."

Presently, the situation has changed. The denominational boundaries have increasingly become porous and flexible, at least in the United States. On the one hand, a century after the beginning of the ecumenical movement, Christians have become even more divided. But on the other hand, the dividing lines no longer coincide neatly with denominational boundaries, but rather with the positions on controversial issues of human sexuality, the ministry of women in the Church, and other social issues. At the same time, non-Orthodox theologians are showing increasing willingness to engage with and incorporate the insights of Orthodox theology. For example, apophatic theology and the concept of deification are no longer perceived as exclusively "Eastern" topics, as they used to be seen in many quarters before. On the contrary, postmodern theologians of all stripes are captivated by the *via negativa*; more remarkably, Catholic, Anglican, Methodist, Lutheran, Calvinist, and Evangelical theologians have recently put forth very appreciative accounts of deification.

There is a growing perception that the Eastern Orthodox tradition has been neglected in the curriculum of Western theological institutions and presently has to be more effectively represented. Forward-looking deans of various theological schools are presently considering concrete ways of institutionalizing such changes. For example, the creation of the endowed chair in Late Antique and Byzantine Christian History for a renowned Orthodox patristic scholar and theologian, Fr. John Anthony McGuckin at Union Theological Seminary, has provided the resources for the establishment of the Orthodox Sophia Institute as a part of the same school.

The fourth and final shift is *from Diaspora theology to convert theology*. Almost without exception, Slavs and Greeks dominated Orthodox theological scholarship in the United States only thirty years ago. In some cases, those Slavs and Greeks were educated and even born outside of their countries of ethnic origin, but their roots still ran fairly deep in their respective ethnic traditions. This situation is rapidly changing. Deep interest in Eastern Orthodoxy has led some non-Orthodox intellectuals to join the Orthodox Church. One might recall such world-renowned scholars as the late Jaroslav Pelikan, metropolitan Kallistos Ware, Richard Swinburne, Fr. Andrew Louth, Fr. John Anthony McGuckin, Norman Russell, Susan Ashbrook Harvey, Edith Humphrey, David Bentley Hart, David Bradshaw, Tristram Engelhardt, and others. I should note that all of these highly influential scholars teach (or have previously taught) at non-Orthodox schools. Converts also predominate among Orthodox graduate students who are currently pursuing their doctorates. For example, out of ten Orthodox doctoral students pursuing their work at Fordham, all are either converts or come from the families of converts. Sociologically, the increasing intellectual presence of converts—I forecast that their influence will increase exponentially in the years ahead—might create some amazing identity challenges for us in the future.

To conclude, world Orthodoxy continues its recovery from an imperial, colonial, and totalitarian past. The traumas of this past are deep and not likely to heal quickly. Orthodox Christian communities in the United States are a microcosm of world Orthodoxy. Originally the results of political upheavals in the home countries, today these communities continue to evolve from largely immigrant bodies to bodies in which much of the leadership is exercised by converts. Today there is a vibrant dialogue between Orthodox theologians and their non-Orthodox friends in the academy and the Church. I expect this dialogue and collaboration to increase and bear many fruits in the future. The time will come when the Orthodox will no longer be too small to be a minority.

NOTES

1. Michael Hollerich, email communication to P. Gavrilyuk, February 20, 2013.
2. Matthew Selby, "Christianity in the Middle East: A Historical Look at the Modern State of the Church in the Place of Its Birth," unpublished graduate paper for the course "Eastern Christianity").
3. For an excellent discussion of this issue, which is largely followed here, see John Jillions, "Orthodox Christianity in the West: The Ecumenical Challenge," in *The Cambridge Companion to Orthodox Christian Theology*, ed. Mary B. Cunningham and Elizabeth Theokritoff (Cambridge: Cambridge University Press, 2008), 276–91.
4. George Florovsky, "A Visit to Anglican Theological Colleges," September 15, 1933, 38 (unpublished typescript in the Georges Florovsky Papers at Princeton University).

18

JUSTICE AND DIVERSITY
A Homogenous Protestant Project?

D. Stephen Long, Southern Methodist University

DIVERSITY, JUSTICE, PROTESTANTISM

My task is to bring together three highly contested terms—diversity, justice, and Protestantism—and make some sense or coherence of the relationship among them. The crucial term is *diversity*; it is also the most recent. *Justice* and *Protestantism* have lengthy histories of use that makes them unwieldy to manage in a brief chapter. However, if we focus on *diversity* and its relationship to justice and Protestantism, then the task becomes more manageable. I will first suggest a range of meanings for the term *diversity*, and then suggest how a (perhaps) Protestant theopolitical vision found in the book of Revelation assists in adjudicating among the range of meanings for *diversity*. I will conclude with some brief attention to the question of justice. What has this theopolitical vision to do with justice?

HOW IS THE TERM *DIVERSITY* USED?

The philosopher Wittgenstein stated that the meaning of a term is in its use. Because I find his statement compelling, I think it insufficient to examine any term simply by providing a definition. Rather than first defining *diversity*, let us ask how it is used in our current context. Diversity is a popular cultural term that is nearly mandatory for any present-day institution. Xavier University's strategic plan, like nearly every strategic plan found in universities, corporations, and government offices, has a plank affirming diversity.[1] Many, if not most, universities affirm their "diversity" as a component of their uniqueness. Let me provide some examples. The strategic plan for arts and science at my own Jesuit institution, Marquette University, has as a core "strategic objective" to "embrace diversity and nurture unique gifts through the Jesuit principle of *cura personalis*." Such statements are, of course, not unique to Jesuit and Catholic institutions; the formerly Protestant now thoroughly secular Northwestern University offers a similar plank in its strategic plan. One of its goals is to "Foster, in international studies and through markets, social structures, and public policy, humanistic inquiry that leads to greater appreciation of different cultures." The third goal of its strategic plan includes "Growing stronger through the richness of our diversity."[2] Another very different kind of university, evangelical Wheaton College, likewise includes an affirmation of "diversity" in its strategic plan. Its fourth goal is to "deepen diversity," and under this goal you find the following statement:

> Yet despite the breadth of the body of Christ, many members of the Wheaton community continue to express a lack of understanding concerning issues of ethnicity and culture, as well as the theology behind current initiatives to promote diversity among students, faculty, staff, and administration on campus. A sincere commitment to diversity should extend to all levels of leadership. Our Savior designed our diversity, and Wheaton College must seek to honor his lordship by diligently pursuing reconciliation and celebrating our unity in Christ.[3]

Two Jesuit Catholic universities as well as a secular and evangelical one, who may not share much in common, share this: diversity is a core strategic objective.

Universities are not the only institutions affirming diversity as part of a strategic plan. Every branch of the U.S. armed forces has a diversity office with a vision or mission statement.[4] Take as an example "The Army's Diversity Vision," which states:

> The Army's diversity vision is to be the national leader in embracing the strengths of diverse people in an inclusive environment. This in-

cludes investing in and managing talent, valuing individuals and developing culturally astute Soldiers and Civilians who enhance our communities and are prepared for the human dimension of leadership and global engagements.[5]

An emphasis on diversity is also integral to business. No one has been better at an "inclusive" work force than a transnational corporation that seeks a global customer base like McDonalds.[6] After several criticisms of its cultural practices (Eric Schlosser's *Fast Food Nation* and Morgan Spurlock's *Super Size Me*), McDonald's corporation hired a "diversity officer," Pat Harris. She implemented several policies of inclusion, including a "Global Inclusion and Intercultural Management Team" in 2009.

The few examples I give could be expanded. I doubt there is a strategic plan or vision statement found in any university, church, government office, or corporation that does not include a "diversity" plank. From the military to government to corporations and universities, "diversity" draws institutions together into a common cultural project. If this sampling of institutions is not exceptional, and I do not think it is, then the first thing that must be recognized about the term *diversity* is its homogenizing force. By that I mean that a primary function of the affirmation of diversity is to ensure sameness across cultural institutions. If I am correct about this function, then the fact that the ubiquitous use of the term diversity actually creates a common cultural project should at least alert us to the fact that the term is being used oddly. When we say "diversity" we mean "sameness."

I do not only mean this as a criticism. The common cultural project the term *diversity* serves is preferable to some alternatives. There are the obvious immoral alternatives: white supremacists, militia groups, and neo-Nazis would not include such a plank in their strategic plans. But other less extreme examples could be provided of groups that explicitly and implicitly exclude precisely the diversities most government offices, corporations, and universities now affirm. Such exclusions have a long history. We find ourselves in a country that was founded upon them: a slavocracy, Native American genocide, patriarchy, and governmental regulations deciding familial structures by outlawing certain practices such as oral sex and homosexuality (laws against these practices were found in every state prior to 1962 and were only decisively rescinded in 2003 when the Supreme Court rejected Texas's sodomy laws in a 6–3 vote). So the ubiquitous inclusion of diversity in strategic plans is an important reminder not to repeat past errors, and that is the first of five uses of the term *diversity* I want to explore.

Diversity as Memory

The ubiquitous presence of "diversity" among U.S. institutions reflects the hard-earned gains of the civil rights movement along with many other liberation movements that challenged, since at least the 1960s, a "Whites only," and predominantly male, culture of power. "Diversity" reminds us of those gains and encourages us not to perpetuate the previous culture. It alludes to a memory, albeit vaguely, that we forget at our peril, a forgetting which is all too easy given the "individualism" still present in popular culture.

Alasdair MacIntyre identified how readily individualism represses memory several decades ago when he set forth a theory of action grounded in a narrative self as opposed to one founded upon "modern individualism." It, he suggested, could not account for the historical particularities of our moral starting point. He wrote:

> For I am never able to seek for the good or exercise the virtues only *qua* individual. . . . It is not just that different individuals live in different social circumstances; it is also that we all approach our own circumstances as bearers of a particular social identity. I am someone's son or daughter, someone else's cousin or uncle; I am citizen of this or that city, a member of this or that guild or profession; I belong to this clan, that tribe, this nation. Hence what is good for me has to be the good for one who inhabits these roles. As such, I inherit from the past of my family, my city, my tribe, my nation, a variety of debts, inheritances, rightful expectations and obligations. These constitute the given of my life, my moral starting point. This is in part what gives my life its own moral particularity.[7]

What matters for moral action are the particular histories that constitute the diverse roles we inhabit. To be born in, or be a citizen of, the United States entails attention to the legacy of slavery, Jim Crow—old and new—and racism. Had we been born in Germany or Africa, our moral starting point would differ. At its best, "diversity" calls us to attend to these histories. But seldom does the affirmation of diversity address these historical specificities. They remain too implicit and vague, so the reason for "diversity" remains unarticulated. When that happens, "diversity," too, easily functions ideologically.

Diversity as Ideology

A second use of diversity is ideological, as if a generic affirmation of diversity suffices to account for our historical inheritances, debts, and obligations. Then "diversity" diverts our gaze from these legacies. Rather than reminding us to examine our particular histories or attend to our concrete situations, it teaches us to forget the conditions that make everyday life possible. Then "diversity" is nothing more than "language on a holiday."

Diversity becomes ideological when it functions contrary to what the term does at its best. Rather than summoning us to be attentive to our histories, it turns us away from them and becomes nothing more than a false voluntarism where the only reason we do not have the inclusive community we desire is due to the bad will of recalcitrant persons who refuse to accept the dominant, common culture of "diversity." Diversity becomes ideology when it reduces to this syllogism:

1. We are a diverse institution.
2. You do not share in our diversity.
3. Therefore, you must be excluded.

Here diversity masks sameness and that makes it ideological. It is a reification in the Marxist sense; it takes something that doesn't actually exist—"our unique diversity"—and falsely assumes it is concrete simply if we say it loudly or frequently. Rather than attending to the specific conditions that prohibit diversity, it diverts attention from them. When this occurs, "diversity" has become nothing more than the ideology found at the food court of any mall, which brings us to a third use of diversity.

Diversity as Market Strategy

In a global market, diversity is a necessary strategy for selling goods and services to as broad a customer base as possible. As I mentioned in the introduction, McDonald's Corporation has a more inclusive and diverse workforce than most other institutions. "Women and people of color make up 73% of McDonald's total workforce, 43% of all franchise staff and 55% of suppliers."[8] If looked upon empirically, this diversity is real; it is not a reification. McDonald's can point to determinate bodily factors—especially color and genitalia, dominant markers of race and gender—and argue that it fulfills the strategic vision of diversity more so than any university. Yet I doubt that any university has McDonald's Corporation in mind when it set its diversity goals. Its "diversity" results not from attention to historical debts, inheritances, expectations, and obligations, but from class differentiation that makes a large pool of unskilled labor power available for the mass production of cheap goods and services. It is the "flat" diversity extolled by Thomas Friedman, who argued that the global market, connecting "all knowledge centers" into a "single global network," flattens the world and links diverse cultures and peoples into a necessary unity. "Diversity" in this sense is necessary for economic growth.

Friedman exhibits this kind of "flat" diversity by citing an African parable translated into Mandarin and posted on the "factory floor" in China by his American friend Jack Perkowski, CEO of ASIMCO technologies:

> Every morning in Africa, a gazelle wakes up.
> It knows it must run faster than the fastest lion or it will be killed.
> It knows it must outrun the slowest gazelle or it will starve to death.
> It doesn't matter whether you are a lion or gazelle.
> When the sun comes up, you better start running.[9]

Business has no choice but to engage in collaborative diversity, argue both Friedman and Perkowski. "Either you get flat or you'll be flattened by China."[10]

Diversity as Global Hegemony

Friedman and Perkowski point to another use of "diversity"; it has become a necessity in the Hobbesian war of all against all that too often defines both the transnational corporation and competing modern nation-states. The mixture of cultures, peoples, and religions they affirm serves the interest of economic growth and global hegemony. Unlike the theological motivation for diversity found in the strategic plans of the Jesuit,

Catholic Marquette and the evangelical Wheaton (*cura personalis*, unity in Christ), the secular Northwestern University explicitly ties "diversity" to "markets." Perhaps it could also be stated, noncontroversially, that "greater appreciation of different cultures" in public policy and international studies is necessary for a hegemonic, global power like the United States. Why is it such a focus in the armed services? Cultural diversity may be a strategic advantage the United States still has over China in their mutual bids for global power. The culture of the United States still assumes *e pluribus unum*. Is it not the case that this use of diversity functions to legitimate rule and the exercise of power? The more inclusive we are, the more right and better means we have to fulfill the mission of American exceptionalism.

Diversity as Epistemology

A very different fifth use of diversity is, I think, unique to the scholarly and intellectual culture of the university. It sets forth cultural diversity, especially the inclusion of formerly underrepresented people, as an epistemology. Diversity fosters a fuller pursuit of knowledge. Although there are many sources for diversity as an epistemology, one undeniable key source is the philosopher Hegel, especially his left-wing inheritors. James Cone notes this important source in his *God of the Oppressed*. He states, "Although God, the subject of theology, is eternal, theology itself is, like those who articulate it, limited by time and history."[11] To defend this epistemological claim, he draws on "Feuerbach, Marx and the Sociology of Knowledge." He cites, with qualifications, the left-wing Hegelian Feuerbach's take on theology—"theology is anthropology"—and states, "It is difficult to ignore the cogency of Feuerbach's logic in view of the obvious sociological context of human speech. What people think about God cannot be divorced from their place and time in a definite history and culture."[12]

Such an epistemological and sociopolitical rendering of diversity owes a debt to a Hegelian politics of recognition, which emerged from his famous discussion of the development of consciousness in the master-slave relationship. Consciousness is not a static, transcendent feature of a human being, but it is mediated through historical interactions whereby one becomes self-conscious and demands the recognition of others, a progressive development where differences increasingly produce unity rather than division. Jean Hyppolite explains well the implications of the master-slave dialectic in Hegel. He writes, "This mutual recognition, in which individuals recognize each other as reciprocally recognizing each other, creates the element of spiritual life—the medium in which the subject is an object to itself, finding itself completely in the other yet doing so without abrogating the otherness that is essential to self-consciousness."[13] Robert Pippin explains the political import of Hegel's mutual recognition: "In political terms what this means is that the true or full exercise of agency by an individual, the possibility of realizing the modern norm of genuinely free activity without which a modern *Gemeinschaft* would not be possible, is only fully 'realized' (*verwirklicht*), if the like capacity of all persons for such agency is recognized, if nothing in my deed implies the contrary, and if that mutuality of recognition is institutionally secured, ultimately in a *Rechtsstaat* [constitutional state]."[14]

If the Hegelian influence on the common culture of diversity is recognized, then it is not contradictory. Recognizing alterity, difference or diversity becomes a common fund for a human agency that reconciles freedom and nature through mutual recognition of differences in a constitutional democracy. Yet Pippin also acknowledges that this mutual recognition is a modern *state* project of grounding freedom in nothing other than its own immanent source, its spontaneity. It needs no theological grounding.

WHAT HAS DIVERSITY TO DO WITH THEOLOGY?

If Pippin is correct, perhaps nothing. Such a political use of diversity intends to avoid theology or any transcendent ground for freedom necessary in a democratic, constitutional state. But the above uses of "diversity" suggest that the term serves differing social formations, and we should at least ask which ones and why. Here I side with Cone's statement: "What people think about God cannot be divorced from their place and time in a definite history and culture."[15] The same should be said of "diversity." What people think about "diversity" cannot be divorced from places and times in definite histories and cultures, and those places and times arise from and serve different social orderings. The question is, which ones? As a common cultural project, "diversity" could serve the social ordering of the modern nation-state, the global market, or a transnational "cosmopolitanism" (the latter does not yet exist despite repeated calls for it since at least Kant). It could serve one, a combination, or all of them. The point here is that diversity is not a neutral term, but one laden with social and political significance; it functions more like a citizenship oath or a creed. To affirm it is not only to affirm "diversity" but also its underlying sociality.

THE BARTHIAN TURN TO ECCLESIOLOGY AND CHRISTOLOGY

Because diversity is not a neutral term but always serves one or more underlying social formations, which sociality it serves matters. It is at this point that theology provides a normative lens that can help adjudicate the underlying sociality, the normative lens of ecclesiology. In the twentieth century, due to the vast influence of Karl Barth's *Church Dogmatics*, Protestant theology underwent an ecclesiological renaissance, especially in theological ethics. Ethics was no longer understood emerging primarily from a "natural," and certainly not a purely natural, realm. Instead, ethics emerges from concrete, particular communities; for Christian ethics it emerges from the Church. Barth, and other Protestant theologians, turned theology away from generic, abstract reason such as natural law as the foundation for ethics and politics and toward more particular, concrete reasons such as Christology and ecclesiology. Being attentive to Barth's Protestant theology provides for a sixth use of "diversity." It emerges from, and serves the ends of, the church as fulfilling God's mission of bringing healing to the nations. It is within and from the worship practices of the Church that we can begin to address the questions that must be addressed about justice and diversity. If we understand diversity as a theological mission essential to Christ's formation of the Church, then we will have means to adjudicate among the range of meanings for "diversity" in our historical context—if we find ourselves in institutions still related to their ecclesial founding. In what follows I will argue that Church-related institutions have a distinct advantage in affirming and understanding why diversity should matter.

WHICH CHURCH?

Three questions immediately arise. First, which Church? Second, is not the Church responsible for exclusionary practices that work against diversity? Third, is not any appeal to the Church as a social reality ordering others triumphalistic? Let me take up these questions by drawing upon the work of the Protestant theologians Stanley Hauerwas and Samuel Wells. Hauerwas is responsible for a significant shift in Christian ethics in the twentieth century, a shift that has not been without its critics both within and without Protestantism. Hauerwas and Wells suggest that the first question, "Which Church?," is "understandable" but unhelpful. They state,

> It is unhelpful because it encourages a sense of finality that diminishes, rather than builds up, the Church. This is a finality that suggests it is possible to 'arrive' at a 'right' church. Such a church would be almost bound to foster pride rather than honesty, complacency rather than confidence. It would resemble a too-tidy dogmatics, in that it would provide such a conclusive guarantee of God that witness would seem unnecessary and service would be neglected. It would misunderstand every aspect of worship.[16]

It misunderstands worship because it fails to see the Church as a project God summons to an end that exceeds its own nature. The all-too-human nature of the Church is called to a perfection it cannot achieve on its own, but without which its earthly life makes little sense. Intrinsic to that calling is "catholicity," which is an anticipated ecclesiological and eschatological form of diversity. It is ecclesiological because it cannot be had without the Church; for the Church is integral to Christ's work. Christ gathers a people from every nation, tribe, tongue, and people into the unity of his body. It is eschatological because it also extends beyond the Church to include all nations. The Church is integral to Christ's work of gathering all people into a unity, but it is always only the first fruits of a new political reality, referred to in Scripture sometimes as a "kingdom" and other times as a "city," that God brings into existence for the healing of the nations.

If the Church were complete and finished in itself, then it would lack the summons to perfection that exceeds its human nature, and would be incapable of reform. If the Church is a project to be perfected, then it must acknowledge its life is a life of repentance, of turning toward what it shall be so that it can be truthful about what it is.[17] Here is where it can affirm better than most other social formations the first use of diversity noted above, diversity as memory. The Church has means for remembering, confessing, and repenting past histories of exclusion. Far from triumphalism, the Church must be humble, for it is always made up of hypocrites who strive to be more than they are, who seek a genuine diversity based on a truthful communion in the midst of our self-deceits.

THE PERFECTION OF THE CHURCH IN THE BOOK OF REVELATION

The genuine diversity of the Church arises from its summons to perfection. The next obvious question is what is this perfection and how does it relate to the various social institutions diversity serves at present. To answer such questions, Protestant theology primarily, albeit not exclusively, turns to Scripture. Two Protestant theologians, the Anglican Oliver O'Donovan and the Anabaptist John Howard Yoder, turn to one of the oddest and potentially dangerous books in the Bible for an answer to this question, the book of Revelation. They offer two overlapping, and yet significantly different, answers as to how the Church in its summons to perfection relates to the diversity of nations, peoples, races, and cultures. O'Donovan presents an "establishment" Protestant vision. The Church makes alliances with national identities. Yoder presents a "Free Church" vision that places more limits on such alliances. Both do so, however, under the influence of Barth's turn toward Christology, ecclesiology, and eschatology, which is why they dare to turn to Revelation for a theopolitical vision that must take into account diversity. Although previous generations read Revelation as escaping social and political questions through an otherworldly apocalypticism, their work recognizes that Revelation offers an important theopolitical vision that gives insight into the relations among the diverse nations and peoples God created. O'Donovan and Yoder provide different interpretations of those relations, but within a common concern that Christ's odd triumph provides the key for any proper social ordering.

For both Yoder and O'Donovan, a central text is Revelation 5, which represents a Christian metanarrative (or what was once considered to be the "anagogical" meaning of Scripture). Here is the ultimate meaning of history contained in a scroll sealed with seven seals and unable to be opened until Christ's Ascension. But now that Christ has ascended, the Lamb who was slain is worthy to open the scroll and to give to John the revelation of the meaning of history. When the scroll is opened, a "new song" cries forth that bears witness to a new "kingdom" served by priests "from every tribe and language and people and nation" (Rev. 5:9–10). The unity found in Christ's triumph is one that includes every nation; it mandates diversity.

What follows the opening of the scroll is a series of "three successive views, each with a cycle of seven visions" where first (Rev. 6:1–8:1) there is "worsening calamities" brought on by an overreaching human political ambition.[18] Second (8:2–11:19), there is "history as a series of judgments invoked by prayer," where God's people are vindicated. The vindication is not found in an otherworldly realm, but in the merging of God's reign and human rule. Thus we find the famous affirmation: "The kingdom of this world has become the kingdom of our Lord, and of His Christ, and He will reign forever and ever" (11:15). A third cycle of seven visions ensues; this time with seven plagues that culminate in the overthrow of "Babylon" (15:1–16:21). "Babylon" represents every political institution that refuses to provide space for the New Jerusalem Christ establishes. Between the second and third cycle comes an allegory explaining the meaning of history. A "woman" gives birth to a "male child who is to rule all the nations with a rod of iron" (12:5). But before this child could rule, he "was snatched away and taken to God and to his throne." The result is that the dragon was defeated in heaven and "thrown down." A voice in heaven proclaims: "They have conquered him by the blood of the Lamb and by the word of their testimony, for they did not cling to life even in the face of death" (12:11). The vision concludes with the "bride of the Lamb," the Holy City made up of the twelve tribes and the twelve apostles; a renewed and restored "polis" where not only the Church and Israel is restored but all the nations "bring their glory into it," excluding only those who "practice abomination or falsehood." The Church must, then, make space for the glory of every nation.

What are the social and political implications for understanding diversity from the Book of Revelation? First, both O'Donovan and Yoder, unlike fundamentalists and dispensationalists, recognize we are dealing here with a unique genre of apocalyptic literature whose purpose is not to provide a blueprint for the end of the world, but what I have termed a "theopolitical vision." Second, for both that theopolitical vision establishes the Church as the primary social formation that allows for the healing of the nations. If the Church is not the Church, then all other social formations lose their proper ordering. The Church belongs to no single nation, race, people, or language; it must be constituted by all of them. This belonging places limitations and obligations on every nation, race, people, and tribe. On the one hand, it relativizes their significance. No single nation or race can make absolute claims for itself, but it also affirms their place in God's good creation. On the other hand, it secures a social and political space for every nation. God provides every nation, race, and tribe with a glory that it brings into the New Jerusalem, which will require hospitality and generosity of each nation. It must welcome others as it itself should expect welcome. But third, how other social formations are rendered intelligible by Christ's odd triumph differs between O'Donovan and Yoder. For O'Donovan the political significance of the apocalypse is that the principalities and powers "have been made subject to God's sovereignty in the Exaltation of Christ." Such subjection is not yet final. He states, "This awaits a final universal presence of Christ to become fully apparent."[19] But it nonetheless has significant political consequences in the present age. The result is the reauthorizing of a "secular authority" that should presume first that Christ has come and second that "the sovereignty of Christ is not now transparent and uncontested." The reauthorized role of the secular authority is to make judgments and offer praise based on these presumptions. In so doing, it must allow for a "certain social space for men and women of every nation to be drawn into the governed community of God's Kingdom, then secular authority is authorized to provide and ensure that space."[20] It is this space that allows for a genuine diversity or catholicity. Any nation or culture that does not allow for the social space by which the diverse nations and peoples of the world can come together into a "Kingdom" that exceeds every nation and people stands against the sovereign rule of Christ. Without such a transnational, Catholic space, the nations cannot be healed.

Yoder, like O'Donovan, recognized the legitimate role of the secular authority in making possible a "social space" for the church.[21] For Yoder, however, this space does not so much reauthorize secular authority as establish limits on it. When the Church seeks to align itself with secular power, it sacrifices its theopolitical vision. Once the "new nation" merged with the old through the marriage of throne and altar, as it did during much of Christendom, the apocalyptic vision was occluded. For Yoder, along with much of the Free Church tradition, the gathered Church sets more limits on secular authority than in O'Donovan's establishment Protestant ecclesiology that makes alliances with it.[22] The Free Church apocalyptic vision does not call persons out of their nations, but it limits how they can participate in the political realm, for they can only do so in terms consistent with the "war of the Lamb," whose decisive criterion is Rev. 12:11: "for they did not cling to life even in the face of death." O'Donovan and Yoder set forth two different Protestant responses to secular authority based on a common reading of Revelation. It is not my task in this chapter to adjudicate between them but to note what they share in common. Christ has triumphed over the principalities and powers in an unexpected way—by being the Lamb who was slain. This victory reorders social life and requires attention to the glory every nation, people, tribe, and tongue contributes to it.

ECCLESIAL TRIUMPHALISM?

If we begin a discussion on diversity with the Church as a project that is being completed as we find in Revelation, then some clarity about the term emerges. It is not primarily a state, market, or cosmopolitan project. It is more important than that. It is a "theopolitical vision" that glimpses how God heals the fractures in God's good creation. Such a theopolitical vision does not need to find the "right" Church, and thus answer the question, "Which Church do you mean?" Any Church that acknowledges it is called to participate in God's holiness and in so doing is capable of acknowledging and confessing its own, and humanity's, failures suffices. Nor does it advocate ecclesial triumphalism. It can look squarely at the sharp criticism brought against it by prophetic voices such as Willie J. Jennings and incorporate it into its analysis. Jennings states, "Christianity in the Western world lives and moves within a diseased social imagination." For him, this diseased imagination is the inversion of hospitality that took place with Christian colonialism.

Jennings traces that imagination not to argue for a post-Christian religion or sustain the Enlightenment's quest for a cosmopolitanism grounded in spontaneous freedom, but instead for a richer diversity that can attend to the historical faults present in the diseased social imagination of Christianity in the Western world. It is the loss of the particular, of Israel, of land, that allowed for the diseased imagination.[23] Thus, a cosmopolitanism that abstracts from the particular does not challenge the diseased imagination. He writes,

> However, rather than building the hope of a cosmopolitanism from the soil of an imagined democratic spirit, I seek a deeper soil. That deeper rich soil is not easily unearthed. It is surely not resident at the surface levels of Christianity and ecclesial existence today. Yet Christianity marks the spot where, if noble dreams join hands with God-inspired hope and presses with great impatience against the insularities of life, for example, national, cultural, ethnic, economic, sexual and racial, seeking the deeper ground upon which to seed a new way of belonging and living together, then we will find together not simply a new ground, not simply a new seed, but a life already prepared and offered to us.[24]

Before this "new way of belonging and living together" can be seeded, it requires "instability" in our current forms of doing so, forms for which too often some of the uses of "diversity" above, especially the ideological, market strategy, and global hegemony, provide nothing but rocky ground. Jennings writes, "The point here is that there is a social and cultural instability engendered by involvement with Jesus before there is the formation of a new coherent community."[25] That instability will include any ecclesiology that cannot acknowledge its diseased imagination by attending in truth to its history. Nonetheless, the soil upon which this new form of belonging grows is not a global market, hegemonic state power, or abstract cosmopolitanism. It is itself theologically particular; it is the body of Jesus. Jennings writes, "Jesus, in forming a new Israel in the midst of Israel, positioned himself as the new source of desire."[26]

ECCLESIAL EXCLUSIVISM?

If the ecclesiological and Christological turn in Protestant theology avoids triumphalism, has it avoided exclusion? Not everyone affirms Jesus as the "new source of desire" who forms a "new Israel" in the "midst of Israel." Although I find the binary exclusion/inclusion ideological and misleading (every form of communication, especially social communication, involves some form of exclusion), the Church is called to a catholicity that excludes on the basis of the truth of communion and not the falsity of division. What gets excluded from the New Jerusalem, or the consummated city of God, is not any single race, tribe, nation, or people, but "falsehood and abomination." The life of Jesus is the basis for the true and the good against which falsity and evil can be identified. What gets excluded is any politics founded on deceit, violence, and conquest. What gets included is the "glory" each nation, race, and people brings to it. Their glory, a glory God distributes abundantly throughout God's good creation, must be welcomed.

JUSTICE?

I have referred to the above position as "Protestant," not because I think it is especially Protestant. I could cite numerous Catholic and Orthodox thinkers who would find such an argument compatible with teachings in their tradition, but I also know Catholic theologians in particular who would challenge this entire approach to the question. Some Roman Catholic theopolitical visions find this analysis too quickly invoking "supernatural" teachings based in faith, especially ecclesiology, eschatology, and Christology, and overlooking the universal intelligibility that nature itself provides and metaphysics can deliver.[27] Justice is a natural virtue that can be set forth without appeal to any particular theological doctrine such as Christology, ecclesiology, or eschatology. The natural virtue of justice rather than Jesus should be the basis for a desire that overcomes exclusions and establishes a diverse, inclusive vision.

It is not only Catholic moral theologians who emphasize nature, the Reformed philosopher Nicholas Wolterstorff does so as well, and against the kind of argument I have set forth in this chapter, where I suggest that Christians should participate in politics by witnessing primarily to a political order founded upon communion, and have said very little about rights or the natural law. In his *Justice: Rights and Wrongs*, Wolterstorff offers a dissenting voice against O'Donovan, MacIntyre, and Hauerwas. They require a "right order" understanding of justice rather than justice as "inherent rights." The "right order" understanding assumes that rights and justice only make sense if we first have a conception of a common good, if we have some "end" or teleology that would give rights their proper ordering to an end. In the case noted above, the end is found in Revelation 21 with its theopolitical vision that then provides a proper social ordering. Wolterstorff's "inherent rights" position claims we do not need any such ordering. Rights naturally inhere in the person. The latter, he suggests, is the true Christian inheritance.[28] Rights do not need a prior order to the good in order for them to be intelligible. Instead, rights are "natural," which means they are not now and never were socially conferred. They do not require historical contexts to render them intelligible. In fact, for Wolterstorff, rights are so basic that we have rights "against God." He writes, "Just as we have moral obligations toward God and God has moral rights against us prior to God's issuing of commands, so too God has moral obligations to us and we have moral rights against God prior to God's making promises to us and covenants with us. I am well aware than many members of the Christian tradition, past and present, will find the latter suggestion abhorrent."[29] It isn't so much that I find this abhorrent as I find it a distortion of the basic teaching of Christianity. Why do I need rights against God unless God is a God whose absolute power threatens me in violation of my moral rights? Who will enforce my rights against God?

Although I do not find Wolterstorff's argument for natural rights compelling, I am sympathetic to arguments for metaphysics found in Catholic teaching. However, too often those arguments ask us to "abstract" from, or "transcend," our particular cultures in order to arrive at the intelligibility of nature, and that, I fear, avoids the significant gains "diversity" brings. Our knowledge is never limited to its cultural and historical contexts. That kind of relativism does not exist; communication renders it false.[30] But God has chosen to give glory to us through the nations and that entails attention to them in their glory and failure. I find compelling Dan Bell's understanding of justice because it can make sense of these historical particularities without abstracting from them. He acknowledges the importance of justice and liberation in contemporary theology, stating, "In [the] recent decade, the claim that the Christian faith is about justice and liberation has achieved the status of a veritable truism. And this is as it should be, for the Word rightly proclaimed is a word of justice and liberation."[31] But he also acknowledges that what justice is must be "discerned" because it is not "self-evident"; it is not easily read off nature as it is or we would not have the troubling histories to which we must attend. Bell argues that modern conceptions of justice, like the ancient *suum cuique* (render to each his or her due), fail to attend to these histories, which clears room for a Christological understanding of justice. He concludes, "Justice and liberation name first and foremost what Christ has accomplished. Christ's work reveals that true justice is formed by charity and that its rule is mercy. Before Christians enact this justice, they receive it as a gift through the liturgical constitution of the Church the Body of Christ. The liturgical reception of justice in turn forms the Church into a servant body that serves the world justly by extending Christ's gift of renewed communion in God."[32]

Perhaps one obvious objection remains. Someone outside the Christian faith, or even Protestantism, could understandably offer an objection along these lines: "Your task was to address diversity and justice from a Protestant perspective. What you have done has little to do with diversity. Instead, you place diversity within particular theological convictions about God, Jesus, the Church and eschatology. How is this diverse?" If you find yourself asking this question, then my primary response would be that we were never discussing diversity in the first place. We were always already mired in ideology.

NOTES

1. One of the planks in Xavier's strategic plan is to "increase ethnic, geographic and international diversity," http://www.xavier.edu/diversity/documents/DashboardHandoutFinal.pdf.

2. http://www.northwestern.edu/strategic-plan/docs/strategic-plan.pdf: "We pay close attention to keeping all those connections strong and are committed unconditionally to providing an optimal environment for every member of our community to learn from and collaborate with others regardless of their similarities or differences. We are unwavering in our resolve that diversity at Northwestern means far more than disparate groups sharing common space. We celebrate and support a new and fully inclusive mainstream and believe that our diversity—in the fullest meaning of that word—enriches all areas of the community. Our vibrancy and vitality derive directly from the breadth of talent, training, and life experience found among our staff, faculty, students, and alumni."

3. http://www.wheaton.edu/About-Wheaton/Leadership/Strategic-Priorities/Deepen-Ethnic-Diversity.

4. http://www.deomi.org/DiversityMgmt/WebResources.cfm.

5. http://www.armydiversity.army.mil/adoAbout/index.html.

6. Aman Singh, "McDonald's Makes Diversity About the Bottom Line," *Forbes*, September 8, 2010, "Women and people of color make up 73% of McDonald's total workforce, 43% of all franchise staff and 55% of suppliers," http://www.forbes.com/sites/csr/2010/09/08/mcdonalds-makes-diversity-about-the-bottom-line/.

7. Alasdair MacIntyre, *After Virtue*, 2nd ed. (Notre Dame, IN: University of Notre Dame Press, 1984), 220.

8. Singh, "McDonald's Makes Diversity About the Bottom Line."

9. Thomas L. Friedman, *The World Is Flat: A Brief History of the Twenty-First Century* (New York: Picador, 2007), 137.

10. Friedman, *The World Is Flat*, 148.

11. James H. Cone, *God of the Oppressed* (Maryknoll, NY: Orbis Books, 1997), 36.

12. Cone, *God of the Oppressed*, 37.

13. Jean Hyppolite, *Genesis and Structure of Hegel's* Phenomenology of Spirit, trans. by Samuel Cherniak and John Heckman (Evanston, IL: Northwestern University Press, 1974), 166.

14. Robert Pippin, *Idealism as Modernism: Hegelian Variations* (Cambridge: Cambridge University Press, 1997), 390–91.

15. Cone, *God of the Oppressed*, 37.

16. They continue, "It would misrepresent gathering if it assumed it was the only community to which people could gather. Reconciliation would become even more problematic, because failure and guilt would seem absurdities in the Right Church. Scripture reading would be impoverished if it suggested the story could be told no other way. Communion would be impaired if it was assumed that divisions were simply the fault of others. Mission would be confused if other Christians were taken to be part of the 'world.' The response to Christians to the brokenness of the Church can only be to be even more committed to worship, witness and service, hoping that in so doing they may form partnerships and friendships that concentrate less on the discordant contexts each is coming from than on the harmonious glory to which each is heading." Stanley Hauerwas and Samuel Wells, eds. *The Blackwell Companion to Christian Ethics*, 2nd ed. (Oxford: Wiley-Blackwell, 2011), 24.

17. See my *The Goodness of God: Theology, Church and Social Order* (Grand Rapids, MI: Brazos Press, 2001) for a discussion of the Christian life as a life of repentance.

18. The interpretation comes from Oliver O'Donovan's 1985 Tyndale Ethics Lecture, "The Political Thought of the Book of Revelation," *Tyndale Bulletin* 37 (1986): 61–93.

19. Oliver O'Donovan, *Desire of the Nations* (Cambridge: Cambridge University Press, 1996), 146.

20. Ibid.

21. Yoder wrote, "The Reign of Christ means for the state the obligation to serve God by encouraging the good and restraining evil, i.e. to serve peace, to preserve the social cohesion in which the leaven of the Gospel can build the church and also render the old aeon more tolerable." John Howard Yoder, *Christian Witness to the State* (Newton, KS: Institute of Mennonite Studies Series, No. 3, Faith and Life Press, 1964), 5.

22. Yoder's self-deception and abuse of authority with respect to his relations with women, especially students, has now become well known. Although it should cause us to rethink his own relation to his work, it does not rule against the work. He was working with a Free Church tradition and not his own idiosyncratic position on theopolitics, although he did have an idiosyncratic position on sex that was not consistent with his Free Church tradition.

23. For Jennings the fundamental problem with Western Christianity was its "jettisoning Israel" then "created a conceptual vacuum that was filled by the European." Willie J. Jennings, *The Christian Imagination: Theology and the Origins of Race* (New Haven: Yale University Press, 2010), 33.

24. Jennings, *The Christian Imagination*, 11.

25. Jennings, *The Christian Imagination*, 264.

26. Jennings, *The Christian Imagination*, 264. Jennings continues, "Rather than follow a historical construct that posits the Jesus movement as simply a reform movement in Judaism or follow a vernacularization thesis that isolates the gospel message into its essential components, which were then reseeded in the cultural/ethnic matrices of various people, Roman, Hellenistic and so forth, I suggest an advent of a new form of communion with the possibility of a new kind of cultural intimacy between peoples that might yield a new cultural politic" (265).

27. Lawrence Dewan, O.P., might raise some critical questions about the emphasis on history, culture, and theological doctrines in discussing what should be a universal question of justice based on reason qua reason. In a lecture addressing the theme, "Philosophical Reflections on Aquinas's Faith and Reason in Dialogue with Asian Cultures," Fr. Dewan wrote, "Now I have been trying to bring out somewhat the role of philosophy in the Holy Teaching and I am insisting on ontology, i.e. a consideration of things from the viewpoint of *being*, and a mode of knowing which is a vision of necessity and with certainty. What sort of relation can such a doctrine have to 'Asian cultures' (and notice the important plural)? I would say that all human beings, of whatever culture, prize true certitude, if it can be had. What Thomas means by scientific knowledge [*scire, scientia*] or philosophy is *something that by its very nature transcends*

what we mean by particular cultures. . . . Again, that means that, while we are right to reflect on our 'cultures,' be they Asian or something else, the goal is to *transcend* mere particular cultures and to know the truth about reality." Lawrence Dewan, O.P., "Faith and Reason from St. Thomas Aquinas," *Science et Esprit* 58, no. 2 (2006): 119–20.The truth about reality can be known through reason qua reason; it does not need the emphasis placed upon history, cultures, and even Revelation noted above. The natural virtue of justice suffices to render each person his or her due.

Likewise the Catholic moral theologian Jean Porter stresses the intelligibility and integrity of nature such that I think she would find it sufficient to provide a reasonable justice universally shared in order to address the vexing questions raised by diversity. In fact, she expresses concern about Catholic theologians like Henri de Lubac, whom I would find sympathetic to my "Protestant" way of developing a theological response to diversity. See her *Nature as Reason: A Thomistic Theory of Natural Law* (Grand Rapids, MI: Wm. B. Eerdmans Publishing Company, 2004).

28. Nicholas Wolterstorff, *Justice: Rights and Wrongs* (Princeton: Princeton University Press, 2008), 4.

29. Wolterstorff, *Justice*, 283.

30. See Sara Coakley's *Christ Without Absolutes* (Oxford: Oxford University Press, 1988), especially pages 1–24 for a profound engagement and critique of "relativism."

31. Daniel M. Bell Jr., "Deliberating: Justice and Liberation," in Hauerwas and Wells, *The Blackwell Companion to Christian Ethics*, 197.

32. Bell, "Deliberating: Justice and Liberation," 210.

19

JUSTICE, DIVERSITY, AND TOLERANCE IN THE JEWISH TRADITION

David Novak, University of Toronto

Thank you very much, Professor Frankel, for your gracious introduction. It is a pleasure to be here at Xavier University and to be back here in Cincinnati.

Now the first time I came to Cincinnati was in 1968 as a rabbi to conduct Jewish High Holy Day services that fall (for a new congregation that did not yet have its own permanent rabbi). At the time, I was the Jewish Chaplain at St. Elizabeth's Hospital, the federal mental hospital, in Washington, D.C. When talking with a colleague, an African American psychiatrist, upon my return from Cincinnati, I noticed that when I mentioned "Cincinnati," her whole demeanor changed and she got a very pained look on her face. That was in 1968, at the height of the civil rights movement, a movement in which my colleague was an active member. Noticing her pain, I inquired as to what I had said that might have elicited that pain. She then told me what the name *Cincinnati* meant to her. She grew up in Michigan, and every year she and her mother would take a train to Alabama to visit her grandmother, who still lived there. Cincinnati was the place where she and her mother had to move into a segregated car. In Cincinnati, she ceased to be a first-class person by being relegated to the segregated car.

I mention this now because the topic this evening, "Justice, Diversity, and Tolerance," begins with justice. Clearly, my colleague, Dr. X, was the subject of a gross injustice in her childhood which, I think, enabled her to develop a better understanding of what justice is, and to act upon that better understanding. But how do we understand justice coming out of an experience of injustice? In the Talmud it is told that when the great first-century sage, Hillel the Elder, was asked by a non-Jew to teach him the essence of the Torah while he stood on one foot, he responded: "What is hateful to you, do not inflict on another person" (*Shabbat* 31a). You shall not do to another person what you wouldn't want done to yourself. This is the negative version of the Golden Rule. The positive version is: "You shall do under others as you would have others do unto you." Some have said that the negative version is more Jewish and the positive version is more Christian. Yet both versions appear in both traditions. Thus the positive version is expressed by the greatest mediaeval Jewish jurist and theologian, Moses Maimonides. The negative version appears in the *Didache*, or the manual instruction, the first post–New Testament Christian work. But there is a difference in the logic of these two different versions of the Golden Rule. As for the positive version, one could say that if you have received just treatment from other humans, if you have been treated fairly by them, you are likely to want to share that positive experience with other people. But if you have been the victim of injustice, it is not at all clear why you should not want to inflict that same kind of injustice on somebody else. In the Talmud (*Yevamot* 118a), the statement that Samson made when he pushed down the pagan temple is quoted: "Let me die with the Philistines" (Judges 16:30). This is taken to be the statement of a person who has suffered and wants other people to suffer along with him. If I am suffering, then you should suffer too. Along these lines, the Anglo-American poet W. D. Auden, in his great poem "September 1 1939" (the day Germany invaded and thus World War II began), wrote: "Those to whom evil has been done, do evil in return." Having suffered injustice often leads you to want to inflict similar injustice on others.

Nevertheless, in the Jewish tradition, it is the experience of injustice that actually is supposed to motivate one not to inflict injustice, but to do the opposite of one's experience. Thus the Bible states: "You shall not oppress the alien, because you know the life of the alien, since you were aliens in the land of Egypt" (Exodus 23:9). That is, you know what it is like to live as an alien in somebody else's society, even though you came to this society as a guest, who should have been treated fairly, but who was in fact enslaved by your hosts. That "misery loves company" is not a maxim you should act upon. The experience of injustice should motivate you to do what is just. In Talmudic logic, one can infer the positive from the negative as well as infer the negative from the positive. From out of the experience of injustice, seek justice.

In the Jewish tradition, this is precisely what we have learned as regards the treatment of the one called the *ger*. The *ger* is usually translated as "sojourner" or "resident-alien." In biblical times, this term denoted a non-Jew living among the Jews, but who was somebody who did not desire to become a full Jew. This was a person living on the sufferance or the official tolerance of the Jewish people. It was the opposite of the experience of the Jews having been slaves rather than sojourners in the land of Egypt, where they had no definite, protected status and thus had no definite rights and duties there. Joseph and his people were enslaved by the Egyptians, though they had not been brought to Egypt as slaves. Yet the Torah demands that Jews not inflict this injustice on anybody else. In the Talmud, this other person is called a *ger toshav*; namely, a resident-alien. In order to become a resident alien in a Jewish society, that person has to choose to accept the duties of a resident-alien and thus obtaining the rights of a resident alien. It is like when I first came to Canada, I became a "landed immigrant," and eventually chose to become a citizen. As a landed immigrant, I had definite rights and definite duties. In this sense, I acquired a legal status similar to that of the ancient *ger toshav*.

When the rabbis were discussing this category of the *ger toshav*, they had to imagine what the rights and duties of this person are, since the Bible does not inform us of what they were. In the Talmud, it is debated as to what these rights and duties actually are. The majority opinion was that these rights and duties were enumerated in the seven commandments commanded to the children of Noah, that is, all humankind (*Avodah Zarah* 64b). This is for many of us in the Jewish tradition (arguable to be sure) the Jewish version of natural law. There are certain kinds of moral norms that are readily accessible by human reason, and have in fact been so accessed in many different cultures. These are the rights and duties to be enforced in any decent human society inasmuch as they are evident to all morally sensitive human persons. The Jewish tradition did not say that these are norms we Jews ourselves have invented, nor are they norms that had been revealed only to the Jewish people. It wasn't that suddenly Jews had power over non-Jews and sat down to decide how to govern these people thereafter. Because these norms are available to human reason, these are norms that people should have known in the first place.

To be sure, in a fully Jewish society, such law-abiding non-Jews are in some sense second-class citizens; nevertheless, their status is such that they have equal civil rights, and that a Jewish polity is obligated to protect them from harm to their bodies and to their property. What the Jewish polity should have been doing was to enforce norms that were already known from time immemorial. In the Jewish tradition, it is taught that this is the law that the Jews themselves were living under before the revelation of the Torah at Mount Sinai. The Torah itself built upon the earlier law, but did not in any way abrogate it. As such, the *ger toshav* had a definite status in this society. The only thing they did not have was the right and obligation of full participation in the religious life of the community.

When the rabbis were imagining how the institution of the *ger toshav* actually functioned at the time when Jews did enjoy sovereignty in the land of Israel, these rabbis were then living under the heel of Roman domination of the Roman province of Palestine. As such, they were thinking retrospectively. Their political status, though, was like that of stateless persons living in a country run according to ad hoc military rule. They were living neither under Roman civil law nor even *ius gentium*, which was Roman law that applied to non-Romans living in provinces that had long been under Roman rule. Judea/Palestine, however, was a military district governed by the whim of the occupying Roman authorities. The fact is, the rabbis were conceiving of how they would treat non-Jews in a sovereign Jewish polity, which they did hope that the Messiah would restore after having eliminated the onerous Roman occupation. Jews living under capricious, often brutal, military rule, nevertheless, wanted to translate into political reality the maxim "what is hateful to you do not do to somebody else." In other words, the unjust rule of the Romans over the Jews should not be something the Jews would inflict over gentiles who will be living in the sovereign domain of the Jews.

Though hypothetical and speculative, this kind of thinking was not just imagination for imagination's sake, but rather imagination that could be translated into political action. This comes out in rabbinic speculation about how warfare was conducted when Jews did enjoy sovereignty in their own land. How would they deal with people whom they had conquered? A story is told in the Jerusalem Talmud (*Sheviit* 36c) that Joshua, who would lead the invasion of the land of Canaan after the death of Moses, which was a war of conquest, sent a message to the residents of Canaan: that they could leave, or wage war, or they could make peace with the people of Israel. Making peace with the people of Israel would require the Canaanites to respect Israeli sovereignty, while at the same time it would not require them to lose their political independence. What were the peace terms? They were the acceptance of the norms of the seven Noahide commandments. In addition, they would have to pay some kind of tax or tribute, which would be tangible evidence of their acceptance of Jewish sovereignty in the land of Israel. In other words, if you respect our dominion, we will respect yours. This, in effect, was preparing Jews for a time when they would have their own polity and their own army. Even conquest was to have a decidedly moral dimension. That moral dimension would make Jewish domination of the land of Israel a negotiated peace rather than raw conquest. The acceptance of just peace terms by the Canaanites would lead to their rights being protected by the Jewish conquerors. Maimonides, who was living under Muslim rule, where Jews (and Christians) had a defined second-class citizen status, that of the *Dhimmi*, seemed to think law-abiding non-Jews in the restored Jewish sovereign polity he hoped and prayed for would have a very similar status. In Islamic law, Jews and Christians enjoy this status because they are living under a law Muslims regard to be binding on all humans.

Actually speaking, this notion that both Jews and non-Jews are subjects of a universal moral law is one that is found in Jewish, Christian, and Islamic writings. Each of these traditions has much more than this minimal law, but not less than it. It is the bottom line that Jews, Christians, and Muslims are not to overcome. It protects particular religious law from fanatics, chauvinists, and racists.

Furthermore, Noahide or natural law was not just the subject of speculation. It played an important role in real human history. In the Middle Ages, in Christian Europe or Christendom, Jews were not citizens of the state. Jews were considered to be a foreign nation that had a contractual arrangement with whoever was the ruler of the society in which they lived. Now, at the time of the French Revolution, there was a historical upheaval that lead to the rise of nation-states in Europe, beginning in France in 1789. These nation-states no longer looked to the Church for their validation. The notion of a state or a nation looking to the Church for its validation was epitomized by the fact that European kings used to be crowned by the Pope. But these new nation-states were "secular," not in the sense of being officially atheistic, but in the sense that they were not governed directly by standards derived from revelation. Thus the French Revolution ended the dominating power of the Catholic Church, but it also eliminated the semiautonomy of the Jewish communities (*kehillot*). Until that time, Jews were not citizens of the country in which they lived.

With the breakdown of the Church's validation of society, secular societies looked elsewhere for their validation. So, for example, Thomas Jefferson, the author of the American Declaration of Independence, spoke of human rights directly endowed by the Creator, without the mediation of any particular historical revelation.

Most Jews in Europe welcomed this revolution, which made them full and equal citizens of the states in which they lived. Right after the French Revolution, Count Stanislas Cleremont de Tonnerre famously stated: "To the Jews as individuals everything; to the Jews as a community nothing." Most Jews welcomed that, yet there were some Jews who did not, especially some rabbis, for they knew all too well that this was the end of their great power in the Jewish community, which was the power to enforce Jewish law. However, when these new nation-states were coming into existence, it was asked: Could Jews become citizens of these nation-states in good faith? The argument against Jewish emancipation was that the Jews were living under a foreign law, one that was at odds with Christian morality. So, even though these states were in fact secular, they were still nominally Christian. How could Jews become members of this kind of state?

Today, the same problem is faced by Muslims. Muslims are asked: If you are living under *Shariah* law, how can you be a citizen of our state in good faith? Do you want to be considered to be foreigners, without the rights of full citizens? So, for example, in Ontario (the Canadian province where I live), several years ago, some members of the Muslim community were actually asking for the right to be governed by *Shariah* law. When the Conservative government seemed to be sympathetic to this view, they were voted out of office. It seems the voters were outraged at the notion that Muslims would want to live according to another law in areas governed by Canadian civil law.

When Jews were petitioning to become full citizens of the Prussian state in the mid-eighteenth century, the Jewish philosopher Moses Mendelssohn argued for the political and legal emancipation of the Prussian Jews as follows: Jews affirm the same natural law and basic moral principles that have governed the society all along, therefore their religious practices alone are basically their private business. In public, Jews are living by the same rational moral standards: natural law or natural rights. Anything in Jewish law that seems to contradict the prevailing moral norms ought to be repealed. Thus the power of *cherem*, which is the power of the Jewish community to ostracize or excommunicate Jews, had to be given up. Religion is now to be a matter of one's own free choice, not something to be coerced by religious authorities. Mendelssohn discusses how both Judaism and Christianity have to be made subordinate to the secular standards of a society that no longer had any particular religious validation. The Jewish idea of natural law, though, could be the basis of the Jewish entry into civil society as full and equal citizens of the state. This was no longer a question of toleration of a minority in a majority state. Rather, it was a claim to justice, a full participation in civil society, without having to give up what makes you different, which is your traditional religious commitment. Previously, a Jew had to be baptized and convert to Christianity in order to enjoy equal rights in any European society.

This accomplished two things. One, it enabled Jews to become citizens of a nation-state, without having to give up their distinctly religious practices. How it worked out in history is greatly debated. What it has also done, at least in principle, has been to enable Jews to ask for acceptance based on criteria of justice rather than mere toleration on the basis of charity. Two, it especially prepares Jews for the situation that we have today in the Jewish State of Israel. That is, it has enabled Jews to deal in a rational, just fashion with those over whom we have power. And I would like to think, despite the problems we do see between Jews and Palestinians in the land of Israel, I still think that if there is good will on both sides, the Jewish tradition has within it the resources to not only recognize the rights of individual non-Jews in the Jewish state (in this case, the Palestinians) but also recognize the collective rights of those non-Jews desiring a state of their own in the land of Israel. So, the speculation of the ancient rabbis about Jewish justice for non-Jews living under Jewish rule could be the source of rational and humane public policy in Israel.

The Jewish view of justice, to be extended toward all those created in the image of God, can be the basis of a program that is both politically and religiously sound and acceptable.

QUESTIONS

1. What is the difference between natural law and religious law? Where does one end and the other begin?

Novak: Natural law deals primarily with interhuman relations. Even before they came to Mount Sinai to accept the Torah, the people of Israel knew the prohibition "Thou shalt not murder." At Sinai, what had been known previously was then written down on tablets of stone. Revealed law, on the other hand, deals much more with the relations between humans and God, mandating such things as Sabbath observance, dietary laws, and forms of worship. This divine-human relationship is one mandated by God for humans, not by humans for themselves and for God. It is from revelation that Jews learn how to celebrate the particular covenantal relationship we directly enjoy with God. This requires direct divine revelation, since it is not a factor in ordinary, general human experience. Natural law, which does operate in ordinary human experience, serves as a corrective to revealed law. Like the conquest of Canaan. The book of Deuteronomy (20:16) says to wipe out all the Canaanites. The rabbis found it preposterous that God would command genocide, so according to what seems like natural law standards, they assumed that this commandment is really provisional. That is, it only would have applied if the Canaanites had refused to accept basic moral law, and if they refused to accept Israelite sovereignty in the land of Israel. In other words, the commandment to wipe out the Canaanites was more of a conditional threat than it was an unconditional imperative. Thus, natural law criteria prevent Jewish law from providing ammunition for fanatics, chauvinists, and racists.

Conversely, the eighteenth-century rationalists (both Jewish and Christian) thought natural law was all you needed, that it is not only necessary for a decent human life, but that it is sufficient for a flourishing human life. Yet natural law, or human rights, is simply not "thick" enough. People need religious celebrations and events, culture, because of their particular history of involvement with each other and involvement with God. Morality is great, but people need something much more substantial to build upon that morality. Rationally evident natural law can give us prohibitions of murder, incest, and robbery, plus the positive commandments to help one another, but it can't tell you how to celebrate your marriage, or the birth of a child, or how to mourn the death of a parent, or what your role is in the cosmic order. That can only come from revelation and the tradition that extends its message and supplements it.

2. What is it in the Jewish or Christian tradition that makes these traditions distinctly Jewish or Christian? Why not just have natural law apart from religious understandings?

Novak: I don't think a Jewish perspective gives one any special understanding of natural law or any special authority to teach it or apply it in the world. In fact, all three monotheistic religions of revelation—Judaism, Christianity, and Islam—teach that there are moral norms that apply to humankind, not because they invented them, but because these religions presuppose them. As humans, we are wired, so to speak, to respect these norms. That is why a lawless mob would have been in no position to accept the higher law of God at Sinai, since they weren't prepared for that acceptance, not having already accepted the more minimal and more general law of God known from creation. Now Jews do have certain insights into that more general law, but so do the other traditions. That is where Judaism, Christianity, and Islam have something very basic in common. This enables Jews, Christians, and Muslims to work together on a number of public moral issues, while still recognizing our more theological differences. Religious traditions do natural law best, however, since they are able to formulate natural law as a minimal condition of human flourishing rather than idealizing it as what is sufficient for human flourishing. This is what distinguishes religious natural law theory from secular humanism and its notions of basic human rights. The greater modesty of the former makes it more viable than the inflated claims of the latter.

3. Aren't the universal norms of which you speak "secular" rather than inherently "religious"?

Novak: I agree that the moral procedures society must implement are secular, but we humans need a metaphysical grounding for our morality. For Jews and Christians, that metaphysical grounding lies in the doctrine that humans are created in the image of God. Without that kind of metaphysical grounding for our morality, in the end our acts become trivial. Yet we do want our most serious acts to have metaphysical significance. All true metaphysics, even the metaphysics of thinkers who did not look to any historical revelation, like Aristotle or Spinoza, have a religious character because they are concerned with how we humans are related to God. This human concern with what is divine, in my Jewish view, is because God is concerned with all humans. That is what being created in the image of God means. This is the sanctity, the essential dignity of the human person, which Pope John Paul II emphasized so often.

4. Do all Jewish thinkers accept the idea of natural law?

Novak: Whether or not Judaism admits of natural law or not is something the late Professor Marvin Fox of Brandeis University and I debated for over twenty years. Truth be told, there is plenty of support for an anti–natural law point of view in the Jewish tradition. There are certain very traditional or "orthodox" Jews who believe everything comes from revelation. In the past, they never entered into any kind of general moral debate. On moral issues, they conversed neither with non-Jews nor even with other Jews less traditional than themselves. Yet with the recent public discussions of biomedical questions, Jews who in the past never talked to anyone outside their circle suddenly, as it were, now go around speaking of "the Jewish view" of X, Y, Z. However, with these traditionalists speaking about the Jewish view on questions like abortion or euthanasia, one could ask: "Are you telling me that the Jewish tradition has authority over me? I'm not Jewish, and even many Jews do not accept the authority of the Jewish tradition on any moral question!" Thus, in order to be accepted in secular public space, any stance has to be rationally arguable. And when it is rationally arguable, you can say that the Jewish tradition is an illustration of a morality that you affirm or ought to affirm. That is quite different from telling a group of Jews when the Sabbath ends or what they may eat and what they may not eat. As such, those holding an anti–natural law position cannot enter anything from the Jewish tradition into public debate without being charged with trying to "ram your religion down the throats of those who do not accept the authority of your religious tradition on any issue."

5. How can natural law thinkers respond to skeptics about natural law, like Richard Rorty? What resources does natural law tradition have about responding to skeptics on natural law, like Rorty?

Novak: It is interesting you mention the late Richard Rorty, who was a colleague of mine at the University of Virginia for the seven-and-a-half years I taught there. We once had a public debate in Charlottesville, Virginia, in the First Presbyterian Church on the question: Can the name of God be invoked in public discourse? According to Rorty, the answer is no, because once you mention God, like uttering "thus saith the Lord," the conversation has ended, because you can't argue against God and expect a religious believer to be persuaded. For him or her, God is beyond argument. But I responded that in mediaeval Jewish thought there is an essential distinction made between the will of God and the wisdom of God. Not eating pork is God's will. But morality comes from divine wisdom. If humans are created in the image of the all-wise God, human beings do have at least some access to that wisdom. We can believe we sometimes know why God willed what God willed. Other times, though, we cannot know why God willed what God willed. In the former case, where God's wisdom is evident, Rorty asked, "Why can't you just say X is a wise or rational thing to do?" I answered that if wisdom is thought, thought requires a thinker. Therefore I can't just speak of *what* is wise. I must also speak of *who* is wise.

Finally, one last word tonight on natural law: the task for a non-Catholic natural law thinker is to convince those in his or her tradition that natural law is recognized by their traditions, that it is not just an apologetic ploy without any real basis in the tradition. Catholic natural law thinkers, who have a tradition in which natural law plays a more explicit role than elsewhere, still have to rethink the whole question of natural law regularly. You can't just quote Aquinas. One of the great Catholic theologians of the twentieth century, the Jesuit priest Bernard Lonergan (who did some of his major work at Regis College of the University of Toronto), once said that there are some ideas that pass from book to book to book without any evidence of ever having gone through a mind. Natural law has to constantly be rethought, and that is the task of philosophers in our respective traditions.

Thank you.

20

UNITY AND RELIGIOUS DIVERSITY IN ISLAMIC THEOLOGY, SHARIAH LAW, AND TRADITION

Muhammad Zia-ul-Haq, University of Islamabad, and Waleed El-Ansary, Xavier Univerisity

Islam offers a unified vision of reality based on the doctrine of *tawhid*, the absolute oneness of God. However, unity does not negate plurality, but places it within a larger context of intelligibility. Similarly, plurality does not mean division and chaos, for unity points to what connects diverse things. Both theologically and as a framework for understanding, unity is distinguished from uniformity, which denotes "a state of bland sameness and oppressive homogeneity."[1] The possibility of "unity-in-diversity" (*al-wahdah fi'l-kathrah*) is essential for understanding to what extent justice is achieved through diversity and to what extent through sameness from the Islamic point of view. According to this perspective, contemporary secular approaches to justice and diversity outlined in the introduction to this volume either deny unity-in-diversity by asserting uniformity on one hand (illustrated by Hobbes) or reducing diversity to division and chaos on the other (illustrated by Lyotard). The ethical question of what justice and diversity ought to be from an Islamic point of view is thus intimately connected to the metaphysical doctrine of unity.

Although diversity takes many forms, this chapter focuses on religious rather than ethnic, cultural, or other types of diversity, because the current discourse on the Islamic tradition makes the discussion of religious differences more urgent,[2] particularly since Islamic civilization is generally acknowledged to integrate a wide range of ethnicities, languages, and cultures.[3] Moreover, religion has returned as a powerful force in many parts of the world,[4] contrary to what was perceived during the waves of secularism in the last century.[5] Indeed, the emerging power of religion in the 1980s prompted Harvey Cox, author of *The Secular City* in the 1960s that highlights the progressive "process of secularization," to admit that the collapse of urban civilization and rise of traditional religions are the two main hallmarks of our era.[6] Diana L. Eck likewise maintains that the challenge today is not so much secularism, but pluralism. In the contemporary urban and global contexts, one faces a new texture of religious diversity with increasing frequency.[7] Ninian Smart cites the rich pluralism inside traditions such as Islam, Christianity, and Buddhism and its implications for mutual understanding as another reason for knowing others.[8] Akbar S. Ahmed similarly points out that nationalism and ethnicity have become weaker with the rise of migration, but that religion can, given the right circumstances, travel and flourish anywhere.[9]

Unfortunately, such religious diversity does not necessarily lead to religious pluralism, for the latter requires much more than tolerance of others living in the same place.[10] Although tolerating a neighbor about whom one is ignorant is better than conflict, it falls far short of pluralism, which requires "acknowledging and engaging differences without any attempt to impose hegemony."[11]

The various responses to and challenges of religious diversity can be understood in terms of competing approaches to comparative religion. At one end of the spectrum is the claim that all the major religions are true.[12] The opposite end of the spectrum claims that all religions are false and that wars, violence, and atrocities are most often perpetrated in the name of God.[13] A third position is the claim that one religion is true and the rest are false, whereas a fourth claims that only one religion is fully true while others are partially true. This last view creates more theological space for the argument that salvation for followers of other religions is possible, conceding some validity to other religious traditions.[14] Indeed, religious diversity has existed throughout the entire history of all the world's major living religions.[15] To clarify these issues from an Islamic perspective, this chapter seeks to identify the rulings of various Islamic disciplines such as theology, Shariah law, Sufism, and philosophy on religious diversity. The chapter concludes by offering a discussion of the question of supersession and its effect on the realization of religious diversity in an Islamic framework.

ISLAMIC THEOLOGY ON RELIGIOUS DIVERSITY

In the midst of distorted images of Islam, understanding the position of Islamic theology and law on religious diversity is of prime importance. Islamic theology asserts that everything except God necessarily exists in multiplicity based on the doctrine of *tawhid*.[16] Religious, cultural, and ethnic diversity is therefore divinely ordained and even ontologically necessary, just as biological diversity is part of God's magnificent design:

> And among His Signs is the creation of the heavens and the earth, and the variations in your languages and your colors: Verily in that are Signs for those who know.[17]
>
> O mankind! We created you from a single (pair) of a male and a female, and made you into nations and tribes, that ye may know (through) each other (not that ye may despise each other). Verily the most honored of you in the sight of Allah is (he who is) the most righteous of you. And Allah has full knowledge and is well acquainted (with all things).[18]

These verses clarify that the divine purpose of human diversity is to foster self-knowledge, which can increase through the encounter of diversity, and mutual understanding for the promotion of harmony and cooperation. Diversity has not therefore been created as a source of social tension, division, and polarization, but to reflect divine infinitude.[19]

> If thy Lord had so willed, He could have made mankind one people: but they will not cease to dispute. Except those on whom thy Lord hath bestowed His mercy: and for this did He create them.[20]

Accordingly, God provided guidance to humankind and created a variety of ways and methods for salvation. The single origin of humanity and the shared content of religions asserting the Oneness of Ultimate Reality suggest that religions could not have been meant to divide humanity, but to encourage competition in goodness and well-being:

> To each among you have we prescribed a law and an open way. If Allah had so willed, He would have made you a single people, but (His plan is) to test you in what He hath given you: so strive as in a race in all virtues. The goal of you all is to Allah. It is He that will show you the truth of the matters in which ye dispute;[21]

Islamic theology asserts that the common core of the messages of all the prophets and messengers was submission to God in the light of divine guidance. All prophets were "muslim" (submitters to God) in the universal sense, for "islam" is not merely the religion preached by Muhammad but was also the religion of all the true prophets of God such as Noah, Abraham, Jacob, Joseph, Moses, and Jesus and their followers.[22]

> (127) And remember Abraham and Isma'il raised the foundations of the House (with this prayer): "Our Lord! Accept (this service) from us: for Thou art the All-Hearing, the All-Knowing." (128) Our Lord! make of us Muslims, bowing to Thy (Will), and of our progeny a people Muslim, bowing to Thy (will); and show us our place for the celebration of (due) rites; and turn unto us (in Mercy); for Thou art the Oft-Returning, Most Merciful. (129) Our Lord! send amongst them a Messenger of their own, who shall rehearse Thy Signs to them and instruct them In Scripture and Wisdom, and sanctify them: for Thou art the Exalted In Might, the Wise. (130) and who turns away from the Religion of Abraham but such As debase their souls with folly? Him we chose and rendered pure In This world: and He will be In the Hereafter In the ranks of the Righteous. (131) Behold! His Lord said to him: "Bow (thy will to Me)": He said: "I bow (my will) to the Lord and Cherisher of the Universe." (132) And this was the legacy that Abraham left to His sons, and so did Jacob; "Oh My sons! Allah hath chosen the Faith for you; then die not except In the Faith of Islam." (133) were ye witnesses when death appeared before Jacob? Behold, He said to His sons: "What will ye worship after me?" They said: "We shall worship thy Allah and the Allah of thy fathers, of Abraham, Isma'il and Isaac, the one (true) Allah. To Him we bow (in Islam)."[23]

Muslim recognition of other religions as legitimate is not limited to Christianity and Judaism, but traditionally extends to major pre-Islamic traditions such as Sabiism,[24] Hinduism, and Buddhism.[25] For example, in the 95th chapter (*surah*) of the Qur'ān, the word *tin* (fig) is mentioned as a symbol of prophethood. Manazir Ahsan Gilani explores this in connection with the unanimous belief of the followers of the Buddha that he received *nirvana*, the first revelation, under a wild fig tree. Gilani considers the mentioning of the fig in the Qur'ān as a subtle way of referring to Buddhism. While the Buddha and Christ represent passive perfection related to withdrawing from the world as a source of dispersion, Seyyed Hossein Nasr argues that the prophet-kings of the Abrahamic traditions represent an active perfection integrating the world around a sacred center, analogous to the roles of Rama and Krishna in Hinduism whose actions and sayings as kings and householders are recorded in the *Mahabhārata* and the *Ramāyana.*[26] The prophets of both Abrahamic and non-Abrahamic religions therefore embody both active and passive types of spiritual perfection. The Qur'ān therefore requires Muslims to hold all prophets in the greatest esteem:

> Say: "We believe In Allah, and in what has been revealed to us and what was revealed to Abraham, Isma'il, Isaac, Jacob, and the Tribes, and in (the Books) given to Moses, Jesus, and the prophets, from their Lord: we make no distinction between one and another among them, and to Allah do we bow Our will (in Islam)."[27]

Islamic doctrine asserts that all nations have received a prophet who both warns the community and bears glad tidings for fidelity to God.[28] It is the confrontation of this universality of revelation with the multiplicity of race, nations, and tribes that necessitates the diversity of revelation.[29]

> Verily we have sent thee in truth, as a bearer of glad tidings, and as a warner: and there never was a people without a warner having lived among them (in the past).[30]

No doubt, Islamic theological discourse often criticizes certain Jewish and Christian doctrines, and there is a debate over the extent to which these theological differences can be reconciled. But this discourse also confirms the message of God contained in these pre-Islamic scriptures.[31] Although God's revealed guidance concerning specific forms of worship, dietary laws, and so forth was modified from time to time, the fundamentals of true religion[32] have always remained the same from the Islamic point of view.[33] As Zafar Ishaq Ansari points out, Muslim scholars generally articulated this principle by distinguishing between *din*, the essential content of religion that remains the same, and *Shariah*, the religious prescriptions for a religious community, which can vary.[34] These prescriptions range from the *Halakah*[35] in Judaism, to *Hodos* in Christianity,[36] to the *Tao* or *Dao*[37] in Chinese religion.[38]

From the Islamic point of view, all who respond sincerely to God's revelation and seek to obey Him are upright and worthy of respect, regardless of the time and place in which they live or the prophet they follow.[39] The religious experience of the Prophet of Islam was distinct in the sense that the Qur'ān was the final revelation, but it was not essentially different from that of other prophets of God in the sense that they each received authentic revelation. Gandhi expressed the same notion when he observed that "revelation is the exclusive property of no nation, no tribe."[40] It is for this reason that the aforementioned verse of the Qur'ān regarding the prophets (and other similar verses) prohibited making distinctions between God's Messengers.[41] Indeed, the Prophet of Islam disliked that he should be considered above Moses and other prophets of God.[42] The relationship between visible diversity, indivisible unity, and divine infinitude can be summed up as follows: Unity ----> Infinitude ----> Diversity.[43]

This principle of unity-in-diversity is especially important in the current context of globalization, since ongoing exposure to multiple worldviews can be profoundly disorienting and lead to physical and mental agitation.[44] The principle of unity-in-diversity explains why religious diversity is part of the divine plan, and suggests that people should not involve themselves in unnecessary disputes over religious diversity in the name of religion.[45]

Many scholars of religious studies have therefore attempted to explore the Qur'ān and *hadith*, which are the recorded sayings of the Prophet of Islam, to account for the richness of Islamic views on religious diversity. Roger Boase, for example, identifies ecumenical[46] aspects of Islam in the following Islamic themes:

1. the primordial religion (*din al-fitrah*); (ii) the right attitude to God—that of an obedient servant (*'abdallah*); (iii) the right attitude to God's creation—that of a custodian (*khalifah*); (iv) the right attitude to others—as equals deserving courtesy and respect; (v) the universality of revelation—that no community on earth has been denied spiritual guidance; (vi) the special status of Jews and Christians as monotheists; and (vii) the duty to engage in dialogue with people of all other faiths and to compete with them in doing good.[47]

He suggests that refuting the prevailing distorted images of Islam in the West may be necessary for conveying the spiritual wisdom of the tradition to help save the planet through interfaith collaboration on global challenges. He points out that much of the Qur'ān advises the Prophet of

Islam and, by extension, every Muslim how they should engage in dialogue with Jews and Christians, and by extension members of other faith communities. He concludes that it has been rightly said: "A Muslim who deliberately rejects the encounter with those of other faiths and other ways of thinking, or even opposes and fights against them, betrays God's cause."[48]

Similarly, Richard K. Khuri maintains that the Prophet of Islam's sustained encounter with the infinite makes interpretational permanence of the Qur'ān impossible, since it is forever capable of generating new interpretations. And since the Qur'ān explicitly recognizes other Abrahamic traditions, it explicitly refers to other ways toward the infinite, in which case one may find implicit Qur'ānic acceptance of all striving for the divine in light of a primordial Islam related to the *fitrah*, or humanity's general and religious disposition.[49] Pluralism is the natural outcome of the encounter between the finite and the infinite, and he concludes that it is not accidental that:

> (a) there are several schools of jurisprudence for the drafting of [Islamic] laws, (b) Muslims were able to engage in Qur'ānic interpretation in a wide diversity of ways for many centuries, and (c) they have managed to co-exist with Christians, Jews, Hindus, Buddhists, Confucians and primordial religions (especially in Africa) in many places over many years.[50]

But if the Prophet of Islam was the last of approximately 124,000 prophets sent by God to humanity, and the scripture of Islam contains the latest and most complete form of revelation enjoying validity until the end of time, does Islam abrogate other religions? Is this why the Qur'ān designates Muslims as "the best community ever brought forth to mankind"?[51] In short, do religions other than Islam still offer salvation to their adherents? Muhammad Khalil ably demonstrates that perhaps the only significant figure in Islamic intellectual history to adopt an exclusivist theological position that denied salvation to followers of other traditions is Ibn Hazm (and interpreting his work in this way is debatable).[52] But Ibn Hazm wrote during a period of intense political and religious conflict in Andalusia, clearly coloring his distressed theological views. Indeed, it would hardly make sense for Islamic law to require Muslims to defend churches and synagogues in order to guarantee that Jews and Christians would go to hell. It is therefore important to consider the question of religious diversity from the point of view of Islamic law, mysticism, and philosophy before returning to the question of supersession.

ISLAMIC LAW (SHARIAH) ON RELIGIOUS DIVERSITY

Islamic law legitimizes religious diversity in the form of various recognitions of non-Muslims. Beyond the basic rights and privileges afforded by citizenship in the Islamic state, certain non-Muslims also enjoy a more fundamental freedom of religion on account of the traditional status of the People of the Book (*ahl al-kitab*); namely, Jews and Christians, as established in the Qur'ān. Such relative equality notwithstanding, certain legal injunctions differ between Muslims and non-Muslims; for example, regarding payment of the religious tax (*zakat*) being incumbent upon all Muslims while non-Muslims pay a nonreligious tax (*jizya*).[53] As for the formal acknowledgment of specific pre-Islamic traditions, the Shariah distinguishes between them based on references in sacred texts to the *Banū Isrā'īl* and Jews (*Yahūd*), Christians (*Nasārā*), Zoroastrians (*Majūs*), Sabiins (*Sābi'a*), and polytheists. Concerning revealed books, the Qur'ān mentions the "scroll of Abraham and Moses" (*suhuf Ibrāhīm wa Mūsā*), "the first scroll" (*al- suhuf al-ūlā*), "the books of ancient people" (*zubur al-awwalīn*), the Psalms (*Zabūr*) of David, and the scroll of Shīth in addition to the Torah (*Tawrāt*) and Gospels (*Injīl*).[54]

Islamic law has always displayed an interest in frankly engaging religions other than Islam, with Judaism and Christianity receiving the greatest amount of attention. Not only were these the major religions faced by Islam in the early stages of its development, but from the Muslim point of view, they have much in common with Islam. And on account of their above-mentioned status as *ahl al-kitab*, any of their adherents falling under Islamic jurisdiction are considered "protected people" (*ahl al-dhimma*). The concept of *dhimma*, which is only mistakenly thought of as an inferior status in Islamic society, is described by al-Zarqa as a juristic description according to which a person is able to "oblige and be obliged."[55] In other words, this status allows a person to enjoy rights and bear obligations.[56] After attaining such legal recognition, non-Muslims become citizens of Islamic states, thereby securing the freedom to practice their respective religions within the protective boundaries of the society, including the maintenance of churches and other places of worship (non-Muslims who were merely visiting enjoyed the status of *mustamin*). Muslims and non-Muslims had social, family, and business connections. Non-Muslims served in the Muslim army, as well as in various administrative and institutional roles, and Muslim men could marry *dhimma* women and consume meat slaughtered by *dhimmis*. Non-Muslims could also enjoy a certain autonomy; not only were their persons and property protected by the state, but they were also permitted to preside over their own cases in accordance with their respective personal laws.[57] All these circumstances required rulings of Islamic law to regulate the conduct of Muslims in their relationships with non-Muslims. From family law to criminal law, procedural matters to commercial law, from non-Muslims living in Muslim societies to Muslims living in non-Muslim societies—on almost every aspect of interfaith life—a variety of opinions is available in treatises of Islamic law regarding followers of religious traditions other than Islam.

The status of *ahl al-dhimma* was explicitly laid down for Jews and Christians by the Qur'ān. Later on, Muslim jurists agreed to extend it to followers of other religions. For example, Uthman, the third caliph, extended this status to the Berbers, as Abdul Malik did later to the Lingayats and Brahmins of India.[58] Hanafī and Mālikī schools of law, as well as some Hanablīs such as Imam al-Awzā'ī (and according to some reports Ibn Hanbal himself), recognize all non-Muslims living in Islamic countries under Muslim rule as *ahl al-dhimma*.[59] For example, Ibn Qudāmah al-Maqdisī, the noted Hanbali scholar, mentions specific Christian denominations such as the Jacobites, Nestorians, Melchites, Franks (*faranjiyya*), Byzantines, and Armenians in his classic legal text.[60] Zoroastrians also came to be treated as *ahl al dhimma* in Islamic law in spite of the problematic nature of some of their beliefs and practices according to many Muslim scholars.

The cornerstone of the legitimacy of religious diversity in Islamic rulings is the principle of "no compulsion in religion" based on the following verse of the Qur'ān:

> There is no compulsion in religion. Verily, the right path has become distinct from the wrong path. Whoever disbelieves in idols and believes in Allah, then he has grasped the trustworthiest handhold that will never break. Allah is all hearing, all knowing.[61]

The various accounts of the circumstances behind the revelation of this verse are significant. According to one account, the verse is related to a pre-Islamic custom (*miqlāt*)[62] among Arab women in which some Ansār women used to declare their children Jews in order to ensure their long life. But after the coming of Islam, some of the Ansār attempted to prevent the loss of their offspring during the expulsion of the Jews for their betrayal of the mutual-protection agreement in the Medina constitution. Not only did they wish for their children to be able to stay, but they were also of the opinion that God had now honored them with Islam, and that it would be appropriate for their sons to embrace the new faith. However, the verse under discussion gave a clear and negative response to their desire to force conversion.[63]

According to another tradition, the verse was revealed in connection with a certain Ansārī called Hasayn (or Abū al-Hasayn), whose two sons were converted to Christianity.[64] The Ansārī father asked the Prophet to pursue them and bring them back to Islam, and these verses were revealed on this occasion. A third report indicates that the verses were revealed when an Ansārī man became frustrated after the failure of his attempt to force his black slave to embrace Islam.[65] Umar b. Khattāb, the second caliph, is reported to have interpreted and implemented this verse in a similar manner in various situations.[66] Many Muslim jurists such as Abū Hanīfa, al-Shāfi'ī, and Ibn Qudāmah maintain that if someone illegitimately forces a *dhimmi* or a *mustamin* to embrace Islam, the latter's conversion is not valid unless they remain a Muslim voluntarily after the coercive force has ceased.[67]

Contrary to criticisms of Islam rooted in the idea of its having spread "by the sword," historically speaking Muslims have largely shied away from forced conversions, due not only to the principle discussed above, but also to their confidence in themselves and the conviction that Islam does not stand in need of the use of such force. As Richard K. Khuri explains, the Muslims were oftentimes without precedent in their openness and generosity toward other religious communities, especially when considered against the situation of many non-Christians and nonconforming Christians in Europe in the wake of its Christianization.[68]

The question of comparative religion is especially acute in situations of Muslims living in non-Muslim majority lands. Khaled Abou El Fadl explains the remarkable diversity of Islamic legal rulings by pointing out that the historical reality of the Shariah defies any attempt to characterize it as a dogmatic monolith.[69]

ISLAMIC SUFI TRADITION ON RELIGIOUS DIVERSITY

Sufism or Islamic mysticism deals with inner dispositions and therefore accommodates a broad range of local differences and manifestations of faith.[70] Indeed, how many Muslims, Christians, or Jews can claim that they truly love God with all their heart, soul, mind, and strength? Or that they truly love their neighbors as themselves? "Although the commandments to love God and to love our neighbors might indeed be an accessible and common ground between all [adherents of different religious traditions], surely the fulfillment of these commandments must remain, for most, a sublime and elusive goal."[71] Only the saint or *walī* can, by God's grace, fulfill these supreme commandments, underscoring the distinction between a commandment and its realization in truly understanding this common ground.

Sufism therefore played a pervasive and unparalleled role in shaping Muslim society and gradually developed into various Sufi orders throughout the Islamic world by the eleventh/fifth century.[72] Sufi teachings have been mainly communicated orally as instruction from spiritual guides to followers, but many of these doctrinal teachings have been compiled into authoritative texts and a scarcer number of manuals of spiritual instruction.[73]

Islamic theology and law do not therefore exhaust Islamic views on religious diversity.[74] Of course, the legal (Shariah), theological, and mystical (*Sufiyya*) dimensions of Islam are not in conflict, but complement one another.[75] Enormously influential Sufi scholars like al-Ghazzali, for example, have been theologians as well as scholars of Islamic law. The difference between these various perspectives according to Reza Shah Kazemi is that Sufism situates the discussion of justice within the wider framework of spiritual virtue, lending the "discourse a dimension of existential depth" and grounding it "in a more organic and all-encompassing framework."[76]

The spirit underlying moral rules and ethical values is strengthened by a commitment to transcendent principles, even though—or precisely because—these principles surpass the realm of action within which those rules and precepts operate. Contemplation and action are seen in this perspective as complementary, not contradictory, as this complementarity goes to the very heart of the Islamic message of *tawḥīd*, of integrating oneness, which is embodied with dazzling evidence in the lives of the Prophet of Islam, his cousin and son-in-law Ali, and other saints of the early Muslim community. Abstract questions of right and wrong come to be rooted in the more definitive principle that emerges in response to the question: What is reality?[77]

In a sense, Sufism moves from a moral to an ontological perspective on justice, relating it to a conception of the good that ultimately depends on a conception of the real, or *tawḥīd*, providing a profound "metaphysics for interfaith dialogue."[78] The great Sufi theoretician Ibn 'Arabi, for example, teaches that God's truth can find expression in the different and even apparently contradictory theological positions of various religions.[79] Contemporary Muslim scholars debate over how to interpret Ibn 'Arabi in this regard, particularly whether or not he claimed that it is obligatory for people in the present age to follow the Shariah brought by the Prophet of Islam as it is the updated version of previous revealed religions.[80] The final section of this chapter returns to the question of supersession, but it is very clear that Ibn 'Arabi denies that previous revealed religions become false. He states:

> All the revealed religions (*shara'ih*) are lights. Among these religions, the revealed religion of Muhammad is like the light of the sun among the lights of the stars. When the sun appears, the lights of the stars are hidden, and their lights are included in the light of the sun. Their being hidden is like the abrogation of the other revealed religions: that takes place through Muhammad's revealed religion. Nevertheless, they do in fact exist, just as the existence of the light of the stars is actualized. This explains why we have been required in our all-inclusive religion to have faith in the truth of all the messengers and all the revealed religions. They are not rendered null (*batin*) by abrogation—that is the opinion of the ignorant.[81]

Sufism also employs the symbolism of other religions to poetically express faith and the rejection of hypocrisy. For example, Mawlana Jalal al-Din Rumi[82] describes religious diversity in a classic story about four quarreling travellers—a Persian, a Turk, an Arab, and a Greek—arguing over how to spend a single coin. Although they all demanded grapes, they were unable to understand this because each spoke a different language. Another traveller who heard them bought grapes to help them understand that they were giving different names to the same desire. Of course, the linguist traveller symbolizes the sage who knows that the travellers inwardly yearn for the same thing, and the single coin symbolizes *tawḥīd*, the ground of all diversity.[83] The sage is therefore necessary to resolve misunderstandings and conflicts, playing the role of peacemaker. Rumi articulates the common essence of all religions in the following verses:

> In the adorations and benedictions of righteous men
> The praises of all the prophets are kneaded together
> All praises are mingled into one stream,
> All the vessels are emptied into one ewer.
> Because He that is praised is, in fact, only one.
> In this respect all religions are only one religion
> Because all praises are directed towards God's light
> These various forms and figures are borrowed from it.[84]

ISLAMIC PHILOSOPHY ON DIVERSITY OF RELIGION

Another line of thought regarding the diversity of religions is found in the Islamic philosophical tradition. Although Islamic philosophy begins with the translation of Greek philosophical texts into Arabic in the ninth century, Muslim philosophers lived in a world where the truths brought by the Qur'ānic revelation and the *ḥadīth* of the Prophet of Islam were given realities.[85] The questions and issues raised by the coming of the Qur'ān and the Prophet established the discursive boundaries of the universe in which Muslim philosophers functioned. They therefore integrated pre-Islamic philosophical traditions into this Qur'ānic and Prophetic framework.[86] Even when the concerns of Muslim philosophers were couched in Greek conceptual terminology, the concerns were strongly shaped by central Islamic issues such as *tawḥīd*, the reality of prophecy as a mode of knowledge, and the creation of an ethically righteous society.

The first major school of Islamic philosophy is the *mashsha'ī* or Peripatetic school, which synthesized Aristotelian and Neoplatonic thought within the matrix of *tawḥīd* and the Qur'ānic revelation.[87] Al-Kindi (d. 260/873), the "philosopher of the Arabs" and founder of this school, espoused the integral nature of Islamic philosophy on the basis of the principle that since God is Truth (*al-Haqq*), all truths come from Him and testify to Him:

> We should not be ashamed to acknowledge truth and to assimilate it from whatever source it comes to us, even if it is brought to us by former generations and foreign peoples. For him who seeks the truth there is nothing of higher value than truth itself; it never cheapens or abases him who reaches for it, but ennobles and honors him.[88]

Regarding the relationship between religion and philosophy, al-Kindi maintained that there are two types of knowledge; namely, divine knowledge (*al-'ilm al-ilahi*) given by God to prophets, and human knowledge (*al-'ilm al-insani*), of which philosophy is the highest form. Since the former can arrive at truths that reason alone cannot reach, al-Kindi claimed that divine knowledge is superior to human knowledge.

Al-Farabi, the next major philosopher of this school, appeared a generation after al-Kindi and maintained that religion and philosophy deal with the same reality but use different methods and languages. Both philosophy and religion "give an account of the ultimate principles of [all] beings . . . the ultimate end for the sake of which man is made [supreme happiness] . . . and the ultimate end of every one of the other beings,"[89] but philosophy provides accounts of these fundamental issues based on "intellectual perception," whereas religion provides accounts based on "imagination" and "persuasive methods."[90] The images and symbols are nevertheless revealed to the prophets along with their inner philosophical meanings, although some of the meanings and symbols may be lost and replaced by man-made metaphors over time.[91]

Because philosophy penetrates the inner meaning of religious images and symbols, it offers a deeper understanding of comparative religion than theology.[92] Osman Bakar explains this delicate point as follows:

> The term used by him [al-Farabi] to refer to religion as distinct from philosophy is *millah* and not *din*. This shows that al-Farabi wishes to contrast philosophy not with a revealed tradition in its totality, but with the exoteric dimension of a revealed tradition. . . . One [kind of philosophy] is what he calls a popular, generally accepted and external philosophy . . . [and he] regards *kalam* as an example of this kind. The other is an esoteric philosophy meant for the elite, a philosophy into which only those who are intellectually and spiritually prepared may be initiated. . . . Furthermore, for al-Farabi this philosophy refers to

that eternal truth or wisdom (*al-hikmah*) which lies at the heart of all traditions.[93]

This does not mean that philosophy can resolve all the theological differences between various religious traditions, but it does mean that philosophy is in a better position to resolve (at least some of) these differences than theology. Al-Farabi nevertheless maintains that some religions may be better than others in terms of the adequacy and effectiveness of their symbols, although he does not criticize any particular religion by name. He states:

> [Symbols may] differ in excellence; some of them are better and more perfect imaginative representations, while others are less perfect; some are closer to, others are more removed, from the truth. In some the points of contention are few or unnoticeable, or it is difficult to contend against them, while in others the points of contention are many or easy to detect, or it is easy to contend against them and to refute them.[94]

In short, the hierarchy of the sciences in al-Farabi's thought positions Islamic theology (*kalam*) and law (*fiqh*) as the "external" or "exoteric" counterparts of the theoretical and practical philosophical disciplines of metaphysics (*al-'ilm al-ilahi*) and politics (*al-'ilm al-madani*), respectively.[95] Because this distinction applies to all religions according to al-Farabi, philosophers within each tradition are the most capable of realizing mutual respect and understanding. Later *mashshai* philosophers such as Ibn Sina, who brought the school to its peak, adopted similar views in this regard.[96]

Islamic philosophy entered a new phase in the thirteenth century with the founding of the School of Illumination, or *Ishraq*, under the towering figure of Shihab ad-Din al-Suhrawardi (d. 1191). He integrated Greek philosophical thought and the wisdom of ancient Persian sages on one hand with *mashshai* thought and theoretical Sufism on the other to forge a new synthesis that was to wield tremendous influence. With Suhrawardi, Islamic philosophy therefore begins to reference the Qur'ān and sunna far more directly.

Moreover, Suhrawardi believed that wisdom, or theosophy, was "revealed by God to man through the prophet Idris, or Hermes," who was therefore the founder of philosophy and the sciences. Seyyed Hossein

Nasr points out that this prophetic wisdom was believed to have been "divided into two branches, one of which came to Persia and the other to Egypt. From Egypt it went to Greece and finally from these two sources, namely Persia and Greece, it entered into Islamic civilization."[97] Since Persian wise men and kings were part of this chain of transmission, pre-Islamic religions play an explicit role in the history of philosophy from an *Ishraqi* perspective, with all this implies for comparative religion.

Suhrawardi accordingly divides the classes of knowers into four categories, the first of which consists of apprentices on the path to knowledge. The second consists of those who have perfected discursive philosophy but are unlearned in the ways of illumination, such as the *mashshai* philosophers, whereas the third consists of those who have not considered discursive modes of knowledge but have attained inner illumination, such as the Persian priest-kings. The fourth category consists of those who have perfected discursive philosophy *and* attained illumination, the theosopher or *hakim muta'alih*. Such a sage would be the most qualified to penetrate the inner unity of the various religious traditions.

The final phase of Islamic philosophy is marked by the seventeenth-century synthesis of Mulla Sadra, who integrates *mashshai* philosophy, *Ishraqi* philosophy, the school of Ibn al-'Arabi and other Sufi theoreticians, and Islamic theology under one philosophical umbrella. Mulla Sadra resolves outstanding philosophical issues such as the question of bodily resurrection on one hand, and situates soteriology with respect to his philosophy of the unity (*wahda*), principiality (*asala*), and gradation (*tashkik*) of being or existence (*wujud*) on the other.[98] He develops his theory of transubstantial motion on this basis to explain the history of religions and cycles of revelation, analogous to an individual whose present adult state is distinct from his or her childhood or adolescent states, yet contains the latter revealing an underlying unity. This synthesis not only has implications for deepening the study of comparative religion, but it also provides a philosophy of nature that can incorporate the findings of modern science into higher orders of knowledge while offering a profound religious critique of secular notions of justice and diversity outlined in the introduction of this volume.

Unfortunately, the last two phases of Islamic philosophy are not as well known in the West as the first phase, because only *mashshai* philosophy had a significant impact on medieval Christian thought.[99] But it is the last phase of Islamic philosophy that holds the most promise for addressing the intellectual challenges of religious pluralism on one hand and responding to modern and postmodern philosophical thought on the other.

SUPERSESSION AND RELIGIOUS DIVERSITY

Although the previous discussion demonstrates that a clear and positive picture of religious diversity emerges from the Islamic tradition, it is important to return to the question of supersession. Tony Bayfield argues that the idea of supersession is not limited to Islam. He points out that many Christians argue for superiority and supersession vis-à-vis Judaism. A similar tendency even exists in Judaism according to Bayfield, and he cites the biblical story of Pinchas, who was appointed the third High Priest of Israel after committing extra-judicial murder in defense of religion—a prominent example of a certain abrogation on an individual level. Bayfield likewise draws attention to contemporary examples of extremism such as Yigal Amir, who, in the name of Judaism yet paradoxically without regard for the law, murdered Yitzhak Rabin, and Baruch Goldstein, who one night after reading the book of Esther murdered a group of Muslims at prayer.[100] Of course, there is a theological difference between Judaism and Christianity in this regard, since the Christian revelation was universal in scope, promising salvation to all believers regardless of birth, whereas the Jews' self-conception was that of a divinely ordained priestly caste for all humanity.[101] It is beyond the scope of this chapter to examine how modern Muslim extremists rationalize violence, but suffice it to say here that traditional scholarship demonstrates how extremists take Qur'ānic verses out of their revealed context and that political, economic, and other factors play a decisive role in this inversion of Islamic principles.[102]

It is also important to point out that the idea of superiority is not limited to religion. Theories such as "the White Man's Burden,"[103] for example, reflect a superiority complex based on racism. Even scholarly exercises such as Samuel Huntington's[104] *The Clash of Civilizations and the Remaking of World Order*,[105] Francis Fukuyama's[106] *The End of History and the Last Man*,[107] and Felipe Fernandez Armesto's[108] *Millennium*[109] are often seen by the Muslims as part of a Western claim of superiority.[110]

The question of religious supersession need not entail the elimination of religious diversity and pluralism, since it is natural for one to prefer one's faith over other faiths. But if one considers that truth is only found in one's own faith and desires to impose this faith on others, this constitutes a clear threat to religious diversity. The idea of the exaltedness of Islam must therefore be interpreted and understood along with the evidence in Islamic sources demonstrating the validity of other faiths. Islam looks on religious diversity as a natural phenomenon, as a concomitant of God's bestowal of free will and choice on human beings. If God in His infinite wisdom did not compel people to embrace a particular religion, how can this be permissible for human beings?[111]

In fact, one of the major justifications for the use of force in Islam is to protect the religious freedom of all people. The Qur'ān says: "And were God not to repel some people by others, cloisters and churches and synagogue and mosques in which God's name is much remembered would have been pulled down."[112] The mentioning of churches and synagogues along with mosques is significant for analyzing the Islamic view regarding religious diversity. Of course, there is a debate over the extent to which theological differences between religions can be reconciled, but the Qur'ān clearly confirms the underlying universality of revelation by recognizing the prophets and scriptures of other religions.[113]

Underlying the supersession question as a determining factor is the more basic attitude taken toward soteriology. Since for most believers what is most fundamentally at stake in the religious life is one's own salvation, the spectrum of possibilities regarding it is no small shaping force when it comes to approaching issues that are scripturally or traditionally ambiguous or controversial. In his *Islam and the Fate of Others*, Mohammad Hassan Khalil provides a very helpful categorization in this regard. Working with the common tripartite division familiar to philosophers of religion, while acknowledging various shades of subtlety, he provides the following basic definitions:

> "[E]xclusivists" maintain that only their particular religious tradition or interpretation is salvific and that adherents of all other beliefs will be punished in Hell. "Inclusivists" similarly affirm that theirs is the path of Heaven but hold that sincere outsiders who could not have recognized it as such will be saved. "Pluralists" assert that, regardless of the circumstances, there are several religious traditions or interpretations that are equally effective salvifically.

Within the inclusivist camp, a distinction can be made between what Khalil calls "limited" and "liberal" strands. The former assert that only those who have not been exposed to the message of Islam may be saved, while the latter claim that it is not mere exposure that is decisive, but rather the exact nature of one's encounter with and response to the message. For the limited inclusivists, the exclusivist argument that the category of the "unreached" no longer exists in modern times is insufficient, and that it is only the rejection of Islam in its "true form" that warrants punishment. The liberal inclusivists, on the other hand, believe that not only must Islam be encountered in an authentic mode, but it must also penetrate the heart, without which genuine acceptance it could not truly be betrayed. Khalil sums up these considerations nicely:

> The debate among inclusivists, then, revolves around the question, What qualifies as a sincere response to the Islamic message upon encountering it? For limited inclusivists, the answer is simple: conversion to Islam. For others, the answer is either conversion or active investigation of the content of the message. . . . But however one qualifies sincere non-Muslims, inclusivists generally agree that these are individuals who never actively strive to extinguish the light of God's message and never take on the rebellious, evildoing, oppressive characteristics of the damned. The God of mercy and justice, so goes the argument, would surely save such earnest non-Muslims, if only through some form of intercession on Judgment Day.

As for the pluralists, diversity of opinion naturally exists in their ranks as well. One might maintain, for example, that while certain religious paths are ultimately equivalent in their salvific efficacy, they are nonetheless unequal as regards the adequacy of their respective truth claims. Other pluralists go further, however, and suggest that the whole truth is not possessed by any one group, a position they find plausible in light of the many irreconcilable differences that characterize the world's religions as well as both the sincerity and self-assurance of believers of all stripes. To acknowledge partiality on its own level is not to deny the integrity or even the existence of the truth, as an epistemological relativist might, but it is rather to indirectly affirm the transcendent nature of God, one of whose names in the Islamic tradition is *al-Haqq*, the Truth. Support for this approach could also be drawn from the *shahadah* itself, which negates all pretenders to absoluteness, not the least of which can be the very forms of religion.

To return now to the discussion of supersession, it is certainly an issue for exclusivists (although there are so few of them in the intellectual heritage, since Ibn Hazm is arguably the only major thinker in this category, as mentioned earlier) and inclusivists. But supersession is arguably a nonissue for pluralists, depending on how they view the question of truth claims above. Indeed, some pluralists argue that just as some Qur'ānic verses have arguably been abrogated by others, but nevertheless remain part of the Qur'ān, supersession cannot eliminate the soteriological efficacy of pre-Islamic revelations. A suggestive analogy can also be found in the phenomenon of human subjectivity itself, in which the present moment of one's experience, while in one sense excluding moments past, does not thereby destroy their reality, which is mysteriously preserved in the present and in part determines its subjective quality.

In light of the preceding arguments, it is now possible to suggest a basic classification of the groups discussed in this chapter according to the above framework. While philosophers and mystics who are concerned with penetrating the inner meanings of revelation will tend to be liberal inclusivists or pluralists, theologians and legal scholars who are concerned with the exoteric dimension will tend to be inclusivists, whether strict or liberal. Such inclinations also incidentally suggest the validity of a more basic metaphysical principle, which is that the passage from the exterior to the interior coincides with a passage from the particular to the universal, or from the relative to the absolute.

In the debate between pluralists and inclusivists, there is also a parallel debate over how to interpret the most prolific of all Sufi writers, Ibn Arabi, and indeed his writings provide an opportunity for profound meditation on the question of universalism in religion. On the one hand he claims preeminence for the Muhammadan path based on its quintessential nature and its status in the economy of revelation, for, in Khalil's summarizing words, it "is like sunlight, while all other divinely revealed religions are like starlight. With the appearance of the former, the latter disappear (which is not to say that they no longer exist) and, if anything, only contribute to the luminosity of the former. The final message is nothing short of exceptional." And "to reject Mohammad's message is to challenge God." But on the other hand Ibn Arabi is not easily confined to inclusivism in light of his transhistorical interpretation of Islam itself.

As Ibn Arabī observes, the term *islām* in the Qur'ānic context (specifically, 3:19) denotes "submission" (*inqiyād*), not reified Islam (3:41). Hence, owing to the wide range of human submissions to the divine and the consequent wide range of manifestations of bliss, there are—on the basis of mystical insight—at least 5,105 "degrees of the Garden," only twelve of which are designated specifically for "the Muhammadan community" (3:42). Hell is the everlasting abode not of anyone who does not identify as a follower of Muhammad but, rather, of those who refuse to surrender to God after the truth has been made clear to them. These are the "guilty ones" (Q. 36:59) who "deserve" their fate.

In the end, what counts for inclusivists and pluralists alike is sincerity and acts in accordance with one's knowledge, regardless of the question of supersession, which could only be a decisive factor for exclusivists. Given the overwhelming emphasis on inclusivity and pluralism in the Islamic intellectual and legal heritage, the basic rule for the recognition of religious diversity is that every follower of any faith considers himself an ordinary creation of God and believes that he or she will be judged before God according to faith and deeds, not according to ancestry. The Qur'ān says:

> This is not the matter of your fancies or the fancies of the People of the Book. And whoever does evil shall be requited for it and shall find for himself besides Allah neither friend nor helper. And whoever does righteous good deeds, male or female, and is a true believer [in oneness of Allah]. Such will enter paradise and not the least injustice, even to the size of a speck on the back of a date-stone, will be done to them. And who can be better in religion than one who submits his face to Allah and he is *muhsin*.[114] And follows the religion of Ibrahim [Abraham] Hanifa. And Allah did take Abraham as an intimate friend.[115]

The circumstances of revelation of these verses show that once Muslims and the People of the Book started claiming superiority with respect to each other, on one hand the People of the Book claimed that their Prophet and sacred scripture came before the Prophet of Islam and the Qur'an, and on the other hand the Muslims claimed that the Prophet of Islam was the final prophet, and that the Qur'ān abrogated previous books. Here the verses revealed and clarified that self-glorification and self-congratulation do not benefit anyone, because nobody becomes superior to anybody else on the basis of conjectures, fancies, and claims.

Instead, everything depends on faith and deeds. No matter how noble and superior one's Prophet and Book may be, it is the faith and deeds of the adherent that will count on the day of Judgement.[116] Ibn Āshūr[117] observed that this verse has decided the disputed claims of Jews, Christians, and Muslims regarding ultimate salvation and clarified that it would be based on good deeds, noble behavior, and following the way of Ibrāhīm.[118]

The idea of religious diversity presented in the verse above is also supported by another verse, which states:

> Those who believe [in the Qur'ān], and those who follow the Jewish [scriptures], and the Christians and the Sabians,—any who believe in Allah and the Last Day, and work righteousness, shall have their reward with their Lord; on them shall be no fear, nor shall they grieve.[119]

The importance of this verse can be understood from the fact that it was revealed twice. This appears to be the only verse in the Qur'ān that has been repeated in exactly the same words. The fact that this verse occurs at the beginning and end of the Prophet's political career means that neither the words nor the purport of these two identical verses were abrogated. This spirit of ecumenism within the Abrahamic traditions, which has been shown in these Qur'ānic verses, retained the potential to assert itself in interfaith relations.[120]

CONCLUSION

Religion is once again gaining prominence as a regulator of individual and collective conduct in contemporary human societies. Although many efforts were made to keep religion out of the public sphere in the last century, it has been reemerging as a powerful force in secular milieux. But whereas before only one or two religions were practiced in a given environment, certain exceptional cases notwithstanding, the modern city is populated by followers of myriad religions. Immigration and globalization have brought people from various cultures and ethnic backgrounds together to form a new, religiously plural culture. This situation obviously demands that the diversity of religions be articulated in a way that helps adherents of various faiths live in an atmosphere of justice and peaceful coexistence instead of extremism and exclusivism. It is also of paramount importance that in the process of working toward such harmony the integrity of the traditions involved is preserved and protected from largely well-intentioned yet ultimately destructive forms of ecumenism, as the compromising of boundaries and therefore religious forms themselves can nullify the ritual efficacy of the latter.

The position of the Islamic tradition on religious diversity should not be confused with the distorted images of brutality, fanaticism, hatred, disorder, and terrorism so prevalent in media portrayals. This chapter presents consistent support for religious unity-in-diversity in Islamic thought from theological, legal, mystical, and philosophical points of view. Monotheism in its purest form asserts the uniqueness of God and the multiplicity of everything else, including religion. Islamic doctrine therefore asserts the universality of revelation and that all nations have been blessed with divine guidance. Religious diversity is thus a natural phenomenon that needs to be respected and protected. Although there is a debate over the extent to which theological differences between religions can be reconciled from higher or deeper mystical and metaphysical points of view, Islamic theology, law, mysticism, and philosophy agree that all major religious traditions express aspects of the truth, that Muslims are obliged by the nature of true belief and therefore by God to respect the followers of other traditions, and that these fellow people of faith may through God's grace attain salvation.

The question of supersession does not imply that previous revelations become false, and Qur'ānic verses indicate that salvation will not depend on the disputed claims of followers of various religions, but on the faith and noble behavior consistent with the way of Abraham. These verses advance the idea that the purpose of religious diversity is to encourage competition in goodness and the well-being of humanity through multiple paths to salvation. This Qur'ānic idea could be used across faiths to advance their adherents' abilities to live together in peace.

NOTES

1. Ibrahim Kalin, "Religion, Unity and Diversity," *Philosophy and Social Criticism* 37, no. 4 (2011): 473.
2. See, for instance, Anna Triandafyllidou, *Addressing Cultural, Ethnic & Religious Diversity Challenges in Europe: A Comparative Overview of 15 Euro-*

pean Countries, February 2011, 1, Overview National Discourses Comparative Country Report, European Commission.

3. For the remarkable range of ethnicities, languages, and cultures comprising Islamic civilization, see, for instance, Seyyed Hossein Nasr, *The Heart of Islam* (San Francisco: HarperOne, 2002), chapter 2.

4. The rise of religion was felt in the 1980s and 1990s, and Harvey Cox, the author of the 1960s *The Secular City*, was forced to write *Religion in the Secular City*. He conceded that the demise of religion had been prematurely announced. See Harvey Cox, *Religion in the Secular City: Toward a Postmodern Theology* (New York: Simon and Schuster, 1984).

5. The late 1960s is marked by the "God is dead" movement, the concept originally coming from German philosopher Friedrich Nietzsche, who spoke in his parable of "The Madman" searching for God. Nietzsche quoted this from his work, *The Gay Science*. He accused all people of being murderers of God. "Where is God?" he cried. "I will tell you. We have killed him—you and I. All of us are his murderers." He also stated, "Gods, too, decompose. God is dead. He remains dead. And we have killed him." This controversial movement was so effective that the *Time* magazine cover of April 8, 1966, was based on the question "Is God Dead?" The article inside that preached the "death of God" inflamed readers. During this period, Harvey Cox began *The Secular City* with the observation that "the rise of urban civilization and the collapse of traditional religion are the two main hallmarks of our era and are closely related." He further observed that "in the urban environment from which the gods have fled, secularism was the dominant world-view, relativising and bypassing religion, renders it irrelevant and a private affair." See Harvey Cox, *The Secular City: Secularization and Urbanization in Theological Perspective* (New York: Macmillan, 1966), 1.

6. Cox, *Religion in the Secular City*, 3.

7. Diana L. Eck, "Is Our God Listening? Exclusivism, Inclusivism, and Pluralism," in *Islam and Global Dialogue: Religious Pluralism and the Pursuit of Peace*, ed. Roger Boase (England: Ashgate Publishing Limited, 2005), 22–23.

8. Ninian Smart, *The World Religions* (Cambridge: Cambridge University Press, 1992), 10.

9. Akbar S. Ahmed, "Clash or Dialogue of Civilizations," in *Islam and Global Dialogue: Religious Pluralism and the Pursuit of Peace*, 110–11.

10. This issue has been separately treated elsewhere under the title of *Towards Advancing Religious Pluralism in Islamic Thought*.

11. Diana Eck, *A New Religious America: How a "Christian Country" Has Now Become the World's Most Religiously Diverse Nation* (San Francisco: HarperSanFrancisco, 2001), 70–71, as quoted in Amir Hussain, "Muslims, Pluralism and Interfaith Dialogue," in *Progressive Muslims: On Justice, Gender and Plu-*

ralism, ed. Omid Safi (Oxford: Oneworld, 2003), 252; Mohammad Hashim Kamali, "Diversity and Pluralism: A Qur'anic Perspective," *Islam and Civilisational Renewal: A Journal Devoted to Contemporary Issues and Policy Research*, Special issue on Islam and Pluralism, 1, no. 1 (October 2009): 28.

12. This is the approach that is adopted by Indian reformer Gandhi and is reflected in his writings on religion that was published under the title *All Religions Are True* (1962).

13. This is the approach of extreme atheists who considered religion as a source of all conflicts and tensions.

14. This is the approach of various extreme exclusivist groups among Christians, Jews, and Muslims who believe that only their religion is correct and others are partly or completely false.

15. See, for details, Ian S. Markham, *Plurality and Christian Ethics* (Cambridge: Cambridge University Press, 1994), 9–10; James B. Wiggins, *In Praise of Religious Diversity* (New York: Routledge, 1996), 5–6.

16. See M. Abdel-Wahab Elmessiri, *Towards a New Islamic Discourse* (Cairo: Ain Shams University, 2007).

17. Qur'ān 30:22. The English translations of Abdullah Yusuf Ali have been used throughout this study.

18. Qur'ān 49:13.

19. Ali S. Asani, "On Pluralism, Intolerance, and the Qur'an," *American Scholar* 71, no. 1 (Winter 2002): 54.

20. Qur'ān 11:118–19.

21. Qur'ān 5:48.

22. See Qur'ān 3:51–52; 6:161–63; 10:83–84 and 90.

23. Qur'ān 2:127–33.

24. Sabiism is among the religions that have been mentioned in Qur'ānic verses; see, for example, 5:69; 2:62; 22:17. Manazir Ahsan Gilani, a famous Indian scholar, in his article titled "Quran Ka sabien," discussed views of Muslims scholars regarding the concept and history of Sabiism. See Manazir Ahsan Gilani, *Maqalat Gilani* (Lahore: Shekh Zaid Islamic Centre, Punjab University, 2004), 14.

25. See Muhammad Hamidullah, *Emergence of Islam* (Islamabad: Islamic Research Institute, 1999), 203.

26. Seyyed Hossein Nasr, *Ideals and Realities of Islam* (Boston: Beacon Press, 1979), 69.

27. Qur'ān 3:84.

28. Qur'ān 35:24.

29. Seyyed Hossein Nasr, *The Heart of Islam: Enduring Values for Humanity* (New York: HarperSanFrancisco, 2002), 6.

30. Qur'ān 35:24.

31. Qur'ān 2:49, 81, 91, 101; 3:50, 81; 4:74; 5:46.

32. Famous Dutch jurist Hugo Grotius in his book *The Truth of the Christian Religion* (published in Latin in 1627) used the terminology *true religion* to distinguish Christianity from Islam and Judaism. Carl Ernst characterizes this book as a "debating manual for European sailors on missions of economic and military conquest and was designed to help them convert the Jew, the Muslim, and the pagan to Christianity." See Carl W. Ernst, *Rethinking Islam in the Contemporary World* (Edinburgh: Edinburgh University Press, 2004), 40.

33. Zafar Ishaq Ansari, "Some Reflections on Islamic Bases for Dialogue with Jews and Christians," *Journal of Ecumenical Studies* 14 (1997): 436.

34. Ibid.

35. It is a terminology that is used in Christianity in the meaning of general principles existing in scriptures. It is legal exposition on Exodus through Deuteronomy. For details, see Stanley E. Porter (ed.), *Dictionary of Biblical Criticism and Interpretation* (New York: Routledge, 2007), 225, 254.

36. This terminology is used in early Christianity in the meaning of "the way," and it describes the actions of the people referred to (having believed, having been saved, having turned to God). See Gerard Mannion and Lewis Mudge (eds.), *The Routledge Companion to the Christian Church* (New York: Routledge, 2008), 12.

37. This word is used in the meaning of road or pathway, respectively. It means the correct or natural way something is done, especially in the actions of rulers and kings. It is one of the basic Chinese philosophical concepts with particular relevance in the Daoist tradition. These concepts are important separately as politico-philosophical and religious terms. See Lindsay Jones (ed.), *Encyclopedia of Religion*, 2nd ed. (New York: Thomson Gale, 2005), 4/2172.

38. Leonard Swidler, "Interreligious and Interideological Dialogue: The Matrix for All Systematic Reflection Today," *Toward a Universal Theology of Religions* (Maryknoll, NY: Orbis Books, 1988), 12.

39. Zafar Ishaq Ansari, "Some Reflections on Islamic Bases for Dialogue with Jews and Christians," *Journal of Ecumenical Studies* 14 (1997): 436.

40. Mahatma Gandhi, *All Religions Are True*, ed. Anand T. Hingorani (Bombay: Bharatiya Vidya Bhavan, 1962), 25.

41. Al Qur'ān 2:136, 285; 3:84; 4:15.

42. Al Bukhari Abu Abdullah Muhammad bin Ismael, *Al Jamiya Al Sahi* (Kitab al-Khusūmāt: Dar Ibn Kaseer, 1987).

43. Ibid.

44. Richard K. Khuri, "True and False Pluralism in Relation to the West and Islam," in *Islamic and Christian Cultures: Conflict or Dialogue*, ed. Plamen Makariev, Bulgarian Philosophical Studies III (Glasgow: Glasgow University Press), 226.

45. Roger Boase, "Ecumenical Islam: A Muslim Response to Religious Pluralism," in *Islam and Global Dialogue: Religious Pluralism and the Pursuit of Peace*, 258–59. For further exploration of religious diversity in Islamic sacred texts and central Islamic doctrines and their implications for the role of Islam as a force for peaceful coexistence, see Muhammad Zia-ul-Haq, "Religious Diversity: An Islamic Perspective," *Islamic Studies* 49, no. 4 (Winter 2010): 498–502.

46. The terminology is used for worldwide or general influence of Christianity. It is derived from Latin *oecumenicus* and Greek *oikoumenikos*. It was used at the Council of Nicaea in 325 CE when the Aryan (and subsequently Muslim) view of Jesus as a human "creature" was condemned as heretical. Roger Boase has justified its use for Islam as the Prophet Muhammad "was sent as a mercy to the worlds," Rahmat lil 'alamin (Qur'Kitab al-Khusūmāt (Qur'ān 21:107).

47. Boase, "Ecumenical Islam," 251.

48. M. Salim Abdullah, "What Shall Be the Answer to Contemporary Islamic Fundamentalism?," in *Fundamentalism as an Ecumenical Challenge*, eds. Hans Kung and Jurgen Moltmann (London: SCM Press, 1992), 71.

49. Khuri, "True and False Pluralism," 235.

50. Ibid.

51. Qur'ān 3:110. For an analysis of this idea and its connection to Muslim polemics against Judaism and Christianity, see Ben Shammai, "Rafiyon ha-behira . . . ," *passim*.

52. Muhammad Khalil, *Islam and the Fate of Others: The Salvation Question* (Oxford: Oxford University Press, 2012).

53. According to Islamic Law, all Muslims male or female, young or old, pay every year at the rate of 2.5 percent on their savings, above the minimum of 25£. See Hamidullah, *Emergence of Islam*, 112.

54. Qur'ān: 3:163; 4:162; 17:55; 20:133; 21:105; 26:196; 53:36; 80:13; 87:18–19; *Māwardi, al-hāwī al-kabīr* 9, no. 226; Ibn Qudāmah, *al-Mughnī* 8, 501, 590; Ibn Qayyim al-Jawziyya, *Ahkām ahl al-dhimma* 2, 432–33.

55. Ahmed M. Al-Zarqa, *Al-Madkhal al-fiqhī al-am*, 6th ed. (1959): 2/737.

56. Mahdi Zahraa, "Legal Personality in Islamic Law," *Arab Law Quarterly*, 203.

57. Ibn Fadlallāh al-Umariy, *al-tarīf bil mustlah al-sharīf*, 142–46.

58. Al-Sarakhsī, *Sharh Kītāb al-siyar al-kabīr li-Muhammad b.al-Hassan al-Shabānī*, Ed.Salā al-Dīn al-Munajjid (9 Cairo, 1971), 4/139; Hamidullah, *Emergence of Islam*, 118.

59. Ibn Qayyim al-Jawziyya, *Ahkām ahl al-dhimma* 1/188.

60. Ibn Qudāmah, *al-Mughnī* 8, 496.

61. Al Qur'ān 2:256.

62. For an explanation of this term, see Ibn Manzū, Lisān al-Arab, s.v. *miqlāt*, 2/72–73.

63. Tibirī, *Jāmi al–bayān*, 3/14–16; Abu Ubaid, *al-Qāsim sim b. Sallām al-Harawī Kitāb, al-nāsikh wa al-mansūkh*, ed. J. Burton, E. J. W. Gibb Memorial Trust (Cambridge: St. Edmundsbury Press, 1987), 96–99; Sunan Bayhaqī, 9/186; Ibn al-Arabī, *Ahkām Al Qur'ān*, 1/233; Ibn al-Jawzī, *Zād al-masīr*, 1/305; Qurtabī, al-Jāmi li *Ahkam al-Qur'an*, 3/256.

64. Tibirī, *Jāmi al–bayān*, 3/15.

65. Tibrisī, *Majma al-Bayān*, 2/305.

66. Ibn Zanjawayhi, *Kitāb al-amwāl*, 1/145.

67. Ibn Qudāmah, *Mughanī*, 8/144.

68. Khuri, "True and False Pluralism," 238.

69. Khaled Abou El Fadl, "Islamic Law and Muslim Minorities: The Juristic Discourse on Muslim Minorities from the Second/Eighth to the Eleventh/Seventeenth Centuries," *Journal of Islamic Law and Society* 1, no. 2 (1994): 171.

70. R. K. Khuri, *Freedom, Modernity and Islam: Towards a Creative Synthesis* (Syracuse: Syracuse University Press, 1998), 224.

71. Michael Allen, "*Theoria* and *Praxis* in Christian and Islamic Mysticism," Barnes Symposium, University of South Carolina, 2009, 2.

72. A. Knysh, *Islamic Mysticism: A Short History* (Leiden: Brill, 2000).

73. Some important manual of Sufism are: Al-Sarrāj (d. 378AH/988CE) *Kitab al-Luma fi al-Tasawwuf'*, ed. R. Nicholson (Leiden: Brill, 1914); Abū Hafs Al-Suhrawardī, *Kitāb 'Awārif al-Ma'ārif* (Cairo: Maktabat al-Qāhira, 1973); Abū Najīb Al-Suhrawardī (d. 563/1168), *Kitāb Adāb al-Murīdīn*, ed. M. Milson (Jerusalem: Institute of Asian and African Studies, 1977); Al-Qushayrī (d. 465/1073), *al-Risāl alat al-Qushayriyya*, ed. N. al-Jarrah (Beirut: Dar Sadir, 2001). See also M. Fakhry, *Ethical Theories in Islam* (Leiden and New York: Brill, 1991); J.-C. Vadet, *Les idees morals dans Islam* (Paris: Presses Universitaires de France, 1995).

74. A. Kevin Reinhart, "Islamic Law as Islamic Ethics," *Journal of Religious Ethics* 11 (1983): 186–203.

75. See, for instance, Seyyed Hossein Nasr, *The Garden of Truth: The Vision and Promise of Sufism, Islam's Mystical Tradition* (San Francisco: Harper Collins, 2008), and Paul L. Heck, "Mysticism as Morality: The Case of Sufism," *Journal of Religious Ethics* 34, no. 2 (June 2006): 256.

76. Reza Shah Kazemi, *Justice and Remembrance* (London: I. B. Taurus Publishers, 2006), 75.

77. Kazemi, *Justice and Remembrance*.

78. See Reza Shah Kazemi, "The Metaphysics of Interfaith Dialogue," in *Paths to the Heart*, ed. James Cutsinger (Bloomington, IN: World Wisdom, 2010); and Reza Shah Kazemi, *The Other in the Light of the One: The Universality of the Qur'an and Interfaith Dialogue* (Cambridge: Islamic Texts Society, 2006).

79. Futuhat, III, 311.23, in Chittick 1994, 155.

80. Muhammad Khalil, *Islam and the Fate of Others: The Salvation Question* (Oxford: Oxford University Press, 2012).

81. Futuhat, III, 153.12, in Chittick 1994, 125.

82. Jalalal-Din Rumi, *Mathnawi*, II, 3681ff.

83. Jeremy Henzell-Thomas, "The Challenge of Pluralism and the Middle Way of Islam," in *Islam and Global Dialogue: Religious Pluralism and the Pursuit of Peace*, 267.

84. F. Hadland Davis, *Wisdom of the East: The Persian Mystics Jalalu'ddin Rumi* (Lahore: SH Muhammad Ashraf, 1967), 102.

85. For a concise overview of Islamic philosophy, see Fuad Naeem and Waleed El-Ansary, "Islamic Philosophy," in *New Catholic Encyclopedia Supplement* (New York: Cengage, 2014).

86. See Seyyed Hossein Nasr, *Islamic Philosophy from Its Origin to the Present: Philosophy in the Land of Prophecy* (Albany, NY: State University of New York Press, 2006).

87. Abdullah Saeed, *Islamic Thought: An Introduction* (London and New York: Routledge, 2006), 95.

88. Translated by R. Walzer in his "Islamic Philosophy," in *The History of Philosophy: Eastern and Western*, ed. S. Radhakrishnan (London: Allen and Urwin, 1953), 2:131.

89. Osman Bakar, *Classification of Knowledge in Islam* (Cambridge: Islamic Texts Society, 1998), 79.

90. Bakar, *Classification of Knowledge in Islam*, 79–80.

91. Bakar, *Classification of Knowledge in Islam*, 74.

92. In this regard, it is important to point out that Islamic theology plays a more limited role in the Islamic intellectual heritage than Christian theology does in the Christian intellectual heritage. Indeed, Islamic philosophy is concerned with many issues that are theological without converting Islamic philosophy into Islamic theology (*kalam*). See Seyyed Hossein Nasr, "Theology, Philosophy and Spirituality," in *Islamic Spirituality: Manifestations*, ed. Seyyed Hossein Nasr (New York: Crossroad Publishing Company, 1997), 393–445.

93. Bakar, *Classification of Knowledge in Islam*, 80–81.

94. Bakar, *Classification of Knowledge in Islam*, 83.

95. Bakar, *Classification of Knowledge in Islam*.

96. From his Siyasat, cited and translated by Fazlur Rahman in his *Prophecy in Islam* (London: George Allen & Unwin, 1958), 40.

97. Seyyed Hossein Nasr, *Three Muslim Sages* (Delmar, NY: Caravan Books, 1997), 61.

98. See Muhammad Rustom, *The Triumph of Mercy* (Albany, NY: State University of New York Press, 2012).

99. See Nasr, *Islamic Philosophy from Its Origin to the Present.*

100. Tony Bayfield, "September 11: The Case Against Us All," in *Islam and Global Dialogue: Religious Pluralism and the Pursuit of Peace*, 195.

101. Alan F. Segal, *Rebecca's Children: Judaism and Christianity in the Roman World* (Cambridge, MA, and London: Harvard University Press, 1986), 180–81.

102. See, for instance, Joseph Lumbard (ed.), *Islam, Fundamentalism, and the Betrayal of Tradition: Essays by Western Muslim Scholars* (Bloomington, IN: World Wisdom, Inc., 2009).

103. British novelist and poet Rudyard Kipling wrote a poem titled "The White Man's Burden: The United States and the Philippine Islands." This poem was published in *McClure's Magazine* in 1899. Through this poem, Kipling urged the United States to take up the "burden" of empire, as heir of Britain and other European nations. The racialized notion of the "White Man's Burden" became a euphemism for imperialism, and many anti-imperialists couched their opposition in reaction to the phrase. The poem coincided with the beginning of the Philippine-American War and U.S. Senate ratification of the treaty that placed Puerto Rico, Guam, Cuba, and the Philippines under American control. Theodore Roosevelt, soon to become vice president and then president, copied the poem and sent it to his friend Senator Henry Cabot Lodge, commenting that it was "rather poor poetry, but good sense from the expansion point of view." See Modern History Sourcebook: Rudyard Kipling, "The White Man's Burden," 1899, Internet Modern History Sourcebook; The US Survey Course on the web. http://historymatters.gmu.edu/d/5478/.

104. Samuel Phillips Huntington (1927–2008) was an influential conservative political scientist whose works covered multiple subfields of political science. He gained wider prominence through his *Clash of Civilizations* thesis of a post–Cold War new world order.

105. Samuel P. Huntington, *The Clash of Civilizations and the Remaking of World Order* (New York: Touchstone, 1996).

106. Yoshihiro Francis Fukuyama (born 1952) is an American political scientist and political economist who is famous for his theory of the worldwide spread of liberal democracies and free market capitalism of the West.

107. Francis Fukuyama, *The End of History and the Last Man* (New York: Avon, 1993).

108. Felipe Fernández-Armesto (born 1950) is a British historian and author of several popular works of history.

109. Felipe Fernandez-Armesto, *Millennium: A History of the Last Thousand Years* (New York: Scribner, 1995).

110. The holders of this thought treat Islam as a dark force in the history, and Muslims treat this theory as a conspiracy against them. See Akbar S. Ahmed,

"America and the Challenge of Islam," *The Hedgehog Review* (Spring 2003): 21–22.

111. Qur'ān 5:51; 6:108; 2:256.

112. Qur'ān, 22:40.

113. Al Qur'ān 2:49, 81, 91, 101; 3:50, 81; 4:74; 5:46.

114. This terminology is used in the meaning of chastity. This is a legal concept describing the personal status of an individual who is free (not a slave) and who either has never committed an act of illicit intercourse or has consummated a lawful marriage to a free partner. See John L. Esposito, *The Oxford Dictionary of Islam* (Oxford: Oxford Press, 2003), 212.

115. Al-Qur'ān 4:123–25.

116. Al-Rāzī, *Al-Tafsīr al-Kabīr*, 11/226; Mufti Muhammad Shafi, *Ma'arif al-Quran*, translated by Muhammad Shamim (Karachi: Maktaaba e Darul-Uloom, 1998), 3/577–78.

117. Muhammad al-Tahir ibn 'Ashur (1879–1973) was an eminent figure in the institution of the Tunisian scholars for most of the twentieth century. He is also highly regarded as a Muslim reformist of the modern era.

118. Ibn Āshūr, Muhammad al-Tahir, *Tafsīr al-Tahrīrwa al-Tanwīr* (Tunis: Al-Dār al-Tūnisiya li-nashr, 1984), 5/208–9.

119. Al-Qur'ān 2:62; 5:69.

120. Sachedina Abdulaziz, *The Islamic Roots of Democratic Pluralism* (Oxford: Oxford University Press, 2001), 33.

IV

Particular Issues in Justice and Diversity: Theology

21

FROM BENEVOLENT TOLERANCE TO HUMBLE REVERENCE

A Vision for a Multicultural Church

Virgilio Elizondo, University of Notre Dame

The church of the United States is rapidly becoming a multicultural and multilingual congregation. It is not strange at all to find a parish where each Sunday Mass is celebrated in a different language. In some of the larger cities, there are easily thirty, forty, to fifty languages spoken. In the past we had national churches to take care of the ethnic immigrants, but today the local parishes are being called upon to welcome immigrants into their ranks. In our seminary in San Antonio, just the faculty is made up of a Pilipino, Vietnamese, Mexican, Mexican American, German American, and Irish American, and the student body is much more diverse.

At the very core of a multicultural church is the original New Testament narrative of the Christian movement: how the slaves, the disenfranchised, the low merchants, the widows, the unemployed, the immigrants, and the socially downcast Galileans found a new and exciting alternative to social life that the world had not imagined possible. In the new community, everyone was accepted with reverence and respect. If the Lord had emptied himself of all social status for them, then they were to do the same for one another. It was the excitement of this new way of life that attracted everyone—even the rich, the righteous, and the mighty, the Jews, the Romans, Greeks, and others. The joyful simplicity of Christians was contagious. Yet it was dangerous, because it dared to transgress all borders for the sake of a new unity.

THE ORIGINALITY OF THE CHRISTIAN MOVEMENT

To best appreciate the challenge and the grace-filled possibilities of the new society, we need to rediscover and make our own the liberating and life-giving *originality* of the Christian movement. It was offered to all peoples, no matter where they came from, a new family name: Christian. It was offered equally to everyone no matter what his or her race or nationality—a new, common bloodstream: the blood of Jesus. It flowed through everyone who joined, producing one close-knit unity: the body of the Lord! Thus the body and blood of Jesus, broken and spilled for the sake of humanity, now rehabilitated a broken humanity racially divided and socially crushed by the human blood that produces everyone's fundamental earthly identity. Peoples of diverse backgrounds, histories, skin color, and heritages could now begin to share in the common story and heritage of Jesus. This new story would not destroy the histories of peoples, but would bring them into a new common space and time. The kingdom of God was now available to everyone.

Christianity produced a new human being who was totally different from the world's ethnicities and nationalities, not by destroying the basic nationality but by transforming the limitations of national identities. Identities were affirmed, but their limitations were destroyed. The early Christians were considered atheists because they refused to recognize the national gods of any nation. Christians had only one God who was truly creator and parent of all. They were respectful of civic authority but refused to accept it as absolute, for they had only one absolute—the unconditional love of God for all human beings regardless of their national or racial identity.

Hence, the Christian identity was the hyphenated identity: Jewish-Christian, Greek-Christian, Roman-Christian. Their identities as Christians made them open to the otherness of others as truly brothers and sisters, all children of the same parent God. The refreshing originality of Christianity is that it transgressed all barriers of separation and division, whether rooted in blood or sacred traditions through the power of unlimited love.

CHRISTIANITY AS DIVISIVE

The Cultural Reality of the United States

Despite the unity in diversity evident among the earliest Christians, historical Christianity has often served more as a basis of exclusion than of welcome. Multiculturalism is rather new in U.S. churches and in society today, yet it is an unquestioned fact of life. Some see it as the new life of the future, while others see it as destructive of all unity—civic, social, and religious. Regardless of how it is understood, multiculturalism is a growing fact of life in the United States and much of the world. Today, as a church, we attempt to break new ground in our understanding of the many aspects and implications of multiculturalism.

The Emergence of a Racist and Segregating Christianity

The U.S. churches are finally coming to grips with the original sin of the great European (and later American) evangelizing efforts that accompanied conquering and colonizing European expansion that began in the fifteenth century. Very simply put, white Europeans saw themselves as godly people while judging all others and their ways as demonic—we the saved, and they the dammed; we the masters, and they the servants or slaves; we the true and beautiful human beings, and they false and ugly human beings; we the possessors and guardians of truth, and they who are enslaved by error.

The white Christian invaders had no doubts about the divine righteousness of their invasion, conquest, and colonization of other people. They never questioned their own superiority. Western culture itself became the great idol of our churches. All had to conform or be cast out. It is the pseudo-divine status of white Western culture that is finally being revealed as the false idol that must be destroyed. It is not Western culture that needs to be destroyed, but its pseudo-divine status that allows it to continue functioning as the unquestioned normative culture and religious expression for all others.

Western theologians still tend to see the Western churches as "the church" while viewing the churches of other people of the world as "local churches." Western tradition is regarded as "Tradition," while everything else is regarded as local tradition. Western theologies are regarded simply as theology, while the theologies and methodologies of other cultures are regarded as ethnic or particular theologies. The West still keeps to itself the right to be the exclusive ecclesial master of the world and guards this right carefully through its universities and publications.

There is no doubt that in the past, and to a large degree today, most of our churches have been mono-churches: monolingual, monocultural, and monoracial. Uniformity and conformity in all things have been the unquestioned norms of acceptance and belonging. These unquestioned norms allowed white churches of the past to justify and legitimize slavery and segregation. In effect, the churches implicitly sacralized fear, dislike, and hatred of others. Separate churches were built to keep diverse people worshipping separately. It has often been observed that eleven o'clock on Sunday mornings is the most segregated hour in America, and that the more churchgoing people are, the more prejudiced they seem to be.

It is out of this scandalous reality of the past that today we are seeking to bring about a new church with a truly multicultural face and heart.

A Graced Opportunity

The undeniable increase in racial and ethnic diversity in the United States poses many potential problems, yet greater than the problems are the opportunities to create something new and life giving on the face of the earth. More and more pastoralists attempt to facilitate a Christian response to the graced opportunities of our multicultural society. However, to promote the emergence of a real multicultural church, we must go from a benevolent tolerance of the otherness of the others to a sincere reverence of others in their otherness.

Before we can embark on pastoral plans that are not merely a benevolent tolerance stemming from guilt feelings about the past, we need to undergo a deep cultural conversion from our previously unquestioned Western paradigm of truth itself—that all truth, whether personal, cultural, technical, natural, or religious, is one, absolute, and complete and therefore can be known in terms of either/or: true or false, good or bad, beautiful or ugly. For such a transformation to take place, we must all die a bit to our collective self-righteousness so that we may be more willing to listen and learn from the others. As communication between persons, cultures, and nations increases, we are becoming aware that it is not possible to reduce truth to one expression. No one has an absolute and exclusive monopoly on truth. We have much to offer one another, if only we can have the humility to reverence and accept it.

MULTICULTURAL CHRISTIANITY AS UNIFYING

How does Christian multiculturalism come about? How do we build churches that welcome all people as they are, not to the degree that they become like the dominant group of the congregation? Do our churches welcome the diversity of God's humanity? Do we merely tolerate diversity, or do we reject it completely? We need to develop a totally new attitude about church, ourselves, and others; a new attitude about the way we see and value the otherness of other persons and peoples. We must decide if we are going to be a tower of Babel of a Pentecost or an assembly of believers.

My experience at San Fernando Cathedral, an active Mexican parish in San Antonio, Texas, since 1731, has been an enriching one. Even though our basic identity is very Mexican, we work hard at welcoming others. We have not found this to be divisive in any way. On the contrary, it continues to be very enriching. On a Pentecost Sunday, we celebrated our worship service in several languages and had the active participation of thirty-three ethnic groups. It was a great experience of the power of Christ bringing us together in ways no human power is capable of doing. The multicultural experience is not easy, but it is certainly exciting and enriching.

In my experience, a truly multicultural parish emerges through three phases, or moments—not necessarily one before the other. The three moments are confession, conversion, and construction.

CONFESSION: NAMING AND CLAIMING THE SIN

The Sin of Dogmatic Ethnocentrism

Most of our churches in the United States came out of the great European colonizing enterprise that started in 1492. The church of that period, because of the Reformation and Counter-Reformation, emphasized dogma and looked at any type of difference as heretical and divisive. This emphasis also dogmatized the cultural and racial ideas of the emerging dominant nations of Europe. "White" and "Western civilization" thus became the dogmatically correct image of the dignified, beautiful, and authentic human being. All others would be looked upon as undignified, ugly (except for the young women of the conquered, who often appeared to the conquerors as more exotic than their own women), and subhuman.

The Catholic and Protestant churches accepted without question the assumption that white Europeans, especially the Anglo-Saxons in North America, were the superior race that had been divinely chosen to be normative of the only true humanity possible or desirable by people in their right minds. Everyone else was considered inferior, heathen, and at best underdeveloped! The benevolent looked on the others as children who needed the loving care and discipline of the white Europeans. The ruthless looked on the others as mere beasts of burden. In many ways, this is still the case today.

Europeans and their American descendants fortified their sense of cultural superiority with the religious conviction that they belonged to the one and only true religion. Throughout history they had fought bloody battles among themselves as to which was the dogmatically correct version of this one true religion, but they never questioned that European Christianity was the one salvation for all the peoples of the world. Of course, "Christianity" meant their own particular understanding of it: Catholic, Lutheran, Methodist, Baptist, and so on.

It was dogmatic certainty intermingled with the European sense of superiority and the European's need for cheap labor that "in good conscience" and with the blessings of religious authorities produced such an incredibly racist and segregated American continent. European immigrants did not hesitate to set up their own churches where they could experience salvation while exploiting and murdering the Natives, the imported Africans, and the conquered Mexicans, without any qualms of conscience.

It is true that some church voices protested loudly, and it is true that church movements have been a part of the force that has attempted to bring about change. But in general, the churches sanctified the white, neo-European culture of the Americas and thus sanctioned contempt for people of other races, cultures, and languages.

For a truly multicultural community to emerge, all are called to recognize their specific cultural sinfulness so that they may repent, receive

God's forgiveness, and begin to create a new way of relating with each other.

The Sin of Arrogant Pride

White Western Christians need to convert from their sins of arrogance and pride. Their righteous sense of superiority has blinded them to their own inadequacies and sinfulness and has kept them from appreciating the treasures God has bestowed on the peoples of the other races and cultures of the world. This unclaimed sin of arrogant and self-righteous pride still allows them to see themselves as human while seeing the others as "cultural groups" or "ethnics."

There is deep and unquestioned Western conviction, bolstered by financial, technological, and military superiority, that the West alone knows the truth, the way, and the life. All others either live in ignorance or at best possess only small bits and pieces of the truth. The minorities might be accepted and enjoyed "folklorically," but the West thinks that it alone knows the right way of life for all who want to be correctly human.

The confession of our cultural arrogance will be the beginning of the liberation from the current ethnocentrism. A collective recognition of our limited view of reality, of humanity, and of God will be the beginning of a new enrichment and source of life that at the present moment seems impossible to imagine.

The Sin of Humiliating Shame

On the other hand, those who have been marginated, brutalized, abused, segregated, put down, ridiculed, or merely tolerated need also to recognize their sin: the sense of inferiority that some come to believe and accept. The victimizer's ultimate triumph is to get the victims to accept the blame for their situation of misery. The sin of the victimized is to accept this as true, resulting in a loss of dignity and self-worth. Attitudes of docility, embarrassment of color and heritage, and the many negative and self-destructive feelings grow out of the inner sense of shame at being who one is. The sin of accepting assigned inferiority leads to a distrust of one's own, a disgust with one's culture and language, and a devastating break with the ways of one's ancestors, for it destroys the inner soul of the person and of the people.

Without confession of our cultural sinfulness, we will at best tolerate one another. We will never enter into a true fellowship among equals, a true family spirit that embraces all as children of the one God. We need to be willing and ready to name and confess our sin so that we may move on to conversion—that is, to a real *metanoia* whereby we will turn our innermost attitudes of life in a radically different direction.

CONVERSION TO THE WAY OF JESUS

Jesus surprised and astounded everyone, rich and poor, sinful and saintly, accepted and rejected, by portraying a totally new vision of the human and the sacred in the very simple and ordinary way in which he related with people and with God in his everyday life. He invited us to share in this new reality that will truly revolutionize our own vision of ourselves, of others, and of God.

Jesus invites us to see ourselves and others in a radically new way through the prism of God's unconditional love for everyone. Through God's love we move from our typical judgmental and conditional tolerance and acceptance of others to the spontaneous joy of discovering our unsuspected sisters and brothers, each one revealing a bit of God's glory. Everyone is invited to convert from pride or shame to a grateful and humble acceptance of who we are and who the other is. This will lead us from either total rejection or benevolent tolerance to a truly humble reverence for one another and an appreciation for the giftedness of each person, nation, and race.

Jesus: The True Image of the Human and of God

The dominant groups of Jesus' day perceived him as a marginal, Galilean peasant. Being Jewish, he belonged to people who were rejected culturally by the powerful Romans. Being from Galilee, he was from a region scorned socially by Jewish officials in Jerusalem, who frequently viewed their coreligionist from Galilee as unknowledgeable and lax in the practice of their faith. And to make things even more interesting, there were rumors about his dubious parentage and scandals about his friendships with prostitutes and public sinners. Thus did the sacred unseen and untouchable God become visible and touchable in the socially, culturally, and religiously rejected Jesus of Nazareth in Galilee!

In the very social-cultural-religious human being that God became, Jesus revealed to us the mystery hidden by humanity's sinfulness since the origins of sin itself: that every human being is of infinite dignity, immeasurable worth, and unique beauty. In its sinfulness, the world constantly creates categories of unworthiness, untouchability, and inferiority, while at the same time creating artificial and often unnatural categories of beauty, importance, dignity, and worth. These sinful categories begin to define the truth of the human and of the divine while in effect hiding (or perverting) the ultimate truth of God and destroying any possibility of human authenticity. Since the escalation of sin (described in Genesis 3–11), this has become the way of the world—the way of men and women throughout history. This was the way Peter was thinking when he wanted a glorious Messiah. This is the way we think when we want only socially acceptable members of the right color and ethnicity in our congregations. But this is not God's way! God creates and loves all of God's children alike.

These human classifications are the sin that brings about the distortion and blindness of the world. In Jesus, God became the nothing of the world so that through Jesus—with him and in him—all might be liberated from their own false notions about themselves and others, and thus come to appreciate people for what they truly are: dignified and beautiful children of God. There is nothing Jesus condemns more than hypocrisy. Sinful people he deals with compassionately; hypocrites he has no stomach for. People who give in to the world's struggles for superiority, honor, artificial beauty, and the like lose themselves to the world and are destructive of self and of others.

The New Image of Self and Others

All are invited to convert—to think and feel in a radically new way so as to belong to God's own family. The rich and mighty are invited to share their wealth and power, while the poor and lowly are assured that they will be uplifted and will receive their fill.[1] The gross inequality of persons is the great sin of the world that prevents the reign of God from coming into existence.

In other words, those who have considered themselves superior are invited to think less of themselves. The righteous are invited to recognize their sinfulness, and those whom society deems unwanted "public sinners" are invited to become aware of their fundamental worth. Those who think of themselves as trash or as nothing are invited to recognize their strength and independence. Thus all are invited to a change of heart and mind. Through baptism we die to the old self to be reborn with the heart and mind of Jesus. We truly become a new creation within the old creation, and thus we are reborn to a new tension. The great difference is that now we know that ultimate triumph is assured and nobody can take it away from us. Hence we can live in peace even within the context of the tensions and uncertainties of the new life of grace.

It is in the very radical acceptance of our personal and collective mystery of giftedness/lack, wealth/poverty, blessing/curse, health/sickness, understanding/blindness, saintliness/sinfulness, truth/ambiguity, knowledge/ignorance that we become truly human. It is in the recognition of our innermost existential poverty as persons, as cultures, and as races that we begin truly to appreciate and welcome the wealth of others. It is in this radical acceptance of God's love for us as we are that we receive the courage to accept ourselves as we are and truly rejoice in the acceptance of others as they are, not as we would like them to be.

Division Because of Unity

In the Gospels, the same Jesus who prays "that all may be one"[2] tell us that he has come to bring about division.[3] These statements seem to contradict each other. Yet in practice it is quite obvious what Jesus is speaking about. Precisely because all are invited in an equal way, those who have usually enjoyed status and privilege will not want to come, not because they are not invited, but precisely because now everyone is invited, especially those considered to be unworthy, unwanted, and untouchable. When the club is made available to everyone, those who took pride in belonging to the exclusive, private club will not want to belong to the new one! In the process of working for the unity of the kingdom, we can expect the scandal, criticism, and persecution of those committed to the empires and sacred institutions of this world. The great paradox is that the call to unity so frequently leads to bitter division!

CONSTRUCTION OF NEW CHURCH BODIES

Each local parish could easily become like a laboratory or greenhouse specimen of the new creation—and is it not in the tiny, invisible cell that new life begins? Prayerful insight, patient trust, and a spirit of welcome are the seeds from which the new creation is born.

Prayerful Insight

Because the unity of the church is not one of men and women but of the Spirit, the work of multicultural unity must begin with sincere prayer that God may enlighten and strengthen us to go beyond our own fears and limitations. It is not through the conclusions reached by rational discourse but by the insight revealed through sincere and prolonged prayer that the new church will be built. Without prayer that truly opens up our minds and hearts to the unconditional love of God in all its consequences, even reading Scripture can simply confirm our distorted notions without giving us insight.

Prayer will bring about a new vision of vision itself, a new understanding of understanding itself, and a new truth regarding the reality of truth. Prayer leads us from narrow tunnel vision to a panoramic one, from isolated to more integrated understanding, and from partial to more complete truth. This does not relativize truth; it amplifies it! This is far more objective than the subjective conviction of one cultural group or another.

Patient Trust

The new multicultural fellowship will not come about overnight. It will take patience with ourselves and with others. We are embarking on something new and deeply personal, yet of planetary implications and consequence. It will not be easy. Even when we are committed to doing it, we will not always know just how to bring it about. Cultural misunderstandings are steeped deep in our historical genes, in fear and misunderstanding. Sometimes signals, gestures, or words will be misinterpreted. Insult will be taken when none is intended, and rejection will be easily experienced.

Trust cannot be mandated. It builds up gradually but can be destroyed in an instant. There is no simple pedagogy for building trust. It takes a lot of love, self-giving, and the willingness to hurt with another and to see and feel in ways we are not accustomed to. It comes about through a lot of careful listening, especially to the silence and absence of those who are marginal or newcomers.

It will take time to build up the trust and confidence that people need to truly be themselves. Everyone has to be able to give up a bit of self to receive much from the others. But in the process of giving and receiving, a new and profound commonality will gradually emerge. In this process, all can truly become one body without anyone having to become like all the others simply in order to belong.

The more each one experiences the willingness of each member to die a bit to self for the sake of others, the more this love will become the new commonality and source of unity for the group. The source of unity will no longer be the racial color, the language, the ethnicity, the social class, the sex or sexual orientation, or even precise religious expression, but the love that allows each one to transgress the taboos that separate us. The new language will be that of agape, which finds ways of communicating through any and all the languages of humanity.

A Welcoming and Inclusive Home

To be truly multicultural, a local parish must visibly reflect the various peoples making up the congregation in every aspect of church life. The very physical surroundings should put us in contact with the places of origin of the various members: pictures, decorations, maps, furniture, and signs in the various languages represented. Efforts should be made to help the members pronounce each other's names correctly. Simple greetings can be learned in one another's languages.

People should be invited to share their personal stories—where they came from, what they left behind, why they came, the struggles it took to get here, how they are getting adjusted, what they miss. Some, like many of our Mexican Americans and Native Americans, never left home but were made foreigners in their own lands. Others might have forgotten the migrations of their previous generations. The story of each one is important. It is by means of personal stories that we break through the stereotypes and begin to know persons as Juan, Mary, Karl, Nindy, Sun Ai, Yong Ting Jin. Through the stories we begin to interconnect on a very personal level.

Parish activities should explore the various diverse and legitimate religious expressions of our one faith. People can experience the excitement of discovering how each expression enriches the ongoing incarnation of our faith. We need to appreciate the ancestral rites of our Asian Christians, the ancestral traditions of our African Christians, the Mestizo Christian traditions of our Latin American Christians. They include such beautiful customs as the Day of the Dead (which is actually the day of the living), La Virgen (which is not understood by North American Catholics or Latin American Protestants), and the crucified Jesus as el Señor del Poder; they also include the community dance and meal rituals of our Native Americans, the icons of Eastern European Christianity, the written alphabetic word for Western Christians, the role of the image-painted word for Christians of hieroglyphic cultures. They should be invited to celebrate each other's feasts, sing their songs, enjoy their foods, and share in their humor.

We must go even further. As Christians, we should lead the way in seeking to truly understand and appreciate all others. If in our minds and hearts we are secure in our own religious conviction, we do not have to be defensive or apprehensive in the face of others. Only one who is insecure will seek to discredit others. Hence, we should present and study the other great religions of the world, not asking whether they are true or false or even if they are a preparation for Christianity, but simply trying to appreciate them as they are. To see the beauty and truth of the others does not deny our own! In fact, it can even strengthen our own and help us to appreciate it more. I have found out in recent years that the more I appreciate the other great religious traditions of the world, the more I come to appreciate and love my own, not because I think we in our faith are better or superior to others, but simply because I have come to a greater awareness of who we are in relation to the others. We need to go beyond the sacralized divisions of the past so that we can become one very diverse and beautiful human family before we destroy one another in the name of the God we confess.

FESTIVE CHRISTIANITY AS PROCLAMATION

The early Christians made many converts through their new life of joy and simplicity. Many of the people Christians encountered had a great deal materially and socially and yet were bored and disillusioned with life. The Christians disregarded social rank and status and were happy because they welcomed everyone alike! *"Never act out of rivalry or conceit; rather, let all parties think humbly of others as superior to themselves, each of you looking to others' interests rather than his own"* (Phil 2:3). All could partake of the Lord's table together—master and slave, citizen and foreigner (Gal 3:28). No matter what their role or status in society might be, within the Christian community they were truly of equal status because here they were brothers and sisters. It was not long before the Christian group was headed by a slave as successor of Peter—Pope Calixtus.[4]

Christians came together not to argue, defend, or try to impose, but simply to sing songs of joy, to tell about the memory of Jesus, to see how they could help one another, and to celebrate their new ritual, the breaking of the bread. In the breaking and sharing of the bread, they transgressed the taboos and celebrated what was now begun in them but would only be fully achieved at the end time—the ultimate unity of humanity. Our multicultural parishes can be the luminous and glorious star whose worship foreshadows the banquet of the eschatological end, anticipating here and now God's ultimate triumph over the divisions of humanity. The parishes where this is beginning to happen are the sparks that will ignite the fires of the new Pentecost of the U.S. church.

NOTES

1. Luke 1:52–54.
2. John 17:11.
3. Luke 12:51.
4. Calixtus I, also known as Callistus, became Pope in 218. He was born a slave and died a Christian martyr in 223.

22

THE COMMON GOOD, FREEDOM, AND DIFFERENCE

Shawn Copeland, Boston College

> This freedom is a funny thing. . . . It ain't something permanent like rocks and hills. It's like manna; you just got to keep on gathering it fresh every day. If you don't, one day you're going to find you ain't got none no more. I'm getting kind of old and I been with you like you say since back in Egypt. It's been kind of tough sometimes. . . . But if you just keep free and be a fine nation of folks I'll feel like I bought something with my life. You done got free of Pharaoh and the Egyptian oppressors, be careful you don't raise up none among yourselves.[1]

The colorful and insightful passage at the head of this chapter comes from the 1939 novel *Moses, Man of the Mountain*, written by African American anthropologist, folklorist, and novelist Zora Neale Hurston. With freedom as its theme, the Exodus story as its dramatic vehicle, and recounted in an African American cultural idiom, the novel forms, according to literary critic Deborah McDowell, a "political allegory analogizing Hebrew oppression in biblical antiquity, black oppression in the contemporary United States, and Jewish oppression in Nazi Germany."[2] The timing of the novel's publication was more than apt, appearing shortly after the infamous *Kristallnacht* pogrom carried out against the Jewish people in Germany and parts of Austria[3] and the intensification of Nazi appeals to racial purity and selective breeding, along with the forced labor, removal, and extermination of non-Aryans. With Hitler's attack on Poland, the probability of a world at war became reality.[4] During the first two years of the conflict, the United States maintained formal neutrality, but this changed with the December 7, 1941, attack on Pearl Harbor. Yet while joining in a war for freedom, the United States overlooked its own enmeshment in the abrogation of the freedom of a significant portion of its citizens.[5] Nearly eighty years after their emancipation from slavery, Jim Crow laws governed social and civic relations of blacks and whites: enforcing "whites-only" housing covenants, redlining, and residential segregation; supporting school segregation, systemic discrimination in employment, economic, and cultural opportunities; prohibiting interracial marriage; and tolerating lynching and targeted violence. Even the nation's armed forces were segregated, until President Harry Truman ended this shameful blot in July 1948 by Executive Order 9981. The story of the oppression, enslavement, and liberation of the ancient Israelites holds a surplus of meaning.[6] Hurston's choice of the Exodus as a means by which to raise and interrogate contradictions troubling the notion, meanings, and exercise of freedom, difference, and the common good was nothing less than brilliant.

In this chapter, I consider some of the difficulties of freedom—the common good, virtue, and difference. It is a way of exploring some perennial moral and social (i.e., political, economic, and technological) questions, such as, "What is the just, the right way to live?" "What is justice?" "How is justice to be realized in a complex social order?" "How might cultural pluralism and difference contribute to the common good?" Or as philosopher Michael Novak asks, "How can one square the common good with personal liberty and cultural pluralism?"[7] As a Roman Catholic theologian, my reflection on these matters aims for clarification of some issues basic in the articulation of a theology of social transformation or a political theology. Three sections comprise the chapter: The first section traces the notion of the common good and some of the ways in which meanings of freedom and virtue have shifted along with it. The second section adverts to the need to grapple with meanings of cultural diversity and difference in our society. The third section offers a brief theological statement on how women and men of faith might influence social (i.e., political, economic, and technological) interactions in realization of the common good.

This chapter presumes: (1) that freedom is an exercise regarding our communal authenticity as a nation and this authenticity depends upon the authenticity of human persons—that is, a concrete, virtuous, self-correcting human living; (2) that the common good is a rich, complex, and pressing problematic realized in and through authentic human relations in society; (3) that we must reject hegemonic meanings of culture in order to engage the differentiated experiences and histories of the peoples of the United States; (4) that the present concrete and existential situation in which we live may be defined as a cycle of decline[8]—a situation so socially (i.e., politically, economically, and technologically) distorted that it deforms us religiously, culturally, intellectually, and morally; (5) that reversal of this cycle entails not only the *recognition* that moral development or character formation has been much overlooked in contemporary social formation, but that new disciplines or habits for ethical and moral thinking, behavior, and action are necessary; (6) that religious faith is integral to the realization of the common good; and (7) that grace is a divine invitation to growth and conversion in society and in history.

FREEDOM AND SLAVERY: THE COMMON GOOD AND VIRTUE

Freedom from enslavement and from political oppression, freedom for equality and human flourishing comprise crucial ends or purposes of government, in particular, a democracy; yet, as the passage from *Moses, Man of the Mountain* suggests and human history demonstrates, the notion, meanings, and exercise of freedom are ambiguous and elusive. Social critic Zygmunt Bauman observes, "Freedom was born as a privilege and has remained so ever since."[9] And sociologist Orlando Patterson puts it bluntly and does so in a way Hurston's characters, Jews, and black Americans would understand: freedom gains its value "as a direct result of the social dialectics of slavery."[10]

FREEDOM AND SLAVERY: PRELIMINARIES

In *Freedom in the Making of Western Culture,* Patterson traces the long history of the development of freedom from ancient Greece to imperial Rome to the rise of Christianity. He distinguishes three aspects of freedom—the *personal, sovereignal,* and *civic*.[11] The *personal* aspect surfaces in such familiar expressions as "I am free and, thus, I can say or do what I wish," or "This is a free country." We speak and act as if the meanings of these expressions were self-evident and required little, if any, explanation or interpretation. On commonsense understanding, they imply a lack of coercion or restraint or interference; at the same time, such expressions intimate that we can do as we please within the limits of others doing the same.

Sovereignal freedom adverts to "the power to act as one pleases, regardless of the wishes of others, as distinct from personal freedom, which is the capacity to do as one pleases insofar as one can."[12] This aspect of freedom implicates desire in two ways: first, it uncovers the fact that we human beings often "desire more than [our] fair share," and second, that many of us "desire to control not only [our] own lives but also the lives of others."[13] Finally, *civic freedom* refers to "the capacity of adult members of a community to participate in its life and governance."[14] Civic freedom involves some sort of political community shaped by reasonably clear definitions of each citizen's duties and obligations as well as rights. Furthermore, civic freedom implies a sense of belonging to a community, whether by birth or adoption, and having a recognized place and/or role in it. Each of these three dimensions of freedom implies some form of social relations, each pertains to the common good, and each of these aspects presents an unruly partner in dialogue about difference and pluralism.

If freedom symbolizes lack of coercion, exercise of personal autonomy, and participation in social and communal life, then slavery denotes force, abrogation of personal autonomy, and social death. Patterson defines slavery as "the permanent, violent, and personal domination of natally alienated and generally dishonored persons."[15] As an extreme form of social, cultural, and personal domination, three factors distinguish slavery from other expressions of asymmetrical and dominative power relations: First, the political setup or organization of a given society forms the context for slavery. Slavery is social: it is political, economic, and public. The slave must be excluded from active political participation, identified as an instrument of the economic order, marked or differentiated in some discernible and public way, and subjected to culturally determined and acceptable use or threat of violence. Second, since slavery sustains itself through persuasion, it includes a psychological element. Through physical or mental intimidation, terrorization, or seduction, the slaveholder seeks to pressure the slave to change or repress the essential way in which she or he understands her or his interests, situation, condition, and very self. At the same time, slaveholders seek to persuade themselves that they are human—and in a way far superior to slaves, that slaves are not human, but a subhuman species made for servile labor. Third, slavery represents "the cultural facet of authority."[16] If culture regards those meanings and values that inform a way of life, and if cultural authority regards the ability to generate, mediate, transmit, and enforce those meanings and values, then slavery debases some of the most crucial philosophical, political, and existential meanings, values, and institutions in a putatively democratic society—in particular, personhood, life, and property. The eighteenth-century philosopher Jean-Jacques Rousseau noted, "to be always the master, the strongest . . . must transform strength into right, and obedience into duty."[17] The "idiom [of slavery] is power;"[18] its grammar violence and coercion; its effective meaning social death.

FREEDOM AND SLAVERY IN THE HEBREW AND CHRISTIAN SCRIPTURES

The desire for freedom has preoccupied human hope from biblical times to the present. The Hebrew Bible testifies to the mighty acts of a God who responded to the pleas of an enslaved people, liberating them from oppression in order that they might live and worship in freedom according to the covenant God would make with them. The Jewish people commemorate this event in the ritual of Passover. The *Haggadah* urges not only the memory of the historical experience of slavery and liberation but also each Jew's personal, immediate, and continuing identification with it: "In every generation let each [one of you] look upon [himself as if he] came forth out of Egypt."[19] Thus, each year the descendants of Abraham gather to drink wine and eat roasted lamb, bitter herbs, and unleavened bread in order to remember, re-appropriate, and hand on this story of Passover, of slavery to freedom:

> A wandering Aramean was my father; and he went down into Egypt and sojourned there, few in number; and there he became a nation, great, mighty, and populous. And the Egyptians treated us harshly, and afflicted us, and laid upon us hard bondage. Then we cried to the Lord the God of our fathers, and the Lord heard our voice, and saw our affliction, our toil, and our oppression; and the Lord brought us out of Egypt with a mighty hand and an outstretched arm, with great terror,

with signs and wonders; and brought us to this land, a land flowing with milk and honey.[20]

In a few verses, the biblical writer captures a people's loss of freedom, experience of bondage and oppression, desire and yearning for freedom. The writer invites us to deeper research into a people's complex history—with one another (Jacob and Esau, Joseph and his brothers), with those outside their kin (the Egyptians), with centuries of imperial affliction and oppression (physical abuse, male infanticide), with social, religious, and cultural suppression, with withering and budding dreams of freedom, with plea and prayer for redemption and freedom.

The dreams, pleas, and prayers of the ancient Israelites were realized in the Exodus-event; with liberation and freedom come responsibilities of memory and action. The book of Deuteronomy sets forth laws regarding the behavior of the ancient Israelites toward servants or slaves in their households.

> You shall not oppress a hired servant who is poor and needy, whether he is one of your brethren or one of the sojourners who are in your land within your towns. . . . You shall remember that you were a slave in Egypt and the Lord your God redeemed you from there; therefore I command you to do this.[21]

This behavior and responsibilities are regulated in absolute terms by a formal covenant made with the Lord God at Sinai. "Only with the covenant," writes Michael Walzer, do the ancient Israelites become "a people . . . capable of sustaining a moral and political history, capable of obedience . . . of marching forward."[22] The laws of Deuteronomy not only codify the people's relationship to God but to one another as well—to a common purpose, a common end, a common good.

In the Christian Scriptures and experience, the notion of *freedom* focuses primarily on Jesus of Nazareth, who is confessed as the Christ of God. "For freedom," the apostle Paul writes, "Christ has set us free."[23] Jesus signifies the contradictions in which freedom is enmeshed: He emptied (kenosis) himself of divinity to show that "whoever wishes to be first among you must be slave of all;"[24] he came "not to be served, but to serve, and to give his life as a ransom for many";[25] he healed and emancipated broken bodies and spirits, yet underwent brutal torture and death on a cross. Jesus was a living parable that challenged slavery and slaveholding. But early Christians adapted and developed codes of household management that prescribed so-called appropriate and acceptable behavior for husbands, wives, children, slaves, and slaveholders.[26] These codes incriminate Christians in slaveholding and, thus, present difficulties not only in understanding Christian thinking about slavery in the Greco-Roman world, but also today. Here are three of those difficulties: First, slavery, the very opposite of freedom, is deployed as a spiritual and theological metaphor to provide "a model of dependence and self-surrender."[27] Second, slavery in the ancient world was a real condition of social death. The early Christian writers used slavery as a metaphor for sin, but it did not occur to them to challenge the cruelty or the existence of slavery. Third, slavery cultivates desire for personal, sovereignal, and civic freedom. But when such desire is so spiritualized, the concrete desire for freedom is subverted and gives way to a damaging detachment from the social matrix and the short- and long-term fate of human persons within it.

REVISITING THE COMMON GOOD: CLASSICAL AND MODERN POSITIONS

This section revisits the positions of selected authors on the notion of the common good in antiquity and modernity.[28] Whereas classical political philosophers set their compass by the ideal, modernity's political philosophers took their bearings by the extreme. Plato and Aristotle, Aquinas and Augustine exemplify the former, Machiavelli, Hobbes, and Locke the latter.[29] Plato and Aristotle, Aquinas and Augustine oriented their search for the right, most just way to live teleologically; that is, by the end or purpose of living. For them, this question was not simply one question among others; rather, it was *the* question to be resolved in living and to be lived up to, for the end of human living was virtuous living. Plato and Aristotle expressed achievement of such a life as the goal of the common good, while Augustine and Aquinas understood that achievement as enjoyment of the gift of Eternal Beatitude.

Machiavelli, Hobbes, and Locke rejected the classical philosophical and theological tradition and reconceived the notion of the common good and virtue. In their new and reduced scheme of practical choices for human living, private or individual advantage displaces the common good, technological possibilities determine the economy, and economic well-being governs the body politic.[30] This reduction and reorientation narrows the "gulf between the is and the ought."[31] Political problems are recast as merely technical ones, and a vocabulary of rights and self-interest circumvents concern for duties, obligations, and the common good.

In the Platonic dialogues, the standard for the common good is the virtuous life lived. The course of one's life is to be charted by seeking after, assenting to, and living in accordance with that which reasonably is most choiceworthy and worthwhile; in other words, striving after and living the virtues. In the *Republic*, Socrates exhorted Glaucon to a life of the pursuit of virtue; the outcome of that quest is the "whole risk for a human being."[32] Indeed, Socrates tells his young friends who have gathered for conversation at the home of Polemarchus:

> Each of us must, to the neglect of other studies, above all, see to it that he is a seeker and student of that study by which he might be able to learn and find out what will give him the capacity and knowledge to distinguish the good and the bad life, and so everywhere and always choose the better from among those that are possible . . . to draw a conclusion and choose between the worse and the better life.[33]

On Socrates' account, justice in the soul and justice in the city are ineluctably related. Justice rises in the soul only when each of its three constituent parts—reason, spiritedness, and desire—performs its own work well and, thereby, serves the health and order of the whole.[34] As a consequence, each citizen is properly ordered toward every other citizen of the *polis*, with each one assigned what is intrinsically good for him and, hence, what is intrinsically good for the city. Each one finds his good in the good of the well-ordered city. The principle of the common good is the virtuous living of the whole community.

While the philosophy of Greek antiquity promoted virtue as both the realization of *man* and *his polis*, the practice of freedom and virtue was strictly proscribed. This tradition accommodated slavery on the grounds that it was natural for some to be slaves and others to be free. Historian David Brion Davis contends Plato supplied the "elements for a theory of intellectual inferiority as the natural basis for slavery" when he argued "a slave might hold a true belief but could never know the truth of his belief, since he was inherently deficient in reason."[35] Plato's philosophy also quartered contempt for women, "categoriz[ing] them together with children and animals, with the immature, the sick and the weak."[36] Even in the *Republic*, with its audacious inclusion of females among the ranks of the guardians, women are undermined. Philosopher Susan Okin points out that before Socrates introduces this revolutionary proposal,

> It is stressed that the impressionable young guardians are at all costs to be prevented from imitating the female sex in what are regarded as its characteristic activities—bickering boasting, uncooperative self-abandonment, blasphemy, and the frailties of sickness, love and labor. Women, easily deceived by worthless guardians, superstitious, prone to excessive grief, lacking in knowledge of what is good for them, and inferior in intellect and in general to men, are no more fit to serve as role models for the chosen youth [of Athens] than are madmen, craftsmen, or slaves.[37]

Aristotle opens his *Nicomachean Ethics* by questioning the proper purpose or end of man.[38] He asks about what is particular to human beings, for life is common even to plants. The function or end or purpose of the human being is to live out, to act out the distinctively rational life. This life as activity has two meanings: activity that is the origin of reasoning and activity that collaborates with reasoning. Corresponding to these two forms of activity are the intellectual and moral virtues, *arête* or the excellences. The end or purpose of man is the human good, the activity of virtue: the activity of the soul in conformity to the practice of virtue in a complete life.[39]

Virtues are concerned with actions and passions and are of two kinds—the intellectual and the moral. The virtues do not exist in human beings by nature, but rather by repeated action, by habit.[40] To attain virtue, a human being must know what he is doing and must do so for its own sake alone and not for any surplus benefit that might accrue. The pursuit and practice of virtue are voluntary and result from decision and choice.[41]

The teaching of the *Ethics* aimed to fit one for life in political community. If the purpose or end of a single individual and the state are the same, that is, virtue, "that of the state seems at all events something greater and more complete whether to attain or to preserve; though it is worthwhile to attain the end merely for one man, it is finer and more godlike to attain it for a nation or for city-states."[42] For Aristotle, the good of a single individual is the same as the good of the state, but it is only in the state that this good can be realized in its fullness.[43] According to Aristotle, "man is by nature an animal intended to live in a polis" and whosoever is without a polis is an aberration or a beast or a god.[44] Although the polis is prior to the individual, the individual does not exist for the end or common good of the state, but the common good poses no opposition to the individual's private good. Constituted, then, by free men of good birth, of good nature, of virtue, of wealth, the polis was the public sphere, the locus of political life.

Aristotle distinguishes among those human beings who are free, those who are slavish by nature, and those who are good individuals. Free persons are capable of orienting themselves and their actions toward the common good of their households and of the state.[45] Slaves lack an innate or natural disposition toward freedom and cannot control their own lives; they have no common share in the responsibility for the household; they have no common share in the state. And "on the level of the master-slave relationship, there is no common good."[46] The free man, the *polites* or citizen, is the one who has the capacity for active participation in political life and, thus, with and for the common good. Nor, is the citizen simply identical with a person who resides in the city-state: women, children, slaves, foreigners, and metics all inhabit the polis without participating as citizens. The citizen in the strict sense is "a man who shares in the administration of justice and the holding of office."[47]

A concept of distributive justice figured prominently in Aristotle's account of the common good. Distributive justice established an equality of proportion between the members of a social body. Those who constituted the polis shared in the obligations, responsibilities, and honors necessary to maintain it, each in proportion to his position in the social order.[48] The determination and realization of the common good entailed the recognition of diversity, as well as ample admixtures of discernment, of sagacity, and of prudence. Finally, Aristotle further distinguished between the good citizen and the good man: the latter is always and everywhere the same, the former relative to the regime. Only in the instance of the best regime is the good man and the good citizen one and the same.[49]

The core of classical teaching on the common good continued, with theological modification, in the work of Augustine and Thomas Aquinas. Their appropriation and transposition of the common good gave full weight to divine revelation, thus sublating the classical notion of the common good to Christianity's promise of a supernatural end for human persons. While neither theologian contested the hierarchy of the social class structures under which they lived, they taught that each human person—male and female, ruler and ruled, free and enslaved, lord and serf—was to live a life of virtue. Augustine held that the good or virtuous, even if poor or enslaved, were free; the wicked or those given to vice and corruption, even if rulers or slaveholders, were enslaved.[50] Augustine and Aquinas wrote of human freedom, primarily, although not exclusively, in relation to will, human choice, virtue, and the human response to and reception of divine grace. While they considered freedom as integral to human nature, most basically, they understood freedom as a gift from God to be exercised in conformity with the divine will. In a lived life of conformity to the will of God, a lived life of virtue and goodness, human beings have and express their true and only freedom.[51]

For Augustine, the common good primarily consists in loving union with God, the Uncreated Common Good, who is the End to whom the human person is ordained. Plato and Aristotle allowed the existence of a life higher than political activity, a life devoted to philosophy, to contemplation. Augustine shares their view, but insists that happiness rests only in the contemplation of God, knowable through divine revelation, grasped in faith, and experienced in the Beatific Vision. Augustine's ethics is an ethic of love: "For if God is man's supreme good . . . to seek the supreme good is to live well, [and] to live well is nothing else but to love God with all the heart, with all the soul, with all the mind."[52]

With Aristotle, Aquinas held that human beings were by nature social: "When we consider all that is necessary for human life, it becomes clear that man is naturally a social and political animal, destined more than all other animals to live in community."[53] Given all that is necessary for human life, one individual alone is not able to furnish himself or herself with all that is necessary; no lone individual's resources are adequate to the complexity and fullness of human life. Nature has destined human beings to live in society; and, by dividing the labor among themselves, each may devote himself or herself to some branch of science, some interest, some occupation. Thus, the communal well-being of a group exists as a *first approximation* of the common good: personal relations, associations, friendships, and, in particular, marriage contribute this end. The welfare of the body politic constitutes a *second approximation* of the common good; its achievement depends upon legislation. Human law is a dictate of practical reason for the common good, framed either by the whole people or by public officials charged with this responsibility. As the end of human living is happiness, law is ordered to the design of all things in order to achieve that happiness, which finds its proximate fulfillment in virtue, the end or purpose of human law.[54] Like Aristotle, Aquinas's discussion of the common good adverts to distributive justice: "a habit whereby a man renders to each one his due by constant and perpetual will."[55] As a general virtue, justice directs the human person in his or her relations with others and with the social whole. Justice is concrete rather than speculative; it governs actions. On his assessment, injustice is a special vice: it holds the common good in contempt and may lead to sin and the disruption of the equality between human persons.[56]

Finally, for Aquinas, the universe is not some self-contained, self-sufficient order: "the whole universe mounts by the inmost desires of every part to an end outside itself."[57] Thus, the *third approximation* locates the common good in the universal goodness of God who, while transcending the created universe, nurtures, sustains, and embraces the whole and all its parts. The theological virtues open the human person to loving relationship with the perfect society, the Trinity. The Aristotelian notion of perfect happiness as contemplation is transformed in light of the Beatific Vision. And the "glow from the heavenly city, far from blurring the earthly city in a haze, makes it clear and real."[58]

The philosopher Leo Strauss situates the break with classical understanding of the common good within the trajectory of political thought initiated in the bold and subtle meditations of Niccolo Machiavelli.[59] Here he counsels rulers on public and private behavior: "It is *not necessary* that a prince should have all of the [good] qualities, but it is certainly necessary that he *appear* to have them."[60] But, it is useful for a ruler to appear "to be compassionate, faithful, humane, upright, and religious" and equally useful to know how should it become necessary to change to the contrary.[61] Further, Machiavelli observes, a wise ruler—one who knows the ways of the fox and the ways of the lion—cannot and should not uphold prior promises if to do so means that the ruler would be disadvantaged or that the conditions leading to those promises no longer existed. "If all men were good, this principle would not be good; but since men are a contemptible lot, and would not keep their promises to you, you too need not keep yours to them."[62] This departure from the classical understanding of virtue is presented in terms of defense of the state, which, carried out by the prince, implies defense of the common good. The well-being of the citizens is identified with the well-being, cunning, and virtue of the prince. Machiavelli continues:

> It must be understood that a prince, and in particular a new prince, cannot observe all those things by which men are considered good, for it is often necessary, in order to maintain the state, to act against your word, against charity, against kindness, against religion. And so, he must have a mind ready to turn itself according as the winds of fortune and the fluctuation of things command him.[63]

The Florentine considered the exhortations and prescriptions of the classical tradition too exacting, too demanding. He opposed its idealism with an approach that sought to replace any imaginary or absolute or transcendent standard.[64] Although he retained the preservation of the common good as the standard for political action, now what counted was the *actual* practice of politics. Machiavelli's new teaching on the common good calls for the reinterpretation of virtue. Classical political philosophy was a quest for a political order most conducive to the practice of virtue, to how human beings *ought* to live together. According to this tradition, the establishment of the best regime depended necessarily upon chance, since the chief ingredient in any regime is the nature of the people available, and that availability is subject to chance: corrupt people will bring about a corrupt regime. What the classical tradition considered elusive, patient of *fortuna* or chance, Machiavelli claimed could be controlled by the use of force: the best regime was not subject to chance and, to use a very modern term, engineered.[65] Strauss observes that what had been for Aristotle an impossibility is for Machiavelli only a very great difficulty. The difficulty can be overcome by an outstanding man who uses extraordinary means in order to transform a corrupt matter into a good matter; that obstacle to the establishment of the best regime which is man as matter, the human material can be overcome because that matter can be transformed.[66]

The ancient connection between virtue as ethical action and custom and law was broken. To quote Strauss again, Machiavelli upended virtue: "Virtue must not be understood as that for the sake of which the commonwealth exists, but virtue exists exclusively for the sake of the commonwealth; political life proper is not subject to morality."[67] Or in Kant's later formulation:

> It only remains for men to create a good organisation for the state, a task which is well within their capability, and to arrange it in such a way that their self-seeking energies are opposed to one another, each thereby neutralising or eliminating the destructive effects of the rest. And as far as reason is concerned, the result is the same as if man's selfish tendencies were non-existent, so that man, even if he is not morally good in himself, is nevertheless compelled to be a good citizen. As hard as it may sound, the problem of setting up a state can be solved even by a nation of devils (so long as they possess understanding).[68]

Machiavelli's "new" teaching spawned the emergence of what is known as "modern" political philosophy, and Thomas Hobbes and John Locke serve as its foremost examples. Hobbes satirized the teaching of classical political philosophy as "books of the old moral philosophers."[69] He denied that human beings are naturally social and political and that true human happiness and true human good are to be found in contemplation.[70] Hobbes describes the mass of humankind as disposed toward a perpetual desire for power that ceases only at death.[71] Nature may have made human beings equal in faculties of body and mind, but the most important equality is the equal ability that each human being has to kill the others. Because human beings live in a constant and perpetual state of fear and danger of death, and because the fear of violent death is a most powerful passion, self-preservation is of utmost importance.[72] Competition, diffidence, and glory intensify this fear. Hobbes writes: "The first, maketh men invade for Gain; the second for Safety; and the third, for Reputation."[73] Enmity and rancor are deemed natural dispositions; every individual is enemy to every other, and men live in a constant state of war or what Hobbes calls the "state of nature":

> Wherein men live without other security, than what their own strength, and their own invention shall furnish them withall. In such condition, there is not place for Industry; because the fruit thereof is uncertain: and consequently not Culture of the Earth; no Navigation, nor use of the commodities that may be imported by Sea; no commodious Building; no Instruments of moving, and removing such things as require much force; no Knowledge of the face of the Earth; no account of Time; no Arts; no Letters; no Society; and which is worst of all, continuall feare, and danger of violent death; and the life of man is solitary, poore, nasty, brutish, and short.[74]

Whether or not such a state of nature all over the world ever existed does not concern Hobbes. The state of nature is a "logical, not an historical hypothesis."[75] It functions, Hobbes asserts, as an "Inference, made from the Passions" in order to conceptualize "what manner of life there would be, where there were no common Power to feare."[76]

To secure their self-preservation and, at the same time, remove themselves from the state of nature, individuals enter into a contract, an artificial, though necessary, compact creating the state. Since human nature makes each individual vulnerable, each one surrenders the natural right to self-preservation and submits to the "common power" required to appease the mass of people and "to direct their actions to the common benefit." Hence, the Commonwealth or great Leviathan, the "Mortall God" to which human beings owe their "peace and defence."[77] The Hobbsean social contract is twofold: (1) the covenant of each member of the civil body with each of the others to acknowledge as sovereign whatever man or assembly of men a majority of their number agrees upon; and (2) the vote determining who or what is the sovereign to be.[78] The state exists not for the good or virtuous life as Aristotle had taught, but for life only.

On Hobbes's account, life is rooted in raw, unrefined passions, the most powerful of which is the fear and danger of violent death. Self-preservation inclines human beings to peace. An individual may do or refrain from doing whatever one can to preserve one's life. As Machiavelli's political theory insinuated, but never explicitly stated, the right to an end implies a right to use the means to attain that end. Unlike the classical teachers who founded the city-state on friendship and virtue, and guided it by reason, Hobbes established the "new" state on enmity and self-regard, and steered it by fear. Like Machiavelli, Hobbes lowered the moral horizon to study things and people as they actually are, not as they ought to be.

John Locke concurred with the Hobbsean concept of the state of nature as a basis for constructing a political theory:

> To understand political power right, and derive it from its original, we must consider, what state all men are naturally in, and that is, a state of *perfect* freedom to order their actions, and dispose of their possessions and persons, as they think fit, within the bounds of the law of nature, without asking leave, or depending upon the will of any other man.[79]

The *Second Treatise on Government* acknowledges a natural state of equality "wherein all the power and jurisdiction is reciprocal, no one having more than another."[80] However, unlike Hobbes's account, Locke's explicitly distinguishes between liberty and license:

> [T]hough man in that state [of nature] have an uncontroulable liberty to dispose of his person or possessions, yet he has not liberty to destroy himself, or so much as any creature in his possession, but where some nobler use than its bare preservation calls for it. The state of nature has a law of nature to govern it, which obliges every one: and reason, which is that law, teaches all mankind, who will but consult it, that being all *equal and independent*, no one ought to harm another in his life, health, liberty, or possessions.[81]

The state of nature produces a kind of perfect equality in which no one has superiority or jurisdiction over another. For Locke, self-preservation holds utmost importance, but unless threatened one may not impair or assault the life, liberty, health of another, or whatever may be necessary to another's preservation. Should an individual transgress the laws of nature, invade the rights of others, do violence or harm to others, those same laws allow punishment of the offender: "in the state of nature, everyone has the executive power of the law of nature."[82] In this way, one man comes to power over another; but that power is neither absolute nor arbitrary; reason triumphs over passion.[83]

Strauss argues that the right to "comfortable self-preservation" stands as the pivot of John Locke's teaching.[84] Each individual has a natural right to the means of life, to the means of self-preservation, to property. Through one's physical or bodily labor and the work of one's hands, whatever an individual removes from out of the common state that nature has provided becomes the property of that individual. No one else has a right to what an individual's labor has achieved. Locke states:

> God gave the world to men in common; but since he gave it them for their benefit, and the greatest conveniences of life they were capable to draw from it, it cannot be supposed he meant it should always remain common and uncultivated. He gave it to the use of the industrious and rational, (and labour was to be his title to it;) not to the fancy or covetousness of the quarrelsome and contentious.[85]

Thus, labor gives rise to the distinction between the common and the private. By labor, one takes what is necessary for self-preservation out of what is common and claims it for one's own.[86] "The great and chief end, therefore of men's uniting into commonwealths, and putting themselves under government," Locke declares, "is the preservation of their property."[87] Thus, civil government comes into existence through mutual contract for the preservation of the means to life—property, since in the state of nature the enjoyment of one's possessions remains uncertain and continually exposed to the avarice of others.

The concept of property forms a central and distinctive feature of Locke's political philosophy. Property antedates civil society and is independent of it; it is an institution of the laws of nature, acquired by man through his labor and the work of his hands. Labor is the only title to property that accords with natural right. Initially, that labor is devoted to meeting sheer physical or vital needs. But soon necessity gives way to comfort: the man subdued in the *Republic* and made virtuous in the *Ethics* now turns to accumulation and luxury.

For Aristotle, the state did not exist for the sake of protection and security alone, but for Locke these were its end, origin, and purpose. Civil society exists for the sake of facilitating the continuing acquisition of property, of money. Man and his possessions moved to the center of the moral universe. Two consequences of Locke's teaching are: first, that the common good is now apprehended in terms of a distinction between the public and private, and the preservation of private possessions now vies for primacy over the common good; and second, commerce and economics, rather than character and virtue, come to occupy a central place in discussions about political things, about the right and the best way to live.

The most famous of all the American state papers, the Declaration of Independence, offers this concept of the morally free individual: "We hold these truths to be self-evident: that all men are created equal; that they are endowed by their Creator with certain inalienable rights; that among these are life, liberty, and the pursuit of happiness." While the U.S. Constitution would detail these inalienable rights, despite protestations to equality, the founding documents were patently selective: only white males owning property or the means thereof were included or eligible for full citizenship. *De facto*, women were excluded, since they were mere extensions of their husbands and fathers; *de jure*, the enslaved Africans were chattel, property, and had no share or participation in personal, sovereignal, or civic freedom; thus the presence of "internal slavery" in a self-professed modern society and the "civic repression" of women.[88]

These new political philosophers argued that the individual human being by nature is complete, independent, prior to, and above society. They conceived of society as an aggregate of autonomous individuals or units cooperating only when the terms of that cooperation advanced the ends or advantage of the parties involved. Such a contractual notion of society displaced the organic understanding held by Aristotle and Aquinas of society as natural to human beings and to our flourishing. The moral fact of civil society was no longer to be understood in terms of obligation or duty, but in terms of *rights*. The citizen no longer correlated personal good with the common good of the social whole, and the standard by which human beings might orient their living was lowered considerably. Virtue was reinterpreted on the basis not of how human beings ought to live, but on the basis of how human beings *actually, in fact*, do live. With this reduction of the moral horizon, self-preservation and the means to it dominate: life *is* solitary, mean, nasty, brutish, and short. The meaning of the common good narrows to a set of entitlements for those who manifest themselves to be the stronger, more powerful, and privileged. The common good was reduced to "the anarchistic conception of individualistic materialism in which the whole function of the city is to safeguard the liberty of each; thus giving the strong full freedom to oppress the weak."[89]

This brief sketch so far has emphasized the shifting, even antagonistic meanings of freedom and slavery, the common good and virtue. Probing these meanings opens a window on the cultural and social orders through which we comport ourselves as historical beings. For Western philosophical concerns and practical political strategies for freedom, the common good and justice have become part of a global conversation. But as Novak states, the current problematic facing liberal societies is that "pluralism seems to render the concept of the common good vacuous" and more amenable to the transient idea of common purpose.[90] Certainly, those who differ one from another may have a common purpose, but even if as he holds, "the chances are overwhelming, at least in genuinely pluralistic societies (of internally various belief systems and perceptual grids)" that people will differ in their understandings of the good—both the common good and their own personal good.⁹¹ But social difference troubles the notion of the common good.

DIFFERENCE

A generic definition of the notion of difference posits some quality or feature of unlikeness among two or more things, events, places, or persons. For instance, the ball used in soccer differs from the ball used in American football in obvious and external features of size, shape, and composition. The soccer ball and the football have different uses and cannot be substituted in playing the sport particular to each. Both a soccer ball and the football and basketball differ from a tennis ball. Still, there is no mistaking tennis for soccer or soccer for tennis. Or consider soccer again: the fans of each team enact various rituals—distinctive hand signals or gestures, face painting or dress—at every game with zany zeal and intensity. Invariably, sports reporters comment on the "religious" fervor of the fans, yet no one confuses these events for the worship of Anglicans or Roman Catholics or Baptists. Some events are so complex that they may prove difficult to distinguish or define. For example, what may be thought to be a war for democracy might, in fact, be a war for oil and dominance.

The social critic Himani Bannerji rightly cautions that we not overlook or erase or elide "distinction[s] between different kinds of differences."⁹² To follow her point, differences that are encoded as gender, race, and class "are structured through power relations."⁹³ In other words, social oppression is one of the differences that power differentials (differences in power and position or status) effect. The political theorist Iris Marion Young extends the notion of social oppression to designate "the disadvantage and injustice some people suffer not because a tyrannical power coerces them, but because of the everyday practices of a well-intentioned liberal society."⁹⁴ Social oppression denotes those "systemic constraints" placed on groups by a few people's choices or policies. The structuring and causes of social oppression are embedded in unquestioned norms, habits, and symbols, in the assumptions underlying institutional rules and the collective consequences of following those rules. It names (as Marion Frye puts it) "an enclosing structure of forces and barriers which tends to the immobilization and reduction of a group or category of people." In this extended sense, oppression refers to the vast and deep injustices that some groups suffer as a consequence of often unconscious assumptions and reactions of well-meaning people in ordinary interactions, media and cultural stereotypes, and structural features of bureaucratic hierarchies and market mechanisms—in short, the normal processes of everyday life.[95]

The practice of civic freedom in the United States, our electoral, legislative, even dissenting procedures, disguise the ways in which oppression structurally or systemically is "reproduced in major economic, political, cultural, and [religious] institutions."[96] At the same time, for too many of our citizens, gender, race, ethno-cultural origin, economic condition, and incarceration proscribe the exercise of personal and sovereignal freedom. Liberal societies may insist on the protection of the rights of individuals, but anti-Semitism, racism, sexism, and homophobia constitute restrictions for individual members of certain social groups in the attempt to exercise that freedom.

While a social group is a collection of people, it is not a collection merely. The notion of social group implies "a specific kind of collectivity, with specific consequences for how people understand one another and themselves."[97] On Young's analysis, basic features shape a social group: differentiation that distinguishes one group from at least one other group through characteristic cultural forms or mores, practices, or way of living; group affinity and preference by members for association with group members; and structuring relations to at least one other group.[98] While group differentiation is never intrinsically oppressive, some groups have been formed out of shared or common experiences of oppression or privilege and/or power structure relations between many groups.[99] A social group may be defined as oppressed when its members as a group experience one of the following five conditions: exploitation, marginalization, powerlessness, cultural imperialism, and violence, each of which severely circumscribes the three constitutive elements of freedom—the personal, sovereignal, and civic.

With the term *exploitation*, Young underscores "that oppression occurs through a steady process of the transfer of the result of the labor of one social group to the benefit of another."[100] The injustice of class exploitation consists not only in gross inequities in the distribution of goods and services in a society but also in structuring damaging relations between social groups.[101] Exploitation has a decisive impact on the common good, which, somewhat inaccurately, is conflated almost exclusively with the economic order; moreover, exploitation circumscribes each of the constitutive elements of freedom—the personal, sovereignal, and civic.

Marginalization stands as a particularly insidious form of oppression, since it seeks to expel an entire group or category of people from meaningful and beneficial participation in the common good, subordinating them to material and/or psychological deprivation, even extermination.[102]

The theory of social relations that Young has delineated locates domination in modern society as a practice. That practice is "enacted through the widely dispersed powers of many agents mediating the decisions of others."[103] Thus, to some extent, many people may hold power in relation to or over others even though they lack deliberative and decisive power over policies.[104] The powerless are those who lack even mediated authority, "those over whom power is exercised without their ever exercising it."[105]

Control and dominance over the means of mediation, interpretation, and communication in a society may be defined as *cultural imperialism*. Cultural imperialism entails not only the "universalization of a dominant group's experience and culture, [but] the establishment of that [experience and] culture as the norm."[106] Often, the cultural products of a dominant group function not only as characteristically their own but as the ideal representative of human achievement as such. Further, Young argues, "The culturally dominated undergo a paradoxical oppression, in that they are both marked out by stereotypes and at the same time rendered invisible."[107] Cultural imperialism defines, positions, and fixes the dominated "other" in a nest of meanings with which they do not identify and which do not reflect their appropriation and interpretation of their cultural, social, aesthetic, or philosophic experience.[108] All too poignantly, women and men of these social groups internalize the dominant culture's "stereotyped and inferiorized images" of themselves, at least insofar as they are forced to react to the behavior of others who are influenced by those images.[109]

Finally, members of oppressed groups suffer *systemic violence*. Members of these social groups live with the dread of random, unprovoked attacks on their persons or property. So, in the United States, Asians, indigenous peoples, women, gay men and lesbians, Arabs, Jews, Puerto Ricans, Chicanos, and black people, nationally, regionally, and municipally, live under such violence and threats of violence—sometimes from one another, sometimes from the dominant group. A key dimension of random, xenophobic violence is its irrationality and unpredictability. It is motivated by the fear or hatred privileged groups experience in relation to these marginalized, powerless social others.[110]

GRACE AND THE COMMON GOOD

In this third section, the driving question is the implication of the gift of divine grace for human living in our social context. This question intends both the cultural and the social; it addresses *structures of disintegration* and evokes *structures of integrity*. Our response depends upon our exercise of free will, upon our concrete personal and communal cooperation with God's gift of grace. For grace is what makes the *difference*; it is the differential in the human effort to realize the common good. On this point, Bernard Lonergan is worth quoting at length:

> Without faith the originating value is man and the terminal value is the human good man brings about. But in the light of faith, originating value is divine light and love, while terminal value is the whole universe. So the human good becomes absorbed in an all-encompassing good. . . . Human development is not only in skills and virtues but also in holiness. The power of God's love brings forth a new energy and efficacy in all goodness, and the limit of human expectation ceases to be the grave. Without faith, without the eye of love, the world is too evil for God to be good, for a good God to exist. But faith recognizes that God grants men their freedom, that he wills them to be persons and not just his automata, that he calls them to the higher authenticity that overcomes evil with good. So faith is linked with human progress and it has to meet the challenge of human decline. Faith places human efforts in a friendly universe; it reveals an ultimate significance in human achievement; it strengthens new undertakings with confidence.[111]

Thus, if we are to advance justice, and so resist decline in our social context, we must develop in attentiveness to differentiated human experience, in understanding the concrete human situation, in reasonableness in our judgments. We must decide and carry out what is good and right in response to the human situation. This development in knowing and doing is the means by which we women and men can take *intelligent control* of cultural and social orders in the realization of the common good. Thus, our personal response to the offer of grace is made manifest in our interpersonal relations and inscribed in our ordering of the social matrix and our understanding that our "good is also God's glory."[112]

Still, our control is flawed, and not only control of that social world: we women and men limp in the disequilibrium of moral impotence. Full self-development and concrete, practical realization of that development in society is a long and difficult process. (Although, it is true, it would be even longer and even more difficult *without* divine grace.) There is a painful gap between the conditioned effective exercise of our freedom and the hypothetical exercise of freedom we would make, if conditions were otherwise. Our own awareness of our own moral impotence heightens the tension between the limitations of *who we happen to be* (conditioned by various social and personal circumstances, psychic development, decisions and actions) and the transcending dynamism toward the person *whom we are called to be*. This data on our moral selves is fraught with ambiguity: on the one hand, there are those occasions that startle and humble us, that remind us that our living is a developing and that we may profit from failure; on the other hand, there are occasions that stand as stark evidence of our eagerness to lower our moral horizon and rest content with ourselves as we are, to lose ourselves in the herd.[113]

When this gap in our knowing (what is good, right, just) and doing (what is good, right, just) spills into institutions, structures, and roles in the social order, our moral failure in converted human living is refracted back to us in those institutions, structures, and roles that constitute the social order. Once the surd or the irrational, once moral impotence and failure become commonplace in the social order, we are pulled down in an undertow, not toward God, but toward the reign of sin.[114] The social surd can be reversed, can become potential good only as we women and men cooperate with the *gift of grace* in the social order—as we meet evil with good, love those who hate us, pray for those who persecute and oppress us. To quote Lonergan again:

> It is not propaganda and it is not argument but religious faith that will liberate human reasonableness from its ideological prisons. It is not the promises [of human beings] but religious hope that can enable [us] to resist the vast pressures of social decay. If passions are to quiet down, if wrongs are not to be exacerbated, not ignored, not merely palliated,

but acknowledged and removed, then human possessiveness and human pride have to be replaced by the charity of the suffering servant, by self-sacrificing love.[115]

Put compactly, the transcendent solution to the problem of the common good is presented to us in the life-death-resurrection of Jesus of Nazareth, the Christ of God. Such love absorbs the irrationality of sin, the contrivance of evil, breaks the cycle of decline that obstructs the concrete realization of the common good in society.

CONCLUSION

I began with a review of the tensions between notions of freedom and slavery and the common good in the Western intellectual tradition; by sketching how oppression, even in a modern liberal society, damages human persons, I hoped to suggest as well how oppression interrupts and distorts the common good. By bringing forward the role of faith, of grace in the social order, I hoped to engage the most basic, constituent—that is, transcendent—dimension of the human spirit.

The difficulties of attempting to live out personal, sovereignal, and civic freedom and virtue in the realization of the common good come to the fore in a conversation between Miriam and Moses: "This freedom is more than a notion," she says. "It's a good thing. It's bound to be a good thing 'cause everybody wants it. But maybe I didn't know what to do with it 'cause I ain't been so happy."[116] Freedom, as Hurston's Moses counsels, *is* a "funny thing."[117] The experience of freedom may leave a people tremulous, tentative, even frightened, or it may leave them exhilarated, heady, even reckless. In the context of Moses's reply, just what it means to be a "fine nation" may imply steering between fearful isolation from others and reckless exploitation of others.

NOTES

1. Zora Neale Hurston, *Moses, Man of the Mountain* (1939; New York: Harper Perennial, 1991), 268.

2. Deborah McDowell, "Foreword: Lines of Descent/Dissenting Lines," in Hurston, *Moses, Man of the Mountain*, xvi.

3. *Kristallnacht*, also known as "The Night of the Broken Glass," was a coordinated attack on Jewish people in parts of Germany and Austria from November 9–10 in 1938 and was carried out by *Die Stumabtellung* (the Storm Detachment or paramilitary Brown Shirts) and non-Jewish civilians. The name *Kristallnacht* comes from the shards of broken window glass that lay in the streets after the windows of Jewish synagogues and Jewish-owned buildings and stores were smashed, and Jewish hospitals, homes, and schools were ransacked. Over one thousand synagogues were burned; more than one hundred Jews were killed in these attacks, and thirty thousand were arrested and placed in concentration camps. See Martin Gilbert, *Kristallnacht: Prelude to Destruction* (2006; New York: Harper Perennial, 2007), and James M. Deem, *Kristallnacht: The Nazi Terror That Began the Holocaust* (Berkeley Heights, NJ: Enslow Publishers, Inc., 2011).

4. As early as the fall of 1933, Adolf Hitler had planned the expansion of Germany through the "dismemberment of the Central European states" and their incorporation into a *Bund* or association; however, this association would consist of conquered and colonized territories, "auxiliary nations, without economies and polities of their own." These nations included Austria, Bohemia, Moravia, and western Poland as well as France, Flanders, Holland, Denmark, Norway, and Sweden, writes Diemut Majer in his *"Non-Germans" under the Third Reich: The Nazi Judicial and Administrative System in Germany and Occupied Eastern Europe with Special Regard to Occupied Poland, 1939–1945* (Baltimore: The Johns Hopkins University Press, 2003), 188–89.

5. It is also well to remember that after the attack on Pearl Harbor, the U.S. government in 1942 ordered the internment of more than 110,000 persons of Japanese heritage living within the continental United States and on the Pacific coast; more than 60 percent of these persons were American citizens. See Roger Daniels, *Prisoners Without Trial: Japanese Americans in World War II* (New York: Hill & Wang, 2004); Ann Whiston Spirn, *Daring to Look: Dorothea Lange's Photographs and Reports from the Field* (Chicago: University of Chicago Press, 2009).

6. Both J. Severino Croatto, *Exodus: A Hermeneutics of Freedom* (Maryknoll, NY: Orbis Books, 1981), 18, and Michael Walzer, *Exodus and Revolution* (New York: Basic Books, 1985), 32, identify Egyptian oppression of the ancient Israelites as linked to state or political power; thus, the Exodus possesses social (i.e., political, economic, and technological) implications and consequences.

7. Michael Novak, *Free Persons and the Common Good* (Lanham, MD: Madison Books, 1989), 20.

8. My use of the notion of decline comes from Bernard Lonergan, *Insight:, A Study of Human Understanding*, 5th ed., rev. aug., *Collected Works of Bernard Lonergan*, volume 3 (Toronto: University of Toronto Press, 1988), 251–63.

9. Zygmunt Bauman, *Freedom* (Minneapolis: University of Minnesota Press, 1988), 9.

10. Orlando Patterson, *Freedom in the Making of Western Culture* (New York: Basic Books, 1991), xv.

11. Patterson, *Freedom in the Making of Western Culture*, 3.

12. Patterson, *Freedom in the Making of Western Culture*, 3–4.

13. Patterson notes: "Sovereignal freedom is always relative. At one extreme stands the person who is absolutely free with respect to another, namely the slave master or absolute ruler; at the other extreme is the person who has no freedom with respect to another, namely, the slave in relation to [the] master. Between the two are all other human beings with more or less power or freedom, with respect to the others." Patterson, *Freedom in the Making of Western Culture*, 4.

14. Patterson, *Freedom in the Making of Western Culture*, 4.

15. Patterson, *Slavery and Social Death: A Comparative Study* (Cambridge, MA: Harvard University Press, 1982), 13.

16. Patterson, *Slavery and Social Death*, 2.

17. Jean Jacques Rousseau, *The Social Contract and Discourses*, Book 1, chapter 3.

18. Patterson, *Slavery and Social Death*, 18.

19. Nahum Glazer, ed., *The Passover Haggadah* (New York: Schocken Books, 1969), 49.

20. *Deuteronomy* 26:5–10.

21. *Deuteronomy* 24:14, 18. All biblical quotations are taken from *The New Oxford Annotated Bible*, New Revised Standard Version, 3rd ed., augmented (Oxford: Oxford University Press, 2007).

22. Walzer, *Exodus and Revolution*, 76.

23. Galatians 5:1.

24. Mark 10:43–44; cf Matthew 20:26–27, Luke 22:26.

25. Mark 10:45.

26. Jennifer A. Glancy, *Slavery in Early Christianity* (2002; Minneapolis: Fortress Press, 2006), 139–52.

27. David Brion Davis, *The Problem of Slavery in Western Culture* (Ithaca: Cornell University Press, 1966), 90.

28. In writing and in speaking, I deploy inclusive or nonsexist language as is appropriate, but in this chapter in citing quotations from the premodern and modern authors, I have not changed their usage of masculine noun and pronouns.

29. My argument here draws on my reading of Leo Strauss and his thesis of "three waves of modernity": Machiavelli begins the first, Rousseau the second, and Nietzsche the third; see *Political Philosophy*, ed. Hilail Gildin (Indianapolis, IN: Bobbs-Merrill, 1975), especially 81–98; see also his *Natural Right and History* (1950; Chicago: University of Chicago Press, 1953), especially 35–119.

30. Strauss, *Political Philosophy*, 123.

31. Strauss, *Political Philosophy*, 91.

32. Plato, *Republic*, trans. with notes and an interpretative essay by Allan Bloom (New York: Basic, 1968), 618c.

33. Plato, *Republic*, 618d, e.

34. Plato, *Republic*, 439d–441a.

35. Davis, *The Problem of Slavery in Western Culture*, 6; see also Gregory Vlastos, "Slavery in Plato's Thought," *The Philosophical Review* 50, no. 3 (May 1941): 289–304.

36. Susan Moller Okin, *Women in Western Political Thought* (Princeton, NJ: Princeton University Press, 1979), 22. It is well to remember that no woman participates in person in any of the Socratic dialogues (even though the high point of the discourse of the *Symposium* is said to come from the mouth of the priestess Diotima).

37. Okin, *Women in Western Political Thought*, 23.

38. All references are taken from Aristotle, *Nicomachean Ethics*, trans. W. D. Ross (Oxford: Clarendon, 1925).

39. Aristotle, *Nicomachean Ethics*, 1094b, 7–9; 1097a; 1098a. Aristotle defines virtue as "a state of character concerned with choice, lying in a mean, i.e., the mean relative to us, this being determined by a rational principle, and by that principle by which the man of practical wisdom would determine it," ibid., 1107a, 1–3.

40. "Actions, then, are called just and temperate when they are such as the just or the temperate man would do; but it is not the man who does these that is just and temperate, but the man who also does them *as* just and temperate men do them. It is well said, then, that it is by doing just acts that the just man is produced, and by doing temperate acts the temperate man; without doing these no one would have even a prospect of becoming good." Aristotle, *Nicomachean Ethics*, 1105b, 5–15.

41. Aristotle, *Nicomachean Ethics*, 1110–13.

42. Aristotle, *Nicomachean Ethics*, 1094b, 7–9.

43. Aristotle, *Politics*, trans. with an introduction, notes, and appendix by Ernest Barker (1946; London: Oxford University Press, 1958): "When we come to the final and perfect association, formed from a number of villages, we have already reached the *polis*—an association which may be said to have reached the height of full self-sufficiency; or rather (to speak more exactly) we may say that while it grows for the sake of mere life (and is so far, and at that stage, still short of full self-sufficiency), it exists (when once it is fully grown) for the sake of a good life," 1252b.

44. Aristotle, *Nicomachean Ethics*, 1253a.

45. Aristotle, *Metaphysics*, trans Hugh Tredennick (1935; 1936; 1947; 1958; Cambridge, MA: Harvard University, Loeb, 1962), 12.10, 3.

46. See Mary P. Nichols, "The Good Life, Slavery, and Acquisition: Aristotle's Introduction to Politics," *Interpretation (A Journal of Political Philosophy)* 11, no. 2 (May 1983): 171–83; see also David Ross, who writes, "It is, though regrettable, not surprising that Aristotle should regard as belonging to the nature of things an arrangement that was so familiar a part of everyday Greek life as slavery was." *Aristotle* (London: Methuen, 1953), 241.

47. Aristotle, *Politics*, 1274b, 32.

48. "As each rival claimant moderates his claim, in the light of the awareness that it can be turned against him, the idea of a common good in which the rival claims can be harmonized emerges. And the idea of the common good necessarily implies both a limitation upon the absolutized claims of each party—including that of virtue—and a priority of the claims of virtue," ibid.

49. Leo Strauss, *What Is Political Philosophy and Other Studies* (1959; Westport, CT: Greenwood, 1973), 35.

50. Augustine, *City of God*, David Knowles (Harmondsworth: Penguin Books, 1972), Book IV, chapter 3.

51. Yet for Augustine, women remained a "special symbol of evil." See Margaret Farley, "Sources of Sexual Inequality in the History of Christian Thought," *Journal of Religion* 56, no. 2 (April 1976): 37. Aquinas argued that regarding individual nature, women are "defective and misbegotten." He maintained that women had souls, but reasoned they did not fully bear the imprint of the *imago dei* or image of God—this was possible only for men (*Summa Theologiae, Pars Prima*. Qs. 90–93).

52. Augustine, *De moribus eccl.*, 1, 25, 46, cited in Frederick Copleston, *A History of Philosophy* (1950; 1952; Westminster, MD: Newman, 1955), vol. 2, *Medieval Philosophy: Augustine to Scotus*, 82.

53. Thomas Aquinas, "On Princely Government," chapter 1 in *Aquinas: Selected Political Writings*, ed. A. P. D'Entreves, trans. J. G. Dawson (Oxford: Basil Blackwell, 1959).

54. All references are taken from Thomas Aquinas, *Summa Theologiae*, trans. Blackfriars (New York: McGraw-Hill, 1966): *S. T.* I-II, q.90, a.2, resp.; a.3, resp.; q.92, a.1, resp., ad.1.

55. Aquinas, *Summa Theologiae*, q. 58, a.1.

56. Aquinas, *Summa Theologiae*, q. 59, a.1.

57. Thomas Gilby, *Between Community and Society: A Philosophy and Theology of the State* (London: Longmans, Green, 1953), 213.

58. Thomas Gilby, *The Political Thought of St. Thomas Aquinas* (Chicago: University of Chicago Press, 1958), 327.

59. Leo Strauss, *Political Philosophy*, ed. Hilail Gildin (Indianapolis: Bobbs-Merrill, 1975). Strauss poses the thesis of "three waves of modernity": Machiavelli begins the first, Rousseau the second, and Nietzsche the third, 81–89; see also his *Natural Right and History* (1950; Chicago: University of Chicago Press, 1953), 35–119.

60. Niccolo Machiavelli, *The Prince* [1513], trans. and ed. Mark Musa (New York: St. Martin's Press, 1964): "It must be understood that a prince, and in particular a new prince, cannot observe all those things by which men are considered good, for it is often necessary, in order to maintain the state, to act against your word, against charity, against kindness, against religion. And so, he must have a mind ready to turn itself according as the winds of fortune and the fluctuation of things command him, and, as I said above, he must not separate himself from the good, if he is able, but he must know how to take up evil, should it be necessary," xviii.

61. Machiavelli, *The Prince*.

62. Machiavelli, *The Prince*.

63. Machiavelli, *The Prince*.

64. Warren Winiarski, "Niccolo Machiavelli," in *History of Political Philosophy*, ed. Leo Strauss and Joseph Cropsey (1963; Chicago: Rand McNally and Company, 1969), 270–71.

65. Machiavelli, *The Prince*: "[M]any have imagined republics and principalities that have never been seen or known to exist in reality; for there is such a gap between how one lives and how one should live that he who neglects what is being done for what should be done will learn his destruction rather than his preservation. . . . It is necessary for a prince who wishes to maintain his position to learn how not to be good, and to use it or not according to necessity," xv.

66. Strauss, *Political Philosophy*, 85.

67. Strauss, *Political Philosophy*, 86.

68. Immanuel Kant, "Perpetual Peace: A Philosophical Sketch," (1795) in *Kant's Political Writings*, ed. Hans Reiss, trans. H. B. Nisbet (Cambridge: Cambridge University Press, 1970; 1977; reprint ed. 1979), 112.

69. All references are taken from Thomas Hobbes, *Leviathan* (1651), ed. Nelle Fuller, *Great Books of the Western World*, vol. 23 (Chicago: Encyclopedia Britannica, 1952); the comparative edition, ed. C. B. Macpherson, *Leviathan* (1968; Harmondsworth: Penguin Books Ltd., 1983), I, xi.

70. Laurence Berns, "Thomas Hobbes," in *History of Political Philosophy*, 356–57.

71. Hobbes, *Leviathan*, I, xi.

72. Hobbes, *Leviathan*, I, xi, 365, 367.

73. Hobbes, *Leviathan* I, xiii.

74. Hobbes, *Leviathan* I.

75. C. B. Macpherson, *The Political Theory of Possessive Individualism: Hobbes to Locke* (1962; Oxford: Oxford University Press, 1964, 1979), 20.

76. *Leviathan* I, xiii.

77. *Leviathan* II, xvii.

78. *Leviathan* II, xvii.

79. All references are taken from John Locke, *Second Treatise on Government* (1690), ed., with an introduction by C. B. Macpherson (Indianapolis: Hackett Publishing Company, Inc., 1980), §4.

80. Locke, *Second Treatise on Government*.

81. Locke, *Second Treatise on Government*, §6.

82. Locke, *Second Treatise on Government*, §13

83. Locke, *Second Treatise on Government*, §8.

84. Strauss, *Political Philosophy*, 89; also, 49–51.

85. Locke, *Second Treatise on Government*, §34.

86. Locke, *Second Treatise on Government*, §28, 35, 43–45.

87. Locke, *Second Treatise on Government*, §124.

88. For a discussion of citizenship, see Derek Heater, *A Brief History of Citizenship* (New York: New York University Press, 2004), 120–29, 77–78, 88–102. Heater writes, although the French Revolution brought the notion of citizenship to European consciousness, "virtually nowhere were slaves, Jews, or women accorded political rights," 80.

89. Jacques Maritain, *The Person and the Common Good*, trans. John J. Fitzgerald (1947; 1966; Notre Dame, IN: University of Notre Dame, 1972), 50; see also Leo Strauss, *The City and Man* (1964; Chicago: University of Chicago, 1978), 82.

90. Novak, *Free Persons and the Common Good*, 20.

91. Novak, *Free Persons and the Common Good*, 21.

92. Himani Bannerji, *The Dark Side of the Nation: Essays on Multiculturalism, Nationalism and Gender* (Toronto: Canadian Scholars Press, 2000), 131.

93. Bannerji, *The Dark Side of the Nation*, 132.

94. Iris Marion Young, *Justice and Politics of Difference* (Princeton: Princeton University Press, 1990), 41.

95. Young, *Justice and Politics of Difference*.

96. Young, *Justice and Politics of Difference*.

97. Young, *Justice and Politics of Difference*, 43.

98. Young, *Justice and Politics of Difference*.

99. Young, *Justice and Politics of Difference*, 47.

100. Young, *Justice and Politics of Difference*, 49.

101. Young, *Justice and Politics of Difference*, 49–50.

102. Young, *Justice and Politics of Difference*, 59.

103. Young, *Justice and Politics of Difference*, 56.

104. Young, *Justice and Politics of Difference*.
105. Young, *Justice and Politics of Difference*.
106. Young, *Justice and Politics of Difference*, 59. Bauman notes for individually successful members of racially or ethnically segregated groups, "there is no 'way out' from the group, however much they desire to get rid of the political, social or cultural deprivations associated with their ethnicity or race," Bauman, *Freedom*, 98.
107. Bauman, *Freedom*, 98.
108. Bauman, *Freedom*, 98. Thus the oppressed experience what W. E. B. Du Bois called "double consciousness." See his *The Souls of Black Folks* (1903; New York: Fawcett Publications, Inc., 1961): "It is a peculiar sensation, this double-consciousness, this sense of always looking at one's self through the eyes of others, of measuring one's soul by the tape of a world that looks on in amused contempt and pity. One ever feels his twoness—an American, a Negro; two souls, two thoughts, two unreconciled strivings; two warring ideals in one dark body, whose dogged strength alone keeps its from being torn asunder," 16–17.
109. Bauman, *Freedom*.
110. Bauman, *Freedom*, 63.
111. Bernard Lonergan, *Method in Theology* (New York: Herder and Herder, 1972), 116–17.
112. Lonergan, *Method in Theology*, 117.
113. Lonergan, *Insight: A Study of Human Understanding*, 622–27.
114. See William P. Loewe, "Dialectics of Sin: Lonergan's *Insight* and the Critical Theory of Max Horkheimer," *Anglican Theological Review* 61, no. 2 (April 1979): 235.
115. Lonergan, *Method in Theology*, 117.
116. Hurston, *Moses, Man of the Mountain*, 262.
117. Hurston, *Moses, Man of the Mountain*, 268.

23

ORDERED JUSTICE AND THE DIVERSITY OF RIGHTS AND NATIONS IN *PACEM IN TERRIS*

Russell Hittinger, University of Tulsa

Beginning on the Feast of Christ the King (October 1942), Archbishop Angelo Roncalli made his annual retreat in Istanbul. The Apostolic delegate to Turkey and Greece selected as a retreat master the Jesuit Father René Follet, who preached on the image of the perfect bishop according to Isidore of Seville.

Roncalli wrote in his diary:

> The Bishop must be distinguished by his own understanding, and his adequate explanation to others, of the philosophy of history, even the history that is now, before our eyes, adding pages of blood to pages of political and social disorders. I want to re-read St. Augustine's *City of God*, and draw from his doctrine the necessary material to form my own judgment.[1]

And so it was here, in Istanbul during World War II, while reflecting on the problem of nationalism, and while reflecting on the bishop as an image of the supranationalism of the Church, that Roncalli resolved to reread St. Augustine's *City of God*. It gave birth to a pattern of themes that would bear fruit exactly twenty years later.

Of course, this Angelo Guiseppe Roncalli would become bishop of Rome in 1958, taking the name John XXIII. He summoned the Second

Vatican Council, died in June 1963, and was beatified during the millennial year, 2000.

Fifty years ago this very week (December 1962)—the fourth year of his pontificate—Pope John assembled a drafting committee for a new encyclical, which would be titled *Pacem in terris* (Peace on Earth).

He typed the following instructions to Msgr. Pietro Pavan of the Lateran, who headed his team of writers:

> Peace is tranquility in the order of things, ordered obedience in fidelity to the eternal law. Order is giving each thing its place, The Peace of mankind is ordered harmony in the home, in the city, in man. Wretched, therefore, is the people that is alienated from God.[2]

These three sentences paraphrase Book XIX of St. Augustine's *City of God*: "Peace is the tranquility of order."[3] As we shall see, peace as tranquility of order is a paradigm of singular importance for his encyclical, especially its teaching on human rights.

So, on the fiftieth anniversary of Pope John XXIII's encyclical *Pacem in terris*, I want to reflect on its teachings: first, by looking back to its place and time in 1962 to 1963; then, by looking around in the encyclical itself; and briefly, looking ahead.

LOOKING BACK

Issued on April 11, 1963, *Pacem in terris* (PT) reflected an acute sense of its own historical moment, both sacred and secular. In about two month's time (from October to December 1962), Pope John:

- *Convened* the Second Vatican Council
- *Wrote* an address in French to "all men of good will" only twenty-four hours after American military forces had gone to DEFCON 2 during the Cuban missile crisis
- Then, having appeared on the cover of *Time Magazine* as the "Man of the Year," *learned* from his physicians of a cancer that would soon kill him.

After receiving the medical report, he set up a drafting committee for the new encyclical. The drafters understood they had only weeks or a couple of months, at best, to finish their work.[4]

So, let us look back.

In the winter of 1962 to 1963, two issues galvanized the attention of the global commons. First, a global division between two highly armed "blocs," a division that began in Europe just after World War II, but which rapidly spread to the rest of the world—to the former colonies, where the "Cold War" was actually a complex skirmish line of civil wars and revolutions, from Southeast Asia to sub-Saharan Africa. Interestingly, except for the very significant admonition that use of nuclear weapons is not a fit instrument for the vindication of justice (PT §127, and §111), the PT does not have very much to say about war, or about the traditional criteria of "just war." (This takes some readers by surprise, but I point out that the encyclical is about peace as tranquility of order.)

The other great issue of the global commons—which, in fact, occupies the far greater part of PT—was the urgent problem of how to achieve political order in an era of very rapid and confusing decolonization. When the UN was established in 1945, 750 million people lived in territories that were not self-governing. By 1960, two-thirds of the new member states were former colonies. In that very year, the General Assembly declared that all peoples have a "right to self-determination," and decreed that "immediate steps shall be taken, in Trust and Non-Self Governing Territories or all other territories which have not yet gained independence, to transfer all powers to the peoples of those territories."[5]

Back then, this was the problem of the so-called Third World—the peoples who belonged neither to the First World of the West nor to the Second World of the Communist bloc. Most of all, the Third World needed to achieve political and economic development within a wider international order. In many cases, these peoples had *de jure* states, with flags and stamps and currencies, but they barely functioned with respect to the minimal requirements of the political. Indeed, it was in 1963 that the long American nightmare in Vietnam began with the assassination of President Diem. In any event, the early 1960s witnessed the largest movement of decolonization and nation building in world history. What we today call globalization began just then (and who could have predicted that China, Korea, India, and Brazil would be the economic masters of a global economy?).

To return to PT, in both the secular and ecclesiastical press, much attention was given to the policy of *aggiornamento*—a bringing-up-to-date. The controversial issue was not (yet) what was going on theologically at the Vatican Council, but rather political collaboration between Catholics and parties on the Left. For all practical purposes, *aggiornamento* was interpreted as "the opening to the Left." In the encyclical, the Pope expressed his hope that Catholics might cooperate not only with nonbelievers but also with adherents of a patently false ideology *insofar as* the cooperation involves "morally lawful aspirations,"[6] especially collaboration in defense of "man's natural rights."[7] The encyclical did not spell out exactly what this meant politically in any particular country.

By and large, the politics of the Cold War determined the way *Pacem in terris* was first received.[8] The *New York Times* (for the first and the last time) printed a papal encyclical in its entirety. The Catholic world was made more than a little nervous by Pope John's words about "collaboration." After all, in 1963, some fifty-five million Catholics were behind the Iron Curtain. The first Catholic president, John F. Kennedy, was notably restrained in his public comments about this part of the encyclical. Italy had the largest Communist Party in Western Europe, and so the Christian Democratic Party was not at all pleased with the Pope's remarks. For its part, the Communist government of Czechoslovakia tried to erect a puppet church called "Pacem in Terris."

As the strange decade of the 1960s unfolded, the encyclical became a kind of icon of the peace and youth movement (it was the good encyclical, in contrast to *Humanae vitae*, the bad encyclical about contraception and sexual morality); conservatives dismissed PT as politically naïve and utopian.

The net effect was that its actual teaching receded from public view, hardly discussed on its own merits. It was celebrated and criticized both for what it said, for what it didn't say, as well as for what people imagined it must have said or not said.[9] It is all the more necessary for us, a generation later, to look carefully at what the encyclical actually said.

While the general reception of PT was appallingly superficial and narrowly political, the bishops at the Vatican Council took the document very seriously. They had just finished the first session of the Council, which had been quickly adjourned for the purpose of electing commissioners who would oversee a new set of schemata for documents. (The Council would eventually issue some sixteen documents, and all of them were being formulated when the encyclical was published.) This allowed the encyclical to exert enormous impact in shaping the agenda between the first and second sessions of the Council (from January to late September 1963). In a very real sense, PT is the first document of the Vatican Council. It would leave its stamp upon several conciliar documents: *Lumen Gentium* on the Church as a sacrament of unity; the decree *Ad Gentes* on missionary work; the decree on ecumenism; and even more indelibly on *Gaudium et spes* and *Dignitatis humanae*.[10]

The Pope and his drafting committee understood that one sentence in particular would have a direct effect on the schemata being drawn by the commissioners: "Also among man's rights is that of being able to worship God in accordance with the right dictates of his own conscience, and to profess his religion both in private and in public" (PT §14). The sentences on the right of religious conscience received more internal discussion and debate than any other theme of the encyclical during its drafting process.[11] In order to allow the Council to exercise its full deliberative weight, however, the sentences on religious liberty were written carefully, even somewhat ambiguously. There can be no question that the Council's doctrine on religious liberty was caused by the dying Pope's own hand in PT.

LOOKING AROUND (IN THE ENCYCLICAL)

I shall now leave behind the historical context and the contemporary events surrounding PT in order to look around in the document itself—particularly its treatment of human or natural rights. And I intend to do so by returning to the Augustinian themes with which we began.

I count some twenty-five discrete rights in sections 11 to 27. In his preface to these sections, the Pope asserts that these are rights that flow inalienably from human nature (PT §9).[12]

They include the right to life, to bodily integrity, to the means that are necessary and suitable for the proper development of life, including the right to security when otherwise deprived of the means to it through no fault of one's own, the right to respect for one's person and reputation, to freedom in seeking truth, and in expressing and communicating one's opinion, to pursuing art within the limits of morality and the common good, and to being informed truthfully about public events. They include too the right to share in the benefits of culture and, therefore, to both a basic education and a technical training in accordance with the educational development of one's country; the right to worship God, both privately and publicly, in accordance with one's conscience; the right to choose freely one's state in life, including the right to set up a family or to follow a religious vocation; and the prior right of parents to support and educate their children. They also include the right to free initiative in the economic field, embracing the right to work; the right to satisfactory working conditions, both physical and moral, and taking account of their special requirements in the case of women; the right to carry on economic activities to the degree of responsibility of which one is capable; the right to a just wage and the right to private property. Finally, they include the right of assembly and association, the right of freedom of movement within one's own country and, when there are just reasons for it, the right to immigrate to other countries, the right to take an active part in public affairs (including women), and the right to juridical protection of one's rights.[13] [14] This was not a sudden eruption of rights talk in magisterial documents. Of the twenty-five rights, the citations are to St. Paul, Church fathers, Thomas Aquinas, and to the encyclicals of modern popes. Only two of the rights have an aspect of novelty: the right of religious conscience (PT §14) and rights of women in the contemporary world (PT §19, but also see §41 and §153).

The most important thing, however, is not the *list of rights*, but the fact that these rights are interwoven according to *six modes of order*. To my knowledge, PT is the only human rights document that explicitly takes this approach. In doing so, PT integrates justice as rights and justice as right order.

The encyclical teaches that peace is richly textured and multilayered order(s):

1. Order in the universe (§§2–3)
2. Order in freedom and conscience that flows from an individual's participation in the eternal law (§§4–7)
3. Order among individual human persons (§§8–10)

§§11–15 begin the list of rights

1. Order between members of a political community and its authorities (§§46–79)

2. Order between political communities (§§80–129)
3. Order that ought to obtain between individuals, social groups, and states to a worldwide community (§§130–45)

In his World Day of Peace Address (2003), marking the fortieth anniversary of *Pacem in terris*, Pope John Paul II said:

> Boldly, but with all humility, I would like to suggest that the Church's fifteen-hundred-year-old teaching on peace as *"tranquillitas ordinis—* the tranquility of order" as Saint Augustine called it (*De Civitate Dei*, 19, 13), which was brought to a new level of development forty years ago by *Pacem in Terris,* has a deep relevance for the world today, for the leaders of nations as well as for individuals. (WDP §6)

John Paul was just right, and he brings us back to the Augustinian themes I mentioned earlier. They must be brought back, front and center, not only because the encyclical was designed just so, but also because the overarching theme of order was ignored, and sometimes outright dismissed, by the generation that first read *Pacem in terris*. For that generation, *order* summoned all of the boogey men of their time and place. Politically, it suggested "law and order," the opposite of social and political change. Socially, it suggested authoritarianism—in the church, in the family, and in the wider society. Philosophically, it suggested cosmological order, and nature herself, which speaks an authoritative word apart from, or even contrary to, human freedom. Order for that generation usually suggested something imposed, despotic, nonparticipatory, and dismissive of human freedom and subjectivity.

Almost immediately, the encyclical was read as a declaration of human rights stripped of the broader context of natural, divine, anthropological, political, and legal modes of order.

To take but one example, let us consider Maurice Cardinal Roy's remarks sent to Paul VI in 1973 on the "Occasion of the Tenth Anniversary of the Encyclical 'Pacem in Terris.'" Cardinal Roy, the former Archbishop of Quebec, was a distinguished churchman. At the time, he was the president of the Pontifical Council on Justice and Peace.[15] In a section titled "A Method for Our Times," the cardinal admitted to being somewhat puzzled by John XXIII's theme of order, especially as it relates to cosmological, metaphysical, and anthropological matters—the first two modes of order in PT. He asked:

Is this answer still valid, ten years later? [Paul VI must have been a little bewildered that an eminent Cardinal would be asking whether the principles of a papal encyclical had become *invalid* in less than ten years!] For today, this idea of nature is very much questioned, if not rejected.... The concept also seems too "essentialist" to people of our time, who challenge, as being a relic of Greek philosophy, the term "Natural Law," which they consider anachronistic, conservative and defensive.... Although the term "nature" does in fact lend itself to serious misunderstandings, the reality intended has lost nothing of its forcefulness when it is replaced by modern synonyms.... Such synonyms are: man, human being, human person, dignity, the rights of man or the rights of peoples, conscience, humaneness (in conduct), the struggle for justice, and, more recently, "the duty of being," the "quality of life." Could they not all be summarized in the concept of "values," which is very much used today?

Incidentally, the word *values* was never used in PT. The term *valori* was superimposed, first in Italian, as headings for newspapers, and through this venue entered into other translations.

Admitting that the very first sentence of PT asserts that peace is "diligent observance of the divinely established order," Cardinal Roy observed: "This word jars the modern mentality, as does, even more, the idea that it summons up: a sort of complicated organic scheme or gigantic genealogical tree, in which each being and group has its predetermined place."[16]

Cardinal Roy completely missed the point of order, so carefully developed by Pope John. Here is my twenty-five-cent explanation of what he missed.

Let us recall Thomas Jefferson's much-quoted sentence, written to the Danbury Baptist Association in 1801, fourteen years after the adoption of the Bill of Rights. "Adhering to this expression of the supreme will of the nation in behalf of the rights of conscience, I shall see with sincere satisfaction the progress of those sentiments which tend to restore to man all his natural rights, convinced he has no natural right in opposition to his social duties."[17] Jefferson here acknowledges the long-recognized tension between *ius* as an individual right demanding satisfaction and *ius* as law, as a public order demanding satisfaction of duties. Jefferson anticipated debates of our own century—certainly the 1960s. One side demanded rights, another side demanded law and order. This opposition ran through cultural, legal, political, and religious institutions.

PT would have us understand that *if* there are natural rights then there is order prior to, and distinct from, the orders we construct or confer. It is a straw man to oppose natural rights and right order. Thus, the importance of the word *endowed*. (The Latin word is *inditum*, something instilled or built into a thing.) Endowment contains *in nucelo* both rights and right order. "We hold these truths to be self-evident, that all men are created equal, that they are endowed by their Creator with certain unalienable Rights, that among these are Life, Liberty and the pursuit of Happiness."

Endowment implies order rather than a merely subjective claim or evaluation. Here, we are in the presence of the strongest relationship between a right and right order—an *inalienable* right, which means that you can't take it and I can't give it. Blessed Pope John uses the word *inalienable* throughout PT. For example: "[The human person] is endowed with intelligence and free will. As such he has rights and duties, which together flow as a direct consequence from his nature. These rights and duties are universal and inviolable, and therefore altogether inalienable."

Now, turning to the encyclical, we find that the charter of human rights (§§8–36) stands between two discussions of divinely created order (§§2–7, 37–38), which serve as bookends. The first is a substantive prelude, while the second is a forceful reminder and admonition. In the prelude, the Pope speaks of the whole created universe, marked by order, intelligibility, and beauty.[18] What emerges "first and foremost" from the progress of scientific discovery, the Pope asserts, is the splendor of creation—an endowment, making possible discovery. It is the same man, made unto the image and likeness of God, who is a part of a vast created order, and who is capable of appreciating and appropriating that order.

As for order *in* human beings, the Pope insists that our participation in divinely established order is more perfect, by virtue of intelligence and a law written in the heart. Human peace, therefore, requires something more than the harmony of physical laws. It requires the tranquility of moral order. The principles of moral order are already reflected, inscribed, instilled in human beings endowed with intellect and will. Everyone can understand, albeit in a rudimentary way, that the *true* governs reason, and that *reason* governs the passions. First we are endowed, not merely with random and sporadic powers, but with order.

Wrapping up the encyclical, the Pope again quotes St. Augustine:

> The world will never be the dwelling place of peace, till peace has found a home in the heart of each and every man, till every man preserves in himself the order ordained by God to be preserved. That is why St. Augustine asks the question: "Does your mind desire the strength to gain the mastery over your passions? Let it submit to a greater power, and it will conquer all beneath it. And peace will be in you—true, sure, most ordered peace. What is that order? God as ruler of the mind; the mind as ruler of the body. Nothing could be more orderly. (§165)

So, rights do not begin in a subjective claim, but with an order—and this order is not alien; it's our very nature, made unto the image and likeness of God, by which we are competent to be provident for ourselves and for others.

It also places certain limits on the legal and political orders that human beings can construct. Consider this passage:[19]

> Governmental authority, therefore, is a postulate of the moral order and derives from God. Consequently, laws and decrees passed in contravention of the moral order, and hence of the divine will, can have no binding force in conscience, since "it is right to obey God rather than men" [citing Acts 5.29]. Indeed, the passing of such laws undermines the very nature of authority and results in shameful abuse.[20] . . . Thus any government which refused to recognize human rights or acted in violation of them, would not only fail in its duty; its decrees would be wholly lacking in binding force.[21,22]

Interestingly, this is precisely the passage that Dr. Martin L. King Jr. quoted from St. Thomas in his *Letter from Birmingham Jail* (April 16, 1963). The day after PT was issued, eight white Alabama clergymen signed a document titled "Call for Unity," affirming the goals of the civil rights movement against legal segregation, but complained about the tactic of civil disobedience. Dr. King countered that one has a moral responsibility not to obey unjust laws, and promptly issued his famous letter five days after Pope John's encyclical. Whether or not King was influenced by the recent encyclical is not important. For our purposes, the important thing is that King argued for an integral unity of rights and right order. Along one front, he chastised white moderates "more devoted to 'order' than to justice." Partisans of "law and order," he said, consider order much too narrowly as the absence of conflict. His audience in the spring of 1963 would have readily understood that the use of force to achieve such a narrow notion of "order" at the Berlin Wall and in streets of cities in Alabama did not have the presumption of justice in its favor. The order to which law pertains cannot be found simply in an uncontested result, but in a result compatible with equity and suitable for a common good. Law moves human agents primarily through obligation, and a law that fails to move its citizens through obligation is scarcely distinguishable from force—a human community moved to and fro chiefly by force is a disordered community.

Dr. King therefore carefully defended rights as having their foundation in law, and in so doing he avoided the trap of putting rights and right order into opposition. Indeed, it is quite telling that in the letter Dr. King was not anxious about a list of rights so much as a spectacle of disorders. Among those that he mentions: the corruption of individual and corporate conscience—and especially of the churches—the use of brutal and arbitrary police powers, the refusal to allow peaceful public assembly, the refusal of political representation at the voting booth, and, finally, the appalling history of using human law to compel both public officials and private citizens to treat one another chiefly on the basis of skin pigmentation, thus reducing PT's second and third modes of order to the first one. Racial segregation is nothing other than government decree compelling citizens (third order) to ignore the endowment that constitutes human beings (second order), and to take as normative the endowments that characterize physical nature (first order). One hardly needs to appeal to a subjective right in order to see that the putative "order" of the law of segregation is a disorder.

The convergence of the two letters (issued only a week apart) is extraordinary. Each letter summarized a common moral teaching, inherited, in its Christian form, by the Pope and Dr. King alike. Each shared the conviction that authentic rights claims and right order are coimplicates rather than opposites, and that the nucleus of both is the anthropological endowment.

Right order also requires respect for the nature of human fellowship. The social principle is one human life participating in that of another, according to various kinds of common good: the family, voluntary societies, the nation-state, to a family of peoples.[23] The term *common good* is used forty-six times in PT. "Now the order which prevails in human society is wholly incorporeal in nature. Its foundation is truth, and it must be brought into effect by justice. It needs to be animated and perfected by men's love for one another, and, while preserving freedom intact, it must make for an equilibrium in society which is increasingly more human in character" (§37). Just as the dignity of a human person is reducible neither to the forces of nature nor the constructions of human art, but rather is *open to reality as a whole*, so, too, human societies are not reducible to the elemental forces of race, class, or historical determinism.

Just as the human person is open to reality as a whole, so too are human societies open to wider orders—to a global order, and to a fully transcendent happiness.[24]

> We must bear in mind that of its very nature civil authority exists, not to confine men within the frontiers of their own nations, but primarily to protect the common good of the State, which certainly cannot be divorced from the common good of the entire human family. (§98)

Here, indeed, we reach one of the most controversial teaching of the encyclical—both then and now; namely, the need for an authority that has "structure and efficacy" for realizing a global tranquility of order in the human family (§136).

Our sobriety and dubiety about the immediate prospects for such an order today should not cause us to impatiently dismiss the principle. It must be discerned through the thickness of human history. The principle is not imposed from the outside, but is detected within other experiences and principles with which we are familiar. The human person is open to reality as a whole. He is not imprisoned either by physical forces or by his own art. Human rights flow from this anthropological principle. And so does the social principle. No true or valid society can pretend to order a human person exclusively to itself. Marriages, families, voluntary societies, nation-states, and so forth, would be grotesque prisons if they made their particular membership the finality of human life. (It was precisely this upon which Roncalli meditated when he considered the problem of nationalism during his retreat in October 1942.) We need to notice that the expanding modes of order continue to track the anthropological principle. Man is open to a universal order—this is his endowment. Therefore, rightful liberties and responsibilities do not begin or stop at the gates of the family or the state.

PT therefore asserts that it is "a postulate of the moral order" that there be authority adequate to coordinating and maintaining the common good (§136). Since human action increasingly pushes beyond the confines of the nation-state and treaties between states, there is need of a module of government to protect the rights and right order of that common good.

LOOKING AHEAD: SIGNS OF THE TIMES

In his opening allocution to the Second Vatican Council, Pope John reminded the bishops that "history is the teacher of life."[25] A common historical experience can have a useful winnowing effect for men and women of good will. For Pope John, the experience of the post–World War II generation provided an opportune moment for setting forth natural law principles governing peace as tranquility of order. The pathologies of totalitarian states were in full evidence; Western Europe was still being rebuilt from the devastation of the war; the Cuban missile crisis had made everyone aware of the need for at least some limits to the use of lethal force, even in defense of a good cause; and the rapid pace of decolonization made it imperative that the new polities be founded on rights and right order.

The decades from 1945 to 1965 provided a crucible of shared experience, generating palpable expectations for political liberty, a common order of rights, and economic development. In the ordinary course of things, moral consensus tied to such moments does not last very long. Across the ocean of human affairs, things change, and the cultural and social signs of the times are not always favorable.

Consider the following passage in the *Confessions*, where Augustine writes:

> Is not this [order] of the universe evident to all whose senses are not deranged: Then why does it not give the same answer to all? Animals, small and great, see it, but cannot ask the question. They are not gifted with reason to sit in judgment on the evidence brought in by the senses. But men can ask the question, so that the invisible things of God are clearly seen, being understood by the things that are made; but by loving these things, they become subject to them, and subjects cannot judge. And these things will only answer the questions of those who are prepared to judge. . . . They look just the same to both, but to

one man they say nothing and to the other they speak. Oh it would be truer to say that they speak to everyone, but are only understood by those who compare the voice which comes to them from outside with the truth that is within. (Conf. X.6)

This is not to say that the basic principles of rights and right order change; it's only to say that our appropriation of them depends on intellectual acuity and moral seriousness.

In 1988, twenty-five years after PT, Cardinal Joseph Ratzinger traveled to England to give the annual Fischer Lecture for the Catholic Chaplaincy at Cambridge University. With a paper titled "Consumer Materialism and Christian Hope," he came prepared to speak about the "characteristic signs of the times." The most troubling sign, he averred, is that "what is moral has lost its evidence."[26] "What was first of all common to all of premodern mankind, however, lies really along the self-same line: the conviction that in man's being there lies an imperative, the conviction that man does not devise morality itself by calculating expediencies; rather, he comes upon it in the being of things."[27]

The key point is reached at the conclusion of the cardinal's prepared remarks. Referring to wisdom traditions in general, he proposed that "morality is not man's prison; it is rather the divine in him."[28] This conviction implies that the whole man is open to reality as a whole. Were this not true, the order of nature would amount to a mere aggregation of "details," and man's own interpretation of these details would amount to partial constructions of his own subjectivity—or, what is more likely, the constructions of social, political, and legal forces. Morality, then, would be a "prison." Perhaps we should go even further to say that whatever is "divine" in man would demand that the individual be emancipated from this prison of mere partialities, which can force but only pretend to bind his conduct. Thus, for the modern person, "morality has lost its evidence." He can "see through" all things but not "see."[29]

And so we have two prelates (Blessed John XXIII and Benedict XI), both devotees of Augustine with strong interest in the theology of history, interpreting the signs under quite different historical skies.

Perhaps the first sign of a changing historical sky was in 1966—the United Nations could reach no moral consensus on a Covenant of Rights, and so it issued two: one on Civil and Political Rights (which emphasized human liberty and limited government); then on Cultural and Economic Rights (which emphasized "new" concerns about class, gender, ethnicity, etc.). The problem was not so much different *lists* of human rights, but different orders that could not be integrated into a single, complex scheme. Can there be tranquility of order if human goods, aspirations, and rights are arrayed in such different, and unintegrated, orders—which is to say different anthropological and moral normativities?

In the discourse about human rights today, we find little consensus regarding what PT proposed as the first two modes of order: order in creation and order in human beings.

While PT was under no illusions concerning the problems of clarifying and instantiating the fifth and six orders (between nations and then with respect to a still-to-be-determined global authority)—everyone knew that it would take a protracted and difficult slog through history to achieve anything resembling an international legal and political order—the first two, however, always were of a different status. For in these, we are dealing with endowments to be discovered and honored. They constitute the anthropological and moral foundation of human rights.

A generation after PT, in the historic democracies of the West, we can see that the first two modes of order (the natural orders) are kept at the most remote periphery of public discourse. To put it bluntly, we are not sure whether human dignity is endowed (in an order prior to our choices) or whether it is constructed (socially, culturally, legally). Many people would say that our first and most abiding right is the right to adopt, construct, and change our own private view of human dignity. And hence, the foundation of rights must be left to private opinion.

On that basis, the human rights project might continue, but its foundation will have to be moved from the natural to the political; it can be no deeper than the fourth order; namely, between citizens and their government. Human rights would be nothing other than what a government confers upon its citizens, or, to say the same thing, what the majority of the citizens can make or allow the government impose as rights. It will go to the courts, who themselves will take stock of what public opinion will tolerate.

In his Address to the UN General Assembly in 2008, Pope Benedict returned to this theme of the moral having lost its evidence. Speaking of the 1948 Declaration, he said:

> However, the results still have not been as high as the hopes. Certain countries have challenged the universality of these rights, judged to be

too western, inspiring a search for a more inclusive formulation. Moreover, a certain propensity towards multiplying more human rights according to the disordered desires of the consumerist individual or from sectarian demands rather than the objective requirements of the common good of humanity have, in no small way, contributed to devaluing them.[30]

"Today," he concluded, "efforts need to be redoubled in the face of pressure to reinterpret the foundations of the *Declaration* and to compromise its inner unity."[31]

Fifty years later, we have good reason to appreciate the encyclical's bid to present rights and right order as integrally related. We also have reason to be sobered by the fickle and uneven paths of human history. PT was initially taken to be a soft, left-liberal encyclical: well intentioned, but rather utopian. As it turned out, the encyclical was far more rigorous and intellectually serious in its understanding of natural, anthropological, and moral order than what the cultural traffic could tolerate. It reads today as a sublimely traditional account of human rights.

NOTES

1. John XXIII, *Journey of a Soul*, trans. Dorothy White (New York: Image Doubleday, 1999), 260–61.
2. Peter Hebblethwaite, *Pope John XXIII: Shepherd of the Modern World—The Definitive Biography of Angelo Roncalli* (New York: Image Doubleday, 1987), 470.
3. Aug., DCD XIX.13. "The peace of the body then consists in the duly proportioned arrangement of its parts. The peace of the irrational soul is the harmonious repose of the appetites, and that of the rational soul the harmony of knowledge and action. The peace of body and soul is the well-ordered and harmonious life and health of the living creature. Peace between man and God is the well-ordered obedience of faith to eternal law. Peace between man and man is well-ordered concord. Domestic peace is the well-ordered concord between those of the family who rule and those who obey. Civil peace is a similar concord among the citizens. The peace of the celestial city is the perfectly ordered and harmonious enjoyment of God, and of one another in God. The peace of all things is the tranquility of order. Order is the distribution which allots things equal and unequal, each to its own place. And hence, though the miserable, in so far as they are such, do certainly not enjoy peace, but are severed from that

tranquility of order in which there is no disturbance, nevertheless, inasmuch as they are deservedly and justly miserable, they are by their very misery connected with order."

4. See Pavan's letter to Loris Francesco Capovilla, the Pope's personal secretary, dated November 23, 1962. Pavan disclosed his first line of thought, which was "to reestablish the great line of encyclicals in argomento di Leone XIII" (mentioning *Sapientia Christianae, Diuturnum,* and *Libertas,* the same trilogy that would become so important for John Paul II). But, Pavan mused, it could be aimed at the entire global situation, teaching not only Catholics but also other Christians and non-Christians. Documento 1, in Alberto Melloni, *Pacem in terris: Storia dell'ultima enciclica di Papa Giovanni* (Rome: GLF, Editori Laterza, 2010), 103–4. At its inception in Pavan's mind, therefore, PT would take the great Leonine teachings on the eternal law, together with the changing tides of history, and allow them to resonate with a much wider audience (*avrebbe una vasta risonanza in tutto il mondo e in tutti gli ambienti*). Drew Christiansen's argument that PT is a kind of "Copernican" revolution turning papal teachings out of their scholastic grounding, and that "natural law is turned upside down," has no basis in either the constitutive history of the document nor in the encyclical itself, which devotes more attention to Aquinas's notion of the Eternal Law than any encyclical between Leo XIII and JPII's *Veritatis splendor*. See Drew Christiansen, S.J., "Commentary on *Pacem in terris,*" in *Modern Catholic Social Teaching,* ed. Kenneth Hines, O.F.M. (Washington, DC: Georgetown University Press, 2005), 225–26.

5. Resolution 1514 (XV), December 14, 1960.

6. PT §159.

7. PT §157.

8. Catholics should do nothing that compromises morality and religion (§157), that one must not forget the possibility and need for conversion (§158), that fruitful cooperation is not a foregone conclusion but must be discerned according to prudence that is itself measured by the principles of natural law and the directives of ecclesiastical authority (§160), and that gradual growth is better than the impetuosity of political revolution (§§161–62). In many countries, the debate seems in retrospect to have amounted to little more than what we would call political "spin." *National Review* dismissed PT as "a venture in triviality." See Richard Brookhiser, *Right Time, Right Place* (New York: Basic Books, 2009), 47. There was also philosophical hand-wringing of a more serious nature, chiefly on the question of whether the Pope was too lenient on Communists and naïve about the aggressive intentions of the Communist ideology. This, in tandem with PT's seemingly ambiguous and soft position on just war, led important Protestant thinkers such as Paul Tillich, Reinhold Niebuhr, and Paul Ramsey to ask whether the encyclical was an exercise in "philosophical anarchism," "natu-

ral law optimism," perhaps "breathing a Pelagian, rather than an Augustinian, spirit." These remarks in Paul Ramsey, "Pacem in terris," in *The Just War: Force and Political Responsibility* (Lanham: Rowan & Littlefield Publishing, 2002), 70–90; first appearing in *Religion in Life* XXXIII (Winter 1963–1964): 116–35. The latter, on Pelagianism, quoting Reinhold Niebuhr in *Christianity and Crisis* (May 13, 1963), 83. See also, Peter Steinfels, "Pacem in Terris: A Retrospective," for the Vincentian Convocation on January 30, 2003, at St. John's University, Vincentian Center for Church and Society, http://www.vincenter.org/convocation/steinfels.html. Also worth noting is Steinfels's passing remarks about how the encyclical was kept at arm's length by some elements of the Left. In two countries, however, the encyclical's bid for more collaboration had significant implications for domestic politics. In Italy, for example, the Church had taken a very strong stance against such collaboration in the elections of 1946 and 1948. The Communist Party actively recruited Catholics, arguing that in the practical order there was no necessary contradiction between supporting desirable political policies and reforms and following the faith and morals of the Catholic Church. It is still debated whether PT did more harm than good in the context of Italian politics. See Elisa A Carrillo, "The Italian Catholic Church and Communism, 1943–1963," *The Catholic Historical Revi*ew 77, no. 4 (October 1991): 644–57. In Czechoslovakia, the government cynically manipulated a high-minded notion of a modus vivendi between Catholics and Communists. In 1951 the government attempted to create a schismatic church, like the one in China, under the rubric of "The Peace Movement of the Catholic Clergy." Under the chairmanship of an excommunicate priest, Josef Plojhar, the aim of the organization was to reduce Christianity to a Social Gospel, which, not surprisingly, turned out to be congruent with the policies of the Communist government. Unable to establish ecclesiastical credibility, it was reestablished as "Pacem in Terris." Eventually, the government made it clear that any attack on "Pacem in Terris" is an indirect attach on the socialist system. See Alexander Tomsky, "Pacem in Terris: Between Church and State in Czechoslovakia," Religion in Communist Lands since its first publication in 1973, Keston Institute (March 10, 1982): 275–82. In only a few years, this question of collaboration and compromise would return not as a conflict between the rivals of the Cold War, but as a conflict between Catholics and secularists over public morality. With *Humanae vitae*, legal abortion, and the collapse of the Warsaw Pact, the terms of this debate will become profoundly reconfigured for a new era of liberalism and public reason.

9. To wit, the doggerel: By now we know the simple trick; / Of how to read Pope John's encyc.; / To play the game, you choose your snippet; / Of "Peace on Earth" and boldly clip it. John Cogley, "In America" (May 18, 1963). Quoted in

Newman, op. cit., 60. http://americamagazine.org/content/all-things/fifty-years-ago-america-playful-poem-pacem-terris.

10. "It is obvious, in the first instance, that the Pope here offers a shining example of everything that he means by his own word, aggiornamento. He situates himself squarely in the year 1963. There is not the slightest bit of nostalgia, nor of lament over the past course of history or over the current situation that history has evoked here on earth." J. C. Murray, "Things Old and New in 'Pacem in Terris,'" *America* 107 (April 27, 1963): 612.

11. See Melloni, ad passim, and the appendices, and Newman's discussion, op. cit., 77–81.

12. So far as I can discern, the terms *natural* and *human* rights are used interchangeably: natural rights (§§12, 13, 20, 28, 30, 157); human rights (PT §§30, 61, 63, 75, 143).

13. Here, I use the very succinct and useful summary by Newman, op. cit., 69–70.

14. My summary leaves to one side the very important corporate rights: church, family, nation, as well as a myriad of other groups that enjoy rightful dignity both in themselves and insofar as they stand toward others according to the principle of subsidiarity. Especially important is §52, where the Pope explicitly affirms the right of peoples to choose their own form of government.

15. Pope Paul VI addressed his letter, *Octogesima Adveniens*, on the eightieth anniversary of *Rerum Novarum* (May 14, 1971), to Cardinal Roy, who, in turn, addressed his thoughts to the Pope on the subject of PT. He was the former Archbishop of Quebec, the first president of the Pontifical Council on the Laity, then, and finally the president of the Pontifical Council on the Family.

16. "Reflections by Cardinal Maurice Roy on the Occasion of the Tenth Anniversary of the Encyclical 'Pacem in Terris' of Pope John XXIII" (April 11, 1973), in Joseph Gremillion, *The Gospel of Peace and Justice: Catholic Social Teaching since Pope John* (New York: Orbis Books, 1976), 556–58.

17. Thomas Jefferson, Letter To Messrs. Nehemiah Dodge and Others, a Committee of the Danbury Baptist Association, in the State of Connecticut (January 1, 1802).

18. Reminiscent of the favorite triad of Augustine: measure, number, order.

19. Also, "It is generally accepted today that the common good is best safeguarded when personal rights and duties are guaranteed. The chief concern of civil authorities must therefore be to ensure that these rights are recognized, respected, co-ordinated, defended and promoted, and that each individual is enabled to perform his duties more easily." Both of which are quoted verbatim by JPII in EV §§71–72.

20. As St. Thomas teaches, "In regard to the second proposition, we maintain that human law has the rationale of law in so far as it is in accordance with right

reason, and as such it obviously derives from eternal law. A law which is at variance with reason is to that extent unjust and has no longer the rationale of law. It is rather an act of violence" (citing S.t. I-II, 93.3 ad 2). §51.

21. For "to safeguard the inviolable rights of the human person, and to facilitate the performance of his duties, is the principal duty of every public authority." Thus any government which refused to recognize human rights or acted in violation of them, would not only fail in its duty; its decrees would be wholly lacking in binding force. §§60–61.

22. We shouldn't overlook the bracing passages quoted from St. Augustine: And just as individual men may not pursue their own private interests in a way that is unfair and detrimental to others, so too it would be criminal in a State to aim at improving itself by the use of methods which involve other nations in injury and unjust oppression. There is a saying of St. Augustine which has particular relevance in this context: "Take away justice, and what are kingdoms but mighty bands of robbers." §98 (*De civitate Dei*, lib. IV, c. 4; PL 41. 115; cf. Pius XII's broadcast message, Christmas 1939, AAS 32 [1940], 5–13). Striking yet another Augustinian theme, in *Mater et Magistra*, having cited the *Confessions* on the inquietude of the human heart, PT includes this admonitory sentence: "Separated from God a man is but a monster, in himself and toward others; for the right ordering of human society presupposes the right ordering of man's conscience with God, who is Himself the source of all justice, truth and love." §215.

23. "And so, dearest sons and brothers, we must think of human society as being primarily a spiritual reality. By its means enlightened men can share their knowledge of the truth, can claim their rights and fulfill their duties, receive encouragement in their aspirations for the goods of the spirit, share their enjoyment of all the wholesome pleasures of the world, and strive continually to pass on to others all that is best in themselves and to make their own the spiritual riches of others. It is these spiritual values which exert a guiding influence on culture, economics, social institutions, political movements and forms, laws, and all the other components which go to make up the external community of men and its continual development." §36.

24. Even if there were an authority competent for ruling a global family, man's perfection would not stop there.

25. *Gaudet Mater* (October 11, 1962), *Sacrosanctum Oecumenicum Concilium Vatican II, Constitutiones, Decreta, Declarationes* (Vatican City: Libreria Editrice Vaticana, 1993), 858.

26. Cardinal Joseph Ratzinger, "Consumer Materialism and Christian Hope," *Teachers of the Faith: Speeches and Lectures by Catholic Bishops*, Foreword by Cardinal Cormac Murphy-O'Connor, ed. Tom Horwood (Catholic Bishop's Conference of England and Wales, 2002), 78–94.

27. Ratzinger, "Consumer Materialism and Christian Hope," 87. The cardinal's speech is an important documentary antecedent to the International Theological Commission's report, *The Search for a Universal Ethics: A New Look at Natural Law* (2008). This document is notable for its serious attempt to readapt the dialogical to the doctrinal facets of natural law and human rights.

28. Ratzinger, "Consumer Materialism and Christian Hope," 92.

29. Ratzinger, "Consumer Materialism and Christian Hope," 90. Quoting C. S. Lewis.

30. Disconnected from the moral sense of values, which transcend particular interests, the multiplication of procedures and juridical regulations can only wind up in a quagmire, which in the end only serves the interests of the most powerful. Above all, this reveals a tendency to reinterpret human rights, separating them from the ethical and rational dimension—which constitutes their foundation and end—in favor of a pure utilitarian legalism.

31. Benedict XVI, Discourse of April 18, 2008, before the General Assembly of the United Nations (AAS 100 [2008]), 335.

24

WAS NATIONAL SOCIALISM POLITICAL RELIGION?

The Transformation of Christianity into a Nazi Religion during the Third Reich

Susannah Heschel, Dartmouth University

As the audience of the Oberammergau Passion Play of 1934 watched Jesus being hoisted on the cross, they thought they saw a parable of the Third Reich: "There he is. That is our Führer, our Hitler!"[1] The identification with biblical imagery continued even after the Nazis were defeated and Germany lay in ruins: in a 1947 letter to a friend, the notorious Nazi theologian and propagandist Wolf Meyer-Erlach wrote, "We are wandering through the wilderness like the Children of Israel. . . . We are like the generation of Israel that was in captivity in Babylon, who had to make bricks in Egypt and were in danger of perishing in the demoralizing service on the front."[2]

How should we evaluate such language? Were religious images invoked because National Socialism was truly perceived by Germans to be a Christian movement, or at least in accord with Christian teachings, or was such language simply empty rhetoric, without political significance?

A discussion has been ongoing for decades about whether National Socialism should be considered a form of "political religion." Yet that discussion has focused on images of Hitler, Nazi propaganda, and the often ecstatic, even messianic enthusiasm for Nazism expressed by Germans and promoted by Nazi propaganda. Hitler's descent from the clouds in Leni Riefenstahl's famous film, *Triumph of the Will*, suggested a messianic or redemptive quality, as if he had been sent from heaven. Some scholars have examined the religious expressions of Nazi leaders and concluded that the Reich itself did not repudiate Christianity, but affirmed and manipulated key images for its own purposes.[3] The political scientist Claus-Ekkehard Baersch has examined the religiosity of Nazi leaders and discovered that Hess viewed Hitler as a deeply religious person, Julius Streicher believed Hitler had God's blessing, Himmler compared Hitler to Christ, and Goering thought Hitler had been sent by God to resurrect Germany. The larger framework of National Socialism as leading a fight against Judaism and Bolshevism also suggested its alignment against Christianity's two "enemies."

Arguments that National Socialism is a form of political religion can be found touted by historians, such as Philippe Burrin, Michael Burleigh, and Saul Friedlaender, among others, though with little attention to what they are trying to convey by using the term, and what it illuminates for historians about National Socialism. For Philippe Burrin, the question is why National Socialism was so appealing to vast numbers of Germans, and his answer implies that it appeals to a presupposed human "religiosity." In Germany, according to Burrin, "feelings and attitudes of exaltation, fascination and reverence, typical of the religious experience were transposed to secular objects."[4] Similarly, the historian Michael Burleigh describes the "diffuse religious emotionality" of National Socialism.[5] Yet identifying passion and enthusiasm as indicators of religion is not persuasive. Such emotional dispositions, described as a crisis in need of redemption, or apocalyptic mentality, are too vague to have explanatory function. Stanley Stowers points out that invocations of "political religion" often imply a distinction between acceptable religion and false beliefs with evil consequences, mimicking theological distinctions between orthodoxy and heresy.[6] Most important, the argument defines religion as emotional experience without ideational content, a definition most scholars of religion would reject. Finally, the argument does not explain why church-going as well as secular Germans found National Socialism appealing.

Invocations of "political religion" do not carry explanatory values, but they do carry theological implications. The term *political religion* was applied to National Socialism by the German political philosopher Eric Voegelin, a conservative Catholic for whom the failure of the German churches to protest during the Nazi era was an abysmal moral capitulation. His assumption is that Christianity is opposed in principle to the crimes committed by the Nazi regime, so that its silence in face of those crimes was a violation of its own moral principles. Yet the problem is more complex than Voegelin perhaps realized. Christianity may not have stood across the fence from Nazi anti-Semitism, but was deeply imbricated in it. Theologians and historians of the German churches continue to debate the connections between Christian anti-Judaism and Nazi anti-Semitism.

Clearly, Nazism was a theological challenge. Particular problems faced Christians who embraced Nazi anti-Semitism. The figure of Jesus was a conundrum: How could a Nazi worship a Jewish god? For a small minority in Germany, the conflict led to a rejection of Christianity and a revival of medieval Teutonic myths and symbols. For others, the answer lay in a redefinition of Jesus as an Aryan whose goal was the destruction of Judaism. Only rarely did a theologian conclude that because Jesus himself was a Jew, Jews should not be targets of persecution, let alone murder.

The Third Reich arrived as a delight to leaders of the so-called German Christian Movement, a significant faction within the Protestant Church that endorsed German nationalism and anti-Semitism. The Nazi regime seemed, at least at first, to promise the sort of overthrow of entrenched authorities and ideas that German Christians hoped to bring about in analogous fashion within the church and theology. As the historian Doris Bergen has carefully delineated, German Christians sought a militarized, manly, anti-Semitic church unleashed from the strictures of what they viewed as pointless doctrines and ecclesiastical discipline, a new Christianity that would play a prominent role in the new Nazi Germany.[7] Yet their expectations of playing an active leadership role in the Reich and the Nazi Party were soon disappointed. Bringing individual regional churches under the control of German Christian pastors and bishops and declaring Christian support for the Führer did not bring the hoped-for admiration from Hitler, nor did it secure positions of authority within the regime for individual pastors and bishops; indeed, theologians were excluded from membership in the SS, much to the disappointment of many pastors, who were limited to "supporting membership." The Nazi disinterest in forging a bond with the church was expressed in a 1936 Nazi Party edict that ordered the removal of the swastika from church altars and the masthead of church publications, leading some pastors to protest, but to no avail.[8]

Although annoyed and even embittered by the lack of enthusiasm from the regime, leaders of the German Christian Movement by no means abandoned the object of their unrequited affection. Instead, they redoubled their devotion to Hitler by speaking, for example, of the "Führer Jesus" and describing Hitler as "God's agent [Beauftragter] in our day."[9] To carve a place for themselves within the Nazi Reich, they emphasized that Germans required both military and spiritual strength, and they would provide the latter. Christianity could not simply be abandoned; they insisted that the German people had a spiritual hunger and that loss of faith was as dangerous as poisoned blood: "The yearning for God in the German people is not a marginal attribute, but makes their blood healthy."[10] In later years, German Christians would describe the war as being fought on both physical and spiritual battlefields; the racial struggle was spiritual as well as physical.

One of the most enthusiastic Nazis among the Protestants was the theologian Walter Grundmann. Born in Chemnitz (Saxony) in 1906, and educated at the Universities of Rostock, Leipzig, and Tuebingen, Grundmann completed his doctorate in 1932 under the renowned scholar of New Testament and rabbinics Gerhard Kittel, a figure who ultimately became one of the most notorious academic supporters of the Nazi regime. Grundmann joined the Nazi Party while a student in Tuebingen, on December 1, 1930. By that time, half of the university student body had joined the Nazi Party, which had arrived in Tuebingen in 1927. Thanks to his early membership in the NSDAP, Grundmann earned the title of an "Alter Kämpfer,"[11] allowing him to wear a lapel pin, the Nazi Party's golden insignia, as well as other privileges. A few years later, he became a "supporting member" of the SS (theologians were not permitted to become full SS members) and of the Nationalsozialistische Volkswohlfahrt (NSV), and he was active as well in the German Christian Movement.[12]

Grundmann's early membership in the Nazi Party earned him prestige during the Third Reich, but that early membership was also the reason the Allies removed him from his professorship at the University of Jena once the Nazis were defeated. An ambitious and cunning political figure within the church, Grundmann was a second-rate scholar who was nonetheless highly prolific, publishing both popular and semiacademic treatises throughout his adult life, until his death in 1974. Indeed, despite his extraordinary efforts on behalf of National Socialism, he was never sanctioned by the church; after the war, he was appointed rector of a Protestant seminary in East Germany, taught at a seminar in Leipzig, and published an enormous array of books, including a three-volume commentary on the synoptic Gospels that were read by pastors in East and West Germany for decades.

Grundmann was a driving force within the German Christian Movement, which continually sought ways to attract the attention of the Nazi Reich. Together with like-minded colleagues—pastors, bishops, and professors of theology—Grundmann came to realize by the mid-1930s that Christianity and National Socialism could best collaborate on the so-called Jewish Problem. In May of 1939, Grundmann became the academic director of the new established "Institute for the Study and Eradication of Jewish Influence on German Religious Life," which flourished though 1945. Financed by donations from regional Protestant churches, most of which came under the control of the German Christian Movement, and by the sale of its publications, the Institute produced a dejudaized, nazified Christian Bible, hymnal, and theology, and sponsored numerous theological conferences and lectures by its members, who included about eighty academics, and numerous pastors, bishops, religion teachers, and lay people. A center of passionate, pseudo-scholarship in the field of theology, this Institute was a powerhouse of anti-Semitic propaganda during World War II, and its members continued to hold flourishing careers in East and West Germany after the war.

The accomplishments of German Christian theologians, organized into a powerful pseudo-research institute, was neglected for the first forty years after the war, as historians of the churches focused instead on those few individual theologians who opposed aspects of the Nazi regime, such as Dietrich Bonhoeffer. "Political religion" should be sought not in a political movement that presents itself as religious, but in the church, which transformed itself via the German Christian Movement into a version of the reigning political ideology.

In a 1933 pamphlet, *Religion und Rasse*, which appeared in abbreviated form in the German Christian publication *Christenkreuz und Hakenkreuz* that same year, Grundmann spoke of "the syphillization of our Volk though Rassenschande, miscegenation, and the hybridization of races" that was destroying its cultural-building capacities. He lauded Hitler's recognition of racial mixing as a "sin against nature and as injustice against the Creator."[13] Although the church's mission was to bring the "message of God to the whole world, to all peoples, to all races, to all human beings," each church was to remain racially distinct, so that "Germanic-Nordic Christianity" would be "different from other races and peoples."[14] But Grundmann hastened to add that his position did not imply that Jesus was a Jew: Jesus called himself "son of man," a title that, Grundmann wrote, was an "expression of old, above all Persian—and that means Aryan—hope for a redeemer and create of a new humanity."[15]

Precisely the combination of pseudo-scholarship—claims that "son of man" is an "Aryan" concept—with Nazi racism drove Grundmann's project and the work of the Institute he directed. Several historians have claimed that Grundmann was mired in traditional Christian anti-Judaism, not Nazi anti-Semitism, yet Grundmann's writings are imbued with Nazi concepts and with an admiration for Hitler that is both political and messianic, reflecting the broader consensus of the German Christian Movement. In 1931, Julius Leutheuser, who served as a pastor and as a leader of a local Nazi Party district in the Werra Valley of Thuringia, wrote: "In Adolf Hitler we see the powers again awakening which were once given to the Savior. For the National Socialists there is the experience of joy that finally one can sacrifice his life for something that will remain. . . . Our way is rough, but one thing we know, that we shall as a result maintain a pure soul. Golgotha is followed by the resurrection. We are still standing on the way to Golgotha. Some will remain on it, but the soul, it cannot be stolen. Into your hands we commend our spirit, for Adolf Hitler, we will gladly die."[16]

For the theologians such affirmations did not seem extraordinary. As a case in point, Grundmann's biography and career are notable for their lack of exceptionalism. Raised in a family that took religion and nation seriously, he came easily to a synthesis of Christianity and völkisch ideology. Nowhere did he encounter a challenge to his views, neither from the church nor from his professors at the university. On the contrary, he was given to feel that he was creating something new and valuable within the field of theology, standing at the pinnacle of German New Testament scholarship and ready to bring into reality the principles that had been articulated inchoate for several generations. If, as he believed, Jesus intended to bring an end to Judaism, and if the gospels had falsified his message in certain places, then it was incumbent upon him and his generation of highly trained historical theologians, Grundmann believed, to amend the text and recover the original, authentic version to Christian believers. The political need for such an authentication made the theological task all the more pressing, and it also enhanced for the theologians of the Institute a sense of their own significance.

After completing his doctorate at the University of Tuebingen in 1932, and his vicariate training in Saxony to become ordained as a Lutheran pastor, Grundmann was assigned to a pastorate in a village, where he remained only briefly. Already gaining a reputation as a strong voice within the church in support of National Socialism, Grundmann was appointed assistant to the bishop of Saxony, Friedrich Coch, who was in the process of reorganizing the church along German Christian lines. As founder and editor of a new church newspaper, which he named *Christenkreuz und Hackenkreuz* (Cross and Swastika), Grundmann began to focus his attention increasingly on Jews and Judaism.[17] During these early years of the Third Reich, there seemed to be no conflict between being Christian and Nazi.[18] Those looking for affirmations of Christianity from Hitler could find them. The *Völkischer Beobachter*, the official newspaper of the Nazi Party, did not hesitate to report that Hitler, in a speech delivered in 1922 in a Munich beer hall, declared, "I say my Christian feelings point me to my Lord and Savior as a fighter (tumultuous, prolonged applause). They point me toward the man who, once lonely and surrounded by only a few followers, recognized these Jews and called for battle against them."[19]

Hitler's words were taken at face value and echoed by German Christians; the pastor Paul Lehmann, for example, wrote that the Nazis had revived the foundational belief of earliest Christianity in divine sonship through Hitler: "We only saw the incarnation of God in Christ, but not the divinization of man brought about by him. The movement of Adolf Hitler allowed us finally to understand again the nobility of spirit of the spiritual Creators of the Occident."[20] While explicit Nazi support for the churches waned quickly during the course of the 1930s, German Christians remained devoted to creating a new kind of church. The German Christian Movement commissioned Grundmann in 1933 to formulate its guiding principles, the so-called Twenty-Eight Theses, which called for a "Rassenkirche," a racial church whose members were united by their "blood and race." He defined Christian experience as the foundation of National Socialism, and Nazism the fulfillment of Christianity. With the Theses,

Grundmann transformed himself into a nationally respected church leader.[21]

Rejecting church doctrine and masculinizing (and militarizing) the imagery and language of the church was relatively easy; ridding Christianity of Judaism was a more difficult task. The central figures of the New Testament were said to be Jews: Jesus, Paul, and the apostles. Baptism had allowed innumerable Jews entry into the church over the course of many centuries. The Old Testament was the foundation of the New Testament. How could Christianity be dejudaized? That was the question facing German Christians, especially after the Nuremberg Laws of September 1935 had not only disenfranchised Jews from Germany but had warned against sexual encounters between Jews and Aryans. Could Christian theology be purified of Jewish "blood"?

By 1936, Grundmann was teaching in the theological faculty at the University of Jena, and two years later he was appointed to a professorship in New Testament and Voelkisch Theology, despite never having written the requisite Habilitation thesis. He was only thirty-two years old, but scholarship was no longer the prime requirement for a professorship in theology at a German university. At Jena, the goal was creating a National Socialist theological faculty, and of the five professors, three were committed Nazi Party members, while the other two were acquiescent.[22] Students were expected to incorporate racial theory into their dissertations, and professors failed theological investigations that were not in accord with anti-Semitic principles. Many theology students were also Nazi Party members and attended classes dressed in their SA uniforms.[23]

Grundmann's scholarly writings functioned simultaneously as interpretations of Christian origins and interpretations of contemporary Germany. In his 1938 book on the divine sonship of Jesus, he insisted that Jesus' teaching was an utter repudiation of Judaism.[24] Analogously, Germans were enacting a collective sonship of the Führer. Jesus' divine sonship meant he experienced an intimacy with God, understanding the Father's wishes and surpassing the need for laws and commands. Germans, too, would understand Hitler's wishes without needing explicit direction. Eradicating the Jews did not have to be proclaimed in order to be understood as Hitler's wish and goal. Moreover, just as the heart overrode the commandments in Jesus' teachings, Germans would know that certain commandments, such as murder, could be legitimately violated.

Grundmann rejected Paul for misunderstanding Jesus' message due to his own Jewish background, and he elevated the anti-Jewish Gospel of John as the better interpretation of Jesus. Although Paul rejected the law, Grundmann could not accept Paul's definition of Christians as the "new Israel"; that smacked of an affirmation of Judaism. The Christian message that Grundmann identified led him to claim that all Christians are united as sons of God, freed from sin and fear of death, a theology better suited to a society at war. Most important, he argued, Jesus taught an eschatology not of a future era, but of a salvation within present history, opening the door to interpretations of Nazism as salvation and Hitler as savior.[25]

In a series of meetings of German Christian representatives from regions throughout the Nazi Reich during the course of 1936 to 1938, a new project was undertaken: establishing an institute, composed of theological scholars and pastors, that would create a new church in accord with German Christian principles. Grundmann had hoped to establish the institute at the University of Jena, where other pseudo-scholarly "research" institutes had been established by professors in various disciplines to carry out "Nazi scholarship," but the disdain for theology on the part of the university rector, Karl Astel, led to its rejection. Instead, the church funded him, and the institute was given offices and room for a library in the villa of the pastors' training center of the Thuringian church, in the city of Eisenach, very close to Jena.

Work to dejudaize Christianity was already underway when the Institute's opening was formally celebrated on May 6, 1939, with ceremonies in the Wartburg castle, a place of important symbolic and historical significance: this was where Martin Luther had received asylum after posting his 95 Theses in Wittenberg. Luther translated the New Testament into German while living in the Wartburg, and the castle took on nationalist significance during the course of the nineteenth century, as members of the German student fraternities held gatherings to proclaim their nationalist, racist, and anti-Semitic convictions. The Institute's opening was marked by string quartets, reading of congratulatory telegrams (from, among others, Julius Streicher, editor of the notorious anti-Semitic weekly newspaper *Der Stuermer*), and lectures. Grundmann gave the keynote address, on "the dejudaization of religious life as the task of German theology and the church." He declared, "The elimination of Jewish influence on German life is the urgent and fundamental question of the present

German religious situation."²⁶ Jews had destroyed völkisch thinking and, with help from Bolshevism, they were now striving for world domination. "For these reasons, the struggle against the Jews has been irrevocably turned over to the German Volk."²⁷ The war against the Jews was not simply a military battle, but a spiritual battle: "Jewish influence on all areas of German life, including on religious-church life, must be exposed and broken."²⁸ That sentence, in turn, became the defining slogan of the Institute, used whenever Grundmann had to explain its purpose.

Institute members were divided into working groups, and their tasks were addressed immediately. One group was assigned the task of preparing a new version of the New Testament (the Old Testament having already been eliminated from German Christian use). Published in 1940, *Die Botschaft Gottes* removed passages describing Jesus' genealogical descent from Old Testament figures, references to Zion, Jerusalem, and the Temple. To distance Jesus from Judaism, the Sabbath was called *Feiertag*, and Passover was called *Osterfest*. Apocalyptic ideas were removed, as well as terms such as *sinner, righteous, repentance*. The epistles of the Jewish convert Paul were abridged, and the Gospel of John, with its strong anti-Jewish motifs, was retained. The following year, the Institute published a hymnal, *Grosser Gott Wir Loben Dich*, containing 339 hymns purged of references to the Old Testament and Hebrew words such as *Hallelujah*, and illustrated with drawings of soldiers carrying guns.

Grundmann and other colleagues from the Institute, such as Wolf Meyer-Erlach, who was also professor of practical theology at the University of Jena, went on lecture tours to Wehrmacht troops in France, Finnland, Ostland, and Ukraine.²⁹ Grundmann described the Institute's work as an effort to reconfigure the consciousness of Europe.³⁰ In a 1942 book he coauthored with Karl Euler, an instructor of the New Testament at the University of Giessen, titled *The Religious Face of Judaism*, they wrote, "A healthy Volk must and will reject Judaism in every form. This reality is justified before history and through history. If someone is upset about Germany's treatment of the Jews, Germany has the historical justification and the historical legitimation for the struggle against the Jews on its side."³¹

The theological problems posed by National Socialism were not always easily resolved. How should a Nazi pray, if prayer implies an attitude of supplication and pathos directly at odds with the manly, militaristic posture promoted by Hitler? The nature of prayer during the Third Reich had to be reconfigured as praise and affirmation rather than atonement and petition. The Nazis formulated short verse as substitutes for Christian liturgy, directed not to God but to Hitler, primarily as expressions of praise for the Führer's beneficent leadership. German Christians wanted to demonstrate that Christian liturgy could be comparably Nazified. They suggested, for example, that religious services should no longer be called "Gottesdienst" (divine service) but rather "Gottesfeier" (divine celebration) because "service" was Old Testament Jewish, while "celebration" was German. Yet such linguistic changes did not resolve all the problems.

Should one pray for Germans and Germany, or for all Christians, even those in countries opposed to the Reich? Could there be prayers for peace, a central theme in Christian scripture and liturgy, when Germany was preparing for war or even at war? Prayers of repentance and requests for divine forgiveness also seemed out of place; *Das Schwarze Korps*, the newspaper of the Sturmabteilung (the so-called Brown Shirts), objected to sinners confessing and asking forgiveness of God on behalf of the Volk.[32] If prayer included entreaties, would that transfer German fate to God's hands? Institute conferences, for example, included the singing of Nazi songs as well as Christian hymns, the Nazi salute as well as a Christian benediction, all expressing triumph.

The Institute also produced a catechism, as well as educational materials for religion teachers. In the catechism, Jesus was defined as "Der Heiland der Deutschen" (savior of the Germans) with the following explanation:

> Jesus of Nazareth in the Galilee proves in his message and behavior a spirit that is in opposition to Judaism in every way. The struggle between him and the Jew became so bitter than it led to his deadly crucifixion. Thus Jesus cannot have been a Jew. Until this very day the Jews persecute Jesus and all who follow him with unreconcilable hatred. By contrast, Aryans in particular found in Jesus Christ the answer to their ultimate and deepest questions. So he became the savior of the Germans.[33]

The catechism omitted traditional doctrinal positions regarding miracles, virgin birth, incarnation, resurrection, and so forth, in favor of positioning Jesus as a human being who struggled on behalf of God and died not only as a martyr but was also a "Sieger" (victor) on the cross, despite being a victim of the Jews. He functioned in that way as a figure with whom Germans could identify in their own struggle against the Jews on behalf of God. This identification is given further impetus in the "Twelve Commandments" presented in the catechism, which include "Keep the blood pure and the marriage holy!" and "Honor Führer and Master!" but omit mention of murder, theft, and, of course, Sabbath observance.

The language of the catechism was subtle by comparison to others. For example, a 1940 catechism, *Ruf an den jungen Morgen*, taught: "Who is the enemy of the German essence? The enemy of the German essence is the eternal Jew. . . . Was Christ a Jew? It is the greatest lie that the Jews have brought into the world, that Jesus is a Jew. . . . What obligations do we have? Jesus' life and teaching is a great challenge against the Jewish spirit. . . . What do we think of the Old Testament? Just as in a field, grain and weeds grow together, so the Old Testament contains good and evil. We have reverence for its eternal truths about God, but we exterminate its Jewish spirit root and branch."[34]

In June of 1942, at an Institute conference in Nuremberg,[35] dejudaization was discussed both in terms of popular liturgy and the problem of the apostle Paul. Hermann Werdermann, professor of Practical Theology at the University of Rostock, warned of the "danger of judaization" in religious instruction that included the Old Testament and Matthew's Gospel. The children's prayer, "I am small, my heart is pure, no one should reside in it except Jesus," based on Psalms 51:10 ("Create in me a clean heart, O God, and put a new and right spirit within me."), was condemned by Werdermann: "Then through that children's prayer a small, self-righteous Pharisee will be raised!"[36] He reiterated those warnings at a meeting in Jena in January of 1943 of the Religious Pedagogy working group, urging that race as the "order of creation" be recognized as the basis of Christian truth and that Jesus be viewed "with German eyes" to see his opposition to Judaism.[37]

Although it was relatively easy to define Jesus as an Aryan, Paul's Jewishness was far less easy to eradicate. In his autobiographical statements included in his writings, Paul is quick to inform his readers that he had been a Pharisee, zealous for the law, prior to his conversion experience on the road to Damascus. The Institute was unsuccessful in redefining Paul. Its version of the New Testament simply excerpted Pauline writings, omitting those referring to his Jewishness, but did not solve the problem conclusively. At an Institute conference held in Nuremberg in June of 1942, theologians Georg Bertram and Theodor Pauls came to the conclusion that "a German faith cannot be based on Paul, because it would then be deformed through his Jewish system of coordinates, and their necessary Germanic foundations would not be able to come into effect."[38] Paul was of mixed race and mixed thinking, combining Pharisaic closed-mindedness with Hellenistic open-mindedness. He was unable to free himself from Jewish ways of thinking, though he managed to preserve the gospel of divine sonship. The question of Paul was never fully resolved.

Finally, in August of 1944, Hugo Pich, a retired pastor who was one of the founders of the Institute, circulated a memorandum calling for a radical purging of Paul. Pich claimed that the Jews were to blame for the assassination attempt on Hitler on July 20, 1944, and for the German war dead. The war, he claimed, was a battle of the German nation against a world Jewry bent on its destruction, while the church, by retaining Paul and his epistles, remained a "breeding ground" for Jewishness.[39] What was needed was the "faith in God" of Jesus, "for which he, in battle against the Jews, went to his death."[40] The church should reject the "Jew Scha-ul with his Jewish-messianic 'Christ'-proclamation."[41]

The reactions to Pich's memorandum were negative. Hugo Rönck, president of the Thuringian church,[42] told Pich that in attacking Paul, he was giving ammunition to the Confessing Church, which long claimed that the German Christians had abandoned Christianity.[43] Johannes Sievers, a pastor and executive director of the Institute, replied that Germany's state of total war had become so drastic that no reconfiguration of the church could be considered at present.[44] Bishop Walther Schultz of Mecklenburg, one of the early and most enthusiastic supporters of the Institute, described Pich as a theological hysteric and urged that his proposal not be adopted as an official Institute policy.[45] Furthermore, Schultz wrote to Rönck, "I consider Pich's observations completely erroneous and moreover an insult to our nation, which is blamed indirectly for having been duped, in its hopeless stupidity and lack of instinct, by some stinking Jew for 1500 years" ("verschwitzem Juden auf dem Leim gekrochen").[46] That Christians might have been duped by believing in Jesus' Jewishness was not considered.

No single demographic or intellectual profile fits the Institute's members. Theologians who joined the Institute represented a spectrum of generational and demographic patterns as well as areas of research within theology. Some were full professors; others were lower on the academic totem pole. Some were Nazi Party members of long standing, while others never joined. Neither age nor geographic location within the Reich seems to have been a determinative factor. What the Institute offered its members was career enhancement and the intellectual tools to racialize their theological research.

Through the Institute, members had the chance to link the theological anti-Judaism that had long pervaded German Protestantism with the racist anti-Semitism promoted by the Nazis and to link their historical claims of the allegedly degenerate nature of Jews in antiquity with the degeneracy of contemporary Jews. Arguments about Jesus' relationship to Judaism were suddenly lifted from the narrow world of gospel interpretation and placed at the center of the Third Reich's politics: solving the "Jewish Problem." Out of the obscurity and political irrelevance of narrow points of theological scholarship, Institute members transformed themselves into experts on the vital problem of ridding Europe of the Jews. The Institute was the theological version of the many racial "research" institutes that flourished in virtually every academic discipline during the Third Reich, creating a widespread project of "Judenforschung" that flourished during the Third Reich and engaged scholars from a wide range of disciplines.[47] Walter Grundmann, as academic director of the Institute, was typical of its members in his academic and political background, and at the same time, he was their inspiration and tireless driving force.

Precisely what academics seek was what the Institute offered: support for publications, conferences to present ideas, gatherings to meet colleagues, and a sense of self-importance. The connections forged through the Institute lasted far longer than the Third Reich. After the war, Institute members wrote letters to denazification commissions on behalf of one another, attesting, falsely, to each other's opposition to National Socialism. Such letters were crucial in attaining denazification clearances. Furthermore, alliances among Institute members continued in joint publications and research projects and in conference and lecture invitations. Even the effort to dejudaize Christianity was not abandoned in 1945, but shifted, with the discovery of the Dead Sea Scrolls in 1948, to claims that the Scrolls represented a non-Jewish, possibly Iranian (i.e., Aryan) context out of which Jesus and his early followers emerged.[48]

What sort of political and social impact did the Institute exert? The archives of the Institute retain a few letters by German chaplains and soldiers, thanking the Institute for its work. A pastor serving as a non-commissioned officer stationed in Ukraine wrote that he read the *Verbandsmitteilungen*, the Institute's newsletter, "with a glowing heart" and rejoiced over the Institute's "blessed progress." A lance corporal wrote: "Everyone has to be liberated from the Jewish delusion, because it is not possible that we in the Third Reich still have Jewish teachings. They must and will be destroyed, at whatever cost. Our struggle will be carried out however necessary. We were born as warriors and, if necessary, will die in battle. We want to open the eyes of our compatriots and liberate them from the Jewish spell, because this is about the well-being and future of our Volk. Our struggle has begun and it will be carried out until the final victory."[49]

The last conference organized by the Institute was held March 22 to 24, 1944, at the Thuringian Pastors' Training Seminary (Predigerseminar) in Eisenach, held despite the bombings that had reached the city, for the purpose of contributing to the "world historical conflict with Jewry for which all the powers of the German soul have to be mobilized," as Bertram wrote.[50] The tone of the conference was shrill in its discussion of Jews, and speakers defined the purpose of the war not in terms of conquest of land or of Bolshevism, but as a war against the Jews. Bertram opened the meeting by declaring: "'This war is the struggle of the Jews against Europe.' That sentence contains a truth that is constantly being newly confirmed by the scholarly work of the Institute. In that way this work is not only a frontal attack, but also securing the stability of the internal front for attack and defense against all secretive Jews and Jewish essence that over the course of the centuries has infiltrated Western culture."[51]

Euler delivered a lecture justifying Nazi policies against the Jews. Echoing by-now-familiar Nazi propaganda, he denounced Zionism, claiming that Jews sought a return to Palestine as a means to achieve "Jewish world rule," and sought equal rights within nations as a "process of destruction" that was the "precondition of the Jewish seizure of world rule." Either the world will be "verjudet" or "entjudet," Judaized or dejudaized, Euler concluded, and there is only one solution to the "Judenfrage," and that is the solution taken by Germany:

We have thrown down the gauntlet with a clear resolution to settle the Jewish question for the entire future. Germany, the land of thinkers and scientists, poets and artists—this land is called by fate to fight to gain the world by fighting what is possible: The solution of the Jewish question! . . . [T]he hour is coming when all choirs and orchestras of the world, together with all those who have lost their lives in the struggle with the Jewish Moloch, will become one in the last hymn of victory, Wake up, the day is coming.[52]

Grundmann's final propaganda publication appeared in 1944 and was written while he was in military service on the Eastern front, a pamphlet defending the Third Reich that was addressed to German troops with little explicit Christian theological content but with an unwavering loyalty to Germany and hatred of the Jews despite the clear evidence that the war was lost.[53] It opens by stating that "the Jew" is "the Antichrist [who] wants to unleash itself (*sich entfesseln*) and overthrow the Reich."[54] He then presents Germany as the savior of Europe against the degeneration of both East and West. Russia disintegrated through military challenges and incompetent leadership centuries ago, while the West disintegrated as a consequence of its liberalism, which permitted the emancipation of the Jews. Thus the war is fought in self-defense against the Jews:

This Western belief system became the pre-condition for the Jews' break-out from the ghetto and their intrusion into Western society with all the devastating consequences of internal and external corruption, of which the Jews are the carriers everywhere. Most of all they pursued the corruption of values and the destruction of awe before the mysteries of life.[55]

Values and awe—here was the religious core of the anti-Semitism and the justification of murder.

To what extent did Grundmann's theology change after 1945? Like other Nazis, Grundmann abandoned the use of certain words: he no longer spoke of German as a "Volk" who were "Aryans," nor did he describe present-day Germans as infected by Jews and their syphilis. However, he continued to describe the dangers of Jews and Judaism in the days of Jesus, using language that carried echoes of his Nazi writings. Judaism was "krank," "gewalttaetig," "fanatisch," "gefaehrlich," for example, and it was the Jews who sought the "Vernichtung" of Jesus. Grundmann's scholarship was never subjected to critical review by colleagues in the field of the New Testament. In the postwar era, he continued to be invited to conferences, and his articles were included in academic anthologies. Even more important, his 1938 membership in the newly inaugurated and highly prestigious Society for New Testament Studies was never revoked.[56] He was East Germany's most exalted theologian and published extensively, including large commentaries on the synoptic gospels that became required reading for pastors in East and West Germany. He traveled extensively, thanks to his work as an informant for the Stasi, the East German secret police, and never expressed a word of regret or remorse over his Nazi activities, nor over the deeds of the Nazi regime.

CONCLUSION

If historians want to view the Nazi regime, in its political goals, propaganda, and ideology, as a form of "political religion," then the collaboration of the German Christian Movement in creating a Nazified Christianity should certainly be understood as its foundation stone. More useful, however, is to understand how the German Christian Movement created a synthesis of National Socialism and Christianity that, in the formulation of Todd McGowan, "provided the conditions for the possibility of National Socialism," specifically in its anti-Jewish policies and actions.[57] Nazi ideology vied with Christianity over anti-Semitism: whose version was superior and most effective. Each helped the other, church and Reich: National Socialism provided the rubrics within which Grundmann could create his Institute and bring into reality the kind of dejudaization that prior generations of Christian theologians could only imagine.

The relationship between Nazism and Christianity was therefore intimate and codependent. Christianity, in its earliest years, proclaimed its supersession of the Old Testament as the foundation of Christian belief that was no longer tenable without its fulfillment in the New Testament. Similarly, National Socialism took up the anti-Semitism of Christianity but elevated it to a more intense level and transformed it from theory to action. Christianity by itself would not fulfill Nazi goals, but without Christian anti-Judaism, Nazi anti-Semitism lost its foundational legitimacy.

In many ways, Grundmann and his colleagues suffered from an unrequited love, never receiving the kind of recognition and honor from the

Reich that they longed for. Yet their contribution to the Nazi regime should not be underestimated. As Grundmann himself asserted, Germany was fighting a spiritual battle as well as a military one, and he and his theological colleagues were leading that spiritual battle. For its part, National Socialism was the military tool of the Institute's goal: eradication of Jews, Judaism, and Jewishness.

ABBREVIATIONS

AAPA: Auswärtiges Amt/Politisches Archiv, Berlin (German Foreign Office archives, Berlin)
  BDC: Berlin Document Center
  ThHStA: Thüringisches Volksbildungsminiseriums (Thuringian Education Ministry archives, Weimar)
  ThLKA: Landeskirchen Archiv, Eisenach (Thuringian Protestant Church archives, Eisenach)
  UH: University of Heidelberg archives
  UL: University of Lund archives
  ZAK: Zentral Archiv der Kirche (Central archives of the Protestant Church, Berlin)

NOTES

1. Dorothy Thompson, "Goodby to Germany," *Harper's Bazaar* 170 (December 1934): 46. On the Oberammergau play, see Saul S. Friedman, *The Oberammergau Passion Play: A Lance against Civilization* (Carbondale and Edwardsville: Southern Illinois University Press, 1984), and James S. Shapiro, *Oberammergau: The Troubling Story of the World's Most Famous Passion Play* (New York: Pantheon Books, 2000). See also Guenter Berghaus, "The Ritual Core of Fascist Theatre," in *Fascism and Theatre: Comparative Studies on the Aesthetics and Politics of Performance in Europe, 1925–1945* (Oxford: Berghahn, 1996), 63.

2. Letter to Schmidt-Clausing, May 26, 1947 (University of Lund, Sweden, archives, Odeberg materials).

3. Claus-Ekkehard Baersch, *Die politische Religion des Nationalsozialismus: die religiöse Dimension der NS-Ideologie in den Schriften von Dieter Eckart, Joseph Goebbels, Alfred Rosenberg und Adolf Hitler* (Munich: W. Fink,

1998); Richard Steigmann-Gall, *The Holy Reich: Nazi Conceptions of Christianity, 1919–1945* (New York: Cambridge University Press, 2003).

4. Philippe Burrin, "Political Religion: The Relevance of a Concept," *History and Memory* 9, no. 1–2 (Autumn 1997): 326–27.

5. Michael Burleigh, *The Third Reich: A New History* (New York: Hill and Wang, 2000), 256.

6. Stanley Stowers, "The Concepts of 'Religion,' 'Political Religion' and the Study of Nazism," *Journal of Contemporary History* 42, no. 1 (January 2007): 24.

7. Doris Bergen, *Twisted Cross: The German Christian Movement in the Third Reich* (Chapel Hill: University of North Carolina Press, 1996).

8. Susannah Heschel, "Church Protests during the Third Reich: A Report on Two Cases," *Kirchliche Zeitgeschichte* 10, no. 2 (1998): 377–88.

9. From "Bericht über die Arbeitstagung der 'Deutschen Christen' Gruppe Rheinland," *Briefe an deutsche Christen* 3, no. 8 (August 1934): 144–46.

10. "Das Gottverlangen im deutschen Volk sei nichts zufälliges, das in ihm das Blut wieder gesund geworden sei," Abschrift betriff. Bericht über DC-Versammlung in Jena am 8. April 1937. ThLKA Eisenach, BK A 124.

11. Grundmann received the membership no. 382544 (BDC Grundmann files).

12. Grundmann joined the SS as a "supporting member" on April 1, 1934 (no. 1032691), and the NSV on July 1, 1934 (no. 1827439). Later, on January 1, 1937, he became a member of the editorial board of the Commission for Protecting National Socialist Writings. Questionnaire signed by Grundmann July 6, 1938. ThHStA in Weimar PA Walter Grundmann, 8807, 68.

13. Walter Grundmann, *Religion und Rasse: Ein Beitrag zur Frage "nationaler Aufbruch" und "lebendiger Christusglaube." Veröffentlichungen der Arbeitsgemeinschaft nationalsozialistischer Pfarrer* 3 (Werdau 1933), 8; appeared in an abbreviated version in *Christenkreuz und Hakenkreuz* 1 (November/December 1933). Cited by Adam, 175. See also that year, idem., "Die nationale Bewegung unter dem Wort Gottes," *Pastoralblätter für Predigt, Seelsorge und kirchliche Unterweisung* 75 (1932/1933), 321–27.

14. Grundmann, "Religion und Rasse, 1," *Christenkreuz und Hakenkreuz* 1, no. 4 (November/December 1933).

15. Grundmann, "Religion und Rasse, 1."

16. Julius Leutheuser, *Peniger Tageblatt* of January 20, 1931; cited by Besier, "German Protestant Churches during the Agony of Weimar," 152.

17. The journal changed its name in 1937 to *Deutsche Frömmigkeit* (*German Piety*), most likely because of a Nazi Party prohibition instituted in 1936 against using the swastika without party approval—a prohibition protested by numerous

pastors who had hung the swastika next to the cross on the church altar. Heschel, "Church Protests during the Third Reich," 377–88.

18. See, for example, Hanche, "Christliche Frauengedanken über Nationalsozialismus"; Börner, "Der Reichsparteitag," 5–6. For a detailed review of Grundmann's articles in *Christenkreuz und Hakenkreuz*, see Roland Deines, "Jesus Der Galiläer: Traditionsgeschichte Und Genese Eines Antisemitischen Konstrukts Bei Walter Grundmann," in *Walter Grundmann: Ein Neutestamentler in Dritten Reich*, ed. Volker Leppin, Roland Deines, and Karl-Wilhelm Niebuhr (Leipzig: Evangelischer Verlagsanstalt, 2007).

19. *Völkischer Beobachter* 13/4/22; cited by Richard Steigmann-Gall, "Was National Socialism a Political Religion or a Religious Politics?," *Religion und Nation, Nation und Religion*, ed. Michael Geyer and Hartmut Lehmann (Göttingen: Wallstein, 2004), 403.

20. Paul Lehmann, *Todeskampf der Christentümer und der gegenwärtigen Wiedergeburt des Urchristentums im deutschen Volk* (1937).

21. Adam, "Der theologische Werdegang W. Grundmanns," 188.

22. Nazi Party members were Grundmann; Heinz Eisenhuth, professor of systematic theology; and Wolf Meyer-Erlach. The other two professors, Karl Heussei, professor of church history, and Gerhard von Rad, professor of Old Testament, were not Nazi Party members, though von Rad had joined the SA in 1934.

23. Herbert von Hinzenstern, quoted by Tobias Schüfer, "Die Theologische Fakultät Jena und die Landeskirche im Nationalsozialismus," in *Thüringer Gratwanderungen: Beiträge zur fünfundsiebzigjährigen Geschichte der evangelischen Landeskirche Thüringens*, ed. Thomas A. Seidel (Leipzig: Evangelische Verlagsanstalt, 1998), 102.

24. Walter Grundmann, *Die Gotteskindschaft in der Geschichte Jesu und ihre Religionsgeschichtlichen Vorausetzungen. Studien zu deutscher Theologie und Frömmigkeit 1* (Weimar: Verlag Deutsche Christen, 1938).

25. Walter Grundmann, *Aufnahme und Deutung der Botschaft Jesu im Urchristentum*, Studien zu deutscher Theologie und Frömmigkeit 3 (Weimar: Verlag Deutsche Christen, 1941).

26. Grundmann's lecture was printed as a pamphlet and distributed through the German Christian publishing house in Weimar, run by Heinz Dungs, himself an Institute member. Six thousand copies were printed, at a cost of 2,070 RM, apparently paid for by Werner, who had promised Grundmann he would distribute the text to pastors within the APU. As announced in the first issue of the *Verbandsmitteilungen*, the Institute's newsletter, membership in the Institute was open to a circle of subscribers, who paid 1 RM and received the newsletter, as well as a discount on Institute publications. ZAK 7/4166, documents 37 and 38.

27. Grundmann, *Die Entjudung des religiösen Lebens als Aufgabe deutscher Theologie und Kirche* (Weimar: Verlag Deutsche Christen, 1939), 9.

28. Grundmann, *Die Entjudung*, 17.

29. AAPA, Sign. R98796, No. 1949, Report (unsigned) of the Institute meeting held in Weissenfels, undated, submitted to General Konsul Wuester at the German Foreign Office.

30. Ibid.

31. Walter Grundmann and Karl Friedrich Euler, "Vorwort," in *Das religiöse Gesicht des Judentums: Entstehung und Art* (Leipzig: Verlag Georg Wigand, 1942).

32. *Das Schwarze Korps*, October 27, 1938; cited by William Helmreich, *The German Churches under Hitler* (Detroit: Wayne State University Press, 1979), 230.

33. *Deutsche mit Gott: Ein deutsches Glaubensbuch* (Weimar: Verlag Deutsche Christen, 1941), 46. The foreword to the catechism was signed by Grundmann, Wilhelm Büchner, Paul Gimpel, Hans Pribnow, Kurt Thieme, Max Adolf Wagenführer, Heinrich Weinmann, and Hermann Werdermann.

34. "Wer ist der Feind des deutschen Wesens? Der Feind des deutschen Wesens ist der ewige Jude. . . . War Christus Jude? Es ist die grösste Lüge, die die Juden in die Welt gebracht haben, dass Jesus Jude sei. Welche Gegenbeweise haben wir? Jesu Leben und Lehre ist eine grosse Kampfansage gegen den jüdischen Geist. . . . Was halten wir vom Alten Testeament? Wie auf dem Felde Korn und Unkraut zusammen wachsen, so findet sich im Alten Testament Gutes und Böses. Vor seinem ewigen Gotteswahrheiten haben wir Ehrfurcht, seinen jüdischen Geist aber rotten wir mit Stumpf und Stiel aus." Wilhelm Gruber, *Rufe an den jungen Morgen: Ein deutscher Katechismus* (1940), 1, 4, 11. Copy viewed at ThLKA Eisenach.

35. The conference took place Monday to Wednesday, June 8–10, 1942, at the Hotel Deutscher Hof in Nuremberg, postponed from a March date due to war exigencies. Notice from Grundmann about postponement of the Tagung, February 25, 1942; UL archives, Odeberg files. Because of the war exigencies, this was not, as usual, a conference open to the public, but open only to members. Its tone was also different. No papers were delivered about Jesus, for the first time, and instead, there was extensive presentation of Nordic literature, with two lectures on the Icelandic hymn, the Völuspa. In addition to theologians, several writers with völkisch connections spoke: Ake Ohlmarks (1911–), Hans Franck (Mecklenburg; 1879–1964), and Wilhelm Kotzde-Kottenrodt. Ohlmarks, a Swede, held a visiting appointment at the Moritz Arndt University in Greifswald. See Åke Ohlmarks and Lars Åkerberg, *Thomas Thorild als Vorläufer der neuzeitlichen Religionswissenschaft* (Greifswald: Veröffentlichungen des Religion-

swissenschaftlichen Instituts der Ernst Moritz Arndt-Universität Greifswald, 1944).

36. Hermann Werdermann (Dortmund), "Die Gefahr des Judaisierens in der religiösen Erziehung und ihre Überwindung," in *Germanentum, Christenum und Judentum*, ed. Walter Grundmann. Studien zur Erforschung ihres gegenseitigen Verhaeltnisses. Dritter Band. Sitzungesberichte der dritten Arbeitstagung des Instituts zur Erforschung des jüdischen Einflusses auf das deutsche kirchliche Leben vom 9. bis 11. Juni 1942 in Nuernberg (Leipzig: Georg Wigand, 1943), 217–48.

37. Five-page report from Institut, Der Pressereferent, Pastor Heinz Dungs, Weimar, dated May 13, 1943. UH archives, PA25: Personalakten: Theodor Odenwald.

38. Theodor Pauls, "Die Ursprünglichkeit des Gotteslobes bei Luther," in *Germanentum, Christenum und Judentum*. Studien zur Erforschung ihres gegenseitigen Verhaeltnisses. Dritter Band. Sitzungesberichte der dritten Arbeitstagung des Instituts zur Erforschung des juedischen Einflusses auf das deutsche kirchliche Leben vom 9. bis 11. Juni 1942 in Nuernberg. Hrsg. Walter Grundmann (Leipzig: Georg Wigand, 1943), 137–92; and Georg Bertram, "Paulus, Judensendling und Christusapostel," in idem., 83–136.

39. Pich, Der Weg zur entjudeten deutschen Reichskirche in der Glaubensgefolgschaft Jesu, 1. ThLKA Eisenach, C III 2a, folder: Institut 1938–1944.

40. Pich, Der Weg zur entjudeten deutschen, 5.

41. Pich, Der Weg zur entjudeten deutschen, 6.

42. Praesidialgesetz makes him a president, rather than a bishop, according to Thuringen church laws dated Feburary 1943, which state that the position of bishop will remain unfilled throughout the war.

43. Letter from Rönck to Pich, dated August 18, 1944. ThLKA Eisenach.

44. Letter from Sievers to Pich, dated August 15, 1944. ThLKA Eisenach.

45. Letter from Schultz to Bertram, dated August 9, 1944. ThLKA Eisenach.

46. Letter from Schultz to Rönck, dated August 2, 1944. ThLKA Eisenach.

47. Dirk Rupnow, "'Judenforschung' Im 'Dritten Reich.' Wissenschaft zwischen Ideologie, Propaganda Und Politik," in *Historische West und Ostforschung in Zentraleuropa zwischen dem ersten und dem zweiten Weltkrieg - Verflechtung und Vergleich*, ed. Matthias Middell and Ulrike Sommer (Leipzig: Akademische Verlagsanstalt, 2004).

48. Susannah Heschel, *The Aryan Jesus: Christian Theologians and the Bible in Nazi Germany* (Princeton: Princeton University Press, 2008), 263–64.

49. Grundmann and Pich, "An die Förderer des Institutes," March 25, 1943, ThLKA Eisenach.

50. Bericht, ThLKA Eisenach, uncatalogued.

51. Bishop Walther Schultz to President Rönck, 2 August 1944 re. Pich's Denkschrift, *Der Jude Schaul*. ThLKA Thüringen, Personalia: Leffler, Grundmann: Institut 1938–1944.

52. ThLKA Eisenach DC, III. Cited by Buss, "'Entjudung Der Kirche': Ein Kircheninstitut Und Die Schleswig-Holsteinische Landeskirche," 175.

53. Walter Grundmann, *Das Reich der Deutschen*, vol. 52, Schriftenreihe zur Truppenbetreuung.

54. Grundmann, *Das Reich der Deutschen*, 4.

55. Grundmann, *Das Reich der Deutschen*, 89.

56. Lukas Bormann, "'Auch unter politischen Gesichtspunkten sehr sorgfaeltig ausgewaehlt': Die ersten deutschen Mitglieder der Studiorum Novi Testamenti Societas (SNTS) 1937–1946," *New Testament Studies* 58 (2012), 416–52.

57. Personal communication from Professor Todd McGowan, University of Vermont, on April 28, 2014.

25

VATTIMO, DIVERSITY, AND CATHOLICISM

Thomas G. Guarino, Seton Hall University

I would like to thank Professor Michael Sweeney of the philosophy department at Xavier University for kindly inviting me to speak in the Ethics, Religion and Society Series, presently examining the notions of tolerance, diversity, and justice. How should these terms be understood, particularly within Catholic institutions?

This evening, I would like, first, to focus on a well-known philosopher, whose thought is popular internationally and who represents a widespread point of view. Secondly, I would like to put his thought into dialogue with insights from the Catholic tradition. Finally, I intend to present some conclusions from this dialogue—highlighting my belief that Christianity has unique contributions to offer contemporary thought on the issues of diversity, tolerance, and justice.

THE THOUGHT OF GIANNI VATTIMO

The philosopher in question is an Italian thinker by the name of Gianteresio (or as he is universally known, Gianni Vattimo).

Born in 1936, Vattimo spent his academic career at the University of Turin, with specialties in hermeneutics and in the thought of Nietzsche and Heidegger. He has been a visiting professor in the United States, having taught at Yale, Stanford, and other institutions. Vattimo has amassed an extraordinary array of publications, both in professional journals as well as in general-interest magazines and newspapers. He is the translator into Italian of Hans-Georg Gadamer's influential work on hermeneutics, *Truth and Method,* and in 2010, he delivered the prestigious Gifford Lectures at the University of Glasgow in Scotland. Vattimo has been a member of the European parliament for many years, and is a philosopher who remains deeply engaged in political issues. Over the last couple of decades, one significant dimension of Vattimo's work has centered on the role of religion in contemporary life and its conjunction with postmodern thought. He describes himself as a thinker who is both a Communist and a Catholic—but, as we shall see, his Catholicism has a unique flavor.[1]

If we try to categorize Vattimo philosophically, we may speak of him as a "postmodern" thinker. But what exactly does that term mean? In truth, almost everyone today considers himself *post*modern because "modernity" has become equated with a bloodless, worldless rationalism that has fallen into deep academic disrepute. Speaking generally, the term *postmodernism* refers to the continually growing critique of Enlightenment construals of rationality. *Modern* rationality is understood as an attemp to pin down reason to the narrowly restrictive canons of empiricism, positivism, and scientism. Consequently, modernity is often equated with a reductive attempt to reduce truth to methodology, particularly those methods and canons associated with scientific inquiry. But this profoundly circumscribed approach to reason leads to the detriment of philosophical wonder, and to the equation of thinking with mere *techné* (or technical skill). It is for this reason that Heidegger famously quipped, "Science does not think."[2] In other words, positivism, with its strong accent on pure methodology, cannot be regarded as thought—as sustained reflection on the nature of truth, or on the relationship between being and history.

*Post*modernity's contemporary ascent, then, is fueled by its opposition to modernity's errors: its simplistic trust in science, its devaluation of the truth mediated by the arts and by tradition, its misunderstanding of historicity, and its marginalization of religion under the banner of the Enlightenment claim that science has unmasked faith as little more than superstitious mythology. Indeed, postmodernity argues that modern forms of rationality are now in deep retreat. One foundation of rationalism—the thesis that faith in God would disappear in the face of continuing education—has now been entirely discredited. And rationalist approaches have hardly solved the intractable problems of human suffering, poverty, and global warfare. In general, modernity's colonization of the world by a luminous scientific reason, apart from religion and tradition, now seems a misguided and constricting dream.

Modernity, of course, was no friend of religious faith. The Enlightenment wished to expel religion from the public square on the grounds that it fomented the passions of men and women, was not supported by empirical evidence, inexorably led to obscurantist dogmatism, and—importantly for us this evening—contributed to loathsome intolerance and injustice. The equation was simple enough: Religious people are by definition dogmatic—fully convinced that they possess the truth—and therefore *ipso facto* intolerant. Consequently, modernity argued that religion's explosive potency could be domesticated and neutered only *by reducing it to an entirely private affair, shorn of any public role in everyday societal interchange.* Vattimo argues, however, that this imperious attitude of modern rationalism has now been exposed as defective. Modernity's exclusion of dogmatic, passionate, and "intolerant" religion in the name of an allegedly objective and disinterested scientific reason is an exhausted project. This is especially the case inasmuch as the profoundly hermeneutical and interpretative character of scientific reasoning itself has been fully unmasked.[3] With the debunking of modernity's pretensions, religion must once again be accorded a central role in society. Religion must be returned, and robustly so, to the public square.

But at this very point the crucial difficulty arises. For while Vattimo insists that religion must be allotted a public, societal role, which *kind* of Christianity is now welcome in contemporary society? Before answering the question, let us examine, even if briefly and within strict limits, Vattimo's signal philosophical idea, known as "weak thought" (*pensiero debole*).

Vattimo argues that if contemporary philosophy has taught us anything, it is that all men and women are deeply enmeshed in history; that is to say, we live and think within particular societal and cultural norms, and only "know" anything within determinate frameworks or paradigms. All human beings, in other words, are swimming in a socio-cultural-linguistic soup; they are profoundly, and inescapably, enveloped by the historicized world. Precisely because of this enmeshment, one must avoid making dogmatic claims to truth, finality, or objectivity. To make such claims is to try to *overcome* the historical and cultural contingency that indefeasibly encompasses us. Indeed, it is precisely historical provisionality and contingency—the intense awareness of our deeply conditioned social location—that must lead to epistemological humility. And so our thought must be "weak" rather than "strong" and dogmatic.

Surely we have learned, Vattimo insists, that there exists no "evidence" that is not itself already implicated in determinate forms of life and in interpretative structures. The meanings of "things" (entities, objects) are only accessible within contextualized frameworks. We possess no clearly available *archai* or undisputed first principles that could settle matters finally, that could offer definitive notions of truth and objectivity that would escape these insuperable limits.[4] This is why hermeneutics has become the new philosophical *koiné*—the common language uniting the educated world—precisely because everyone now recognizes that there are no "answers" to the most fundamental questions—there exist only widely divergent interpretations.[5]

Given these epistemological principles, it is essential that men and women show tolerance for every nonviolent point of view. Why is this the case? Because the major questions before us—What is the meaning of life? By which values should we live? What are the ethical foundations of a just society?—cannot be solved simply by attending to states of affairs, as if the world provided solutions to these pressing questions. On the contrary, these are all matters of continuing—and deeply historicized—interpretation, both individually and in diverse communities. Consequently, there should reign the widest possible tolerance for a plurality of opinions and lifestyles—and this for the sake of equality and justice.

The Internet serves as a good example of what Vattimo and postmodernity are driving at. We may pose to the web a range of questions: What is the nature of humanity? Which values are ultimate? Is there a God? Do we know anything about him? The web will respond with millions of answers, delivered in milliseconds. And this is precisely Vattimo's point: In these innumerable responses, we have the multivalent, infinitely interpretable world on full view. The Internet, with its inexhaustible explanations of reality, makes patently clear that *we reside in a world of competing and proliferating interpretations without a defined center*. And so, once again, this unlimited interpretative plurality must give rise to an unfettered tolerance of any nonviolent point of view. Only in this way can a truly just society be achieved.

Religious thought, however—which is almost invariably dogmatic thought—insists on objectivity and final truth, thereby "freezing" and "congealing" the process of interpretation. But this insistence on finality and ostensive truth is "strong thought" par excellence, tending toward (physical or spiritual) aggression and intolerance. Thinking that is genuinely tolerant—and therefore just—acknowledges the deeply interpretative nature of human life and discourse. *And such recognition must "weaken" and "lighten" our sense of the finality of being and truth.* This weakened notion of truth—necessarily encased by provisionality—gives us a clue to the kind of religion Vattimo sanctions.

An example will illustrate the point. Vattimo contrasts the Christian crucifix and the Muslim chador (the chador is one type of long garment worn by Muslim women). Vattimo argues that the crucifix, which is usually found in the public buildings—classrooms, courtrooms, and municipal centers—of countries with a Catholic heritage is entirely acceptable within European society. The chador, however, should be opposed. Is this a case of blatant anti-Muslim prejudice? Not at all. Vattimo reasons, rather, that in the contemporary world the crucifix has lost its strength and power. The ubiquitous symbol now blends into the background like wallpaper, reduced to a cultural accoutrement. But the chador (like the niqab) represents an aggressive and exclusive truth claim. It is a clenched fist waved in the face of society; we have the truth and you do not. As such, it is an intolerant symbol and must be excluded from public life.[6] This tableau gives us some inkling of Vattimo's understanding of religion and its role in the contemporary world. As previously noted, the Torinese claims he is a Catholic-communist.[7] In truth, Vattimo is interested in only two words from the Catholic tradition, words he takes to be conjunctive with his postmodern philosophical project: *caritas* and *kenosis*.

Caritas, of course, within the usual Christian lexicon, refers to charity and selflessness, to the supernatural love poured into the human heart by the action of the Holy Spirit, uniting human beings to both God and neighbor. But for Vattimo, Christian *caritas* can only be properly understood as tolerance in the widest possible sense. To exercise charity is be nonjudgmentally tolerant of every (nonviolent) viewpoint; it is to accept the world as a vast interpretative bazaar, to unreservedly embrace hermeneutical pluralism, and to countenance every creative interpretation of life. The truly charitable person is the one imbued with "weak thought," who offers no definitive, metaphysical-moral assertions, who renounces claims about the *ontos on*, reality as such.

The other word from the Christian vocabulary that is important to Vattimo is *kenosis*, which comes from St. Paul's letter to the Philippians. Paul says of Jesus, "Though he was in the form of God, he did not deem equality with God something to be grasped out, but he emptied himself, taking the form of a slave" (Phil 2:5–11). This notion of God "pouring himself out" or "emptying himself" is attractive to Vattimo since he reads this as manifesting a "weakening" of God himself. St. Paul's letter offers us a parable about God's renunciation of authority and power. And this biblical story of divine weakness and renunciation is entirely conjunctive with Vattimo's own *pensiero debole*; that is, the philosophical abjuration of any strong metaphysical or moral position. Insistence on the truth of one's viewpoint—the very definition of dogmatic, metaphysical, and representational thought—violates the Christian parable of God become man, a story about the relinquishment of divine power in favor of weakness.[8]

Postmodern philosophy is, for Vattimo, the philosophical transcription of the truth of Christianity. Postmodernity distills for us, rationally, what Christianity says in narrative style. In the Torinese's telling, Christian faith—with its emphasis on *caritas* and *kenosis*—ultimately underwrites the sublation of Christianity itself by the philosophical idea of weak thought.[9]

NIETZSCHE'S INFLUENCE ON VATTIMO AND POSTMODERNITY

Before placing Vattimo's thought in dialogue with Catholicism, I would like to mention, even if briefly and incompletely, the genealogy of much postmodern thinking. Both Friedrich Nietzsche and Martin Heidegger have had a profound influence on Vattimo's thought. This evening, I will limit myself to discussing a few salient points on the nineteenth-century thinker.

Nietzsche's influence on postmodernity, and, therefore, his influence on contemporary notions of tolerance and diversity, can be summed up by two of his favorite axioms (both of which are deeply inscribed in Vattimo's philosophy):

- There are no facts—only interpretations. And this, too, is an interpretation!
- The world has become a fable.

What do these maxims mean?

Nietzsche's first aphorism is found in his *Nachlass* or *Late Notebooks*.[10] His point, of course, is that "facts" are inexorably embedded in contingent perspectives. To speak of facts in the sense of *facta bruta* is borne of an extraordinarily naïve epistemology. "Evidence" is always riddled with theoretical commitments, prior suppositions, and background assumptions. Facts only come to life—are only properly understood—within particular contexts. Insofar as all observers are embedded in preexisting socio-cultural-linguistic worlds, there exist no universal or unambiguous warrants for truth. This is the point of Nietzsche's famous dictum, "God is dead." God can no longer serve as a first principle for truth because God, too, is an interpretation. It is precisely for this reason that in contemporary academic discussions one often hears the phrase: "it's interpretation all the way down."[11] This sentence simply confirms Nietzsche's point: all "facts" are inextricably bound to interpretative frameworks. And the ontological cash value of this is that we cannot say in any definite way that something is true or false. For if evidential warrants and criteria for truth vary from community to community—even from person to person—then how can anyone place boundaries on diversity or tolerance? *We must live with a vast panorama of interpretations concerning truth and meaning.*

For understanding Nietzsche's second aphorism, "the world has become a fable," we need only turn to the tale he relates in *The Twilight of the Idols*.[12] Nietzsche tells us that the "truth" or the "true world" was first promised to the wise man, the follower of Plato. Gradually, the truth became more unattainable. It was promised to the Christian who committed himself to living an ascetical and virtuous life. Later, in Kantian philosophy, the true world became entirely unknowable and unattainable since the noumenal world (reality itself) entirely escaped humanity's cognitive grasp. Today, Nietzsche concludes, the idea of a "true world" no longer even serves a purpose. It is a superfluous idea, best abolished. The truth, for Nietzsche, is that there is no truth—at least in the sense of discovering some reality or criterion that serves as a preexisting norm for human meaning and action. The task of contemporary men and women is to *create* truth and meaning through their personal interpretations. Indeed, this is the characteristic hallmark of the *Übermensch*—the Overman who has the fortitude to establish, through creative imagination, the self-propelled truth and meaning of the world. This is why Nietzsche is fond of saying that contemporary man "is rolling from the center toward X."[13] We are deracinated beings—existing apart from a *logos*-structure to the world—always rolling toward X, the unknown world of the future.

A final parable revelatory of Nietzsche's (and Vattimo's) thought may be found in *Thus Spoke Zarathustra*. Nietzsche sees some passing priests (who are meant as placeholders for traditional Christian morality) and says of them:

> I am moved by compassion for these priests. . . . He whom they call Redeemer has put them in chains; in chains of false values and delusive words. Would that someone would yet redeem them from their Redeemer! . . . They thought they were sleeping on an island, but it was a sleeping monster. . . . Eventually, the monster comes and wakes and devours what built huts upon it. Behold the huts which these priests built![14]

Traditional Christians, in other words, have built their houses on what they thought was firm bedrock, *terra firma*—the reality of God and Christ, of truth and morality. In fact, what they took for unshakeable rock was in reality a monster who will awaken and devour them. Who is this ravenous beast? It is, of course, historicity and contingency. Nietzsche's point is that there exists no such reality as ontological bedrock that reaches down to the foundations of truth, the *ontos on*, reality itself. No one can claim to have found the truth, or the "secret of life." That is why the world has become a fable. The truth is that there is no truth.

Now, for both Nietzsche and Vattimo, these kinds of doubts about truth, meaning, and objective reality, about the *logos*-structure of the world, are not worrisome; on the contrary, they are *liberative and emancipatory* precisely because they overcome the "neurotic" desire for objective, metaphysical reality, thereby unleashing Promethean freedom.[15] We gradually come to acknowledge that we are the *creators* of truth and meaning rather than their discoverers. And obviously, if creative interpretation is a vast and limitless spectrum, then boundaries cannot be placed on tolerance and diversity.

This is why Vattimo is convinced that those who make strong, metaphysical claims for truth inexorably stifle tolerance and diversity; they offer only bellicose assertions for dogmatically held beliefs, when, in fact, the sovereign human will empowers each person to seize his own life, to mold it and shape it as he sees fit, apart from predetermined structures—apart from assertive claims about "the truth" or about a stable and unchanging "human nature." Nietzsche concludes by saying (in a perspective that Vattimo makes his own) that this sanctioning of unlimited perspectives should not be discouraging but should lead to optimism: "Who will prove to be the *strongest*? The most moderate, those who have no *need* of extreme articles of faith." That is, the strong person is the one who welcomes unlimited pluralism, the one who renounces ontological and moral foundations, the one who accepts a life of risk, contingency, and change.[16]

In summary: For Vattimo and postmodern thought generally, the accent is placed on the subject's own intense, form-shaping role; the human being, not an antecedent structure, nature, or objective truth, is the measure of all things. Any insistence on a discernible *logos*-structure of the world—a world mediating preexistent truth and meaning—is an enemy of emancipatory freedom since it tries to shape the subject according to a priori norms. Only the autonomous person in his or her sovereign liberty is the proper locus of truth, thereby allowing for unlimited diversity and, so, egalitarian justice.

BENEDICT XVI AND THE FORM OF THE WORLD

Now, to Vattimo's and Nietzsche's postmodern point of view, I would like to juxtapose the philosophical position staked out by Pope Benedict XVI in two of his most impressive and noteworthy speeches: one at Westminster Hall in London and the other at the Bundestag in Berlin. These talks are significant insofar as they deal, unmistakably, with the issues of tolerance, diversity, and justice. In both of these speeches, Benedict is speaking to civil authorities and to academics. His primary concern is this: How do contemporary states build a just and tolerant society?

It should first be stated clearly that Pope Benedict, in all of his writings, defends a "healthy secularity" or what he has called *laïcité positive*. He is certainly not asking for a confessionally religious society or a sacred public square. On the contrary, the state is understood as a secular entity possessing its own (relative) autonomy. Indeed, one theme found throughout all of Benedict XVI's writings is that there exists a (relatively) autonomous natural order.[17] This autonomy of the created estate is fully affirmed at Vatican II:

> "By the autonomy of earthly affairs, we mean that created things and societies enjoy their own laws and values." And again, "By the very fact of their creation, all things are endowed with their own stability, truth, goodness, their own laws and their proper order." (*Gaudium et spes*, no. 36)

These statements clearly display the classical Catholic theme that the natural sphere possesses an integral excellence and intrinsic stability, even apart from revelation. And it is precisely within this natural sphere that Benedict points to the world itself as message bearing. As opposed to Nietzsche, Vattimo, and postmodernity generally, the Pope argues that the world has a form, a *logos*-structure, which allows us to discern elements of truth and meaning. It is just this point that the Pope hammers home in his two speeches to civil authorities: *meaning and truth are discoverable within nature and society.* It is not a matter of the individual creating a world on the basis of his or her sovereign will; it is a matter, rather, of discovering the intelligibility, the disclosure, already embedded in the very form of the world.

Let us examine Benedict's comments more closely. In 2010, at Westminster Hall in London, before the most distinguished academic and political classes of British society, the Pope stated:

> The fundamental questions at stake in Thomas More's trial continue to present themselves . . . as new social conditions emerge. . . . By appeal to which authority can moral dilemmas be resolved? These questions take us directly to the foundations of civil discourse. [For] if the moral principles underpinning the democratic process are themselves determined by *nothing more solid than social consensus, then the fragility of the process becomes all too evident—herein lies the real challenge for democracy.* (emphasis added)

The Pope is asking, in other words, by which precise warrants do we reach the fundamental truths about morality and justice guiding society?

Is it on the basis of consensus alone? And is this a solid enough foundation? He then asks the British to examine their own history:

> A positive illustration of this is found in one of the British Parliament's particularly notable achievements—the abolition of the slave trade. The campaign that led to this landmark legislation was built upon firm ethical principles, rooted in the natural law, and it has made a contribution to civilization of which this nation may be justly proud.

The Pope continues:

> The central question at issue, then, is this: where is the ethical foundation for political choices to be found? The Catholic tradition maintains that the objective norms governing right action are accessible to reason, [even] prescinding from the content of revelation.

Benedict XVI is here arguing that there is a *natural visibility* to truth that allows meaning to be perceived within the world itself. There is a discernible "form"—and so a discernable truth—mediated by the world which is not simply the result of the individual's creative self-definition or self-interpretation. For Benedict, the truth has a natural visibility and intelligibility that should aid us in the creation of a just and properly tolerant society.

I would like to cite one last speech by Pope Benedict, delivered to the civil authorities in Berlin in 2011, where he again drives home his point about the visibility of truth mediated by the form of the world:

> For most of the matters that need to be regulated by law, the support of the majority can serve as a sufficient criterion. Yet it is evident that for the fundamental issues of law, in which the dignity of man and of humanity is at stake, the majority principle is not enough. . . . [Christianity] has pointed to nature and reason as the true sources of law . . . which naturally presupposes that both spheres are rooted in the creative reason of God.

In a clever rhetorical move, the Pope then points to the ecological movement—which is particularly strong in Germany—as offering a clue to the rediscovery of the meaning and truth inherent in the world itself:

> Young people [in Germany] had come to realize that something is wrong in our relationship with nature, that matter is not just raw material for us to shape at will, but that the earth has a dignity of its own and that we must follow its directives. . . . The importance of ecology is no longer disputed. We must listen to the language of nature and we must answer accordingly. Yet I would like to underline a point that seems to me to be neglected, today as in the past: there is also an ecology of man. Man too has a nature that he must respect and that he cannot manipulate at will. Man is not merely self-creating freedom. Man does not create himself. He is intellect and will, but he is also nature, and his will is rightly ordered if he respects his nature, listens to it and accepts himself for who he is, as one who did not create himself. In this way, and in no other, is true human freedom fulfilled.

In both of these talks, Benedict's point is unmistakable: We do not simply interpret the world as we wish, according to the dictates of our sovereign will. Rather, the world is disclosed to us with a preexisting form that is ours to cultivate and to perfect. *Kosmos* and *physis* truly teach us something about the human person and his proper flourishing. And to follow this teaching is human emancipation—not Promethean freedom directed by an imperious volition.

For Vattimo and Nietzsche, of course, the world is a multicultural Babel, an irreducible web of interpretative plurality. There exists no fundamental architecture of man or the world that in itself discloses meaning and truth. Indeed, to speak of "human nature," in the sense of the preexisting and normative contours of reality, is the enemy of freedom, precisely because it constricts personal creativity. After all, how can I act autonomously—and so freely—if I must discover a preexisting truth about the world and about human nature itself? Benedict, however, insists that one "receives" truth and meaning by attending to the form of the world and of the human being.

Between the position championed by Pope Benedict and that championed by Nietzsche and Vattimo, one may see the contemporary contest over notions of tolerance, diversity, equality, and justice.

SPOILS FROM EGYPT

At the end of this brief investigation, we may legitimately ask: How should the notions of diversity and tolerance be operative in Catholic universities—and in Christian institutions at large? I offer a final thought this evening—reprising an insight that resounds throughout the Christian tradition.

The Catholic Church has never ceased learning from secular society and from non-Christian thinkers. In early Christianity, when the surrounding culture was largely pagan, this issue was felt with more intensity than we feel it today—at least until very recently. The earliest Christians unceasingly asked: What is the relationship of the Church to the contemporary (and often hostile) culture? Should Christians read pagan literature? Should they be influenced by Plato, Aristotle, and Marcus Aurelius? Should the disciples of Christ bear arms in service to the pagan Roman Empire? These were pointed and irrepressible questions.[18]

Origen, an early third-century theologian, was crucially thoughtful on this issue. He wrote in response to Celsus, a Greek thinker who lived at the end of the second century and was a determined opponent of Christianity. One of Celsus's complaints was that Jews and Christians refused to melt into the larger culture of the empire; both groups insisted on their uniqueness and distinctiveness. Celsus finds Judaism and Christianity equally distasteful, but Judaism at least has the merit of possessing a tradition and history. Christianity, on the other hand, is virtually a new religion.

In his reply to Celsus, Origen says, "We are careful not to raise objections to any good teachings, even if the authors are outside the faith . . . nor do we seek to overthrow statements that are sound" (*Contra Celsum*, VII, 46). Origen then offers a biblical image in support of this assertion, saying that just as the Israelites took gold and silver from the Egyptians for the Exodus—and used these precious metals for God's service by fashioning sacred vessels—so, similarly, Christians should take gold and silver from pagan authors, using their philosophical insights for the glory of God. This trope, "spoils from Egypt," has been a central one throughout Christian history. Insights and ideas may be appropriated from the surrounding culture—even from the most ardent enemies of Christianity—but these ideas must be disciplined and molded by biblical faith.[19]

At the same time, Origen issues a warning: "Rare are those who take only what is good and useful from the surrounding [Hellenic] culture. Many men take ideas that are deeply out of harmony with the Christian faith. And then, instead of forging instruments for God's service, they build only the golden calf at Bethel."[20] Origen's point, of course, is that Christians can and should make use of insights and wisdom from every quarter. However, if these conclusions are not molded and disciplined by the Christian faith, they can easily become deformed, distorted, and idolatrous. Augustine, Basil, and Aquinas later appropriated Origen's image of "spoils from Egypt."

While numerous Christian thinkers could be cited on just this point—St. Thomas preeminently—I limit myself to mentioning the nineteenth-century historian John Henry Newman. Newman reprises the "spoils" imagery in his own terms, telling us that the Church is a "treasure house . . . casting the gold of fresh tributaries into her refiner's fire, or stamping upon her own, as time required it, a deeper impress of her Master's image."[21] The Church, in other words, draws wisdom from every quarter, purging it of dross, then stamping the purified substance with the image of Christ. All ideas and concepts must ultimately be subordinated to biblical truth.

Newman offers still another biblical image illustrating how the Church uses insights drawn from the surrounding secular culture. In response to those who argued that Catholicism is simply a mélange of Old Testament ideas mixed with pagan philosophy, Newman responds, "They [his opponents] cast off all that they find in Pharisee or heathen; we conceive that the Church, like Aaron's rod, devours the serpents of the magicians." Newman's reference here is to Exodus 7:9, where Aaron's rod turns into a serpent—and gobbles up the serpents of Pharaoh's magicians. In a similar way, the Church assimilates, biblically disciplines, and profitably uses every form of thought. Newman concludes by stating that no matter the falsehood attached to a particular philosophy, the Church can always extract good from evil because she is heir to the Lord's promise: "If they [his disciples] drank any deadly thing, it should not hurt them."[22]

CONCLUSION

The history of the Church offers us rich instruction as to how concepts such as "diversity" and "tolerance"—or any other secular philosophical or political idea—should be received by a Catholic and Christian institution. There exists a good deal of shared space between Christians and the secular world—a shared political order, shared learning, and, at least to some extent, a shared social morality. St. Augustine, in the *City of God*, thinking about the Church's relationship to the pagan Roman Empire, says that Christians often make use of the same goods as non-Christians, but with a "different faith" and a "different hope" (*De civ. Dei*, 18, 54). Similarly, Vatican II says that the Church looks with great respect on all that is true, good, and just in the institutions that the human race has established (*GS*, no. 42).

But granted this legitimately shared sphere, the enduring question remains: How are contemporary philosophical and political ideas purified, perfected, and strengthened both by reason and by the light of faith? How do Christians bring the salt and light and power of the Gospel to secular ideas? How do we ensure that the political order does not sacralize itself, precisely because the political order can never be ultimate and must always be chastened and refined by the Gospel of Jesus Christ? How, to again quote the council, are the achievements of the nations illumined by both reason and revelation so that the may be "healed and perfected to the glory of God" (*Lumen gentium,* no. 17).

Ultimately, Catholicism, and Christian institutions generally, cannot allow their fundamental principles to be dictated by a non-Christian, secular culture. Much less should such institutions think that tolerance, plurality, and justice can only be achieved where one finds the dissolution of strong Christian principles. Catholicism must ensure that the ideas and concepts its institutions use and embrace are fundamentally shaped by the light of rightly ordered reason and by the divine wisdom revealed in ancient Israel and, uniquely, in Jesus of Nazareth.

NOTES

1. In the following section, I rely on material found in Thomas G. Guarino, *Vattimo and Theology* (London: T & T Clark, 2009), and "Return of Religion in

Europe? The Postmodern Christianity of Gianni Vattimo," *Logos: A Journal of Catholic Thought and Culture* 14 (Spring 2011): 15–36.

2. See Martin Heidegger, *What Is Called Thinking?*, trans. J. Glenn Gray (New York: Harper and Row, 1968), 8. For a recent comprehensive look at Heidegger's critique of scientific thinking, see *Heidegger on Science*, ed. Trish Glazebrook (Albany: SUNY Press, 2012).

3. The deeply hermeneutical character of science, of course, is a thesis propounded by Thomas Kuhn in his well-known manifesto, *The Structure of Scientific Revolutions*, 2nd edition (Chicago: University of Chicago, 1970). I have treated Kuhn's thought at greater length—and its relationship to philosophical and theological reasoning—in "Rahner, Popper and Kuhn: A Note on Some Critical Parallels in Science and Theology," *Philosophy and Theology* 8 (1993): 83–89, and in "Rosmini, Ratzinger and Kuhn: Observations on a Note by the Doctrinal Congregation," *Theological Studies* 64 (2003): 43–68. Vattimo argues that science thinks it grasps objective data but fails to acknowledge the sociocultural horizons that inexorably envelop it. See his *A Farewell to Truth*, trans. William McCuaig (New York: Columbia University Press, 2011), xxxii.

4. This is why Vattimo says that truth, understood in an objective, descriptive, or representational sense, is an illusion. See Gianni Vattimo, *Della Realtà: fini della filosofia* (Milan: Garzanti, 2012), 75. For a more elongated treatment of this point, see his *A Farewell to Truth*, 1–46.

5. For Vattimo's most recent remarks on hermeneutics as the world's philosophical *koiné*, see *Della Realtà*, 28–30.

6. See Gianni Vattimo, *After Christianity*, trans. Luca D'Isanto (New York: Columbia University Press, 2002), 95–102.

7. Most recently, see Vattimo, *Della Realtà*, 11.

8. I have used the words *parable* and *story* here because Vattimo makes no commitment to biblical truth. Indeed, his foundational principle of *pensiero debole* does not allow him to say that the Scriptures offer representational truth or metaphysical bedrock. For the Torinese, the *norma normans* for religion is always philosophical reasoning, particularly the "emancipatory" thought of Nietzsche and Heidegger.

9. Of course, this kind of philosophical sublation of religious faith by philosophy is the quintessential Enlightenment move, which is why I have wondered to what extent Vattimo's thought—at least on the issue of religion—differs from modernity itself. This is a legitimate question even if the Torinese has told us that a true "overcoming" (*Überwindung*) of the past is impossible, opting instead for a *Verwindung* (alteration, healing) of it. See Guarino, *Vattimo and Theology*, 7–8, 145–47.

10. Friedrich Nietzsche, *Writings from the Late Notebooks*, ed. Rüdiger Bittner, trans. Kate Sturge (Cambridge: Cambridge University Press, 2003), 139, no.

7 [60]. The same text may be found in his *The Will to Power*, tr. Walter Kaufman and R. J. Hollingdale (New York: Random House, 1967), 481.

11. For example, see Brice Wachterhauser, "Getting It Right: Relativism, Realism and Truth," in *The Cambridge Companion to Gadamer*, ed. Robert J. Dostal (Cambridge: Cambridge University Press, 2002), 52–78.

12. Friedrich Nietzsche, *The Twilight of the Idols*, R. J. Hollingdale (London: Penguin, 1990), 50–51.

13. Nietzsche, *The Will to Power*, no. 1 of *European Nihilism*.

14. Friedrich Nietzsche, *Thus Spoke Zarathustra*, tr. Walter Kaufmann (New York: The Viking Press, 1966), 91 (with translation slightly altered).

15. For Vattimo on the "neurotic" desire for metaphysical objectivity and representational truth, see *Della Realtà*, 30, 44–45.

16. See Nietzsche, *Writings from the Late Notebooks*, 121, no. 15. Of course, there are other influences on Vattimo and postmodernity besides Nietzsche, particularly the thought of Martin Heidegger. For more on Heidegger's influence on Vattimo, see Anthony C. Sciglitano, "Gianni Vattimo and St. Paul," in *Paul in the Grip of the Philosophers*, ed. Peter Frick (Minneapolis: Fortress Press, 2013), 117–42.

17. I have examined Pope Benedict's notion of "healthy secularity"—and its theological roots in the distinction between nature and grace—in "Nature and Grace: Seeking the Delicate Balance," *Josephinum Journal of Theology* 18 (2011): 150–62.

18. For an excellent analysis of the relationship between the early Christians and the surrounding secular culture—particularly how shared secularity was understood—see Robert A. Markus, *Christianity and the Secular* (Notre Dame: University of Notre Dame, 2006).

19. I analyze the history of Christian reflection on "spoils" in *Foundations of Systematic Theology* (New York: T & T Clark, 2005), 269–311.

20. "Letter to Gregory," *The Ante-Nicene Fathers*, 4 (Grand Rapids: Eerdmans, 1956), 393–94.

21. John Henry Newman, *An Essay on the Development of Christian Doctrine* (London: Longmans, Green & Co., 1894), 382.

22. Ibid., 441. In the twentieth century, Henri de Lubac, the well-known Jesuit historian, continued to defend the spoils trope, arguing that if the salt of Christianity is to maintain its tang, there must occur a continual appropriation of new ideas. Cyril of Alexandria rightly made use of Plato, as did Ambrose of Seneca, Aquinas of Aristotle, and Matteo Ricci of Confucius. This assimilative daring, de Lubac insists, must be duplicated in our own day, with ideas harboring even Marxist and Nietzschean elements finding a place in some new theological synthesis, for "in the Church, the work of assimilation never ceases, and it is never too soon to undertake it!" See Henri de Lubac, *The Drama of Atheist*

Humanism, tr. E. Riley (London: Sheed and Ward, 1949), vi. Of course, with the prior tradition, de Lubac also insists that the Church must purify and discipline every form of thought, deepening it and bringing it to successful issue. See Henri de Lubac, *Catholicism*, tr. L. Sheppard (New York: Longmans, Green & Co., 1950), 116, 144, 152.

26

RESPECTING GAY PEOPLE

Justice and the Interpretation of Scriptural Traditions

Kwame Anthony Appiah, New York University

Scriptural argument is important to all Americans, whether or not we are religious. After all, we are fellow citizens with a shared responsibility for the republic, and a significant number among us believe that the scriptures matter in thinking about how to carry out that shared responsibility. Interpretations of the scriptures thus have consequences for many matters of great public controversy.[1]

I'm going to consider one such question: How should Christians approach the biblical passages that pose an apparent obstacle to acceptance of lesbian and gay sex? But I am not going to try to answer it. Instead, I want us to think together about how a Christian faced with these scriptures might reasonably address it. We owe our fellow citizens consideration of the views they reasonably entertain, so one task for all of us—including non-Christians—is to try to understand the views of someone who makes reasoned appeal to scripture.

What do I mean by "scripture"? There are central written texts, supposedly inspired by gods or holy men, in each of the world's great religions. The Sanskrit sutras are holy because they record the sayings of the Buddha; Taoism has many writings ascribed to divinities, though the Dao De Jing, its best-known text, is the work of a human author; and the Bhagavad Gita, which is central to Hinduism, records a conversation between the god, Lord Krishna, and the prince Arjuna.

But in the Abrahamic religions—Judaism, Christianity, and Islam—there's a rather more specific understanding of the key religious texts, which grows out of the Jewish understanding of the Hebrew Bible—composed of the Torah, the Prophets, and a third group of Writings, canonized in rabbinic Judaism by the third century CE. A similar status was eventually accorded to some Hebrew scriptures and some New Testament writings in Christianity, as it changed from a Jewish sect to a new universal religion; and the Qur'an, in Islam—which grows against the background of Jewish and Christian faith in the Arabian peninsula—has a special place as part of God's unfolding revelation to humankind.[2]

Not only are these scriptures regarded as divinely inspired, they have a central place in the life and belief of the faithful, and reading and interpreting them have always been a central part of their lives. This is particularly evident in Judaism, since the Torah is full of detailed instruction in moral and ritual matters; indeed, the distinction between moral and ritual concerns, as we shall see, is not always easy to draw in the Torah.[3]

So Christianity starts with the Jewish idea of scriptures as authoritative divinely inspired guides to human life, whose paradigm is the very explicit instruction of the Torah.[4] So how can a Christian know which texts to regard as scripture in this way?[5] The texts that are treated as scriptural in the New Testament—by preceding them with the formula "It is written"[6]—are Jewish scriptures, whose status *as scriptures* reflects the developing understanding of Jews around the time of Christ.[7] So the question of why the books of the New Testament should also be regarded as scriptural needs attention.

Much of the Torah consists of instructions delivered by Moses to the Israelites on how to conduct themselves in virtue of Yahweh's special covenant with them. And the Prophets were called by God to instruct the twelve tribes. So the contents of the "Law and the Prophets" are essential (if true) to guiding the life of the children of Israel. But that's no guarantee that the writing down of the texts was itself divinely guided. So that someone who reads these texts as evidence of God's will for the Jews might wonder if those who wrote it down misunderstood their oral sources or those who transmitted the texts introduced errors of transcription. And indeed, we see in the Dead Sea Scrolls that extremely devout Jewish scholars felt free to adjust the very words of the scriptures in accordance with their developing understanding of the Law, in the century before Christ's birth.[8]

The New Testament has at his heart the Gospels—recording Christ's life—and the exposition of the meaning of his life in the work of some of the leaders of the early church. But there are many texts from this period reporting and interpreting this good news that are not found in Christian Bibles. In fact, the idea of *a* Bible—a single list or canon of writings with an authoritative written version—was absent when the individual books of the Bible were written, so the Bible itself doesn't tell believers how it should be read: scripture is a biblical concept, but the Bible is not. So the Bible cannot be the sole source of Christian understanding; and the churches have always taught, beginning with the preaching of St. Paul, that the members of the post-Apostolic Christian community had access to evidence—including the oral testimony of the life of Christ and other evidences of God's work in history—which showed them how to conduct their lives. From the very beginning, St. Paul taught Christians to believe that they were the "body of Christ," and whatever he meant by this exactly, it suggests that the experience of the church in history is itself a part of God's self-revelation. We should also recall that in the early church, especially among the Apostles, prophesy was believed to be still alive, so that divinely inspired messages came from out of the mouths of people other than the Messiah.

If the scriptures are divinely inspired, God inspired them in order to assist us. And, on relatively uncontroversial Christian assumptions, this means that the guidance it offers, when properly understood, is authoritative. We come now, then, to the question that arises for someone who regards the Christian Bible as scriptural in this way: How are we to seek that proper understanding?

The challenges begin with the fact that the scriptures were written in languages that no modern people speak as their mother tongues: ancient Hebrew; κοινή Greek—in the case of 2 Maccabees and the New Testament; and biblical Aramaic, in the case of Daniel, Ezra, and a single sentence in Jeremiah. Jesus himself spoke a later form of Aramaic, which is also something we may have to bear in mind. Though someone of his background would have known some Greek as well, New Testament and other records of his sayings are presumably Greek translations of things said in Aramaic and Hebrew. A modern Christian will know the scriptures, therefore, through layers of translation.

You might think that this is not such a difficulty. We need only work from a text that says in English what the original text said in Hebrew or

Aramaic or Greek. All we need, that is, is to start with the best translation of the best text. But that is not so easy. First, the sources for modern Bibles are manuscripts that are divergent. Sometimes, settling the text will matter a lot. In the church in which I was raised, we often discussed when women could speak in church, and in particular 1 Corinthians: "The women should keep silence in the churches. For they are not permitted to speak, but should be subordinate, as even the law says. If there is anything they desire to know, let them ask their husbands at home. For it is shameful for a woman to speak in church."[9] We would have been saved much trouble had we known and accepted the view of the distinguished Dominican New Testament scholar Jerome Murphy-O'Connor—a specialist on 1 Corinthians, in particular—who has argued that this passage is a "post-Pauline insertion."[10]

But a second problem is not with the idea of the best text but with the idea of the best translation; and that is a subject that I, as a philosopher of language by training, have thought about a good deal.

What we translate are inscriptions, things written by men and women, and those inscriptions are the products of intentional human actions, which, like all such actions, are undertaken for reasons. Since reasons can be complex and extensive, grasping an agent's reasons can be a difficult business; we can easily feel that we have not dug deeply enough when we have told the best story we can. Still, there is a familiar basic thought here: written statements do ordinarily propose themselves as motivated, at least in part, by a desire to express a certain specific thought, and it is, roughly, the same thought for each inscription of the same form. This distinguishes written statements from many other kinds of action where we cannot usually tell just from the form of the act—the shape of the thing the agent does—just why he has done it. This is easy enough to explain. What is distinctive about speech and writing as kinds of action is that they are *conventional*, and the thought we normally take someone to be intending to express in uttering a sentence is the thought that the conventions of language associate with it, its *literal* meaning. Learning the grammar and the lexicon of a language is learning a complex set of instructions for generating acts that are standardly intended to achieve their effects in others who know the same instructions . . . because they recognize those intentions. If we are to translate an ancient text, we must begin by trying to reconstruct these intentions.[11]

If the literal meaning of an utterance is a matter of what intentions a speaker would ordinarily be taken to have in uttering it, then a literal translation ought to be a sentence of, for example, English, that would ordinarily be taken to be uttered with the intention that the original, say, Greek or Hebrew, sentence was conventionally associated with. But if you cannot conventionally communicate a certain literal intention in language A and you can in language B, then the translator cannot produce a literal translation: no word for "burnt Sienna," no translation of "the tablecloth is burnt Sienna."

Of course, many, many things we say and write are not actually meant literally. Take some of the poetry in the Bible. When you read:

> I am very dark, but comely,
> O daughters of Jerusalem,
> like the tents of Kedar,
> like the curtains of Solomon (Song of Solomon 5)

you are not meant to assume that the author was a woman who wanted you to believe that she was really like a dark tent, even in color. You will recognize, instead, that this is a poetic form. And one of the things you can conclude, as a result, is that the writer may not even be a woman or black or beautiful, since you may be being asked to imagine these words in the mouth of someone a possibly male writer has invented.

So the first immediate consequence of this recognition is that the normal literal intentions are, so to speak, canceled. Still, the poet intends that, starting with the literal meaning—starting with that "cancelled" literal intention—and building on a mutually known fact, you can work out something that she *does* intend to communicate: an idea, a picture, a mood, a feeling . . . something other than what would be communicated by someone saying these words in a normal context literally.[12]

In order to begin to have an understanding of the scriptures, we must first know the language well enough to be able to identify what the intentions conventionally associated with each of its sentences are; we must begin with the literal meanings of words, phrases, sentences. More than this, in understanding the scriptures, we must grasp not merely the literal intentions but the whole message that would be communicated by the utterance of the sentence in more ordinary settings; metaphor, as it occurs in the scriptures, works only because it also occurs outside it. This is a historical inquiry, and it may be that the available evidence simply will not allow us to identify either the literal meaning or the intended sense of a metaphor, whose understanding relies on the mutual expectations of readers and writers of a particular language and culture.

Now a successful translation aims not just to construct a text that reproduces the implied intentions of the author but, more, to produce something that shares the central literary properties of the object-text; and, as is obvious, these are very much more than its literal meaning. A competent translation aims at producing a text whose relation both to the literary and to the linguistic conventions of the culture of the translation is relevantly like the relations of the object-text to *its* culture's conventions.

So we may choose, rightly, to translate a term in a way that is unfaithful to the literal meaning because we are trying to preserve formal features that seem more crucial, that gets us closer to the overall significance of the original. But even if we did not have to make such choices, even if we could, *per impossibile*, meet all the constraints of literal and figurative meaning and all the literary conventions, we would not have produced the perfect translation. We could aim higher, trying to echo literary qualities of the object-text that are not a matter of the conventions.

So that the reason why we cannot speak of the perfect translation here is not just that there are desiderata that cannot all be met, it is rather that there is also no definite set of desiderata. A translation aims to produce a new text that matters to one community the way another text matters to another, but texts matter for many reasons, and it is part of our normal understanding that there can always be new readings, because new things can come to matter about a text, so there are new reasons for caring about new properties. There can be no perfect translation of a scripture—or anything else of interest—in this sense.

One simple reason, as we have seen, is that some scriptures are poetry. Because the poetry is shaped by much more than its function in communicating literal thoughts, and because the features of the language that it is written in—beyond the capacity to convey propositional thought—are not duplicated in other languages, there simply is no such thing as a perfect translation of such scriptures. Perhaps this is why, in Islam, it is said that you cannot truly address the Qur'an except in its original language. Perhaps this is also why Robert Frost—exaggerating, I think, but not hugely—said that poetry is what gets lost in translation.

Faced with the task of using the divinely inspired texts in these ancient languages to guide your life, then, you will have to start with imperfect translations. But at key points, it may be necessary to learn about the original texts for at least four reasons we can now identify.

First, your translation may rely on an original text that is corrupted, as Professor Murphy-O'Connor believes many Greek texts of 1 Corinthians are. Second, the translator may have been working with a word that has no proper corresponding English word. Third, the historical evidence necessary to work out what this text would have conveyed to a reader at the time of its inscription may be unclear or unavailable. And fourth, the translation may have been shaped by the translators' legitimate desire to produce a text that has some of the literary properties of the original, and, for this, the literal meaning may not have been the main point.

These issues arise for the reading of any ancient text, whether or not it is scriptural. Once we take account of the fact that these are scriptures, however, further issues come into view. And I want now to make two philosophical claims, one about interpretation, and one about morality.

About interpretation I say: each passage needs to be read in a way that makes best sense not just of the scriptures taken as a whole, but in the light of our whole understanding of the world. In philosophical jargon, I am suggesting a coherentist epistemology for scriptural interpretation.

The claim about morality is that moral truths are just that, truths. Moral beliefs, that is, can be correct or incorrect; they are not just opinions or preferences that we are free, either individually or as a community, to make up as we please. And just as I am proposing a coherentist approach to the epistemology of interpretation of scripture, so I propose a coherentist picture of moral epistemology. In constructing our moral views, we must try to make them cohere to the greatest extent possible, again not just with one another but also with our other nonmoral beliefs.[13] Rationality requires us, I claim, to try to make our moral beliefs coherent, not just with one another but also with the rest of our understanding of the world.

Coherentists face an inevitable problem because of the holistic character of this standard of judgment. If what matters is coherence, then we have to think, in the end, about everything, and we cannot think about everything at once. We have to start *somewhere*. John Rawls proposed a method that met this difficulty. What he suggested was that we should move back and forth between particular judgments and general principles, trimming each to the other, until we reach what he called a "reflective equilibrium." If our general views come into conflict with too many particular judgments, we may have to abandon them. If our particular views cannot be made consistent with our general principles, however, we may have to abandon the particular views instead. At reflective equilibrium, our intuitions and our theory will cohere.

It is here that the character of the texts as scriptures is central. They are divinely inspired and authoritative guides to Christian life. If the advice they gave us were contradictory, they could not serve this function. As Justin Martyr put it almost two millennia ago in his Dialogue with Trypho: "If there be a pretext for saying that [a Scripture] is contrary to some other, since I am entirely convinced that no Scripture contradicts another, I shall admit rather that I do not understand what is recorded."[14] We can interpret *ordinary* texts as inconsistent, since there is no difficulty in believing that human authors might have incoherent beliefs, or might have changed their minds in the course of writing, or might be attempting to deceive us. So the best interpretation of them may be that some of what they say is false. But none of these is an attitude we can adopt toward the scriptures, taken as divinely inspired. We have many possible ways of responding to an apparent contradiction, though. One would be to revisit the various possible reasons for rejecting a translation that I have canvassed: concluding that the passage is not, in fact, scriptural, or admitting, with Justin, that we do not understand what the text says.

But another would be to read some scriptures as containing guidance as to how we should interpret others, giving priority to the words of Christ and (perhaps) to the Apostles who knew him. The scriptures are an unfolding body of texts, received in human history, addressed to those to whom they were first revealed, and their message for us, now, might not be what it was for them. One obvious suggestion here is that the Hebrew Bible was addressed to the children of Israel, and that both Christ and St. Paul suggest that Christ's incarnation changed the situation, in ways that mean, in particular, that some prescriptions of the Torah no longer apply, or no longer apply in the same way, or do not apply to Gentile Christians, those whose connection to God is through the New Covenant, not the Old. This view is adumbrated within these New Testament scriptures, in a way that reflects the history through which they were brought together as *the* book, the Bible.[15]

The canonical New Testament was not regarded as scripture in the first centuries of the life of the church. Only gradually did the idea of a fixed canon, with a preference for texts of Apostolic authorship, develop.

(And some of the fathers of the church clearly were influenced by mistaken beliefs about the authorship of the texts that became canonical.) When Athanasius transmitted the list—the canon—of the New Testament that we now largely accept in the mid-fourth century in his 39th Festal letter, he included the Book of Revelation, but this inclusion was contested in various parts of the Christian world, in part because its author was not an Apostle, and Revelation is not included as part of the cycle of New Testament readings in the Eastern Orthodox churches even today.[16] And what should we say about the Epistle to the Hebrews or the Pastoral Epistles (1 and 2 Timothy and Titus), whose acceptance relied to some extent on the mistaken belief that they were written by St. Paul?[17] In recalling the complexity of the issues in the history that produced the canon we now accept, we should remember as well that there was never agreement among Christians—either in the first few centuries of the life of the church or later—about exactly which *texts* of the books on the canonical lists should be accepted; and current biblical scholarship has a vast database of texts and variants from which to work. Jerome Murphy-O'Connor is not straying from any orthodoxy in denying that some passages in some versions of 1 Corinthians are scriptural; he *would* be if he rejected the whole epistle.

The coherentist holds that our interpretation of the scriptures must both fit with other scriptures and whatever else we know. Christians who seek a proper understanding of homosexuality must try to establish a reflective equilibrium among texts that seem to be about homosexuality, other texts, and our wider knowledge of the world beyond the texts. We can start from any of these and seek to reconcile it with the others.

But one natural place to start is with what Christ himself says in the Gospels, because Christ is, on a Christian understanding, the central focus and authority of the whole Bible. After scouring the canonical Gospels, you might observe that Christ said nothing about homosexuals. But that would be, at best, very misleading. For—to insist on the obvious—homosexuals are men and women, and everything he says about human beings applies to gay men and women too. The familiar general moral teachings of the Gospel therefore clearly apply to the treatment of lesbians and gay men.

In the synoptic Gospels, as we have seen already, Christ regularly identifies the core of the Jewish tradition, the Law and the Prophets, with two commandments: to love God and to love your neighbor. Both of these are clearly rooted in the Hebrew Bible, the first being a synopsis, so to speak, of the first few Ten Commandments having to do with our relation to God, and the second—which is to be found, in pretty much these words, in Leviticus—could be seen to underlie those of the Commandments that have to do with our treatment of others.[18] But in other places, as in Matthew 5 immediately after the Beatitudes, Christ contrasts his attitude with an older Jewish attitude, urging his followers to out do the scribes and Pharisees in following the law.

This question is important because Christ's view *appears* at least to contrast strongly with that of the texts he himself treats as scripture. Leviticus 19:18, for example—which contains the prescription to "love your neighbor as yourself"—is followed by Leviticus 19:19, which reads: "You shall keep my statutes. You shall not let your animals breed with a different kind; you shall not sow your field with two kinds of seed; nor shall you put on a garment made of two different materials." And this seems like a paradigm of the sort of law of Moses (like the prescription of male circumcision) that Christ never directly endorses—except, perhaps, by implication, as when he says in Mathew 5:18, "For truly I tell you, until heaven and earth pass away, not one letter, not one stroke of a letter, will pass from the law until all is accomplished." And St. Paul, as you know, went on to suggest that Christians were freed from the ritual dimensions of Jewish practice by Christ's fulfillment of the Law.[19]

At any rate, Christ also gives the Old Testament idea of a neighbor a radical twist both in the parable of the Good Samaritan and in Matthew 25, where he says that anyone who has fed the hungry, clothed the naked, cared for the sick, and visited those in prison will "inherit the kingdom," because doing these things for "the least of these who are members of my family" is doing it for him.[20] So that the point, in effect, is that anyone who is *literally* near us, whether or not they are of our kin or kind, is owed the love that people spontaneously give to those who are *figuratively* close to us. He also urges his followers regularly to manage their own lives by avoiding judging others: in Matthew and Luke, Christ says, "Judge not and"—or "so that"—"you will not be not judged."[21] This is the message of what he *says*. But in consorting with prostitutes and tax collectors, in being gracious to Gentiles and to sinners, he embodies a picture of what it is to recognize the dignity of every human being, each of whom is made—according to the Jewish understanding he inherited—in the image of God. St. Paul gives a fair reading of this strand of Christ's moral teaching, at least as it relates to our treatment of one another, when he says, in Galatians 5:14, "For the whole law is summed up in a single commandment, 'You shall love your neighbor as yourself.'" For someone who recalls the banned garments of mixed materials in Leviticus 19:19, this is bound to sound like a revisionary view of the Law.

We already have an opportunity to apply the coherentist strategy of seeking reflective equilibrium, by noticing that this Gospel picture coheres with a picture of the moral life that we can have, as St. Anselm would have said, *remoto Christo*; that is, independently of the evidence of Christ's life.[22] For what the Universal Declaration of Human Rights calls the "recognition of the inherent dignity and of the equal and inalienable rights of all members of the human family" is surely part of the shared moral understanding of all morally responsible human beings today. And to recognize dignity is, conceptually speaking, to recognize the right to certain forms of respect. The UDHR calls this recognition the "foundation of freedom, justice and peace in the world," and, because, as I said a while ago, lesbian and gay people are members of the human family, this right to respect belongs to them, too. Our morality is in this way coherent with the Gospels; and, of course, therefore, vice versa.

I want to make one further point about our modern understanding of sexuality, which is not moral but psychological. We now recognize that homosexuals are people who experience their erotic attachments to those of their own gender as given, in the sort of way that the erotic attachments of those whose preference is for the other gender are natural to them. Gay men and lesbians do not choose their erotic preferences, any more than straight or asexual people do. What they have to do is to decide how to *act* in light of their desires.

Nowadays, even someone who thought sex between people of the same gender was wrong could think committed, loving relationships between two people were a human good. And many of us also believe that erotic life is a good, at least when embedded in such relationships, which last ideally "till death do us part."

This is a modern conception, as I say. The idea that some people were born with a disposition that expresses itself in erotic longing for members of the same gender is not one that all societies have had. There is no sign of such a conception in the Hebrew Bible, so far as I can see, and very little suggestion of it in the New Testament, except by inference in one passage I shall discuss later. The Hebrew Bible does have the idea of long-term relationships of love between men and between women—David and Jonathan and Ruth and Naomi spring to mind—but these relationships are not erotic. David's erotic life famously includes his adulterous heterosexual relationship with Bathsheba, and Naomi is a widow, who works hard to find a husband for her widowed daughter-in-law, Ruth.

So let me now turn, at last, to those scriptural passages allegedly focused on how Christians should regard homosexual acts. My interest, as I say, is not in settling what they mean but in showing how these ideas about scriptural interpretation might be brought to bear.

I do not need to discuss the passages in Genesis about the sin of Sodom, because, despite their centrality in later Christian condemnation of homosexual practices, proper attention to the text and its historical meaning makes it clear that it is simply not about them.[23] The most relevant Old Testament passages are two in Leviticus. "You shall not lie with a male as with a woman; it is an abomination" (Leviticus 18:22), and "If a man lies with a male as with a woman, both of them have committed an abomination; they shall be put to death; their blood is upon them" (Leviticus 20:13).

Our task is to make this passage coherent with other biblical passages and with the moral understanding I just sketched. We should first explore what the central term of condemnation here—*abomination* or, in the Hebrew, *toevah*—actually means. The root sense of the word is something that is disgusting or loathsome. At the end of Leviticus 18, all the things that have been described in the chapter—incest, sex with a menstruating woman, adultery, sacrificing children to Moloch, bestiality, alongside "lying with a male as with a woman"—are declared to be abominations; and the penalty for them is being "cut off from their people." In Leviticus 20, where the penalty is set higher, the context is also a condemnation of adultery, incest, and bestiality, and now the penalty for all of them is death.

These are not the only things condemned in the Torah as abominations. Deuteronomy 14:3 says any of the animals banned on the list that follows is *toevah*: animals that have split hooves but don't chew the cud, animals from the sea that don't have fins and scales, anything that "dies of itself," and "a kid cooked in its mother's milk" as well as a dizzying list of flying animals.[24] Sacrifices of "an ox or a sheep that has a defect, anything seriously wrong" (Deuteronomy 17:1); remarrying a wife you divorced who has since married and divorced someone else (Deuteronomy 24:4); and those who use dishonest weights and measure in trade are also on the list of abominations.

What is clear, then, is that something may be *toevah* because it breaches rules of ritual purity (the list of proscribed animals, the imperfect animal sacrifices) as well as because it is morally wrong (dishonesty, incest, bestiality).[25] So one question about how these passages should be understood is whether homosexual acts (and remarrying a divorced woman) belong with the former or with the latter.[26]

There are many other questions we might ask about these passages as well: What exactly is so bad about a man's lying with a man "as with a woman"?[27] Is it that he is treating a man as if he were a woman? If so, might there be forms of sexual relations between men that are permissible, in which men clearly treat each other as men? If the issue is homosexuality, why is there no mention of sex between women? This is only the beginning of a conversation.

These are the only passages to rely on in the Hebrew Bible if you are seeking an explicit proscription of homosexual acts. When we turn to the New Testament, there are essentially three passages to consider,[28] and together they nicely exemplify the major possible strategies for reconciling a text with our broader understanding.

They are all in Pauline Epistles. The first of them I want to consider briefly is 1 Timothy 1:10, in which the word ἀρσενοκοίται(ς) occurs in a list of "lawbreakers and rebels, the ungodly and sinful, the unholy and irreligious." This epistle and the other two so-called Pastoral Epistles were accepted into the canon in part because they were thought to be by St. Paul. But many modern scholars are persuaded they are not by St. Paul and also of a later composition. So you could adopt the approach of ignoring this passage as not scriptural, which, as I said toward the start, is always one of the possibilities.

But even if we were to set 1 Timothy aside for this reason, there is a second, canonical epistle, whose Pauline authorship is pretty secure, which contains ἀρσενοκοίται, alongside another term that has been thought to be a way of referring to those who engage in homosexual acts, namely μαλακοί. And that is 1 Corinthians 6:9, which lists these two among the many sinners who will not enter the kingdom of God.[29]

There has been much scholarly discussion of both these terms. Μαλακοί uncontroversially means a weak or soft man, but it is unlikely, as John Boswell argued many years ago, that it could have meant, as some have suggested, a man who took the passive role in homosexual sex.³⁰ The reason, as he argued, is that while many forms of behavior (from being unflappable to being disposed to masturbation to wearing women's clothing) could be regarded as unmanly in the Hellenistic world, having sex with men—as Hercules, among the mythical, or Alexander, among the historical, did—was not one of them. And indeed, the fathers of the church after St. Paul tended, as Boswell also points out, to associate μαλακοὶ with "masturbation or general moral laxity." Even if, despite this, you thought that μαλακοὶ meant someone who is passive in homosexual sodomy, St. Paul would, of course, be condemning only one kind of homosexual act in using this word, or, at most, people disposed to that act, not homosexuals in general, understanding that term in the modern way I sketched earlier. But this is not surprising, given that the whole modern idea of homosexuality was absent, as I have said.

Ἀρσενοκοῖται poses even greater challenges. To begin with it is not a word that is attested in Greek before St. Paul uses it in these passages. So we begin with a puzzle about why St. Paul doesn't talk about homosexuality, if that is what he wants to do, using language that is more familiar, especially given the vast body of writing about male-male eros in the Greek corpus.

The word's roots are a Greek prefix meaning "male" and κοῖται, which is associated with the word for "bed," and so might be translated helpfully as bedder; that is, someone who takes another person to bed.³¹ Now you might think that it is obvious that a word that is effectively "male-bedder" must mean someone who beds men. Boswell has an English analogy that shows why this is not so obvious an inference: "lady killer," he points out, is ambiguous between "a lady who kills," where lady is the subject, and a "person who kills ladies," where lady is the object. And after reviewing many compound words in Greek beginning with ἀρσεν- (and the related ἄρρην-), he concludes that the meaning "male sexual agents"—where ἀρσεν- makes the man the subject—is more likely. I myself think that Paul's coinage is less puzzling when you recall that the Septuagint version of Leviticus 19:22 contains both ἄρσενος and κοίτην, which suggests, at least, that Paul, a Greek speaker who presumably had access to the Septuagint, had this passage in mind.³² Which means, of course, that the relevant Old Testament and New Testament passages are connected.

But whatever he did mean—whatever the literal intention that St. Paul used the word with—it is very unlikely that his readers would have understood him to be talking about people engaging in homosexual acts; the reason is simple. There is extensive discussion of such acts in κοινή Greek, but, Boswell writes, "*no* previous or contemporary author used [this word] in a way which clearly indicated this connection." And indeed, as he also points out, when Chrysostom in the fourth century (who did write extensively about sex between men) comments on these exact passages, he does not mention homosexuality at all.

So this second text exemplifies both the case where we are dealing with a term that has no translation in our language and the possibility that the attempt to find a literal intention for a word will fail for lack of historical evidence.

Our final text is Romans 1:26–27, which translates:

> For this reason God gave them up to dishonorable passions. Their women exchanged natural relations for unnatural, and the men likewise gave up natural relations with women and were consumed with passion for one another, men committing shameless acts with men and receiving in their own persons the due penalty for their error.

This is the only passage in the Bible that can be construed as involving voluntary homosexual sex between women as well as between men. It is from an epistle whose canonicity has never been seriously put in question. And I am aware of no argument that the text is corrupt. On the other hand, the point of the passage, placed here towards the start of an epistle to the church at Rome, is to rehearse the history of Gentile lack of faith. The evidence of God's existence is available to all, and yet people have failed to accept Him. As a result, women and men have taken up unnatural sexual practices. It is difficult looking back through a millennium of teaching about natural law, influenced profoundly by St. Thomas's reading of Aristotle, not to see the talk of acts "παρὰ φύσιν," against nature, as wrong in themselves, as violations of natural law. But St. Paul uses the very same expression later in the Epistle, in Romans 11, to describe God's action in adding the Gentiles to the Jewish tradition, grafting them, as he says, using a metaphor from viticulture, onto the Jewish stock, "παρὰ φύσιν." Far from being wrong, this is an act of divine grace. So it seems reasonable, at least, to read Paul as seeing the evidence of infidelity in men and women turning away in their lust from what is natural to *them*; just as they have turned away from the evidences of God's existence that should naturally have led them to Him. If that is so, then it is at least *possible* to read this passage as critical of homosexual sex only when it is not natural to the person who engages in it. Though, that it *could* be natural to someone is an idea that St. Paul clearly nowhere expresses.

But if you see the scriptures as created by God to guide us, and if you believe, as I do, that they can only be interpreted as a whole and in coherence with your other views, then you will think that the fact that this passage *could* be interpreted in this way should incline you to do so if your other beliefs about the scriptures and morality require it. If the interpretation seems strained in isolation, as it does to some, that strain must be weighed against the strain of thinking that Christ Jesus who came into the world to save sinners and who commanded us to love all those who came near us would have condemned those whose natures lead them to express erotic desire in the context of a loving relationship with a person of their own gender.

In seeking to bring coherence to their moral beliefs, the historical experience of the church, and a developing understanding of the scriptures, I believe this is one of the possibilities that people of faith can reasonably be drawn to consider. But my main purpose here is not to persuade you of that, because the process of seeking reflective equilibrium in our judgments on these matters obviously requires consideration of many more issues and texts than I have been able to mention. What I do hope to persuade you of is that seeking coherence in this way is a method that will allow each person and each community to seek an understanding both of the scriptures they revere and of the moral life.

NOTES

1. I should note that there are contemporary Christians who may not regard the Bible as scripture in this sense. For some of them, these texts are historically distorted reflections of God's word, and so some parts may be rejected as inconsistent with Christ's moral teaching, in the sort of way that some of the early Christian writings were rejected in the next few centuries, and I don't wish to take sides in this dispute. I am approaching a question that arises for those who regard the Bible as scripture in the sense I am discussing. I *will* mention later some views about the canonization of the Christian Bible that see that process as

centrally about the developing self-understanding of the church. In traditions like that, there is a place, at least in principle, for a continuing reassessment of the canon.

2. Because Muslims believe it was dictated to the Prophet by the Angel Gabriel, learned by his early followers orally, and then transcribed, the words of the Qur'an, like the inscriptions on the tablets that Moses brought down from Sinai, are literally given from on high.

3. My understanding of the issues of the history of the biblical texts that I address by way of example in this chapter derives largely from Lee Martin McDonald, *The Biblical Canon: Its Origin, Transmission, and Authority* (Grand Rapids, MI: Baker Academic, 2007). I rely on him for most historical claims about texts, though, of course, I have examined some of those to which he refers for myself. Once again, what matters for my purposes is only that these are views that a reasonable Christian might hold, not that they are uncontroversially true. But this reading is very much a Protestant reading, and I am not going to discuss current Roman Catholic views about the formation of the biblical canon. (Many people are not aware that the Old Testament canon is different for Roman Catholics and Lutherans: Tobit, Judith, 1 Maccabees, 2 Maccabees (which is in Greek), Ecclesiastes, The Song of Songs, Baruch (including the letter of Jeremiah), and parts of Daniel and Esther are Apocrypha for Lutherans. These differences derive from Luther's having rejected those texts from the Septuagint that were not in the Jewish canon recognized by the rabbis in his day. He did not, apparently, know, that *that* canon was decided after the time of Christ. Luther also had doubts about some New Testament books—including Hebrews and Revelation, in part on theological grounds.

4. In Judaism both the five books of Moses and the wider body of the Tanakh (the Hebrew Bible as a whole) can be referred to as the Torah, as can oral traditions, and the Mishnah in which they were recorded and the Talmud and the Midrash; so the word has both narrow and broader senses.

5. The Book of Revelation might be thought to claim scriptural status for itself in Book 1 verse 3: "Blessed is he who reads aloud the words of the prophecy, and blessed are those who hear, and who keep what is written therein." But you have to regard it as authoritative already to take this claim seriously.

6. Γέγραπται.

7. The interpretation of Christ's many citations of the Psalms, for example, depends on a detailed knowledge of them. When, on the cross, he says in Hebrew, "My God, My God, why hast thou forsaken me?" he is quoting Psalm 22, which contains these words: "a company of evildoers encircles me. My hands and feet have shriveled; I can count all my bones. They stare and gloat over me; they divide my clothes among themselves, and for my clothing they cast lots." This will sound to many like a foreshadowing of the crucifixion; especially if

you translate the passage here rendered as "My hands and feet have shriveled," as some translations including the King James Bible do, as "They pierced my hands and my feet."

8. This distinguishes the Torah, by the way, from the Qur'an, which contains this promise in Surah 15, verse 9: "We have sent down the Qur'an Ourself, and We Ourself will guard it." This has been interpreted as guaranteeing the word-for-word reliability of its text. *The Qur'an*, trans. M. A. S. Abdel Haleem (New York: Oxford University Press, 2004).

9. 1 Corinthians 14:34–35. In this talk I will use the Revised Standard Version Catholic Edition, http://www.biblegateway.com/versions/Revised-Standard-Version-Catholic-Edition-RSVCE-Bible/, accessed September 30, 2013. For reasons I discuss here, I do not mean to suggest that we should take its text as authoritative.

10. "I have accepted 1 Cor 14:34–35 and 2 Cor 6:14–7:1 as post-Pauline insertions." Jerome Murphy-O'Connor, "The Non-Pauline Character of 1 Corinthians 11:2–16?," *Journal of Biblical Literature* 95, no. 4 (December 1976): 615.

11. I'm relying here on the ideas of H. P. Grice. See H. P. Grice, "Meaning," *Philosophical Review* 66, no. 3 (July 1957): 377–88. For details see Anthony Appiah, *Assertion and Conditionals* (Cambridge: Cambridge University Press, 1985).

12. This is clearly important to reading the Gospels, by the way, since Christ quotes the poetry of the Psalms more often than any other Jewish scripture.

13. I should perhaps add that I am not suggesting a coherence theory of moral *truth*. The issue is not what it is for a moral claim to be true but what it is for a moral belief to be *rational*. On the question of the correct account of moral truth, I will remain agnostic.

14. *Anti-Nicene Fathers*, 1:65.2, http://www.ccel.org/ccel/schaff/anf01.viii.iv.lxv.html.

15. The process of settling which writings should become part of the official scriptures—the process of canonization—took place against the background of the assumption that the early church—though centrally focused on the life and teaching of Christ—should continue to regard the Jewish scriptures as divinely inspired guides to life as well. This posed a central difficulty because both Christ in the Gospels and St. Paul *appeared*, at least, to deny that the Law and the Prophets were to be interpreted literally, at least by those followers of Christ who were not themselves Jewish. In some places in the Gospels, as in Matthew 5, Christ appears to have a more demanding interpretation of the law than the texts of the Torah literally understood prescribe, as when he says in Matthew 5: 27–28: "You have heard that it was said, 'You shall not commit adultery.' But I say to you that everyone who looks at a woman with lust has already committed adultery with her in his heart." And on the other hand, Christ seems often to

overrule Mosaic law, in effect if not explicitly, about the woman taken in adultery, that those without sin should cast the first stone; or when, in various places, he identifies the core of the law with two commandments: to love God and to love your neighbor. St. Paul in Galatians 3:14 says, " Christ hath redeemed us from the curse of the law." And in Galatians 3:24–25, "Therefore the law was our disciplinarian until Christ came, so that we might be justified by faith. But now that faith has come, we are no longer subject to a disciplinarian." There are thus a variety of possible attitudes to the ritual dimensions of Jewish law, as opposed to the moral ones; and, as I argue in the text, this distinction is itself not always clear.

16. A careful review by Lee Martin McDonald of the various canonical lists from Eusebius, along with patterns of reference to New Testament writings among the fathers of the early church, suggests, "The most common criteria employed in the canonical process include apostolicity, orthodoxy, antiquity, and use" (McDonald, *The Biblical Canon*, 405). If this is how the canon was actually decided, there are, of course, questions about each of these criteria; it is, for example, clear that the fathers believed that some texts were written by Apostles that were not. There is reasonable ground for doubting that John and Matthew were written by the Apostles of those names. As for orthodoxy, if a text could be rejected in the first century because it failed to fit with the church's developing understanding of the meaning and message of the life of Christ, then, of course, there might be reasons to reject it for the same reason in the church's experience since then. Antiquity is a problem for those of the canonical books, like the Epistles to Timothy, that are almost certainly later than some of the early Christian writings that were rejected. As for use, the acceptance of the Epistle to the Hebrews, which Paul certainly did not write (and which does not claim to be authored by him), in the life of the early church seems to have weighed heavily in its canonization, which is reasonable enough if you conceive of the experience of the church as the continuing life of the body of Christ. But this example shows that the question which texts should be accepted as scripture can depend, in the end, on arguments that are as much theological as historical; which fits, of course, with my coherentist claim that we must make sense of the scriptures in the light of everything we know. (Eusebius apparently included Revelation in his list because Constantine wanted it, not because he has great respect for it himself.)

17. See Bart D. Ehrman, *Forged: Writing in the Name of God—Why the Bible's Authors Are Not Who We Think They Are* (New York: Harper Collins, 2011), 277.

18. "You shall not take vengeance or bear a grudge against any of your people, but you shall love your neighbor as yourself: I am the Lord" (Leviticus 19:18).

19. Christ mentions circumcision once, in John 7:22, as an example of something permitted on the Sabbath. But he insists that, while Moses "gave" it to the Jews, it was "from the patriarchs," which makes it unclear what he thinks its standing is; and St. Paul thought it was clearly a part of the law that did not apply to Gentiles, which was the decision made in the Council at Jerusalem in Acts 15 (though this retains a more ritual proscription of blood and, in some texts, of "strangled things").

20. "'Come, you that are blessed by my Father, inherit the kingdom prepared for you from the foundation of the world; for I was hungry and you gave me food, I was thirsty and you gave me something to drink, I was a stranger and you welcomed me, I was naked and you gave me clothing, I was sick and you took care of me, I was in prison and you visited me.' Then the righteous will answer him, 'Lord, when was it that we saw you hungry and gave you food, or thirsty and gave you something to drink? And when was it that we saw you a stranger and welcomed you, or naked and gave you clothing? And when was it that we saw you sick or in prison and visited you?' And the king will answer them, 'Truly I tell you, just as you did it to one of the least of these who are members of my family, you did it to me'" (Matthew 25:34–40).

21. Matthew 7:1; Luke 6:37.

22. In the preface to *Cur Deus Homo*, Anselm says he has written two books, "Of which the first . . . with Christ out of view, proves by necessary reasons that it is impossible for any man to be saved without him. . . . Now in the second book similarly, as if nothing were known about Christ, it is shown with no less obvious reason and truth, that human nature is instituted in such a way that every man should enjoy a blessed immortality." "Quorum prius . . . remoto Christo—quasi nunquam aliquid fuerit de illo—probat rationibus necessariis, esse impossibile ullum hominem salvari sine illo. . . . In secundo autem libro similiter, quasi nihil sciatur de Christo, monstratur non minus aperta ratione et veritate, natura humanam ad hoc institutam esse, ut alliquando immortalitate beata totus homo . . . frueretur." S. Anselmi Cantuariensis Libri Duo, *Cur Deus Homo*, ed. Hugo Laemer (Berlin: Sumtibus Gust. Schlawitz, 1857), xv–xvi.

23. You will recall that the "men of Sodom" ask Lot to give up two guests who are staying with him "so that they can know them." Lot refuses, and the Sodomites try to break down the door. The two guests, who are angels, then blind the men of Sodom and allow Lot and his family to escape. "Then the LORD rained down burning sulfur on Sodom and Gomorrah" (Genesis 19:24). As is very evident from this brief retelling of the story, there are two serious offenses here: first, a breach, to put it mildly, of the laws of hospitality (which have continued to be of central importance in the lives of people in the Middle East until this day) and, second, humiliation and assault through rape. The fact that the rape in question is of men by men is part of what is humiliating about it. But

it is hard to see that we can draw any inference about an attitude to voluntary sexual relations between people of the same sex from this passage. And, indeed, as David Greenberg has pointed out, the first writers to "assert unambiguously that the Sin of Sodom involved homosexuality" were the Jewish writers Philo and Josephus in the first century of the Common Era. In identifying the meanings of a text, I argued earlier, we need to begin with its literal meanings; given the fact that these are constituted by conventions in the communities who use the terms, the fact that for many centuries no one in those communities interpreted the passages as being about sex is powerful evidence against an interpretation that does so.

24. "the eagle, the vulture, the osprey, the buzzard, the kite of any kind; every raven of any kind; the ostrich, the nighthawk, the sea gull, the hawk of any kind; the little owl and the great owl, the water hen and the desert owl, the carrion vulture and the cormorant, the stork, the heron of any kind; the hoopoe and the bat."

25. In fact, this is suggestively like a list of taboos, which will in many societies include both certain forms of food and certain immoral acts.

26. The issue of the divorce is moot for Christians, of course, since Christ explicitly says that remarriage after divorce (which he says is permissible if your wife is unfaithful) is adultery (Matthew 5:31).

27. After all, in other places in the Hebrew Bible, people "lying with" doesn't get qualified in this way.

28. It has recently been argued that Matthew 19:11–12, which is about eunuchs, is relevant as well. "But he said to them, 'Not everyone can accept this teaching, but only those to whom it is given.' For there are eunuchs who have been so from birth, and there are eunuchs who have been made eunuchs by others, and there are eunuchs who have made themselves eunuchs for the sake of the kingdom of heaven. Let anyone accept this who can." This is not quite as crazy as it might seem—equating men without normal sexual organs to homosexuals might seem like the worst kind of conflation of issues. But it occurs after a discussion of marriage and divorce and in response to a suggestion from the disciples that celibacy might be the best option. So the thought that some people might naturally (from birth) or as a result of a physical change (by castration) abstain from heterosexual marriage is definitely there. So you could suppose that a homosexual, on the modern understanding, was someone who was from birth inclined against heterosexual sex in a similar way. But if Christ had been suggesting that, why does he go on to talk about castrating yourself "for the sake of the kingdom of heaven." The point about eunuchs, natural or artificial, is what they don't do, not what they do do.

29. "Do you not know that wrongdoers will not inherit the kingdom of God? Do not be deceived! Fornicators, idolaters, adulterers, male prostitutes, sodom-

ites (οὔτε μαλακοὶ οὔτε ἀρσενοκοῖται), thieves, the greedy, drunkards, revilers, robbers—none of these will inherit the kingdom of God" (1 Corinthians 6:9–11).

30. John Boswell, *Christianity, Homosexuality and Social Tolerance* (Chicago: Chicago University Press, 1980), Appendix 1.

31. St. Paul uses the verbal form *κοίταις* in Romans 13:13, which the King James Bible nicely translated as "chambering," which in Elizabethan English had the sense both of sexual indulgence and effeminacy, rather like μαλακοί.

32. "καὶ μετὰ **ἄρσενος** οὐ κοιμηθήσῃ **κοίτην** γυναικός βδέλυγμα γάρ ἐστιν." I don't know why Boswell doesn't mention this.

27

HOMOSEXUALITY AND THE WORD OF GOD

Mary Healey, Sacred Heart Seminary

In an August 2013 interview with the Jesuit magazine *La Civiltà Cattolica*, Pope Francis famously stated:

> The church's pastoral ministry cannot be obsessed with the transmission of a disjointed multitude of doctrines to be imposed insistently. Proclamation in a missionary style focuses on the essentials, on the necessary things: this is also what fascinates and attracts more, what makes the heart burn. . . . We have to find a new balance; otherwise even the moral edifice of the church is likely to fall like a house of cards, losing the freshness and fragrance of the Gospel.

The Pope's advice serves as a salutary caution for anyone setting out to discuss the biblical teaching on homosexuality.[1] It suggests that to be fruitful, such a discussion cannot be confined to examining biblical prohibitions of homosexual conduct. One must also ask: What does the word of God say to those who experience same-sex attraction? Is the biblical teaching on homosexuality compatible with the "freshness and fragrance" of the good news of Christ? What is its place in relation to "the essentials" of the Gospel? In what follows I hope to clarify what Scripture says about homosexuality in light of these questions.

HOMOSEXUALITY IN THE OLD TESTAMENT

Four passages in the Old Testament directly refer to homosexual behavior: two narratives (Gen 19 and Judg 19) and two legal texts (Lev 18:22 and 20:13). To be interpreted properly these passages must be viewed within the broader context of biblical teaching on sexuality, the foundations of which are laid in the creation narratives of Genesis 1–3.

The Creation Account: Genesis 1–3

Although Israel's creation stories belong to the cultural matrix of the Ancient Near East, even a cursory comparison of the Genesis narrative with the myths of the surrounding pagan cultures reveal the absolute distinctiveness of its portrayal of God.[2] The gods of the Canaanites, Egyptians, Assyrians, and Babylonians related to the natural world in a highly sexualized manner, and were promiscuous and polymorphous in their sexual behavior. Their erotic activity and cosmic conflicts spawned the world.[3] Religious rites were primarily for the purpose of inducing fertility (both human and agricultural) and were often orgiastic; cultic prostitution played a prominent role.

In stark contrast, the God of biblical revelation is utterly transcendent. There is no hint of sexual activity in God. The world originated not out of divine copulation or struggle, but simply by the utterance of God's word, which brought all things into being out of nothing.[4] All that exists exists solely as a result of God's free and sovereign will. The effect of this biblical doctrine of creation was to demythologize sexuality. Sexuality does not belong to the divine sphere but to the created order willed by God. Sexuality and the covenant founded on it, marriage, are a gift of God, "sanctified by the fact of creation itself and subject to God's holy laws."[5] As part of God's created order, sexuality "receives, in the very act of its creation, a constitutive nature which needs to be respected if man and society are to flourish."[6]

Each of the two biblical creation accounts (Gen 1 and 2) depicts in its own way God's design for humanity.[7] In Genesis 1 the creation of sexually differentiated human beings and the divine blessing of fertility appear as the very pinnacle of God's creative work (1:26–28). The supreme importance of this step is highlighted by a pause in the rhythm of the six days. Instead of simply speaking a word of command, God makes a solemn decision: "Let us make man . . . " God then creates human beings, male and female, in his image and after his likeness. He blesses them, commands them to be fruitful, and gives them dominion over all other animate beings; that is, they are appointed as his royal representatives over all creation.

There is a curious oscillation in this text between the singular and plural, in regard to both God and human beings. The very foundation of Israelite religion is absolute monotheism (Deut 6:4), yet Genesis 1:26 posits a plurality in God: "Then God said, 'Let *us* make man in *our* image, after *our* likeness.'"[8] In the next statement the plural becomes a singular: "So God created man in *his* own image, in the image of God *he* created him." Likewise the human being created in God's image is irreducibly both a collective singular ("he created *him*") and a sexually differentiated plural ("male and female he created *them*"). The point, although it remains only implicit in the text, is that the interpersonal communion made possible by the differentiation of the sexes is intrinsic to human existence, and is somehow essential to man's being created in the image of God. God's desire for an image of himself in the world is realized not in the creation of isolated individuals but of a man and woman who are to unite in marriage. Moreover, their union is to be fruitful, giving rise to the primordial human community, the family. As Saint John Paul II pointed out in his reflections on this text, "Man . . . is, in fact, 'from the beginning' not only an image in which the solitude of one Person, who rules the world, mirrors itself, but also and essentially the image of an inscrutable divine communion of Persons."[9]

Whereas Genesis 1 presents a rhythmic, highly structured account of the creation of the whole cosmos, Genesis 2 describes from a more concrete and existential perspective the origin of humanity, the crown of God's works. Here God forms man (*'adam*) from the dust of the earth and breathes into him the breath of life (Gen 2:7). God's remark, "It is *not good* that the man should be alone; I will make him a helper fit for him" (Gen 2:18), is in striking contrast to the repeated refrain in chapter 1: "God saw that it was *good*." It emphatically asserts what Genesis 1:27 already implied: man is not made for solitude; essential to human nature is interpersonal communion. Following this remark, God presents each of the animals to Adam in search of the suitable "helper." Narrative suspense is created, as none of the animals is found capable of the communion for which the man longs.

At the culmination of the narrative, God finally acts to resolve the crisis by putting the man into a deep sleep, taking one of his ribs, and fashioning it into a woman. It is of pivotal significance that God does not simply fashion another *'adam*, a replica of the first, but a complementary being from Adam's side—one who is different yet intimately related to him, with whom he yearns to be *re*united.[10] In a scene with strong nuptial overtones, God presents the woman to the man, and he responds with an outburst of delight: "This at last is bone of my bones, flesh of my flesh; she shall be called Woman, because she was taken out of Man" (Gen 2:23).[11] As John Paul II observes, the narrative depicts a moment of existential self-discovery. The man recognizes that the woman—unlike the animals—is his equal, a person like himself, to whom he can give himself in love and who can freely receive and reciprocate this gift. Through her, he comes to recognize the deepest purpose of his existence: to share in an exchange of love in which the gift of self is freely given and received. In this perspective the meaning of the woman's designation as "helper" becomes clear: she helps the man recognize and fulfill his true vocation; namely, to love.[12]

By accenting the male-female distinction, the text conveys that it is precisely through *the complementarity of their bodies*—their sexual differences that render union possible—that the man and woman realize their vocation to interpersonal communion. Through their bodies, they each recognize the other as equal and yet irreducibly other. Their bodies are designed to be joined in a sexual union that expresses and embodies a union at the deepest level of the person. As John Paul II points out, the body has an intrinsically "spousal" quality; it is apt for marital union. "The human body, with its sex—its masculinity and femininity . . . contains, 'from the beginning,' the 'spousal' attribute, that is, *the power to express love: precisely that love in which the human person becomes a gift* and—through this gift—fulfills the very meaning of his being and existence."[13] Genesis thus affirms the only sexual "orientation" with which human beings are created: the orientation to spousal communion with the opposite sex that is inscribed in the body, male or female.[14] *Sexual union* properly speaking is in fact not possible with a person of the same sex, even if various forms of erotic activity are possible.

Genesis goes on to show the relevance of this defining moment of self-discovery for all future marital relations: "Therefore a man leaves his father and his mother and cleaves to his wife, and they become one flesh"

(2:24). Marriage is depicted in covenantal terms; that is, it is a kinship bond created by solemn commitment.[15] Sexual union is the bodily expression of that covenant by which a man and a woman give themselves to one another wholly and irrevocably. The Israelite prophetic tradition will invest the marital covenant with a profound theological significance: it is the earthly image of the spousal love between God and his people.

Through this narrative, Genesis gives symbolic expression to the truth that is imprinted in the human body and is therefore in principle accessible to every human being: the intrinsic meaning of sexual union is to signify and enact the marital covenant between a man and a woman. Marriage is therefore the only appropriate context for sexual expression. And it is only the union of a man and a woman that is able to "multiply and fill the earth" with new life.

The biblical authors are well aware, however, that sexual desires and behaviors often fail to correspond with the divine plan. In fact, a major aim of the creation narrative is to explain the origin of the *disharmony* that exists in human relationships and in the world. This explanation is given in the story of the fall in Genesis 3. In contrast to the myths of the surrounding cultures, Genesis grounds the disorder in the world not in Fate or the caprice of the gods, but in human free will. Adam and Eve choose to distrust and disobey God, placing themselves outside of his gracious plan for human life. Not incidentally, the first consequence of their sin is a loss of sexual innocence: "they knew they were naked" (3:7). They intuitively recognize that sin has brought about a distortion whereby sexuality can become a means of self-gratification rather than self-gift: love twisted into lust. Moreover, sin brings a disturbance in the marital relationship itself—instead of mutual self-donation, there are tendencies toward distrust and disunity (3:12), exploitation and dominance (3:16). The rest of the book of Genesis displays the manifold forms of disorder that sin introduces into human relationships.[16]

The Sodom Story: Genesis 18–19

With this foundation in mind, we can turn to the biblical passages that directly concern homosexual behavior. The most well known is the story of the destruction of Sodom and Gomorrah in Genesis 18–19.[17] It is unfortunate that this passage so often takes center stage in debates about Scripture and homosexuality, since it is a narrative and thus does not in itself provide a norm of conduct. To add to the difficulty, the passage does not explicitly name the wrongdoing for which these cities are punished. Was it homosexual behavior, or was it hostility toward strangers (sometimes described as "inhospitality") and attempted gang rape?[18] Many recent commentators argue for the latter, holding that only centuries later did homosexual behavior become prominent in explanations of the sin of Sodom.[19]

One clue for interpreting the story is provided by the context in which it appears. The story is part of a tightly woven literary unit that begins with Yahweh's visit to Abraham and Sarah at the oaks of Mamre, promising the birth of their son (Gen 18:1–15), and concludes with the account of Lot's incestuous relations with his daughters (19:30–38). The episode is thus framed by contrasting references to sexual relations. The first, that of Abraham and Sarah, depicts a married couple who trust in God and conform to his plan, leading to great blessing in the birth of their son Isaac and ultimately the people of Israel. The other, that of Lot and his daughters, is about distrust in God (cf. 19:31) and disorder in sexual relationships, leading to future troubles in the birth of Ammon and Moab, ancestors of Israel's historical enemies. This frame provides an important clue for interpreting the story itself.

Another suggestive parallel is that both the Mamre and Sodom scenes involve a divine visitation. In one, the Lord is welcomed with extraordinary humility and hospitality; in the other, the Lord (represented by the angels) is treated with extraordinary contempt and hostility. In fact, this parallel provides the deepest clue to the meaning of the story. The fundamental question is how human beings will respond to God.

Finally, a third significant parallel is between the Sodom episode and the account of Noah and the flood (Gen 6–8). Both depict catastrophic destruction as a result of grave evil. In both cases, the evil includes both sexual immorality and violence; and in both, God mercifully spares one man and his family.[20]

The Sodom story itself has three scenes: Abraham's intercession for Sodom and Gomorrah, the arrival and attempted assault of the angelic visitors in Sodom, and the destruction of the cities (18:16–19:29).[21]

In the first scene (Gen 18:17–33), Yahweh considers whether to inform Abraham of the coming judgment: "Shall I hide from Abraham what I am about to do, seeing that Abraham shall become a great and mighty nation, and all the nations of the earth shall bless themselves by him?" (Gen 18:17–18).[22] This question recalls God's promise to Abraham that he would be a source of blessing to all nations (12:3; cf. 22:18), and implicitly places Abraham's prayer for Sodom in that context. His role, presaging the role of his descendants, is to intercede for those who are estranged from God and his ways. Despite the patriarch's bold negotiations, however, the city is found to be lacking even a minimal number of righteous people for whose sake it could be spared.

In the second scene (Gen 19:1–11), the two angels arrive in Sodom and are welcomed by Lot, who clearly means to offer them protection. But the men of the city surround the house and demand, "Where are the men who came to you tonight? Bring them out to us, that we may know them" (19:5).[23] As often in the Old Testament, here the verb "to know" (*yada'*) has an obvious sexual connotation:[24] they want to have sexual relations with the two visitors. This is confirmed a few verses later by Lot's offer to hand over his "two daughters who have not known man" (19:8), indicating that he recognizes their motive as lust. The narrator leaves unsaid whether Lot is bluffing or actually intends to carry through on his shocking offer, but in either case he seeks to prevent the homosexual rape of his guests.[25] The fact that Lot begs the men of Sodom to accept this substitute shows that the offense is not *only* violent sexual coercion, since this would occur in either case.

Lot's plea, "do nothing to these men, for they have come under the shelter of my roof" (19:8), shows that the crime is made incalculably worse by the fact that it would be perpetrated against guests, who have a right to expect protection and care from their hosts. It is important to note, however, that hostility toward strangers is presented not as the townsmen's motive, but as an exacerbating factor in their crime. The townsmen refuse Lot's offer of his daughters, confirming that their motive is specifically homosexual lust. But at the root of all is their rejection of God, as evidenced in their contemptuous behavior toward God's angelic messengers.

In biblical tradition Sodom becomes a symbol of depravity and consequent divine judgment. But again, what precisely is the depravity associated with Sodom? The prophet Isaiah hurls the epithets "Sodom" and "Gomorrah" at the Israelites in prophetic indictment, then proceeds to accuse them of bloodshed, injustice, oppression, and corruption (Isa 1:10–23; cf. 3:8–9). Jeremiah speaks of Jerusalem becoming "like Sodom" because of its adultery (i.e., infidelity to the spousal covenant with

Yahweh), deceit, and siding with evildoers (Jer 23:14). Ezekiel describes Jerusalem as having outdone in evil her "sister Sodom," who was guilty of pride, gluttony, prosperous ease, and failing to aid the poor and needy (Ezek 16:49).[26] These passages make clear that the sin of Sodom consisted of a whole range of vices, especially sins of social injustice. On the other hand, it would be a mistake to infer that homosexual behavior was not part of the picture. Immediately following the list of sins just mentioned, Ezekiel states, "They were haughty, and did an abomination before me; therefore I removed them" (16:50), probably alluding to the passages in Leviticus that speak of sexual misconduct as an "abomination" (see below).[27]

In later Jewish references to Sodom, the emphasis on homosexual conduct becomes more pronounced.[28] Two New Testament texts reflect this emphasis. The letter of Jude states that the people of Sodom and Gomorrah "indulged in sexual immorality and went after other flesh" (Jude 7, literal translation),[29] which probably refers to homosexual conduct (or, less plausibly, to their unwitting attempt to engage in sexual relations with angels). The second letter of Peter speaks of Lot's distress at "the licentiousness of the wicked" and God's judgment on the Sodomites as a warning to "those who indulge in the lust of defiling passion and despise authority" (2 Pet 2:7, 10). For those who accept these texts as part of Sacred Scripture, they must be recognized as giving an authoritative interpretation of the sin of Sodom. The question of Sodom's sin is thus not either/or but both/and. Their sexual misconduct was part of a larger pattern of pride, greed, and selfishness—all rooted in arrogant disregard for God and his will.

In the Synoptic Gospels, Jesus takes up the tradition of Sodom as the epitome of evil leading to divine judgment, but he concludes with a twist that probably shocked and offended some of his listeners: those who refuse to accept his apostles sent to preach the gospel will fare worse than the people of Sodom. "If any one will not receive you or listen to your words, shake off the dust from your feet as you leave that house or town. Truly, I say to you, it shall be more tolerable on the day of judgment for the land of Sodom and Gomorrah than for that town" (Matt 10:14–15; Luke 10:12; cf. Matt 11:23).[30]

Jesus thus affirms Jewish tradition regarding the gravity of the sin of Sodom, while at the same time relativizing it. Although Sodom's sexual immorality, violence, and hostility to God's angelic messengers were

The Prohibitions of Leviticus 18 and 20

The two Old Testament texts directly prohibiting homosexual acts are in Leviticus, in a section of laws that scholars call the Holiness Code (Lev 17–26) because it contains detailed prescriptions for living as God's holy people.

> You shall not lie with a male as with a woman; it is an abomination. (Lev 18:22)

> If a man lies with a male as with a woman, both of them have committed an abomination; they shall be put to death, their blood is upon them. (Lev 20:13)

Both texts appear in lists of sexual offenses including adultery, bestiality, various forms of incest, and child sacrifice.[31] Homosexual sex is not singled out as the only sexual act that is gravely sinful. Rather, all these acts are an abuse of sexuality, departing from God's intention for marriage as revealed in Genesis 1–2 and instead pursuing erotic pleasure for its own sake. All are described as characteristic of the Canaanites and the reason for their expulsion from the land. God warns Israel, "Do not defile yourselves by any of these things, for by all these the nations I am casting out before you defiled themselves; and the land became defiled, so that I punished its iniquity, and the land vomited out its inhabitants" (Lev 18:24–25). Chapter 18 simply proscribes the acts; chapter 20 specifies the punishment for each. The penalty in most cases is death, underscoring the gravity of the offense.[32]

The offenses are summed up as "abominations" (*to'evot*) in 18:27, 29, although only homosexual acts are singled out as "an abomination" (*to'evah*) in the singular (18:22; 20:13). The Hebrew term signifies that which is abhorrent, and is therefore incompatible with the holiness required of God's people. Throughout the Old Testament it is used for egregious sins, including idolatry, sexual immorality, and various forms of social injustice.

The Torah, however, also uses "abomination" for various forms of ritual impurity, including unclean animals (Deut 14:3),[33] sacrificing a blemished animal (Deut 17:1), and intercourse with a menstruating woman (Lev 18:19, 29). Thus the argument is often made that the prohibition of homosexual conduct belongs to the category of laws concerning ritual purity, not morality.[34] Unlike sin, ritual impurity is morally neutral and can result from involuntary acts (e.g., menstruation, nocturnal emission of semen) or even from morally good acts (e.g., marital sexual relations, burying the dead). These purity laws, it is argued, are based on prerational, culturally conditioned taboos that are now recognized as obsolete.[35] Moreover, the New Testament affirms that the Mosaic purity laws have been abrogated in Christ (Mark 7:18–19; Acts 10:15; 15:19–21).[36]

The problem with this argument, however, is that it would have to be equally applied to the laws against adultery, incest, and bestiality. Yet few would want to argue that these are based on obsolete, culturally conditioned taboos. Rather, all of these prohibitions, as applying to free human acts, belong to the moral law that orders sexual conduct according to God's design. The fact that they are listed alongside ritual purity laws, in a code that does not sharply differentiate between the cultic and the moral, cannot mean that they are obsolete. In fact, the only Mosaic law regulating sexual conduct that clearly relates to ritual purity, the prohibition of intercourse with a menstruating woman (18:19; 20:18),[37] also has a moral foundation. Walter Kaiser argues that this rule embodies the principle that "no husband has sovereignty over his wife or her body, but that ultimately all is owed to God."[38] Even within marriage, the sexual instinct is not given free reign but is subject to limits. The self-restraint required during this period helps ensure that sexual union is ordered to the Creator's intention for life-giving spousal union.

Another line of argument seeks to uncover the implicit motives underlying the Levitical rules against homosexual acts and show that they no longer apply in a modern context.[39] Some authors hold that what made homosexual acts particularly egregious was their subversion of male status; that is, they treated a man as if he were a woman, thereby depriving him of his superior, active role.[40] Although that concern is prominent in other Ancient Near Eastern legal codes,[41] there is no evidence that it plays a role in the biblical texts. Although the Torah assumes a patriarchal social context, it contains no laws to safeguard male superiority. In fact, such reasoning would render other parts of the Torah inexplicable, particularly the affirmation that men and women are equally created in the image of God and given collective rule over creation (Gen 1:26–28), and the relegation of the husband's "rule" over his wife to the tragic consequences of the fall rather than to the original order of creation (Gen 3:16).[42]

Still others argue that Leviticus 18:22 and 20:13 refer only to exploitative forms of same-sex eroticism. However, the prohibitions are absolute, penalizing both parties. There is no exception for mutual consent.[43] They apply equally to Israelites and to resident aliens (Lev 18:26). Nor are there any grounds for limiting the prohibition to male cult prostitutes, as some authors have claimed, since Leviticus 18:22 and 20:13 simply use the Hebrew term for "male" (*zakar*), not "male cult prostitute" (*qadesh*), nor "boy, youth" (*na'ar*).[44]

JESUS' TEACHING ON SEXUALITY

Jesus' moral teaching, like all his teachings, is part of his proclamation of the good news of the kingdom. In him, the kingdom is at hand: God's promises are fulfilled, the curse of sin is broken, death is destroyed, Satan is conquered, and humanity is at last reconciled to God. All his sayings on sexual morality need to be read within the context of this "good news."[45]

The argument is frequently made that since Jesus said nothing explicit about homosexual relationships, he therefore would have had no objections to them, or would even have approved of them provided that they take place in loving, committed relationships.[46] But this argument from silence quickly collapses since by the same reasoning, Jesus would also have approved of incest, bestiality, and other sexual behaviors condemned in the law of Moses but not mentioned by him. Jesus' silence must be interpreted within the context of first-century Judaism, which unequivocally held to the law's prohibition of nonmarital sexual activity.[47] Jesus did not hesitate to challenge certain elements of tradition surrounding the law in his day (Mark 2:23–28; 3:1–5; 7:9–23). But far from relaxing the moral law, he makes its demands even more stringent.

In the Sermon on the Mount, Jesus affirms the continuing validity of the law: "Think not that I have come to abolish the law and the prophets; I have come not to abolish them but to fulfill them. . . . Whoever then relaxes one of the least of these commandments and teaches men so, shall be called least in the kingdom of heaven; but he who does them and teaches them shall be called great in the kingdom of heaven" (Matt

5:17–19). He then goes on to explain how this fulfillment "demands a surfeit, not a deficit, of righteousness."[48] Speaking with an authority that puts him on a par with the divine Lawgiver, Jesus pronounces six antitheses that deepen and interiorize the law: "You have heard it said . . . but I say to you . . ." In the second antithesis he sets a higher standard of sexual purity than the law had demanded: "You have heard that it was said, 'You shall not commit adultery.' But I say to you that everyone who looks at a woman lustfully has already committed adultery with her in his heart" (Matt 5:27–28).[49] Not only the act itself but also the desire for it must be rooted out.

There is not the slightest indication that Jesus approved erotic behavior condemned in the law of Moses. In another saying, Jesus reaffirms that disordered sexual conduct originates in the heart: "What comes out of a person is what defiles him. For from within, out of the heart of man, come evil thoughts, sexual immorality [*porneiai*], . . . adultery, . . . debauchery. . . . All these evil things come from within, and they defile a person" (Mark 7:20–23). The term *porneiai* encompasses sexual immorality in general, including homosexual acts and all the other sexual behaviors forbidden in the Torah.[50]

Two further sets of Gospel passages are crucial for interpreting Jesus' astoundingly high standards for sexual morality: his teaching on God's original intention for marriage and his personal interaction with sexual sinners.[51]

GOD'S INTENTION FOR MARRIAGE

Jesus' most extensive teaching on marriage occurs, ironically, in the context of a discussion about divorce (Mark 10:2–12; cf. Matt 19:3–9). In response to a question from the Pharisees as to whether divorce for any cause is justified, Jesus appeals to what God intended "from the beginning." He quotes from both creation accounts. The first quotation, "he made them male and female" (Gen 1:27), affirms God's creation of men and women as gendered beings who are called to fruitful sexual union. The second describes God's purpose for this sexual complementarity: "For this reason a man shall leave his father and mother and be joined to his wife, and the two shall become one flesh" (Gen 2:24). Jesus thus reaffirms the teaching of Genesis that the differentiation of the sexes is for the purpose of the one-flesh union that is the bodily expression of the marital covenant between husband and wife. Moreover, by the very fact of appealing to humanity before the fall, Jesus implies that from now on, *God's original intention* is the true standard for sexual union and marriage. Although Moses had allowed divorce and remarriage as a concession to "hardness of heart" (Mark 10:5), that concession has been annulled since the era of the dominion of sin is over. Now that Christ has come, there is a new reality at hand—the kingdom of God—bringing a new power to live according to what God intended from the beginning. As Jesus has already suggested, this new reality will come about through his passion and resurrection (Mark 8:31–9:1).

Christ's words in the Sermon on the Mount calling for sexual purity in thought and deed are not, then, merely the expression of a lofty ideal, a goal toward which we should aim. They are authoritative and efficacious words; they have power to accomplish what they demand, for those who accept his call.[52] John Paul II comments:

> *Only in the mystery of Christ's Redemption do we discover the "concrete" possibilities of man.* It would be a very serious error to conclude . . . that the Church's teaching is essentially only an "ideal" which must then be adapted, proportioned, graduated to the so-called concrete possibilities of man. . . . But what are the "concrete possibilities of man"? And of *which* man are we speaking? Of man *dominated* by lust or of man *redeemed by Christ?* This is what is at stake: the *reality* of Christ's redemption. *Christ has redeemed us!* This means that he has given us the possibility of realizing *the entire* truth of our being; he has set our freedom free from the *domination* of concupiscence. And if redeemed man still sins, this is not due to an imperfection of Christ's redemptive act, but to man's will not to avail himself of the grace which flows from that act. God's command is of course proportioned to man's capabilities; but to the capabilities of the man to whom the Holy Spirit has been given; of the man who, though he has fallen into sin, can always obtain pardon and enjoy the presence of the Holy Spirit.[53]

Mercy for Sexual Sinners

The second set of key texts are those in which Jesus reaches out to those branded as sexual sinners, particularly the "woman of the city" in Luke

7:36–50, the Samaritan woman in John 4, and the woman caught in adultery in John 8:1–11.[54] There is no mention of homosexual behavior, probably because it was rare in first-century Judaism,[55] but Jesus offers forgiveness to all without exception. The Gospels depict Jesus not only unhesitatingly associating with "tax collectors and sinners," but even seeming to prefer their company.[56] He clearly had a special compassion for those who had engaged in sexual sin and had experienced the resultant social ostracism.

These episodes are sometimes taken as an indication that Jesus was indifferent to sexual immorality. But such a reading is only possible by distorting the texts as well as ignoring Jesus' explicit moral teachings. These passages "no more suggest that Jesus was soft on sexual sin than do the stories about Jesus' fraternization with tax collectors insinuate an accommodation to economic exploitation."[57] In response to the Pharisees' complaint that he ate with sinners, Jesus reveals his true motive for welcoming sinners. He is the physician who has come to heal:[58] "Those who are well have no need of a physician, but those who are sick; I have not come to call the righteous, but sinners to repentance" (Luke 5:31–32).[59] His mission is not merely to accept all in love, but to *heal* all of their debilitating moral sickness by calling all to repentance—including, ironically, the Pharisees who deem themselves righteous.

Numerous other passages confirm that Jesus invites people not simply to enter the kingdom but to become "fit for the kingdom" (Luke 9:62) through faith and repentance manifested in a changed life.[60] He tells the adulterous woman, "Neither do I condemn you; go, and sin no more" (John 8:11). He compares the tax collectors and prostitutes to a son who first refused to do his father's will, but then "repented" and did it (Matt 21:28–32). He tells a parable about a wedding banquet to which all are invited, but the guests must put on a "wedding garment," which symbolizes righteous conduct (Matt 22:1–14). Nowhere is there the slightest indication that Jesus endorsed a way of life contrary to the moral law.

On several occasions, however, Jesus indicates that spiritual pride and the self-righteousness that precludes repentance are a more formidable barrier to the kingdom than sexual sin: "Truly, I say to you, the tax collectors and the prostitutes go into the kingdom of God before you. For John came to you in the way of righteousness, and you did not believe him, but the tax collectors and the prostitutes believed him; and even when you saw it, you did not afterward repent and believe him" (Matt 21:31–32).[61]

The Gospel's high standards of sexual morality may at first seem to threaten the possibility of human happiness for some. But all the limits Scripture places on human conduct are for the sake of something greater. The Gospel reveals that there is a personal relationship available to all that is satisfying beyond our wildest expectations, a spousal relationship with Jesus himself, the divine Bridegroom (Matt 9:15; John 3:29). Those who are not called to an earthly marriage are not denied happiness or intimate spousal love. The Gospels depict in a variety of ways the joy of those who encounter Jesus and experience his unconditional love and forgiveness, imparting the grace to begin a new life. Their reactions include celebratory feasting (Mark 2:14–15), following Jesus on the way of discipleship (Luke 8:2), extravagant expressions of love in response to his love (Luke 7:36–50), and exuberant proclamation of the good news to others (John 4:29)—all signs of the messianic joy of the kingdom.

PAULINE TEACHING ON SEXUALITY

Three passages in the Pauline literature explicitly mention homosexual conduct: two lists of vices (1 Cor 6:9–11; 1 Tim 1:9–11) and a lengthy reflection on the moral consequences of idolatry (Rom 1:18–32).[62] As with the Old Testament and Gospel texts, these need to be interpreted within the broader context of Paul's teaching on marriage. Paul's vision of the exalted meaning of marriage is most fully developed in Ephesians 5:21–33;[63] he offers his most detailed practical advice concerning sex and marriage in 1 Corinthians 7.

In his exhortation to husbands and wives in Ephesians 5, Paul cites Genesis 2:24: "For this reason a man shall leave his father and mother and be joined to his wife, and the two shall become one flesh." He then adds: "This is a great mystery, for I am speaking of Christ and the church" (Eph 5:32). With this statement, Paul brings the institution of marriage to a whole new level of significance. Marriage is not only part of God's original design for humanity, it is a mystery[64] that already from the beginning of time pointed in a veiled way to the fullness of God's plan of salvation. The prophets had described God's love for his people as that of a bridegroom,[65] but Paul invests the nuptial imagery with a deeper import. "Creation itself is a prophecy of redemption. This means that in the corporate reality of man and woman, as Genesis describes it, is already present in a proleptic symbol the unity of Christ and the Church."[66] All marriages, whether between Christians or not, are an earthly image of, and in some way participate in, the ineffable mystery of Christ's love for his people.[67]

Such Were Some of You: 1 Corinthians 6:9–11

Paul's earliest mention of homosexual conduct occurs in 1 Corinthians, in a section in which he addresses scandalous conduct that the Corinthian community has tolerated in its midst, particularly incest and lawsuits against one another in pagan courts. Many of the Corinthian Christians were Gentiles who had undergone a radical conversion from the sexually permissive lifestyles that were common in Greek culture. As in other letters, Paul takes pains to show them that their former conduct is utterly incompatible with their new life in Christ.[68] In our passage he admonishes:

> Do you not know that the unrighteous[69] will not inherit the kingdom of God? Do not be deceived: neither the sexually immoral, nor idolaters, nor adulterers, nor passive homosexual partners [*malakoi*], nor men who lie with males [*arsenokoitai*], nor thieves, nor the greedy, nor drunkards, nor revilers, nor robbers will inherit the kingdom of God. And such were some of you. But you were washed, you were sanctified, you were justified in the name of the Lord Jesus Christ and in the Spirit of our God. (1 Cor 6:9–11, author's translation)

Paul's sharp warning, "Do not be deceived," indicates that it is in fact possible for Christians to deceive themselves regarding sin and its devastating consequences. In the case of serious sin, the consequences are eternal: those who persist in these sins will be excluded from the kingdom of God. Of the ten terms on the list, four refer to sexual conduct, and a fifth, idolatry, is closely linked to sexual immorality, as will be seen below.[70]

Two terms refer explicitly to homosexual conduct.[71] *Malakos* is literally "soft, delicate" (cf. Matt 11:8), but in ancient Greek was used for men or boys who played the passive role in homosexual relations.[72] The translation "boy prostitutes" (for example, in the NAB) inordinately narrows the meaning, since there is no evidence that the term was limited either to adolescents or to those who sold their services.[73] The translation "effeminate" is also inaccurate, since Paul is not speaking of a personality characteristic but of sinful acts. The second term, *arsenokoitai* (literally, "men who lie with males"), was probably coined by Paul himself, combining two terms used for the prohibition of homosexual acts in the Septuagint translation of Leviticus 18:22 and 20:13: *arsēn* ("male") and *koitē* ("lying" or "bed"). Thus, *malakoi* and *arsenokoitai* together refer to the two partners in same-sex relations.[74]

But the warning is not complete without the jubilant exclamation of verse 11: "Such were some of you. But you were washed, you were sanctified, you were justified in the name of the Lord Jesus Christ and in the Spirit of our God." No matter what their past misdeeds, those joined to Christ through faith and baptism have been liberated from bondage to sin and brought into life-transforming communion with God. They are no longer under the domination of sinful impulses. They belong to the "fellowship of redeemed sinners, who praise the mercy of God."[75]

As numerous exhortations throughout Paul's letters make clear,[76] this new freedom in Christ does not mean that disordered sexual desires simply disappear. Paul "was not guaranteeing former adulterers that they would never again experience sexual desire for people other than their spouse, or former thieves and swindlers that they would never again be tempted by material possessions."[77] It *does* mean there is a new power within Christians, the Holy Spirit, to resist these impulses and live a holy life in accord with God's will (cf. Rom 8:4, 14). As in Jesus' teachings, so in Paul's letters, the Gospel demands the purification not only of deeds but also of desires. "Those who belong to Christ Jesus have crucified the flesh with its passions and desires" (Gal 5:24; cf. Col 3:5). Thus there is no justification for the claim that Paul would allow for the indulgence of same-sex erotic desires, no matter how deeply rooted and longstanding those desires may be.

The admonition of 1 Corinthians 6:9–11 is followed by an exhortation to sexual purity (6:12–20).[78] Like Jesus, Paul grounds the norm for sexual behavior in God's original intention for marriage: "the two shall become one flesh" (v. 16; Gen 2:24). The ultimate rationale for fidelity to that divine intention is the inconceivable dignity of the human body as revealed in Christ. The body is created to be the dwelling place of the triune God. A Christian's body is united with the body of the risen Christ (v. 15) and is a temple of the Holy Spirit (v. 19), in which God the Father is to be glorified (v. 20).

God Gave Them Up: Romans 1:24–27

Romans 1:24–27 is Paul's most extended discussion of homosexual conduct. It is part of a long argument in which he describes the human condition apart from Christ: all human beings, Jews as well as pagans, are under the power of sin and in radical need of redemption (1:18–3:20). The fundamental sin that underlies all others, according to Paul, is suppression of the truth about God. That is, people ignore the evidence that creation itself gives to the Creator God, and instead of honoring God they worship idols of their own making. In response to that willful blindness, God "gave them up" to degrading passions (a refrain repeated in vv. 24, 26, 28). Idolatry thus leads to sexual immorality, of which Paul presents homosexual conduct as a prime example, though it is by no means the only example.

> Therefore God gave them up in the lusts of their hearts to impurity, to the dishonoring of their bodies among themselves, because they exchanged the truth about God for a lie and worshiped and served the creature rather than the Creator, who is blessed forever! Amen.
>
> For this reason God gave them up to dishonorable passions. Their women exchanged natural relations for those that are contrary to nature, and the men likewise gave up natural relations with women and were consumed with passion for one another, men committing shameless acts with men and receiving in themselves the due penalty for their error. (Rom 1:24–27)

What Paul is describing here is a general societal deterioration that occurs as a result of rejection of the truth about God. He describes it in three stages. The first stage (1:24–25) involves general sexual permissiveness, in which people indulge their lustful desires and engage in sexual relations outside the covenant of marriage. Paul probably has in mind fornication (sex between unmarried people), adultery, prostitution, and other sexual sins, all of which dishonor the body (cf. 1 Cor. 6:18).

The second stage (vv. 26–27) involves homosexual acts: women engaging in sexual relations with women, and men with men. Paul implies that the "exchange" of natural relations for unnatural (v. 26) is a direct result of the "exchange" of God for idols (v. 25; cf. v. 23)—in this case, the idol of sexual pleasure.[79] But a key question in interpreting this text is: What does Paul mean by "natural" (*physikos*) and "contrary to nature" (*para physin*)? The claim is often made that the phenomenon of homosexual orientation was unknown to Paul, and that therefore what he says here is addressed only to those who are heterosexual by nature yet engage in homosexual acts; it has no relevance to those who are oriented by nature to the same sex.[80] But the phenomenon of an exclusive or predominant attraction to the same sex was in fact well known in the ancient Greco-Roman world and likely familiar to Paul.[81] More importantly, there is no evidence at all that Paul would have understood what is "natural" as constituted by the inclination or desires that a person experiences. Otherwise one would have to recognize a "natural" orientation to other forms of sexual sin—not to mention envy, deceit, boasting, and other sins mentioned in the same passage (1:29–31).[82] Rather, "natural" means living in harmony with the order of things willed by the Creator.[83] In this context, it means living in accord with God's design for sexuality as revealed in both creation and Scripture; namely, the one-flesh union of man and woman in marriage.[84] Homosexual conduct, like idolatry, is a rejection of God's plan for human flourishing. Paul repeatedly highlights the fact that such conduct profoundly demeans the dignity of those who practice it, whether men or women (vv. 24, 25, 27, 28).[85]

The third stage (vv. 28–32) involves a general loss of humanity, as people fall into deeper enslavement, no longer able to check their evil desires. It is important to recognize that Paul is not speaking of the moral decline of any given individual, but rather that of a society that has systematically refused to acknowledge God. It is also crucial to note that Paul does not single out people who engage in homosexual conduct while letting others off the hook. Rather, his indictment is aimed at all who dishonor God by ignoring his design for the human body.

CONCLUSION

The biblical teaching on homosexual conduct, interpreted impartially, is deeply challenging to modern sensibilities. Since today there are people with same-sex attraction for whom it seems innate and unalterable, the assumption is often made that to take the biblical teaching at face value is to condemn such persons to a life of loneliness, frustration, and unfulfillment. But this assumption is incompatible with the witness of the New Testament. Same-sex attraction is simply one form of the disorder that is in every human heart due to the fall, although it can bring with it particularly difficult crosses. The Gospel proclaims not only the forgiveness of sin but also the healing of all these forms of disorder and the power to live a transformed life in communion with God and others. The key to this progressive transformation is coming to know one's identity as a beloved son or daughter of God (cf. Rom 8:13–16), which in turn takes place through intimate union with Christ.[86]

Love for others entails treating them with kindness and respect, while not denying, either outright or by implication through silence, aspects of truth that are challenging or controversial. For Christians, love demands giving witness to the full truth of God's purposes for humanity revealed in creation and Scripture. A Christianity that preaches high standards of sexual morality without imitating Jesus' warm welcome of sinners is hypocritical and unattractive. A Christianity that proclaims mercy toward sinners without calling them to repentance and holiness of life is deceptive and self-deceiving. And a Christianity that proclaims mercy and upholds high moral standards but without making available the power for healing and transformation is impoverished and burdensome, "holding the form of religion but denying its power" (2 Tim 3:5). But a Christianity that proclaims and lives by the full truth of the word of God is an invitation to joy and the fullness of life.

NOTES

1. It is important to bear in mind that the Bible does not use the modern term *homosexual*, referring to a condition or a category of people. Rather, Scripture refers to those who engage in same-sex erotic *acts*.

2. This paragraph and the next draw from Joseph C. Atkinson, *Biblical and Theological Foundations of the Family: The Domestic Church* (Washington, DC: Catholic University of America, 2014), 22–32.

3. In an Egyptian creation myth, for example, the god Re recounts: "Then I copulated with my own fist, I masturbated with my own hand. I ejaculated into my own mouth. I exhaled Shu the wind, I spat Tefnut the rain" (Victor H. Matthews and Don C. Benjamin, *Old Testament Parallels*, rev. ed. [New York: Paulist, 1997], 8). Likewise in a Babylonian creation myth the god Marduk

conquers the goddess Tiamat, crushes her skull, splits her body in two, and forms heaven and earth from the halves (ibid., 16). In a Hittite myth, "the god Kumarbis bites the male generative organs of Anus who consequently is impregnated with three gods" (Atkinson, *Foundations*, 28).

4. The doctrine of creation *ex nihilo*, which developed gradually in biblical tradition, appears in Isa 44:24; 2 Macc 7:28; Rom 4:17.

5. Edward Schillebeeckx, *Marriage: Human Reality and Saving Mystery* (London: Sheed and Ward, 1965), 15.

6. Atkinson, *Foundations*, 50. This created order is part of the foundation for the biblical teaching on justice (Hebrew *tsedeqah*, translated as "righteousness" or "justice"; *dikaiosynē* in the Septuagint). In biblical thought, justice is always defined relationally: to be just is to be in right relationship, first with God and then with fellow human beings. Justice toward God entails honoring him as God, which even prior to the Mosaic law entailed living in accord with his ways (cf. Gen 6:9; 18:19).

7. Biblical scholarship ascribes the creation account to two different strands of Israelite tradition: Genesis 1 is generally attributed to the Priestly writer (P), Genesis 2 to the earlier Yahwist writer (J).

8. The usual Hebrew term for God, *'elohim*, is a grammatical plural, but when referring to Yahweh it is always used with verbs or modifiers in the singular. Various explanations of the plural in Genesis 1:26 have been proposed, such as the suggestion that God is addressing his heavenly retinue, as in Job 1:6. However, Atkinson (*Foundations*, 54) points out two problems with this approach: "Thematically, the essential point of the Genesis narrative is that it is *only* God who creates. To introduce an angelic court is possible, and even to address it is plausible; but to make them agents of creation is neither. Secondly, there is a problem with associating the image in which man is made with anything other than God. . . . If the dialogue partners were angels, then the image would be a confused hybrid of a divine-angelic nature. But the Scriptures strongly affirm that it is only in the image of God that man is made." The tension remains unresolved in Genesis, but in light of the New Testament it may be recognized as a foreshadowing of the revelation of God as a trinitarian communion of persons.

9. John Paul II, *Man and Woman He Created Them: A Theology of the Body*, trans. Michael Waldstein (Boston: Pauline, 2006), 163.

10. Robert A. J. Gagnon, *The Bible and Homosexual Practice: Texts and Hermeneutics* (Nashville: Abingdon, 2001), 60–61; Francis Martin, *Sacred Scripture: The Disclosure of the Word* (Naples, FL: Sapientia Press, 2006), 201.

11. Here for the first time the human being (*'adam*) is designated a man (*'ish*), in distinction from the woman (*'ishshah*), implying that prior to this scene *'adam* represents undifferentiated human nature.

12. The term "helper" (*'ezer*) has sometimes been misread as implying the wife's role as servant to her husband. But in nineteen of the twenty-one Old Testament instances, the term is used for God (e.g., Ps 10:14; 30:10; 54:4; Isa 63:5); to "help" man discover his vocation to love is a quasi-divine role.

13. John Paul II, *Man and Woman*, 185–86.

14. The contemporary term *sexual diversity* is thus a misnomer; Scripture and the human body itself attest rather to the sexual *polarity* of male and female.

15. The terms *bone* and *flesh* in Genesis 2:23 allude to the kinship bond formed by covenant; cf. 2 Sam 5:1; 19:13. For the meaning of covenant as a kinship bond, see Scott Hahn, *Kinship by Covenant: A Canonical Approach to the Fulfillment of God's Saving Promises*, Anchor Yale Bible Reference Library (New Haven/London: Yale University Press, 2009), 3–4.

16. The first report of *sexual* disorder per se is the brief account of Lamech, the first polygamist (4:19–24). Although the Bible nowhere explicitly condemns polygamy, it implicitly censures this violation of God's design for marriage by portraying Lamech as a man without restraint in regard to both sex and violence. The Old Testament's tolerance of the polygamy of patriarchs and kings is an example of God's concession to human weakness as the moral understanding of the unity and indissolubility of marriage developed gradually.

17. Due to space limitations I will pass over the story of the rape of the Levite's concubine in Judges 19, which has many similarities to Genesis 19.

18. Hospitality in this context does not of course bear its modern sense of good manners, but the solemn obligation to help and protect aliens, who were particularly vulnerable in the ancient world.

19. E.g., Phyllis Bird, "The Bible in Christian Ethical Deliberation concerning Homosexuality: Old Testament Contributions," in *Homosexuality, Science, and the "Plain Sense" of Scripture*, ed. David Balch (Grand Rapids: Eerdmans, 2000), 142–76.

20. In addition, both stories "are followed by the hero's intoxication with wine and the disgraceful actions of his children" (Gordon J. Wenham, *Genesis 16–50* [Word Biblical Commentary; Nashville: Thomas Nelson, 2000], 40–45). Lot (like Noah) behaves righteously in one instance, but unrighteously in another.

21. Wenham notes that the story is arranged as a palistrophe; that is, as a series of scenes and then parallel scenes in inverse order, such that the second half is a mirror image of the first half (*Genesis 16–50*, 40–45). The central scene marks the turning point of the story. In this case, there are eleven scenes, at the center of which is the announcement of the destruction of Sodom in 19:12–13.

22. God concludes, "No, for I have chosen him . . . "—literally, *I have known him*, a common expression for the covenant relationship (cf. Exod 33:12, 17; Hos

2:20; 13:5) and perhaps an ironic contrast with the exploitative and violent "knowing" demanded by the Sodomites in 19:8.

23. The emphatic expression "the men of the city, the men of Sodom, both young and old, all the people to the last man" (19:4) is not meant to be taken literally but is standard Semitic hyperbole, reinforcing the general wickedness of the city already mentioned in Genesis 13:13; 18:20. For similar examples see Joshua 10:40; Judges 20:26.

24. Cf., e.g., Genesis 4:1, 17, 25; 24:16; 38:26.

25. Lot's horrifying offer is evidently based on his assumption, within the cultural context, that although heterosexual rape is a grave evil (cf. Gen 34), it is still a lesser evil than homosexual rape of guests. If Lot is bluffing, he may intend to shame the townsmen into reconsidering their action; this is how the first-century Jewish historian Josephus interprets it (*Jewish Antiquities* 1.11.3). Either way, Genesis in no way condones Lot's attempt to deal with the situation. In the parallel story in Judges 19, the atrocity is actually carried out: the Levite hands over his concubine to gang rape.

26. Likewise Wisdom 19:13–14, an apparent reference to Sodom, speaks of treating guests with hatred. Sirach 16:8 says God "spared not the neighbors of Lot whom he abhorred for their pride," where the Greek verb for abhorred (*ebdelyxato*) is related to the noun *bdelygma*, "abomination." See Gagnon, *The Bible and Homosexual Practice*, 85.

27. Although most English translations render it as a plural, *to'evah* ("abomination") in Ezekiel 16:50 is in the singular, as in Leviticus 18:22 and 20:13. See Gagnon, *The Bible and Homosexual Practice*, 79–85.

28. Philo says of the Sodomites, "Not only did they go mad after women, and defile the marriage bed of others, but also those who were men lusted after one another, doing unseemly things, and not regarding or respecting their common nature" (*On Abraham* 135); Josephus recounts that "when the Sodomites saw the young men to be of beautiful countenances . . . they resolved themselves to enjoy these beautiful boys by force and violence" (*Jewish Antiquities* 1.11.3). See also *Jubilees* 16:5–6; 20:5–6; *Testament of Levi* 14:6; *Testament of Benjamin* 9.1; *Testament of Naphtali* 3.4, which describe Sodom's sin in a more general way as lust and sexual immorality.

29. Most major English translations render this difficult phrase "pursued unnatural desire" (ESV) or "practiced unnatural vice" (NAB) or something similar.

30. In a separate saying, Jesus adds, "For if the mighty works done in you [Capernaum] had been done in Sodom, it would have remained until this day" (Matt 11:23).

31. The last item may appear to be unrelated, but in the biblical mindset it is not: to offer one's child, the fruit of sexual union, in sacrifice to Molech (done for the sake of agricultural prosperity or military success) is not only a grave act

of idolatry but a grave act of rebellion against the Creator's plan for sexual union. The analogy to abortion (often done for the sake of convenience or to avoid financial stress) is inescapable.

32. It is important to recognize that, as the Catechism notes, the Old Testament books "contain matters imperfect and provisional" (CCC 122). They contain God's temporary provision for a society that as yet had little understanding of the dignity of the person and no infrastructure for maintaining justice and good order in the family and community. Already by the time of Christ, many of these penalties were no longer carried out. Jesus himself refused to invoke the death penalty in a case where the Law of Moses called for it (John 8:3–11). Christian tradition has always held that the judicial penalties belong to that part of the Law of Moses that has been abrogated by Christ (see note 36).

33. Cf. also Leviticus 11:13; 20:25 where a different word for "abomination," *sheqetz*, is used of unclean birds.

34. E.g., Bird, "Ethical Deliberations," 150–57.

35. Dan O. Via, in Via and Robert A. J. Gagnon, *Homosexuality and the Bible: Two Views* (Minneapolis: Fortress, 2003), 5–8.

36. Catholic tradition recognizes a distinction between three kinds of Mosaic precepts, as articulated by Thomas Aquinas: "We must therefore distinguish three kinds of precept in the Old Law; viz. 'moral' precepts, which are dictated by the natural law; 'ceremonial' precepts, which are determinations of the Divine worship; and 'judicial' precepts, which are determinations of the justice to be maintained among men" (*Summa Theologiae* I-II, q. 99, a. 4). The judicial precepts include the penalties applied to various offenses. Whereas the ceremonial and judicial precepts have been abrogated by Christ, the moral precepts remain valid.

37. Leviticus 15:19–24 deals with the ritual impurity resulting from menstruation. Later Jewish tradition, extrapolating from other purity texts, prescribed that after menstruation a woman is restored to the status of purity by immersion in a *mikvah* (ritual bath). According to Michael Kaufman, "Judaism understands that the ritual, properly observed, elevates conjugal relations from an act of self-gratification to a meaningful, blessed mitzvah devoted to the service of God—a joyous, sacred physical-spiritual union of body and soul" (Kaufman, *Love, Marriage, and Family in Jewish Law and Tradition* [Northvale, NJ: Jason Aronson, 1996], 197, quoted in Atkinson, *Foundations*, 144).

38. Walter C. Kaiser, *Toward Old Testament Ethics* (Grand Rapids: Zondervan, 1991), 199, quoted in Atkinson, *Foundations*, 144.

39. For examples see Gagnon, *Bible and Homosexual Practice*, 128–42.

40. Martti Nissinen, *Homoeroticism in the Biblical World* (Minneapolis: Fortress, 1998), 42–44.

41. See Gagnon, *Bible and Homosexual Practice*, 44–56.

42. See Gagnon, *Bible and Homosexual Practice*, 141, who also points out that if male status were the issue, "We would expect the authoritative role of 'judge' Deborah in Judges 4 to have been 'judged' an abomination in ancient song and subsequent narrative tradition."

43. As Gagnon points out, the absoluteness of the stance against homosexual conduct distinguished Israel's law code from those of the surrounding cultures, just as Israel's absolute monotheism stood out against the polytheism of its neighbors. Gagnon, *Bible and Homosexual Practice*, 131.

44. Homosexual cult prostitution was a recurring problem in Israel's history, as evidenced by the explicit prohibition in Deuteronomy 23:17–18 and the reports in 1 Kg 14:24; 15:12; 22:46; 2 Kg 23:7. But none of the behaviors listed in Leviticus 18 and 20 have a specifically cultic reference.

45. For the purposes of this chapter I will prescind from the question of which of the sayings recorded in the Gospels can be traced back to the historical Jesus and to what degree they have been shaped by the redaction of the Evangelists. The source of Christian faith is the canonical Jesus, the Jesus presented by the fourfold Gospel witness, not speculative reconstructions of historical criticism, which are always subject to revision.

46. See, for example, Via, *Two Views*, 39.

47. Gagnon notes that "Jews in the period from 200 B.C. to A.D. 200 viewed same-sex intercourse as a prime example—most often *the* prime example—of Gentile sexual depravity. Cf. *Letter of Aristeas* 152; *Sibylline Oracles* 3:184–87, 596–600, 764; 5:166, 430; *Sentences of Pseudo-Phocylides* 190–92, 212–14; *Wisdom of Solomon* 14:26; Philo, *Abraham* 135–37, *Special Laws* 1.325, 2.50, 3.37–42, *Contemplative Life* 59–62; Josephus, *Jewish Antiquities* 1.200–1, *Against Apion* 2.199, 273–75; *Testament of Levi* 17:11; *Testament of Naphtali* 3:4; *Second Enoch* 10:4; 34:1–2; *Mishnah Sanhedrin* 7:4" (Gagnon, *Two Views*, note 60, posted online at http://www.robgagnon.net/2VOnlineNotes.htm; accessed June 26, 2014).

48. Joseph Ratzinger (Pope Benedict XVI), *Jesus of Nazareth*, vol. 1, trans. Adrian J. Walker (New York: Doubleday, 2007), 102.

49. As certain texts in the law already implied, God's concern is not merely with external behavior but with the interior movements of the heart (Exod 20:17; Deut 10:16; 30:6; 2 Sam 11; Prov 6:25; Sir 9:5).

50. See "πορνεία," in W. Arndt, F. W. Danker, and W. Bauer, *A Greek-English Lexicon of the New Testament and Other Early Christian Literature* (Chicago: University of Chicago Press, 2000).

51. The claims regarding a supposed erotic dimension to Jesus' relationship to the "beloved disciple" in the Gospel of John, or the centurion's relationship to his slave (Matt 8:5–13), are without foundation. See Innocent Himbaza, Adrien Schenker, and Jean-Baptiste Edart, *The Bible on the Question of Homosexuality*,

trans. Benedict Guevin (Washington, DC: Catholic University of America Press, 2011), 107–14.

52. The epistles of Paul speak of this power as the Holy Spirit, who enables Christ's followers to live lives of radical holiness (Rom 15:16; 1 Cor 6:11; 2 Thes 2:13; 1 Pet 1:2).

53. John Paul II, *Veritatis splendor*, 103.

54. The double standard by which women were held accountable for sexual sin far more often than men prevailed in first-century Judaism as in most other premodern cultures, as the behavior of the scribes and Pharisees in John 8:3–11 makes especially evident.

55. See Gagnon, *Bible and Homosexual Practice*, 159–63.

56. Matt 9:10–11; 11:19; Mark 2:15–16; Luke 5:30; 7:34; 8:2; 15:1–2; 19:1–10.

57. Gagnon, *Two Views*, 70.

58. As his interlocutors were probably aware, by identifying himself as the physician, Jesus is claiming a divine prerogative (cf. Exod 15:26).

59. The versions in Matthew 9:13 and Mark 2:17 lack "to repentance"; Luke has added this phrase precisely to preclude the misunderstanding that Jesus invited sinners into the kingdom without calling them to conversion of life.

60. Matt 7:21-27; Luke 15:7, 10; 18:10-14; 19:2-9; 24:46-47; John 5:14.

61. Cf. Matt 12:24–32; Luke 7:29–30; 11:42–52.

62. Again for reasons of space I will pass over the 1 Timothy passage, which is similar to 1 Cor 6:9–11.

63. Biblical scholars are evenly divided as to Pauline authorship of Ephesians; see Harold W. Hoehner, *Ephesians: An Exegetical Commentary* (Grand Rapids: Baker Academic, 2002), 9–20. Whether Paul was the author or not, Ephesians represents an authentic development of Pauline theology and a part of the Scriptures recognized as canonical by the Church.

64. The Greek term used here, *mysterion*, is translated *sacramentum* in Jerome's Vulgate translation; thus this text provides the basis for the Catholic understanding of marriage as a sacrament.

65. See, for instance, Jeremiah 3:20; Isaiah 54:5–7, 10; 62:4–5; Hosea 2:16–20.

66. Martin, *Sacred Scripture*, 218.

67. See Mary Healy, "St. Paul, Ephesians 5 and Same-Sex Marriage," in Robert Fastiggi, Jane Adolphe, and Michael Vacca (eds.), *St. Paul, Natural Law and Contemporary Legal Theory* (Lanham, MD: Lexington Books, 2012), 147–59; also published in *Homiletic and Pastoral Review*, May 2011.

68. Cf. Rom 6:12–21; Gal 5:16–21; Eph 2:3; 4:17–24; Col 3:5–10; 1 Thes 4:3–8.

69. The Greek word is *adikoi*, which can also be translated "unjust" and has the same root as *dikaiosynē* (see note 6 above).

70. The first term, *porneia*, was used broadly for any sexual activity outside of marriage.

71. It is important to underscore that Paul is not referring to people who have same-sex attraction, but to those who engage in same-sex behavior. Today there is a greater recognition that such behavior is not merely a choice but can stem from inner wounds and compulsions that are difficult to resist. Nevertheless, Paul proclaims Christ's victory on the cross as offering healing and liberation from *all* the disorder in human desires (both sexual and otherwise), which are ultimately rooted in the fall, and providing the grace to resist temptation and live chastely. "No temptation has overtaken you that is not common to man. God is faithful, and he will not let you be tempted beyond your ability, but with the temptation he will also provide the way of escape, that you may be able to endure it" (1 Cor 10:13).

72. See Raymond Brown, *An Introduction to the New Testament* (New York: Doubleday, 1997), 529; Gagnon, *Two Views*, 82. Philo of Alexandria uses the cognate nouns *malakotēs* and *malakia* to describe the effeminacy of passive homosexual partners (*On Abraham* 136; *Special Laws* 3.37–42).

73. See Gagnon, *Bible and Homosexual Practice*, 306–12.

74. The same two terms appear in the vice list of 1 Timothy 1:9–10, which lists behaviors contrary to "the law"—that is, the Mosaic law—in an order roughly corresponding to the Decalogue.

75. George Montague, *First Corinthians* (Catholic Commentary on Sacred Scripture; Grand Rapids: Baker Academic, 2011), 105.

76. Romans 6:12–14; 13:14; Galatians 5:16; Ephesians 4:22; Colossians 3:5–8.

77. Gagnon, *Two Views*, 84.

78. See Montague, *First Corinthians*, 106–12, for a helpful commentary on this passage.

79. The close link between idolatry and sexual immorality is a prominent theme in the Old Testament. Here Paul seems to be borrowing especially from Wisdom 13–14.

80. Via, *Two Views*, 15; Nissinen, *Homoeroticism*, 57–88.

81. See Gagnon, *Bible and Homosexual Practice*, 380–92.

82. Moreover, the phenomenon of an exclusive or predominant attraction to the same sex was in fact well known in the ancient Greco-Roman world and likely familiar to Paul. See Gagnon, *Bible and Homosexual Practice*, 380–92.

83. Joseph Fitzmyer, *Romans*, Anchor Bible (New York: Doubleday, 1993), 286.

84. As Paul's reference to idolatrous "images" of various creatures in v. 23 echoes Genesis 1:26, so his description of relations between "females" and between "males" in vv. 26–27 alludes to Genesis 1:27. See Himbaza, Schenker, and Edart, *Question of Homosexuality*, 95–98.

85. Romans 1:27 is the sole direct reference to lesbian relations in the Bible.

86. It is ironic that the Last Supper scene in which the "beloved disciple" leans on the breast of Jesus (John 13:23–25) is falsely claimed as having erotic overtones. Rather, it depicts the experience of Christ's unconditional, self-giving love that is available to every disciple, and is precisely the means of *liberation* from disordered erotic desires.

28

HOW (NOT) TO DEBATE CHRISTIAN SEXUAL ETHICS

Mark D. Jordan, Harvard University

I am tired of quarreling over homosexuality, but I have more to confess than fatigue. I have come to doubt our motives for rehashing the same old arguments, whether in churches or in public squares. On melancholy days, I worry that all the loud arguments persuade no one and harm many. They harden positions while feeding anger. On days darker still, I conclude that the purpose of rehashing arguments is precisely to make people angrier—since both religion and politics, for some Americans, appear to consist mainly of righteous indignation. I then conclude despairingly that churches shout about sex because few people listen when they talk gently about anything else, especially God.

Those are, I confess, the despairing days. Since I have spent my adult life teaching Christianity and trying to live it, I am not eager to concede that religion can fairly be reduced to rage or repression. I do remain convinced that our grinding debates over homosexuality show that something has gone badly wrong in how we proclaim moral conclusions from Christian faith, especially with regard to sexuality. So let me describe our predicament again—less confessionally this time.

Some political campaigns that seek to decriminalize same-sex relations or to legalize same-sex marriage assume a narrative about the task at hand. The story goes something like this: "We have our view, which we know to be right. People on the other side cling irrationally to a contrary view, which we know to be wrong, if not evil. Our aim is to win enough votes to beat the other side. So we will deploy all the techniques we can conceive or purchase to move enough undecided people to our side. Then we'll exert ourselves to deliver them and our already committed 'base' to wherever votes will be cast or the decision will be made." I caricature, but not by much. I do of course acknowledge that there are counterexamples to my caricature—like the Campaign for Southern Equality, which begins from a position of deep respect for its political adversaries as it tries to engage them. Still, too much of our notion of public "debate" around issues of gender and sexuality assumes this tactical model of poll-and-media electioneering.

The model is wrong. It is wrong tactically, even when it wins, because it ignores long-term change when it focuses only on the shifts of that fleeting entity, opinion. The model of electioneering is also wrong ethically. Even if it can avoid authorizing deceptive rhetoric, it fails to acknowledge the troubling implications of its own claim that the laws have been badly mistaken. To say that a society has distorted an important moral issue should lead to sharp questions about the whole of moral formation in that society. If it has been badly wrong, it doesn't need just to change specific laws or particular attitudes. It has to ask what went wrong with the whole of its moral culture.

Wanting to lead discussion beyond reiterated controversies, I don't mean to abandon my views about sexual justice. Do I think that same-sex activities between consenting adults should be legal? Yes. Do I think that the 2003 Supreme Court decision in *Lawrence v. Texas* was right to strike down sodomy laws? Yes. Was I glad to get the news about the decision? Yes, indeed. I worked hard on my contribution to an *amicus* brief for the case, and on the morning the decision was announced, I joined the crowds that began to gather along Castro Street in San Francisco. At one point I was watching a volunteer paste up announcements of a rally to be held in the evening. An older man came up to ask what was going on. When he heard the news, he began to cry. He said, "I never thought I'd live to see the day." That's how I felt that June morning. But my gladness was tempered by the memory of how long the law had been wrong and how many lives had been mangled by it. The Court's decision could not erase the Court's past injustice, nor could it remake as if by magic the situation of moral education in America.

I hold analogous views about the issues debated in Christian churches. Do I think that same-sex relations can be justified under natural and divine laws—by appeal to divine creation and by anticipation of redemption? Yes. Should openly homosexual women and men be ordained to the Christian priesthood or ministry? Yes. Should Christian churches welcome and bless same-sex couples? Yes. Am I grateful that some Christian churches have corrected their moral teaching and enriched their liturgies to offer these blessings? Yes. Still my gladness is tempered by the sober memory of all those centuries in which Christian churches taught wrongly on all these topics, with violent consequences for their members and for any others who happened to fall under their power. It is not enough to correct an unjust church teaching and then forget it. Christians have always to ask why the official teaching went wrong and why the powerful means of moral formation available to Christian communities did not prevent the error or correct it sooner. How can communities instructed by the scriptures, shaped by the sacraments, and led by the Holy Spirit have gotten sexuality so wrong? If the question reaches beyond sexuality, it must be asked insistently about sexuality—where the errors have been not only significant and persistent but also full of consequences for every believer and many nonbelievers.

The polemical framing of our tiresome debates has many negative consequences for our moral thinking about sexuality. I will name three. (1) The framing tends to measure thinking or speaking terms only of its usefulness to debate—indeed, of how much it contributes to one side or the other. This criterion flattens language both by polarizing possibilities and by insisting that every position be an adamant solution. (2) The polemical framing makes the articulation of a winning position the sufficient end of moral analysis. This removes from sight whether ethics "succeeds" when it wins the debate—rather than leading on to larger questions about the causes of moral error or the larger aims of moral education. (3) The framing of our debates about sexuality tends both to separate these topics from others in theology and to insist that they can be fully articulated in presently available terms. The reification of our terms of debate not only detaches sexuality from the rest of theology, it removes it from the slow development of theological inquiry, from the continuing education of the Christian people.

So tonight I refuse to rehash the familiar arguments. They deserve more than rehashing in any case. Over the past sixty years or so, scholars have built up an enormous library on homosexuality and Christianity, whether considered biblically or ethically or historically or scientifically. This scholarship is there to be read in the libraries, and its major works should be read by anyone concerned with these topics. But I want now to do something different. I want to try to retrieve some of the moral questions excluded by our manner of debating homosexuality, especially questions about moral formation or education. I will attend just to three words that we regularly use in debate to describe what moral education should encourage or remove. Two words are about encouragement: toleration and appreciation for diversity. The third word is about what education is meant to remove: homophobia. But my whole aim is not to stop with first hearings of these words—not to assume that we know what these words mean or which moral judgments they encode. I want to take these words out of the polemical present of our repetitive debates and back into the longer span of theological thinking. In a longer discussion, I would do the same with the term *homosexuality* and, indeed, with *sexuality* itself. For the moment, translating three terms will be work enough. So let me continue to speak of homosexuality and sexuality with deliberate vagueness.

I will translate the terms *tolerance, appreciation for diversity*, and *homophobia* backward into the framework of a single work with a privileged position in many theological traditions, the *Summa of Theology* by Thomas Aquinas. I am not trying to reconstruct Thomas's teaching on same-sex desires or actions. Nor am I trying to assess his relation to the current positions of the Roman Catholic "magisterium." I am translating three key terms in our debates back into Thomas in order to stop our harmful repetitions by troubling our assumptions about the ethics of debating sex.

TOLERATION AND APPRECIATION FOR DIVERSITY

We Americans like to tell the story of the growth of our religious toleration. It often features principles enunciated by John Locke, Thomas Jefferson, James Madison, or George Mason, then a string of legislative acts, executive policies, or Supreme Court decisions meant to apply them. The story is of course more complicated than that, and the present result is much more unsettled—especially in constitutional law. It would be more accurate to say that a complex and poorly known political past has left us confused over religious toleration. This confusion sometimes expresses itself as a tepid open-mindedness: "You can fancy whatever you like about God because all religions are just private feeling anyway." On this view, the only thing that toleration really requires is that religions should play well with each other and stay out of adult politics.

Even this dilute notion of toleration mixes the deep with the superficial. The desire for an end to wars of religion was indeed one of the strong motives for advocates of religious toleration. I take their desire as urgent and honorable. I also remember that when American Catholic thinkers had to reconcile our constitution's first amendment with official Catholic teaching that seemed to contradict it, they appealed precisely to the common good of civil peace. This is what John Courtney Murray does when he argues that Roman Catholics should regard constitutional separations of church and state not as articles of faith, but as "articles of peace in a pluralist society."[1] To reach this conclusion, Murray invokes England's long and bitter experience with religious controversy. He quotes Samuel Johnson on the "39 articles" of the Church of England as "articles of peace."[2] He could just as well have quoted the greater Anglican divine, Richard Hooker, whose masterwork, the *Laws of Ecclesiastical Polity*, is a sustained plea not to destroy civil society by religious zealotry.

I want to affirm these arguments for peace at a moment when some Americans seem eager to split the country just to vindicate their brand of orthodoxy. But then I want to notice different and perhaps stronger arguments that depend on meanings of "toleration" found in some traditional theological texts—and notably in Thomas Aquinas.

What is toleration in Thomas? In one famous passage, he asks whether a Christian ruler should "tolerate" Judaism—that is, whether the ruler should permit Jewish ritual practice.[3] The answer—perhaps it will surprise—is that these practices should be tolerated either so long as some good comes from them or whenever suppressing them would cause harm. In other words, Christian governments should permit religious practices that they believe to be false and spiritually dangerous in view of the society's common good. That agrees with Murray, but there is more in the passage. Thomas's basic argument for toleration is that human government should imitate the divine, which evidently permits evils in the universe for the sake of greater good. For a human ruler to try to stamp out all evils would be to try to govern better than God does. Arguing this point, Thomas mentions a particular example, which he takes from Augustine: if political regimes were to do away with prostitution, Augustine says, the world would be convulsed with lust. I do not want to ask at the moment whether Thomas is right to hold that prostitution should be legalized. I want only to notice that when he argues for religious toleration, he assumes that Christian rulers should refrain from enforcing basic principles of sexual morality in order to preserve civic peace. It would not take a very clever Thomist to apply this text to some of our present debates about same-sex marriage.

Readers of Thomas who are asked about toleration often turn to this passage, but it is only one piece of his teaching on toleration as a virtue. For him, toleration is closely related to the virtue of fortitude or courageous strength. According to a definition that Thomas cites, toleration is actually a main part of fortitude.[4] Speaking in his own voice, Thomas describes the toleration of evils as the crowning moment of the virtue patience.[5] He associates it with martyrdom, but also with austerity of life.[6] And so on. In all of these passages, Thomas is not recommending masochism. He is arguing that suffering certain evils can contribute to spiritual growth.

Now I take a step that Thomas does not take in his writings. He does not extend the notion of civic toleration to the legalization of same-sex acts. I argue that we should—and according to several of his moral principles. In a religiously plural democracy, Christians should tolerate religious diversity not just to keep the peace but as a positive practice of patience both outside and inside churches. Whatever else our homosexuality debates might be, they are now religious debates. Reporters and bloggers may pretend that these debates pit the religious against the secular. In fact, they oppose Christian to Christian. A growing number of historically important churches teach that same-sex relations are not just tolerable, but morally equivalent to any other sexuality created by God. A growing number of individual Christians in all denominations are coming to the same conclusion—not by lapsing from faithful practice, but because of their faithful practice. To advocate for toleration in these debates is to advocate for the practice of patience *among Christians*. Why should a Christian be patient with one another? For many reasons, according to Thomas, but not least so that she can hear whatever God might be saying through the person she regards as her enemy.

We Americans live in a fantastically impatient culture. Such a culture is not congenial to Christianity. For Thomas Aquinas, as for most of the theological traditions, patience is the essence of our earthly condition. In old images recalled by Vatican II, Christians are "the pilgrim people of

God," as we say in English, and their union is "a pilgrim church."[7] To be a pilgrim requires patience, because no pilgrim has reached her goal. The Christian task in history is to seek God, not to pretend to inhabit the heavenly city. Patience with strife, even within Christian community, is the very condition of pilgrimage.

If we want to practice toleration in our debates over sexuality, if we want our debates to encourage toleration, we should keep this older view of virtue in mind. Toleration is not bland indifference to what people believe. Neither is it the impossible wish that religions should stay out of politics. Christian toleration requires instead that any advocacy be tempered by the humility appropriate to learners still on pilgrimage through salvation history. From that humility, it is a short step to a theological appreciation of diversity.

In our debates, "diversity" is another confused word—and on occasion deliberately confusing. It is often only a euphemism that lumps together kinds of people who have suffered social exclusion or stigmatization—as if only some minority were diverse, while the majority were obviously not. By a similar fallacy, only some people are supposed to possess sexuality or gender or race or class. In order to translate the term backward into the theological tradition, I need to use it more precisely—and more candidly—to mean morally significant differences among human beings.

Human diversity is one segment of the greater diversity of creation. If you ask "Why did God create so many different things?," Thomas Aquinas has a clear answer: to display God's beauty.[8] A world with many different creatures, of widely varying capacities, is a more beautiful world. Not coincidentally, it is also a better image of God, since no single creature or kind of creature, no matter how magnificent, can capture more than a sliver of divinity. The general rule applies to human differences. Not all our differences are divinely created, of course. Some differences among us result from social injustices or fundamental decision. We dispute, of course, about whether a particular difference is created, imposed, or chosen. At the heart of debates over homosexuality is the dispute, whether same-sex desire is a difference created by God or by the disorder of sin. So any moral evaluation of diversity has to begin from discernment—which is to say, from humility before creation.

Thomas applies this principle of respect for divine diversity at many places, including to polygamy, which was a divinely approved marital arrangement at a certain stage of history.[9] He does not apply it to homosexuality. On the contrary, he holds a very restricted view of the morally permissible uses of human genitals. He classifies most forms of human sexual contact not only as sinful but also as vice against nature.[10] Yet here again we ought to extend the Thomistic account of appreciation for created diversity to include human sexuality. Most Christian churches have done something like this in the last hundred years. Indeed, even "conservative" Roman Catholic pastoral theology now approves some marital acts that were once classified as "sodomy," a term that means nothing in particular so that it can terrify the imagination in general.[11] More startling examples of changed sexual teachings are available in conservative Protestant churches: recall the marriage manuals of Marabel Morgan or Beverly LaHaye.[12]

Growing appreciation for sexual diversity in the great majority of churches is not just a concession to social changes or medical discoveries. It is also a growth in the virtue of appreciating divine creation. The created order expresses God. So we should ask of sex—as of any created difference—what it shows us about God. As we learn more about sexual differences, we should keep asking what more we are learning about God. This is true not just for physiology but for psychology. If our capacities for erotic experience were created by God and not by sin, then they must function in the long moral education that leads us back to God. It is not enough for theologians to excuse sexual pleasure as if it were a vaguely distasteful necessity for getting a nasty chore done. A theology of sex must be able to say what the creation of sex in all its diversity *shows* about God, as it must be able to help Christians learn from sex something for their pilgrimage. Refusing to ask this sort of question brings me to my third current term—to *homophobia*.

HOMOPHOBIA

Homophobia is a recent word, though actually a bit older than many people assume. It flickered into print in the early part of the last century as a medical or quasi-medical term.[13] Still the current meaning of *homophobia* appeared only toward the end of the 1960s. The rediscovered term is frequently traced to George Weinberg, a psychologist who claimed to have applied it then to negative attitudes he found among his teachers and fellow students. Weinberg devoted the first chapter of a 1972 book to this kind of homophobia.[14] By then, another psychologist had already provided a diagnostic tool for finding it.[15] The term passed almost immediately from psychological sources into the speech of gay and lesbian communities.[16]

"Homophobia" looks like a clinical diagnosis. Its components imply that it designates a pathological fear of "homo"—that is, of homosexuality or homosexuals. So the term sometimes blends with an older notion of "homosexual panic." This panic was supposed to be a quasi-psychotic fear in reaction to unwanted homosexual advances—or else an acute anxiety state with delusions that one was thought to be homosexual.[17] It is wise to pause before importing any unexamined clinical terms into Christian theology. It is especially important to pause in this case, because *homophobia* seems an especially clear example of an unexamined judgment masquerading as a diagnosis. It unifies with a supposedly clinical precision what are in fact quite different acts, opinions, and dispositions. You can see this by noticing the contexts in which "homophobia" is actually used. It is typically associated with notions like prejudice or oppression. Those associations hardly help to specify the term's meaning, since most people are also unclear about what they think prejudice is—or where social oppression comes from. If homophobia is a prejudice, does that make it an opinion? A condition of ignorance? A feeling? A psychological immaturity or maladjustment? A vice? A sin?

These questions are not just a moralist's quibble. If we want to argue against homophobia as a moral evil, or if we want to lead people out of homophobia by "diversity training," we should be able to say what kind of thing we imagine it to be. Only then could we propose the sort of moral education capable of addressing it.

What in fact is supposed to be wrong with speaking or acting "homophobically"? Some would say that there is nothing wrong with it. The word *homophobia*, they would continue, is just a way of smearing people who judge that homosexuality is sinful or socially harmful. I am willing to agree up to a certain point: I do think that "homophobic" is sometimes used just as an insult. But I would not agree with the implied conclusion—that the acts or attitudes labeled "homophobic" are in fact principled conclusion or bold tenets of faith. I have not found most condemnations of homosexuality to be motivated by a dispassionate love of truth. Perhaps some pure souls enter these debates with perfect equanimity, motivated only by a rational desire to follow the evidence wherever it leads. There may be such souls—but in more than two decades of debating, I am not sure I have met one. My typical experience is that even the most serious arguments against homosexuality arise from mixed motives, some of which are ignoble. The term *homophobia* tries, however badly, to register those other motives. So while I consider the term misleading, I refuse to dismiss it as only an insult. There is much besides pure philosophy or stainless doctrine in arguments against homosexuality. We need some way to talk about that admixture.

Which morally doubtful motives might push someone to condemn homosexuality? That question has attracted a number of answers. Perhaps the most frequent points to sexual disgust. People are said to argue against same-sex practices because they find them disgusting. There are two problems with this answer. First, it is hard to think of any sexual act that is now performed exclusively by homosexuals. Things that homosexuals do are also done by heterosexuals. So the disgust cannot be at the act, but at the people doing the act—which sends us in other directions, say, to gender hierarchies. The second problem with pointing to sexual disgust as the motive under homophobia is that disgust is hardly directed only at homosexuals. Many people condemn sexual practices or desires that they do not share, and some people experience extreme disgust at quite common practices—indeed, at the very idea of sex. So sexual disgust cannot explain the particularity of the reaction to homosexuality.

A second common explanation of homophobia points to fear. The suffix of "-phobia" is obviously trying to name that, however confusedly. Let me set aside psychological models of phobias in order to begin sorting the kinds of fears that are commonly supposed to lurk under condemnations of homosexuality. There are a lot of them. First, fear of the unknown or unfamiliar. Never forget how much people do not know about other people's sexual desires or practices, even with the Internet. Then, second, fear of something desired that is also forbidden. Our desires can scare us—whether they are morally acceptable or not. Desire can generate fear, and fear can fuel desire. But these are many other fears. In societies or groups that stigmatize same-sex relations, feeling sexual desire for a person of the same genital configuration brings fear of the loss of social relations or economic status, fear of being cast out by your family or losing your job. Again, for the believer in a religion that condemns same-sex desires or practices, feeling the desires brings the fear of eternal separation from God—or, at very least, the fear of being cast out from the religious community that has nurtured you.

Fears swirl around condemnations of homosexuality. The clumsy word *homophobia* tries to get at them, but it does so by mistaken analogy to clinical pathologies. It would be better to describe the fears by less misleading terms—and perhaps even by some of the traditional distinctions in theological analyses of fear. Only then could we begin to think through some of the consequences that follow from the range of fears mislabeled "homophobia." For example, even if you hold that homosexual genital relations are sinful, or that homosexual inclinations are objectively disordered, it is hard to justify the severe penalties levied historically against the commission or suspicion of same-sex acts or feelings—execution, judicial torture, banishment, lengthy imprisonments or involuntary hospitalizations, cruel medical procedures. This century-spanning desire to punish, to exclude, to destroy queer bodies—that is not any fear, that is a dangerous and despicable fear acting itself out as institutionalized violence.

Traditional moral analyses of fear might help us to appreciate the deep sources of that violence. They might also help us to think its relation to the positive principles of toleration and appreciation for diversity. Even someone who thinks that homosexuality is sinful and that all sexual acts should be confined to marriage might agree that a violent response to homosexuality is disproportionate—and so a sin against both Christian love and pagan justice. But suppose, if only for a moment, that same-sex desire is part of divine creation and that homosexuality is no more intrinsically sinful than heterosexuality. How would we analyze what we now call "homophobic" violence then? We would have to add that the reaction is a violent refusal of the created order, that it is a sin against nature so far as it rejects what God intends in creating sexual diversity. If God created same-sex desire, then wanting to punish or eradicate that desire is wanting to undo God's will. Rejection of God's order is the basis of any sin. What would distinguish homophobia, always supposing that homosexuality is divinely created, would be its resort to often horrific violence, both personal and institutional, in order to undo part of God's creation. That violence, which often dresses itself up in language about nature, may well be a violent rejection of the nature God created.

Just here you may suspect that I have gone through all these translations just to make an overly clever joke. I seem to have taken the traditional category of the sin against nature and flipped it around, so that it now applies to those *attacking* same-sex love rather than to those *practicing* it. I assure you, I am not joking. If homophobia is the fearful and violent impulse to eradicate divinely created difference, then it is a sin. Indeed, it is a serious sin. Serious sins cannot be healed by a few quick sessions of training. They require all the means of Christian moral formation.

You see, I hope, how pressing on some of our common terms leads us out of the polemical frame of our repetitive debates to more important moral questions—and to a call for more serious moral response.

DEBATES AND FORMATION

In this chapter, I have for the most part set aside questions about whether certain sexual acts are intrinsically good or bad, permissible or sinful. I have bracketed them for two reasons. It is not possible to address those questions seriously outside an incarnational moral theology that begins with the creation of embodied souls, moves through their education by word and sacrament, and ends with a meditation on resurrection. You cannot detach Christian sexual ethics from the rest of theology—not if you want to think it adequately. I also bracketed those familiar questions about same-sex acts in order to bring to light moral doubts about our current ways of debating them. Even if you believe that homosexuality is a sin, you can commit worse sins than homosexuality by how you argue against it. How we debate sometimes matters more than what we debate—for the common good of civil peace, but also for our own progress toward the highest good.

The point is made sharply by the great Dominican Thomist Francisco de Vitoria. Having performed a scorching analysis of the main Spanish justifications for colonizing the so-called New World, Vitoria sketches a few arguments that actually could be justifications. He then reminds his readers that he is speaking hypothetically and subject to the "limitation that [colonization] be done for the good and benefit of the [indigenous peoples], and not only for the profit of Spaniards. In this is the whole danger to souls and to salvation."[18] There are serious questions about homosexuality to be raised from Christian tradition—and, I believe, answered from it. Too often, they are raised for motives other than the good and benefit of the people they are supposed to save. In this—and not in sexual sins—is the greater danger to souls and to salvation.

NOTES

1. Versions of the essay were published under various titles beginning in 1954. I follow John Courtney Murray, "Civil Unity and Religious Integrity: The Articles of Peace," in his *We Hold These Truths: Catholic Reflections on the American Proposition* (New York: Sheed & Ward, 1960), 78.

2. James Boswell, *Life of Johnson: An Edition of the Original Manuscript*, ed. Marshall Waingrow (Edinburgh: Edinburgh University Press, 1994), 54.

3. Thomas Aquinas, *Summa theologiae* 2–2.10.11.

4. The definition comes from Macrobius and is discussed by Thomas at *Scriptum Sent.* 3 d.33 q.3 a.3 qc.2 arg. 1 and *Summa theol.* 2–2 q.128 art.1 arg.6, ad 6.

5. Thomas Aquinas, *Summa theol.* 2–1.66.4 ad 2; compare his *Super Col.* cap.1 lect.1.

6. Thomas Aquinas, *Summa theol.* 2–1.102.4 ad 4.

7. *Lumen Gentium* nos. 7 (*in terris adhuc peregrinantes*), 14 (*Ecclesiam hanc peregrinantem*), 48 (*Ecclesia peregrinans*), 68 (*peregrinanti Populo Dei*).

8. Thomas Aquinas *Summa contra Gentiles* 2.39–45; much more briefly, *Summa theol.* 1.47.1.

9. In his commentary on the *Sentences*, for example, Thomas says that the prohibition against many wives belongs to the natural law not as a primary or fundamental teaching, but only as the kind of inference that can change with historical circumstances. The need for high rates of reproduction among the Israelites justified polygyny and concubinage for them. See *Scriptum in Sententiis*, 4.33.1.1 corp, ad 1 and ad 2, and 4.33.1.2 corp and responses to the counter-arguments.

10. Thomas Aquinas, *Summa theol.* 2–1.154.11, where the "vice against nature" includes masturbation (*immunditia* or *mollities*), bestiality (*bestialitas*), same-sex genital contacts (*vitium sodomiticum*), or any genital activity that does not "serve the natural manner of copulation," either because it involves an instrument (*instrumentum*) not intended for copulation or because it belongs to one of the "other monstrous and bestial manners of copulation."

11. For example, John F. Kippley, *Sex and the Marriage Covenant: A Basis for Morality*, 2nd ed. (San Francisco: Ignatius Press, 2005), 45–46. Authoritative treatments of the definition of sodomy are rather more complicated that Kippley allows. Consider, for example, the argument by the "Salmanticenses" in *Cursus theologiae moralis* 6.7.5.1: semination in the "inappropriate vessel is not 'essen-

tially required'" by the "notion (*ratio*) and metaphysical essence of sodomy." When there can be in principle no procreative mixture of seed, simple "penetration of the vessel" is enough. Ejaculation only becomes an issue in determining the degree of sodomy, whether it is imperfect or perfect—that is, incomplete or complete. See *Collegii Salmanticensis Fratres Discalceatorum . . . Cursus theologiae moralis*, vol. 6 (Venice: Nicolaus Pezzana, 1724), 165, col. a, ¶87.

12. Tim and Beverly LaHaye, *The Act of Marriage* (Grand Rapids: Zondervan, 1976); Marabel Morgan, *The Total Woman* (Old Tappan, NJ: Revell, 1973), and *Total Joy* (Old Tappan, NJ: Revell, 1976).

13. It was also used comically as a fancy way of saying contempt for men—or so it seems in the 1920 example that the OED takes from *Chambers's Journal*. For medical uses, see "Homophobia Called Curable," *American Spectator* 138 (January 7, 1937): 114.

14. George Weinberg, *Society and the Healthy Homosexual* (New York: St. Martin's Press, 1972), chapter 1.

15. Kenneth T. Smith, "Homophobia: A Tentative Personality Profile," *Psychological Reports* 29 (1971): 1091–94.

16. For two examples out of hundreds, see the review of Fassbinder by Thomas Waugh in *Body Politic*, December 1, 1972, 8, or the letter to the editor by "Stephen" in *Body Politic*, January 1, 1973, 23.

17. H. T. Chuang and D. Addington, "Homosexual Panic: A Review of Its Concept," *Canadian Journal of Psychiatry* 33, no. 7 (October 1988): 613–17; Vernon Rosario, "Rise and Fall of the Medical Model," *Harvard Gay and Lesbian Review* 6, no. 4 (October 31, 1999): 31.

18. Francisco de Vitoria, *De indis*, sect. 18, as in *Obras de Francisco de Vitoria: Relecciones teologicas*, ed. Teofilo Urdanoz (Madrid: Biblioteca de Autores Cristianos, 1960), 725.

29

NOT JUST LOVE

The Anthropological Assumptions of Catholic Teaching on Same-Sex Attraction and Activity

John Grabowski, Catholic University of America

I am indebted to Dan Grabowski, Rebekah Grabowski, Christopher Klofft, and Thomas Petri, O.P., for helpful comments and suggestions on earlier versions of this chapter.

INTRODUCTION

Our popular culture proclaims with increasing energy and confidence the ascendancy and momentum of what has come to be identified as the "LGBT" (or "LGBTQLMNOP") cause. Hit songs preach the message of accepting and celebrating diverse sexual orientations, telling individuals that they were "born that way."[1] Others capture the increasingly popular portrayal of acceptance of gay relationships and marriage as an issue of justice, intoning that it's the "same love" that draws same-sex couples together as their opposite-sex counterparts.[2] Such views are not limited to entertainers and the media who cover them; journalists, bloggers, and public intellectuals add their voices to the growing chorus of tolerance that can be surprisingly intolerant of those with opposing views. We are told that "marriage equality" and other LGBT issues are the civil rights issues of our time with the implication that those who oppose them are bigots who will ultimately be found on the wrong side of history.³ The advancing tide of state and judicial approval of same-sex marriage and repudiation of "defense of marriage" statutes can be understood as civil law catching up to where the culture went some fifty years ago with the widespread acceptance and use of contraception and the adoption of "no fault" divorce by many states.⁴ With the abandonment of both the link between marriage and procreation and a real notion of marital permanence, marriage has been increasingly conceived as a private arrangement ordered only to the happiness of individuals who enter it.

What is perhaps more surprising is the way in which revisionist Catholic moral theologians have increasingly echoed and advanced the ideas of the wider culture, albeit in more nuanced ways. Catholic teaching on sexuality has been subject to new and critical scrutiny across the board since the forceful backlash against *Humanae vitae*'s reassertion of the tradition's opposition to contraception in 1968,⁵ but most early Catholic revisionist thought in the period following the encyclical focused on arguing for exceptions to what had been regarded as exceptionless moral norms prohibiting contraception, masturbation, sex outside of marriage, and homogenital activity. So, the typical argument ran, sexual activity by homosexual persons in a stable, committed relationship was nonideal, but it was better than imposing mandatory celibacy on persons acting in accord with a stable orientation they did not choose.⁶ Now, however, one increasingly finds revisionist moral theologians who assert the "naturalness" of homogenital activity for those persons who have a homosexual orientation, cast doubt on the link between sex and procreation even within the natural world, and argue that justice requires evaluating same-sex relationships on exactly the same basis as those between opposite-sex partners.⁷ The Church's teaching is discounted as culturally and scientifically outdated and hurtful in its exclusion of same-sex-attracted people from the fulfillment offered by caring and committed sexual relationships.

This chapter seeks to offer a critical evaluation of these arguments and their assumptions with a view to uncovering the sharply differing conceptions of the human person and of the concept of justice at work in them as opposed to those found in official Catholic teaching on homosexuality. It is the contention of this chapter that, while revisionist analyses tend to view persons as individuals whose identity is largely shaped by sexual desire and whose activity must be evaluated according to standards of justice understood as fairness, Catholic teaching resists these reductions, advancing an anthropology that sees human dignity as grounded in a shared human nature instantiated in sexually diverse persons called to lives of justice shaped by Trinitarian love.

This chapter will proceed by first providing an overview of some important and influential recent Catholic revisionst approaches to same-sex attraction and activity: Todd Salzman and Michael Lawler's idea of "sexual orientation complementarity," recent challenges to the idea of sexual dimorphism in the natural world and hence in human relationships, and Margaret Farley's justice-centered evaluation of same-sex and opposite-sex relationships on equal terms. It will then critically evaluate these arguments, with a view to surfacing some of their anthropological and ethical assumptions and how these differ from those found in the Catholic theological tradition as well as recent Church teaching. The concluding section of the chapter will aim to show that Catholic teaching points to the need for a clear articulation of a common human nature, the reality of sexual differential as an essential feature of human personhood, and an understanding of justice that can account for both unity and difference among persons.

SOME RECENT REVISIONIST ARGUMENTS ON SAME-SEX ATTRACTION AND ACTIVITY

Salzman and Lawler's "Sexual Orientation Complementarity"

In 2008, Todd Salzman and Michael Lawler of Creighton University published a volume titled *The Sexual Person: Toward a Renewed Catholic Anthropology*. In it they sought to promote a critical dialogue on Catholic teaching on sexuality, teaching that they argued was still rooted in a classicist view of the world dominated by a deductive understanding of human reason and a static understanding of nature.[8] The work endeavored to give a comprehensive treatment of the history of Catholic teaching on sexual issues, the current divisions within Catholic moral theology, and an array of contemporary issues that bear upon sexuality—issues of sexual equality, contraception, cohabitation, reproductive technologies, and homosexuality. While many of the positions that the work advanced and even the methodology that it used proved to be controversial,[9] it is the novel treatment of sexual orientation and same-sex activity that is of interest here.

Appropriating the notion of sexual complementarity found in magisterial teaching on sexuality, these authors seek to invest it with new meaning. Catholic teaching, they claim, rests on an understanding of this reality that prioritizes "heterogenital and reproductive complementarity"—the physical differences of men and women that capacitate them for procreation.[10] In opposition to this, they advance what they call "personal complementarity," which can account for the multiple dimensions of sexuality—interpersonal, affective, and even parental. This "personal" focus can accommodate sexual orientation as a part of a "holistic" understanding of complementarity as a basis for discerning the truly human character of sexual acts. The "heterogenital complementarity" valorized in Church teaching is "necessary" but "not sufficient" in order "to realize a truly human act" since: "Heterosexual rape and incest take place in a heterogenitally complementarity way, but no one would claim that they are personally complementary."[11] Traditional arguments against same-sex activity are dismissed as irrelevant or even discriminatory.[12] Instead, for persons with a homosexual orientation, if the actions are otherwise just and loving,[13] Salzman and Lawler argue, "For those who are by 'nature' homosexual . . . homosexual acts are natural, reasonable, and moral, and heterosexual acts are unnatural, unreasonable, and immoral."[14]

Two observations are worth making at this point. First, it is evident that the term *natural* here is being used to describe that which is experienced by individuals as in accord with their own individual desires and sense of self. As will be shown below, this is a very different understanding than that found within the Catholic tradition. Second, there is a significant disjunct between "the personal" and the physical in Salzmann and Lawler's anthropology.[15]

NATURE AS RAINBOW: THE CHALLENGE TO SEXUAL DIMORPHISM

If Salzman and Lawler's work tends toward a privatized account of nature shaped by individual experience, other recent revisionist works have argued against the priority of sexual dimorphism on which Catholic sexual teaching rests. This is the thrust of many of the essays in the ecumenical and interdisciplinary 2010 volume *God, Science, Sex, Gender: An Interdisciplinary Approach to Christian Ethics* that was based on a series of symposia held at Loyola University in Chicago in 2007.[16]

At the heart of the argument is the iconoclastic work of evolutionary biologist Joan Roughgarden, who argues against the accuracy of the "sexual selection" paradigm, which has driven biological theory on sexual behavior since Darwin.[17] Surveying evidence from the world of nature, she argues against the existence of universal roles for male and female members of species, for the existence of multiple genders within the sex of various animals, for the presence of both sexes in plants and fish, and for frequent homosexual activity in many animal species. She proposes instead a theory of "social selection" in which gender flexibility and homosexual behavior is understood as a common and integral part of the natural world.

The point of this research, however, is not just to revise biological theorizing but to draw out implications for human life and behavior. Thus, Roughgarden argues: "Both science and religious doctrine are complicit in the persecution of gay, lesbian, and transgender people. Indeed, to some, being unnatural is sinful in itself."[18] To the contrary, she asserts: "Homosexuality is not against nature, it is an adaptive part of nature."[19] Building on this line of argument, the editors of the volume, Patricia Beattie Jung and Anna Marie Vigen, argue that discoveries in the sciences, the relativization of procreation as a purpose for human sexual activity, and the fact that there are some 5.5 million intersexed persons in the world today all serve to call into question the sexual dimorphism upon which traditional Christian teaching rests.[20] Like the work of Salzman and Lawler, the thrust of this volume serves to undercut the idea of a shared human nature that could be the basis of moral judgment,[21] but it broadens this into a critique of a sexually dimorphous order within the natural world as a whole. Diversity and difference are the order that the natural world displays. Human sexual diversity is a part of this larger complex whole.

Farley's "Just Love"

Perhaps the most influential recent revisionist argument on the subject is that put forward by Margaret Farley, R.S.M., in her 2008 work *Just Love:*

A Framework for Christian Sexual Ethics.[22] Like Salzman and Lawler's work, this text received praise in some academic circles but drew a negative evaluation from Church authorities.[23] Like Salzman and Lawler, she privileges the role of experience in her invocation of "the Wesleyian quadrilateral" of authority;[24] however, more than them she sees this experience as largely provided by the testimony of gay men and women themselves.

As she has argued for some time, Farley sees scripture and tradition as ambiguous and inconclusive as sources for a moral evaluation of present-day same-sex relationships.[25] However, while she finds that the sciences contribute useful information to understanding the reality of sexual orientation and preference, she also finds them to be inconclusive for formulating criteria for a moral evaluation.[26] She therefore turns to experience to determine whether such activity can conduce to human flourishing. And by experience she specifies that she means "primarily the testimony of women and men whose sexual preference is for others of the same sex."[27] However, this determination of human flourishing is not completely subjective since for Farley sexual activity in same-sex relationships must conform to more general standards of justice that bear upon the evaluation of sexual activity in any relationship. Such standards flow from the reality of the individual person in his or her autonomy and relationality as well as the individual's social location. The specific norms by which any sexual activity should be evaluated include the following: the prohibition of unjust harm, the free consent of sexual partners, respect for the mutuality and equality of these partners, some form of commitment, fruitfulness, and social justice.[28]

Like many other feminist theorists, Farley has adopted the common post-Kantian understanding of justice as fairness.[29] In other words, justice demands that all sexual relationships be evaluated by exactly the same criteria—whether between gay or straight people, married or unmarried. When sexual activity between same-sex partners fulfills these criteria, it can be considered "just"; as to whether it contributes to their personal fulfillment, we should listen to the testimony of their experience and take their word for it. Like Salzman and Lawler, she does not see the body as playing a significant role in her understanding of personal flourishing, and she prioritizes experience in moral evaluation. Even more than them she dispenses with the concept of a shared nature as a basis for ethical consideration, and to this she adds the focus on justice understood as fairness to equal and autonomous individuals.

ANALYSIS AND CRITIQUE

A full analysis of the preceding arguments is beyond the scope of this chapter. Indeed, given the highly polarized nature of the debate, virtually any statement at all on this topic is likely to be contested and controversial rather than "a last word." Instead, these reflections will aim to further uncover some of the presuppositions of the above arguments with a view to contrasting them with those underlying official Catholic teaching on same-sex attraction and activity. Of particular concern for this treatment are the notions of person and nature, the status of sexual difference and attraction within them, and how these bear upon an understanding of justice.

"Shades of Gay"? The Mutability of "Sexual Orientation"

Much like the ideas found in popular advocacy for LGBT causes, in differing ways the various revisionist arguments considered above presuppose the a priori nature and fixity of sexual orientation. Sexual orientation is conceived as a given, prior to any choice, volition, or activity for both same-sex-attracted and opposite-sex-attracted people.[30] Sexual activity for same-sex-attracted people is simply action in accord with who they are and as such it can be deemed "just" or indeed, wholly "natural."

However, this assumption is open to question on a variety of grounds. First, not only are the causes of sexual orientation themselves disputed,[31] there is simply no one agreed-upon definition of the concept. In fact, some have argued that the very concept of sexual orientation is a modern invention dating from the nineteenth century designed to serve as a placeholder for a conventional morality in a culture that had largely abandoned a Christian framework for thinking about sex.[32] Second, even scientific accounts of sexual orientation have recognized varying degrees of malleability within it, often viewing it as a continuum and acknowledging that individuals can and do act sexually in ways that differ from their primary orientation for extended periods of time.[33] Third, there is also evidence that sexual attraction and inclination can be shaped and altered over time by behavior.[34] Fourth and even more controversially, there are groups that argue for the possibility of long-term change of same-sex attraction in individuals through therapeutic intervention.[35] Others dispute this claim and argue that these efforts actually cause harm to those who undergo them.[36] But in spite of the highly contested nature of the data and the categories in which to interpret them, these factors indicate that sexual orientation is neither univocal in its meaning nor immutable in its impact on human behavior.

It is true that in its recent teaching the Church has acknowledged the reality of same-sex attraction as an unchosen reality for many people.[37] However, the way in which it has done so is instructive in a number of ways. First, the Church in its official teaching has resisted the reduction of the person to their sexual inclinations, speaking of "homosexual persons" or "persons with homosexual tendencies" (as opposed to "homosexuals"), and it has acknowledged that the number of such persons "is not negligible."[38] In insisting that "[i]t is deplorable that homosexual persons have been and are the object of violent malice in speech or action . . . [and that] the intrinsic dignity of each person must always be respected in word, action, and law," the Church has highlighted the importance of using language in ways that fosters just social relations.[39] Second, while acknowledging deep-seated homosexual tendencies in some people, magisterial teaching has also resisted the deterministic assumption that this inclination must be expressed in sexual activity that reflects it. All persons have disordered inclinations, including sexual ones, but these do not compel action based on them.[40] Third, the Church's official teaching has not univocally used the language of "homosexual orientation," though this can be found within it. As seen in the preceding analysis, it also speaks of "inclinations" or "deep-seated tendencies" to describe the reality of same-sex attraction.

What these observations make clear is that in the Church's view a person is more than his or her desires or inclinations. Having disordered inclinations is a shared human condition for those living within a fallen world.[41] Same-sex-attracted persons are not morally culpable for inclinations that they did not choose. Like their opposite-sex-attracted brethren, they are morally responsible for what they do with their disordered inclinations. Further, they have the same dignity and the same capacity for growth in virtue and holiness that all human beings possess.

In light of these considerations, Salzman and Lawler's novel language of "sexual orientation complementarity" can be understood to be problematic in a number of respects. It ignores the malleability of "sexual orientation" observable in both human behavior and scientific data. Furthermore, it reifies sexual attraction or inclination, making it an intrinsic and defining feature of personhood, more basic than physical sexual difference. This in turn seems to obscure the insight that the identity of the person and his or her corresponding dignity is greater than his or her dominant sexual attraction. Finally, it reduces the category of nature and "the natural" into an individually constituted reality.

While the Church's teaching on sexual orientation has undergone development in recent decades, its opposition to same-sex activity has been a constant feature of its teaching from the beginning. This is because it has understood in light of the witness of both scripture and human reason that such activity "closes[s] the sexual act to the gift of life" and "do[es] not proceed from a genuine and affective sexual complementarity."[42] That is to say, such activity is violation of both the procreative nature of sex and union of equally human but sexually differentiated persons.

"Birds Do It . . . ": Sexual Dimorphism in Nature and Human Nature

The appeal to the procreative purpose of sexuality recalls the traditional category of "sins against nature" as a way of characterizing sexual acts that in themselves are not apt for procreation.[43] But it is precisely the concept of the "natural" that arguments such as those of Salzman and Lawler seek to reclaim by arguing that same-sex activity can be natural for same-sex couples who have "sexual orientation complementarity." This dissolution of the category of nature seems to be intensified by the argument that the order of the natural world is shot through with diverse sexualities and same-sex activity. However, this argument too is in need of closer examination.

Even in the volume that emerged from the Loyola colloquia, there were those who questioned Roughgarden's extrapolations from outliers of diverse sexual manifestation in nature and animal behavior to an alleged rainbow of sexual diversity shining through the whole of the natural world.[44] The reaction of most of her fellow evolutionary biologists to her work has been even more critical.[45] In point of fact, the overwhelming majority of literature in evolutionary biology turns on the basic and widespread nature of sexual dimorphism as the driver for mating and sexual behavior. Proponents of this growing discipline tell us that mating strategies of modern men and women (including same-sex-attracted ones, albeit in different ways) are largely a genetic imprint left by the evolutionary history of our early human ancestors.[46] Furthermore, even if one accepts some diversity of sexual behavior in the animal world, it remains a stark biological fact that sexual dimorphism is the basis of the continuation of almost all animal species—at least mammalian ones. Offspring can come into the world naturally only through the union of male and female. Whether explicated in biblical or Aristotelian terms, this teleology apparent in both animal and human sexuality is an inescapable one.

It also remains true philosophically that observable biological phenomena are not the same as "nature" in a metaphysical sense. For Saint Thomas and the Catholic moral tradition, "nature" refers to a set of properties or inclinations that a thing characteristically pursues for its fulfillment and that identify it as a member of a species.[47] To discern this nature one must abstract from individual instances of action to the inclinations at which they aim. In the case of human nature, these inclinations are spiritual realities apprehended by reason—not merely biological or psychological impulses. Furthermore, these inclinations belong to humanity as a species—not simply to individuals. While individual persons possess human nature, this is as a shared set of goods toward which they are inclined.

Salzman and Lawler's "sexual orientation complementarity" represents an effort to overwrite and reconstitute this common human nature with the same-sex attraction experienced by individuals. Roughgarden's coloring of the natural world with the hues of the LGBT rainbow is an attempt to write sexual diversity into the whole of nature, further dissolving the duality of sex that the Church sees as basic to humanity and to creation as a whole. Ultimately these efforts fail to understand the concept of nature and a natural order that is at the basis of Catholic moral reasoning. And it is not just the Church's moral doctrine that turns on the concept of nature—this is true of its teaching in its doctrines of human solidarity, original sin, the Incarnation, and the redemption.[48]

Justice Beyond Sameness

Recent Catholic teaching has insisted on the goodness and profound significance of the sexual differentiation of male and female created in the image of God as "two equally valuable but different expressions of the one nature of humanity."[49] Responding to the growing modern confusion about sex differences caused in varying ways by second-wave feminism, the sexual revolution, the current dissociation of sex and gender, and its own internal controversy following *Humanae vitae*, the Church has repeatedly affirmed the goodness and profound significance of sexual difference.[50] Created together in the image of God (Gen. 1:27), men and women are both fundamentally equal as human yet irreducibly different as persons. As noted above, this difference is sometimes described in the language of "complementarity." Thus, the *Catechism of the Catholic Church* teaches: "Man and woman were made 'for each other'—not that God made them half-made and incomplete: he created them to be a communion of persons, in which each can be 'helpmate' to the other, for they are equal as persons ('bone of my bones . . .') and complementary as masculine and feminine."[51] Hence male and female together are in the image of God who, as Revelation discloses to us, is also a communion of persons in the mystery of His Trinitarian life.[52]

Throughout his pontificate Pope John Paul II sought to deepen the Church's awareness of the goodness and the profound anthropological significance of sexual difference. In his weekly general audiences that have come to be known as the Theology of the Body, he spoke often of the "originality" of men and women in their existence as persons:

> [T]he knowledge of man passes through masculinity and femininity, which are, as it were, two incarnations of the same metaphysical solitude before God and the world—*two reciprocally completing ways of "being a body" and at the same time of being human*—as two complementary dimensions of self-knowledge and self-determination and, at the same time, *two complementary ways of being conscious of the meaning of the body.*[53]

The bodily differences of men and women reveal unique ways of existing as a person within a shared human nature. As the late Pope says: "Their unity *denotes* above all *the identity of human nature; duality on the other hand, shows what, on the basis of this identity, constitutes the masculinity and femininity* of created man."⁵⁴ Yet these differences are themselves a summon to communion with others through the sincere gift of self in love—a reality that John Paul II described as "the spousal meaning of the body."⁵⁵

Persons are not autonomous individuals whose identity is conferred by their desires or self-creating subjects who create themselves *ex nihilo* by their choices. Pope Benedict XVI in his final Christmas address to the Roman Curia made the point forcefully in remarks that deserve to be cited at length because of their profundity. Commenting on the famous phrase of feminist thinker Simone de Beauvoir, "one is not born a woman, one becomes so," he observes:

> These words lay the foundation for what is put forward today under the term "gender" as a new philosophy of sexuality. According to this philosophy, sex is no longer a given element of nature, that man has to accept and personally make sense of: it is a social role that we choose for ourselves, while in the past it was chosen for us by society. The profound falsehood of this theory and of the anthropological revolution contained within it is obvious. People dispute the idea that they have a nature, given by their bodily identity that serves as a defining element of the human being. They deny their nature and decide that it is not something previously given to them, but that they make it for themselves. . . . The words of the creation account: "male and female he created them" (Gen 1:27) no longer apply. No, what applies now is this: it was not God who created them male and female—hitherto society did this, now we decide for ourselves. Man and woman as created realities, as the nature of the human being, no longer exist. Man calls his nature into question. From now on he is merely spirit and will. The manipulation of nature, which we deplore today where our environment is concerned, now becomes man's fundamental choice where he himself is concerned. From now on there is only the abstract human being, who chooses for himself what his nature is to be. Man and woman in their created state as complementary versions of what it means to be human are disputed. But if there is no pre-ordained duality of man and woman in creation, then neither is the family any longer a reality established by creation.⁵⁶

The separation of "gender" from sex begun in second-wave feminism thus acts as a solvent to the very concept of human nature and of sexually differentiated and irreducible persons created in the image of God. This "profound falsehood" reduces human beings to self-created spirits whose bodily and sexual reality is shaped by either uncontrollable desire or an act of the will. The end result is a seemingly endless array of "genders" constituted by an individual's sexual preferences.[57]

A concept of justice invoked as a source for the moral evaluation of human sexual activity must be able to account for the basic equality of dignity and rights of all persons grounded by a shared human nature *and* the irreducible differences between men and women as persons that are the basis of marriage itself both naturally and sacramentally.[58] To abstract from the concrete realities of human nature and personhood is to invoke a concept of justice which is itself an abstraction. The concept of justice invoked by Farley and by Salzman and Lawler, who rely on her, presupposes a view of persons as autonomous and largely self-creating subjects who must be treated as basically interchangeable. Justice understood as mere fairness must abstract itself from the contingencies of difference and the body and view all individuals, relationships, and sexual activity on equal and interchangeable terms. Conversely, the concept of justice defended by the Church is specified by reference to the body, by sexual difference and its life-giving potential, even while defending the dignity and rights of persons grounded in a shared human nature. But more than this, it is specified by the demands of justice toward the Creator who made male and female in his own image and endowed them with the capacity to become co-creators with Him in the generation of new human life.[59]

CONCLUSION: TOWARD A TRINITARIAN ACCOUNT OF JUSTICE AND LOVE

Alasdair MacIntyre famously argued that the concepts of justice and rationality require a tradition to render them intelligible.[60] The analysis above supports this contention in regard to the application of justice to an evaluation of same-sex attraction and activity. However, it would specify this further by noting that the concept of justice requires an anthropology to concretize it and that this anthropology is itself embedded within a larger understanding of the world and its relationship to its Creator.[61]

Revisionist arguments to justify same-sex activity end up making autonomy, desire, and choice the hallmarks of personhood. Ironically, in the promotion and celebration of sexual diversity, certain differentiating features of personhood—most notably bodily sexual difference—are suppressed by a cookie-cutter approach to justice as fairness between autonomous individuals. Sexual acts by same-sex-attracted persons must be evaluated by the same criteria as those by opposite-sex-attracted persons. The problem created by the fact that only those in the latter group can actually marry can be solved by either reducing marriage to just another form of commitment or redefining marriage to accommodate same-sex couples. The problem that only sexual acts by men and women are capable of generating new human life can be addressed by seeing procreation as just one form of a larger "fruitfulness" inherent to any interpersonal love. These arguments seem to oscillate between a monist reduction of persons to a basic interchangeable identity and an atomist fixation on difference.[62]

Ultimately, the anthropology proposed by Catholic teaching on same-sex attraction and activity reflects its integrative approach to the person and the universe. Male and female, procreation and interpersonal union, person and nature, equality and difference are all held in a fruitful tension. From the vantage point of the Church's theological tradition, this fruitful tension finds its source in the mystery at the heart of all reality—the revelation of God as a Trinity of Persons. Human sexual dimorphism and the I-Thou communion of love of which it is the basis finds its completion in the I-Thou-We community of the family. This is but a created reflection of the eternal communion of Persons of Father, Son, and Holy Spirit who are irreducibly distinct in their mutual relations while each possesses the fullness of the one divine nature. Both unity and difference are equally basic.[63] Justice in relations between persons must account for these realities, as must the love that is justice's completion. Sexual expression by same-sex-attracted individuals or unmarried opposite-sex-attracted individuals falls short of the full measure of love.

NOTES

1. This was the name of a chart-topping album and single released by the performer known as Lady Gaga in May 2011. A section of the song lyrics convey the relevant message: "Whether life's disabilities / Left you outcast, bullied or teased / Rejoice and love yourself today / 'Cause baby, you were born

this way / No matter gay, straight or bi / Lesbian, transgendered life / I'm on the right track, baby / I was born to survive." http://www.metrolyrics.com/born-this-way-lyrics-lady-gaga.html (accessed June 4, 2014) for complete lyrics. She has subsequently started a charitable foundation by the same name. See http://www.huffingtonpost.com/news/born-this-way-foundation/ (accessed June 4, 2014).

2. This was the name of a popular song released by Macklemore and Ryan Lewis in 2012. The entire song is an *apologia* for the immutable nature of same-sex attraction, the need for equal treatment of same-sex-attracted persons in society, and a polemic against conservative and especially religious opposition to such views. See http://www.metrolyrics.com/same-love-lyrics-macklemore-ryan-lewis.html (accessed June 4, 2014) for the song's lyrics.

3. There is even an online journal of news and opinion titled "The New Civil Rights Movement." See http://thenewcivilrightsmovement.com/ (accessed June 4, 2014).

4. This is the opinion of Catholic journalist and pundit Phil Lawler. See his piece, "Three Important Perspectives on Same-Sex Marriage," available at http://www.catholicculture.org/commentary/otn.cfm?id=978 (accessed June 8, 2014).

5. For an overview of this reaction, see my analysis in *Sex and Virtue: An Introduction to Sexual Ethics*, Catholic Moral Thought Series (Washington, DC: CUA Press, 2003), 10–22.

6. In regard to the justification of sexual activity by same-sex-attracted individuals, some used the language of ontic or premoral evil of Catholic proportionalism to justify these exceptions, while others used the language of a "relational responsibility" approach to justify such compromises. For an example of the first approach, see Philip Keane, S.S., *Sexual Morality: A Catholic Perspective* (Mahwah, NJ: Paulist Press, 1977), 71–91. An example of the second approach is provided by the work of Charles Curran in the 1970s and 1980s. See, for example, his "Moral Theology, Psychiatry and Homosexuality," in *Transition and Tradition in Moral Theology* (Notre Dame, IN: UND Press, 1979), 59–80, and "Moral Theology and Homosexuality," in *Critical Concerns in Moral Theology* (Notre Dame, IN: UND Press, 1984), 73–98. For an overview of these and other positions in Catholic theology in the post–*Humanae vitae* debate on this issue, see James P. Hanigan, *Homosexuality: The Test Case of Christian Ethics* (New York: Paulist, 1988).

7. An early example of some of these views can be found in the thought of Gregory Baum, who argued that having homosexual orientation could be considered akin to being left-handed—it is neither good nor bad, just different. See his essay "Catholic Homosexuals," *Commonweal* 99 (February 15, 1974): 479–81. More current examples of these positions will be provided below.

8. *The Sexual Person*, Moral Traditions Series (Washington, DC: Georgetown University, 2008), 1–3. The arguments of the book were reprised in text-

book form in their *Sexual Ethics: A Theological Introduction* (Washington, DC: Georgetown University, 2012).

9. On September 15, 2010, the USCCB Committee on Doctrine issued a public statement calling attention to problems of both methodology and conclusions in Salzman and Lawler's text (including but not limited to those on same-sex relationships). See "Inadequacies in the Theological Methodology and Conclusions of *The Sexual Person: Toward a Renewed Anthropology* by Todd A. Salzmann and Michael G. Lawler," available at http://www.usccb.org/about/doctrine/publications/upload/Sexual_Person_2010-09-15.pdf (accessed June 8, 2014). Especially problematic in this work's method is the weight given to experience—understood both social scientifically and anecdotally. For a critique of this trend in this work and revisionist moral theology generally, see my "Catechesis and Moral Theology: Toward a Renewed Understanding of Christian Experience," *Nova et Vetera* 13, no. 1 (2015, forthcoming).

10. *The Sexual Person*, 140–43. They point out that the term *complementarity* is a relatively recent addition to the vocabulary of Catholic teaching, appearing in Pope John Paul II's (1981) Apostolic Exhortation, *Familiaris consortio*, no. 19.

11. *The Sexual Person*, 149.

12. They write: "Relying on the historical critical method espoused by the Magisterium, we have demonstrated that traditional interpretations of scripture condemning homosexual acts lack legitimacy." They go on to describe the "rhetoric" of this teaching as "entrenched, and sometimes discriminatory and hurtful." *The Sexual Person*, 232.

13. They rely heavily on the work of Margaret Farley for their arguments concerning justice. Her work will be considered below.

14. *The Sexual Person*, 233.

15. The USCCB analysis frames this dualistic tendency well: "In their view, personal complementarity is independent of bodily complementarity, and exists even when contradicted by bodily non-complementarity. The implication here is that the personal and the bodily are separable. Rather than an integral part of the human person, the human body becomes merely an instrument of the human spirit, an instrument that can be manipulated according to one's desire" (15).

16. Chicago: University of Illinois Press, 2010. The essays represent a variety of disciplines: science—particularly evolutionary biology—philosophy, theology, ethics, and literature.

17. See her "Evolutionary Biology and Sexual Diversity," in P. B. Jung and Aana Marie Vigen, eds., *God, Science, Sex, Gender* (Chicago: University of Illinois Press, 2010), 89–104. This essay is a resume of her book *Evolution's Rainbow: Diversity, Gender, and Sexuality in Nature and People* (Oakland: University of California Press, 2009).

18. "Evolutionary Biology and Sexual Diversity," 101. Her focus in these comments was on the controversy over same-sex marriage and the ordination of openly gay clergy in the Episcopal and Anglican churches.

19. "Evolutionary Biology and Sexual Diversity," 103.

20. See their "Introduction," in *God, Science, Sex, Gender*, 1–19, esp. 6–8.

21. Vigen in her conclusion to the volume notes: "After reading and reflecting on the array of analyses offered in this volume, I am not sure how much can be said definitely of an 'essential human nature' whether in biological, theological, philosophical, or ethical terms." See "Conclusion," 256.

22. New York: Continuum, 2008.

23. In addition to receiving critical acclaim by some scholars and reviewers, the work was awarded the Louisville Grawemeyer Award in Religion in 2008. On June 4, 2012, the Congregation for the Doctrine of the Faith (CDF) published a notification on Farley's book, citing both general and specific problems in the work. For the text of the notification, see http://press.catholica.va/news_services/bulletin/news/29292.php?index=29292&lang=en (accessed June 13, 2014).

24. This approach purports to offer four complementary sources of authority for approaching and evaluating moral questions: experience, scripture, tradition, and reason. In addition to Salzman, Lawler, and Farley, this approach can be found in the work of Lisa Sowle Cahill and the more recent work of Charles Curran. See Charles Curran, *Catholic Moral Tradition Today: A Synthesis* (Washington, DC: Georgetown, 1999), 48. Cf. Michael G. Lawler and Todd Salzman, "Human Experience and Catholic Moral Theology," *Irish Theological Quarterly* 76 (2011): 35–56.

25. See *Just Love*, 273–80. She offered similar arguments in her earlier essay "An Ethic for Same-Sex Relations," in *A Challenge to Love: Gay and Lesbian Catholics in the Church*, ed. Robert Nugent (New York: Crossroad, 1984), 93–106.

26. See *Just Love*, 280–86.

27. See *Just Love*, 286–88; the citation is from 286.

28. See *Just Love*, 208–32. By "fruitfulness," Farley does not necessarily mean procreation as an end of sexual activity. All persons, including gays, lesbians, and ambiguously gendered persons, can "participate in the rearing of new generations" and the fruitfulness "of all interpersonal love" (227). For an extended reflection on what she means by "commitment," see her earlier work *Personal Commitments: Beginning, Keeping, Changing* (San Francisco: Harper & Row, 1986).

29. For a more extensive utilization of this understanding of justice in a feminist context (which Farley cites in her work), see Susan Moller Okin, *Justice, Gender, and the Family* (New York: Basic Books, 1989).

30. Salzman and Lawler offer this definition of sexual orientation: "a psychosexual attraction (erotic, emotional, affective) toward particular individual *persons* of either the same or the opposite sex, depending on whether the orientation is homosexual or heterosexual." *The Sexual Person*, 65 (emphasis in original; citing Robert Nugent).

31. After reviewing evidence for a variety of theories explaining the bases of sexual orientation both biological (such as genetic and neuro-hormonal) and developmental (such as the psychoanalytic explanation of a disruption in a child's relationship with a parent that interferes with the development of gender identity, which is a component of sexual attraction and identification), Gerald Coleman wisely concludes that: "[N]o one theory of homosexuality can explain such a diverse phenomenon." See the overview he provides in *Homosexuality: Church Teaching and Pastoral Practice* (New York: Paulist, 1995), 48–55; the citation is from 54. Though Coleman's treatment is a bit dated, Salzman and Lawler make a similar point: "Concerning the genesis of homosexual and heterosexual orientations, the scientific community generally agrees that there is no single isolated cause. The experts point to a variety of genetic, hormonal, psychological, and social '*loading*' factors, from which the orientation may derive." *The Sexual Person*, 65 (emphasis in original).

32. Michael Hannon writes in a provocative recent essay: "Contrary to our cultural preconceptions and the lies of what has come to be called 'orientation essentialism,' 'straight' and 'gay' are not ageless absolutes. Sexual orientation is a conceptual scheme with a history and a dark one at that. . . . Over the course of several centuries, the West had progressively abandoned Christianity's marital architecture for human sexuality. Then, about one hundred and fifty years ago, it began to replace that longstanding teleological tradition with a brand new creation: the absolutist but absurd taxonomy of sexual orientations. Heterosexuality was made to serve as this fanciful framework's regulating ideal, preserving the social prohibitions against sodomy and other sexual debaucheries without requiring recourse to the procreative nature of human sexuality." See "Against Heterosexuality," *First Things* 241 (March 1, 2014): 27–34; the citation is from pages 27–28. Similar critiques of the concept of sexual orientation have been put forward by gay academics.

33. Thus the widely used scale developed by Kinsey and his associates in 1948 envisions sexual orientation as a 7-point scale with 0 being an exclusively heterosexual person and 6 being exclusively homosexual with many gradations (representing most of the adult population) in between. The Klein Sexual Orientation Grid (KSOG) takes this further, factoring in sexual desire and arguing that orientation can and does change over time. See Fritz Kline, *The Bisexual Option* (New York: Arbor House, 1978). Many recent studies document the fluidity of sexual orientation and attraction among persons belonging to these various

groups. See, for example, J. D. Weinrich and Fritz Klein, "Bi-Gay, Bi-Straight, and Bi-Bi: Three Bisexual Subgroups Identified Using Cluster Analysis of the Klein Sexual Orientation Grid," *Journal of Bisexuality* 2 (2002): 109–39; O. F. Kernberg, "Unresolved Issues in the Psychoanalytic Theory of Homosexuality and Bisexuality," *Journal of Gay and Lesbian Psychotherapy* 6, no. 1 (2002): 9–27; and Neil and Brian Whitehead, *My Genes Made Me Do It: A Scientific Look at Sexual Orientation*, 3rd ed. (2013), available at http://www.mygenes.co.nz/download.htm (accessed June 13, 2014).

34. Nicanor Austriaco, O.P., argues that sexual orientation can be understood in Thomistic terms as a *habitus* formed from the matrix of disposition, choice, and action. See his essay "Understanding Sexual Orientation as a *Habitus*: Reasoning from the Natural Law, Appeals to Human Experience, and the Data of Science," in *Leaving and Coming Home: New Wineskins for Catholic Sexual Ethics*, ed. David Cloutier (Eugene, OR: Wipf & Stock, 2010), 101–18.

35. For an overview of such "reparative" or "gender-affirming" therapies, see Joseph Nicolosi, *Shame and Attachment Loss: The Practical Work of Reparative Therapy* (Downers Grove, IL: IVP Academic, 2009). See also the report by the National Association for the Research and Therapy of Homosexuality (NARTH), "What Research Shows: NARTH's response to the APA Claims on Homosexuality," *Journal of Human Sexuality* 1 (2009): 1–121. For an overview of clinical issues in treating same-sex-attracted persons that is open but not limited to this reparative approach, see the thoughtful analysis provided by Philip Sutton, "Who Am I: Psychological Issues in Gender Identity and Same Sex Attraction," in *Fertility and Gender: Issues in Reproductive and Sexual Ethics*, ed. Helen Watt (Oxford: Anscombe Bioethics Centre, 2011), 70–98.

36. See Salzman and Lawler, *The Sexual Person*, 65. For a clinical perspective opposed to that of NARTH, see the American Psychological Association (APA) report *Appropriate Therapeutic Responses to Sexual Orientation* (Washington, DC: APA, 2009), 1–130.

37. See, for example, the CDF, Declaration on Sexual Ethics (*Persona humana* [1975]), no. 8; CDF, *Letter to the Bishops of the Catholic Church on the Pastoral Care of Homosexual Persons* (1986), no. 3. For an overview of Church teaching on same-sex attraction and activity and its pastoral implications, see the balanced overview provided by Coleman, *Homosexuality*. See also John F. Harvey, *Homosexuality and the Catholic Church: Clear Answers to Difficult Questions* (Westchester, PA: Ascension Press, 2007). For more concise treatments, see Grabowski, *Sex and Virtue*, 335–40; and William E. May, Ronald Lawler, and Joseph Boyle, *Catholic Sexual Ethics: A Summary Explanation and Defense*, 3rd ed. (Huntington, IN: Our Sunday Visitor, 2011), 286–96.

38. See the *Catechism of the Catholic Church* (*CCC*), 2358–59. The citation is from the Second Edition, Libreira Editrice Vaticana, English translation by the USCC (Washington, DC: USCC, 1997), 566.

39. CDF, *Letter* (1986), no. 10. See also the excellent discussion of the power of language and the need to avoid reductive or denigrating epithets for same-sex-attracted people (even when these come from within the gay community) provided by Coleman, *Homosexuality*, 30–32.

40. As Coleman observes, "A person can be homosexual in orientation without having acted on this psychosexual attraction" (*Homosexuality*, 16). The same could be said for heterogenital activity outside the context of the marriage covenant.

41. Official Church teaching has described this inclination as an "objective disorder" (see the CDF *Letter*, no. 3; *CCC*, 2358) insofar as it inclines persons toward activity that the Church understands to be disordered. However, as Coleman, notes, the Church does not teach that homosexual persons are themselves disordered. See his thoughtful analysis of this language in *Homosexuality*, 94–96.

42. *CCC*, 2357. Salzman and Lawler complain that this "affective complementarity" is really just a way of referring to heterogenital complementarity for reproduction (see *The Sexual Person*, 146–49), but their own "holistic complementarity" prescinds from bodily sexual difference altogether.

43. See, for example, Thomas Aquinas, *Summa theologiae* (hereafter *ST*), II-II, q. 154, a. 12.

44. Terry Grande, Joel Brown, and Robin Colburn, in their essay "The Evolution of Sex," *God, Science, Sex, Gender*, 105–22 argue against Roughgarden that, a few exceptions notwithstanding, "the existence of sexual dimporphism is a fact" (116). They also disagree with her contention that sex selection is defunct, arguing that it is obvious throughout the natural world though it can be extended by "social selection" in higher animals and humans (117–18).

45. Roughgarden herself attributes the reaction to *Nature's Rainbow* by her peers to homophobia. See "Evolutionary Biology and Sexual Diversity," 102.

46. See, for example, David Buss, *The Evolution of Desire*, revised ed. (New York: Basic Books, 2003); and Helen Fisher, *Why We Love: The Nature and Chemistry of Romantic Love*, reprint ed. (New York: Holt, 2004). Cf. David Blankenhorn, *The Future of Marriage*, rpt. ed. (New York: Encounter Books 2009), 11–68.

47. On the inclinations of human nature in the teaching of Saint Thomas, see *ST* I-II, q. 94, a. 2. John Paul II acknowledged: "The Church has often made reference to the Thomistic doctrine of natural law, including it in her own teaching on morality." *Veritatis splendor*, no. 44. The citation is from the Daughters of Saint Paul edition, Vatican translation (Boston: St. Paul Books and Media,

1993), 59. For an excellent overview of Aquinas's conception of the inclinations and their function in his ethic of virtue, see Servais Pinckaers, O.P., *The Sources of Christian Ethics*, trans. Mary Thomas Noble (Washington, DC: CUA Press, 1995), 400–56.

48. This point is forcefully argued by John Finnis against attempts by revisionist thinkers to argue for a concept of human nature as mutable. See his "The Natural Law, Objective Morality, and Vatican II," in *Principles of Catholic Moral Life* (Chicago: Franciscan Herald, 1980), 113–49, see esp. 141–42.

49. This is the expression of Walter Kasper in his essay "The Position of Women as a Problem of Theological Anthropology," trans. John Saward, in *The Church and Women: A Compendium*, ed. Helmut Moll (San Francisco: Ignatius Press, 1988), 58–59.

50. The contentious debate that started with the issue of birth control quickly spread to other issues of sexual ethics. In this same period, the Church has been further polarized by ongoing arguments in favor of the ordination of women, which have not been entirely resolved by authoritative statements by the magisterium in *Inter insignores* (1976) and *Ordinatio sacerdotalis* (1994). At the same time, it is true that there are persons with physically ambiguous sexual characteristics (the "inter-sexed" persons mentioned above) and those who experience a disconnect between their physical sex and their psychological experience of themselves as persons—sometimes called transgender persons. A treatment of these complex phenomena would require a separate essay. Here I would simply note that the focus in Catholic teaching is on the typical manifestation of sexual difference within humanity, not on these exceptional cases that account for some 1/1400th of the current human population.

51. *CCC*, 372, 95.

52. Of course, this does not mean that God is male or female. As a divine and spiritual being God transcends the distinctions of biological sex. However, both Scripture and the Church's tradition have analogously applied qualities of human masculinity to femininity to God *simpliciter* or to the Persons of the Trinity. See *CCC*, 370, and John Paul II, Apostolic Letter, *Mulieris dignitatem*, no. 8.

53. The citation is from *Man and Woman He Created Them: A Theology of the Body*, trans. Michael Waldstein (Boston: Pauline, 2006), 10:1, 166. Emphasis in original.

54. John Paul II, *Man and Woman*, 9:1, 161. Emphasis in original. The same focus on the mutual relation and irreducible difference of men and women as persons within a shared human nature can be found in his more weighty teaching in the Apostolic Letter *Mulieris dignitatem*, no. 10. This distinction between person and nature as a key to understanding sexual difference has been highlighted in recent Catholic theological reflection on sexual difference. In addition to Kasper's essay cited above, Michele Schumacher speaks of "one nature in two

modes"; see "The Nature of Nature in Feminism, Old and New: From Dualism to Complementary Unity," in *Women in Christ: Toward a New Feminism*, ed. Michele Schumacher (Grand Rapids: Eerdmans, 2004), 38–41. Put more sharply, one might speak of sexual difference as accidental on the level of nature but essential to existing human persons. Cf. Grabowski, *Sex and Virtue*, 110–11.

55. Waldstein in the index to *Man and Woman* (682–83) notes that this term is an important and wide-ranging one in the Theology of the Body catecheses, appearing some 117 times. For an overview of the range of meaning of the term as employed in these catecheses, see Earl Muller, S.J., "The Nuptial Meaning of the Body," in *John Paul II on the Body: Human, Eucharistic, Ecclesial.*, Festschrift for Avery Cardinal Dulles, S.J., ed. John McDermott, S.J., and John Galvin, S.J. (Philadelphia: Saint Joseph's University Press, 2008), 87–120.

56. The French is *on ne naît pas femme, on le deviant*. See Pope Benedict XVI, "Address of His Holiness Benedict XVI on the Occasion of Christmas Greetings to the Roman Curia" (December 21, 2012). Available at http://www.vatican.va/holy_father/benedict_xvi/speeches/2012/december/documents/hf_ben-xvi_spe_20121221_auguri-curia_en.html (accessed June 4, 2014). Thus, Catholic new feminists reacting to de Beauvoir and her impact on modern thought argue for the need to reunite these realities. See Beatriz Vollmer Coles, "New Feminism: A Sex-Gender Reunion," in *Women in Christ*, 52–66.

57. A sign of such confusion can be witnessed in the recent decision by Facebook to gives its users some fifty different options for their gender self-identification. On this, see Aimee Lee Ball, "Who Are You on Facebook Now? Facebook Customizes Gender with 50 Different Choices," *New York Times*, April 4, 2014, available at http://www.nytimes.com/2014/04/06/fashion/facebook-customizes-gender-with-50-different-choices.html?_r=0 (accessed June 14, 2014).

58. This is why the Church can simultaneously defend the basic human and civil rights of same-sex-attracted persons while resisting the claim that their inclination bestows on them a right to redefine marriage that has God as its author. See the CDF's *Non-Discrimination against Homosexual Persons: Some Considerations Concerning the Response to Legislative Proposals*, nos. 12, 15. Surely all persons—including same-sex-attracted persons—need friendship, love, and communion with God and with other human beings. Yet contrary to the messages preached by our popular culture, neither friendship nor personal fulfillment requires sexual expression.

59. For an analysis of the demands of "justice toward the Creator" in the context of a personalist analysis of sexuality, see Karol Wojtyla, *Love and Responsibility*, trans. H. T. Willets (San Francisco: Ignatius, 1981), 211–61.

60. See his *Whose Justice? Which Rationality?* (Notre Dame: University of Notre Dame Press, 1989).

61. One problem with Salzman and Lawler's dismissal of the Catholic natural law tradition as being embedded in a "classicist" worldview as opposed to their own "historically conscious" one is that they ignore the historicist presuppositions imbedded in this schema that Bernard Lonergan imported into theology from Vico and Hegel. That is, they fail to acknowledge themselves as part of a historically situated (and hence limited) tradition.

62. The problem of whether sameness or difference was more basic to reality—known as the problem of the One and the Many—was one of the oldest philosophical conundrums to bedevil the ancient world.

63. This can be understood as Christian revelation's response to the ancient problem of the One and Many and its replication in modern debates about the status of sexual difference. See John S. Grabowski, "Mutual Submission and Trinitarian Self-Giving," *Angelicum* 74 (1997): 499–500.

INDEX

abortion, 109, 143, 185, 240–241, 248, 258, 404
Abraham, 164, 338, 410, 413, 414, 428, 429, 459, 552, 578
Ackerman, Bruce, 99, 102, 104, 110
Adams, Robert, 214
African-American, 175, 178, 179, 181, 208–221, 224–225, 227, 240, 241, 281, 395, 453, 455, 457, 475
Ahmed, Akbar, 407
Al-Farabi, Abu Nasr, 420, 420–421, 421
Al-Ghazzali, Abu Hamid, 417
Al-Kindi, Abu Yusuf Ya'qub, 419, 420
Al-Suhrawardi, Shihab ad-Din, 421–422
Allen, Jeffner, 249
Allen, Prudence, 258, 264
Alvare, Helen, 268
Amato, Paul, 319
Anderson, Ryan, 285–287, 287, 288, 289, 291, 292, 293–294, 295, 297–298, 301–302
animals, xii–xiii, xxiv, xxxiii, 65, 67–68, 214, 463, 465, 563, 575–576, 619, 623
Anscombe, Elizabeth, 19, 26–27, 212
Ansari, Zafar Ishaq, 411
Anselm of Canterbury, 561
Apel, Karl-Otto, 49–50
Appiah, Anthony, 309
Aquinas, Thomas, xxi–xxiii, 19–34, 336, 340, 351, 405, 461, 464–466, 472, 491, 546, 617, 618, 619, 621

Aristotle, xi–xiii, xiv–xv, xvi, xix–xx, xxi–xxiii, 3–17, 27, 32, 52, 160, 196, 217, 312, 325, 349, 367, 403, 461, 463, 463–465, 467, 469, 471, 472, 545, 565
Armesto, Felipe Fernandez, 423
Arrow, Kenneth, 112
Arthur, John, 208, 211, 213, 228
assimilation, 44, 49, 52, 166, 175, 367, 546
Athens, xxvi, 166, 167, 345
Auden, Wystan Hugh, 395
Audi, Robert, 110–111
Augustine, St., 167, 168, 340, 345, 348, 400, 461, 464–465, 487, 488, 493, 496, 499, 500, 546, 547
Aurelius, Marcus, 545
autonomy, 31, 39, 43, 46, 49, 52, 53, 74–76, 108, 133, 136, 138, 141, 196, 240, 414, 458, 472, 541, 544, 620, 626, 627

Bachiochi, Erika, 258–259, 268
Baersch, Claus-Ekkehard, 509
Bakar, Osman, 420
Balthasar, Hans Urs von, 267–268, 352
Bannerji, Himani, 473
Barry, Brian, 99
Barth, Karl, 381, 383
Bayfield, Tony, 423
Beauvoir, Simone de, 248–249, 626
Bell, Dan, 389
Bellarmine, Robert, 351

Benedict XVI, Pope (Joseph Ratzinger), xxxi, 353, 354, 500, 501, 541–542, 543, 544, 626
Bentham, Jeremy, 59–60, 62, 67
Bergen, Doris, 511
Bertram, Georg, 520, 523
Berube, Michael, 25
Boase, Roger, 412
body, xxv, 147, 170, 199–200, 202–203, 251, 260, 262, 264, 265, 286, 288, 301, 311, 320, 320–321, 322, 323–324, 326, 352, 364, 382, 387, 389, 442, 452, 468, 553, 576–577, 582, 589, 590, 591, 620, 625, 627
Boswell, John, 563–565
Bradshaw, David, 370
Buddhism, 168, 407, 410, 413, 551
Burleigh, Michael, 510
Burrin, Philippe, 510
Butler, Sara, 268

capitalism, xviii, 25, 87, 140, 188, 194, 198, 203, 287, 299
Carpenter, Dale, 43
Carson, Thomas, 207, 221
Catholicism, x, xxiii, 172, 176, 181–182, 202, 267–268, 280, 335–354, 360, 364, 367, 369, 373, 374, 378, 388–389, 399, 405, 446, 453, 456, 473, 490, 533–547, 604, 605, 607, 621–628
Celsus, 545
charity, 31, 66, 83, 281, 389, 401, 537. *See also* love
Chesterton, Gilbert Keith, 340, 341, 348, 351
Christianity:, xx–xxiii, 165, 168, 170, 171, 178, 196, 336, 345, 348, 360, 361, 367, 386, 388, 401, 403, 407, 411, 414, 416, 423, 442–443, 446, 453, 457, 464, 533, 535, 538, 545, 552, 574, 601, 603, 606; Christianity and National Socialism, 509–525
Chrysostom, John, 363, 565
Church, 135, 162, 164, 172, 181, 187, 267–268, 280, 336, 337–338, 347, 350–354, 359–370, 375, 381–387, 389, 399–400, 413, 414, 424, 441–454, 487, 490, 493, 497, 509–525, 545, 546–547, 553, 558, 566, 587, 601, 602, 605, 606, 607–608, 616, 618, 619, 622, 623, 624, 625, 627, 628
citizenship, 4, 11–12, 14–15, 19, 31, 50–51, 74, 75, 84, 107–108, 109–112, 115, 115–116, 117, 123–124, 126–128, 133–135, 138, 148, 160, 172, 179, 194, 198, 277–280, 282, 285, 346, 348, 376, 380, 397, 398, 399–401, 414, 453, 455, 458, 462, 464, 466, 471–472, 474, 496–497, 501, 551
Cixous, Hélène, 145
class, 8, 21, 67, 82–83, 83, 87, 114, 115, 181, 188–189, 192, 195, 197, 198, 241, 245, 246, 259, 319, 377, 395, 398, 412, 452, 464, 473, 474, 497, 500, 620
Classical (pre-modern) period, 28, 61, 171, 196, 336, 340, 343, 344, 345, 353, 461–469, 500, 542, 617
Clement of Alexandria, 340
Cohen, Joshua, 99, 102, 110
colonialism, 145, 159, 220, 370, 386, 443, 445, 489, 499, 534, 625
communion, 339, 347, 360, 363–364, 365, 366, 382, 387, 388–389, 575–576, 589, 591, 625, 628
community, 4, 6, 8, 11, 16, 24, 30, 31, 61, 75, 90, 92, 182, 243, 319–320, 323, 325, 328–329, 354, 366, 377, 384, 387, 398, 400–401, 411, 413, 417, 427, 441, 446, 453, 458, 462, 463, 493, 588, 606, 610, 618, 628. *See also* communion; unity.
Cone, James, 379, 380
Confucius, 345, 413
Constantine I, Emperor, 361
constitution, 110, 116, 117, 133–134, 138, 163, 175, 242, 278, 282
consensus, x–xi, xvii–xix, xxvi, 48–49, 106–108, 109, 125, 134, 135–136, 139, 143, 146, 148, 299, 317, 327, 499, 500–501, 514, 542
contraception, 240, 248, 258, 490, 615
contract, xv, 14, 28, 31, 32, 47, 53, 101, 126, 129, 403, 469, 471, 472
Cornell, Drusilla, 249
Corvino, John, 310, 311, 313, 314, 314–319, 321, 322, 324–325, 326–329
cosmopolitanism, 25, 42, 45, 179, 380, 386–171

INDEX

Coulanges, Fustel de, 168
Cox, Harvey:, 407
culture, ix, 21, 23, 26, 33, 39, 40, 52, 107–108, 114, 124, 135, 145, 165–166, 169, 170, 175, 176, 177, 184–185, 197, 198, 219, 221, 241, 248, 254, 256, 260, 266, 268, 281–282, 303, 312, 315, 317, 318, 325, 327, 328, 340, 341, 350, 352, 353, 365, 373, 376, 377, 378–380, 383, 384, 389, 397, 402, 407, 428, 443, 444, 446, 447, 450, 453, 456, 457, 458, 475, 491, 523, 545–546, 547, 555–556, 574, 577, 588, 602, 606, 615–616, 621; multiculturalism, 21, 25, 49, 165, 281, 341, 441–454, 544

Dante degli Alighieri, 171
Darwin, Charles, 91, 171, 619
Davis, Angela, 225, 245
Day, Dorothy, 92, 328
Delmar, Rosalind, 238
Demacopoulos, 368
democracy, xv, xviii, 4, 7–8, 14–15, 94, 102, 107, 114, 117, 123–148, 160, 161, 164, 172, 181, 193–194, 196–198, 244, 280, 282, 350, 380, 387, 457, 458, 473, 501, 542, 606
deontology, 39–53, 100, 217. *See also* Kant, Immanuel.
Derrida, Jacques, 22, 123–148, 190, 194, 196, 200–201
Descartes, René, xi, xvii, 52, 201
Dewey, John, 81, 85–94
Diamond, Irene, 182, 200
dignity, 32, 34, 138, 214, 215–216, 223, 230, 254, 258, 267–268, 282, 327, 347, 403, 447, 449, 498, 501, 560–561, 589, 590, 622–623, 627
discrimination, xiv, 115, 117, 164, 184, 220, 246–247, 262, 266, 281, 309, 310, 455. *See also* prejudice.
dogma, xx–xxi, 51, 343, 363, 382, 416, 445–446, 535, 537, 538, 541
Dulles, Avery Cardinal, 336
Dworkin, Ronald, 99, 102, 104, 110, 230

Eberle, Christopher, 111, 112
Eck, Diana, 407

economics, xvi, 6, 33, 84, 86, 87, 88, 92, 94, 114, 127, 175, 177, 249, 253, 278, 282, 320, 362, 377, 378, 387, 423, 455–456, 458, 461, 471, 474, 489, 491, 499, 500, 586, 611. *See also* wealth.
education, ix, xii, xviii, xxiii, 25, 25–26, 71, 72, 81, 83, 88, 90, 92, 172, 190, 195, 196–198, 237, 240, 243, 244, 248, 256, 282, 340, 364, 491, 534, 536, 602, 603, 608, 609, 612
El Fadl, Khaled Abou, 416
Engelhardt, Tristam, 370
epistemology, 27, 230, 378–380, 539, 557
equality, ix, xii, xv, xix, xxi, xxiii, 4–8, 11–12, 16, 28, 32, 34, 47, 50, 66–69, 74, 83, 92, 101, 108, 114, 116, 123, 124, 126–128, 129, 132, 135–136, 138, 139, 140, 142, 145, 146, 148, 171–172, 192, 194, 196, 198, 219, 223, 237, 240, 241, 242, 244, 245, 246, 247, 255, 256, 258, 259, 263, 267, 269, 277, 281–282, 285, 298, 309, 312, 314, 327, 398, 400, 401, 414, 425, 442, 448, 449, 450, 453, 457, 464, 465, 468, 470–468, 471, 495, 523, 536, 544, 561, 576, 582–583, 615, 617, 620, 623, 625, 627, 628
essence, xii, xix, xxi, 44–45, 47, 81, 130, 138, 142, 187, 190, 194, 196, 198, 200, 210, 229, 237, 288, 290, 297, 303, 316, 324, 327, 336, 339, 364, 379, 381, 395, 403, 405, 407, 418, 494, 520, 523, 575, 606, 617. *See also* nature.
ethnicity, ix, xiv, xxiv, 25, 39, 124, 146, 165, 175, 177, 179, 180, 182, 183, 184, 219, 278, 281, 350, 359, 365, 366–367, 370, 374, 387, 407, 409, 428, 441, 442, 443, 444, 445, 447, 449, 452, 500; ethnocentrism, 138, 445–446, 447
Euler, Karl, 518
exclusion, xiv, 115, 117, 136, 161, 163, 164, 172, 182, 241, 256, 263, 287, 295, 297, 301–302, 311, 312, 314, 315, 316, 317, 320, 324, 324–325, 326, 365, 375, 377, 382, 384, 387, 388, 413, 425, 426, 427, 428, 443, 444, 450, 458, 471, 535, 537, 588, 604, 607, 611, 616
exploitation, 6, 8, 124, 176, 220, 241, 446, 474, 478, 577, 583, 586

family, xiii–xiv, xix, 44, 46, 172, 179, 184, 198, 237–278, 239, 240, 243, 244, 246, 247, 249, 251, 256, 257, 258, 265, 268, 269, 279, 281–282, 286, 293, 294, 296, 298, 299, 300, 304, 311, 312, 315, 316, 320, 323–325, 370, 375, 376, 414, 442, 448, 449, 453, 491, 493, 497, 498–499, 560–561, 575, 610, 626, 628
Farley, Margaret, 617, 617–620, 627
feminism, 27, 59, 145, 181, 187, 190, 195, 196, 199, 200, 202–203, 203–204, 237–270, 620, 625, 626
Feuerbach, Ludwig, 379
Finnis, John, 102
Firestone, Shulamith, 249
Florovsky, Georges, 367
Foucault, Michel, ix, 200, 202, 219–220
Fox, Marvin, 404
Fox-Genovese, Elizabeth, 249
Francis I, Pope (Jorge Bergoglio), 573
Frankfurt School, 49, 175
freedom, 27, 30, 31, 42, 45, 46, 47, 52, 53, 61, 74–76, 88, 101, 105, 106, 108, 113–114, 116, 117, 123, 124, 126, 127–129, 132, 133–136, 138, 139–140, 142, 143, 145, 148, 160, 168, 175, 184, 185, 189, 198, 209, 241, 244, 248, 252–253, 254, 255, 256, 257, 263, 269, 282, 329, 345, 347, 350, 361, 364, 367, 379–380, 383, 386, 400, 401, 414, 424, 455–478, 491, 492, 493, 495, 497, 520, 540, 541, 544, 557, 560–561, 574, 576, 577, 582, 585, 589, 620. *See also* liberty.
Friedan, Betty, 248
Friedlaender, Saul, 510
Friedman, Judge Bernard, 300
Friedman, Thomas, 377–378
Freud, Sigmund, 199, 201, 340, 345
Frye, Marion, 473
Fukuyama, Francis, 423

Gadamer, Georg, 533
Gallagher, Maggie, 285
Gaus, Gerald, 99, 102, 111, 112
gender, ix, x, xiv, xvi, 43, 82, 86, 115, 124, 125, 135, 147, 159, 163, 181, 184, 192, 194, 197–200, 204, 237, 246–247, 255, 257, 260, 262, 263, 267, 268, 294, 377, 473–474, 500, 561, 566, 584, 601, 607, 610, 618–619, 625, 626
George, Robert, 285–286, 287, 288, 289, 291, 292, 293–294, 294, 295, 297–298, 301, 301–302, 302–303
Gandhi, Mahatma, 411
Gilligan, Carol, 250
Girgis, Sherif, 285–304
Glasgow, Joshua, 207–230
Glendon, Mary Ann, 268
globalization, 140, 412, 428, 489
Godwin, William, 59, 61, 64, 69
goodness, xii, xiii, xv, xxi, xxiv, 4–16, 19–34, 40, 45, 49, 50–51, 60–62, 66, 68, 70, 72–76, 83, 89, 94, 105, 106, 109, 115, 117, 124, 125, 126, 128, 129, 130, 132, 134–135, 136, 141, 143, 160, 168, 172, 193, 195, 198–199, 203, 211, 214, 214–215, 216, 217, 228, 254, 255, 278, 279, 281, 282, 291–292, 294, 296, 302, 319, 320, 323–324, 325, 326, 347, 354, 367, 388, 409, 418, 427, 429, 444, 462, 463, 464, 466, 469, 474, 477, 478, 520, 546, 547, 575, 581, 605, 612, 624, 625; common good, 4, 6, 8, 13, 14, 16, 30, 116, 237, 257, 263, 269, 309, 310, 317, 318, 346, 388, 456–478, 491, 496, 497, 499, 605, 612; comprehensive good, 123, 133, 136, 140, 141, 143, 146, 148, 323; diversity of goods, 19–34; greater good, 68, 70, 71, 73, 605; human good, 23, 24, 313, 323, 463, 468, 476, 500, 561; public good, 193, 286, 311, 313; instrumental good, 33, 254; personal good, 228, 472; social good, 76, 81; supreme good, 581, 612
grace, 168, 337, 339, 346, 350, 352, 364, 417, 429, 442, 444, 450, 456, 464, 476–478, 565, 587
gratitude, 31, 32, 278–279, 281, 448, 602
Grotius, Hugo, 27, 40–42, 43–44, 52
Grundmann, Walter, 512–525

Habermas, Jürgen, 49, 161, 201
Hare, R. M., 69–72, 76, 100–101, 101
Harnack, Adolf, 343
Hart, David Bentley, 370
Harvey, Susan Ashbrook, 370
Hauerwas, Stanley, 382, 388

INDEX

Heenan, Cardinal John, 348
Hegel, Georg Wilhelm Friedrich, 45, 201, 379, 380
Heidegger, Martin, 533–534, 538
Herder, Johann Gottfried, 44–46, 52
hermeneutics, 49, 127, 129, 130, 136, 533, 535, 536
heterogeneity, 21, 22, 123–124, 125, 137, 139, 140, 141, 143, 146, 147
heterosexuality, 289, 298, 316, 325, 561, 590, 610, 611, 618
Hildebrand, Dietrich von, 344
Hillel the Elder, 395
Hinduism, 194, 410, 413, 551
Hitler, Adolf, 455, 509–525
Hobbes, Thomas, xi, xv–xix, 41, 43, 165, 378, 407, 461, 468–469, 470
Hodge, John, 239
Homer, 171
homogeneity, xiv, 19, 21, 124, 128, 136, 140, 146, 185, 375, 407
homophobia, 220, 474, 603–604, 621–624
homosexuality, 163, 247, 312, 375, 559, 561, 562, 563–565, 565, 573–574, 577, 579–584, 585, 587–591, 601–603, 606–607, 609–612, 616–619, 622
Hooker, Brad, 72–73, 74, 76
Hooker, Richard, 605
hooks, Bell, 238–241
Horace (Quintus Horatius Flaccus), 167
hospitality, 20, 29, 30, 31, 138–140, 145, 146, 384, 386, 577, 578
Hume, David, 44, 53, 59
Humphrey, Edith, 370
Huntington, Samuel, 423
Hurka, Thomas, 214
Hurston, Zora Neale, 457, 478
Husserl, Edmund:, 21
Hutcheson, Francis, 59
Huxley, Aldous, 348
Hyppolite, Jean, 379

Ibn 'Arabi, Abu 'Abd Allah Muhammad, 418, 422, 426–427
Ibn Ashur, Muhammad al-Tahir, 427
Ibn Hazm, Abu Muhammad, 413, 426
Ignatius of Antioch, St., 350
Ignatius of Loyola, St., 348

immigration, 178, 183, 277–282, 366–367, 428, 441–454, 464
inclusivity, 111, 112–113, 139, 241, 295, 300–301, 302, 314, 374–375, 377, 378, 388, 418, 424–427, 452–453, 501
institutions, ix, xviii, 26, 34, 44, 48, 83, 85, 87, 88, 105, 106, 108, 109, 112–114, 117, 124, 126, 184, 185, 203, 207, 208–209, 216, 219, 220, 222–227, 230, 246, 249, 269, 278, 279, 280, 281, 282, 294, 303, 310, 315, 318, 340, 341, 350, 351, 368, 370, 373–377, 379, 381, 383, 384, 398, 415, 450, 458, 471, 473–474, 477, 494, 533, 545, 547, 587, 611
Islam, xx–xxiv, 143, 165, 168, 169, 196, 364, 398–399, 403, 407–429, 552, 556

James, William, 59, 88–94, 159
Jefferson, Thomas, 400, 494, 604
Jennings, Willie, 386
Jerusalem, 166, 167, 178, 338, 360, 384, 387, 448, 518, 555, 579
Jesus of Nazareth, xxi, 340, 349, 352, 359, 387–390, 410, 411, 442, 448–449, 450, 453, 454, 460, 478, 509, 511–512, 513–514, 516, 516–522, 524, 538, 547, 553, 566, 580, 583–592
John XXIII, Pope (Angelo Roncalli), 87, 487–502
John Paul II, Pope (Karol Wojtyla), 33, 254, 255, 257, 268–269, 353, 403, 493, 575, 576, 585
Joyce, James, 202–203
Judaism, xx–xxiii, 165, 168, 228, 401, 403, 404, 410, 411, 414, 423, 509–525, 545, 552, 583, 585, 605; Jewish people, 167, 179, 184, 228, 338, 395–405, 411, 428, 442, 448, 455, 459, 509–525, 552, 559–560, 580, 605; anti-semitism, 179, 228, 474, 509–525
Jung, Patricia Beattie, 619
Jungmann, Joseph, 338, 339, 340
Justin Martyr, 558

Kaiser, Walter, 582
Kant, Immanuel, 19, 20–21, 27, 33, 34, 39–53, 63, 100, 160, 187, 190, 198, 199, 201, 214, 216, 218, 254, 380, 467, 539, 621. *See also* deontology.

Kazemi, Reza Shah, 417
Kearney, Richard, 22
Khalil, Muhammad Hassan, 413, 424, 425, 426
Khuri, Richard, 413, 416
King, Martin Luther, 135, 496–497
Kittel, Gerhard, 512
knowledge, xv, xvii, xviii–xix, 43, 62, 69, 112, 126, 138, 139, 189, 201, 291, 364, 378, 379, 389, 409, 419, 420, 422, 427, 450, 559, 625
Knox, Ronald, 345
Koppelman, Andrew, 287, 289
Kupperman, Joel, 26

labor, xiii, 142, 161, 181, 195, 196, 243, 247, 255, 256, 269, 270, 278, 377, 446, 455, 458, 463, 466, 470–471, 474
Lacan, Jacques, 198, 199
language, xvii–xix, 20–21, 23, 25, 50, 51, 100, 109, 116, 124, 165, 177, 180, 190–193, 196, 199, 247, 261, 265, 297, 317, 342, 343, 344, 346, 350, 353, 359, 377, 383, 384, 407, 409, 418, 420, 441, 445, 446, 447, 452, 509, 516, 520, 524, 536, 553, 554–555, 555, 556, 564, 565, 603, 611, 622, 623, 625
Larmore, Charles, 99, 102, 108, 111, 117
law, xv–xix, xx–xxi, 6, 8, 12–13, 15–16, 19, 26, 29–30, 40–42, 44, 46, 49, 63, 81, 83, 85–86, 100, 110–112, 114, 115, 125, 132, 133, 135–136, 138, 140, 147, 165, 167, 168, 168–170, 179, 181, 193–194, 198, 242, 254, 282, 285, 289, 290, 292, 294, 298, 301, 309, 310, 312, 313, 314, 315, 316, 317–318, 325, 340, 346, 349, 375, 381, 388, 397, 401, 402–405, 408–409, 411, 413–415, 417, 464, 466, 467, 469–470, 471, 490, 492, 493, 494, 495, 496–561, 565, 574, 581, 581–582, 583, 584, 586, 602, 604, 605, 615, 622
Lawler, Michael, 617–620, 623–624, 627
Leibniz, Gottfried Wilhelm, 164
Leutheuser, Julius, 514
Lewis, Clive Staples, 168, 344, 345
liberty, xv, xvi, 47, 50–51, 59, 75, 81, 107, 115, 117, 127, 135, 138, 196, 277–278, 279, 281–282, 456, 470, 472, 491, 495, 499, 500, 541. *See also* freedom.
liberalism, 25, 48–53, 102, 105, 107–110, 114, 116–117, 125–129, 132–137, 140–143, 175–176, 184, 203, 240, 425, 426, 472, 473–474, 478, 502, 524
liberality, xxi, 6, 31, 32
Locke, John, 47, 461, 468, 469–471, 604
Lonergan, Bernard, 405, 476, 477
Loury, Glenn, 225
Louth, Andrew, 370
love, 22, 31, 216, 254, 267, 270, 287, 294, 302, 303, 304, 311, 315, 316, 318, 322–323, 328, 345, 365, 417, 442, 448, 449, 450, 451, 452, 453, 465, 477, 478, 497, 525, 537, 559–560, 561, 566, 576–577, 586, 587, 592, 609, 611, 615, 616, 619, 625, 627, 627–628. *See also* charity.
Luther, Martin, 91, 517
Lydon, Mary, 202–203
Lyotard, Jean-François, xi, xvii–xix, 407

Machiavelli, Niccolò, 461, 466–468
MacIntyre, Alasdair, 23–25, 31, 34, 349, 373, 388, 627
MacKinnon, Catherine, 246
Madison, James, 162, 604
Maimonides, Moses, 395, 398
Maritain, Jacques, 344
Marquard, Odo, 159
marriage, 225, 248, 249, 255, 264, 285–304, 309–329, 351, 385, 402, 456, 465, 498, 519, 574, 575, 576–577, 581, 582, 584–585, 587, 589, 590, 601, 605, 607, 611, 615–616, 627
Marxism, 175, 187, 200–201, 230, 245, 377, 379. *See also* socialism, , 87, 146
Maurin, Peter, 350
McDowell, Deborah, 455
McGowan, Todd, 525
McGuckin, John Anthony, 370
McLanahan, Sara, 319
McWhorter, John, 219–220
Meezan, William, 319
Mendelsohn, Moses, 401
mercy, xxi–xxiii, 31, 389, 585, 589, 592
Meyer-Erlach, Wolf, 509, 518
.
Mill, James, 59

Mill, John Stuart, 52, 59–63, 64, 66, 68, 74, 171
minority, 184, 187, 278, 325, 354, 359, 361, 362, 367, 370, 376, 607
modernity, xi, xvii–xviii, 19–20, 21, 26–29, 31, 33, 40, 41, 103, 162, 164, 165, 172, 181, 198, 243, 336, 340, 341, 343, 345, 348, 351, 378, 379–380, 380, 389, 422, 423, 425, 428, 461, 467, 468, 471, 475, 478, 494, 500, 534–535, 553, 561, 563, 582, 591, 621, 623, 625
Moi, Toril, 200
Moore, G. E., 100–101, 101, 172
Moses, 169, 340, 398, 409, 410, 414, 455, 457, 478, 552, 560, 583, 584
Montesquieu, Charles-Louis de Secondat, Baron de La Brède et de, 44
motherhood, 189, 243, 245, 248–249, 251, 254, 255, 256, 260, 262, 264, 265, 267, 298, 318
Murphy-O'Connor, Jerome, 553, 557, 558
Murray, John Courtney, 304, 605
mysticism, 351, 352, 369, 413, 417, 426, 427, 429

Nagel, Thomas, 99, 102
Nasr, Seyyed Hossein, 410, 421
National Socialism:. *See* Christianity and National Socialism
nationalism, 138, 178, 198, 365, 407, 487, 498, 511
nature, xii–xvi, xix, xxi–xxii, 6, 9–15, 19–20, 23, 30, 40–42, 44–48, 72, 81, 83, 86, 88, 91, 100, 101, 103, 106, 108, 117, 126, 129, 142, 166, 168, 171, 211, 213–214, 237, 238, 242, 243, 244, 254, 260, 264, 266, 267, 268, 269, 270, 285, 289, 289–290, 292, 294, 301, 302, 303, 311, 312, 322, 323, 324, 325, 337, 340, 348, 348–349, 363, 364, 380, 381, 382, 388–389, 399, 401, 402–404, 422, 424, 429, 444, 462, 463–465, 468–472, 490, 491, 495, 496–498, 499, 500, 501, 502, 513, 522, 536, 541, 541–542, 543, 544, 561, 565–566, 574, 575, 590, 602, 607, 611, 616–617, 617–619, 620–621, 623–625, 625–627, 628. *See also* essence.
Newman, John Henry, 349, 546

Nietzsche, Friedrich, 200–201, 533, 538–541, 542, 544
Novak, Michael, 456, 472
Nozick, Robert, 99, 102
Nussbaum, Martha, 108, 287, 294

O'Donovan, Oliver, 383–385, 388
Okin, Susan, 462
oppression, xvi, 187, 190, 193, 196, 213, 220, 238–240, 246, 262, 278, 279, 362, 379, 396, 407, 455–456, 457, 459–460, 472, 473–475, 477, 478, 579, 609
order, 15, 28–29, 31, 42–43, 47, 51, 83, 94, 105, 109, 111–112, 127, 134, 136, 137, 138, 144, 239, 282, 323, 324, 346, 380, 383, 384, 388–389, 402, 423, 456, 462, 464, 465, 467, 472, 476, 477, 478, 488, 489, 492–493, 494–502, 520, 541, 544, 547–566, 574, 577, 578, 582, 584, 589, 590, 591, 607, 608, 623, 624
Origen, 347, 545–546
otherness, xxi–xxiii, 123, 125, 137–145, 145–147, 166, 187, 194, 196, 198, 200, 379–380, 408, 442, 444, 445, 448, 475, 576

Papanikolaou, Aristotle, 367
Patterson, Orlando, 457–458
Patton, Paul, 200
Paul, St., 169, 170, 335–336, 339, 343, 345, 347, 348, 349, 350, 351–352, 353, 460, 464, 516, 517, 518, 520, 520–521, 538, 553, 558, 560, 563–565, 587–591
Pauls, Theodor, 520
peace, 42, 46, 52, 84, 167, 195, 200, 251, 398, 488, 489, 490, 492, 493, 494, 495, 499, 519, 561, 605–606, 612
Pelikan, Jaroslav, 370
peoples, 12, 42–43, 43, 48, 84, 123, 135–136, 148, 172, 177, 377, 378, 382, 383, 384, 428, 442, 445, 446, 447, 452, 475, 489, 497, 513
Peter, St., 165, 449, 453
Phillips, John Bertram, 343
Pich, Hugo, 521
Pieper, Josef, 32
Pinker, Steven, 230
Pippin, Robert, 379–380
Pius XII, Pope, 352

Plato, x, 25, 160–161, 196, 325, 345, 419, 461, 462, 465, 539, 545
pluralism, 49, 103, 105, 124, 125, 133, 136, 159–160, 163, 311, 407–408, 413, 422, 424, 427, 456, 458, 472, 541, 606
Plutarch, 312, 325
postmodernity, xi, xvii–xix, 20, 22, 24, 25, 188, 190, 195, 197, 198, 203, 204, 343, 369, 454, 514, 533–534, 536, 538, 541, 542
poverty, xv, 7, 33, 59, 65, 66, 198, 241, 448, 449, 450, 464, 534, 579
power, ix–x, xv, xvi, xix–xx, 81, 86, 117, 135, 138, 142, 143, 163, 167, 172, 175, 185, 197, 200, 220, 224, 243, 245, 246, 249, 251, 252, 254, 257, 268, 336, 347, 349, 361, 373, 377, 378, 384–385, 387, 397, 399, 400, 401, 428, 442, 445, 448, 449, 458, 468, 469–470, 472, 473, 474, 475, 489, 496, 497, 537, 538, 541, 584–585, 589, 590, 591–592, 602
prejudice, 71, 185, 219, 220, 246, 278, 341, 444, 537, 609
privilege, ix–x, xvi, xviii–xix, 141, 161, 184, 239, 257, 265, 282, 362, 414, 450, 469, 472, 474, 475, 604, 619
procreation, 260, 264, 286, 289, 291, 292, 295, 296, 297, 303, 311, 320, 321, 323, 615–616, 618, 619, 623, 627. *See also* reproduction.
prophecy, xi, 81, 87–89, 91–94, 165, 169, 171, 351, 354, 386, 410, 410–411, 411–412, 412–413, 416, 417, 418, 419, 420, 421, 424, 427, 428, 552, 552–553, 559, 576, 579, 583, 587
Protagoras, 161
Protestantism, xxiii, 41, 117, 178, 181, 183–185, 280, 340, 341, 365, 373–390, 446, 453, 511, 512–513, 522, 607
Pufendorf, Samuel, 27, 41

racism, 67, 92, 124, 178, 194, 203, 207–230, 350, 376, 399, 402, 423, 442, 443, 444, 445, 446, 455, 474, 497, 509–525
Rahner, Karl, 351
rape, 198, 199, 214, 246, 577, 579
Rauch, Jonathan, 287, 319

Rawls, John, 39–40, 43, 47–53, 99–117, 123–148
Raz, Joseph, 102
reason, xii–xv, xix, 26, 27, 41, 43, 45, 47–48, 50, 67, 69, 81, 83, 90, 109, 110–112, 113, 114, 115–117, 125, 126–128, 133–136, 140, 142–143, 145, 160, 168, 190, 194, 198–200, 203, 214, 215, 251, 261, 341, 345, 347, 349, 381, 397, 420, 462–463, 465, 469, 470, 476, 495, 534–535, 547, 617, 623, 624
reciprocity, 5, 34, 45, 128, 133–135, 142, 217, 379, 470, 576, 625
Regnerus, Mark, 298–299
relativism, 15, 16, 138, 353, 389, 425
reproduction, xiii, 240, 249, 258, 286, 287, 288–289, 289–290, 291, 292, 302, 303, 303–304, 321, 322, 328, 617–618. *See also* procreation.
respect, 21, 29, 51, 52, 53, 135, 138, 142, 159, 160, 208, 213, 215–216, 220–228, 240, 248, 251, 255, 256, 265, 313, 341, 347, 359, 366, 367, 398, 403, 411, 412, 421, 429, 441, 442, 491, 497, 544, 547, 561, 574, 592, 601, 607, 620, 622
revolution, 88, 160, 170, 180, 189, 198, 239, 240, 246, 361, 362, 366, 399, 400, 448, 462, 489, 625, 626
Rich, Adrienne, 203
Ricoeur, Paul, 29, 34
Riefenstahl, Leni, 509
rights, xv–xvi, 27, 30, 43, 47, 50, 59, 63, 65, 67, 75, 81, 83, 88, 109, 114, 127–128, 135, 138, 141, 142, 181, 189, 194–195, 196, 203, 208, 217, 223, 237, 240, 241, 242, 244, 248, 253, 265, 277, 282, 313, 318, 336, 346, 376, 388–389, 395, 397–398, 398, 400, 400–401, 402, 403, 414, 443, 458, 461, 469, 470, 471–472, 474, 487–502, 523, 561, 579, 602, 616, 627
romanticism, 44, 108, 194, 286, 287, 294, 299, 300, 304, 310, 311, 314, 316, 318
Rome, xxvi, 167–168, 171, 176, 177, 340, 345, 457, 565
Rönck, Hugo, 521
Rorty, Richard, 100–101, 405
Roughgarden, Joan, 619, 623
Roy, Maurice Cardinal, 493, 494

INDEX

Rousseau, Jean-Jacques, 47, 93, 137, 169, 458
Rufus, Gaius Musonius, 312, 325
Ruddick, Sara, 251, 260
Rumi, Mawlana Jalal al-Din, 418
Russell, Norman, 370

Sadra, Mulla, 422
Salzman, Todd, 617–620, 623–624, 627
Sandefur, Gary, 319
Scanlon, T. M., 50–51, 99, 102
Schneewind, Jerome, 27–28
Schiltz, Lisa, 268
Schmemann, Alexander, 364
Schultz, Bishop Walther, 521
Second Vatican Council, 336, 349, 350, 351–352, 487, 488, 490, 499, 541, 547, 606
secularity, 21, 39, 51, 110–111, 134, 164, 171, 175, 240, 294, 335, 336, 348, 364, 373, 374, 378, 384–385, 399–400, 401, 403–404, 407, 422, 428, 488, 490, 510, 541, 545, 546, 547, 606
segregation, 281, 395, 443–444, 446, 447, 456, 496–497
Sen, Amartya, 99, 102, 112–115, 117
Seneca, Lucius Annaeus:, 167
sexism, 239–240, 241, 246, 248, 253, 255, 260, 301, 343, 474
Shakespeare, William, 179, 342
Shestov, Lev, 166
Sidgwick, Henry, 65, 70, 75
Sievers, Johannes, 521
Singer, Peter, 59, 65, 65–69, 71, 72, 73, 74, 75, 76, 230
slavery, 11, 15, 31, 49, 161, 172, 180–181, 221, 239, 242, 281, 376, 379, 396–397, 416, 441, 443, 444, 453, 456, 457–460, 462–463, 464, 471, 472, 477, 478, 538, 543
Smart, Ninian, 407
Snaith, Norman, 335
social science, ix–xi, 48, 102, 175, 250, 262, 299, 315, 319, 352, 379
Socrates, 59–60, 312, 325, 345, 455–457
Solomon, David, 27, 28
Sommers, Christina Hoff, 244, 246
Spinoza, Baruch, 403
Stein, Edith, 270

Stoicism, 169, 177, 325, 345
Strauss, Leo, 466, 467, 470
Sullivan, Andrew, 287
Swinburne, Richard, 370

Tannen, Deborah, 250, 265, 266
Taylor, Charles, 19, 20, 21, 27
Taylor, Paul:, 219, 230
Tertullian, Quintus Septimius Florens, 166, 347
Tessman, Lisa, 230
tolerance, 25, 47, 49, 50–52, 162, 163, 175–176, 177, 178, 179, 180, 181, 184–185, 188–189, 190, 194, 198, 203, 336, 346, 395, 397, 408, 444, 448, 533, 535, 536–537, 538, 539, 540–541, 541, 543, 544–545, 547, 604, 615
translation, problem of, 23, 190, 196, 494, 553–555, 556–557, 558, 565, 588, 611
Tufts, James Hayden, 81–85, 87–89, 91, 92, 94
Turner, Denys, 22

unity, xiii, xv, xviii, xxi, 21, 74, 105–106, 108, 123, 124, 125, 128, 134, 141, 146, 166, 286, 286–287, 287–303, 311–327, 340, 344, 346, 349, 350, 363, 364, 364–365, 377, 378, 379, 382, 383, 407, 411–412, 422, 429, 441, 442, 443, 450, 451, 452, 454, 465, 490, 496, 502, 575, 576–577, 584, 587, 590, 591, 606, 610, 611, 617, 625, 628. *See also* communion; community.
university, ix, x, xi, xiv, xvi, xviii, xx, 21, 341, 373–374, 375, 377, 378, 379, 512, 514
utilitarianism, 19, 20–21, 27, 34, 59–76, 90, 101, 127, 142, 216, 344

Vallier, Kevin, 111
Vattimo, Gianni, 533–544
Vigen, Anna Marie, 619
violence, 86, 125, 196, 199, 387, 408, 423, 455, 458, 468, 469, 470, 474, 475, 536, 537, 578, 579, 580, 602, 611, 622
virtue, xii, xxiii, 3–17, 19, 20, 27–34, 44, 52, 53, 83, 100–101, 162, 163, 207–208, 211, 212, 213, 214–219, 222, 223, 226, 230, 251, 270, 336, 341, 346,

388, 417, 456, 457, 461–467, 469, 471, 472, 478, 606, 607, 622
Vitoria, Francisco de, 612
Voegelin, Eric, 510

Walt, Johan van der, 142
Walzer, Michael, 460
Ware, Kallistos, 370
wealth, xiii, 4, 7, 32, 177, 180, 223–224, 240, 245, 268, 449, 450, 463
Weber, Max, 159
Weinberg, George, 608

Wells, Samuel, 382
Werdermann, Hermann, 520
Whitman, Walt, 91
Wittgenstein, Ludwig, xvii, 373
Wolterstorff, Nicholas, 111, 112, 388–389

Xenophanes, 312, 325
xenophobia, 175, 362

Yoder, John Howard, 383–385
Young, Iris Marion, 473, 474–475, 475

ABOUT THE CONTRIBUTORS

INTRODUCTION

Michael Sweeney is a professor of philosophy at Xavier University. He received a BA and an MA in philosophy from Marquette University, an MA in medieval studies from the University of Toronto, an STB from the Pontifical Gregorian University in Rome, and a PhD in philosophy from the Catholic University of America. From 2011 to 2015, he directed the Ethics/Religion and Society Program at Xavier University. The 2011–2014 Ethics/Religion and Society Program lecture series on "Justice, Tolerance and Diversity" was the origin of this volume. He has been a Fulbright Scholar in Moscow, Russia. He is the author of two books: *Srednevekovaya Khristyanskaya Filosofiya* [*Medieval Christian Philosophy*], trans. A. K. Lyavdanski (2001) and *Politicheskaya Filosofiya Srednikh Vekov* [*Political Philosophy of the Middle Ages*], trans. A. K. Lyavdanski and M. B. Kravchenko (2006).

PART I: JUSTICE AND DIVERSITY FROM DIVERSE PHILOSOPHICAL PERSPECTIVES

Peter Simpson teaches philosophy and classics at the Graduate Center in the City University of New York. He received a BA and MA in classics from Oxford University and a PhD from Victoria University, Manchester. He previously taught at the Catholic University of America, University College Dublin, and Manchester Polytechnic, United Kingdom. He has been a Rhodes Scholar and a Fulbright Scholar. His publications include *Goodness and Nature: A Defense of Ethical Naturalism* (1987); *The Politics of Aristotle*, translated with introduction, analysis, and notes (1997); *A Philosophical Commentary on the Politics of Aristotle* (1998); *On Karol Wojtyla* (2001); *Vices, Virtues, and Consequences* (2001); translation of Suarez, *Defense of the Faith*, vol. 1 (2011); translation of Suarez, *Defense of the Faith*, vol. 2 (2012); translation of and commentary on *The Eudemian Ethics of Aristotle* (2013); translation of and commentary on *The Great Ethics of Aristotle* (2014); *Political Illiberalism: A Defense of Freedom* (forthcoming).

Thomas Hibbs taught at Boston College for thirteen years and is currently Distinguished Professor of Ethics & Culture and Dean of the Honors College at Baylor University, where he also directs the Great Texts Program and the Baylor Interdisciplinary Core. He received his BA and MA in philosophy from the University of Dallas and an MMS and PhD from Notre Dame. His writings include *Dialectic and Narrative in Aquinas: An Interpretation of the* Summa Contra Gentiles (1995); *Shows About Nothing: Nihilism in Popular Culture from The Exorcist to Seinfeld* (2000); *Virtue's Splendor: Wisdom, Prudence, and the Human Good* (2001); *Aquinas, Ethics, and Philosophy of Religion: Metaphysics and Practice* (2007); *Arts of Darkness: American Noir and the Quest for Redemption* (2008); and, in addition to scholarly articles, numerous popular book and film reviews.

Aaron Szymkowiak teaches philosophy at Xavier University. He received a BA in philosophy from Penn State, an MA in political science from Penn State, and a PhD in philosophy from Boston University. He has published on Kant and Hutcheson; articles on Thomas Malthus and Adam Smith are forthcoming.

Raymond Hain teaches philosophy at Providence College. He received his BA from Christendom College and his PhD from the University of Notre Dame. He was a postgraduate student at Blackfriars Hall, Oxford University. His publications are in the area of ethics, and he is the editor of *Ethics and Culture: Essays in Honor of W. David Solomon* (forthcoming).

James Campbell is the Distinguished University Professor at the University of Toledo. He has been a Fulbright Lecturer at the University of Innsbruck (1990–1991) and the University of Munich (2003–2004). He received a BA from Temple University and a PhD from SUNY/Stony Brook. His books include *The Community Reconstructs: The Meaning of Pragmatic Social Thought* (1992); *Understanding John Dewey: Nature and Cooperative Intelligence* (1995); *Recovering Benjamin Franklin: An Exploration of a Life of Science and Service* (1999); *A Thoughtful Profession: The Early Years of the American Philosophical Association* (2006).

Paul Weithman teaches philosophy at the University of Notre Dame, where he is also director of the Philosophy, Politics and Economics Program. He received his BA from Notre Dame University and his PhD from Harvard University. His books include *Religion and the Obligations of Citizenship* (2002) (awarded the NASSP book award, 2003); *Why Political Liberalism? On John Rawls's Political Turn* (2010); ed., *Religion and Contemporary Liberalism* (1997); ed., with Henry Richardson, *The Philosophy of Rawls*, volumes 1-5 (1999); ed., *Liberal Faith: Essays in Honor of Philip Quinn* (2008).

Fred Evans is a professor of philosophy and coordinator of the Center for Interpretive and Qualitative Research at Duquesne University. He received his BA and MA in philosophy from Indiana University and his PhD in philosophy from the State University of New York at Stony Brook. He also has an MA in psychology from the University of Regina in Canada and worked for an nongovernmental organization in Laos during the 1970s. Among his many publications are *Psychology and Nihilism: A Genealogical Critique of the Computational Model of Mind* (1993); *Chiasms: Merleau-Ponty's Notion of the Flesh*, eds. Fred Evans and Leonard Lawlor (2000); *The Multivoiced Body: Society and Communication in the Age of Diversity* (2008; 2011).

PART II: PARTICULAR ISSUES IN JUSTICE AND DIVERSITY: PHILOSOPHY

Rémi Brague is emeritus professor of medieval and Arabic philosophy at the University of Paris I and the Ludwig-Maximilian-Universität of Munich where he held the Romano Guardini chair. He has been a visiting professor at Penn State, Boston University, Boston College, and the Universidad de Navarra. He received his PhD from the Université Paris-Sorbonne (Paris IV) and is a member of the Institut de France (Academy of Moral and Political Sciences). Among his works translated into English are *On the God of the Christians: (and on one or two others)* (2013); *The Legend of the Middle Ages: Philosophical Explorations of Medieval Christianity, Judaism, and Islam* (2011); *Eccentric Culture: A Theory of Western Civilization* (2009); *The Law of God: The Philosophical History of an Idea* (2008); *The Wisdom of the World: The Human Experience of the Universe in Western Thought* (2004).

Camille Paglia teaches at The University of the Arts, Philadelphia. She received her BA from Binghamton University and her PhD from Yale University. A cofounding contributor to Salon, she is also on the editorial board of Arion. Her books include *Sexual Personae: Art and Decadence from Nefertiti to Emily Dickinson* (1990); *Sex, Art, and American Culture* (1992); *Vamps & Tramps: New Essays* (1994); *Break, Blow, Burn: Camille Paglia Reads Forty-Three of the World's Best Poems* (2005). Most recently she is the author of *Glittering Images: A Journey through Art from Egypt to Star Wars* (2012).

Gayatri Chakravorty Spivak is director of the Center for Comparative Literature at Columbia University. She received an undergraduate degree in English at the Presidency College, Kolkata, under the University of Calcutta; her PhD in comparative literature is from Cornell University. Her scholarship has been honored around the world. Among her many publications are translation of and introduction to Derrida's *Of Grammatology* (1976); *In Other Worlds: Essays in Cultural Politics* (1987); *Selected Subaltern Studies* (1988); *Outside in the Teaching Machine* (1993); *The Spivak Reader* (1996); *A Critique of Post-Colonial Reason: Toward a History of the Vanishing Present* (1999); *Death of a Discipline* (2003); *Other Asias* (2007); *An Aesthetic Education in the Era of Globalization* (2013).

Jorge Garcia is a professor of philosophy at Boston College and a fellow of the Du Bois Institute at Harvard University. Previously he taught at Rutgers University, Georgetown University, and the University of Notre

Dame. He writes on ethics, medical ethics, and race. He is the author of *The Heart of Racism: Essays on Diversity, Race, and Relativism* (2012) and more than eighty articles.

Laura L. Garcia is a scholar in residence at Boston College; she has taught at Boston College, Calvin College, the University of Notre Dame, the University of St. Thomas, the Catholic University of America, Georgetown University, and Rutgers. Her BA in philosophy is from Westmont College and her PhD is from the University of Notre Dame. She is a manuscript referee for Blackwell Publishers, Catholic University of America Press, *The Thomist Faith and Philosophy*, *International Philosophical Quarterly*, *Christian Scholars Review*, *Theoretical Medicine and Bioethics*. She edited and introduced *Truth, Life and Solidarity: The Impact of John Paul II on Philosophy* (2010) and is the author of more than thirty articles on ethics and feminism.

Robert P. George is the McCormick Professor of Jurisprudence at Princeton University. He founded and directs the James Madison program at Princeton. He received a BA at Swarthmore, a JD from Harvard Law School, an MTS from Harvard Divinity School, and a DPhil from Oxford University. He has been a member of the United States Commission on Civil Rights, the President's Council on Bioethics, the Council on Foreign Relations, and a Judicial Fellow at the Supreme Court. He has received the Presidential Citizens Medal and a Bradley Award for Civic and Intellectual Achievement. His many publications include *Making Men Moral* (1995); *Great Cases in Constitutional Law* (2000); *In Defense of Natural Law* (2001); *Clash of Orthodoxies: Law, Religion and Morality in Crisis* (2002); *The Meaning of Marriage: Family, State, Market, and Morals* (2006); *Body-Self Dualism* (2007); *Embryo: A Defense of Human Life* (2008).

John Corvino teaches philosophy at Wayne State University. He received his BA from St. John's University and his PhD from the University of Texas. He is the author of *What's Wrong with Homosexuality?* (2013); with Maggie Gallagher, *Debating Same-Sex Marriage* (2012); editor and contributor, *Same Sex: Debating the Ethics, Science, and Culture of Homosexuality* (1997).

Sherif Girgis received his BA from Princeton and won the 2007 Dante Prize. As a Rhodes Scholar, he received an MPhil from Oxford University. He is currently completing a PhD in philosophy at Princeton and a JD from Yale. His is coauthor with Robert George and Ryan Anderson of the much discussed *What Is Marriage? Man and Woman: A Defense* (2012).

PART III: JUSTICE AND DIVERSITY FROM DIVERSE THEOLOGICAL PERSPECTIVES

Peter A. Huff teaches theology at the University of Mary. Previously he held the T. L. James Associate Professor of Religious Studies Chair at Centenary College of Louisiana; from 2010 to 2013 he held the Besl Chair at Xavier University, a visiting chair in the Ethics/Religion and Society Program. He received degrees from the Cleveland Institute of Music, Mercer University, Southern Baptist Theological Seminary, and Indiana University; he received his PhD in historical theology from Saint Louis University. Professor Huff has been a significant contributor to dialogue between Christians and Buddhists and between Christians and Mormons. His books include *Allen Tate and the Catholic Revival* (1996); *What Are They Saying About Fundamentalisms* (2007); ed., *Knowledge and Belief in America* (1995); *Tradition and Pluralism* (2008), and most recently, two books on the Second Vatican Council: *Vatican II: Its Impact on You* (2011) and *The Voice of Vatican II: Words for Our Church Today* (2012).

Dr. Paul L. Gavrilyuk is a professor of theology at the University of St. Thomas. He received a BS from the Moscow Institute of Physics and Technology and an MTS and PhD in theology from Southern Methodist University. As an Eastern Orthodox historian and theologian, he offers courses in the history of Christian doctrine, Christianity in late antiquity, liturgical studies, and Russian religious thought. He has lectured in Italy, France, Belgium, Russia, Ukraine, and Kazakhstan; he has been a visiting professor at Harvard Divinity School. His recent publications include two books: *The Suffering of the Impassible God: The Dialectics of Patristic Thought* (2004; 2006) and *Histoire du catéchuménat dans l'église ancienne* [*A History of the Catechumenate in the Early Church*] (2007), which was originally published in Russian in 2001. His scholarly articles have appeared in *The Journal of Theological Studies*, *Scottish Journal of Theology*, and *Vigiliae Christianae*.

D. Stephen Long is Cary M. Maguire Professor at Southern Methodist University. His BA is from Taylor University and his doctorate is from Duke University. He is an ordained United Methodist and served in Honduras and North Carolina. His books include *Living the Discipline: United Methodist Theological Reflections on War, Civilization, and Holiness* (1992); *Tragedy, Tradition, Transformism: The Ethics of Paul Ramsey* (1993); *Divine Economy: Theology and the Market* (2000); *The Goodness of God: Theology, Church and Social Order* (2001); *John Wesley's Moral Theology: The Quest for God and Goodness* (2005); *Calculated Futures* (2007); *Theology and Culture* (2007); *Speaking of God: Theology, Truth and Language* (2009); *Christian Ethics: Very Short Introduction* (2010); *Hebrews: A Theological Commentary on the Bible* (2011); *Keeping Faith: An Ecumenical Commentary on the Articles of Religion and Confession of Faith in the Wesleyan Tradition* (2012); *Saving Karl Barth: Hans Urs von Balthasar's Preoccupation* (2014).

David Novak is chair of Jewish studies, a professor of religion, and a professor of philosophy at the University of Toronto. He completed his undergraduate studies and an MHL (master of Hebrew literature) at the University of Chicago; his rabbinic diploma is from the Jewish Theological Seminary of America, and his doctorate in philosophy is from Georgetown University. He is a Fellow of the American Academy for Jewish Research and the Academy for Jewish Philosophy, a member of the Board of Consulting Scholars of the James Madison Program in American Ideals and Institutions at Princeton University, and has been a Fellow at the Woodrow Wilson International Center for Scholars in Washington, D.C. He delivered the Lancaster/Yarnton Lectures at Oxford University and was a Charles E. Test, MD Distinguished Visiting Scholar at Princeton University. Professor Novak is the author of sixteen books, including *In Defense of Religious Liberty* (2009); *The Jewish Social Contract: A Essay in Political Theology* (2005); *Talking with Christians: Musings of a Jewish Theologian* (2005); *Natural Law in Judaism* (1998); *Leo Strauss and Judaism: Jerusalem and Athens Critically Revisited* (1996); *The Election of Israel: The Idea of the Chosen People* (1995).

Covenantal Rights: A Study in Jewish Political Theory (2000) won the award of the American Academy of Religion for best book in constructive religious thought in 2000. He has edited four books and is the author of over two hundred articles in scholarly and intellectual journals.

Muhammed Zia ul-Haq is a professor in and dean of the Faculty of Shariah and Law in the International Islamic University of Islamabad. He received a BA in Islamic studies from Bahauddin Zakariya University, Multan, Pakistan; an MA in Arabic from the University of the Punjab, Lahore, Pakistan; an MA in Islamic studies from Bahauddin Zakariya University, Multan, Pakistan; his doctorate in comparative *Fiqh* (Islamic law) is from the Institute Superieuer Du Theologie, Ezzituna University, Tunis, Tunisia. He is the author of eleven books and numerous articles in Arabic, Urdu, and English. During the 2012–2013 academic year, he was a Fulbright Scholar at Xavier University.

Waleed El-Ansary holds the Helal, Hisham and Laila Edris El-Swedey University Chair in Islamic Studies at Xavier University; he previously taught at the University of South Carolina. He received an MA in economics from the University of Maryland and a PhD in human sciences from George Washington University. He has been a consultant to the Royal Court of Jordan and to the Grand Mufti of Egypt. He is the coeditor of *Muslim and Christian Understanding: Theory and Application of "A Common Word"* (2010). Two books are forthcoming: *The Spiritual Significance of Jihad in Islamic Economics* and *Not by Bread Alone: E.F. Schumacher and the Perennial Philosophy*.

PART IV: PARTICULAR ISSUES IN JUSTICE AND DIVERSITY: THEOLOGY

Virgilio Elizondo is an endowed professor in pastoral and Hispanic theology at the University of Notre Dame. He received a BS in chemistry from St. Mary's University; an MA in pastoral studies from the Ateneo University, Manila; and an STD/PhD from Institut Catholique, Paris. The recipient of numerous honorary degrees, he is widely recognized as "the father of U.S. Latino religious thought." His books include, with Gustavo

Gutierrez and Timothy Matovina, *Beyond Borders: Writings of Virgilio Elizondo and Friends* (2009); *Galilean Journey: The Mexican-American Promise* (2005); *God of Incredible Surprises* (2003); with John Francis Burke, *Mestizo Democracy: The Politics of Crossing Borders* (2003); *The Future Is Mestizo: Life Where Cultures Meet* (2000); with Timothy Matovina, *San Fernando Cathedral: Soul of the City* (1998); with Timothy Matovina, *Mestizo Worship: A Pastoral Approach to Liturgical Ministry* (1998); *Guadalupe: Mother of the New Creation* (1997); *Christianity and Culture: An Introduction to Pastoral Theology and Ministry for the Bicultural Community* (1978).

Shawn Copeland is a professor of theology at Boston College. She previously taught at Yale Divinity School, the Institute for Black Catholic Studies, Xavier University of Louisiana, and at Marquette University. Her BA is from Madonna College and her PhD is from Boston College. She is the former president of the Catholic Theological Society of America. Her books include *Enfleshing Freedom: Body, Race, and Being* (2010); *The Subversive Power of Love: The Vision of Henriette Delille: The Madeleva Lecture in Spirituality* (2009); with LaReine-Marie Mosely and Albert Raboteau, *Uncommon Faithfulness: The Black Catholic Experience* (2009).

Russell Hittinger is William K. Warren Professor of Catholic Studies and a research professor of law at the University of Tulsa. He previously taught at Fordham University and at the Catholic University of America, and has taught as a visiting professor at Princeton University, New York University, and Charles University in Prague. He is on the governing board of Pontificia Academia Sancti Thomae Aquinatis (Pontifical Academy of St. Thomas Aquinas) and a member of the Pontifical Academy of Social Sciences. He is one of two lay academics in the world to serve as ordinarius in two Pontifical academies. He chairs, with Ambassador Mary Ann Glendon (Harvard), the Catholic Social Thought Project, Lumen Christi Institute, University of Chicago. His books include *Paper Wars: Catholic Social Doctrine and the Modern State* (forthcoming); *Thomas Aquinas and the Rule of Law* (2007); *The First Grace: Rediscovering Natural Law in a Post-Christian Age* (2003); *A Critique of the New Natural Law Theory* (1987).

Susannah Heschel is the Eli Black Professor of Jewish Studies at Dartmouth College and has held visiting professorships at Princeton, Tufts, the University of Frankfurt, the University of Edinburgh, and the University of Cape Town. Her award-winning publications include *Abraham Geiger and the Jewish Jesus* (1998) and *The Aryan Jesus: Christian Theologians and the Bible in Nazi Germany* (2010). Her edited works include *Moral Grandeur and Spiritual Audacity: Essays of Abraham Joshua Heschel* (1997); with David Biale and Michael Galchinsky, *Insider/Outsider: American Jews and Multiculturalism* (1998); with Robert P. Ericksen, *Betrayal: German Churches and the Holocaust* (1999).

Thomas G. Guarino teaches theology at Seton Hall University and is a Fellow of the Center of Theological Inquiry at Princeton and on the board of the Center for Catholic and Evangelical Dialogue. He received his BA from Seton Hall, an STB from the Pontifical Gregorian University in Rome, and an STD from the Catholic University of America. Among his writings are *Vincent of Lerins and the Development of Christian Doctrine* (2013); *Vattimo and Theology* (2009); *Foundations of Systematic Theology* (2005); *Revelation and Truth: Unity and Plurality in Contemporary Theology* (1993).

Kwame Anthony Appiah teaches in the Department of Philosophy and the School of Law at New York University; he previously taught at Princeton. He received a BA and PhD in philosophy from Cambridge University. He was elected to the American Academy of Arts and Sciences, the American Philosophical Society, and the American Academy of Arts and Letters; he is a member of the Advisory Board of the United Nations Democracy Fund and chair of the Board of the American Council of Learned Societies. Among his academic books are *In My Father's House: Africa in the Philosophy of Culture* (1992); *Color Conscious: The Political Morality of Race* (1996); with Peggy Appiah and Ivor Agyeman-Duah, *Bu Me Bé: The Proverbs of the Akan* (2002); *Thinking It Through: An Introduction to Contemporary Philosophy* (2003); *The Ethics of Identity* (2005); *Cosmopolitanism: Ethics in a World of Strangers* (2006); *The Honor Code: How Moral Revolutions Happen* (2010); *Lines of Descent: W. E. B. Du Bois and the Emergence of Identity* (2014). His other writings include three novels.

Mary Healey teaches sacred scripture at Sacred Heart Major Seminary in Detroit; she previously taught at Ave Maria University and Christendom College. She received a BA from the University of Notre Dame; an MA in theology from the Franciscan University of Steubenville; an MA in philosophy from the Catholic University of America; an STL from the International Academy of Theology in Gaming, Austria; and an STD. from the Pontifical Gregorian University in Rome. She is general editor, with Dr. Peter Williamson, of the *Catholic Commentary on Sacred Scripture* and chair of the Doctrinal Commission of International Catholic Charismatic Renewal Services in Rome; in 2014 she was appointed by Pope Francis to a five-year term on the Pontifical Biblical Commission. She is the author of *The Gospel of Mark* (2008) and *Men and Women Are from Eden: A Study Guide to John Paul II's Theology of the Body* (2005) and the editor of three books.

Mark D. Jordan is Andrew W. Mellon Professor of Christian Thought in the Harvard School of Divinity. Professor Jordan writes on sexual ethics. He received his BA from St. John's College and his PhD from the University of Texas. Among his awards are the John S. Guggenheim Memorial Foundation Fellowship, a Fulbright-Hays grant (Spain), and a Henry Luce III Fellowship in Theology. His publications include *The Invention of Sodomy in Christian Theology* (1997); *The Silence of Sodom: Homosexuality in Modern Catholicism* (2002); *The Ethics of Sex* (2001); *Telling Truths in Church: Scandal, Flesh, and Christian Speech* (2004); *Rewritten Theology: Aquinas after His Readers* (2005); *Blessing Same-Sex Unions* (2005); *Authorizing Marriage? Canon, Tradition, and Critique in the Blessing of Same-Sex Unions* (2006); *Recruiting Young Love: How Christians Talk about Homosexuality* (2011).

John Grabowski teaches theology at the Catholic University of America. He received his BA from the Franciscan University of Steubenville and his PhD from Marquette University. He and his wife were appointed to the Pontifical Council for the Family by Pope Benedict XVI in the fall of 2009, where they serve as a member couple. He is also currently serving as a theological advisor to the U.S.C.C.B. Committee on Laity, Marriage, Family, and Youth. He wrote the Foreword to the 1997 English edition of Pope John Paul II's *Theology of the Body*. He is the author of *Sex and Virtue: An Introduction to Sexual Ethics* (2003).